PENGUIN BOOKS

THE GATE OF HEAVENLY PEACE

Jonathan D. Spence was born in England in 1936 and educated at Winchester College and Cambridge University. He came to the United States in 1959 to continue his graduate studies at Yale University, whose faculty he joined in 1965 and where he is now George Burton Adams Professor of History. He lives in Woodbridge, Connecticut, with his wife and two sons. Professor Spence is also the author of *Ts'ao Yin and the K'ang-hsi Emperor: Bondservant and Master; To Change China: Western Advisors in China 1620–1960; Emperor of China: Self-Portrait of K'ang-hsi;* and *The Death of Woman Wang. To Change China, The Death of Woman Wang, Mao Zedong,* and *Treason by the Book.*

聽

1926 元

THE GATE OF HEAVENLY PEACE

The Chinese and Their Revolution
1895–1980

JONATHAN D. SPENCE

PENGUIN BOOKS

PENGUIN BOOKS
Published by the Penguin Group
Penguin Books USA Inc., 375 Hudson Street,
New York, New York 10014, U.S.A.
Penguin Books Ltd, 27 Wrights Lane,
London W8 5TZ, England
Penguin Books Australia Ltd, Ringwood,
Victoria, Australia
Penguin Books Canada Ltd, 10 Alcorn Avenue,
Toronto, Ontario, Canada M4V 3B2
Penguin Books (N.Z.) Ltd, 182–190 Wairau Road,
Auckland 10, New Zealand

Penguin Books Ltd, Registered Offices:
Harmondsworth, Middlesex, England

First published in the United States of America by
Viking Penguin Inc. 1981
First published in Great Britain by
Faber and Faber Ltd 1982
Published in Penguin Books 1982

26 25 24 23 22 21 20 19 18 17 16

LIBRARY OF CONGRESS CATALOGING IN PUBLICATION DATA
Spence, Jonathan D.
  The gate of heavenly peace.
  Bibliography: p.
  Includes index.
  1. China—History—20th century. 2. China—
History—1861–1912. I. Title.
[DS774.S59 1982] 951 82-5245
ISBN 0 14 00.6279 3   AACR2

Printed in the United States of America
Set in CRT Palatino

Map by Anita Karl/James Kemp

Pages 513–16 constitute an extension of the copyright page.

This book is dedicated
to my mother,
with love

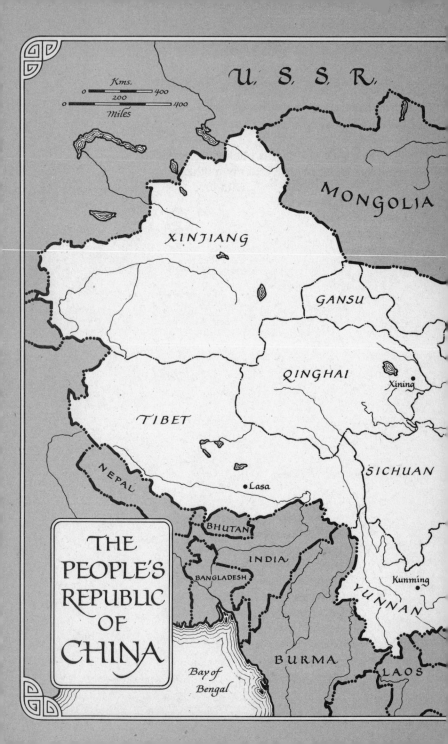

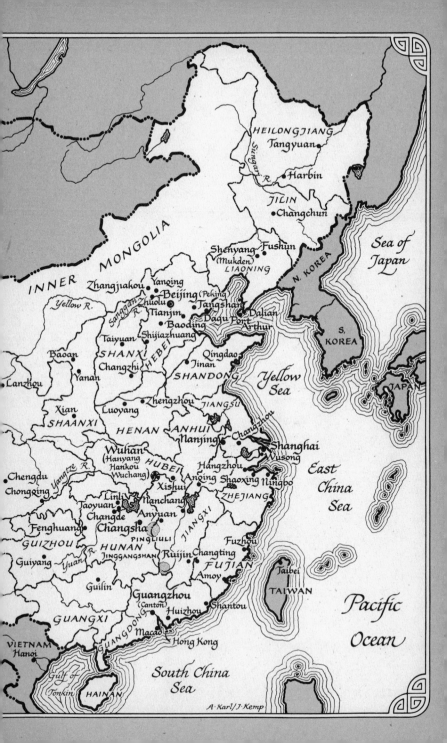

Contents

List of Illustrations

For sources of illustrations see page 470.

Acknowledgments

My very special thanks go to two people who helped me consistently with this book: Monica Yü, my patient language guide and literary detective, and Antony Marr, the most ebullient and efficient of curators. I am also deeply grateful to Merle Goldman, Michael Lestz, and James Cole for their shrewd and usefully critical readings of the draft manuscript, and to Parker Po-fei Huang for checking many poems with me.

Not only friends and colleagues at Yale but also many other scholars gave generously of their time, their written materials, or their bibliographic expertise. My thanks to Jean James, Robert Hegel, and Bonnie McDougall; Joey Bonner, Anita Chan, Jonathan Unger, and John Burns; David Goodman; Nancy Levenberg and John Bryan Starr; Cheng Pei-kai, Stephen Hay, and Sherman Cochran. I am also grateful to the Whitney Griswold Fund in the Humanities at Yale for a grant to begin the work on this book; to Leo Lee for lending me his transcripts of the Xu–Elmhirst correspondence; and to Ingeborg Wald for locating and making available copies of the Straight Family Papers at Cornell University dealing with Elmhirst. I first aired various ideas concerning themes in this book in public lectures at Cornell and the University of Kansas at Lawrence; my thanks to the audiences there for provocative and often stimulating questions. Shen Congwen also graciously gave me an evening of his time during his visit to the United States, with

Hans Frankel helping as interpreter, to confirm many details of his life before 1949.

My thanks, too, to those who made typescripts out of my various inscrutable longhand drafts: Mary Garrison, Florence Thomas, Laura Boucher, Mary Whitney, and especially Katrin van der Vaart, who in addition to typing also prepared the draft index.

A book like this, attempting an overview of a massive and complicated subject, inevitably depends heavily on the work of other scholars. As well as thanking all the publishers who gave permissions for printed matter to be reproduced—a complete listing of all such permissions begins on p. 513—I would like to acknowledge my special debt to those scholars who have explored, in books or in dissertations, the individual Chinese figures whose lives constitute this book: in particular, the work of Hsiao Kung-chuan, Lo Jung-pang, and Eve Armentrout-Ma, on Kang Youwei; on Lu Xun, William Lyell and the translations of Yang Hsien-yi and Gladys Yang; on Qu Qiubai, the studies by Tsi-an Hsia, Paul Pickowicz, Li Yu-ning, and Marián Gálik; on Xu Zhimo, the work of Leo Lee, Cyril Birch, and Gaylord Leung; Kai-yu Hsu on Wen Yiduo; Nieh Hua-ling and Jeffrey Kinkley on Shen Congwen; Prudence Chou, Ranbir Vohra, and Paul Bady on Lao She; and Chang Jun-mei, Gary Bjorge, and Yi-tsi Feuerwerker on Ding Ling. I have tried, in the notes and bibliography, to give a comprehensive sense of my debts to other writers—often young scholars—who currently are making the field of modern Chinese studies in the United States such an extraordinarily lively and exciting one.

And, finally, my thanks to my editor, Elisabeth Sifton, constantly supportive yet constantly questioning.

J. D. S.

Yale University
March 1981

Preface

The Gate of Heavenly Peace guards the southern approach to the former imperial palace complex in Beijing. Until China's last dynasty fell in 1912, it was through this gate that the main axis of the Emperor's power was believed to run, as he sat in his throne hall, facing south, the force of his presence radiating out across the courtyards and ornamental rivers of the palace compound, passing through the gate, and so to the great reaches of countryside beyond. During the teens and twenties of this century the gate ceased to have either a clear defensive or a clear symbolic function, though it bore quiet witness to the new paradoxes that were beginning to dominate Chinese life: north of the gate the corrupt court of the abdicated Emperor lived on in twilight grandeur behind their walls, struggling to survive amidst turbulent warlord regimes; in front of the gate, using it as marker and meeting place, political activists, students, and workers gathered in vocal demonstrations to protest the ineffectualness of their nominally republican regimes in the face of foreign imperialist aggression, only to be dispersed with clubs or with gunfire.

After the Second World War and the Communist victory of 1949, the Forbidden City area became a museum. The crowded alleys in front of the gate were leveled, and a massive parade ground was created; in the center of the vast space rose the simple monument to the martyrs of the revolution, flanked by the blank-faced, austere public buildings of the new People's

Republic. During the Cultural Revolution of 1966 the gate, dominated now by an immense colored portrait of Chairman Mao Zedong, became a reviewing stand in front of which marched the Red Guards, a million or more strong. And in the late 1970s, as the Maoist posters were one by one taken down, a new generation of demonstrators assembled in the space between the gate and the mausoleum housing Mao's embalmed corpse to protest the restrictions on thought and movement imposed by Mao's successor governments.

Thus while the name of the gate, with its rich historical echoes and its evocations of a timeless sphere beyond politics, has seemed across the last century to bring a promise of solace to the Chinese people dreaming of escape from current realities, the gate itself in the same period came to stand implacably for the power of the state: the state that sought sometimes to prevent such dreams, sometimes to coopt them, and sometimes wavered uncertainly before their unpredictable force.

In the period between the 1890s and the 1980s there were few years when China was not shaken by internal dissensions or foreign assaults, and whether they wished it or not, few Chinese could avoid being touched in some way by violent pressures for change. They lived in a world that was ideologically speculative, politically tumultuous, and economically precarious, so that creative survival, if one were not to rely on chance alone, demanded both adaptability and courage.

A single focus for the Chinese revolution appears elusive as one looks back across the twentieth century; one sees, rather, an overlapping series of quests, some of which were abandoned long before they were attained, others of which failed after seeming to be almost within the seekers' grasp, while yet others were gained, albeit in fleeting or in altered form. The pressures of Chinese modernizers between 1895 and 1900 did push the reigning Qing dynasty to change the shape of government and education in more drastic ways than had been attempted for almost a millennium; the assaults by constitutional reformers and political revolutionaries of many camps did lead to the Qing dynasty's collapse in 1912; and the incentive to exploration provided by that collapse did lead to new structures in politics and new expressiveness in literature and art. At the same time, passions were aroused that could be stilled only through violence, and the great tragedy of the struggle between the Communist Party and the Nationalist Guomindang dominates Chinese history between 1924 and 1949. During that struggle, and to the loss of the nation, despite endless protestations to the contrary each of these major political parties grew narrow-minded and ingrown, saw vision succumb to the organizational needs of the moment, and employed weapons of censorship, harassment, intimidation, and death.

These weapons continued to be used both in Taiwan and in the People's Republic after 1949: inside China, as the immensely ambitious program of redistributing land to the poorer peasants and landless laborers was carried through in the early 1950s, only to be reversed (or "carried to a higher stage") in the rural collectivization movements that ended private ownership of any sizable tracts of land at the end of that same decade, tensions developed within the society that could not be solved by suasion alone. The Communist Party device of mass campaigns inevitably, it seems in retrospect, threw intellectuals, industrial workers, peasants, and finally the party cadres themselves into new cycles of utopian hope and brutal coercion.

This book is about a small number of the Chinese men and women who were caught up in this process of violence and renewal, and it is my hope that a description of their lives will serve to introduce the reader to the extraordinary sequence of events that are often loosely lumped together as constituting the "Chinese revolution." Each of these lives had its own shape and force, and they are not presented here in the spirit of "group biography," as that genre is often practiced nowadays. What I wish to convey, rather, is something of the difficulties of the day-to-day decisions that each of these people had to make, the confusing contexts in which they operated, the intrusions of outside events upon them when they sought to remain sheltered, and the responses of outside agents when they made their occasional bold decisions to act.

The Chinese who tell their story in these pages are not the major political leaders whose names have come to define our sense of modern China. Though leaders of the Nationalist Guomindang Party such as Sun Yatsen and Chiang Kaishek, and Communist leaders like Mao Zedong and Zhou Enlai, are discussed to some extent, I have preferred to concentrate on certain other individuals whose lives were not so obviously central to the course of the revolution but who nevertheless described their hopes and their sorrows with particular sensitivity, and whose personal experiences help to define the nature of the times through which they lived. The main narrative line is carried by three people. The first is the scholar Kang Youwei, trained in the canons of traditional Confucianism, who became a spokesman for radical reform as the Qing dynasty drew to its close in the late nineteenth century, and after political failures and exile sought in utopian speculation a solace for his current sorrows. The second is Lu Xun, who studied medicine in Japan as a young man and then, after switching his allegiance to the realm of literature, came to be the most articulate spokesman for the thwarted longings of his students and his countrymen during the 1920s. The third is Ding Ling, educated as a girl into the emancipated world of the "new" China after the Qing dynasty fell, who became both a writer and a political activist and had to learn the hard way how great were the dissonances between her own creative talents and the criteria for artistic life that were imposed, seriatim, by both the Guomindang Nationalists and the Communists.

The lives of Kang, Lu, and Ding span the entire period of modern Chinese history. Kang Youwei, born in 1858, died in 1927, as the Communists were struggling to obtain leadership over peasant insurrections and urban strikes, thus initiating their first great trial of strength with the Nationalists. Lu Xun, born in 1881, died in 1936, as the Communists, apparently broken by the Nationalist Party, managed to survive their Long March of retreat to the barren northwest of China, while Japan completed her preparations for invasion. Ding Ling, born in 1905, survived house arrest in the 1930s, "reform through labor" in the 1940s and the 1960s, and prison in the 1970s, to rejoin the political hierarchy being redefined by Vice-Premier Deng Xiaoping in 1979. I have set these three main stories in a frame of chronological history, where they are echoed by other lives—presented here as secondary to the narrative but in no way deemed of lesser significance—such as those of the early woman revolutionary Qiu Jin, the warlord soldier Shen Congwen, the young Marxist Qu Qiubai, the Western-educated poets Xu Zhimo and Wen Yiduo, the satirical novelist Lao She, and the young protester of the 1970s, Wei Jingsheng.

Taken as a whole these people show—as vividly, I hope, as the many thousands of other Chinese of similar talents and experiences who were *not* chosen might have done—how flexible, how courageous, and how subtle the Chinese response to crisis in our own time has been. The willingness to make political commitment when such commitment was obviously dangerous, the determination to hope even when hope seemed futile, the sheer energy and bravado hurled into the task of surviving in a disintegrating or murderous world—all can be found repeatedly in the Chinese I have considered here, and may help to banish any simpler clichés concerning Chinese apathy, or the narrow range of Chinese vision, that have so long dominated our Western consciousness.

The Chinese whose thoughts, words, and actions constitute the heart of this book were all intellectuals in some form or other, yet though they could not speak at first hand for workers or peasants, they were far from being mere spectators. At their more strident or ineffective moments, certainly, one can see them as being in some senses parallel to the members of the chorus in a Greek play, watching in horror and fascination the tragic working out on center stage of a conflict between mortals and gods, the end of which has been long foretold. Yet though the cultured voices of these Chinese may seem at times too piercing, and their gestures too ritualized, they still possess the essential power—denied to the traditional chorus—of leaving their apparently allotted space and marching to the center of the stage. It is often true that those who do this die earlier than the others—"before their time," to use a simple phrase—but one cannot deny that they often show a startling wisdom, the wisdom of those who have seen the hidden directions of this particular play, who have understood that this is not the kind of drama in which those who stay on the periphery will be left in peace.

Note on Pronunciation

The system of romanization used in this book is Pinyin, now slowly gaining acceptance as the standard international form for rendering written Chinese. In general, the Pinyin names are pronounced roughly as written, but there are some important exceptions:

Q: This letter in Pinyin has the sound of a hard *ch*; thus Qing (dynasty) is pronounced *Ch*ing and the name of the Marxist Qu Qiubai is pronounced *Ch*ü (with an *ü* sound) *Ch*iubai.

X: In the old Wade-Giles system this letter was rendered as *hs*—that is, by placing an aspirant before an *s* sound to give a slight hiss. The writer Lu Xun's name is thus pronounced Lu *Hs*un, and the poet Xu Zhimo's *Hs*ü Zhimo.

C: C at the beginning of a Pinyin cluster has the force of *ts*; thus Shen Congwen is pronounced Shen *Ts*ungwen.

Also following Pinyin, Mao Tse-tung becomes Mao Zedong, Chou En-lai becomes Zhou Enlai, and Peking and Canton become Beijing and Guangzhou. The only exceptions to Pinyin usage followed here are in the form Yangtze River, and in the widely recognized names Chiang Kaishek and Sun Yatsen, since those in any case render southern dialect pronunciation, not the original Mandarin.

All references in the notes and bibliography follow the forms used by the author *being cited*. Thus we inevitably will find such references as "For more on Ding Ling, see Chang Jun-mei's *Ting Ling*"; "On Qu Qiubai's early years see Li Yu-ning's essay on 'Ch'ü Ch'iu-pai.' " In the current stage of Chinese romanization there seemed no alternative to this rather ungainly approach save total chaos.

What could a man require more from a nation so pliant and so prone to seek after knowledge? What wants there to such a towardly and pregnant soil, but wise and faithful labourers, to make a knowing people, a nation of prophets, of sages, and of worthies? We reckon more than five months yet to harvest; there need not be five weeks, had we but eyes to lift up, the fields are white already.

John Milton,
Areopagitica

THE GATE OF
HEAVENLY PEACE

·1·

AROUSING THE SPIRITS

In the early spring of 1895, a party of Japanese troops boarded and searched a Chinese steamer as it sailed through the North China Sea. The high-handed action was typical of the kind of thing that had been happening since Japan had defeated Chinese land and naval forces in the brief war waged between August 1894 and February 1895; in that war, ostensibly fought over the two countries' spheres of influence in the Korean peninsula, the effectiveness of Japan's newly modernized armed forces, supported by a restructured economic and industrial base, had been overwhelmingly demonstrated.

One of the passengers on the steamer, the scholar Kang Youwei, felt the insult to China's sovereignty with special keenness; Kang had been sending letters and memoranda to the court of the ruling Qing dynasty for almost a decade, urging that economic and military reforms be instituted in China, and now the worst of his fears about the results of the rulers' apathy were realized: "I was enraged when the Japanese came and searched our ship," he wrote later in 1895; "if the court had listened to my advice earlier, we would not have had to endure such humiliations." Kang's anger was real enough, but he was rather ingenuous in believing that the rulers in Beijing—whose Qing dynasty had ruled over China since 1644—would heed the advice of a scholar-teacher from south China who held no bureaucratic office and had no relatives serving in senior government posts. Nevertheless Kang was correct in sensing that the Japanese victory proved that the dynasty was in danger of collapsing; though no Chinese could dare to say such a thing openly, Kang Youwei did tell those students from his Guangzhou academy who were with him on board the ship that China's case must now be considered similar to that of Turkey: they were two large, sick nations with proud traditions, preserved in their helplessness by foreign powers that exploited them.[1]

The impact of the incident was heightened for Kang Youwei by the fact that at the time he encountered the Japanese he was en route to Beijing to sit for the highest level of the state civil-service examinations. The purpose of these triennial examinations was to select the most brilliant of China's Confucian scholars for a lifetime of service in the imperial bureaucracy, but the reality that Kang experienced when he finally reached Beijing made a mockery of these claims: the examination cells in which the tests were to be held were dilapidated and filthy; the city was full of rumors of corruption and malfeasance in the selection of the final rosters of candidates (charges that were leveled particularly in the case of students from the Guangzhou area); even the sedan-chair coolies who carried the students to the examination halls were rioting for better pay, and stole grain and other supplies.[2] Beijing itself was awash with the wreckage of humanity: "No matter where you look in Beijing," Kang wrote that May, "the place is covered with beggars. The homeless and the old, the crippled and the sick with no one to care for them fall dead on the roads. This happens every day. And the coaches of the great officials rumble past them continuously; they are as indifferent as the local officials are in the rest of the province."[3]

Kang Youwei was thirty-seven years old in 1895. At one level his upbringing had been similar to that of many wealthy Chinese of the time. He had memorized the shorter Confucian classics by the age of ten, coached by tutors and a stern but affectionate grandfather; he had passed the local-level examinations at fifteen and proceeded to prepare rigorously for the higher levels of the state examination system; at eighteen he had been married to a young woman three years his senior, to whom he had been "engaged" when he was seven and who had been chosen for him by his parents; he traveled regularly to local shrines and towns near Guangzhou, recording his visits in poems; he rebelled, at intervals, against the exhausting drudgery of mastering the highly formulaic "eight-legged essay" system on which success in the examinations depended, and hence withdrew at intervals either into the realm of pure textual scholarship or into the peaceful world of Buddhist meditation.[4]

But at the same time his character developed in unusual directions and fate brought him special sorrows and special opportunities. His father was at home, sick with tuberculosis, all through Kang Youwei's tenth year, and so at a time when fathers in Chinese traditional society were often far from home on official business, Kang and his father could spend every day together. To Kang in later life, this year of 1867 appeared "like a dream," as he recalled sitting with his father in a small pavilion, keeping off insects and trying to make him comfortable, fetching his cane or holding the basin into which his father coughed his life away. Kang's only brother, Guangren, was born in July that same year, and seven months later their father was dead. Kang, the oldest surviving son, put his knowledge of Confucian rituals to practical use as he attended to his father's funeral; at the same time he became precociously aware of fine economic distinctions as he watched the family slide into genteel poverty.[5]

Through ceaseless historical and philosophical reading during his teens and early twenties, Kang developed a sublime self-confidence in his destiny and in his power to mold the future. He came to feel that he "stood, towering and lofty, above the common people," as he put it, "associating myself with the great and good men of the past,"[6] and began to believe it was his destiny to become one of the great sages of China. Particularly after his revered grandfather was accidentally drowned in 1877, and Kang undertook a prolonged period of study of Buddhist sutras, his introspection grew deeper: "For a whole month I stayed up all night and let my mind wander freely. I thought of heaven and of the world of men, of the greatest joy and of the greatest sorrow which I might experience as tests of my character. At first wild thoughts crowded my mind like demons, but later my nightmares ceased and I felt spiritually transcendent, carefree and at ease."[7] Such freedom brought a growing sense of social responsibility: "Thinking of the misery and hardship in the life of men, I believed that heaven had endowed me with the intelligence and ability to save them. I turned my thoughts toward commiserating and sympathizing with the people in society, and made it my mission to take part in worldly affairs."[8] In 1879 he was astonished during his first visit to Hong Kong (a British colony since 1842), especially by "the elegance of the buildings of the foreigners, the cleanliness of the streets, the efficiency of their police"; this positive impression of Western influence was bolstered by a visit to Shanghai, the booming cosmopolis that had been declared an international treaty port after China's defeat by the British in the Opium War of 1839–42, and Kang began to read Western scientific books in translation and to draft plans for saving China by applying Western political and economic concepts.[9]

Many Chinese scholars had been developing plans for such "self-strengthening" through partial adaptation of Western technology—military, industrial, and scientific—but Kang absorbed these initiatives and then moved past them into his own visionary realm. By the time of his journey to Beijing in 1895, he had formed an extraordinary blend of ideology and practice: he had written letters and drafted petitions urging railway development and military reform on the bureaucracy and the Emperor; he had protested the Empress Dowager Cixi's decision to spend money badly needed for China's military defense on her own palaces; he had developed local military organizations to repel bandits; he had organized societies to stop the practice of binding women's feet.* In a series of private academies that he founded—he was constantly looking for larger premises and shifting from street to street in Guangzhou until he acquired the space, the prestige, and the continuity he

---

* In foot-binding, first practiced in the eleventh century A.D., the feet of young girls were tightly strapped in cloth so that they would remain small. Tiny feet were regarded as erotically stimulating, and by the nineteenth century the custom had become common throughout China despite the pain it caused.

wanted by taking out a ten-year lease on a section of the Confucian temple—Kang had assembled around himself a group of dedicated students. These young men were instructed in a curriculum of Confucian learning that might, if pursued with application, bring them success in the national civil-service examinations; at the same time they helped Kang with the research on which he based his innovative and iconoclastic studies of the Confucian canon. This research, culminating in *A Study of Confucius as a Reformer*, a book that he drafted between 1886 and 1889, was designed to show among other things that buried inside the original texts written by Confucius before they had been adulterated by later hands was a faith in the need for change and development. Such an interpretation meant that the new institutional and scientific elements being introduced by the Western powers could be seen as having antecedents in the Chinese tradition, and thus need not be simply rejected out of hand in an attempt to preserve some original Chinese "purity."[10]

Though influential scholars in Guangzhou and elsewhere denounced these works in critiques that Kang described as "vicious and unbearable," his own students found him a brilliant and inspiring teacher, one who permanently changed their way of looking at the world. Kang, in turn, was eager for the prestige that accrued to him from these talented followers; he openly searched for men of resolution who would help him in his great task of "bringing his ideals to fruition," and he mourned those who died prematurely almost as if they had been members of his own family.[11] Together with his students he pursued a course of study that added Western sciences to the infrastructure of Confucian scholarship, and he encouraged a range of vivid speculations whose origins could be found in Buddhist doctrines and in the outer fringes of Western astronomy. Thus Kang Youwei's sense of the relativity of size (to which he was drawn by observations through a microscope) and his sense of the relativity of speed (to which he was drawn by study of electricity and the speed of light) led him to speculate on the possibilities of endless subdivision or endless expansion, to the infinite variety of things, and to what he called "the intermixture and interaction of primeval influences in which one can foresee the dawn of the millennium." He summarized the content of this teaching, and the private intellectual context within which he placed it, in a passage written at the end of 1895:

For the Way that we followed we took the primal force as the essence of all things, and the balances of *yin* and *yang* as defining their mode of operation. As all the basic principles of existence had their *yin* and *yang* characteristics, so in nature could one find eight basic correlations: in the atmosphere warmth and cold, in energy attraction and repulsion, in matter solids and fluids, in forms square and round shapes, in light white and black colors, in sound clear and harsh notes, in bodies male and female sexes, and in the soul its spiritual and its sentient components.

I believed that other worlds exist in other universes, in other galaxies—worlds like our earth, worlds that parallel our physical selves, worlds of the soul, and worlds within our blood corpuscles. These are the correlations of the worlds. Thus, when I discoursed on the world, I approached the topic in terms of courage, propriety, a sense of righteousness, wisdom, and benevolence; when I discoursed on the sages of the past, I approached the subject from the point of view of the Three Historical Levels; and when I looked to the future, I based my views on the concept of the Three Stages of Human Development. I made benevolence the center of my philosophy, which was to follow the will of heaven in bringing about unity on this earth by drawing together all nations, races, and religions. I also speculated on the changes in the speech, writing, food and drink, clothing, and housing of mankind after the world is united, on equality for men and women and universal laws for everyone, so that a paradise on earth for all men might be attained.

My speculations went further. I imagined what it would be like five hundred or a thousand years hence, what kind of future world it would be, what changes would have taken place in the soul of man, in human anatomy, in communications with the moon and the stars. I speculated on climates, objects, beings, governments and culture, rites, music and literature, dwellings, and food that might exist on other stars and in other worlds, and wondered whether distant universes would follow their natural courses or deviate, and whether they would live or die. My thoughts wandered far into the mystery and infinity of space and time. I gathered the deep and more abstruse statements in the classics and in other philosophic works, examined hidden meanings in Confucianism and Buddhism, studied new ideas developed in China and in the West, traced the evolution of man and nature, compared the tenets of various religions, pored over maps of the world, reviewed the present and the past in order to see the pattern of the future. . . .

Every day the salvation of society was uppermost in my thoughts, and every moment the salvation of society was my aim in life, and for this aim I determined to sacrifice myself. Since there were an infinite number of worlds, great and small, I could only console and try to save those on the world where I had been born, those I met along the way, those I had a chance to grow close to. Each day I would call to them and hope that they would listen to me. I made this my guiding principle and my goal.[12]

The thousands of other examination candidates who crowded to Beijing in the springtime of 1895 might not have shared the expansiveness of these long-range dreams for the world, but they did share with Kang Youwei a sense of urgency over China's predicament and a profound sense of humiliation and frustration. These men—ranging in age from their early twenties to their mid-fifties, for the highest levels of examinations often took decades to pass, and Kang Youwei as a candidate of thirty-seven would in no way have seemed old—had come of age in an era during which China was undergoing an apparently unending series of defeats. Before succumbing to the Japanese in 1894, Chinese forces had been defeated by the British in 1842, by the French and British jointly between 1856 and 1860, and by the French again in 1884. For more than thirty years officials eligible by rank to send in "memorials"—the carefully formulated state documents, transmitted to the Emperor, in which policy recommendations could be presented for possible implementation—had been suggesting various ways to meet the foreign threat. Some of these suggestions, having to do with arms manufacture, foreign-language training, the dispatch of students abroad, the development of steamships, had been carried through to a certain extent, even if grudgingly; but progress was slow, for though the traditional bureaucracy *could* adapt, it generally regarded change as detrimental to good order, and the Empress Dowager Cixi, who had acted as regent for fifteen years while her nephew Guangxu was reaching maturity, though eager to preserve the Manchu ruling house on the throne by strengthening its economic base and opposing the Western powers, could not afford to alienate the senior members of her bureaucracy, whether Chinese or Manchu.[13]

Yet however patient, or inhibited, this new generation of Confucian scholar-students might have been, they could not but react with amazement and anger when the terms of the peace treaty finally negotiated between China and Japan at Shimonoseki reached Beijing by telegram on April 15, 1895: China had been forced to cede both southern Manchuria and Taiwan to the Japanese, and had agreed to pay a colossal indemnity, equivalent to two hundred million ounces of silver. Japanese industries were also to be allowed into the rich Yangtze Valley area. Within hours of hearing this news, Kang Youwei and some close friends were circulating a petition urging rejection of the treaty; within days they had drafted a statement to the Emperor in the form of a memorial almost eighteen thousand characters long, cosigned with the names of more than a thousand examination candidates drawn from all eighteen provinces of China proper. The crowded meetings at a local temple in Beijing, the hurried lobbying with senior officials, the long lines of men patiently queuing outside the government bureaus to make their feelings known, the willingness of students to commit themselves in public to an antigovernment stance even while competing in the government exams— all these circumstances made it, in the words of one contemporary observer, an unprecedented example in China of patriotic and emotional expression. In his own memoirs, Kang noted that "to gather an assembly of more than a thousand men in this way was something that had never happened before in this dynasty." And Liang Qichao, a close friend and former student of Kang Youwei's, who had been with him on the steamer when it was boarded by the Japanese and who worked day and night for thirty-six hours making copies of the giant document, found that the whole direction of his life had changed; his brother wrote that "from that time onward one can say his student days were over."[14]

The document that Kang drafted was a cry for change, directed in part to the young Emperor Guangxu, in part to the Emperor's sixty-year-old aunt, the Empress Dowager Cixi, who held much of the real power in the state, and in part to the senior officials at the Qing dynasty court. What Kang Youwei and his cosigners were requesting—albeit in the most courteous language possible—was a complete transformation of China's economic and educational system. After reviewing the various defeats that had made China's nineteenth century so bleak, Kang pointed to China's own history for one encouraging sign to the future. In the past, he noted, the most skillful emperors had never regarded their country's laws and customs as frozen; on the contrary, the founders of the Han dynasty (in 206 B.C.), of the Ming dynasty (in A.D. 1368), and of the Qing dynasty (in the mid-seventeenth century) had all adjusted to new circumstances by establishing new institutions, and had employed new men drawn from outside conventional bureaucratic channels. The Japanese had acted similarly in their dramatic Meiji Restoration reforms of the 1860s and 1870s.

Such personnel and institutional flexibility would "arouse the country's spirits," wrote Kang; similarly, moving the capital away from Beijing would "strengthen the country's base." Beijing was hopelessly vulnerable, too near the sea to be easily defended, and hence constantly luring the emperors into making foolhardy concessions to foreign powers—"to preserve this insignificant ten-mile span of city we have given up thousands of miles of territory." Just as previous emperors had changed institutional modes, so had they changed their capitals when strategic considerations called for it. For the Qing court in the 1890s, of all the possible choices in the far north, the south, or the far west, the city of Xian in Shaanxi province seemed the best to Kang; in this inland center of power, once the base of the Qin dynasty (in the third century B.C.) and site of the great capital of Changan during the Sui and Tang dynasties (between the sixth and ninth centuries), the Chinese armies could muster in depth, and commerce and transportation routes could be reopened in naturally protected and distant fastnesses that Japanese troops would never dare to penetrate.[15]

In another section of the document, which Kang headed "Increasing the Country's Power," he urged a return to the ideal of the "people under arms" that had once been a feature of China's earlier regimes and was now the basis for success of the Western countries that bordered on the Atlantic. The Qing state needed a better regular army of strong young soldiers (as the Emperor Kangxi had suggested two centuries before, Kang noted), which could be combined with local militia forces into a truly effective military system. The troops of this revivified army should draw on the best military technology: Chinese infantry should have small arms and rifles such as the German Mauser, the French Chasseur, the British Martini gun, and the American Hotchkiss and Remington; Chinese artillery should have heavy guns made to the same standard as those manufactured by the Krupp company. What China could not initially manufacture herself she should purchase at intelligently competitive rates—for instance on the international Hong Kong arms market—rather than at inflated domestic prices. And the Chinese should be aware of how swiftly military technology changed: in the Franco-Prussian War of 1870–71, guns had been able to fire ten rounds a minute; by the time of the Russian clash with China in the 1880s, there were guns able to fire thirty rounds a minute; and now (as the Chinese had learned at their cost) the Japanese had guns that could fire sixty rounds a minute. If China herself could not muster enough technically skilled persons, then she should call on the four million Chinese who lived overseas in Southeast Asia—who felt China's humiliation all the more keenly for looking on from the outside, but remained Chinese at heart and would be eager to help her regain her lost prestige.[16]

These opening sections of the memorial must have been startling enough reading for conservative officials in the bureaucracy, even those who had known the various reformist arguments of the previous thirty years; but, Kang pointed out, they were really only preambles, temporary expedients proposed in response to enemy pressure. The only hope for China's future lay in a full "self-strengthening program" that would reform the basic governmental structures of the country. "When objects get old, they break. When institutions get old, they are corrupted." Therefore the Emperor must move boldly in at least six areas of fundamental importance. First, the Qing government must increase taxes and raise more domestic revenue. The current government receipts were at the level of only seventy million ounces of silver a year. Such a sum was quite inadequate—it would take every ounce of the current seventy-million-a-year income for three years just to pay off the Japanese indemnity demands from the last war, for example. By drawing on rich gentry households and merchants, by developing state banks and extending transport systems, there was no reason that China's revenues could not exceed a hundred million ounces of silver a year. Second, China must develop a national railway network—for national defense, to open up border regions, and to stimulate commerce. Third, the Qing government must encourage the machine industry and develop shipping. Fourth, China must exploit her own vast mineral resources—the copper of Yunnan, the coal and iron fields of Shanxi and Guizhou, the lead in Shandong and Hubei, the tin in Jiangxi and Hunan, the many resources of Sichuan—for "if we don't open them up, then others will." Fifth, the Chinese currency system must be unified and stabilized; and sixth, an effective national postal system must be set up.[17]

At this point Kang interjected a note of caution. These six reforms would strengthen the nation, he said, but of themselves they could not alleviate the suffering of the Chinese poor.

> China's population was more than four hundred million in the Daoguang reign [1820–50], and in the several decades of prosperity since then,* the population has increased further. Yet our industry and trade have not flourished; the people's lives have grown harder and more constricted; some have emigrated to other countries, there to live as slaves, and others have stayed but have become thugs who prey upon the local villages. Even though the foreigners are not now attacking, our internal troubles are serious. Our nation is founded upon people—if we cannot think how to foster those people, then we ourselves destroy our own foundation.[18]

---

* A rather euphemistic remark in view of the civil and foreign wars that had wracked the Qing since 1839.

Thus Kang led into the last part of his memorial, which he described as a four-part program for "helping the people's livelihood." In agriculture, he saw the need for much greater sophistication if China was to do well in a competitive world market where even Chinese staples such as silk were being challenged by Italian, French, and Japanese manufactures, while tea was being produced with success in India and Ceylon. China needed to set up agricultural societies and training schools to develop higher levels of rural skill, to diversify further into forestry and fisheries, and to investigate new products. In industry, the Chinese must learn from the Western development of steamboats, rails, and telegraphs, which had so boosted Western power in the previous decades—and must transcend the fairly limited interest in innovations that had been expressed by such Confucian statesmen as Zeng Guofan in the 1860s and 1870s, and instead concentrate on building centers for advanced training in modern technology. These centers, in turn, would draw on students well educated in mathematics and mechanics. The constructive interaction of ingenuity and education could most graphically be seen in the United States, where thirteen thousand patents a year were issued for new industrial inventions, as opposed to the hundred or so issued in Russia.[19]

As to foreign trade, obviously China had to meet the competition from the West and Japan by developing her own products, by boosting indigenous Chinese trading companies, studying Western mercantile methods, translating Western commercial texts, and developing the teaching of "merchant skills." China could not forever use the excuse of the deleterious opium trade to explain her ineffectiveness in current markets, since imported textiles accounted for far more of China's adverse payments balance than opium itself. In a kind of hymn to Western technology, unprecedented in any Chinese official document, Kang listed for the Emperor some examples of what China was buying from the West in the 1890s:

> In addition to the fifty-three million ounces of silver we
> spend on foreign cottons, we buy such items of ordinary
> use as heavy silk, satins, woolens, fine silks, gauze, and felt;

umbrellas, lamps, paint, suitcases and satchels; chinaware, toothbrushes, toothpowder, soap, and lamp oil. Among co-mestibles we buy coffee, Philippine and Havana cigars, cig-arettes and rolling paper, snuff, and liquor; ham, dried meats, cake, candy, and salt; and medicines—liquid, pills, powders—as well as dried and fresh fruit. We also buy coal, iron, lead, copper, tin, and other materials; wooden utensils, clocks, watches, sundials, thermometers, barome-ters, electric lamps, plumbing accessories, mirrors, photo-graphic plates, and other amusing or ingenious gadgets. As more households get them, more people want them, so that they have reached as far as Xinjiang and Tibet.

China must stem this spending by developing her own indus-trial base.[20]

In suggesting plans for helping the rural poor in China, Kang cited a number of foreign examples—from Siberia to Missis-sippi, Borneo, Brazil, and Canada—as he looked to resettle-ment programs (whether penal and compulsory, or voluntary and commercially motivated) that would induce the Chinese to colonize their own frontier areas. Such a policy would reverse the pattern of overseas emigration among China's very poor, which had led to the exploitation of coolie labor in the United States* and to the eviction of other Chinese from their homes and jobs in Australia and Southeast Asia. For the criminals, there should be rehabilitation through work training, and for the disabled or seriously diseased, a system of hospices.

Kang's lengthy document closed—as was fitting for an exam-ination candidate—with a broad overview of problems in Chi-nese education, from the stilted formalization of examination prose to the low appropriations for library budgets. Again, he drew on many examples from foreign states—India, England, Bismarck's Germany, Japan—but as if realizing that too many of his arguments drew on foreign examples, Kang included a ringing reaffirmation of Confucian moral values and their cru-cial importance to the survival of a vigorous China. Kang, a brilliant Confucian scholar himself (albeit one known to be

---

* The first restrictive action against the immigration of Chinese laborers into the United States had been taken by President Chester A. Arthur in 1882, and had been renewed in stronger terms by President Benjamin Harrison in 1892.

both iconoclastic and eccentric), even suggested that the Emperor encourage the sending of eminent Confucian scholars to the West—thus reversing the apparently inexorable flow of Western missionaries bent on converting the Chinese to Christianity. Though Kang probably was not aware of it, a similar suggestion had been made by Leibniz almost exactly two hundred years earlier, in the full flush of his enthusiasm for Chinese Confucian values. Kang went beyond Leibniz, however, in suggesting that the Chinese not only spread the teaching of the Confucian Way but also seek to establish major Confucian academies overseas—any scholar attracting over a thousand students to such an institution should be rewarded, he thought, with hereditary noble rank.[21]

This outspoken and original document had a checkered life. The powerful official Sun Yuwen, who in 1895 was concurrently a grand councilor and president of the Board of War, was a backer of ratification of the treaty with Japan and also, allegedly, a leader among the corrupt elements in the bureaucracy. He actively spoke out against the student signatories of Kang's memorial, and sent his agents to stir up rumors among the students to inhibit them from signing; he also ordered large placards criticizing those who opposed the treaty to be conspicuously posted around Beijing. Thus when Kang presented his memorial at the Censorate office on May 2—this being the office that could forward his document to the Emperor—the staff there refused to accept it for transmittal. However, the signatories were apparently not directly penalized, since many of them did pass the senior examinations—along with Kang Youwei—even though their names were known to the authorities; and at the end of May, Kang resubmitted an amplified version of the same memorial. This time it reached the Emperor, who read it in early June and ordered copies made and circulated among his senior advisers; he also sent a copy to the Empress Dowager and ordered one to be kept on file in the Throne Hall. Buoyed by this favorable reception, Kang submitted yet another massive reform memorial in July, but after a series of delaying maneuvers by conservative officials it was effectively blocked and never reached the Emperor.

Kang stayed on in Beijing for three more months, continuing

to press for modernization and reform in any way he could: he printed a newssheet for circulation among senior officials in the capital, giving information on foreign educational, military, and political events; he founded a Society for the Study of National Strengthening; he had a lengthy interview with the Emperor's tutor, believed to be a backer of reform; he met with the influential British missionary-reformer Timothy Richard; he collected foreign books from the British and American ministers in Beijing; and he dispatched a friend to buy more Western materials in Shanghai, having discovered to his disgust that there was not a single good map of the world for sale in the Beijing bookstore district. Unexceptionable as these activities may sound, they were unpopular in many political circles, and Kang was eventually forced to leave Beijing in October under mounting threats of being prosecuted as a troublemaker. As for observable practical achievement in Beijing during these busy months, only one suggestion initiated by Kang managed to travel through all the bureaucratic channels and actually get implemented: Kang had noted the filthy and unkempt condition of the Beijing streets (indeed had graphically reported on the corpses of famine victims and beggars one found there), and he finally got a detailed memorial on this subject submitted to the Emperor. The Emperor authorized repairs, but the order was held up in committee at the Board of Works, which had jurisdiction over such matters; when they grudgingly released it, it was held up again by a local official in the Censorate; when action at last was taken, only one small section outside the Xuanwu Gate was in fact repaired.[22]

One other of Kang's ideas was picked up in a rather unlikely fashion, however, by a man whom Kang disliked intensely and had branded as one of the "most arrogant men in the government"; this was the censor Chu Chengbo. Chu, presumably influenced by Kang's ideas for using the overseas Chinese to serve the state, sent in a memorial in July 1895 asking the Emperor to permit Chinese traders to take over the various arsenals and dockyards that the government had built over the past thirty years, so that they would be run on innovative and commercial lines. In an enthusiastic response of August 1895, the Emperor said that the Chinese in Southeast Asia, Australia, and the western United States should be permitted to form syndicates to take over such operations, either by buying leases to the government enterprises or by buying the enterprises outright. They would also be permitted to establish new plants if they so chose, borrowing Chinese government funds for the purpose. "Everything is to be done after the manner of foreign countries," explained the Emperor, "where the mercantile and trading classes are permitted to do as they please." Though the idea of using overseas Chinese to help the state was not a totally new one, such dramatic and enthusiastic espousal of it was highly unusual; in ensuing years the Qing court began to woo the overseas Chinese systematically, bringing in large influxes of foreign capital to develop nascent Chinese industries.[23]

A very different approach to the overseas Chinese was that taken by Sun Yatsen. Eight years Kang's junior, Sun was also born near Guangzhou, but to economic and social circumstances that were worlds away from Kang's. Sun grew up in a peasant family, in a densely populated area where land was scarce and the living hard. From here, Chinese had been emigrating in large numbers to Southeast Asia and the United States for nearly half a century; two of Sun's uncles had died in California during the gold rush, and his elder brother had emigrated to Hawaii. Since Sun's own father was making a precarious living by combining jobs as an agricultural laborer, a tailor, and a village watchman, Sun Yatsen was sent to Hawaii, where his brother had prospered and become an influential businessman. Thus it was that Sun, who would have had no chance of a decent education had he stayed in Guangdong province, was enrolled in the British-run Iolani School, whence he moved to Oahu College; in 1886 he left Hawaii and returned to study Western medicine, first in Guangzhou under an American doctor and afterward with the British in Hong Kong.[24]

By the time of the Sino-Japanese War, Sun had developed into a polyglot hybrid: only partially educated in the Chinese classics, he was a skillful surgeon, a baptized Christian who knew how to speak English and to play cricket, and he had built up a wide circle of acquaintances among the semi-Westernized Chinese of Hawaii, Hong Kong, and Macao, and among Western doctors and missionaries, while still keeping close to his own kith and kin among the farming people of Guangdong. Though his experiences ended by making him react violently against the religious superstitions of his native village—he had even, in iconoclastic zeal, desecrated the local temple during one visit at home—he was eager to apply his new-won skills to helping China. Convinced that Western power sprang from an imaginative use of human talent in conjunction with free trade and exploitation of natural resources, rather than merely from ships and guns, Sun had written a lengthy memorandum on the subject, which he tried to present to an influential official in 1894. But the official, distracted by the outbreak of war with Japan, had rebuffed him. By the end of 1894, accordingly, Sun was disgusted with the Manchu court's weakness in opposing the Japanese, impressed with British efficiency and sense of purpose, and utterly unsure of the course he should himself pursue.

While Kang Youwei had concluded that he should concentrate on persuading the Emperor to press through reforms, and thus make China strong while also preserving the Manchu dynasty, Sun Yatsen took an utterly different approach, and decided that the Manchu regime would have to be overthrown before China could become strong. In November 1894, as a first step toward achieving that overthrow, Sun founded a small revolutionary group in Hawaii which he named the Revive China Society. Dedicated to the goal of ousting the Manchus and adapting Western scientific and industrial skills to strengthen the nation, the society also had a broadly republican aim, though this was not strongly emphasized in Sun's first manifestos. (Sun was perhaps influenced here by the example of Hawaii, which had become a republic in the summer of 1894.[25]) By the summer of 1895, Sun had attracted about one hundred and twenty recruits, who paid five dollars each in initiation fees, and gathered another seven hundred dollars or so by selling "revolutionary bonds" that he promised to redeem at ten times the face value once a rising against the Manchus had succeeded. A few other members sold off shops or land, and he could expect some further aid from his brother, yet it seems an absurdly tiny base from which to launch a rebellion.

Sun seems to have counted largely on the support of members of secret societies. These semisecret or secret organizations in China, bonded by religious, economic, and localistic ties, and sometimes engaged in illicit or criminal activities, were pledged—by long-standing tradition—to expulsion of the foreigners (be they Manchu or Western) and to the restoration of Chinese sovereignty. The societies had become particularly promising allies by mid-1895 because many of their members had been recruited into the Qing armies and thrown into the war with Japan. Now demobilized, often with months of pay in arrears, they formed a reservoir of semitrained, disaffected, and volatile manpower. Coordinating his plans with a handful of secret-society leaders from a base in Hong Kong, aided by six members of the Revive China Society who had followed him from Hawaii, Sun laid his dramatic plans for an October rising in Guangzhou, which would spread across China, forcing the collapse of the Manchus and the establishment of a Chinese Republic. The Qing officials in Guangzhou learned of the projected coup and rounded up and executed many of the conspirators before a shot had been fired. Sun escaped and fled first to Macao and then to Hong Kong; pressured by the Qing, the British ordered him to leave, and he moved on to Japan, to Hawaii, and in the summer of 1896 (furnished now with false papers which stated that he had been born in Hawaii), to San Francisco to seek more funds and recruits.[26]

Kang Youwei was back in Guangzhou by November 1895, but he did not refer to Sun's abortive rising either in his writings or in any conversations that have been recorded. Instead he put the finishing touches to his *Study of Confucius as a Reformer* and embarked on a series of new projects, one being a book on the Meiji reforms in Japan, the other an elaborate scheme to open up a "new China" in Brazil—which, covering latitudes similar to China's and being comparatively underpopulated, seemed to Kang an ideal future homeland for Chinese emigrants.[27] He visited Hong Kong with his younger brother, Guangren, and founded a reform magazine in Macao; he traveled to the western province of Guangxi, where he tried and failed to interest the officials in the city of Guilin in constructing modern streets; he returned to Beijing and founded a study society for natives of Guangdong resident in Beijing and persuaded the government to donate books on various modern topics to it; responding to the latest military and diplomatic disaster for China, in which the Germans had seized the Shandong city of Jiaozhou as a naval base, Kang and some friends formed the Know Our Humiliation Society; having come to admire the efficiency of the Japanese and the power of the British, he suggested to the court a grand alliance of China, Japan, and Britain that would resist further Russian and German advances; and with friends in Beijing he drafted proposals to bring economics and the natural sciences into the curriculum of the state examination structure.[28]

The life of reading and argument had its occasional bursts of excitement. With only one day's notice, for example, in January 1898 Kang was summoned to appear before some of the most powerful officials in the empire to explain his views on the need for institutional reforms. The interview began inauspiciously when one of the senior Manchu officials present said firmly, "The laws of the ancestors cannot be changed." Kang, according to his own account, responded, "The laws of the ancestors were designed for the administration of the land of the ancestors. Now if we cannot even defend the land of the ancestors, how can we talk of their laws?"[29] Kang outlined his views for fiscal and educational reforms at some length, and was told to write them out formally. The finished document was finally submitted to the Emperor Guangxu in March. As the court struggled with new foreign threats—the British were now demanding a base at Weihaiwei in northern Shandong, the Russians the two harbors of Dalian and Port Arthur in southern Manchuria—Kang's suggestions were sidetracked; so he filled the time by planning to organize the candidates who had once again gathered for the triennial examinations in Beijing. With the help of his brother, Guangren, and his able student and friend Liang Qichao, he formed in Beijing the Society to Preserve the Nation, which was harassed by unsympathetic officials but received new life when the Emperor heard of it and expressed his belief in its patriotic intent. But Kang grew convinced that there was little more to be achieved in the capital and in mid-June 1898 made ready to return home to his students in Guangzhou.

Kang always tried to accept life's sudden dissonances, and was fatalistic about change; he had written once: "I said to myself if things were proceeding too easily, something untoward was bound to happen."[30] So now, just as he was about to leave, he received a letter from his daughter in Guangzhou warning him that there was an epidemic near his home and he would do better to stay on a few days in Beijing. His departure delayed by that crucial moment, there came an edict summoning him to appear in audience with the Emperor at the Summer Palace. As he told his daughter in a hurried letter, in which he sent a hundred dollars to be shared with his wife and family and referred to a similar incident that had occurred the year before: "Last year when I was ready to come home, it was the First Minister who detained me; this year, it is the Emperor. How truly strange!"[31]

Kang's June audience with the Emperor Guangxu made a deep impression on him, and he was henceforth never to waver in his affection and admiration for this ruler, even though Guangxu as a Manchu might more logically have been associated with the whole corrupt and ineffective Manchu court, which many Chinese besides Sun Yatsen were beginning to feel had to be overthrown before China could regain her rightful place in the world. But Kang felt that Guangxu had reached out to him personally, and that in doing so he had had the courage to defy his aunt, the Empress Dowager Cixi, who had seemed consistently opposed to modernization and reform. Thus for Kang it was undoubtedly also symbolically significant that the audience took place in the Summer Palace, west of Beijing, rather than in the Forbidden City. For the new Summer Palace rose near the site of the old one, which had been destroyed by British and French troops when they occupied Beijing in 1860, as a reprisal for the Chinese murder and detention of their diplomatic envoys; to raise the money to rebuild the palace complex the Empress Dowager had plunged into debt and mortgaged desperately needed revenues. Kang's opening remarks to the Emperor Guangxu could not have been more apposite in this locale, as he described the problems confronting China:

> It is like a large building that, because its timbers have decayed, is about to fall down. If small patches are made to cover up the cracks, then as soon as there is a storm the building will collapse. It is therefore necessary to dismantle the building and build anew if we want something strong and dependable. To lay a foundation, the area of the land, the height of the building to be constructed, the number of bricks and tiles, the sizes of the windows, doors, and balustrades, the amount of plaster, nails, bamboo, and other items must all be planned and estimated as parts of the overall design before purchasing the materials and hiring the laborers. This is the only way that a building can be constructed. If any one part of the general plan is neglected, the building cannot be properly constructed; and even if constructed, it cannot resist a storm.[32]

In the two and a half hours that followed, Kang repeated the substance of his 1895 memorial, adding the thought that there would have to be widespread changes in government personnel if reform was to go forward; using the present officials, with their outdated education and lack of sensitivity to reform, would be "like climbing a tree to catch fish."[33]

After the audience, Kang wrote a brief, excited letter to his mother, emphasizing how rare it was for someone of his junior status ever to see the Emperor: "To be received in audience! There has been nothing like this since the 1850s. I have been away from home six months and I think often of you and regret our separation, but am sure when you hear this news it will be some consolation. And what comes next? If I do not come home but am kept in Beijing, then I will have you come here. I am really fine!—as is Guangren, who is also here and very well."[34]

At about the same time he took his brother, Guangren, for a long walk in the beautiful Western Hills near Beijing to think through the options before them. The relations between the two had always been close, ever since Kang Youwei at ten years old had begun to look after the seven-month-old in response to his father's deathbed wish. He had seen the young boy through a childhood plagued by many illnesses, and helped with his education; then watched him develop into an outspoken young man never afraid to "shout aloud" the truth as he saw it. Guangren had studied Western medicine at the Anglo-American hospital in Guangzhou (where Sun Yatsen had worked for a while) before proceeding to try to open a medical school of his own in Shanghai. Guangren was very much a man of the new China that Kang was hoping to build, in that he was at once a hard worker and an idealist, although he did not share his elder brother's interest in political activity.[35] The two men were aware of their fairly dangerous situation: it was obvious that conservative forces were prepared to oppose the Emperor, and there were disquieting evidences that the Empress Dowager might launch a countercoup. She had maneuvered to have one of her close associates put in command of extra troops in northern China, for one thing, and the Emperor's reform-minded former tutor had been forced out of office. Kang himself was dogged by threats of assassination and was constantly spied on. A flurry of letters between Guangren and other members of the Kang family suggests that they may have been planning a possible escape route to Macao if things got too dangerous. They were also in touch with Chinese friends living in Victoria, Canada.[36]

The sequel to the imperial audience must have astonished Kang. For in a dizzy spate of reform activity during the summer of 1898—often following the exact recommendations made by Kang, to whom he had given an official appointment as secretary in one of the Beijing bureaus—the Emperor issued edicts abolishing the formalistic "eight-legged essay" system, establishing a national university, converting local temples into schools, setting up one group of local bureaus to develop Qing commerce and others to develop agriculture and industry. Kang urged the Emperor onward by summarizing in book form the startling achievements of the Meiji Emperor in stimulating Japan's modernization; as a counterexample he explained how the Polish court, utterly misled by foolish conservatives (in

Kang's reading), had finally seen their country partitioned by Russia, Prussia, and Austria.[37] As the reforms were promulgated, advice poured in to the Emperor. Kang wrote with amusement but also with obvious approval of the Qing dynasty equivalent to the "big-character posters" that were to dominate a later revolutionary age; among the messages reaching the court, he wrote, "some were by country folk and fishermen, written on sheets of paper two feet high," but the Emperor merely smiled at this gracelessness and read them all the same; Kang also applauded the Emperor's refusal even to censure those who criticized the imperial person, since "having opened up the way for public opinion to reach the throne, it would not be right to reprimand them and so block their views."[38]

With the rapid promulgation of these new policies the Emperor needed new men to help him; innovative senior appointments might have been blocked in the bureaucracy (with or without the Empress Dowager's pressure), but Guangxu avoided this particular confrontation by appointing several young reformers as secretaries in the central policy-planning office known as the Grand Council. Here, though their nominal rank was not high, they would be ready for consultation when required, just as Kang Youwei was. Among these new appointees was the twenty-three-year-old chairman of the Reform Society in Kang Youwei's home province of Guangdong; another, Tan Sitong, aged thirty-three, was an outstanding scholar and philosopher and a student of the martial arts, who had developed a deep interest in Western science and mathematics. Tan was an admirer of Kang Youwei and a friend of Kang's student Liang Qichao, and he had been instrumental in setting up reform societies and newspapers in Hunan province, where he had helped to make the city of Changsha a center of innovative thinking. He had great prestige among the younger radicals but was suspect to older officials in Hunan because of his outspokenness and the irregular pattern his career had followed.[39]

By the time Tan received the Emperor's summons and made the long journey from Hunan province to Beijing, it was already September, and the reforms that he had hoped to assist the Emperor in implementing had begun to arouse more and more opposition, both in Beijing and in the provinces. Tan had referred to the timing of the Emperor's invitation as being like "life revealing itself when one is despairing unto death," but both he and his young colleagues had no sense of how to proceed in the complex world of imperial politics; Kang Youwei himself worried that the whole reform group were too frail to bear the burdens placed on their shoulders.[40] Driven to panic by the opposition they were encountering, and more and more fearful that the Empress Dowager might move against them and the Emperor, they tried to preempt her by staging a coup of their own. In assessing the potential loyalties of certain senior military officers in the case of a showdown between the Emperor and the Empress Dowager, the reformers were taking the gravest risks of being betrayed and charged with treason should things go awry. Anticipating the worst, Kang tried to persuade the Emperor to leave Beijing, on the pretext of making an inspection tour of his domain. Beijing, wrote Kang, was a city "with walls that are crumbling, air filled with dust, the water of its springs polluted, its inner pulses ravaged, its once-regal spirit vanished." The capital's conservative atmosphere, the presence of large numbers of ineffective but still dangerous troops, the many officials whose livelihoods were threatened by any attempt to streamline bureaucracy and cut sinecures— all made change difficult. The Emperor should therefore move—not to Xian in the west, as Kang had suggested in 1895, but to Shanghai. For Shanghai, though it was a center of Western power, was a vast and bustling entrepôt, a center for technical change and new ideas, a place, as Kang told the Emperor, that was "open and untrammeled."[41]

Before any such elaborate plans could be carried out, the opposition struck back. Troops led by officers loyal to the Empress Dowager moved on Beijing; secretly warned by friends, Kang fled to Tianjin on September 20, 1898, and thence—on a British ship—to Shanghai and Hong Kong. The Emperor was placed under arrest on an island in the palace grounds on the twenty-first. That same afternoon, Beijing police surrounded the Guangdong provincial club, where Kang and many of his Guangzhou friends had often stayed; finding Kang gone, they arrested his younger brother, Guangren. On the twenty-second, Kang's close friend Liang Qichao, having tried unsuccessfully to get help from the Japanese legation for the Kang faction, escaped from Beijing and was taken aboard the Japanese cruiser *Ōshima*; later that day the city was cordoned off and further escape routes closed. On the twenty-fourth, Tan Sitong, having refused to leave Beijing in words that later became famous to the generations of new China—"I wanted to kill the robbers, but lacked the strength to transform the world. This is the place where I should die. Rejoice, rejoice!"—and having tried to rescue the Emperor from his palace prison by means of local swordsmen-braves, was also arrested. Kang's younger brother, Guangren, together with Tan Sitong and four other young reformers selected from those who had been rounded up in Beijing, were given a cursory trial on September 27 on treason charges of having tried to incite a military coup. At four o'clock the trial was interrupted by an order—presumably from the Empress Dowager—for their immediate execution. The six were beheaded that evening.[42]

"I lost a wing," wrote Kang Youwei, in anguish at his brother's death.[43] We can only guess at the extent of his grief, which was compounded by many elements: Kang had obviously asked his younger brother to stay on in Beijing, apparently hoping Guangren would pack up the books and personal property Kang himself had had to leave behind in his hurried flight—at the very best interpretation this was a betrayal of his childhood promise to his father to look after Guangren; Kang's carelessness in having Guangren associated with his own extremist image was also a contributing factor; furthermore Guangren's death was pointless in the worst sense, a random casualty on a revolutionary course that was not yet clearly charted; Guangren had been involved only peripherally, if at all, in any activities against the state. When Guangren died, at the age of thirty, leaving an eight-year-old daughter and no son, Kang, who had no son, either, became the only surviving male in the main family line. In a brief, bitter poem of regret (which despite the anguish of the context is larded with classical allusions to earlier palace coups), Kang further lamented that he had not even been able to give his brother a decent burial:

> You kicked in the palace door in broad daylight,
>   they cordoned off the city:
> At the execution grounds blood spurted on court robes.
> For a hundred years in the night rain your spirit will grieve
> And, tragically, be untended on Qing Mountain.[44]

There was no way that Kang, preoccupied with his own survival and the safety of the rest of his family, could get his brother's body from Beijing—a loyal servant from the Guangdong provincial club roughly sewed the head back on to the body and gave the corpse a temporary burial. Kang's wife, his secondary consort, and his daughters, warned by a telegram from Beijing, had managed to reach Macao on September 25; other friends got his mother to Hong Kong on the twenty-seventh, and Guangren's widow and daughter joined her three days later. All the Kang family holdings and houses, and Kang's own splendid library, were confiscated by the state. Of the family's melancholy reunion, Kang wrote a month later: "My mother and her maid were crying softly, overcome by sadness and anxiety. When I saw her, I told her that I had been both unfilial and unable to save China, and I had placed her in grave danger. Although by the grace of heaven she was now safe, I had still caused her considerable grief. My unfilial act reached up to heaven."[45] In a strangely successful act of deception, designed to spare his mother even greater grief, Kang and his family concealed her son Guangren's death from her, and she was persuaded to believe that he had become a monk and withdrawn from the world.[46]

Even after this disastrous series of catastrophes to himself, his immediate family, and his Emperor, Kang seems to have kept his hopes high, and he was buoyed up by the hospitable welcome (backed by cash gifts) that he received from wealthy Chinese sympathizers in Hong Kong. In October 1898 he was further cheered by a telegram from the Japanese prime minister, Ōkuma Shigenobu, inviting him to Japan and offering him assistance; this heightened Kang's admiration for the country that had defeated his own, which itself shows how easily the reformers were able to separate out aspects of modernization from elements of nationalism when they chose to do so. Sun Yatsen, who was in Japan at this time, endeavored to set up a meeting with Kang Youwei, but Kang turned down the opportunity, presumably to underline the fact that he considered himself still a loyal minister of the Emperor Guangxu, whereas Sun, by his actions in 1895, had proved to be an insurrectionary.

Yet if Kang had hoped to receive Japanese backing at the highest level for his plans to restore the Manchu Emperor to active power, such expectations were shattered when the Ōkuma ministry fell on October 31, five days after his own arrival in Japan.[47] So in the spring of 1899 Kang set sail from Yokohama on a Japanese ship, with the long-range goal of getting to Washington and persuading President McKinley to restore the Emperor. Since he was not able to get permission to travel in the United States, however—the American authorities wanted an official guarantee of Kang's character, which of course the Qing were not about to give—he landed at the port of Victoria, in Canada. The lieutenant governor of British Columbia gave him an interview, the Chinese community in Vancouver was warmly welcoming, the prime minister gave him tea in Ottawa, and Canada's governor-general, the Earl of Minto, invited him to a ball. Yet it soon became apparent that the Canadians were in no position to offer Kang any substantive help; nor, it turned out, would the British, though Kang's visit to London (where he arrived at the end of May) had the effect of getting a motion concerning British intervention in China brought up before the House of Commons by Sir Charles Dilke, leader of the Liberals. After eight hours of lively debate, in which some members of Parliament described the Empress Dowager and her cohorts as "corrupt and besotted individuals" while others were influenced by charges that Kang himself had been guilty of "injudicious conduct," and the strategic need to hold Russian ambitions in the Far East in check through a strong, modernized China was carefully considered, the motion was defeated by only fourteen votes.[48]

Thus ended Kang's search for international backing at the highest level. He was now seriously short of funds, and had no choice but to turn to the overseas Chinese community and walk the sometimes demeaning and always demanding path of revolutionary fund-raising that Sun Yatsen had been treading for three years. Kang returned to Canada from England in the summer of 1899 in a sober mood. He was able to settle comfortably in Victoria, where he founded his own group—named, after much debate among his supporters, the Society to Protect the Emperor, to highlight its goal of supporting Emperor Guangxu in his attempt to establish a modernizing constitutional monarchy. But Kang could not ignore the commercial interests of most of his backers, and the constitution of the society was also geared to the goal of developing and protecting Chinese business groups overseas. Nor, indeed, could Kang afford to ignore the close-knit ties of Chinese overseas brotherhoods (the so-called tongs, with which Sun Yatsen had already established contact during his travels in 1896). The Canadian groups had close ties with the Chinese in the United States, since they were experts at running illegal Chinese immigrants across the border in defiance of the American exclusion laws—thus Kang accepted the designation as a "dragon head" of the powerful Elder Brothers' Society, and received more than seven thousand dollars in donations and the use of an island retreat.[49]

It had been an extraordinary introduction to life in those foreign nations which he had admired and written about for so long, and to those overseas Chinese whose industry he had believed must be harnessed by the Qing state. In a poem written in Canada on the August 1899 celebration of the imprisoned Emperor's birthday, Kang caught many elements of his and China's paradoxical plight:

Far across the seas we celebrate Your Majesty's birthday,
The dragon banner unfurls above the white men's buildings.
White people, clinking their glasses, assemble grandly beside us;
While the yellow race squeeze, with lighted lanterns, through
    narrow lanes.

The lord on high grants You life, and has pity on us here below.
A petty official, prostrate, in tears, lies in bitter obscurity.
From this distant Canadian island I gaze toward Beijing:
Waves around the Emperor's palace-prison; how often I return
* in my dreams.*[50]

·2·

VISIONS AND VIOLENCE

By the late 1890s the frustration and anger expressed in 1895 by the sons of the elite had spread outward and downward through Chinese society. In the process, important values had shifted. Though the need for national regeneration was clear, there was a growing hostility to Western or Westernized-Japanese modes, especially among those Chinese who felt that foreigners not only had brought commercial and territorial demands but also had corroded the moral atmosphere of China. Foremost among the corroders, they believed, were Christian missionaries, who had followed hard on the heels of opium traders and foreign troops. This anti-Christian sentiment, coupled with anger at the persistent Western incursions into northern China in 1898, was woven through with strands of Chinese martial-arts and folk-religious traditions to produce the phenomenon known as the Boxers. Starting in the provinces of Shandong and Hebei, surreptitiously backed by the very government officials who were meant to suppress them, and then openly endorsed by the Manchu ruling house they had initially claimed they wished to overthrow, the Boxers burst into violent activity in 1900, sacking churches and killing missionaries and their Chinese converts; in June their forces converged in a protracted siege of the foreign diplomatic legation quarter in Beijing, which lasted until allied troops entered the city in mid-August.

Both Kang Youwei and Sun Yatsen saw these upheavals as

offering a good environment for the realization of their own ambitions. Early in 1900 Kang Youwei, who had left Canada and, after brief visits to Japan and Hong Kong, was now settled among some of his wealthy backers in Singapore, was deeply alarmed by new rumors that the Empress Dowager Cixi was again planning to debar the ousted Emperor Guangxu forever from his throne and to install a younger Manchu prince in his place. Kang mobilized the support of tens of thousands of overseas Chinese through his Society to Protect the Emperor to deluge the court in Beijing with telegrams of protest. In the spring of 1900, after protracted correspondence with Liang Qichao and other supporters in Southeast Asia, Canada, and the United States, as well as with friends within China (the offices of a Shanghai photographic-supply store were used as a front through which mail could pass from Kang to his collaborators on the mainland), Kang determined to attempt an armed insurrection. A sense of urgency was added to his planning by the fear that Sun Yatsen might manage a successful rising of his own in Guangdong province; to counteract this, Kang decided to launch a series of coordinated risings at Hankou (in the Yangtze River tri-city area known as Wuhan) and in Anhui province. Liang Qichao, who had been cautious about the feasibility of such a rising—he had written to Kang that he "wished to fly, but had no wings"—was reassured by the fact that some major secret-society leaders within China had shifted their allegiance from Sun to Kang, apparently encouraged by the news of the enormous gifts (in excess of three hundred thousand dollars) that overseas Chinese had made available to Kang.[1]

As his choice to lead the risings, Kang settled on the Hunanese reformer Tang Caichang, who had been a close friend of Tan Sitong's and had worked with Liang and some of the martyred 1898 reformers on a range of educational projects. Tang agreed to work with Kang, although he had a difficult time reconciling local goals and revolutionary aspirations with Kang's continually stated aim to preserve and restore the Emperor Guangxu to power, especially since both the Emperor and the Empress Dowager had fled to Xian in northwestern China as the Boxer crisis spread; in the event, Kang Youwei's lack of ex-

perience led to Tang's downfall, for desperately needed supplies and funds, which were allegedly going to be smuggled
into China via a dummy hardware company in Hong Kong and
the revolutionary associate's photography shop in Shanghai,
never materialized. In early August, after the Anhui groups rebelled—without orders—ahead of the scheduled zero hour, the
entire plot rapidly unraveled. On August 21, thirty of the Hankou leaders, including Tang Caichang, were arrested before firing a shot, and summarily executed by the Qing authorities.[2]

Even while Kang's supporters were being rounded up and
executed in Hankou, Sun Yatsen was proceeding with his own
plans for another armed uprising, in the area of Huizhou, one
hundred and fifty miles east of Guangzhou. Ever since the de-
bacle of his 1895 Guangzhou uprising, Sun had been working
ceaselessly to strengthen his base of support among overseas
Chinese and among the secret societies inside China. He had
been greatly aided in this task by the attempt made by the staff
of the Qing legation in London during 1896 to kidnap him
during one of his fund-raising trips to that city, and to ship him
back to China for trial and certain execution. This episode,
which Sun only narrowly escaped, brought him worldwide
publicity when it was recounted in the British press, and effectively made up for whatever humiliation he had suffered the
year before. Sun also benefited from this period in London by
embarking on a wide course of reading in the British Museum,
during which he laid the groundwork for a more systematic
ideology for his Revive China Society that was to take him beyond the basic goals of anti-Manchuism and republicanism toward a policy aimed at preventing the formation of great
monopolistic landholdings in China. (Sun was especially influenced by the socialist tax-equalization and land-redistribu-
tion theories of Henry George, and had also refined some of
these theories during 1899, in protracted discussions with Liang
Qichao and other Chinese radicals exiled in Japan.[3])

But as Sun, from his bases in Japan and Taiwan, followed the
progress of the Boxer risings and Kang Youwei's failed insurrection during late 1900, he had little opportunity to spread
word of these new ideological interests; he concentrated, instead, on giving maximum encouragement to the Triad secret-

society members in the Huizhou area, who rose in force in October 1900 and fought with remarkable bravery against the Qing armies. They had received some money, munitions, and advice from Sun's associates, but mainly they fought on their own terms with arms captured from the Qing forces, and under their own slogans. Claiming that their primary goal was to "protect the foreigners and exterminate the Manchus" (in a deliberate reversal of the slogans used by the Boxers in the north), the rebel forces also promised to "institute beneficial reforms and throw the country open to the trade of the world." Their armies, though unable to seize the major city of Huizhou itself, were nevertheless disciplined, effective in smaller skirmishes, and attracted wide support among the local peasantry. The rebels might have spread over Guangdong province and even into Fujian, to the northeast, had Sun been able to come up with the extra stores of cash and munitions he had promised them; but cheated by one of his gun-running intermediaries, misled by vacillating Japanese supporters on Taiwan, and unable to conceive a successful and sustainable military strategy for the rebellion as a whole, Sun saw the rising slowly fizzle and die. At the end of October those participants who had not been killed and were known to the Qing forces, and hence could not melt back into the countryside, escaped to Hong Kong by junk.[4]

Sun responded to these renewed failures by pressing vigorously to find new insurrectionary opportunities and to tap new sources of funds. These tasks were made harder for him by Kang Youwei's scholarly prestige among the overseas Chinese communities, and Sun continued to lose political followers to Kang's Society to Protect the Emperor—even Sun's own elder brother in Hawaii joined the society for a brief period. Yet Kang was apparently too dejected by the human cost of the Hankou and Anhui risings, and too unsure of his own political direction, to press his own suit with real determination. Thus in a poem written in late 1900 he lamented the death of Tang Caichang, who had been only thirty-three—clearly this reawakened memories of Kang's own dead younger brother, and of Kang's partial responsibility for that death.[5] And insofar as his Society to Protect the Emperor had a platform, it remained a broadly nationalist and cultural one, aimed not against the Manchus but rather at redressing the inferior position of the Chinese in the world. The charter stated that the society hoped to gain better commercial and legal standing for the Chinese and to elevate them to a level "equal that of any other civilized race," while the general political goal was "to impress upon the Chinese people the urgent need of a revival of reform in governmental affairs of China."[6]

The Hankou disaster made a deeper rift among Kang's various followers than the Huizhou failure did among Sun's. For Kang, it brought into question the whole policy of working with secret societies inside China; and in the years after 1900 Kang seems to have yielded to pressures from the Canadian Chinese for developing the Society to Protect the Emperor into a major commercial operation, with overseas banking, real-estate, and transportation interests. In the long run, such profits were intended to benefit the restoration of Emperor Guangxu's power, but in the short run they made Kang and his supporters appear merely mercenary. There were also serious differences with his leading surviving disciple and lieutenant, Liang Qichao, who, though he had not followed up on his stated intention of retiring to become a monk after Tang's arrest and execution, made a series of speeches to the Chinese in Australia in late 1900 suggesting that Emperor Guangxu might serve in China after a *republican* revolution—presumably as president of a new republic rather than as a constitutional monarch.[7] Such statements obviously suggested profound indecision about where the Society to Protect the Emperor should focus its sights.

Furthermore the Singapore base was growing dangerous for Kang Youwei: though the British government officials had been courteous and protective, his most powerful Chinese backer, Khoo Seokwan, who was reputed to have contributed a quarter of a million Singapore dollars to the Hankou rising, broke with Kang after the rising's failure; several of Khoo's most influential followers shifted toward Sun Yatsen's group, as charges of incompetence and even embezzlement were leveled at Kang; Khoo himself responded to Kang's failure by repledging his loyalty to the Manchu government, for which gesture the gratified court rewarded him with an honorary official rank.[8]

Since the summer of 1900 Kang had either believed, or pretended to believe, that Sun Yatsen had hired assassins to murder him. Since the Qing government had put a price on his head of 140,000 taels (a tael being equivalent to an ounce of silver at this time), Kang's fears were not unreasonable, and the governor of Singapore supported him by having several of Sun's representatives jailed. When Sun then appeared in person in Singapore to obtain his friends' release, Kang was able to persuade the governor to have Sun deported and refused readmission to Singapore for a period of five years.[9] Nevertheless Sun maintained considerable influence among the Singapore Chinese community even during his enforced absence, thanks to his use of skillful agents loyal to the Revive China Society, who continued to preach the anti-Manchu message. One of these men, a fugitive from Sun's failed Huizhou uprising, was a Guangdong native with extended secret-society contacts; he was particularly successful in rallying the Singapore Chinese behind Sun's banner not only because of his persuasive oratory but because he used his medical skills to set up free clinics for patients with venereal diseases, which brought him a following among the poor Chinese laborers, secret-society members, and prostitutes of the area. Sometimes under cover of "educational" activities, sometimes by direct persuasion, these supporters of Sun's spread the anti-Manchu and republican message widely, so that the newly designed revolutionary flag of "blue sky, white sun, and red earth" flew at meetings from Kuala Lumpur to Penang.[10]

Kang was tired, sick, and depressed during this period; a move from Singapore to Penang failed to cheer him, and in December 1901 he left Penang to take a trip to India with his younger daughter, Tongbi. After some weeks of touring, they settled in a rented house in Darjeeling, the renowned resort for jaded British administrators of India and their families, in the foothills of the Himalaya. Here, with Tongbi, he walked and rode in the mountains and drew refreshment from the air and the great snowy vistas. But the problems of China followed him: Liang Qichao and many of Kang's former supporters were now calling for an anti-Manchu policy, and even for the establishment of a revolutionary government in southern China, or else for the establishment of an independent regime in Guangdong province. In two careful and lengthy letters written to Liang and to the overseas Chinese, Kang reasserted the need for gradualism if China was to avoid being partitioned by the major Western powers and Japan. A restored emperor, even though Manchu, working constructively with Chinese and Manchu officials, could establish a strong and legitimate government. To leap from autocracy to a republic would not be possible without chaos, wrote Kang, developing arguments that he had been thinking through for at least a year concerning both the inevitability of eventual democratic forms and the need to pass through each measured historical stage.

Kang bolstered his argument partly by reference to the French Revolution and the evolution of British and American government, but also by drawing on the only Confucian source that referred in some detail to developmental progress in human history. Since the time of Confucius in the fifth century B.C., Chinese historical accounts and analyses tended to be cyclical in structure, using the idea of repeated dynastic cycles as a political model and emphasizing movement from *yin* to *yang* and back in ceaseless oscillation rather than dialectical progression. But at intervals over this long period of time occasional scholars had pointed to a small group of early texts that gave a very different picture; one of these was a commentary on the Confucian *Spring and Autumn Annals*, and one a section within the *Book of Rites*. In the "Gongyang" commentary on the *Spring and Autumn Annals* the claim was made that Confucius had believed in a broad movement across time and history, in which mankind had moved from an Age of Disorder, through an Age of Ascending Peace, to an Age of Universal Peace. In the "Liyun" section of the *Book of Rites* one could also find indications that Confucius had envisioned a future Great Community (Datong) in which the conventions of family and of the state would no longer obtain. Kang seized on these texts both to explain the motion of human history and to oppose the increasingly impatient political stand of his own followers. He reinterpreted Confucius to suggest that the developments he presented lay in the future: China had come through the Age of Disorder, in this interpretation, but could not simply leap into the Age of Universal Peace without first joining the Western powers and Japan in the slow move through the Age of Ascending Peace. There were thus no shortcuts to the Great Community, although in reflecting on that Great Community one could begin to plan the future of a better and happier world.[11]

As he walked in the mountains around Darjeeling with his daughter Tongbi, Kang completed a synthesis of these allegedly Confucian ideas with ideas from the Buddhist tradition and from those parts of the Western utopian literature that had been made available to him in Chinese translation; among these latter one can trace elements from Étienne Cabet's *Voyage to Icaria*, which had been published in 1840, John Fryer's *Homely Words to Aid Government*, which was published in Chinese in 1885, and Edward Bellamy's *Looking Backward*, published in the United States in 1888 and available in a Chinese version by 1892.[12] (Though Kang did not himself mention Bellamy by name, his disciples Tan Sitong and Liang Qichao both read *Looking Backward* in translation during the 1890s; Tan Sitong had written that the world projected by Bellamy had "almost the image of the Datong" that one could find in the "Liyun," while Liang Qichao called it one of the most important books he had read on the West.[13]) And it was in Darjeeling, late in 1902, that Kang finished his astonishing *Book of the Great Community* (*Datongshu*).

The time spent in this beautiful mountain retreat (time financed in part, perhaps, with money originally raised for the disastrous 1900 Hankou risings, which Kang's enemies claimed had never been satisfactorily accounted for) was liberating for Kang. It was here, he stated, that he was at last able to write a longer poem in homage to his martyred younger brother that he had felt closed up within him for four long years;[14] and it was here that he not only found the words to describe the future but also examined his own past for the origins of certain darker visions that had been with him for decades. He had long felt, he wrote in his preamble to the *Book of the Great Community*, that "our whole world is nothing but a world of grief and mis-

ery, and its inhabitants are nothing but grieving and miserable
people. The living beings on this earth are all destined for
slaughter. The azure heaven and the round earth are no more
than a great slaughter-yard, a great prison."[15] He now traced
the origins of this vision to the fact that when he was a child
little more than ten years old he saw a lantern-slide show of the
town of Sedan after the French troops had been defeated there
by the Prussians—"the corpses stretched out among the grass
and trees, the houses all charred ruins"—which made him
aware that he manifested his oneness with the universe by
sharing in its suffering.[16] As he grew up, this sense of unity
grew, through age, through study, and through exercise of
imagination:

> I was born on this earth, so I come from the same womb as
> humans in all countries, even though our body types may
> be different. I know of them and so I love them. I have
> drunk deeply of the intellectual heritage of ancient India,
> Greece, Persia, and Rome, and of modern England, France,
> Germany, and America. I have pillowed my head upon
> them, and my soul in dreams has fathomed them. With the
> wise old men, noted scholars, famous figures, and beautiful
> women of all countries I have likewise often joined hands,
> we have sat on mats side by side, sleeves touching, sharing
> our meal, and I have grown to love them. Each day I have
> been offered and have made use of the dwellings, clothing,
> food, boats, vehicles, utensils, government, education, arts,
> and music of a myriad countries, and these have stimulated
> my mind and enriched my spirit. Do they progress? Then
> we all progress with them. Do they slide backward? Then
> we all slide with them. Are they happy? Then we are happy
> with them. Do they suffer? Then we suffer with them. It is
> as if we were all parts of an electrical force which intercon-
> nects all things, or partook of the pure essence that encom-
> passes all things.[17]

All the world's sorrows, Kang thought, could be subsumed
under six categories: those that come from our biological
frailty, from natural disasters, from accidents of status within
society, from restrictions imposed by institutions, sufferings
because of human emotions, and sufferings springing from
high responsibility. If we looked more carefully at the nature

of each category we would see that each springs from the boundaries that humans have erected around and between themselves—boundaries of family, gender, class, nation, occupation, and laws; if mankind could eliminate these boundaries, we should enter the world of the Great Community.[18] With skill and forethought, mankind could perhaps remove these boundaries, one by one.

The end of nationhood was to be accomplished by gradual federations (Kang saw the United States and Germany as models of smaller units coalescing into larger ones) rather than through the internecine wars that could be seen as the harsher side of natural selection. Democracy as opposed to autocracy was a healthy sign, for varied constitutions, labor unions, and socialist organizations all promised escape from the self-centeredness of the nation-state. Nation-states would gradually coalesce into larger units, as Russia absorbed Eastern Europe, Brazil the other Latin American nations, Germany took over Scandinavia and the Low Countries, and a Muslim empire was forged of Turkey, Persia, and India. But these great confederations would not stay forever separate; they would slowly draw together under the pressures of a world parliament, which would attain unifying force through economic sanctions, a patrolling navy, and a universal language designed by musicians and philosophers. When these trends were accompanied by the universal disarmament of all former nations, then the Great Community would be attained. (Kang considered that the planets and star clusters, however, were beyond human management. In one aside, he followed various nineteenth-century theorists in expressing the belief that there were currently wars on Mars, as elsewhere in outer space, but felt such struggles would continue forever—apparently without involving our earth.[19])

The Great Community would end the class distinctions that sprang from slavery, caste systems, or the remnants of aristocratic and feudal institutions. In a world with industrialized production, however, the problems would be more difficult, for as factories grew ever huger and communications more sophisticated, "the disparity between poor and rich will be like the distance between sky and sea." Kang did not think struggle could be avoided: "Those who are unequal, cry out. This is a natural consequence, and hence recently there have been increasing battles between labor unions and capitalists in Europe and America. Only the sprouts have appeared as yet, but soon more and more unions will be formed, and I fear we will have tragedies of blood and iron. This struggle will not be one of strong states confronting the weak, but between those who are poor and those who are rich. A hundred years hence this will be the problem demanding the whole world's attention."[20] The only way to ameliorate these tensions, thought Kang, would be to eliminate the family, so that the principle of private property no longer dominated people's thoughts.

Slowly and methodically the rulers would also end the distinctions of race that currently separated the world into black, brown, yellow, and white. Kang did not think simple legislation would solve this: "With the noble intention of liberating the black slaves, Lincoln assembled the troops and shed blood, yet to this day the American people do not admit the equality of black people. They do not permit black people to eat with them or sit with them; they do not permit black people to ride first class on ships or trains; they do not let black people enter hotels; black people who have been elected to minor office are still kept down by the Americans."[21] The reasons, thought Kang, were due to profound antipathies concerning physical appearance, body smell, and cultural behavior; such antipathies would disappear only when the causes had been eradicated through programs of geographical relocation to induce changes in physique and pigmentation, and by encouragement of racial intermarriage on a global scale. In cases of incorrigible wickedness or incurable disease, sterilization drugs would be administered. Such a blending and purging would lead finally to a Great Community with only one race; Kang made it clear that he felt the inexorable laws of natural selection would lead the race to have the physical aspects of the former white race and the mental skills of the yellow race.[22]

The abolition of administrative boundaries would follow from the absence of nations. With the world divided on mathematically precise lines based on the latitude/longitude grid (to facilitate social intercourse while abolishing the nationalism of frontiers), all people would be linked by a complex network of electrical communications, managed by the Great Community's government, perched high on a mountaintop in clear, healthful air. How to choose this government was a problem: Kang was not impressed by what he had heard of political elections; he described them as a "world of darkness," where plotting, assassinations, or bribery through free handouts of food and drink often led to the choice of the undeserving and involved a corruptive aspect of competition.[23] It is worth remembering this suspicion of elections—as opposed to the administration of the overall system of government in the West—since they had never been held in China and were to be held rarely in the future. Perhaps Kang was influenced here by the views of another member of the group of progressive Hunan reformers, Huang Zunxian, who after a stint as Chinese consul in San Francisco in the 1880s offered, in verse form, his view of an American election:

> *One day in a theater,*
> *An audience of a thousand assembles;*
> *Black leather chairs are set out in rows,*
> *In ascending levels like a flight of stairs;*
> *A myriad brilliant lights*
> *Shine upon velvet curtains.*
>
> *A drunk-looking man mounts the stage*
> *And starts to speak with a tongue protruding.*
> *His whiskers are curled and yellow,*
> *His eyes blink like a hawk's*
> *Out from his open mouth pour the words*
> *A torrent belching forth without ceasing.*
> *He laughs and the roof tiles fly;*
> *At his anger the pillars shake and crack.*
>
> *At times the crowd responds, "Aye, aye!"*
> *At times they cry out, "Nay, nay!"*
> *As emotions grow they are roused like thunder*
> *And set a pounding rhythm of applause.*
> *At the end, all raise their hands on high*
> *Clear proof this party stands as one.*[24]

Kang's projected solution was to have elections to senior executive offices conducted solely by telephone; the results would be binding, though those chosen to be heads of the twenty ministries would initially decline their posts out of politeness. Most of the Great Community's ministries were pragmatically labeled (Health, Industry, and so on), but the last three showed Kang's vision of humankind's improvement: the Ministry of Encouraging Knowledge, the Ministry of Teaching the Way, and the Ministry of Utmost Happiness.[25] While specific ministries would handle the distribution of resources, free compulsory education to the age of twenty, and the focusing of economic life and technology around great self-governing farm units in the countryside, these last three would see to the evolving wisdom of humankind: it would be their task to end the invidious distinctions between town and country, to prevent excessive idolization of any specific individuals, and to discourage both laziness and the competitive instincts among the new free peoples of the world.[26]

Perhaps Kang's most moving (and most original) reflections concerned the problems of abolishing the two other "boundaries" in the Great Community, the boundaries of the family and the boundaries of gender. Though he was sympathetic to the original protective roots of the family, and saw how the clan system had made China populous and fostered filial piety, he found it to have become destructive, to have induced crucial economic and social divisions within society, and to have hindered the implementation of standardized education and child-rearing practices. In the Great Community, the family would be replaced by institutions that would follow each human being from just after conception (freely arrived at by free adults) to the grave. The care would start in a Human Roots Institution, where pregnant women would be cherished and instructed, and attended by skilled female doctors. Infant rearing, nurseries, primary and middle and senior schools would lead, at the end of life, to public sanatoriums and homes for the poor or terminally ill. The last in the sequence of institutions would be the public crematorium.[27]

Implicit in this whole structure was the equality of men and women, the boundary between them being as great as any of the others that Kang wanted to shatter. We can guess that much of what Kang wrote here came from the heart and was no mere projection into the future, for his own family experiences had been troubled and varied, and gave him ample knowledge of female suffering and potentiality. For example, he had been old enough to see the difficulties his widowed mother faced after the death of his father, and he himself had been charged with looking after his baby brother—that martyred brother whose widow and young daughter were now also his family responsibilities. Of his three sisters, one had died at the age of two; one was compelled at an early age to marry her sick fiancé, who died nineteen days later, leaving her a childless widow for forty-three years, while her money was wasted by her late husband's clansmen; one was left a widow with three small boys and died young, in great unhappiness. "Her exertions and her anxieties hastened her death," wrote Kang. "I was two years older than she; we loved each other and enjoyed each other's company. She had a good memory, was quiet, and was untiring in her desire for learning. She died in poverty and I, being far away, could not help her."[28] As young men, both Kang and his brother had struggled actively to end foot-binding, and had founded public societies to give support to those who wanted to ban the practice. Kang refused to allow his own daughters to have their feet bound—and it was certainly because of this decision that Tongbi was now free to walk with him in the mountains instead of hobbling around with her mother in Hong Kong. Kang's own arranged marriage to Zhang Miaohua had apparently been fairly happy at first; but three of their five children (two girls and a boy) died in infancy, leaving Kang two daughters. In 1897, just before he was forty, he took a secondary consort named Liang, who bore him a son in Penang.[29] His wife was left to look after her mother-in-law in Hong Kong during Kang's travels; possibly Kang took his consort Liang with him to India, though he makes no mention of her. It is to his daughter Tongbi that the poems written in Darjeeling make constant and loving reference. Kang obviously admired Tongbi greatly and treasured her company, yet he took the painful decision of sending her off to study in Europe and the United States when she was still only seventeen. "It is such a long journey for a young girl," he wrote in a farewell poem, "but a step forward for women's rights." (Not a step forward for Kang's own independence, however, as he immediately called for his other grown daughter, Tongwei, to come and join him.[30])

These family details lay in the background of Kang's finest passage on women in the *Book of the Great Community*:

> In the more than ten thousand years of human history, taking all nations of the whole earth together, incalculable, inconceivable numbers of people have had human form and human intelligence; moreover, each man has had some woman with whom he was most intimate, whom he loved the most. Yet men have callously and unscrupulously repressed women, restrained them, deceived them, shut them up, imprisoned them, and bound them. Men have prevented them from being independent, from holding public office, from being officials, from living as citizens, from enjoying participation in public meetings. Still worse, men have not let them study, or hold discussions, or make a name for themselves, or have free social intercourse, or enjoy entertainments, or go out sightseeing, or leave the house. And worse even than that, men have forced them to distort and bind their waists, veil their faces, compress their feet, and tattoo their bodies. The guiltless have been universally oppressed, the innocent universally punished. Such actions have been worse than the worst inhumanity. And yet throughout the world, past and present, for thousands of years, those whom we call good men, righteous men, have been accustomed to the sight of such things; have sat and looked and considered them to be matters of course, have not demanded justice for the victims or offered to help them. This is the most appalling, unjust, and unequal thing, the most inexplicable theory under heaven.
>
> I now have a task: to cry out the natural grievances of the incalculable numbers of women of the past. I now have one great desire: to save the eight hundred million women of my own time from drowning in the sea of suffering. I now have a great longing: to bring the incalculable inconceivable numbers of women of the future the happiness of equality, of the Great Community and of independence.[31]

To achieve the equality that Kang saw as the ultimate goal, the Great Community would insist on everyone's having absolute equality before the law, in elections, in education, and in holding office—though women must have served in the Human Roots Institution, in the child-rearing institutions, or in one of the old-age institutions before holding office. Men and women would dress identically at all public functions, to avoid unnatural discriminations. When education was completed, at the age of twenty, any man or woman could undertake a marriage contract—such contracts could not be for less than a month or for more than a year, though they could be renewed. Homosexuals would also be permitted to sign such contracts with one another. Aware that highly educated and happily employed women might choose not to have children, thus threatening the eventual survival of the species, Kang urged that everything possible be done to make their pregnancies pleasant and fulfilling: as well as having a beautiful environment they might have lovers in the early stages of pregnancy and use mechanical pleasure devices after delivery if they so chose. In the Great Community, the universality of desire would be recognized.[32]

Despite the sustained brilliance of Kang's rhetoric, the apparent clarity of these visions, and the emotional commitment he seemed to bring to the effort to attain their realization, he was not able to combine his thoughts on the Great Community with the world of real politics in which he was forced to operate. After Kang had finished his *Book of the Great Community* and left Darjeeling in the spring of 1903, he traveled widely throughout Southeast Asia, Europe, and Canada—and also now in the United States, which he was at last able to enter on a tourist visa in 1905, describing himself as a teacher and journalist and styling himself "Professor Kang." He continued to urge the overseas Chinese to support Emperor Guangxu and the establishment of a reform-minded constitutional monarchy in China;[33] he also continued to press the primacy of the Confucian value system in public, and claiming that his ideas of the Great Community were "too advanced for the times," he shared them with only a few favored students, and refused to have the entire book published.[34] Had he been known more widely as the advocate of such ideas, he would surely have built up a following among the new generation of radical Chinese students, restless and angry since the Boxer Rebellion and the allied occupation of Beijing in 1900, who were now openly

beginning to discuss problems of republican organization, socialism, and rights for women. Kang's own great scholarly
prestige, his reputation as a leader during the 1898 reforms,
and his unabashed interest in industrialization and capitalism
always assured him of considerable support among the better-
off and more conservative overseas Chinese. But it was Sun
Yatsen who began to speak more effectively to the issues of
social revolution, drawing on parallels from within European
societies, and explaining to students that since China was a
country that had "not yet applied machinery to the land" and
where "the productive forces still depended on human labor
and were not all in the hands of the owners," they might be
able to carry through revolutionary change before the gap between rich and poor grew as wide as he saw it in Europe and
the United States.[35]

Kang's friend and former student Liang Qichao, who turned
thirty in 1903, was torn about where his ideological loyalties
should lie. While Kang worked in Darjeeling, Liang was living
in exile in Japan, and it was here that he began to develop ideas
for saving China through the marshaling of her total citizenry
around the concept of a rejuvenated nation-state. The world
dominated by foreign imperialist forces required new organizational forms undreamed of in traditional Confucian and imperial China: Liang saw that the motivating force of modern
history was becoming "the citizenry's struggle for survival,
which is irrepressible according to the laws of natural selection
and survival of the fittest"; successful participation in this
struggle would call for a politically active nation exercising
popular sovereignty; the powerful voice of Rousseau offered an
antidote to traditional despotisms and the "slavish mentality"
of the Chinese people. This slavishness, he wrote in a letter to
Kang Youwei during the hectic year of 1900, had led to "the
catastrophic culmination of the corruption and degeneration
that have afflicted China in the past few thousand years." The
"illness," he continued, "cannot possibly be cured without
taking the medicine of liberty."[36]

Yet Liang did not make the jump over to Sun Yatsen's camp
that might have been expected to come from such sentiments.

The case of Meiji Japan, he wrote in an essay, showed that one could have social revolution without dynastic overthrow; and to counter arguments, such as Sun's, which insisted on the need for anti-Manchu revolution, Liang in 1902 wrote a biography of the guillotined Girondist Mme. Roland, presenting her as a central heroine of the French Revolution whose ideal of liberty was destroyed, along with her own life, in the dark forces the revolution had unleashed. Such revolutions, he commented, were deluges that smashed the dams and swept away the good along with the evil.[37]

When Liang finally visited the United States in 1903, his lingering admiration for democracy was quashed; he saw the system there as dominated by corruption and spoils: elections were too frequent, too corrupt, too focused on short-run aspects of popularity to bring forth leaders who could handle the crucial long-range problems. Men of high caliber tended to shun political life, and most presidents were mediocre people. What there was that was strong in American democracy was localistic and deeply rooted, and could not be easily adapted to other countries.[38] In a protracted visit to San Francisco's Chinatown—typical of the communities in the United States where the Chinese had congregated since the great period of emigration in the 1860s and 1870s—Liang found exemplified the worst aspects of Chinese familism, selfishness, and mob rule. Such a people, he concluded, could not yet be ready for full democracy; they needed the strong hand of the state to dominate and guide them. The Chinese, he wrote at the end of his American travels, could forget Jean Jacques Rousseau and George Washington; instead, they should find inspiration in the stern and effective legalists of their own ancient tradition, or in the lives of leaders such as the Spartan Lycurgus and England's Oliver Cromwell.[39] Thus even as Kang Youwei was breaking his own European journey to visit the docks in Holland where Tsar Peter the Great had gone to study shipbuilding more than two centuries before, Liang returned to him in spirit, writing that the reforms being carried out in Russia showed the effectiveness of autocracy, and arguing that social Darwinist ideas supported national centralization of power. "It is not the obscurantists who will be the ruin of China," he wrote at this time, "but the progressives."[40] And in an even more reflective vein: "The sacrifices of 1793 in France were rewarded only in 1870, and the rewards did not measure up to the expectations. If we now seek to purchase liberty at the price of infinite suffering, it may not be attained after seventy years, and even if it is, what will have happened to our ancestral country?"[41]

Even if Liang had returned, after flirting with more extreme solutions, to Kang Youwei's view that China was not ready for sudden change, and that constitutional monarchy—if need be, still under Manchu control—was the surest road to modernization and growth, many of their former friends could no longer subscribe to such views, or to their apparent approval of Russian autocracy.

By 1903, detailed information on the Russian revolutionary movement, particularly its nihilist and anarchist strands, was available in Japan; from there it made its way to China, often in the form of translations from the Japanese, which were avidly read. Such works presented the basic ideas of Herzen, Chernyshevsky, and Bakunin, and described their passionate convictions in a world where violence and idealism necessarily coexisted;[42] the need for such convictions seemed especially acute to many young Chinese, who were also aware of the demands Russian imperialism was now making on China, notably in the region of Manchuria. Ou Qujia, for example, who had once been a student of Kang Youwei's and was actively involved with him in both the 1898 reforms and the 1900 rising, urged separatism for southern China in his pamphlet *The New Guangdong;* like Liang, he castigated the Chinese for their slavishness and their "quietistic passivity"; after 1902, when he was ostensibly working in San Francisco for Kang's Society to Protect the Emperor, he was a decisive force for moving the California members of that organization in a dramatically more revolutionary direction, by harping on elitist ideas about South Chinese racial superiority.[43] Another young activist, Qin Lishan, who had been a reformist student in Changsha during the days before 1898 when Liang Qichao and Tan Sitong had been lecturing there, and had also led one wing of the abortive 1900 uprising for Kang, was so moved by the stories of Russian intellectuals leading the masses during the 1901 strikes and riots against the Tsar in Moscow and St. Petersburg that he wrote vividly of the need for Chinese scholars to seize their destiny in a similar way. Impatient with Kang's refusal to work with the uneducated Chinese masses, Qin went on to undercut seriously Kang's position among the Chinese in Southeast Asia.[44] A third former follower, Han Wenju, who had first studied with Kang in 1891 and had been an organizer of the 1900 rising from a base in Macao before coming to an extremist anti-Manchu position, wrote a long commentary in 1903 on the first Chinese novel to deal with anarchist and revolutionary themes; he noted that many nihilist ideas grew out of Hegel, Marx, and Saint-Simon and were similar to the ideas concerning the Great Community in the "Liyun" chapter of the *Rites* (which Kang had used as a springboard for his own utopian work). Han also unequivocally urged a revolutionary assault on Manchu autocracy: "Of all the cases of corruption and disorder in the world, there is none which did not originate in the autocratic form of government. It's like being tied up with dozens of ropes—autocracy being the main rope. If you cut it, the rest will fall away. Otherwise you can't untie yourself in a hundred days."[45] The attempted reforms of 1898 in which Kang had worked with Emperor Guangxu had often been referred to as the Hundred Days of Reform, and Han may have been sniping at Kang here; but the focus of his remarks was Sofya Perovskaya, the Russian anarchist who had been executed in 1881 for her part in the assassination of Tsar Alexander II, and it was obvious that Han applauded her deed.

Sofya Perovskaya provided a spellbinding model for Chinese protorevolutionaries. Born into a wealthy family (both her grandfather and her father were powerful officials in the Tsarist regime), she had found a "second family" among radical students in reading groups in St. Petersburg and then in the communal society of the Chaykovists. With her skill at disguises and at outwitting the Tsarist police, her important intellectual contacts with Kropotkin, her work among peasants as an inoculator against smallpox, her devoted volunteer teaching of poor industrial workers living in appalling conditions, her dramatic escape after her first arrest in 1873, and her eventual commitment to the terrorist organization known as Narodnaya

Volya (the People's Will), her life encapsulated all the elements of self-sacrifice and danger. And it was almost impossible not to be moved by her part in the assassination of Tsar Alexander: Sofya positioning the assassins after the Tsar changed his projected route; Sofya calmly waving a white handkerchief as the Tsar's sleigh and the accompanying Cossacks came racing down the frozen canal; the first, misthrown dynamite bomb; the second, clutched by Grinevitsky, killing the assassin himself and fatally wounding the ruler; Sofya's arrest and her composure at the trial; Sofya dying on the gallows at the side of her lover, the serf's son Andrey Zhelyabov, when she was only twenty-seven.[46]

Debate over assassination was common in China at the turn of the century, and even those supporting the reformist side argued that assassination might induce leaders to make beneficial changes. There are hints that Kang, in the dark period after his brother's death, held discussions on the feasibility of assassinating the Empress Dowager; and Liang Qichao pointed to the possible advantages of assassination in certain contexts. In 1904 a former student of the Changsha reformers would have successfully killed the ex-governor of Guangxi province (who had taken a pro-Tsarist stance over Russia's claims in Manchuria) had he not, in his excitement, forgotten to release the safety catch of his revolver; and a close friend of Kang's tried to assassinate the Empress Dowager in 1906, for which act he was arrested and murdered in prison.[47]

Another member of the same group went considerably further in homage to what he understood as the Russian model, forming a so-called assassination squad among Chinese studying in Japan, and studying bomb manufacture with a chemist from Guangzhou then living in Yokohama. After his return to China he recruited a student named Wu Yue, who in 1905, in seeming imitation of Grinevitsky's act, threw himself clutching a bomb in the path of five imperial commissioners. These men had been dispatched by the Empress Dowager to study foreign constitutional governments. Wu was killed instantly, and two of the commissioners were injured. In a testament that Wu had written before this assassination attempt, he made it clear that he was not acting against the commissioners themselves but attempting to provoke the Manchu government into ever greater acts of repression so as to stimulate a revolutionary counterresponse by patriotic Chinese.[48]

A different (yet in some respects parallel) example of the shift toward extremism can be seen in the Shanghai newspaper *Subao*, one of the many new journals concerned with reform, modernization, and international news that were slowly changing Chinese intellectual life. Between 1899 and 1902, writings by Kang Youwei and by Liang Qichao often appeared in *Subao*; the paper also discussed such topics as the importance of protecting the Emperor Guangxu against the Empress Dowager, and urged the establishment of a constitution for China. By 1902, however, after the Empress Dowager had tried to preempt some of the opposition to her rule by ordering the restructuring of China's educational system and the introduction of Western learning into the curriculum of the new schools, the *Subao* editors began to appeal for readership among the new generation of radical students who were now enrolling. In 1903 they made *Subao* the semiofficial organ of the Shanghai Patriotic School. This institution, with the addition of the newly founded Shanghai Patriotic Girls' School, became a focus for discussion of revolutionary theory in central China; and as *Subao* grew better known it began to draw correspondence from all over China. By the summer of 1903 it was printing articles that openly praised the assassination methods of the Russian nihilists and recommended the killing of Manchus; it suggested that the overthrow of the Emperor would be as easy, for four hundred million Chinese, as "pushing over a rotten tree." In another article, attacking Kang Youwei for his continued support of the Manchus, the *Subao* writers referred to the Emperor by his tabooed personal name, and also described him disrespectfully as a "despicable wretch."[49]

It was one of the central ironies of foreign imperialism in China that writing such violent anti-Manchu propaganda was comparatively safe as long as it was done from Shanghai's foreign concession areas, where the Qing police could not make arrests without consulting with foreign consular staff and the Shanghai Municipal Council. Hence it was in this same base in 1903 that another violent critic of the Qing dynasty, Zou Rong, issued his own book-length manifesto entitled *The Revolutionary Army*. Zou, who was originally from Sichuan province and had received a year of advanced education in Japan, was a great admirer of the 1898 martyr Tan Sitong, though he had no time for Kang Youwei's reformist views, and he had become a close friend of the most radical *Subao* writers.[50] In his manifesto, which he wrote at the age of eighteen, Zou Rong invoked the spirits of Washington and Rousseau just as Liang Qichao was urging Chinese youth to reject these models; Zou called on his Chinese countrymen to dare to be free, to seize back their own beautiful land for themselves, and to "cleanse themselves" of two hundred and sixty years of Manchu rule:

> How sublime is revolution! How majestic!
> For this I march the length of the Great Wall, scale the Kunlun Mountains, travel the whole of the Yangtze, and follow the Yellow River to its source; for this I plant the banner of independence and ring the bell of freedom. My voice reechoes from heaven to earth, I tear my lungs to shreds in crying out to my fellow countrymen: Listen! Our China must have revolution today! If we are to throw off the Manchu yoke, we must have revolution today. We must have revolution if China is to be independent. We must have revolution if China is to take its place as a powerful nation on the globe, if China is to survive for long in the new world of the twentieth century, if China is to be a great country in the world and play the leading role. Oh, revolution, revolution! My fellow countrymen, are there any of you—the old, the middle-aged, those in their prime, the youth, the children—be they men or women, who will speak out for revolution or bring the revolution to fruition? My fellow countrymen, assist each other and live for each other in revolution. Today I cry out at the top of my voice to spread the message of revolution throughout the land.
> Revolution is a universal rule of evolution. Revolution is a universal principle of the world. Revolution is the essence of the struggle for survival or destruction in a time of transition. Revolution submits to heaven and responds to men's needs. Revolution rejects what is corrupt and keeps the good. Revolution is the advance from barbarism to civilization. Revolution turns slaves into masters.[51]

Zou Rong mocked his countrymen for the servile way in which they had accepted Manchu domination over their country: they were worse off than prostitutes, he wrote, for even prostitutes got decent handouts and had a chance to marry their clients. The Chinese were no better than horses, resting docilely between their master's legs; they were like cattle, who gratefully accepted the "nurture" offered by their masters, although this "nurture" represented but a fraction of the results of their labor. Those Chinese who served the Manchus as senior ministers—especially those who had helped to suppress the great Chinese rebellions in the mid-nineteenth century—were the "butchers" of their race. The Chinese, with their pigtails and peacock-feather decorations, had accepted Manchu dress and now submitted to the mockery of the world. Nothing could ever make up for these centuries of indignities, not even if "when my fellow countrymen urinated, the Manchus drank off the last drops, or after my fellow countrymen defecated, the Manchus licked them clean."[52]

Zou surveyed for his readers the achievements of the British, French, and American revolutions, and pointed with a kind of anguished triumph to the ultimate battle that had to be waged between the yellow and the white races. Like Kang, he saw these two races as the pinnacle of the human evolutionary process, but he went beyond Kang in separating out the Chinese from all others (Tibetan, Cochinese, Mongol, Tungusic, and Turkic) as being specially poised against the whites, "poised for the fight, undertaking battle in the world of evolution, the great arena where strength and intelligence have clashed since earliest times, the great theater where for so long natural selection and progress have been played out."[53] In a closing passage, Zou called for expulsion of the Manchus, execution of the Emperor, establishment of an elected general assembly, military service for all males, equality of rights between men and women, the guarantee of freedom of speech, thought, and the press, the right to reject by force a government that violated the people's rights, and establishment of a constitution and units of local self-government based on the American model.[54] The Chinese should be proud of being called the Yellow Peril, he ended: "You possess the right of the sacred race! You possess government; run it yourselves. You have laws; guard them yourselves. You have industries; administer them yourselves.

You possess armed forces; order them yourselves. You possess lands; watch over them yourselves. You have inexhaustible resources; exploit them yourselves. You are qualified in every way for revolutionary independence."[55]

The Revolutionary Army was printed and distributed in the International Settlement of Shanghai in the spring of 1903. Shortly after its appearance it was warmly reviewed in *Subao*. Angered and humiliated by what they considered to be treasonous writings, the Qing authorities asked to have Zou Rong and the *Subao* staff extradited to Chinese courts for trial and punishment; British officials had acceded to a similar request in 1900, when Tang Caichang had sought shelter in the British concession after the abortive Hankou rising. But by 1903 the Westerners were more resistant to Qing pressures, and by a curious coincidence they were strengthened in their decision not to hand over Zou Rong and the *Subao* editors, since at precisely this time they learned that a Chinese journalist, formerly a close friend of that same Tang Caichang's, had just been beaten to death by the Qing police in a Beijing jail. So they insisted that Zou Rong be tried in what was known as the Mixed Court of the International Settlement, where Chinese official observers were present but the trial took place according to the premises and practices of Western law. As a result Zou—who could have expected a death sentence from the Qing—received a two-year jail sentence for issuing inflammatory writings. Yet even this light sentence was too much for his weak health, and he died in prison during the spring of 1905.[56]

Zou was only nineteen years old at his death, and his early demise increased his already considerable fame. Sun Yatsen in particular saw the power and usefulness of Zou's message, and his supporters printed and distributed thousands of free copies of *The Revolutionary Army* (retitled *The Fight for Survival*) in the Singapore area. Sun himself had eleven thousand copies of the book printed in San Francisco when he was visiting there in 1904.[57]

Zou Rong had harped—to great rhetorical effect—on the need to mobilize the four hundred million Chinese to seize their own freedom and expel the Manchus and other foreign powers. Kang Youwei had called on the eight hundred million women in the world to work together to end their own subjugation. In 1904 a young woman, Qiu Jin, took the logical step of combining the nationalist and the feminist issues by concentrating on the plight of the two hundred million women within China itself.

Qiu Jin described this plight, in an essay published in the autumn of 1904 in one of the new radical Chinese journals appearing in Japan, in terms of her own personal experience of what such subjugation could mean.

> We, the two hundred million women of China, are the most unfairly treated objects on this earth. If we have a decent father, then we will be all right at the time of our birth; but if he is crude by nature, or an unreasonable man, he will immediately start spewing out phrases like "Oh what an ill-omened day, here's another useless one." If only he could, he would dash us to the ground. He keeps repeating, "She will be in someone else's family later on," and looks at us with cold or disdainful eyes.
>
> Before many years have passed, without anyone's bothering to ask if it's right or wrong, they take out a pair of snow-white bands and bind them around our feet, tightening them with strips of white cotton; even when we go to bed at night we are not allowed to loosen them the least bit, with the result that the flesh peels away and the bones buckle under. The sole purpose of all this is just to ensure that our relatives, friends, and neighbors will all say, "At the so-and-so's the girls have small feet." Not only that, when it comes time to pick a son-in-law, they rely on the advice of a couple of shameless matchmakers, caring only that the man's family have some money or influence; they don't bother to find out if his family background is murky or good, or what his character is like, or whether he's bright or stupid—they just go along with the arrangement. When it's time to get married and move to the new house, they hire the bride a sedan chair all decked out with multicolored embroidery, but sitting shut up inside it one can barely breathe. And once you get there, whatever your husband is like, as long as he's a family man they will tell you you were blessed in a previous existence and are being rewarded in this one. If he turns out no good, they will tell you it's "retribution for that earlier existence" or "the aura was all wrong."[58]

In this essay Qiu Jin was protesting injustices that had existed for centuries, and the nature and vigor of her protest indicates another of the many crosscurrents in the spreading flood of the Chinese revolution. The growing number of girls' schools in China, the influence of Western missionary teachers and of Chinese reformists, the founding of hostels for women and of clubs to promote the marriage of those with unbound feet, the return of the first Chinese women college graduates from overseas, the publication of magazines and newspapers focusing on women's issues, the translation of books and pamphlets about Western feminist leaders—all contributed to the radical nationalism of the day.[59] In other essays Qiu Jin invoked Mme. Roland, along with Sofya Perovskaya and Catharine Beecher, and in dozens of her poems we find her emphasizing the need for a new women's spirit. Yet, like Kang Youwei, she tried hard to avoid overreliance on Western models, and found echoes of this spirit in China's past, as she celebrated heroic women in Chinese history and pointed to occasions when they had had the courage their male contemporaries lacked.[60]

The sentiments in her 1904 essay were thus products both of the times and of her own personal experiences. According to some sources, her father had been kindly and indulgent to her, but the attack on insensitive fathers in her essay does not seem to have been entirely rhetorical. We can gauge something of her negative feelings toward her deceased father from a letter she wrote in 1905, in which she pointed out that if the family would only stop spending so much on the sacrifices to his memory, then they'd all have enough to eat.[61] On foot-binding, the strength of her emotion suggests that her own feet had been bound as a girl, and some of her poems imply that she had unbound her feet herself in later life; in another poem, she wrote that "as long as we have these tiny three-inch feet we can do absolutely nothing. We must abolish the practice."[62] As for arranged marriages, she once told her brother that most of her own personal troubles sprang from the central fact that she had not been free to choose her own husband and the one she had ended up with was not a decent man.[63] Her feelings about the merchant husband from Hunan province whom her parents had compelled her to marry were expressed beyond any ambiguity when she left him, her young son, and her daughter in the summer of 1904 and took ship (with what money she could scrounge together) for Japan.[64] In an eight-line poem written after she left Beijing, called simply "Regrets: Lines Written En Route to Japan," Qiu Jin summed up her life at twenty-six:

> *Sun and moon have no light left, earth is dark;*
> *Our women's world is sunk so deep, who can help us?*
> *Jewelry sold to pay this trip across the seas,*
> *Cut off from my family I leave my native land.*
> *Unbinding my feet I clean out a thousand years of poison,*
> *With heated heart arouse all women's spirits.*
> *Alas, this delicate kerchief here*
> *Is half stained with blood, and half with tears.*[65]

The Chinese students studying in Japan, among whom Qiu Jin now found herself, were in a paradoxical situation. By leaving home they had deliberately turned their backs on the traditional pattern of the Confucian educational system, and though in many cases they had been chosen for study abroad by senior Qing officials in their home provinces, and received comfortable stipends as long as they enrolled in an accredited Japanese school and followed a formal course of study, their chances of getting regular employment when they returned to China were by no means assured. They were closely watched by representatives of the Qing government in Japan, and they were expected to behave with decorum; yet at the same time they were subjected to an extraordinary flood of new ideas and experiences and were made acutely aware of the weakness of the Qing dynasty and its backwardness in comparison to the Meiji government in Japan. When the Japanese defeated the Tsarist armies in the war of 1904–1905 and prevented their encroaching farther into Manchuria, the admiration of these Chinese students was unbounded. Japan's victory demonstrated with renewed vividness how the Meiji reforms had strengthened the entire nation, and in rejoicing that an Asian nation had at last defeated a major European power, the Chinese felt that much of the shame over their own defeat at the hands of the Japanese in 1894 was expunged. In a poem in heroic vein Qiu Jin praised the Japanese victory over the "powerful, devious, and absolutely untrustworthy Russians," who had seized Chinese territory despite the protests of the whole world; she contrasted them with the unified front of the Japanese, in which the country rose up as one and women volunteers serving with the Red Cross were allowed to accompany their men to war.[66] In Japan, too, she found friends among the exiled leaders of the anti-Manchu risings. Qiu Jin had been in Beijing during the Boxer Rebellion and had witnessed the shame of the allied occupation of the city; now, as she read the magazines published by Chinese student groups in Japan, she was presented with emotion-charged essays that attacked the Manchus as being of racial stock inferior to the Chinese, that exalted the act of assassination as a means of arousing the people to revolutionary action, and that extolled the example of Sofya Perovskaya. In poems of her own, Qiu Jin began to invoke the spirit of Rousseau and the Polish patriots who had struggled for their freedom, and saluted Wu Yue for his assassination attempt on the five Qing commissioners and for attempting to bring some spirit back to the Chinese people, who had been "dead for more than two hundred years."[67]

The Chinese studying in Japan often clubbed together according to provincial origin; hence Qiu Jin, who had been born in Zhejiang province, had married a Hunanese, and then had lived as a young mother in Beijing, met and became active with people from all these areas. While she was technically enrolled in the Aoyama Vocational Girls School in Tokyo, she spent more time with an activist group that named itself the Group of Ten, as well as working with a society of women progressives and writing essays for *The Vernacular Journal*, which had been founded by Chinese students in Tokyo seeking to develop a forum for radical ideas that could be used to combat the reformist proposals of Kang Youwei's followers. She joined an overseas branch of the Triad secret society in Yokohama, and in the summer of 1905 she was admitted to the ranks of the Revolutionary Alliance, a new, centralized organization formed by Sun Yatsen and his supporters from a number of heretofore competing anti-Manchu revolutionary groups.[68]

She was not sure how to define her identity as a woman rev-olutionary. On one level she glorified the martial arts, marks-manship, and bomb making of her male comrades; in tender poems she also spoke of her women friends and their own needs and aspirations. At some stage, in Tokyo, she had herself photographed in male Western attire—dark three-button suit, wing collar, soft cloth cap, dusty walking shoes—and holding a cane. In a wry poem she commented on this person she saw gazing back at herself:

> *Who is this person, staring at me so sternly?*
> *The martial bones I bring from a former existence*
> *   regret the flesh that covers them.*
> *Once life is over, the body itself will be seen*
> *   to have been a deception,*
> *And the land of ours that has not yet emerged,*
> *   that will be real.*
> *You and I should have got together long ago,*
> *   and shared our feelings;*
> *Looking out across these difficult times our*
> *   spirits garner strength.*
> *When you see my friends from the old days*
> *Tell them I've scrubbed off all that old mud.*[69]

Despite the excitement of discovering a new mode of exist-ence, she was constantly short of money in Japan and felt the pain of the separation from her family. But when her elder brother Yuzhang, apparently responding to her mood of dejec-tion, wrote to her on behalf of the family, suggesting that she return to China and make up with her former husband, Qiu Jin's response (dated June 19, 1905), in which she summarized her views of her former husband's character, was violent:

That person's behavior is worse than an animal's. I have never known human shamelessness like it. Now that he has seized my remaining jewelry, how can we even think of him as being a human? He treats me as less than nothing, and I am sure that the reason for his taking my money and pos-sessions is that he wants to finish me off. My treatment in that household was worse than a slave's; the poison of hatred has eaten deeply into me. If I am treated decently I respond decently; if I am treated as being of no account, then I respond in the same way—it's not that I have no feelings. When I think of him my hair bristles with anger, it's absolutely unbearable.

Send my sister to try to get my money back—if he won't give it up, then sever all relations. I have thought this through fairly thoroughly: rather than be treated as a slave, why should I not stand up for myself? Henceforth I am going to try to support myself through my own efforts; why should I be somebody's wife? Besides which, we hate each other so much that nothing good could come of it. There has been no letter from him for a year, he has shown no respect to his seniors in my family, and I have also heard that he has taken a new wife.

If any of the sentiments I have just expressed prove to be mere rhetoric, may the gods above abandon me. If I progress even one inch, I shall never let his family name be used on top of mine. If I cannot progress even that inch, and am unable to support myself, then I shall sue him to get back my son, my daughter, and my property. If the suit fails, then I shall die.[70]

In early 1906 Qiu Jin did in fact return to China, but not to her former husband or her family. Instead, she went to the Shanghai area, where she had formed close friendships with some of the revolutionaries, and where she could be confident of a sympathetic audience in a lively intellectual and political milieu. The prosecution of Zou Rong and the *Subao* writers had not dampened desires for radical change, which could be sought in a multitude of directions and in new schools of every persuasion. In Shanghai a group of radical teachers and intellectuals, several of whom had also studied in Japan, had tried to coordinate the various anti-Qing forces in the city into the Restoration Society (Guangfuhui). "Restoration" in this context had the revolutionary overtones of battling for popular and national sovereignty and had nothing to do with the "restoring" of the Emperor Guangxu, still being sought by Kang Youwei. The goal of the Shanghai group was fundamentally anti-Manchu, and was succinctly expressed in their blood oath (which echoed the words of a Song dynasty patriot repelling Jurchen invaders in the twelfth century): "Restore the Chinese race, and recover our mountains and rivers." In 1905, Restoration Society members were active in boycotts directed against American businesses, in protest against the ratification by President Theodore Roosevelt of even more stringent laws against Chinese immigration into the United States. In 1905 and the following year the society's ranks were swelled by contacts in nearby regions of northern Zhejiang province, and in late 1905 many of the members then in Japan joined Sun Yatsen's Revolutionary Alliance, as Qiu Jin had done.[71]

From the time of her return to China, Qiu Jin was in conflict, pulled by the sometimes parallel but more often divergent demands for gradualist reforms of benefit to women on the one hand and for violent revolutionary change on the other. She told her close friend the famous woman calligrapher Wu Zhiying that she felt herself to be different from the other youthful revolutionaries of her day: "Women must get educated and strive for their own independence; they can't just go on asking the men for everything. The young intellectuals are all chanting, 'Revolution, Revolution,' but I say the revolution will have to start in our homes, by achieving equal rights for women."[72] It was in this vein that she founded and wrote for *The Chinese Women's Journal* in Shanghai, taught at a local girls' school near the city, and translated selections from Japanese works on health care and nursing—as if she accepted her own calculation that a slow shift of women's position in the society, if undertaken through education, would take several decades.[73] Yet at the same time she felt drawn to the life of violent revolutionary activism, was attracted by those selfsame young people who cried, "Revolution!" and feared lest life was racing past her. We know from one of her poems that she felt old at twenty-seven, and sick at heart that she had "accomplished nothing."[74]

At this juncture Qiu Jin's career intermeshed with that of a cousin, a fellow native of the prosperous Zhejiang city of Shaoxing, named Xu Xilin. Xu, thirty-three years old in 1906, had had a restless and varied career that had taken him to Japan and had led him into the ranks of the Restoration Society (though he refused to join Sun Yatsen's Revolutionary Alliance) and then into the edges of the military and police bureaucracy. Leaders in the Restoration Society were eager to foment a rebellion in Zhejiang and thought that both Xu Xilin and Qiu

Jin might be capable leaders. The idea appealed to them, for each had a full measure of that recklessness which one can find among certain people in any revolutionary situation: this is not that neglect of consequences to oneself which is needed to lead organized forces into war, or even that desperation necessary to charge police lines or storm barricades, but, rather, a reckless-ness concerning all possible consequences, which invites discovery and punishment even as it seems to promise inviola-bility. Thus, although the "revolutionary forces" they could call upon in Zhejiang consisted of little more than a loose con-federation of partially Westernized intellectuals, a few students returned from Japan, some members of local secret societies in alliance with salt smugglers, and perhaps some disaffected sol-diers in the provincial garrison forces, both Qiu and Xu pro-ceeded to act as though they were the ones who controlled the situation while the Qing dynasty had no resources left whatso-ever.[75]

In reality, the Qing state was still a powerful force. It may have been thwarted in the *Subao* case, but it maintained effec-tive military and police powers in most of the cities and coun-tryside of China, and had indeed increased its military strength in the years since 1901 by organizing a number of New Armies along Western lines and updating their drill, logistics, and ar-maments. The idea of sending a mission abroad to study con-stitutional systems had not been abandoned after Wu Yue's assassination attempt: with two new commissioners replacing those who had been injured, the group of five men traveled to the United States and Europe and in 1906 reported back, albeit in guarded tones, recommending a transition to some form of constitutional monarchy; plans were beginning to be formu-lated for the convening of provincial and national assemblies. In 1905 the imperial system of competitive examinations based on the Confucian classics was abandoned by the Qing court, opening the way for reform of the school system and curricula throughout China, for the development of a major university in Beijing, and for more government sponsorship of student study overseas. In many areas government control of the economy was also strengthened, as more state-directed but merchant-run companies were founded and the railway network was gradually extended. The only benefit that Xu and Qiu might derive from these reforms was that they constituted an argument to many Chinese nationalists against gradualism, for gradualism might enable the Manchus to reestablish their position, bolstered now with new techniques and resources.[76]

In these circumstances Qiu Jin played out the final act in her drama. The actual setting was the Datong School, an institution that exemplified both the boldness and the impracticality of the Zhejiang revolutionaries. (Though the Chinese ideographs spelling out the school's name were pronounced the same as those for Kang Youwei's Great Community, they were written differently, and the school was in fact named for a small village west of Shaoxing city, where there happened to be a convenient empty warehouse.) It had been established by Xu Xilin in the early summer of 1905 as a front organization to conceal the stocks of guns and ammunition he had purchased in Shanghai that spring, and the first program organized by the school— with official blessing—was a six-month training session for rural militia organizers, though it also offered classes in English, Japanese, physics, and art. The "students" were recruited as much as possible from sympathetic secret-society members in the Shaoxing area.[77]

After Xu left the Datong School in late 1905, a succession of leaders and as many quarrels weakened it considerably, but in 1907 Qiu Jin was appointed to the faculty, a job she combined with directing a local girls' school and a physical-education association in Shaoxing. She used this latter as yet another front to establish contacts with troops in the New Armies in the province.[78] Far from attempting to pose as a retiring schoolteacher, Qiu Jin drew adverse attention from the conservative local elite by riding into town astride a horse, dressed in Western male attire, and by encouraging her girl students to engage in military drills. Qiu had been given the task of coordinating secret-society activities with the Restoration Society's risings and with Xu Xilin; this task proved difficult, however, since Xu was some distance away, having accepted the directorship of the police academy at Anqing, to the west, in Anhui province. Qiu Jin did draw up elaborate plans for the military organization, down to details of uniforms and of their flag—which she envisioned as being a giant version of the ideograph for "Han Chinese," in black, sewn onto a pure white ground.[79] She also held a number of meetings, raised funds, and tried to keep communications open by courier. But in reaching out to the broader masses who might have supported a revolution she had no experience whatever. Perhaps the closest she had come to the Chinese working poor was when she was crammed in among the coolies while traveling third class to Japan, but then—as she told her friend Wu Zhiying—she had always carried a dagger for protection.[80] Her sense of separation from the common herd can be gauged from an image in one of her poems in which she playfully suggested that she must have been a water lily in a previous existence, since she was the sort of person "who can jump into the filthy water and still stay pure."[81] In Zhejiang, at any rate, she was never able to reach down beyond the level of the local secret-society leaders, though the province was ripe for social violence: a desperate peasantry had endured a succession of near-famine years, poor conditions in the province were exacerbated by the presence of thousands of refugees from outside Zhejiang, and the poorer townsmen of Shaoxing had rioted twice for food in 1907.[82]

In the meantime, the Qing authorities were alarmed both by rumors of activities at Qiu's school—which they searched several times in the spring and summer of 1907—and by the possibilities of trouble at Anqing. In late June 1907, Xu was alerted to danger by the extraordinary fact that he was ordered to arrest himself—as head of the police academy he had been given the order to round up all the suspects on a list of names obtained by the government, a list that included a coded version of his own name. His response was to try to swing his Anqing academy behind him by a violent revolutionary act. On July 6 he was able to shoot and kill the Manchu governor of Anhui province at the academy's graduation exercises, but only about thirty men joined him for what was meant to be the outbreak of the revolution proper. They fought for four hours, were arrested, interrogated briefly, and executed. At the request of the murdered governor's family, Xu's heart was cut out and offered to his victim's memory.[83]

Qiu Jin learned of these events in Anqing by reading the

Shanghai newspapers, but she disdained all suggestions that she flee the Datong School, although her arrest was almost a certainty. Government troops did indeed arrive in Datong on July 13. Qiu Jin and a handful of her students tried to fight off the troops but she was soon cornered and arrested. After interrogation under torture, she was beheaded on July 15.[84] Other secret societies and groups of salt smugglers, who fought in scattered risings that year, were also suppressed, though often after costly and protracted battles. The Zhejiang risings ended like all the others attempted by Sun Yatsen and Kang Youwei in the previous nine years.

With great regularity in her early poems, Qiu Jin had used her own family name of Qiu, which in Chinese has the literal meaning of "autumn"; and in scores of punning or alliterative lines that linked "Qiu" to the words for rain and wind, she evoked the chill dampness of the season, which seemed a fitting commentary on her own depressed existence as a young married woman. This period had been succeeded by one in which she showed a more spirited self-consciousness concerning her roles as a woman, and which in turn led to the heights of revolutionary bravado. But in the moments before her execution Qiu Jin wrote a final line of verse that returned to the earlier themes and because of its resonance ensured that her sorrowing side rather than the analytical or martial one would live on more vividly in the memories of her people: "Autumn rain, autumn wind, they make one die of sorrow."[85]

·3·

WANDERINGS

Qiu Jin had read of Xu Xilin's death in a Shanghai newspaper; Lu Xun read of the death of both in the Tokyo newspapers. As a fellow native of Shaoxing he could not help being affected by the news, and he attended a general meeting called by Zhejiang province students in Tokyo to mourn the two martyrs and to vilify the Manchus publicly for their cruelty; at that meeting, after a hectic debate, the students decided to send a telegram to Beijing protesting the inhumane executions.[1] This was a moderately courageous act, since if the Qing authorities disapproved of the students' behavior they could cut their stipends and order them back to China. Lu Xun, however, did not sympathize deeply with either of the revolutionary victims: he had seen the Chinese students who had traveled with Xu Xilin to Japan in 1905 and had been repelled by their behavior; he had also found it repugnant that Xu, claiming to be so revolutionary, had brought along with him to Japan special embroidered shoes for his wife's bound feet. Lu had also had some discussions with Qiu Jin while she was studying in Tokyo and had not been very impressed. He felt that the reason she acted so recklessly in Shaoxing was that she had been overidolized by wildly applauding Chinese students at her public lecture appearances in Japan the year before. She was "clapped to death," he remarked to a friend.[2]

The remark is sardonic, uncompromising, and perceptive, three traits that were to inform much of Lu Xun's later writings about cultural and political change. Lu Xun had been born in 1881, a few years after Qiu Jin, and had come to Japan at the age of twenty-one. His previous education had combined traditional classical training for the state exams, wide reading in Chinese fiction and folktales, and intensive study of English at the Westernized Nanjing Naval Training School and of geology and mineralogy in the Nanjing School of Mines. In Nanjing, along with the excitement spread by the ideas of Kang Youwei and Liang Qichao, there was, for Lu, the discovery of Thomas Huxley, whose *Evolution and Ethics* was made available during his school days in Yan Fu's classical Chinese summary and translation. As Lu Xun recalled this moment from his late teens:

> On Sunday I rushed down to the southern suburb of the city and bought a copy. It was a thick lithographed edition on white paper and sold for exactly five hundred cash. I opened it and looked in; it was printed in very good characters. The book began: "Huxley, his back to the mountains and facing the plains, sat alone in his room in southern England. Beyond his threshold the various views were all in order like the threads on a loom. He then began to imagine what the scenery had been like before the Roman general Caesar arrived in England. He hypothesized that there had been nothing but the untouched wild grasses."[3]

Lu Xun was captivated and read the book straight through. To this introduction to the fierce struggles in a world dominated by the forces of natural selection he added more varied aspects of European culture as newly published translations by the late-Qing writer Lin Shu, in classical Chinese, led him to the world of Sherlock Holmes, Rider Haggard,* and Alexandre Dumas's *La Dame aux Camélias.*[4]

In Japan, Lu Xun was torn by conflicting currents of doubt concerning the self, Chinese cultural identity, and the future of the Chinese nation which afflicted most Chinese students there,

---

* Haggard already had an astonishing reputation in China by 1900; his novel *Joan Haste* brought him even greater fame with the Chinese reading public in 1905. Lin Shu once grouped Haggard with Shakespeare as "the exceptional geniuses of a great civilized nation."

and he groped for new ways to express himself. Initially he was drawn by the claims that Liang Qichao was making for the role of literature in society. Liang, since 1896, had been recommending the reading of vernacular fiction by the populace, stating that such books could "awaken a sense of national shame" by depicting such themes as "the shameful ways of the bureaucracy, the ludicrous stupidities at the examination halls, the inveterate habit of opium smoking, the cruel torture of foot-binding."[5] (Since Lu Xun's own grandfather had had his bureaucratic career ruined and been sentenced to death for attempting massive bribery in the provincial state examinations—Lu himself had had a stand-in take the examinations during his own absence—and since Lu's father was an opium addict and his mother had caused a scandal by unbinding her own feet, he might well have been moved by this passage.[6]) After the collapse of the Hundred Days of Reform in 1898, Liang had sought exile in Japan, where he became a firm believer in the importance of the "political novel"; originally an import to Japan when the works of Bulwer-Lytton and Disraeli were translated, to great popular acclaim, the genre then drew several influential Japanese public figures to try their hand in the 1880s and 1890s. Liang may have been influenced by this combination of the successful holding of public office with the writing of political fiction, for in 1902 he began his own new journal, *New Fiction*, in Yokohama with a ringing declaration of fiction's power to "renovate" morality, religion, manners, the arts, and a nation's character.[7]

Lu Xun was stimulated to write a story for the Zhejiang students' magazine on the "Spartan spirit" as exemplified by the stand of Leonidas and his men against the Persians at Thermopylae; and he heeded Liang's words on the potential importance of science-fiction works by condensing and translating into Chinese (from Japanese translations) Jules Verne's *From the Earth to the Moon* and *Journey to the Center of the Earth*. In a slightly more scholarly vein he pieced together two factual articles, one on geology and one on Mme. Curie's work with radium.[8] Though not, as far as we know, joining any of the revolutionary Chinese organizations in Japan, he went to various rallies, and heard Chinese radicals rail at the Empress Dowager and the Chinese minister in Japan, and submit to deportation as a result.[9] And he cut off his queue.

The queue—that long pigtail of hair worn by Chinese men during the Qing dynasty—had been forced on them at the time of the Manchu conquest of China in the 1640s, when this adoption of the Manchu tribal hairstyle was seen as fitting evidence of Chinese acceptance of Manchu rule. Though the queue had been worn, even if sometimes grudgingly, for more than two centuries, it became a symbol of shame to Chinese nationalists in the late nineteenth century, especially to those who traveled abroad. Lu Xun mocked those Chinese students in Japan who kept their queues coiled up on their heads, "so that their hats stood up like Mount Fuji,"[10] though he knew that many were justifiably worried that they would be pinpointed as potential revolutionaries if they returned to China without them. (The martial young Chiang Kaishek had to be especially cautious in military school after cutting off his queue; the fiery nationalist Zhang Binglin, who had publicly cut off his queue at a Shanghai rally, had been jailed along with Zou Rong in the *Subao* case; while Sun Yatsen's revolutionary colleague Huang Xing decided to keep his intact while he was in Japan so that he could return safely to China.[11]) In later years Lu Xun vowed that he had cut off his queue for neither aesthetic nor revolutionary reasons, but simply because it was "inconvenient"; yet at the time he was obviously impressed by the significance of his own action. Like Qiu Jin after she had dressed in her Western clothes, the shorn Lu Xun at once had his photograph taken, and he inscribed a poem on the back of it for one of his closest friends:

My heart has no way to dodge the arrows loosed by love of country;
Storms weigh down like boulders and darken the gardens of my homeland.
I pass my message to the chill stars, for my people don't heed my sorrow.
I pledge to make my own blood my offering to my native land.

The poem is in classical Chinese form, and the sentiments are nationalist, but the poem also borrows its arrow image from

the romantic hero of Byron's "Lara," which Lu Xun was reading at the time.[12]

After learning enough Japanese to read and take notes, Lu
Xun made the decision to stay on and study modern medicine.
The lure of this particular vocation had previously attracted
Kang Youwei's brother, as well as Sun Yatsen, whose motives
seem to have been the generalized goal of attaining a specific
expertise that would help in China's modernization. Lu Xun
shared that to some extent. As he wrote later: "I dreamed the
beautiful dream that on my return to China I would cure patients who, like my father, had been wrongly treated; and if
war broke out, then I would serve as a doctor in the army and
simultaneously strengthen my countrymen's faith in reform."[13]
Yet Lu Xun's decision had further and deeper causes. His father had not just been "wrongly treated"; he had in fact spent
many years as an increasingly sick invalid, squandering large
sums of money on extravagantly prescribed herbal medicines
that the young Lu Xun often had to collect from the drugstore
(after first visiting the pawnshop to get some money to pay for
them). It is also known that Lu Xun had suffered, as an adoles-
cent, from severe toothaches—traditional doctors had pointed
out to him an interconnection between the teeth and the
kidneys, and between the kidneys and the male sex organs,
hinting clearly that self-abuse was the cause.[14] Such misinfor-
mation was harmful and embarrassing, and the incident may
have convinced Lu Xun of the need to strike out at such ignorance. As far as modernizing went, he also had the courageous
example of his mother, for in her mature years she had boldly
risked family and public censure by unbinding her own feet.[15]
In the broader sphere, in conversations with his friends Lu Xun
was already exploring the whole question of modernization in
its symbolic dimensions, as he argued endlessly about the ways
of curing "the sickness of the Chinese people."[16]

While she was in Japan, Qiu Jin had been buoyed on waves
of optimism concerning the Japanese victories over the Russians in 1905, but to Lu Xun the conflict was more ominous and
more ambiguous. In 1904 he had chosen to enroll at the medical school in the northern Japanese town of Sendai because he
wanted to avoid the company of other Chinese students (and

also because the school was free), but the obvious corollary of
this decision was loneliness. Furthermore, the town was a staging center for Japanese troops and equipment, and he felt
harassed by the Japanese students; he also had language difficulties, problems with his lodgings, and was even accused of
collusion with his instructors in passing his basic exams.
Though he passed all the key subjects (doing well in anatomy,
satisfactorily in physiology, and rather less well in dissection
and German), he decided to drop out of school in 1905, during
the second year of his training.[17] As Lu Xun himself described
the formative moment that led to this decision:

> In our second year we had a new course, bacteriology. All
> the bacterial forms were shown in slides, and if we com-
> pleted a section before it was time for the class to be dis-
> missed, some news pictures would be shown. Naturally at
> that time they were all about the Japanese victories over the
> Russians. But in these lantern slides there were also some
> Chinese who had acted as spies for the Russians and were
> captured by the Japanese and shot while other Chinese
> looked on. And there was I, too, in the classroom.
>   "Banzai!" The students clapped their hands and cheered.
> They cheered everything we saw; but to me the cheering
> that day was unusually discordant. Later, when I came back
> to China, I saw idlers watching criminals being shot, who
> also cheered as if they were drunk. Alas, there is nothing
> one can do about it. At that time and in that place, however,
> it made me change my mind.
>   At the end of my second year I called on Mr. Fujino to
> tell him I was going to stop studying medicine and leave
> Sendai. A shadow crossed his face, and he seemed on the
> point of speaking but then thought better of it.
>   "I want to study biology, so what you have taught me, sir,
> will still be useful." As a matter of fact, I had no intention of
> studying biology; but seeing he looked rather sad I told this
> lie to comfort him.[18]

Obviously the visual impact of these photographs had some
of the same shock value for Lu Xun that the sight of Sedan's destruction had had for Kang Youwei some thirty years earlier,
but Lu Xun was not just reacting to suffering itself: he was
reacting to the apathy and inertia on the Chinese faces. As he
explained the moment in another essay, the sight of the photo-

graphic slides of his countrymen had convinced him that medical skills were not so important as he had imagined:

> The people of a weak and backward country, however strong and healthy they may be, can only serve to be made examples of, or to witness such futile spectacles; and it is not necessarily deplorable no matter how many of them die of illness. The most important thing, therefore, was to change their spirit, and since at that time I felt that literature was the best means to this end, I determined to promote a literary movement. There were many Chinese students in Tokyo studying law, political science, physics, and chemistry, even police work and engineering, but not one studying literature or art.[19]

Before he set out to try to launch this literary movement, however, Lu Xun returned home to Shaoxing in 1906 for a denouement that would have aroused as much sardonic comment from Qiu Jin as her own death did from Lu Xun: he submitted tamely to an arranged marriage with a girl he barely knew, conducted in full ritualistic terms. The episode has grotesque aspects, since the chosen bride was so small as to appear deformed, and Lu Xun (who took part in the ceremonies wearing, it appears, one of those fake queues that so smacked of hypocrisy to him) may never have consummated the marriage. Certainly he never referred to it in his writings, the couple had no children, and he went so far as to taboo the two ideographs of his wife's name from use in his literary work (as one was meant to do for the unmentionable personal names of reigning emperors).[20]

Soon after the ceremony Lu Xun returned to Japan with his younger brother, leaving his new wife behind. He embarked on an eclectic and far-reaching program of reading, focusing especially on two categories of materials: those from countries suffering foreign occupation or threatened by disintegration, and those which showed the strength of the individual spirit and will.

The constant threat of dismemberment or partition that weak nations faced in a world dominated by the strong had been regularly mentioned by Kang Youwei, Zou Rong, and Qiu Jin, all of whom warned either directly or obliquely that unless the Chinese state were reformed it might well disintegrate under the pressures from foreign powers. The new vernacular journals and newspapers, addressing a wide audience of potential and actual Chinese nationalists, discussed such topics as the way that Russia, Prussia, and Austria carved up Poland between 1772 and 1795; the fate of the Jews and the possibilities inherent in the Zionist movement; and the problems that blacks faced in the United States (even elaborating on such specialized areas as the work-study program at Tuskegee Institute, in Alabama).[21] Picking up on such currents, Lu Xun and his brother concentrated particularly on literature from Russia, Eastern Europe, and the Balkans, carefully translating (usually from prior German translations) such poets as the Polish Adam Mickiewicz and the Hungarian Sándor Petőfi.[22] Some of their ideas on these countries crystallized during informal lectures given by the radical Zhang Binglin which Lu and his brother attended each Sunday in Tokyo. Zhang, a brilliant polemicist and editorial writer for *Subao*, who was bitterly hostile to the Manchus and hated Kang Youwei for what he considered gradualist and pro-Manchu attitudes, had been released from prison in 1906 after serving a three-year term in Shanghai along with Zou Rong and others accused in the *Subao* case. Though Lu Xun found Zhang's classical essay style almost impossible to comprehend, he so admired Zhang's poems of homage to Zou Rong—written while Zhang was in prison and published in a Japanese newspaper—that he committed them all to memory.[23] Lu Xun's brother recalled of these Tokyo lectures that "Zhang regularly incited people against the Manchus, and used to lecture on the topic. Later, as I paid attention to the literature of national revolution I came to connect this literature with that of weak and small peoples. Among works by Dutch, Polish, Jewish and Indian writers several described the decayed conditions of those countries, and others described their tragic loss of independence. When I read these they had a deep effect upon me."[24]

The threat of weakness could also have the positive effect of bringing out new dimensions of the individual will, as Qiu Jin had shown in her own life, and many other authors had shown in their lives or in their work. In essays written in Japan during

1907 and 1908, Lu Xun dealt at length with European writers who "were firmly determined to rebel, who devoted their energy to action and ran counter to the common disposition of their contemporaries." Lu Xun called such men the "Mara" poets, ascribing to them the awesome powers associated with the Buddhist god of destruction and rebellion of that name.[25] Mickiewicz and Petőfi were in this category, and the true archetype for Lu Xun was Byron; others were Shelley and Pushkin, Lermontov and Gogol, Ernst Arndt and Karl Körner. Lu Xun's thinking about these "Mara" poets was influenced by his readings in Nietzsche and Ibsen, and by his feeling that he was living in a world where a balanced combination of intellect and emotion was no longer possible. One must therefore throw one's weight behind the "superhuman willpower" that could be called forth from the emotional realm, and pursue moral and aesthetic rather than material values. "If we want to work out a policy for the present," he wrote, "we must examine the past and prepare for the future, discard the material and elevate the spirit, rely on the individual and exclude the mass. When the individual is exalted to develop his full capacity, the country will be strengthened and will arise. Why should we be engrossed in such trivialities as gold, iron, congresses, and constitutions?"[26] At the end of his essay on the "Mara" poets he asked: "Where are now the warriors of the world of the spirit? Where are those who raise their voices for truth, who lead us to goodness, beauty, strength and health? Where are those who utter heartwarming words, who will lead us out of the wilderness? Our homes are gone and the nation is destroyed, yet we have no Jeremiah crying out his last sad song to the world and to posterity."[27]

These and other essays of the same period show that Lu Xun was a believer neither in Kang Youwei's plan for industrialization and constitutionalism nor in the more democratic and socialist aspects of Sun Yatsen's Revolutionary Alliance platform, which would permit the masses a voice in the political sphere. Those parts of the West that had experienced the recent benefits of material progress had already experienced materialism's evil consequences, wrote Lu Xun: "Mind and spirit progressively deteriorated; aims and taste degenerated into vulgarity."

At the same time, one had to "exclude the mass" because "right and wrong cannot be decided by the People"; they could offer no more than pressure to conform, though in the simple riches of their folk tradition there lay some hope for a purer understanding of nature and a deeper aspiration toward the absolute—purer and deeper, at least, than anything the traditional Chinese gentry could offer.[28]

Thus Lu Xun had moved beyond politics as he had moved beyond medicine. Knowing various figures in both the Restoration Society and the Revolutionary Alliance, he did not choose to join their parties. His goal was nothing less than to bring out the reserves of willpower latent in the Chinese people, to imbue his countrymen with the heroic and demonic strength to change their destiny. But in this realm, as he labored, everything began to go awry: the teacher from whom he was taking special classes in Russian tried to commit suicide, and the classes were discontinued; a literary magazine Lu Xun tried to found, ambitiously called *New Life* (the title taken from Dante's *Vita Nuova*), folded before the first issue; a proofreading job taken to earn extra money collapsed when the printers got into difficulties; and the two cherished and beautifully edited volumes of stories translated from German, Russian, and other sources—on which he had set such store as a means of transforming Chinese consciousness—sold a total of about twenty copies each in Tokyo when they were published in 1908, and about the same number in Shanghai, out of an initial printing run of fifteen hundred.[29]

When Lu gave up his work in Japan and returned to China to take up a teaching job in Hangzhou in 1909, it was with hopes most deeply muted. He soon moved from Hangzhou back to his hometown of Shaoxing; there he was a popular teacher (rather strict: he forbade his students to cut off their own queues) and was regarded as particularly bold for the way he was willing to discuss problems of sexual reproduction in his physiology lectures. But he did not write.

Liang Qichao also believed in writing as a means of transforming the Chinese people, and at the turn of the century, just around the time Lu Xun first arrived in Tokyo, he began writing a novel called *The Future of New China*. In form it was a futuristic political satire, drawing on a variety of strands, from Bellamy's *Looking Backward* (which Liang had seen in Chinese translation) to current Japanese novels set in the future; Liang may also have been influenced by Kang Youwei's utopian visions, which were being given final form in the *Book of the Great Community*. Liang sets the action of his novel in 1962, as the Chinese people are celebrating the fifty years that have passed since a "new order" was established in China. An elderly narrator lets his thoughts drift back to 1902, when a young constitutionalist and a young revolutionary, both recently returned from Europe, debate the future course of China. At this point Liang apparently got stuck—not surprisingly, in view of the very pressing problems that he and Kang Youwei faced from Sun Yatsen—and he abandoned the novel after four chapters in order to concentrate on political work and on the editing and publication of political journals.[30]

From the time that Kang came down from Darjeeling, in 1903, through to the final collapse of the Qing dynasty in 1912, he and Liang were to be constantly seeking an answer to the conundrum of gradualism versus revolutionary activity; the difficulty of this was increased by Sun Yatsen's pointed attacks on Kang's supporters as "criminals" and pro-Manchu "racial traitors" as well as by the Manchus' own swing toward reform, which undercut Kang's complaints against them. An additional problem was the reformers' constant shortage of the money they needed to keep their hopes alive.

Obviously the name of the Society to Protect the Emperor had to be changed, despite the depth of Kang's emotion associated with it. Among the Chinese in Canada and the United States, the name China Reform Association came to be used instead. In 1906, as the Manchus prepared the commission of five to go abroad to study foreign constitutions with a view to possible change in China, Kang accepted the inevitable, and adopted the name of National Constitutional Association. Liang, however, preferred yet another name, the Imperial Constitutional Association; the upshot was that, though finally the "Protect the Emperor" name was dropped, all three others stayed in circulation among the overseas Chinese. To add to the confusion, Liang founded yet another group, initially based in Tokyo, named the Political Information Society, to work for the establishment of a Chinese national assembly, a strong and independent judiciary, more local autonomy, and greater reciprocal rights for China in foreign relations. These were planks that Kang, too, could endorse, but since Liang and others wanted to have this organization directed from within China proper, neither the still-exiled Kang nor Liang himself could head it. So it was with another reformer as "secretary-general," and with the backing of local merchants and scholars, that the society opened its doors in Shanghai early in 1908. Kang and Liang were not without competition, since several other clubs and societies with rather similar names and goals, run by Chinese entrepreneurs and gentry, had recently been established.[31]

For some time now, Kang's organizations overseas had shown a more martial face and continuing evidence of strong financial backing. One proof of this was the rebuilding of the San Francisco headquarters of the Society to Protect the Emperor, which had been destroyed in the great earthquake of 1906: within months the necessary money had been collected from over one hundred and fifty individual donors (offering contributions that ranged from five to four hundred dollars); one of the donors was the founder of the Guangzhou Bank, another a wealthy Chinese who was an important figure in the Fresno gambling world, and a third the head of one of the major "fighting Tongs."[32] Such swift and enthusiastic support was backed by an imposing infrastructure of military schools run by the China Reform Association; these schools functioned successfully in at least twenty-one American cities. Uniformed Chinese cadets, armed with discarded National Guard weapons, met weekly to sing the school song (composed by Kang) and to drill under orders of American instructors. In Los Angeles the Chinese students of the Western Military Academy marched proudly in the Pasadena Tournament of Roses Parade with their "general," the flamboyant writer and military theorist Homer Lea; in New York the Third Chinese Regiment was reviewed by Kang Youwei on Mott Street during his 1905 trip, after which he traveled in a coach drawn by white horses to a reception at the Waldorf-Astoria.[33] In terms of specific Confucian ideology—as if echoing Kang's dream for Confucian academies to be built in the West, which he had presented to the Qing rulers in 1895—a Chinese graduate student at Columbia University founded the Association of the Confucian Religion in New York City, to foster knowledge of the sage's teachings. (This association prospered and later moved, first to Shanghai and then to Beijing. Oddly enough, major contributors were awarded the status of "life members" in homophonic ideographs for the Western phrase—as "laifu meibo"—rather than an honorific Chinese term.[34])

A major area of further political activism came through Kang's energetic attempts to modify the United States Chinese exclusion laws, and President Theodore Roosevelt granted him an interview to discuss the problem; failing any change, Kang and many Chinese worked successfully for a time to encourage a boycott of American goods among overseas Chinese and in China itself, a movement that was surprisingly successful and showed the strength of Chinese nationalism. Friends of Qiu Jin's backed the boycott in Shanghai, where it continued until 1907. Only slowly did Chinese enthusiasm wane, after the Americans in turn began to boycott Chinese-owned businesses.[35]

Kang was also, as always, writing a stream of essays and books on reform, focusing especially on issues of bureaucratic organization and recruitment, on scientific education for Chinese citizens, and on structures for local self-government. In the summer of 1908 he and Liang published a manifesto which they addressed to the Qing government in the name of the Chinese communities in two hundred cities around the world. It can stand as an accurate summary of the stage Kang's political thinking had reached after his varied experiences in exile: convocation of a national assembly to achieve genuine constitutional rule; retirement of the Empress Dowager, and removal of the court eunuchs from all positions where they might influence political decisions; an end to discrimination against Han Chinese in favor of Manchus in bureaucratic assignments; res-

toration of Emperor Guangxu to power as a constitutional
monarch; transfer of the capital from Beijing to a new site in
the Yangtze Valley region; abolition of the provincial governor-general system and its replacement by a system of smaller
regional administrative zones that could be more effectively
controlled by the central government; and establishment of
special bureaus to attend to China's peripheral areas such as
Manchuria, Mongolia, Tibet, and Xinjiang, while increasing
the military power of China through universal conscription,
naval development, and construction of major munitions factories. When these measures were vigorously championed by
the new Political Information Society, the Kang-Liang front organization in Shanghai, the Qing court responded by arresting
several of its members and ordering the society suppressed.[36]

One might have thought the goals in this manifesto—with
the exception of the clause on Emperor Guangxu's becoming
constitutional monarch—could be accepted by most Chinese,
whether overseas or at home, but in fact the tensions between
Kang's supporters and Sun Yatsen's had continued to grow
more bitter with the years and there was little possibility for a
meeting of minds. Battles were fought not just with words in
pamphlets and newspaper articles but for control of those
newspapers themselves—for instance, Kang's supporters took
over a paper of Sun's in Singapore, and Sun's supporters
ousted Kang's from one in San Francisco.[37] Other battles were
fought for leadership of the military cadet groups in the United
States, for access to funds in Chinese enclaves all over the
world, for support among foreign communities and by foreign
governments, for control over management of secret societies
and benevolent associations. In 1906 Sun's supporters went so
far as to accuse Kang's daughter Tongbi, then a student in
Hartford, Connecticut, of deliberately defrauding overseas
Chinese. Kang ordered them sued for libel in the Hong Kong
courts and eventually won his case.[38] Kang's organizations
controlled more money because they were especially strong in
the United States and Canada, where trading ventures sponsored by the Society to Protect the Emperor and the China Reform Society initially made hundreds of thousands of dollars,
most spectacularly in real-estate ventures in Mexico, but also

through banking, trade, and restaurants. But Kang and his assistants also drained those funds by establishing more new schools and newspapers than they could well afford and by making a number of overoptimistic investments, including major ones in Chinese railways and in a streetcar concession in Torreón, Mexico. With the collapse of the Mexican President Porfirio Díaz's regime in 1910, Kang was deprived of most of the resources remaining that had not been lost to absconding associates, through carelessness, or as a result of Kang's own extravagance.[39]

One cannot calculate the costs of Kang Youwei's peregrinations between 1904 and 1910, but they must have been enormous: Herculaneum, Pompeii, and Rome; Milan, Paris, Berlin, Copenhagen; West Point, Yellowstone National Park, Salt Lake City, Monte Carlo, the Alhambra, Fez; Uppsala and Trondheim; Kandy, Luxor, Jerusalem, Constantinople—these are only a fraction of the places he visited, and in many of them he stayed in the most luxurious hotels. Why did he travel so much? Partly because he felt homeless and restless, as he admitted to Liang Qichao. Partly because as of 1907 he had a new companion, a seventeen-year-old Chinese girl from Guangdong province who had settled with her family in the United States. With delightful candor (in the very spirit that Kang Youwei had exhorted the world's women to adopt) she had offered herself to Kang as consort (his third), companion, and secretary, after being passionately impressed by his photograph. (They traveled everywhere together, lingered awhile on a little island Kang had bought off the Swedish coast, and had a son in December 1908.)[40] But almost certainly the main reason that Kang Youwei traveled in this way is that he was either consciously or subconsciously emulating Confucius, the sage he had admired so deeply since his youth and had written about so provocatively. Confucius had wandered, also in seeming randomness, among the fragmented states of fifth-century B.C. China. Seeking a worthy ruler to employ him and finding none, he had spent his peripatetic life in writing, teaching, and reflecting on the problems of human life and politics in this troubled world. At almost every place Kang himself visited, he wrote elegant, classical poems, often very long, not just celebrating the scenery but reflecting on the history of each area and its possible lessons for the present or the future.[41] A wondrous flight by balloon, high above the roofs of Paris, brought reflections on fate and Napoleon's power; a visit to the Netherlands brought reflections on Peter the Great's ship-building apprenticeship; the sight of Constantinople brought joy at the Ottoman empire's restoration of constitutional government, and regret that this achievement still eluded China; the massed mourners at noon beside the Wailing Wall in Jerusalem brought thoughts on human sorrows and on the weak or fragmented nations of the world, which China might well soon join, and on Kang's own thwarted hopes:

Solomon built this three thousand years ago,
At the foot of the Wall crowds of men and women still cry out;
Each noon hundreds throng through the narrow streets,
Stand pressed against the Wall and weep, tears flow like springs.

Their treasures sent to Rome, how can we tell their sorrows?
It was during the time of the Han dynasty, the details are lost in the
*   mists of the past.*
We too have faced disasters in our two thousand years as a nation,
Foreign invaders brought chaos to China, laid waste our capital under
*   stormy skies.*

There is no way I can avoid getting caught up in my feelings for people,
And it was for my country's sake that I brought sorrows to self and fam-
*   ily.*
I weep for my brother, for my friends, on the cloudy execution grounds,
I weep for their bodies unburied, and our three ancestral graves all now
*   defiled.*

One can never abandon one's native country or rest forever undisturbed;
I remain always a Chinese man, looking in the direction of my former
*   home.*
Eyes askance I weep under the coverlet, my spirit torn by doubts,
And seek just to tell my fellow patriots what these Jews are like.[42]

Sun Yatsen, too, was endlessly wandering: in Japan, in Southeast Asia, in Europe, in Canada, and in the United States. But he showed a fixity of purpose in his assaults on the Man-

chu regime that far exceeded Kang Youwei's. In the years between 1905 and 1910—quite apart from the failed risings in
Anhui and Zhejiang provinces, where Qiu Jin and Xu Xilin had
been killed, and in which his Revolutionary Alliance was only
peripherally involved—Sun was in some way connected with
half a dozen attempted risings in areas as varied as Manchuria,
Guangdong, Guangxi, and Hunan. The combinations of forces
involved in such risings constantly changed, depending on the
availability of funds, the nature of the local power structure,
and the speed of the Qing response. At Pingliuli, on the border
between the provinces of Hunan and Jiangxi, in central China,
dissident coal miners, secret-society members, and mutinous
soldiers sparked a rising in December 1906 which the Revolutionary Alliance and local radical students tried to join and direct; had they been successful, they would have forged a
formidable cross-class coalition, but local Qing forces were too
strong and the groups fragmented.[43] In Manchuria, during the
spring of 1907, a youthful supporter of Sun's tried to win the
allegiance of mounted bandits in the Manchurian-Korean border region, but was foiled by Qing troops.[44] In December 1907
Sun and other neophyte military leaders tried to move from a
base near Hanoi to join up with a larger group of mountain
guerrillas in Guangxi province; that failing, and Sun's having
been deported by the French, in March 1908 other Revolutionary Alliance members made a strike into western Guangdong province with two hundred Chinese revolutionary troops;
that failing also, the revolutionaries tried during April to link
with another small rising farther west, in Yunnan province.
Again they were foiled, and the French deported the remaining
Revolutionary Alliance members whom they could identify.[45]
In November 1908 members of the Revolutionary Alliance,
having successfully infiltrated the ranks of several brigades in
the Guangdong New Army, were partly responsible for starting
a mutiny near Guangzhou, in an attempt to capitalize on the
unrest caused by the recent deaths of the Emperor Guangxu
and the Empress Dowager. However, the mutiny did not
spread and enough troops stayed loyal to the Manchus to suppress the mutineers.[46]

These ceaseless failures led to arguments within the Revolutionary Alliance concerning Sun's abilities, and to a number of demands for his resignation or replacement, as well as to his being abandoned by many influential members of the Restoration Society. The failures also caused some revolutionaries to return to their earlier belief in the need for assassination of senior Manchu figures in order to spark massive reprisals that would in turn lead to revolt. In this spirit the Revolutionary Alliance veteran Liu Sifu lost all the fingers of his left hand in an unsuccessful attempt to kill a senior general in Guangzhou, and Sun's friend Wang Jingwei attempted to blow up the Manchu regent in Beijing (he was arrested before the attempt, though not executed).[47]

Yet Sun's very tenacity brought him a steady stream of new followers, and he was always able to get enough funds from overseas Chinese—whether in Singapore, Hawaii, or Vancouver—to keep some of his revolutionary newspapers in circulation and to make some arms available to his supporters. Particularly after 1908, with the death of Emperor Guangxu, closely followed by that of the Empress Dowager, and the establishment of a new Manchu regency ruling in the name of the boy-emperor Puyi, the main reason for continuing to give support to any Manchu monarch was eroded and Kang Youwei's supporters in the United States began to melt away; this was important to Sun, who had always had to yield to Kang's superior organization there, and he was able to move into the vacuum. A pro-Sun Youth Party founded in San Francisco in 1909 brought him new support among students, laborers, and schoolteachers; in October of that same year he traveled to New York, where he received enough offers of loyalty to found a small revolutionary cell. This in turn led to contacts with secret-society elders in Boston and with prorevolutionary Chinese Christians in Chicago. One of the Chinese translators working for the Canadian immigration staff was also won over, and could thus ease entry for Sun's supporters into North America.[48]

Though Sun had to be careful of the entrenched and powerful secret societies, which were still in general loyal to Kang Youwei and continued to believe in the measured political and commercial operations with which Kang was associated, Sun's youthful supporters charged into the breach with their new radical journals, accusing the elder generation of reformers of being "mice and cattle." They backed feminist causes, sponsored plays written by and for Chinese women, and invoked the powerful image of Qiu Jin in their cause. In their political statements they set forth frankly what Sun Yatsen's party had come to stand for: strong belief in democratic government, vigorous nationalism, some backing for socialist theories, and implacable hostility to Kang Youwei.[49] During the early months of 1911 Sun raised some seventy thousand dollars from the Chinese in the United States and Canada, a staggering sum in view of his decade-long record of failures; he sent this money to Hong Kong, where his lieutenants were planning their largest and most ambitious rising to date. The Guangzhou uprising of April 1911 once again followed the strategy of combining Revolutionary Alliance members in a coordinated rising with sympathizers inside the Guangzhou New Army units; but though this joint force stormed the offices of the governor-general and fought vigorously, there had been massive security leaks, many of the expected sympathizers from army units outside the city never joined, and Sun's supporters were suppressed by troops loyal to the government. Nearly one hundred revolutionaries were killed, and the Revolutionary Alliance network in Guangdong province was wrecked.[50]

The mere fact that so many risings could take place year after year illustrates the desperation that many Chinese felt. Frustrated by their country's weakness as a power in the international order, and tempted to blame the Manchus for that weakness, they were also alarmed by the burgeoning military and institutional power that the Manchu regents for Emperor Puyi were developing: the New Armies (despite infiltration by members of the Revolutionary Alliance) promised to give the Qing quite a new kind of power base; the newly organized cabinet form of government was dominated by Manchus, and might soon bring provincial administrations more tightly under Manchu control; while the Manchu attempt to centralize China's diffuse and ineffective railway network, which at one level could be seen as an intelligent and much-needed reform, was also vigorously protested as evidence of a Manchu deter-

mination to undermine provincial autonomy even further and
to break the influence of an emergent Chinese entrepreneurial
class. Sun Yatsen was thus riding a wave of broadly diffused
anxiety and anger, and the Revolutionary Alliance was too
small an organization to represent (let alone contain) the conflicting interests of emancipated students, local gentry, merchants, women, and overseas Chinese.[51]

Sun did try to respond to the new scale on which anti-Qing
feeling was manifesting itself by abandoning the "southern
strategy" by which he had used base areas in Hong Kong,
Hanoi, or Singapore to foment internal revolt, and in mid-1911
he ordered a new committee of the Revolutionary Alliance to
be formed farther north, in Shanghai. Staffed by revolutionaries from the central provinces of Hunan and Hubei, this
committee had the direct goal of encouraging risings in the
members' home provinces, especially in Wuhan (the tri-city
area comprising Hankou, Hanyang, and Wuchang), where its
members worked vigorously to foster contact with the New
Army units in the region. But Sun's influence was limited, and
when revolutionary troops in Wuchang mutinied on October
10, 1911, fearing arrest after an accidental bomb explosion had
alerted Qing police to their activities, there were no senior Revolutionary Alliance members in the area. When they finally got
there (disguised as Red Cross workers), they found the revolutionary forces under the command of a senior former Qing
army officer. They lost the foreign-concession and commercial
center of Hankou after two weeks' heavy fighting, and lost the
major industrial city of Hanyang also, after three weeks more
of intense battles with Qing troops, but these events triggered a
series of mutinies, risings, and defections throughout China
that brought down the Qing dynasty.[52]

Sun Yatsen, who heard the news of the tri-city risings while
he was traveling by train between Denver and Kansas City on
one of his fund-raising trips, did not at once return to China.
Instead—and this only highlighted the importance of the European presence in China—he traveled to Europe in an attempt to
present the republican case persuasively and to prevent any of
the European governments from intervening on the side of the
Qing dynasty. Having received guarded, but to him encourag-

ing, indications of support, he returned to China, reaching Shanghai on December 25, where he received a tumultuous welcome. A week later he traveled to Nanjing; on January 1, 1912, he was named provisional president of the Republic of China.

This arrival of Sun's had little in common with Lenin's triumphant journey to the Finland Station in 1917, though each was returning from protracted exile as head of a revolutionary party that had brought down a mighty ruling house. It is true that the Revolutionary Alliance had contacts in many parts of China: with officers and men in the New Armies, with secret-society leaders, with powerful members of merchant associations, with students, and with the elected representatives of the new provincial assemblies of China, which had first met on a formal basis in 1909. But as a leader Sun had little control over the power seizures that took place after the Wuhan fighting sparked risings across the land. In southern China, for example, though Guangdong province was controlled in part by members of the Revolutionary Alliance or by militarists sympathetic to them, much of the power in the neighboring province of Guangxi was held by a bandit leader–turned–soldier who had actually suppressed the Revolutionary Alliance's risings, while the military governor of Yunnan province was a deeply loyal student of Liang Qichao's and a firm believer in the Japanese martial spirit.[53]

The picture was no clearer in central China. In Hunan province, power ended up in the hands of the scholarly president of the Hunanese assembly, after members of a society in favor of constitutional monarchy had had the leading members of the Revolutionary Alliance assassinated. In Hubei province the new military governor was a career officer with a long history of anti–Revolutionary Alliance activities, who had consented to lead republican forces only under threats of physical coercion. Shanghai, at least, was controlled by Chen Chimei, a capable military officer who had joined the Revolutionary Alliance in Tokyo; but Chen did not countenance other radical allies, especially the members of the former Restoration Society, and he had their most important spokesman assassinated in early 1912.[54] (China's future leaders played their first minor roles in these troubled days: Chiang Kaishek, born in Ningbo, and educated at a military school in Tokyo, where he became a passionate admirer of Zou Rong's *The Revolutionary Army* and joined the Revolutionary Alliance, rose along with his commanding officer, Chen Chimei, and became a regimental commander in 1911 while still only twenty-four; Mao Zedong, son of a Hunan farmer, aged eighteen and a student in Changsha in 1911, joined the Hunan Army at this time, though he saw no active military service, just the bodies of those former revolutionaries cut down in the streets by the military men of the dawning Republic.[55])

The more northerly provinces were directly or indirectly under the control of Yuan Shikai. Yuan, formerly commander of the powerful and modernized Qing military force known as the Beiyang Army, had been the officer responsible for arresting the 1898 reformers and breaking the Emperor Guangxu's power in that year. He had himself been forced into retirement by the Manchu regents for the boy-emperor Puyi after the deaths of Guangxu and the Empress Dowager in 1908, on the spurious ground that he had a serious foot ailment that prevented him from carrying out his duties. But the senior officers commanding the other New Army units in northern China were personally loyal to Yuan, and when the 1911 fighting erupted in Wuhan these troops refused to obey the Qing court and remained largely inactive; Yuan, in addition, "regretfully" refused the Manchu orders that he return to active duty by declaring that his foot ailment was still too serious! While the Beiyang Army dawdled, the Manchus finally agreed to Yuan's conditions for leading his troops against the revolutionaries: the Manchus should convene a national assembly, organize a cabinet responsible to that assembly, sanction political parties, declare a general amnesty, and confirm Yuan as supreme military commander. That agreed to, the Beiyang Army recaptured Hankou and Hanyang from the Revolutionary Alliance forces, and the Manchus named Yuan prime minister of the provisional parliament in Beijing; but at the same time the delegates in central China elected Sun Yatsen provisional president in revolutionary-held Nanjing. Delicate and protracted negotiations among Yuan, Sun, and the Manchu regents ensued; the conclusion was the abdication of the Manchu regime on February 12, 1912, followed the next day by Sun's resignation as provisional president. On February 15 Yuan was elected provisional president of China by the Nanjing assembly, to serve until such time as a constitution could be promulgated and national elections could be held.[56]

In the summer of 1911 Kang Youwei had rejoined Liang Qichao at Liang's Japanese home in Hyogo prefecture. "For thirteen years, in Hong Kong and Singapore, I've been living apart from you," wrote Kang in the colophon to a reunion poem, "and it has been eight years since I saw you in person. Your son and daughter, born in Japan, don't even recognize me. Seeing each other again, it's as if I were dreaming." The reunion was initially a happy one: Kang brought his young consort with him, and had the bittersweet satisfaction of seeing his dead brother's daughter enrolled as a student in the Japanese Women's University.[57] But the news of the October rising in Wuhan and the violence that accompanied it horrified him and destroyed his hopes for a peaceful transition to constitutional monarchy. He wrote to a friend who had sent a telegram about the risings:

> Hearing that the upheaval is so great causes me terrible pain. I've been meaning to write to you but couldn't bring myself to do it. The Wuhan army could not strike up to the north after the initial uprising because they thought they'd be prevented by the government land and naval forces, so they could not press forward. They didn't realize that the government lacked sufficient confidence in its New Army troops to transfer them to the front. Furthermore the government lacked arms, and money for the troops' salaries, and wasted a week or more; on top of which the motor vehicles were too small to tow the artillery. So they told every locality to look out for itself and the whole country has descended into chaos.[58]

Kang reached, as so often, for foreign parallels and found three that were mutually reinforcing in their bleakness: the example of France showed the futility of high revolutionary expectations; the example of India illustrated what happened to a nation divided; and if republican government had worked in the United States, as Kang had to admit it had, that was only because the population was small at the time of the American Revolution, and English democratic traditions were deeply rooted in the society—neither condition pertained in China.[59] Therefore, again, Kang clung to hopes for restraint; where once, sixteen years before, he had warned the Emperor that misplaced reforms would be like climbing trees to catch fish, now he wrote that for China to plunge into revolutionary democracy was like asking a savage to fly an airplane.[60]

Liang Qichao shared Kang's doubts—though in his case, being deeply aware of the divisions between Sun and other members of the Revolutionary Alliance, he feared that a neater parallel to China would turn out to have been the recent case of the Mexican Revolution: there Francisco Madero, having successfully ousted President Porfirio Díaz, ended by fighting against Emiliano Zapata.[61]

Over the next few months Liang and Kang played out the last moves in their attempt to have some kind of gradual transition in China's government. Since a full constitutional monarchy seemed impractical in the current revolutionary situation, Kang elaborated a different theory, which he called "token monarchy in a republic." Under this system the monarch would give continuity to the state through hereditary leadership, but would in fact be no more powerful "than a religious image in a temple, made of clay and wood." Either the Manchu boy-emperor could serve in this role, thought Kang, or perhaps the lineal descendant of Confucius, who bore the hereditary title Duke Kung. Kang wrote to the revolutionary leaders urging this system, and to other friends in both northern and southern China.[62]

Liang Qichao developed an even more elaborate plan: working through contacts in the Beijing Imperial Guards, he would try to foment a palace coup that would install the boy-emperor's uncle—brother of the deceased Emperor Guangxu—as prime minister of China. The Chinese official considered most responsible for alienating the Chinese gentry from the regime could then be executed, the Emperor would publish a "confession of his errors," and the Manchus would adopt Chinese surnames. Faced with the prospect of a new unified national government, the Revolutionary Alliance would see the disastrous effects of continued armed uprising, and a China true to at least some of Liang and Kang's values would be preserved. In November 1911, after the Qing court, pressured by some of the radical officers in the northern army, lifted the ban of exile from Kang and Liang, Liang made a rapid visit to Manchuria to discuss these ideas with army leaders, some of whom had been radical students in Japan and had worked with him. But the mission turned out to be frustrating and dangerous: one of his key contacts was assassinated, other officers who attempted a mutiny in northern China were executed, and the area around Fengtian in southern Manchuria was threatened by bandits. Liang's friends warned him to flee, and only ten days after he had arrived he returned to Japan. An attempt to develop a second plan, to hold Guangdong province loyal to Kang and Liang's forces, ended in similar frustration and failure.[63]

Once the Manchu ruler abdicated in February 1912, Kang seemed to accept the inevitable. He wrote to his overseas Chinese supporters that, though he deeply regretted the "tragic bloodshed," there was now a republic in China; they should close ranks in a new National People's Party and take an active part in the work of national reconstruction. And he encouraged a friend of his in the overseas Chinese community to take up a seat in the new parliament, even though the situation was fraught with difficulty. Kang himself, however, did not return to China but continued his life of study and reflection in Japan. His relations with Liang now grew quite strained. Liang had flatly turned down invitations to serve in the "cabinet" of Yuan Shikai under the dying Qing regime, but a stream of letters kept urging him to separate himself from Kang and to return to China and serve in the new Republic. By the spring of 1912, as he moved toward a decision, he and Kang had a more or less open rift; Liang pushed ahead, and in October 1912 he finally left Japan for China.[64]

Liang's return to his homeland, after all the dramas that had led up to it, turned out to be curiously unpleasant. After a very rough trip from Japan, cooped up in the cramped cabin of a tiny ship where there was no room even to pace on the deck and enjoy the sea air, Liang found that the ship simply stopped outside the harbor of Dagu because of strong winds in conjunction with adverse tides that made it impossible to enter the shallow harbor. For three infuriating days all Liang could do was look over the water toward a strip of Chinese shore. As he wrote to his daughter on the third of those days:

> It's now the eighth, and we are still sitting just off Dagu. Fifteen years ago, in my hasty flight from China, I hid out here for eleven days. . . . For more than a decade I've been hoping to return to my own country and for the past several months I've been getting my plans together. How could one guess that, after all that, I'd spend another three days on this shallow sheet of water a few feet wide that might as well be a thousand miles. Nobody has the faintest idea when we will ever get ashore. I don't think you can find these kinds of shallow-water harbors anywhere else on the globe except in this venerable and great country of ours. Shut up here in this cabin day after day, I know nothing of what is going on in the world: Has chaos in Beijing thrown everything topsy-turvy? Have several countries collapsed elsewhere in the world?[65]

It was a depressing portent of the muddles and frustrated hopes that Liang and so many others were to meet in the years ahead; depressing, too, for those gathered on the shore, waiting to welcome the exile home.

Lu Xun, teaching in Shaoxing, began to write about the revolution when it first erupted, though he could not find much drama in it. Most people simply followed the pattern established in the Zhejiang capital city, Hangzhou, where the Manchu garrison had surrendered to Chinese revolutionary troops on November 6 after two days of desultory fighting. The provincial assembly, where gentry and merchant interests predominated, was the only organized civilian institutional body and took the lead in declaring provincial independence; its members joined forces with New Army units (many of whom had previously joined the Revolutionary Alliance) and some local secret-society forces to disarm Qing government troops and take control of the province's railways. After the assembly had elected Zhejiang's new governor—a well-liked member of the gentry who had once led a successful protest against the Qing government's railway policy in his province—a series of appointments was made to deal with the armed forces, finance, education, and industry. In a few cases new officials were also sent out from Hangzhou to replace dismissed Qing prefects in the smaller cities, but in most areas the local landlords and gentry who had been strongest in the late Qing dynasty consolidated their control over the structures of government. In Shaoxing the former Qing prefect was in fact retained as head of the new civil government. Merchants were influential in the reorganization, but so were several radicals who had been connected with the old Datong School. And when disorder in the surrounding countryside became so acute that the citizens decided they needed a separate military governor, the man they got was the same secret-society leader who had been Qiu Jin's revolutionary contact in 1907, a man named Wang Jinfa.[66]

Lu Xun described how a friend from his Japan days came to call on him in some excitement, saying they should go out to take a look at "free" Shaoxing:

> So we walked through the streets, and saw white flags everywhere. But though outwardly all was changed, beneath the surface all went on as before; for this was a military government organized by a few of the old-style gentry. The chief shareholder in the railway company was head of the administration, the moneylender had become director of the arsenal. . . . As soon as a few youngsters raised an outcry, Wang Jinfa came in with his troops from Hangzhou—in fact he would probably have come even if there had been no outcry. After his arrival he was surrounded by a crowd of idlers and new members of the revolutionary party, and reigned supreme as "Military Governor Wang." In less than ten days most of his men in the administration, who had arrived in cotton clothes, were wearing fur-lined gowns although it was not yet cold.[67]

In a short story which he completed early in 1912, Lu Xun set out to capture this vision of a revolution that didn't happen, although the anticipation and anxiety about its being about to happen were genuine enough. The story—to which he never gave a title—describes the rebellion through a child's eyes: the narrator is a nine-year-old boy, who develops his perceptions partly from his own observations and partly from listening to the words of two key speakers. One of these is the man who teaches him the Confucian classics, a pedantic and worldly scholar irreverently named "Master Baldy"; the other is "Old Wang," the doorkeeper at the child's family home, patient, kind, who long ago saw the "Longhaired" bandits (as the Taiping rebels in the 1860s were known, from their refusal to wear the Manchu queue) when they briefly seized the city of Shaoxing.

The little group, sitting outside on a summer's evening, is startled by the news that the "Longhairs" are coming. The child knows enough to realize these cannot really be the Taipings, who were defeated and died long ago, but since they are "rebels"—of whatever kind—the mention of their coming is enough to stir the populace to desperate and contradictory activity:

> I noticed that there were more people on the road than ants on an ant hill. They all seemed frightened and were wandering about as if they couldn't decide which way to go. Most were carrying things, though a few were probably preparing to flee the impending difficulties. I noticed that among them were quite a few people from He market who were apparently fleeing to Wu town; the residents of Wu town, on the other hand, were obviously fleeing in the direction of He market! Old Wang told me that he had been through this kind of thing before and there was no reason to get excited prematurely.[68]

Old Wang's comment is firmly rooted in his own past experiences: "How many times have I heard people say, 'The Longhairs are coming,' " he tells the listening boy. "When the Longhairs really *did* come, it was terrifying. But what did it amount to, after all?"[69] Yet Lu Xun is no sentimentalist about "age-old peasant wisdom" or any similar cliché; the narrator lets us know that long ago Wang's father made money out of feeding those same Longhaired rebels in his hometown, while Wang and the other villagers chased the defeated Taipings with spades and hoes, fighting each other for the loot that the fleeing rebels dropped. Thus Wang's sense of survival is not so different from Master Baldy's, which Lu Xun develops in a paragraph that is an early crystallization of his feeling of contempt for the Confucian gentry-scholars; he was to develop and refine that contempt in his writings for the rest of his life:

> People used to say that my teacher, Master Baldy, was the wisest man in all Wu town. They really had something there, for he could have lived in any age of chaos and come through it without the slightest scratch. From the time when Ban Gu created the universe on down through generation after generation of fighting and killing, through alternations of peace and war, through the waxing and waning of dynasties, Master Baldy's forebears had never laid down their lives to preserve a government, nor had they lost their lives by joining rebel causes. Their line had survived down to this very day and now one of them, Master Baldy, was an honored teacher who expounded to mischievous students like myself on the wisdom of Confucius—a man who had been able at the age of seventy to follow all of his heart's desires without exceeding the proper bounds of morality. If one were to explain Baldy's talent for survival on the basis of the modern theory of evolution, then one might attribute his talent to racial heredity. But in retrospect, as I see it today, his peculiar talent must have been gained entirely from books.[70]

In the event, as Lu Xun tells it, the rebels don't come. Perhaps there never were any, perhaps it was only a rumor caused by refugees from some other catastrophe. It's late, the talk languishes, the child goes to the bedroom that he shares with his amah, a warmhearted old family servant named Li. Lu Xun ends his story, and his first major fiction, with a dialogue of dreams and rebels that is surely an allegory concerning China and 1911:

> As I put my head down on the pillow I heard the rain come down harder and beat against the giant leaves of the banana palm in front of my window. I remember thinking how much it sounded like crabs crawling across the sand.
>
> "Don't hit me, Master Baldy, I promise that I'll prepare my lesson next time. . . ."
>
> "Hey, what's going on here? Are you dreaming?" Amah Li came to my bed and patted me on the back. "With all

that shouting of yours you scared me right out of my own nightmare. What are you dreaming about?"

"Oh, it was just a dream. It didn't really happen. Amah Li, what were you dreaming about?"

"I was dreaming about the Longhairs. I'll tell you about it tomorrow. It's almost midnight. Go to sleep now, go to sleep."[71]

·4·

THE FAR HORIZON

Like the little boy in Lu Xun's story, Shen Congwen was nine years old in 1911. He, too, had been raised on dramatic tales of the Longhaired rebels (his grandfather had fought them and his father loved to talk of them), but when the revolution came to his hometown of Fenghuang, in the western part of Hunan province, the reality transcended any previous mythologies.[1] At first the child was aware simply of unusual numbers of people hurrying in and out of the house; then he saw his father cleaning a rifle while one of his uncles sharpened a sword, heard voices stammering in impatience and excitement, watched his brothers and sisters being sent off to the countryside with their nursemaid. And though he had no idea exactly who was fighting whom or why, he knew that something had gone wrong when his father left one night and returned the next morning to sit in his chair, silent, his head hanging down.

The boy heard an uncle talk of four hundred heads piled in the market square, and of the evidence of other executions in the form of long rows of severed ears hanging on cords outside the magistrate's office.[2] The sight of these heads, and the blood, became central to his memories of this time, for as soon as his father heard that none of the heads displayed in the square belonged to a relative, that the shops were all reopening and crowds of the curious were gathering to take a look, he asked his son if he would like to go along as well. Shen Congwen said that he would. As he later recalled the experience:

> The arcade was covered with heads, and more were hanging from the slats of the scaling ladders. These ladders were made of new bamboo—the rebels used newly cut bamboo from the mountain, and nailed slats horizontally across the ladder poles. I was amazed and did not understand why all these people had been killed; I didn't understand why all these people had had their heads cut off. Not long after, I discovered strings of ears, a strange-looking sight which not many see in a lifetime. My uncle asked me, "Little one, are you afraid?" I answered as best I could, "No, I'm not."
>
> I had heard many stories of battles and killings which always mentioned "heads piled up like mountains, blood flowing to become a river," and when I went to the opera, I had heard songs about "thousands of troops and horses, both sides fighting to the death." I had seen a wooden human head on a red tray in the opera in which Qin Qiong, a legendary hero, wept over his friend's head, but I had never seen a real human head severed in battle. Now there were so many heads in such a big heap, and every one of them dripping blood, freshly cut from human necks. I was not afraid, but I didn't understand why these people had let the soldiers behead them. I suspected there had been some mistake.
>
> Why had they been beheaded? I was uncertain, and when I returned home, I asked my father. His answer was "Revolution," which was not a satisfactory answer at all.[3]

Insofar as one can piece together the background to this and the subsequent slaughter, it would appear that Shen Congwen's father, together with other members of their clan and some of the gentry in their area, had joined forces with the local Miao tribesmen in an attempt to storm Fenghuang's city walls with scaling ladders, seize the government buildings, and oust the Qing magistrate. When this attempt was foiled, the defeated gentry claimed to be innocent bystanders in an uprising by the Miao villagers, and they watched passively as the Miao were systematically rounded up and executed. Shen commented:

> Soon there were too many prisoners for the local guards to manage. It seemed that all the prisoners from the Miao

villages would have to be beheaded. The local officials, when they reported to the governor, would usually say the revolution had been planned by the Miao tribes. The local officials were required to destroy everyone found to be revolutionary. Many people were arrested; most were very simpleminded—not clever enough to plead innocent—but the executioners themselves seemed frightened by all the killing. Several powerful local gentry who had secretly conspired with people outside the city to revolt, but who had not been discovered by the officials, sent a petition to the governor to ask that limits be set on the killing, and that there be some selection: those who deserved execution should be killed, but the innocent should be released. Every day, one or two hundred innocent farmers were arrested.

The officials would not let them all go, nor did they want to kill all of them. The dilemma was soon solved by arranging a procedure for selection, the responsibility for which was assigned to the Heavenly King worshiped by the local people. The soldiers led the prisoners to the temple, to the main chamber, where each was made to cast a pair of bamboo rods: one face up and one face down was "regular," and the prisoner was released; both faces up meant one was *yang* fodder, and also meant release; both faces down meant *yin* fodder, and that the prisoner was condemned to die. Life or death depended on the cast. Those who were to die went to the left; those who were to live went to the right. A man who had been given two chances of three to live remained silent when it was determined he had to die; he lowered his head and walked to the left.[4]

Shen Congwen's matter-of-factness in the face of so much killing may not be a later pose. Fenghuang, where he was raised, in western Hunan, near the border with the two neighboring provinces of Sichuan and Guizhou, was, like so much of rural China, long accustomed to violence. It was an upland area of forests and swiftly flowing rivers, in which Chinese immigrant settlers jostled for land with the indigenous Miao peoples, while the older Chinese families often sought military careers, as did most of the men in the Shen clan. Shen Congwen received some schooling in classical Chinese from local tutors, but had long periods of free time in which to roam the alleys and riverbanks, to watch the scores of craftsmen as they went about their business, and to observe nature in all her richness of hillside and stream. He also watched spellbound, hour after hour, as patient cattle were killed in the slaughter yards; he studied the prisoners in the local jail as they shuffled, with their manacled feet, off to a day of heavy labor; and he played on the city execution grounds with neighborhood children.[5]

Fenghuang had none of the obvious signs of modernizing change—steamships, trains, electricity—that were becoming so prevalent in eastern China; it was in a different universe even from Changsha, where the reform academies had flourished in the 1890s and where the Revolutionary Alliance was active after 1905. One contact with this outside world did come through the powerful family of Xiung Xiling, also of Fenghuang—Shen Congwen's mother's younger sister had married into that family. Xiung Xiling had been an active member of the Changsha reform academies, had traveled in the entourage of the five commissioners who went to Europe and America to study foreign constitutions, and after his return had kept in close touch with Liang Qichao during Liang's years of exile in Japan.[6] Typical of the aspects of European culture that had reached western Hunan was the fact that one of Xiung's brothers had commissioned an equestrian portrait of himself dressed as Napoleon and hung the painting in his mansion (his wife was painted as Josephine in a companion portrait). The Xiungs also owned a set of Lin Shu's translation of Dickens, as a delighted Shen Congwen was soon to discover.[7]

Shen's father, too, had traveled and must have had a fairly intimate knowledge of the force of foreign firepower: at the time that the Boxer Rebellion broke out in northern China during 1900, he had been an officer on active duty at the Dagu forts, which guarded the approaches to Beijing from the sea. After the Boxers besieged the legations in Beijing, the foreign powers prepared a relief force; this joint force defeated the Qing troops at Dagu, and the Manchu commanding officer committed suicide in shame. Shen's father, though uninjured in the fighting, was forced to retire, and returned home under something of a cloud.[8] There is no record of the stages by which he came to adopt an anti-Qing position, but when the circles of revolt had finally spread out from Changsha and reached the western Hunan hills in March 1912, Shen's father stood among the dignitaries on the rostrum in Fenghuang to welcome in the new Republic, and to vilify the former Qing magistrate. It was a grand occasion, and overhead flew a white flag, painted with the bold ideograph for "Han Chinese" (as Qiu Jin had envisioned it five years before). Yet Shen Congwen recalled it all with sadness, for his father put himself up as a candidate for the elections to the Hunan provincial assembly and lost; humiliated and angry at the defeat, he left his family and returned to Beijing, to try to resume his military career, and did not see his son again for twelve years.

After his father had gone, Shen Congwen slowly learned to assess the changes that the revolution had brought to Fenghuang. The patterns of military life, the Chinese domination over the Miao minority peoples, the rituals at the offices of the new republican officials—all these seemed to continue almost exactly as before; the most important change that he noticed was that local Fenghuang families now held office as both civil magistrates and military garrison commanders. Whereas by Qing law such officials had had to be appointed from outside the province, now in the Republic the local elite solidified their hold on the power structure and the lesser families began at once to feel their exactions.[9] Since Shen Congwen's family lost out in this shift, he clearly did not approve, but he could do nothing about it, just as he could do nothing to dislodge from his memory what he called the "vividly imprinted picture" of the thousands of local peasants who had been killed; his own personal solution, after a few more years' desultory schooling, was to join one of the small local armies that dominated his particular sector of western Hunan. In this, like millions of other young Chinese, he was merely living with the realities caused by the erosion of central control and China's slow slide toward warlordism.

In Shaoxing, Lu Xun had sensed the same hollowness at the center of the revolution, and one small incident that he records was a microcosm for the next decade of troubles. In 1912 the new revolutionary government of Shaoxing appointed Lu Xun principal of the local high school. In line with the spirit of the times, he fostered and encouraged a school newspaper. Within a few weeks the student writers for the newspaper expressed their own emancipation by criticizing certain policies of Shaoxing's new military governor, Wang Jinfa, along with most of the other civil officials in the area and, for good measure, their friends and concubines. After a few days of this, Wang sent the student leaders five hundred dollars, which they accepted, telling Lu Xun that they considered the money to be the military governor's way of buying "shares" in the paper. Having accepted the money, the students renewed their abuse. This time Wang sent a detachment of troops, who smashed up the newspaper's offices and roughed up the staff. One of the paper's backers was bayoneted in the attack, and, as Lu Xun sarcastically noted:

> He flew into a fury. Of course, one couldn't blame him—it was rather painful. After his fury subsided, he took off his clothes and had a photograph taken to show the wound, which was about an inch across; he also wrote an account of what had happened, which he circulated everywhere, to expose the tyranny of this warlord government. I doubt if anyone has kept that photograph. It was so small that the wound was practically invisible, and without an explanation anyone seeing it would be bound to take it for a nudist photograph of some rather eccentric and romantic fellow.[10]

In this incident—the "romantic and eccentric" elements notwithstanding—deeply significant issues of freedom of expression, corruption, and violence lay buried; transposed to the national scene, these same elements affected all China's modern history.

When Yuan Shikai had been named provisional president of China in February 1912, following the abdication of the last Manchu ruler and Sun Yatsen's abandonment of the presidential title, he had agreed to Sun's request that the formal inauguration of the new presidency be held in Nanjing, and Sun's supporters in the provisional assembly also voted to make Nanjing the new national capital. This was more than symbolic, for Nanjing was the center of Sun Yatsen's strength, well away from Yuan Shikai's Beiyang Army base, and it was also a city rich with historical overtones, having been the original capital of the Ming dynasty during the fourteenth century. But the idea of moving the capital was resented by many Chinese (and by most foreign diplomatic representatives), and when, in late February, a number of mutinies among the troops in the Beijing region erupted, Yuan claimed that the unrest in the army made it essential for him to stay in the north, and he insisted that he be inaugurated there. The inauguration took place in Beijing on March 10 and the idea of moving the capital was dropped.[11]

Having failed in these preliminary moves, Sun's supporters tried to hold Yuan in check through the promulgation of a provisional constitution that gave major power in the state to the premier. The premier was to be chosen from a cabinet that was itself to be drawn from the political party holding the most seats in the two houses of the National Assembly. The president would then become more a figurehead than chief executive of the nation. In an attempt to make these ideas into a political reality, the former Revolutionary Alliance was reorganized into a broad-based political party, now called the National People's Party—the Guomindang—the same name that Kang Youwei had briefly thought of adopting for his own organization.

The chief force behind the new party was Song Jiaoren, a young but long-standing member of the Revolutionary Alliance, who had been trained in law in Japan, had tried to exploit the Manchurian bandit risings in 1907, had participated in the 1911 Guangzhou uprising, and had helped found the central Revolutionary Alliance headquarters in the summer of 1911. Ebullient, tough-minded, and not overscrupulous, Song directed the overall campaign for the Guomindang as well as running for election in his home province of Hunan. He criticized Yuan Shikai for keeping too much power in his own hands, and called for a curb on presidential powers and the institution of a truly democratic republic in China. Sun Yatsen took only a limited part in the campaign, and it was mainly due to Song that the newly formed Guomindang decisively defeated the other major political parties in the February 1913 national elections, winning 269 out of the 596 seats in the House and an absolute majority in the Senate. As the triumphant Song Jiaoren was about to board the train at the

Shanghai Station on March 20, 1913, en route to take up his new parliamentary duties in Beijing—he was still only thirty years old, and widely expected to be China's new premier—he was gunned down by an assassin and killed.[12]

Though there was an outcry at this murder, and evidence that the trail of those responsible led back to Yuan Shikai himself, other politicians were eager to benefit from any discomfiture to the Guomindang. Chief among these were the leaders of the Progressive Party, a merger formed by three smaller parties that had been defeated in the 1913 elections. The most influential intellectual in this group was Liang Qichao. Liang had been bitterly disappointed at his party's electoral defeat; as he wrote in a letter to his daughter two days before Song was killed: "Our party has lost! I am totally exhausted. What can one do with a society like this one? I'm really sorry I ever returned [to China]. There are other things that pierce my heart, but these I cannot tell you about. Yet though I am so depressed, I have to keep on with my newspaper writing, even if I cannot reveal the worst things there, either. I've been holding my pen for two hours without being able to write one word, already the sky is lightening and I just go on sitting here vacantly."[13] The bitterness of his reaction, like that of Shen Congwen's father, suggests that in this first election many Chinese were not able to separate out the inevitable frustrations of party politics from questions of personal humiliation and loss of face, thus lending some substance to Kang Youwei's warnings that China was simply not ready for democracy at this time. But Liang also was convinced that opposition parties in the election had used both physical violence and corruption to gain their own ends, and since he had never shown any affection for Sun, he was willing to acquiesce in later actions by Yuan Shikai against the Guomindang.[14]

So was Liang's former colleague from the Changsha reform society days, Xiung Xiling, who had already served as finance minister in the first provisional government, of 1912. When Yuan Shikai pressed ahead, in the spring of 1913, to raise a so-called Reorganization Loan of one hundred and twenty-five million pounds sterling from a consortium of foreign banks, the Progressive Party backed his decision. The Guomindang, however, protested fiercely and vigorously, for they feared this act would place China's new regime firmly in the hands of foreign financial interests. Yuan's response was to ban any further political activities by the Guomindang, to dismiss any provincial governors known to be Guomindang supporters, to have Xiung installed as premier, and to order two of his strongest military units south to attack Nanjing, the bastion of Guomindang power.

The city fell, after hard fighting, on September 1, 1913. Less than two weeks later Xiung formed a cabinet, which included Liang Qichao as minister of justice, and in early October this cabinet managed to maneuver a new presidential election law through the National Assembly that led to ratification of Yuan's title as president of the Republic. In early November the same cabinet cosigned Yuan's order for the dismissal of all remaining Guomindang supporters from the National Assembly and the arrest of any Guomindang members in Beijing. Sun Yatsen, who had been trying to rally support from other provincial governors, saw his military hopes for success vanish. In December 1913 he sought political asylum in Japan.[15]

Liang Qichao, so long a stalwart battler for moral principle and constitutional reform, now found himself tangled in the skeins of political expediency. One could claim that the provincial governors who had opposed Yuan and declared their provinces "independent" of the central government had betrayed their trust; one could argue that a duly elected National Assembly had confirmed Yuan "legally" as president; one could certainly say that the Xiung cabinet had desperately important financial, legal, and administrative business to conduct, and that even after the dismissal of the Guomindang members the National Assembly was still the only forum in which the cabinet could operate. But after Yuan dismissed what was left of the National Assembly in January 1914, Liang must have needed tortuous internal arguments to justify his serving on Yuan's Council of State. Nevertheless Liang did so, and continued to work for Yuan (albeit with increasing misgivings) until the president showed unmistakably that he intended the final political coup: the installation of himself as a new emperor of China.[16]

Yuan's move was a curious combination of his own personal ambition coupled with his sense that a monarchy might solve the intractable problems of political legitimacy and financial viability that faced the new government of China. His own inability to see that the legitimate airing of public grievances was not necessarily intended as a personal assault on his own integrity had already led to the collapse of elected institutions; and the plea bargaining among semiautonomous provincial and subprovincial units that had marked the new Republic had ensured that no adequate unified financial-planning or revenue-collecting system was instituted. Yuan was eager to centralize the government and to strengthen China through military and educational reforms, but such reforms were extremely expensive and the taxes to pay for them were bitterly resented both by members of the elite (who were asked to pay the most) and by the rural and urban poor (who saw none of the projected reforms as being of any advantage to them personally).[17] The result was disaffection in the provinces and, on Yuan's part, ever-growing reliance on foreign loans for survival. But, especially after the outbreak of war in Europe in July 1914, Britain, France, Germany, and Russia had no spare resources to apply to China, and the dominant foreign presence in China became that of Japan. The Japanese government had not initially looked favorably on the formation of the Chinese Republic, but they rapidly came to see that they could exploit the situation to their own advantage by trading off major financial loans for territorial and economic concessions inside China. As Yuan grew ever more desperate for money, their demands grew harsher. Finally on May 7, 1915, in the so-called Twenty-one Demands, Japan pushed for further special economic privileges in Manchuria, Shandong province, and the Yangtze Valley, for the right to lease agricultural lands in Manchuria and reside there with extraterritorial legal status, and for permission to station Japanese police on Chinese soil. Despite Chinese outrage, and a well-organized attempt to water down the demands, Yuan had to yield to Japanese pressure; paradoxically, the episode made him more than ever determined to increase the central power of the Chinese state by reestablishing the monarchy, with himself as ruler.[18]

In some ways, the logic of Kang Youwei's arguments had pointed in the direction that Yuan decided to follow, for Kang had warned ceaselessly of the impracticality of a republic at this stage of China's historical development, and in essays with self-defining titles such as "China Cannot Escape the Situation in Central and South America" he continued to push for the form of government he described as "token monarchy within a republican system." In a journal he founded (bearing the sage-like name *Compassion*) he also wrote vigorously in support of establishing Confucianism as a state religion, to give some continuity and stability to Chinese beliefs; Yuan did reestablish elements of the ritual side of Confucian thought, and even conducted ceremonies in the former Qing Temple of Heaven. Yet Kang, looking at China from his base in Japan, was terribly conscious of his country's weakness. He warned of the danger of overreliance on foreign loans, of the danger of federalism, of the gravity of the cultural perils that China faced as she jettisoned her own values in favor of Western ones, and of the probability that the current government of "bandits and beggars" would lose control of China's peripheral but vital areas: Tibet, Mongolia, Turkestan, and Manchuria.[19]

By the strangest of ironies—in no sense does it seem to have been by design—Kang at last returned to China from Japan in December 1913, at the very moment that Sun Yatsen, forced once more into exile, fled from China to Japan for the second time in his life. Kang's visit was for the purpose of burying his mother, deceased at eighty-three years of age, in the family burying place in Guangdong province. He laid her to rest with her martyred son, Guangren, whose remains, unknown to her, had been lying for more than a decade in a temporary grave in Macao. Early in 1914 the Beijing government ordered that Guangren, Tan Sitong, and the four other martyrs of the 1898 reform movement be honored throughout China and their deeds recorded for posterity; if Yuan Shikai had seen this as a means of placating Kang Youwei, he was disappointed, for when he asked Kang to serve the Chinese government in Beijing in some capacity, Kang rejected the overture. Instead he settled down in rented quarters in Shanghai to resume a life of writing and scholarship; his somber feelings were accentuated by the fact that within the year both his elder sister and his young Chinese-American consort, who had been with him on so many travels, also died.[20]

During the years 1912–14 Kang and Liang, as far as we know, did not have much contact with each other. But they were both outraged by the presumptuousness of Yuan's imperial restoration attempts of 1915 and issued angry public denunciations. Both placed their hopes for defeating Yuan on Cai E, a former reformer, now the military strongman controlling the provinces of Guizhou and Yunnan; Kang urged General Cai, in a long letter, to seize Sichuan province as well and make it a base of operations for his National Protection Army. With the rich resources of Sichuan behind him, wrote Kang, with a reformed financial structure, and following the tenets of Confucianism, General Cai could successfully strike back at Yuan. Liang Qichao tried to marshal a similar grouping of forces in the Guangdong area to back General Cai, since he felt the southeast was the key base for a successful counterstrike, and contained several worker and terrorist groups ready to die if necessary to destroy Yuan's henchmen. Though General Cai did not oust Yuan from power, he did wage battles in western and central China that seriously weakened Yuan's position.[21]

Thus did Liang and Kang both become involved in those same murderous intricacies of warlord politics that they had urged China for so long to avoid. The death in mid-1916 (from natural causes) of the angry and disappointed Yuan Shikai ended this particular crisis; in line with the provisions of the 1913 Constitution he was succeeded by the vice-president, and the National Assembly members dismissed in 1914 were reconvened, but China was no nearer to having strong central leadership or financial solvency. In early 1916 Kang wrote to another militarist, General Zhang Xun, a central China warlord whom Yuan Shikai had honored with the title inspector general of the Yangtze provinces, pointing out to him that Yuan Shikai's imperial pretensions marked a pivotal moment in China's chances for survival; "the Qing house" was "inescapably connected" with such imperial restoration attempts. "What," Kang asked, "are the general's thoughts on this?"[22] The hint could hardly have been broader, since General Zhang was known to have been fiercely loyal to the Manchus ever since he had been specially honored by the Empress Dowager for his help to her family during the Boxer rising. General Zhang had also fought tenaciously in 1911 to hold Nanjing for the Qing against the revolutionary forces, and though unsuccessful then, he had been rewarded by Yuan Shikai and had held on to much of his army; it was he who had seized Nanjing in the summer of 1913 and driven out the Guomindang, and throughout this period he had kept his own queue and ordered all his troops to do the same. Kang, perhaps seeing in the general's loyalty an echo of his own never-lost affection for the late Emperor Guangxu, and realizing that this might be his last chance to ensure that the developmental stages he believed to be essential for China's survival were properly followed, continued to keep in touch with Zhang through the year 1916.

General Zhang's ambitions were becoming well known in China, and even high-school teachers and students criticized him in essays and poems. For example, the earliest known work by Zhou Enlai, later premier of the People's Republic of China, at this time an eighteen-year-old student in the Nankai Normal School, in Tianjin, was just such a protest poem; written in oblique tones, since direct criticism of a warlord would have been too dangerous, it is dated September 1916:

> Over our vast land the storm-clouds rise,
> All of us sunk in gloom, who dares speak out?
> Now, to intensify our pain, autumn's come:
> The chirping of crickets is too much for my ears.[23]

Hoping to make some political capital from these disturbances, Sun Yatsen returned from Japan to Shanghai in the summer of 1916, as the leader of a reorganized and disciplined Guomindang, now formally named the Revolutionary Party. He aimed to bring some meaning back to the Constitution by drawing together a new coalition of those interested in suppressing militarism, so that a semblance of legitimacy would return to China's disintegrating republican structure. But neither Sun nor the protesting students had much effect on the current militarist mood, and in the middle of June 1917 General

Zhang Xun led his army into Beijing. On June 27 Kang Youwei also returned to the city, at General Zhang's invitation, by train; he gazed with deep nostalgia at the familiar buildings, walls, and palaces, which he had not seen since he fled from China in 1898. In the evening light they glistened, under a sky cleared by rain.[24] Inside the Forbidden City the deposed Emperor Puyi, now aged eleven, was living with his tutors and family, sustained by a generous stipend provided by the republican government. During the next four days, as General Zhang began negotiations with ex-Emperor Puyi's entourage, Kang Youwei journeyed to the Summer Palace, where once the Emperor Guangxu had received him in audience, and visited the Temple of Confucius and the zoo. On July 1 General Zhang announced that Puyi had been restored to the throne, and invited Kang to attend him at his "court." In the draft of a poem (which he never completed) an excited Kang celebrated the moment: at last, after six years of constant turbulence, the country could rest at peace as the imperial banners waved again.[25]

Kang Youwei was given the official title of a deputy director in the Emperor's advisory council. Just as he had in the Hundred Days of Reform in 1898, he drafted a score of reform edicts and proposals, designed to strengthen the bureaucracy and make China into a valid constitutional monarchy. Kang's stated foreign model on this occasion was the British one of 1660 when, following the death of Cromwell, the British had restored Charles II to the throne, showing that an ordered constitutional monarchy could follow hard upon a republican period.[26] But while Kang had his thoughts directed on his "token monarchy" concept, which would function only under the aegis of a strong and independent parliament, both General Zhang and most of Emperor Puyi's advisers envisioned the abolition of all the republican forms and a restoration of full imperial power. Kang was kept out of the Emperor's inner circle and grew increasingly disappointed; cries of anger from all over the country greeted this new restoration, and the very warlords who had promised General Zhang their support now made haste to withdraw it. The denouement could hardly be better pictured than it was by Kang in the prose introduction to a classical poem that he wrote that same month:

On the eighteenth Pan Shien and Wei Chiliang flew a plane up from the Nanyuan airfield and bombed the palace, killing three people. Everyone at court was greatly alarmed. At dawn on the nineteenth Prince Chun summoned me to the palace, sending me a sedan chair with two bearers from the Forbidden City, but they failed to wait for me long enough, so I had to walk. After I reached the Donghua Gate I found it closed and had to ask for entrance repeatedly until the guards, seeing my [court] hat and robes, finally let me enter. In the palace, all was confusion. Prince Chun ordered me [and Zhe] to go to the foreign legations to discuss our travails and see if the ambassadors would protect the palace. Zhe would return and report to the prince, while I stayed on in the embassy.[27]

So it was that, as the opposition to General Zhang hardened and the gunfire of rival armies could be heard rumbling over the city of Beijing, Kang sat quietly in the American legation and read the proofs of his book on the Confucian *Spring and Autumn Annals*.[28]

In the course of these three years, from 1914 to 1917, Kang and Liang had negotiated or corresponded with fifty or more senior military officers. These men were the most visible part of the warlord structure, often controlling tens of thousands of troops and dominating territories as large as countries. Their backgrounds were endlessly varied: many had come up by the route of Qing military academies and service in the Beiyang Army under Yuan Shikai; many had also received advanced military training in Japanese staff schools or with Japanese forces in the field; a few had studied in Germany. Some had been bandits who had been given regular commissions in the Qing armies to keep them quiet, or else had drifted from banditry into control of territory in the political vacuum that developed in 1912. Some had been members of the Revolutionary Alliance, some of the Restoration Society, some of radical establishments such as the Datong School; some had fought loyally for the Qing, others for Yuan Shikai first on the Qing and then on the republican side, others had been staunchly loyal to Sun or to one of his lieutenants. Many, despite the apparently fragmentary nature of their activities, were fiercely nationalist. Some were Christian. There were those who sought the highest offices in China—as president, premier, cabinet minister, provincial governor—and attained them (though usually fleetingly); others were content with a local base that might furnish revenues from opium smuggling, transport dues, or rural taxes, or else perhaps lived on semilegalized handouts from other military commanders or local district governments.[29]

The lower levels of this military life were vividly described by Shen Congwen, who, after his childhood induction into the world of revolution, served during his teens as a private soldier and clerk in one of these smaller military units in his home terrain of western Hunan; like others before and after him, in many times and places, Shen found army life to be one of general boredom punctuated by bouts of random violence. The main efforts of the Hunanese soldiers were directed to supporting themselves and their officers, and to guarding their base areas against bandit depredations. They lived usually in small market towns, billeted in temple compounds or other public buildings. Food was simple but adequate; there was some physical exercise and drill, but target practice with live ammunition was almost unknown because of the shortage of both rifles and bullets. Wages were low, three or four dollars a month, but a reasonable diet was provided. Education was limited to occasional exhortations on patriotism and duty from the officers; illiteracy was almost total, and quite simple literary skills could lead swiftly to preferment, though paradoxically some older-generation scholars with considerable learning had drifted into the ranks, and the young Shen was able to develop a passion for traditional calligraphy that stayed with him the rest of his life. Random assignations with local women were not allowed, but to relieve the monotony soldiers visited prostitutes, frequented gambling dens, engaged in drinking bouts, and watched executions.

Executions were particularly popular with the soldiers because they were usually followed by a party that supplemented their simple rations. If the victim had been a deserter, then the joy was increased, since a bounty would be paid to the unit. The executions were most often of those alleged to be bandits, men (and occasionally women) brought in by the rural militia from the neighboring hills and villages; the soldiers usually accepted the charge of banditry without further scrutiny, and would carry out the executions by beheading on market day, when there would be a large crowd present. The prisoners were often beaten up or tortured before being killed, and their demeanor under stress was a basic topic of conversation among the soldiers, each victim being the subject of admiration or contempt according to circumstances. Shen records that these killings were commonplace; twenty or thirty would be killed even in the quietest months, but the number might rise to hundreds or even to two or three thousand after a major outbreak of bandit activities or during a "pacification" campaign. Bandit forces, to reverse the coin, might ambush roving patrols (though because of this the troops rarely went on patrol!) or seize merchants and foreign missionaries, who might be either killed or ransomed. On occasion entire military units might be wiped out in ambush, as happened to one unit that Shen had served in shortly before.[30]

Shen gave an unforgettable view of the small confrontations of this period, off the national stage, in an autobiographical vignette that he entitled "The Chief," since it focused on Shen's dealings in western Hunan with the head of his commanding officer's bodyguard, an ex-bandit chief named Liu Yunting. After giving up banditry and joining the regular army, Liu served his commander faithfully until he seduced a female bandit captive held by a neighboring unit, hoping to help her escape and recommence his previous bandit life in the mountains. The act was discovered and the woman executed; several days later, Liu was arrested by his commanding officer, just as he was preparing to leave camp with Shen on a travel passport that had been issued jointly to them. Describing how Liu begged for mercy and was rejected by his commander, Zhang, Shen closes the account with these words:

> The chief heard the commander's verdict and no longer called out for justice, but smiled at the men in the two buildings and suddenly became more relaxed. "Fine, Commander. Thank you for looking after me for so many years. Good-bye, brothers." Then, after a pause, he added, "Com-

mander, you're really a dreamer. Others have offered six thousand dollars to get me to kill you, but I wouldn't do it."

Commander Zhang seemed not to hear and turned away to order the adjutant to buy a good coffin. Then the chief was hustled out the main gate and I never saw him again. That afternoon I boarded the [river]boat. My passport had originally had two names on it, but the chief's name had been scored out with red ink. The passport went through many bad rapids with me, and five days later, when I arrived at Baojing, I handed it in to the adjutant for cancellation.

Some three years later, in Zhenzhou in Hunan, the talented and uncommon Commander Zhang and several of his orderlies were invited for a drink by a certain Captain Tian from divisional headquarters. As they entered the Gaopinger Gate along with four sedan-chair bearers, they were cut down by machine-gun fire even before the welcoming trumpets had stopped sounding. The bodies were casually dumped into a ditch, and it was two months later before they were buried.

As for that Captain Tian of divisional headquarters who had assassinated him, it turned out that one year later, in the very same city, a unit commander sent by Ye Kaixin, the Hunan chairman, using the same ruse of inviting him as a guest, assassinated him in the narrow street in front of the Confucian temple.[31]

The deliberately terse language is ideally suited to presenting the cycle of violence to which Shen and others grew accustomed, violence that had been prevalent enough in the nineteenth century but seemed to grow ever worse in the years after 1911.

Kang Youwei assessed the death toll of the first two years of China's revolution at twenty million. He took this figure from Japanese sources and it may be vastly exaggerated, since the Japanese had their own reasons for making the deaths look as numerous as possible: the more the Chinese destroyed themselves, the more the Japanese could pose as purveyors of order and rationality as they increased their own economic and political investments in China and in Manchuria. But even a figure one-tenth as high is bleak enough, and in the context quite conceivable: if we try to calculate the victims of the Guangzhou insurrections, the Manchus cut down with their families when defeated by the Chinese nationalist armies, the Miao rounded up and killed in Hunan and elsewhere, the workers and troops who lost their lives when Yuan Shikai ordered his Beiyang Army to seize Hankou and Hanyang from the Revolutionary Alliance, the citizens and troops killed in the two prolonged assaults on Nanjing in 1911 and 1913, the battles among secret societies for local control, and the deaths of those countless refugees who ran, terrified, from "He market" to "Wu town" (as Lu Xun had put it)—we are presented with cumulative evidence of violence and death that had moved beyond any rational justification, even in the grandiose terms of a final attainment of national order.[32]

For some Confucian scholars of the old school, adjustment to this world was completely impossible. Liang Ji, a fine scholar and retired minor official, made this point with ultimate clarity when he drowned himself in a Beijing lake, just before his sixtieth birthday, in November 1918. His death had an upsetting effect on many people because his final writings made it clear that his decision to take his own life was made out of disgust with both the old order and the new; Liang Ji felt that, just as few men had been willing to sacrifice themselves in loyalty to the ousted Qing, so, too, would no one sacrifice private interest to serve the new Republic with integrity. Liang Ji had been a passionate amateur of Beijing opera and he used the decline in the opera's standards as his index to what had gone wrong with the world: moral and aesthetic standards of performance had fallen because society was in decline, and the audience could not even see that the standards *had* deteriorated. They lived in a world in which the old Confucian values, summarized in the four ideographs "loyalty, filial piety, chastity, and righteousness," had been supplanted by the four new values of "eating, drinking, amusement, and pleasure."[33]

Though Lu Xun was not deeply impressed by Liang Ji's death—he alluded to it rather sarcastically in later writings—his own anger and disgust with the state of China had reached such a point by late 1918 that when he looked for a metaphor to describe his country's intellectual state he chose the image of syphilis. His medical training in Japan and his Shaoxing teaching of classes on human reproduction ensured that his bleak metaphor was not casually chosen: Lu intended to drive home the idea that the rottenness within the Chinese people had become congenital, that there were now "dark and confusing elements in the blood vessels." If there was to be any hope for China (arsphenamine under the brand name "606" *had* been used with some success in actual cases of syphilis), it could come only from a total cleansing of these blood vessels which, by extension of the metaphor, constituted the living force of the Chinese consciousness.[34]

Lu Xun wrote also of the terrible sense of hopelessness that overcame him as he worked at a boring desk job in Beijing—Shaoxing teaching now abandoned—and sat at home by night patiently deciphering and copying old inscriptions from classical sources. "What's the use of copying those?" a visiting friend who had shared his radical interests in the old Japan days asked him one night. "There's no use." "In that case, what's your reason for copying them?" "There's no reason."[35] In fact, the only internal justification for this scholarship, as Lu Xun saw it, was as an opiate against the waves of loneliness that overwhelmed him, a loneliness that, as he wrote in one image, "coiled around my spirit like a huge poisonous snake." And this sense of loneliness, in turn, sprang from a feeling of futility that had been growing ever stronger since the failure of his various literary ventures in Japan: "At first I could not grasp the reason for these feelings, but then I came to see that if a man's endeavors meet with approbation, then he can advance to a new stage, and if they arouse opposition, then he can fight back; but to issue your clarion call to those living in your own time and have them make no response at all, to receive neither their approval nor their opposition, that is like being left standing in a boundless desert, one has no idea what to do, that is the real pity of it!"[36]

Lu Xun stated later that his decision to try once more to write was made in the belief that though he himself could now have little effect on the world (and wanted little) he might nevertheless "encourage those fighters galloping on in loneliness, so that they do not lose heart."[37] These "fighters" were men such as Chen Duxiu and the other editors of *New Youth*, the political and literary review that Chen had founded in Shanghai in 1915.

This review became the focal point for an all-out assault on the entire system of Confucian values, an assault that was intensified after Kang Youwei continued to insist that Confucianism as a state religion might strengthen China and fill the moral emptiness that was such a terrible part of current life.[38] Chen argued in 1916 that Confucian belief could not be combined with Western thought in a fruitful new synthesis: "If we want to build a new society according to the Western model in order to survive in this world, the basic task is to import the *foundation* of the Western society, that is, the new belief in equality and human rights. We must be thoroughly aware of the incompatibility between Confucianism and the new belief, the new society, and the new state. We must courageously decide to throw away that which is incompatible with the new belief, the new society, and the new state!"[39] Chen Duxiu had no simple illusions that this would be easy to do; indeed, his own attempts to apply social Darwinist theories to China convinced him that China's weakness and inadaptability might well lead to its extinction, and this dejected view was supplemented by his conception of how difficult it was to attain a valid nationalism. Such nationalism, he believed, must contain the emotional elements of patriotism, but these must be linked to reason, a consciousness of the ends to which patriotism was directed. It was also in 1916 that he wrote to a friend:

> My pessimism is not caused by the lack of quick success in our undertaking, but has developed from an awareness of the hopelessness of our catching up with European and American civilizations. They are progressing hundreds of miles each day, while we are left far behind. Most of our people are lethargic and do not know that not only our morality, politics, and technology but even common commodities for daily use are all unfit for struggle and are going to be eliminated in the process of natural selection. Although there are a few awakened people in the country, who can save us from the fate of perishing?[40]

Both Chen Duxiu and Lu Xun were fully aware that for the massive new urban reading public, partially trained in the new schools that had been founded around the turn of the century, and slowly growing used to a factory- or office-oriented work-week, the old values continued to have resonance. Indeed much of the popular fiction coming out in such magazines as the leisure-oriented *Saturday* (*Libailiu*), or in popular novels with print runs of over a hundred thousand copies in some cases, took a deeply conservative view with respect to traditional Chinese values: these writings mocked superficial Westernization and in some cases were specifically and dramatically anti-imperialist; their authors catered directly to a public that was both fascinated and repelled by warlordism and political corruption by producing social and "exposé" novels that served to reaffirm traditional values of service and commitment; and even the madly popular new genres of romantic love stories were read as surrogates for action rather than as instigators of change in women's status.[41]

Lu Xun clearly believed that the *New Youth* editors and writers must be feeling that same loneliness he had experienced after his failures in Japan. Yet at the same time he was ambivalent about whether it was any service to jolt the Chinese masses out of the complacency that such escapist literature seemed able to induce, since the reality they would have to face was so appalling. As he put it in a conversation with one other editor of *New Youth*, "Imagine an iron house without windows, absolutely indestructible, with many people fast asleep inside who will soon die of suffocation. Since they will die in their sleep, they will not feel any of the pain of death. Now if you cry aloud to wake a few of the lighter sleepers, making those unfortunate few suffer the agony of irrevocable death, do you think you are doing them a good turn?"[42] The editor replied that one must, nevertheless, make the attempt, for one could not be sure that there was no chance of escape whatsoever for those trapped in the iron house.

The image chosen here by Lu Xun surely came from one of his profound and frightening teenage memories, from the moment when his father lay dying and a neighbor, Mrs. Yan, who was attending the sickbed, insisted on burning paper money and copies of a Buddhist sutra to accompany the dead man to the underworld, while at the same time urging the young Lu Xun to hold his father back on earth as long as possible:

"Call him!" said Mrs. Yan. "Your father's at his last gasp. Call him quickly!"

"Father! Father!" I called accordingly.

"Louder! He can't hear. Hurry up, can't you?"

"Father! Father!!"

His face, which had been composed, grew suddenly tense again; and he raised his eyelids slightly, as if in pain.

"Call him!" she insisted. "Hurry up and call him!"

"Father!!!"

"What is it? . . . Don't shout. . . . Don't. . . ."

His voice was low, and once more he started panting for breath. It was some time before he recovered his earlier calm.

"Father!!!"

I went on calling him until he breathed his last.

I can still hear my voice as it sounded then. And each time I hear those cries, I feel this was the greatest wrong I ever did my father.[43]

Such recollections were harrowing, but Lu Xun found the strength to draw on them, to use creatively "the things I have been unable to erase from my memory," as he put it.[44] The result was a spate of writing that led him to produce, in just a few years, many of the finest short stories in the history of modern Chinese literature. Lu Xun wrote now in the vernacular cadences of spoken Chinese, freely and sharply, as opposed to using the difficult classical language in which he had written as a youth. By incorporating snatches of dialogue, colloquialisms, and descriptive passages, and creating a world where pain and regret were immediate and convincing, he became the first major serious writer to cut into the popular-fiction market of the weekly magazines. Between April 1918 and April 1919 he produced three stories that complemented one another in presenting a picture of the Chinese as a people corrupted by their culture, encrusted with harmful superstitions, grown casually cruel out of habit. The Chinese were a cannibalistic people, he wrote in "Diary of a Madman," and if you looked carefully you could read the words "eat people" scrawled between the lines of their classical texts; they were a spuriously moralistic people, he wrote in "Kong Yiji," who abused the trappings of learning to cheat each other; they were a people so shortsighted and narrow-minded, he wrote in "Medicine," that they would betray to the Qing executioners the youngsters who tried to liberate them. These stories had overtones and influences from many writers Lu Xun admired, particularly Gogol and Andreyev, but much more profound were the echoes of his youth: the wineshop and teahouse gossipers in Shaoxing, the harried journeys to the pawnshop as a child and the visits to the pharmacy for outlandish herbal "remedies" for his constantly ill father, the unimaginative Confucian teachers of his schooldays, the heart plucked still warm from the executed body of Xu Xilin in 1907, the young Qiu Jin with her futile yet haunting message, the silent Chinese on the Sendai lantern slides watching the execution of their compatriots.[45]

In "Medicine," finished in April 1919, such traceable images are prominent. The story starts on an autumn dawn with the ideograph for autumn, "Qiu" (also the ideograph of Qiu Jin's surname), and the narrative is dominated by the offstage presence of a revolutionary martyr called Xia Yu: the ideographs "Xia" and "Yu" echo the ideographs in Qiu Jin's name. The story itself concerns the parents of a child dying from consumption; in line with local superstitious beliefs, they seek to cure him by feeding him fresh human blood, in this case by means of a steamed wheat-flour roll that has been dipped in the blood of the newly beheaded young revolutionary Xia Yu. The family name of these parents and their sick child is "Hua," the ideograph for "China." The townspeople have no sympathy for the dead revolutionary Xia Yu and mock him posthumously when they learn that he had even tried to convert his jailer to his views; and they praise for his foresight the clansman who, to save his own hide, betrayed Xia Yu to the Qing police. In one teahouse scene Lu Xun is careful to insist that a "twenty-year-old" in the story is at one in his narrow mentality with the "graybeards" of the town; in other words, youth in itself does not hold the answer to solving China's problems.

As the story closes, two old women converge on the town graveyard. One is Mother Hua, whose son Shuan has died of consumption despite the steamed roll dipped in blood that she fed to him; the other is the dead revolutionary's mother, the widow Xia. Neither knows the identity of the other.

Outside the west gate and lying close to the foot of the city wall was a piece of land that had always been government property. Diagonally across it ran a narrow crooked path, which, starting as a shortcut trodden out by the shoes of passers-by, had ended by becoming a natural boundary. On the left of the road were burial mounds of criminals who had been executed or had died from exposure in jail; on the right was a burying ground for paupers. Both sides were already crowded with rows and files of mounds like the ceremonial cakes at a rich man's birthday party.

It was unusually cold at the spring festival this year. The buds on the poplars and willows were scarcely half the size of a grain of rice. Not long after daybreak Mother Hua stood before a fresh grave on the right-hand side of the path. She set out four plates of food and a bowl of rice, wept awhile, and burned sacrificial money. Then she sat mutely on the ground, apparently waiting for something, though she could not herself have told what it was she expected. A faint breeze ruffled her thin hair, whiter by far than it had been the year before.

Along the path came another woman, whose hair was also half white, wearing a ragged coat and skirt. She carried a round broken basket that had once been red lacquer, and a string of sacrificial paper money. She had to rest every few steps. Suddenly she saw Mother Hua sitting on the ground watching her. She hesitated and an embarrassed flush spread over her pale thin face. Then, summoning her courage, she made her way over to a grave on the left-hand side and put down her basket.

This grave was in the same row as that of Little Shuan, separated only by the narrow path. Mother Hua watched the woman set out her four dishes of food and the bowl of rice, saw her stand and weep and then ignite the paper money. "There must be a son," she was thinking to herself, "in that grave, too." The old woman had been moving about, looking things over, when suddenly her arms and legs began to flap around, she stumbled back several steps and stood staring in amazement.

Mother Hua feared that the woman was going insane from grief, and she felt constrained to rise, cross the path, and speak to her. "Old woman," she said quietly, "don't take it so hard. Let's go back home."

The woman nodded, but her eyes remained in a fixed stare. "Look!" she stammered. "Look, what's that?"

Mother Hua followed her pointing finger and her eyes fell on the grave in front of them. It was ugly enough, with patches of yellow dirt where the grass had not grown. But a closer look produced a shudder of astonishment, for there, clearly encircling the rounded tip of the grave, was a wreath of red and white flowers.

Even to their age-dimmed eyes the flowers were quite distinct. There were not many of them; they were somewhat wilted; but they were arranged very regularly in a perfect circle. Mother Hua took a hasty look at her son's grave and at the others, but she saw nothing beyond a few bluish wildflowers braving the cold here and there. She was overcome by a sudden feeling of emptiness and didn't want to look any closer. The other old woman went nearer to the grave and regarded it carefully, muttering to herself: "They have no roots. They don't seem to have grown of themselves. But who could have come here? . . . Children wouldn't play here. . . . Relatives stopped coming long ago. . . . What can have happened?" She stood lost in thought and suddenly broke out in a sobbing cry: "Oh, my son Yu! They all wronged you! And you can't forget it. Are you still grieving? And is this a sign from the spirit world you give me so that I will know?" Looking about her she could see nothing but a black crow sitting on a leafless tree. "I know now," she continued. "Oh, my son Yu! They murdered you. They'll get their punishment someday, for heaven knows all. Just close your eyes. . . . But if you are really here, if you are listening to me, give me a sign . . . make that crow fly on to your grave."

The breeze had died away. The blades of dry grass stood up stiffly like copper wire. The quivering sound of her voice echoed more and more faintly on the air and was gone. All around was the stillness of death. The two women stood in the withered grass gazing up at the black crow; and the crow, with head tucked in, sat on the branch as though it were cast in iron.

A long time passed. Slowly the number of people coming to the graveyard increased; some were old, some young, as they moved in and out among the grave mounds.

Without understanding why, Mother Hua felt she had been relieved of a great burden and decided she wanted to leave. Turning to the other woman she said, "It's time for us to be getting back."

The old woman sighed and listlessly gathered up the dishes of food. She hesitated a moment more, then walked slowly away. "What can it all mean?" she mumbled to herself.

They had gone not more than twenty or thirty steps when

a loud caw sounded behind them. With a jerk, they turned their heads to look and saw the black crow spread its wings, tense its body, and fly like an arrow toward the far horizon.[46]

By the spring of 1919, then, Lu Xun was saying that the revolution had been either useless or misconstrued, depending on one's angle of vision: Xia's blood had not saved the dying child Hua Shuan, and the Chinese people had been unable to see any other significance in Xia's sacrifice. Yet Lu Xun was also saying that there was a trace of hope, even if that trace was so faint and so ambiguous that it could be presented only through elusive symbols. Someone, after all, had placed that circle of flowers on the dead revolutionary's grave, flowers red as the blood on the steamed bread, and red as the flag of the Bolshevik revolution. Little Shuan's mother did cross over that narrow path, from her own side among the paupers on the right, to stand beside Xia's mother on the left. And the crow, though it could not be persuaded to give the specific sign requested, nevertheless took flight, swiftly and with apparent purpose, in the direction of some distant objective.

Lu Xun was evasive about whether that distant objective was some form of socialist revolution for China, but the realities of current events soon made that evasiveness irrelevant to many. "Medicine" appeared at the same time that *New Youth* ran its first comprehensive issue on Marxism, and while young Chinese were first learning that at the Paris Peace Conference, which settled the issues of the First World War, China's claims had been callously brushed aside by the Western powers. Thus Lu Xun's message was swept up into the general rush of socialist and anti-imperialist action and rhetoric that inaugurated a new period in China's ongoing revolution.

Socialist theory, at some level of rigor, had been espoused by a small number of Chinese since the first decade of the twentieth century. A Chinese delegate had been present informally at the meeting of the Second International at Brussels in 1909, there had been socialist study societies in Shanghai, and an official Socialist Party had been formed at the time of the 1913 elections (though it claimed to be educational rather than political, and so did not run candidates for office). In France, also, Chinese students interested in anarchism had become knowledgeable about socialism and formed their own societies in conjunction with a successful work-study program. Their numbers grew dramatically after 1917, when China's decision to enter the First World War on the side of the Allied powers—a decision dictated by China's desire to force the cancellation of Germany's concessions and special privileges in her territory—brought two hundred thousand or more Chinese laborers to France, to work in war industries or to assist the Allies with trench digging, transportation, and construction projects behind the lines. Some of these Chinese were literate on arrival, and many more became so through special army training programs; thus in France more and more Chinese both came into contact with socialist theory and were able to gauge the impact of the Bolshevik revolution on the Allied war effort.[47] Before the dissemination of Lenin's writings on imperialism, it was not easy for radical Chinese activists to make the connection between socialist and anti-imperialist politics, and indeed many had been deeply impressed by President Wilson's Fourteen Points on the rights of self-determination for small or weak nations and were convinced that the United States would ensure that other Allied powers respected Chinese sovereignty. Few knew that the Chinese administration in Beijing that came to power after the failure of General Zhang's restoration attempt had returned to the unpopular policies of Yuan Shikai and had signed away crucial rights in the Shandong peninsula and in the city of Qingdao to the Japanese in return for a fresh round of massive loans in 1918; even those who knew of those dealings were unaware of the secret commitments that had been made by Great Britain and France to Japan, with respect to the latter's special situation in China.[48]

Much of the information on the last phase of these negotiations at Versailles reached China via telegrams sent from Paris by Liang Qichao. Liang, despite (or perhaps because of) his political involvements, had been as dismayed as anyone by the growing evidence of China's weakness on the international scene, and had traveled to Europe in late 1918 to assess the situation there and, if possible, exert some pressure on the Chinese delegates. After his beatific voyage over calm seas, with time for reading and reflection and "no trouble from the affairs of the world, just spending each day with the bright sky and the colors of the sea," his only worry was that "after reaching land again I might never recapture this happiness."[49] London in February 1919, with a "sun like blood" struggling through heavy fog, with inedible food and a freezing hotel room, jolted him sharply back to reality, and left him with the thought that "if this is what it's like *after* the war, one can imagine what things were like *during* the war." Yet English stoicism in the face of these deprivations impressed Liang, and he contrasted their frugality with the waste that one saw everywhere in China.[50] When he reached France in March, however, his thoughts took a new tack as he confronted the destructive folly of war. He expressed his sense of shock and confusion in a postcard to his daughter:

> We left Paris at seven in the morning on March 7, and got to Reims at eleven o'clock. Reims used to be a major city with over a million inhabitants, now only a few thousand are left. None of the buildings in the center of town is intact. This was the most famous city in early French history, founded in the third century, and has a gate honoring the Roman Emperor Augustus; the cathedral is also famous, as a perfect example of the Gothic style—building started in the twelfth century and was completed in the sixteenth, the outer walls being decorated with over twenty-five hundred stone sculptures, lined up in rows. The Germans bombarded it three times, in 1914, 1916, and 1918; the cathedral was hit repeatedly and over half destroyed.[51]

In later letters and essays Liang returned to this theme of disillusion over the loss of life and cultural destruction of the war, a disillusion encompassing not only Germany but all the Western nations that fostered a climate in which such outrages took place. And his own disgust was compounded by the slowly emerging story of private deals in the past and pusillanimity in the present that led to the Allied powers' final rejection of China's pleas and the honoring of Japan's demands: in a spate of telegrams to political colleagues in China, Liang warned that this was a "once-in-a-thousand-years opportunity" for China to demand her international rights; if she could not make her point now, how could she ever claim a right to independence among the countries on this earth?[52]

When the news that the final Versailles decisions had gone against China was published in a Beijing newspaper on May 1, 1919, it had an effect that echoed and amplified the response of Kang Youwei and the examination students to news of Japan's treaty terms at Shimonoseki twenty-four years earlier. But the protest that spilled out into the streets of Beijing in the form first of a massive demonstration and then of riots on May 4 gave its name to a new epoch in China's history, an epoch in which China's indigenous cultural yearnings were combined with a new international political awareness and a new and wider social consciousness. Perhaps this was the truest and most generous interpretation of Lu Xun's symbol of that distant horizon to which flight was possible, for with this sense of political recommitment came, despite the anguish and anger, a renewed joy in the possibilities of the human self. The international and solipsistic flavor of this exaltation was caught in a poem by the young Guo Moruo, at this time studying in Japan to be a doctor—like the young Lu Xun fifteen years before—as he took a break from his medical texts and walked along a beach with his little son, Ah-ho:

> Ah-ho, where is the blue sky?
> He points to the azure expanse overhead.
>
> Ah-ho, where is the earth?
> He points to the islands in the sea.
>
> Ah-ho, where is your Daddy?
> He points to a bird flying in the air.
>
> Aha! So I am that flying bird!
> I am that flying bird!
> Watch me outfly the white clouds,
> Watch me race against the gleaming sails,
> And see who flies the higher,
> See who speeds the faster.[53]

·5·

THE LAND OF HUNGER

Conceived of narrowly, as a political "incident," the crisis of May 4, 1919, could be summarized by the events that took place between one-thirty and five-forty-five on that particular afternoon. Assembling at the Gate of Heavenly Peace, on the southern edge of the Forbidden City, some three thousand students representing thirteen colleges and universities of Beijing began a patriotic protest march to the foreign diplomatic quarter. Many carried small banners with nationalistic and anti-Japanese slogans: "Return Qingdao to Us," "Refuse to Sign the Peace Treaty," "Boycott Japanese Goods," "Down with the Traitors"; others distributed broadsheets, of which twenty-five thousand copies had been run off that morning by a local printer, protesting Japan's commercial and territorial claims on Shandong in more detail and urging the Chinese people never to surrender their rights.[1]

Refused admission to the diplomatic quarter by the police, the students changed their route of march to the house of the minister of communications, Cao Rulin. Cao, who was concurrently the director of the Chinese state bank, had been chosen as a target because he was known to be pro-Japanese: he had negotiated the Twenty-one Demands in 1915, helped to arrange the massive new series of Japanese loans in 1918, and was now urging Chinese ratification of the Treaty of Versailles.[2] The students failed to find Cao—he slipped out through a back door—but they broke into his house, set parts

1. Sun Yatsen (second from left) and three radical student friends, photographed around 1887, probably in Hong Kong. The group were known informally as the "four great bandits."

2. Tan Sitong in 1898, shortly before his execution

3. Kang Youwei in 1903, the year after he finished the *Book of the Great Community*

4. Liang Qichao in 1903,
aged thirty

5. Zou Rong, author of
The Revolutionary Army, around 1903

6. Lu Xun in Tokyo, 1904,
after cutting off his queue

7. Qiu Jin in male attire, probably in Japan, 1905

8. Lu Xun in Tokyo, 1909

9. Sun Yatsen as provisional president of the new Chinese Republic, January 1912

10. Song Jiaoren, leader of the Guomindang 1913 election campaign, shortly before his assassination

11. Yuan Shikai as president, around 1914

12. Liang Qichao in Europe, 1919

13. Kang Youwei, around 1920

of it afire, and beat up some of Cao's family and friends whom they found hiding there. As the gathering started to disperse, the police finally took firmer action, arresting thirty-two of the students and taking them off to jail.

This incident appears trivial on the surface, but its repercussions were immediate and far-ranging. The Beijing students not only received strong support from their own teachers and their popular university chancellor, Cai Yuanpei (the brilliant scholar and volatile Restoration Society leader of Qiu Jin's Shanghai days in 1906, who had departed to study for a Ph.D. in Germany and had returned to rise swiftly in the Chinese academic hierarchy), but also held together with remarkable tenacity and skill, forming their own amalgamated student union so as to exert maximum pressure on the government. Since May 7 had been unofficially declared across China to be National Humiliation Day, in memory of Yuan Shikai's acceptance of Japan's Twenty-one Demands on that day four years before, the effect of the demonstration on Chinese students outside Beijing was immediate. A clumsy government attempt to impose a news embargo on the details of the incident failed utterly, and within a day, students in Tianjin, in Shanghai, and then in a spreading circle of other cities, began to plan their own strikes and protests. In Japan, too, thousands of Chinese students demonstrated in Tokyo and were dispersed only after repeated police and cavalry charges that left twenty-nine students seriously injured.[3]

Telegrams of outrage—whether about the Chinese government's willingness to compromise on the Japanese situation or about its conduct in arresting the students—poured into Beijing. Sun Yatsen urged that all the students be exempted from punishment because of "their patriotic sentiments." Kang Youwei, already in a state of intellectual excitement because he had seen in the founding of the League of Nations the first step on the road toward his Great Community, described the students' demonstration as the first valid expression of "people's rights" since the inauguration of the Republic in 1912; he called it "a rare and precious event" and likened the students to those twelfth-century Song dynasty patriots who had also protested their government's weakness in the face of foreign aggression.[4]

Though a harried government ordered the release of the thirty-two students—they were escorted triumphantly back to their campuses by fellow students in a cavalcade of thirteen automobiles—there was no way that the burgeoning movement could now be contained, especially after one of the students died from injuries received during the demonstration. In other cities more student unions were formed, and these began to cooperate with other economic and social groups. In Shanghai sixty-one schools and colleges sent delegates to the same union and joined with merchants and workers in planning boycotts and strikes; after they had established their own "labor department" for liaison with the working people, they attracted more than one hundred thousand participants to a rally at the end of May. Dockers in Chinese ports refused to unload Japanese goods, shops agreed not to sell them, and in Hangzhou the rickshaw pullers refused to transport Japanese nationals. Teaching faculties were not slow to follow with their own organizations; the teachers at Beijing colleges and normal schools combined their forces in a teachers' union by the middle of May.[5]

The sense of excitement was increased by the sudden resignation of Cai Yuanpei, chancellor of the National University of Beijing, the most prestigious institution in the country. Cai had consistently backed the students' right to self-expression and had protested to the government when the thirty-two were arrested, but he had also been a firm believer that the university must be a center for culture and research and that students must study. His resignation message began with the enigmatic remark "I am exhausted! 'Those who killed your horse are the children by the road.'" Educated Chinese knew that Cai was referring to an old and touching fable in which the story is told of an official showing off a particularly handsome horse that has rarely been seen in public; as the children by the side of the road applaud in excitement at the sight, he rides the horse faster and farther until it drops dead of exhaustion.[6] Did this elliptical message mean that Cai Yuanpei thought he was that horse and his students those children? Or, as some thought, did the horse stand for the unpopular pro-Japanese ministers whom the president of China refused to dismiss in the face of public clamor? Perhaps Cai Yuanpei did not want to be "clapped to death," as Qiu Jin had been in 1907, according to Lu Xun's mordant comment at the time; or perhaps he did not want to be a party to the government oppression that he thought must surely follow. Already in the tri-city area of Wuhan, the pro-Japanese military governor was showing grim sternness toward the student demonstrators; he ordered his troops to break up all large assemblies, hundreds of students were beaten up by his troops and at least one was shot, and all public protests ceased after his order that any student making further anti-Japanese speeches would be executed.[7]

The president of the Republic, Xu Shichang, continued to think that the students should return to class and that China should go ahead and ratify the Versailles agreements. President Xu, who had come to office in the troubled months after the suppression of General Zhang's Manchu-restoration attempts, had been a close associate of Yuan Shikai's, and though like Chancellor Cai Yuanpei he was a brilliant scholar (the two of them were among the few men holding high offices in the Republic who had been members of the intellectually prestigious Hanlin Academy during the Qing dynasty), his interests were firmly on the side of traditional classical learning, and against the use of the vernacular language and the studies of radical social theory, modern law, and social science that were flourishing at the National University.[8] So he continued to support the pro-Japanese ministers and to refuse to order the Versailles delegates not to ratify the treaty; when the students responded with a total boycott of classes, he ordered the arrest of all those participating in further demonstrations.

The student response was brilliantly successful. Refusing to be intimidated, they took to the streets in small squads of a dozen or so, lecturing and exhorting people in parks and on street corners to keep up pressure on the government against ratification and to boycott Japanese goods, and daring the government to arrest them. "There are two sources of world civilization: one is the study, the other is the prison," wrote Chen Duxiu, the former editor of *New Youth* who had recently been made dean of students at Beijing National University. "We the youth must make up our minds to enter the prison once out of the study, and enter the study once out of the prison. Only these provide the most lofty and sublime life. And only those civilizations born in these two places are true civilizations with life and value."[9] As the government arrested the first group of students, thousands more started to picket in the streets, this time carrying bedding and food in backpacks to show their readiness to go straight to jail. The government arrested four hundred and fifty. Next day, even more were in the streets, and as the number of those arrested passed the eleven-hundred mark and every jail in Beijing was filled, the government had to take over entire university buildings and convert them to temporary prisons. Despite often grim conditions in these makeshift quarters, the students refused all the outside offers of funds that were pressed on them by sympathizers—Liang Qichao's brother, for example, was politely turned away when he offered one group a thousand dollars contributed by merchant groups in Guangzhou—and thus avoided the appearance of venality that Lu Xun had noted so caustically among his young student newspaper editors in Shaoxing during the revolution.[10]

Renewed waves of protest on behalf of the Beijing students spread over China, exceeding even those after May 4. In Tianjin an enormous coalition of more than one hundred and seventy educational, economic, and religious groups formed the Combined Alliance for National Salvation; the political excitement was so great that Zhou Enlai broke off his studies in Japan and returned to Tianjin to head the journal of the expanded student union there. Shortly thereafter the various city-based unions were affiliated into one Student Union of China. In Shanghai, sympathy strikes were declared in more than forty businesses and factories, and some fifty thousand workers from textile mills, foundries, rail and train lines, cigarette factories, and the docks responded by leaving their jobs.[11]

At first the demonstrations had been largely conducted by male students, but as more and more of the men were jailed by the government, the women students began to demonstrate on their own—a new and startling development. In Tianjin, women students and teachers had already formed an Association of Patriotic Women Comrades and a special speech-writing corps (in which the normal-school student Deng Yingchao, later to marry Zhou Enlai, was one of the leaders); now, in Beijing, a hundred women demonstrated on June 4 at the first arrests of their male comrades, and on June 5 more than a thousand women assembled to protest in front of President Xu's residence.[12] Finally the president acted, and on June 10 he accepted the resignations of Cao Rulin and two other ministers most notorious for their pro-Japanese stance; even though he continued to hesitate over a specific order to the Chinese delegates at Versailles that they not ratify the treaty, those same delegates—impressed by the news of the protests in China, inundated by more than seven thousand telegrams, and physically harassed by Chinese students in Paris—finally did not sign at the closing Versailles ceremonies on June 28.[13]

That outcome, so long desired by so many, was at best symbolic, since the Chinese refusal to ratify the treaty did not substantially affect Japan's de facto position in China. But the movement begun in these months of May and June continued, and had an incalculable effect on education, on labor organizations, on the attitudes of intellectuals toward their country and toward themselves. There were many indicators of this shift: four hundred or more journals, written in the vernacular and devoted to culture and politics, were founded in this same period; hundreds of new schools, often with radical curricula, were set up; problems of international politics and of domestic social organization began to receive intensified scrutiny.[14] *New Youth* magazine, which had not previously had a specific political focus (at least not one articulated in any formal way), came out with a fresh and idealistic manifesto late in 1919. Among other things, this stated:

> We believe that the moral progress of mankind should expand to a standard above the life based on animal impulse; therefore, we should extend a feeling of friendship and mutual assistance to all peoples of the world. But toward aggressive and possessive warlords and plutocrats we must be hostile.
>
> We advocate mass movement and social reconstruction, cutting off relations completely with past and present political parties.
>
> Although we do not believe in the omnipotence of politics, we recognize that politics is an important aspect of

public life. And we believe that in a genuine democracy, political rights must be distributed to all people. Even though there may be limitations, the criteria for the distribution will be whether people work or not, rather than whether they own property or not. This kind of politics is really inevitable in the process of introducing the new era and a useful instrument for the development of the new society. As for political parties, we also recognize them as a necessary device for political practice, but we shall never tolerate membership in parties that support the interests of the few or of one class rather than the happiness of the whole society.

We believe that politics, ethics, science, the arts, religion, and education should all meet practical needs in the achievement of progress for present and future social life.

We have to give up the useless and irrelevant elements of traditional literature and ethics, because we want to create those needed for the progress of the new era and new society.

We believe that it is requisite for the progress of our present society to uphold natural science and pragmatic philosophy and to abolish superstition and fantasy.

We believe that to respect women's personality and rights is a practical need for the social progress at present, and we hope that they themselves will be completely aware of their duty to society.[15]

This last injunction was particularly pertinent, because the record of change for women in China had been decidedly mixed. Despite some advances in education for women, some changes in the legal structure to prevent the worst injustices to widows, and a growing emphasis on ending the practices of foot-binding and female infanticide, most of the abuses—pinpointed by Qiu Jin and by Kang Youwei almost twenty years before—were still omnipresent. Furthermore, many of the promising initiatives taken just before the 1911 revolution had petered out in the ensuing warlord years. A number of women's military and Red Cross units, formed at the height of the 1911 revolutionary excitement, had been disbanded shortly thereafter. For a brief moment in Guangdong province some women had been permitted to vote and to participate in the provisional assembly, but such activities ceased after the Guomindang dropped its planks on women's rights, which the Revolutionary Alliance had originally espoused. Extensive and aggressive lobbying in the Nanjing provisional assembly by Chinese suffragists in 1912 had won publicity but no effective results. And other promising ventures, such as the formation of women's insurance groups to give them access to education, and the attempt to form women's banks by pooling the proceeds of sold jewelry, had collapsed completely.[16] In 1914, also, the cause of women's education had been publicly deprecated by the minister of education, leading to some further setbacks. (The minister, Tang Hualong, was later assassinated by a Chinese barber in Victoria, Canada.)[17]

At the same time, however, some positive signs continued. As more schools for girls and women were founded, society grew more willing to tolerate and even encourage such new establishments, and a fresh pool of emancipated teachers (both men and women) swiftly emerged to staff them.[18] Popular accounts of heroines in other nations and romantic stories about Chinese women were widely read, and so were Qiu Jin's poems, which had been published almost immediately after her death in 1907 and were soon brought out again in a new and expanded edition. From the founding of *New Youth* in 1915, Chen Duxiu had championed the cause of women's rights, and in 1918 he ran a complete vernacular translation of Ibsen's *A Doll's House* in the magazine (the play had first been discussed by Lu Xun in one of his Japanese essays written in 1907); the play became immediately popular, and the name of its heroine, Nora, gradually became a potent one in China, as Sofya had been a decade before.[19]

As Shen Congwen had been an involved observer of the intricacies of the warlord world in western Hunan province, so was Ding Ling an involved witness to the struggles of women in Changsha and in the smaller country towns a hundred miles or so down the Yuan River from the areas where Shen was stationed. Born in 1905 in the north-central Hunan town of Anfu, to a large and moderately prosperous landowning family, Ding Ling, also like Shen, was destined to become one of her country's foremost writers and to live on into the 1980s in the People's Republic of China.[20] Like Shen, too, she wrote vividly of the 1911 revolution, describing it partly through a child's eyes and partly in terms of the stories her mother told her. She remembered how she was frightened, along with the other children, at the rumors that the Longhaired bandits were coming, and how they stood nervously in the garden as the adults discussed the alarming astronomical portents visible in the night sky. The central memory of revolution to her mother was of sudden silence, or rather the ending of an accustomed noise, for in the market square, where they had yelled all day for custom, the sedan-chair carriers now worked silently and ceaselessly, too busy with ferrying the rich out of the city and down to their country relatives to have the time or the necessity to seek further business; hundreds of other bearers came in from the countryside to benefit from this sudden boom, but there was work for all. Ding Ling and her family watched carts loaded with household possessions being hurried to safety, heard the townsmen (even as they fled) speculate that they should be all right since theirs was a little place and not worth attacking, heard, too, of the increase in fares on all the riverboats, heard sounds of distant gunfire, and saw the first young men of the scholar-gentry class strolling the streets without their queues and were told, "They must be revolutionaries."[21]

Ding Ling's father, who had been a student briefly in Japan, had died while she was still very young, before 1911, and in later accounts he figures vaguely, an ineffective and generous man who gave away family possessions on whim to relatives and casual acquaintances. Ding Ling herself, in later life, could never quite recall his face, though she would struggle mentally to do so. But her relationship with her widowed mother was close, and became even more so after her mother made the courageous decision to leave the shelter of the sprawling, half-empty complex of buildings that constituted the family's ancestral home and to seek a modern education, first in the new school for girls that opened in Changde, and later in the provincial capital of Changsha.[22]

Though modern education was only just beginning to reach Changde, the city of Changsha had been a leading center of radical thought during the 1890s, when Tan Sitong, Liang Qichao, and other leading reformers had taught there. But even after Tan's execution and Liang's exile it continued to be a lively educational center, containing some of the best schools in central China, as well as being a pioneering center for women's education.[23] In her reconstruction of her mother's school life in Changde during 1911 and in Changsha (at the First Girls' Normal School) during 1912 and 1913, Ding Ling shows much of the pressures and excitement that gripped these women—aged anywhere from the early teens to the forties—as they tried to prepare themselves for a life in the new China.[24]

To Ding Ling's mother, already thirty when she first entered school, came a slowly growing sense of the outside world, of China's humiliations at the hands of foreign powers, and of the need for internal reform and self-strengthening; many of her women friends articulated their desire to "rescue" China.[25] Students who had grown up in homes among opium-smoking relatives (even ten-year-olds smoked on occasion) could join in the debates on the harmfulness of opium addiction with melancholy satisfaction, and shared the excitement over the more radical journals that reached Hunan from Shanghai.[26] Some invoked the heroic image of Qiu Jin as an example to women of the day, but others argued the cause of education against that of violence; as one young woman put it, "If you look at what has happened since the Restoration Society was founded, so many times they've tried uprisings, but there has been no single example of success, the only result was that a few people had their heads cut off."[27] By the end of their first year in Changde, a group of seven women—Ding Ling's mother at thirty being the oldest, and her closest friend, Xiang Jingyu, at seventeen being the youngest—had drawn up a solemn manifesto in which they pledged to devote themselves to constant study so as to achieve equality between men and women and to rescue their country through education.[28]

The younger children, allowed to sit in sometimes as the adults were talking, got used to arguments about education and their future roles, and learned to give patriotic responses to their half-bantering interlocutors. A little girl is told, "We must give you a proper education, you must stop setting high store by the male and undervaluing the female. . . . Little one, wouldn't you like to study? Wouldn't you like your auntie to buy you a candy?" "I want to study, but I don't want any candy; I want a foreign steamship," replies the child, who has seen a detailed model of a foreign passenger liner in the house of one of her mother's friends.[29] At the same time Ding learned how great the gulf had been between the education and expectations of men and women, how her mother's younger brother sailed out into the world of business and learning while her mother stayed at home, trained only in embroidery. Now, as her widowed mother struggled with her schoolwork, Ding could see how she survived by selling off bits of land, or from the proceeds of the hundred little chicks that the old family maid managed to raise, along with a few piglets and vegetables. The vulnerability of those chicks emerging from their shells was to seem to Ding a fitting image for a girl child born in such a place and time.[30]

Most harrowing, however, was watching a mother's pain and tenacity as she unbound her feet. Ding Ling later recorded her mother's accounts of her first days in the school, as the country women, already dazed by the experience of the entrance examinations, the preparations, and the unfamiliar surroundings, struggled to stop the tears from flowing down their faces as they stood on their bound feet during the seemingly endless introductory ceremonies, suffering every kind of rage and humiliation along with the physical pain.[31] A modernized educational curriculum presented these women with a dramatic challenge, in that it offered gym classes to all students yet at the same time excused all with bound feet from attendance. Given courage by some of her radical friends with normal feet, Ding Ling's mother determined to attend the gym classes despite the mockery of many of her schoolmates; removing the layers of cloth wrappings, taking the first anguished steps, bathing her feet in cold water every night to lull the pain, exercising regularly, she found that her feet slowly began to straighten out, and finally she was able to wear regular footwear like her friends and teachers.[32] The upshot of this tenacity for Ding Ling's mother was that by 1914, when she had no more money left to pay for school expenses, she was able to get a teaching job in an elementary school at Taoyuan, not far from Changsha; she taught there for several years until she was promoted to direct the women's school in Changde where she had begun her own education.[33]

Such a slow and steady struggle was in itself a kind of victory, and enabled Ding Ling, precociously literate and unhampered by bound feet, to entertain exalted ideas of her own potential. For a while, she stayed on at the Changsha elementary school attached to the First Girls' Normal School, where her mother had studied; then, for a time, she moved back to Changde to be with her mother, before returning around 1919 to study in Changsha. During these years of her adolescence a profound influence was her mother's close friend from that earlier sworn band of seven young women in Changde, Xiang Jingyu.[34] Xiang, once the youngest of that group, and naively excited by their program for national survival, had now become a strong-minded and talented woman, trained at Changsha's finest advanced school for women—the Zhounan Girls' Middle School—which she and her friends made a center for political activity. With her friend Cai Chang, and encouraged by the school's radical director, she developed a Women's Work and Study Group, along the lines of the Society for Work and Study in France, which Mao Zedong had organized with Cai Chang's brother Cai Hesen in the leading male school. The young women joining Xiang's group were prepared to embark on the journey to France so that they could be the spearhead of China's latest generation of self-strengtheners, both by attaining advanced training and by learning patterns of self-reliance and self-sufficiency through a program of labor. Xiang talked often and at length with Ding Ling about her plans, and when she made the long journey by steamer and sailing vessel back upriver to her own home, she would often stop over with Ding and her mother at Taoyuan. The women students at Taoyuan and the Zhounan School were also the leaders as the May Fourth Movement spread out to Hunan, and under the aegis of the United Student Alliance (which Mao Zedong had formed) they organized Committees of Ten to Save the Nation, which traveled around the province to develop patriotism and a sense of purpose among Hunanese youth.[35]

Along with patriotism came a growing sense of the meaning of freedom for women, sparked in part by essays in *New Youth* and similar magazines that analyzed the patterns of women's dependence in Chinese society, criticized conventional marriage patterns, and spoke out for a variety of patterns of cohabitation or free love. Ding Ling was finally able to escape an arranged marriage that elders in her late father's clan had set up for her by so outraging her future in-laws by her radical behavior that they felt it better not to have their son associate with her: along with Yang Kaihui (her friend and the daughter of one of Changsha's leading teachers) she insisted on enrolling in a previously all-male high school that had only just been made coeducational, an act of bravado finally accepted by her mother but not by the rest of the family. And while still only fourteen years old, Ding Ling also lobbied, vocally but unsuccessfully, among the Hunan provincial authorities to grant equality of rights to women, and to enable women legally to inherit property. When Xiang Jingyu, Cai Chang, and their other friends left Changsha for French language training in Beijing and then traveled to Paris in 1919, Ding Ling and her mother did not have the money to accompany them, though they continued to keep in touch through letters.[36]

Yet the extraordinary articulateness, energy, and courage of these young women could not hide the fact that adverse pressures within Chinese society continued to be so strong that, despite the trends toward partial emancipation, countless other women kept their own feet bound and bound those of their daughters, acceded quietly to the marriages arranged for them, and, if widowed, meekly lived the life of "chastity" that local custom demanded. Woman's inferior status was even "proved" afresh, at intervals, but now the pseudoscientific language of Westernized science and mathematical formulas was adopted to supplement the older Confucian canons of hierarchy and obedience.[37]

In an essay in *New Youth* titled "My Views on Chastity," written in 1918, Lu Xun held up these muddled attitudes about women to ruthless scrutiny, pointing out that the current one-sided view of chastity for women (when it was not demanded of men) had all the logic of Kang Youwei's insistence on restoring the Emperor, or of those spiritualists who wished to invoke the spirit of the ancient philosopher Mencius to solve China's problems. He asked pointedly:

> In what way do unchaste women injure the country? It is only too clear today that "the country is faced with ruin." There is no end to the dastardly crimes committed, and war, banditry, famine, flood, and drought follow one after the other. But this is owing to the fact that we have no new morality or new science and all our thoughts and actions are out of date. That is why these benighted times resemble the old dark ages. Besides, all government, army, academic, and business posts are filled by men, not by unchaste women. And it seems unlikely that the men in power have been so bewitched by such women as to lose all sense of right and wrong and plunge into dissipation.[38]

Arguments based on *yin* and *yang*, continued Lu Xun, were obviously "gibberish," since even if there were such principles, one could never "prove" one sex to be superior to the other; only a country such as China could "create such a perverted morality, which becomes more exacting and cruel with each passing day."[39] The existing system had placed outrageous demands on Chinese women for millennia, and though one could not correct past abuses, at least one could work to stop their recurrence:

> These women are to be pitied. Trapped for no good reason by tradition and numbers, they are sacrificed to no purpose. We should hold a great memorial service for them.
> After mourning for the dead, we must swear to be pure, intelligent, brave, aspiring, and progressive. We must tear off every mask. We must do away with all the stupidity and tyranny in the world that injure others as well as ourselves.
> After mourning for the dead, we must swear to get rid of the meaningless suffering that blights our lives. We must do away with all the stupidity and tyranny that create and relish the sufferings of others.
> We must also swear to see to it that all mankind knows legitimate happiness.[40]

Expostulation about such hypocrisy was not confined to a small elite of writers clustered in Beijing or Shanghai. Thus when Miss Zhao of Nanyang Street in Changsha committed suicide in 1919 because she absolutely refused to marry Mr. Wu of the same city, as her parents insisted, there were those willing to take up the cause dramatized by her death, and to try to make a constructive lesson out of it. Among them was Mao Zedong, now a young man in his mid-twenties, who had left his father's farm in central Hunan to come to Changsha to study, and in the process had walked out on the arranged marriage with the daughter of a neighboring family that his parents had long since negotiated. Instead, Mao had met, and was later to marry, Ding Ling's friend and fellow activist Yang Kaihui. Yang Kaihui's father was the neo-Kantian philosopher Yang Changji, with whom Mao had spent several years studying ethics at the Changsha First Normal School, and from whom he absorbed several crucial ideas concerning the self-realization of the individual and the individual's responsibilities to society. Mao would also (one assumes) have read Yang's 1915 article on the Chinese family in which he praised the rights enjoyed by women in the West and the possibilities of freely choosing marriage partners there. Yang also pointed in the same essay to the dangers of having arranged marriages for the mentally and physically weak, who in actuality should not be allowed to perpetuate those weaknesses.[41] Perhaps in unconscious resistance to the eugenic ruthlessness of this view, Mao's first youthful essay, published in *New Youth* in 1917, had been on physical training and the need to strengthen the bodies of the Chinese people through vigorous exercise and martial training, to wipe out the old Chinese ideals of "white and slender hands," "slow gait and grave, calm gaze," and to substitute instead a creative "savagery" that would enable one "to leap on horseback and to shoot at the same time; to go from battle to battle; to shake the mountains by one's cries, and the colors of the sky by one's roars of anger; to have the strength to uproot mountains like Xiang Yu and the audacity to pierce the mark like You Ji."[42]

But such romantic and dramatic ideas of self-transformation could not save Miss Zhao, for she was one of the unlucky ones, although in courage, no doubt, she was the equal of teenagers like Ding Ling and Yang Kaihui. As Mao Zedong wrote in an essay for a Changsha newspaper in 1919, Miss Zhao died because she was caught "in three iron nets that composed a kind of triangular cage": the three nets were *her* family, the Wus (the family of the intended groom), and Chinese society itself. However obdurate the Zhaos and Wus might have been, "if in society there had been a powerful group of public opinion to support her, if there were an entirely new world where the facts of running away from one's parents' home and finding refuge elsewhere were considered honorable and not dishonorable," then the young woman would have lived. She died "because of the darkness of the social system," added Mao, and because of "the negation of the individual will." If there were simple conclusions to be drawn, they were that society must change but also that suicide—however much one might respect it in this case—was not an adequate answer. It was just because "suicide results from the fact that society deprives people of all hope," wrote Mao, "that we should struggle against society in order to regain the hope we have lost. We should die fighting."[43]

One wonders if Qu Qiubai read this article, for his mother had killed herself in 1915, when he was sixteen years of age, by carefully scraping the red phosphorus heads off a box of matches and then swallowing the powder, helping it down with a glass of wine. In her case, too, the reasons for the act of desperation were as complex as Chinese society itself: she had married ("well," one would have initially said) an educated man in one of those old Jiangsu landed families that had been the backbone of the scholar-gentry class in the Qing dynasty and that (as Shen Congwen had noted in the case of his own province), after the 1911 upheavals, had often added political power to their economic strength. But her husband was lazy and extravagant, unable either to extract more money from the land or to find a job in the new republican or provincial bureaucracy. He had given a good primary education to Qu Qiubai but then, as the money dwindled, he had drifted off to another province to find teaching work, on a salary so small that he could send no remittances home to his wife. Exhausted by the struggle to raise the six children he had left her with, forced to care for her partially paralyzed mother-in-law, surrounded by a mounting sea of debts, and constantly sniped at by her husband's relatives for her poor domestic management and her lack of filial piety, Qu Qiubai's mother one day could bear no more.[44]

Qu Qiubai was overwhelmed by his mother's death—he had rushed back from school at the news, in time to see her body with the accompaniments of the suicide still scattered around it—and utterly unsure about his own future. Almost without resources, he drifted to Wuhan, where he was given some financial help by relatives, and by 1916 he had moved on to Beijing. There, too poor to pay any admission fees or tuition at the regular universities, he entered the five-year Russian Language Institute, newly established under the aegis of the Ministry of Foreign Affairs; the institute was not only tuition-free but also provided a small stipend and the promise of employment, after graduation, in government, in the diplomatic service, or on the Chinese Eastern Railway.[45] Qu had been well educated in classical Chinese, especially poetry, and had a deep personal interest in Buddhism, but according to his later recollections he had no knowledge of Russian literature before entering the institute in 1917 and had paid no attention to the revolution in Russia. If he had any ideology, it was "anarchism of the Tolstoy type."[46]

For three years in Beijing, Qu led a lonely life of intensive study, working eleven hours a day at the Russian and French studies demanded by the institute, and on his Buddhist and classical Chinese philosophical texts; these latter, he believed, would help him at what he called the "transcendental" level of serving humanity through attaining true altruism.[47] His only social contacts were among his fellow students of Russian and with a small group that met in the office of the chief librarian at Beijing National University, Li Dazhao, for informal discussions of problems of Marxist theory. Mao Zedong, who had come to Beijing after graduating from the Changsha First Normal School, was working as an assistant librarian under Li at this time, and also attended the meetings. From Li's presentations of Marxist theory Qu could garner some solace in a world that he had thus far seen as largely negative—the corrupt bureaucrats of Beijing depressed and angered him, the jealousy and hatred within his extended family had baffled him and left him with a feeling that "The meaning of life was absolutely obscure."[48] Li, even though his own studies of Russia and Marxism were at their inception, presented his younger Chinese listeners with the encouraging view that Russia was an example of a country that had been able to benefit from its late entry into the modern world: "Just because of its comparative slowness in the evolution of civilization," wrote Li in July 1918, "there existed surplus energy for development"; China, by implication, could take heart from this. Four months later Li presented a view that the "victory of Bolshevism" was inevitable; victory would sweep away warlords, bureaucrats, and capitalists alike. In rhetoric echoing Zou Rong's of fifteen years before, he wrote: "Every place in the world will see the victorious flag of Bolshevism, and hear the triumphal song of Bolshevism. The bell of humanitarianism is sounding. The dawn of freedom has arrived."[49] Qu remained cautious, and continued to see more likelihood of liberation through Buddhism: "I believed that the world was to be saved through the practice of Bodhisattvahood and that everything was impermanent, including the social system."[50]

For Qu it was the demonstrations on May 4, 1919, rather than these abstract discussions, that galvanized him to action and changed the direction of his thoughts. In the first days of May, according to his later memories, he was something of a reluctant participant, who became a delegate representing the Russian Language Institute only because it was a "job which no one else wished to take";[51] but after he had marched in the May 4 rally, taken part in the June rallies also, and been jailed along with hundreds of other Beijing students for three days, he felt as if "sucked into a whirlpool" and together with a small group of friends in Beijing "joined the movement with an unbelievable fury." He was now twenty years old, and in later writings he described the effect of the demonstrations on his own thinking:

> We were all aware of the deep-seated maladies of the society to which we belonged but were yet ignorant of their cure. Feelings alone, however, ran so strong that restlessness could no more be contained. That was, so far as I can see, the real significance of the student movement. There

was a demand for change, and that demand erupted in an outburst. It had then at least its shocking and rousing effects, for as Kropotkin said, "One riot does more than many thousands of books and pamphlets."

The patriotic movement had actually a deeper meaning than mere patriotism. The taste of colonialism in its full bitterness had never come home to the Chinese until then, even though we had already had the experience of several decades of foreign exploitation behind us. The sharp pain of imperialistic oppression then reached the marrow of our bones, and it awakened us from the nightmares of impractical democratic reforms. The issue of the former German possessions in Shandong, which started the uproar of the student movement, could not be separated from the larger problem.[52]

In the course of the next few months, Qu immersed himself in the worlds of political journalism and social activism; these endeavors were fostered not only by the general ambience of "May Fourth radicalism" and of the earliest Marxist study groups but also by such social-reformist-inclined institutions as the Chinese Y.M.C.A., which in the context of a reactionary and warlord China had considerable influence.[53] To his earlier concentration on classical Chinese philosophy and Buddhism, and to his growing absorption in Marxism, Qu now added a developing interest in the works of Bertrand Russell. The fascination with Russell, many of whose works were translated into Chinese at this time, was not surprising, if one considers that Russell's work in mathematical logic meshed with the effort made by many Chinese (aroused by Chen Duxiu's calls that they now study "Mr. Science" and "Mr. Democracy" instead of Confucius) to achieve a deeper understanding of Western scientific concepts; furthermore, Russell's reflections on the world of appearance and the nature of reality often coincided to a startling extent with the concerns of Buddhist philosophy, while his pacifism and political radicalism impressed those already attracted to the socialist experiments in the Soviet Union.[54]

Russell came to China on a lecture tour in late 1920, just after visiting the Soviet Union, as one of several famous figures sponsored by the Society for Lectures on the New Learning. This group, formed to bring influential Western intellectuals to

China, had been established by Liang Qichao after he had returned from France and decided to devote the rest of his life to scholarship and teaching rather than to politics; an indication of Russell's popularity in China at this time can be seen from the fact that there was both a Russell Study Society and a *Russell Monthly* (*Losu yuekan*), and his lectures on the possibilities of social transformation were enthusiastically received. Russell was accompanied by his lover, the young sociologist Dora Black, whose public lectures at women's schools and to anarchist groups—in which she made no secret of her relationship with Russell, praised the Soviet Union for reforming relations between the sexes, and told Chinese youth to strike out boldly against old marriage patterns and to find their psychological and economic freedom—were also most effective.[55] The message that both Black and Russell carried was of course radical in the Chinese context, and deeply resented by Chinese conservatives; but it had its disturbing side to certain Chinese leftists, also. To Mao Zedong, for example, who attended the lectures Russell gave when he moved on from Beijing to Changsha (lectures that Ding Ling probably also heard), the persuasiveness of Russell's arguments that communism might be achieved without violent revolutionary upheaval—by means of education and enlightened persuasion—was alarming. In vigorous letters of refutation that he sent to Cai Hesen and his other Hunanese friends, now studying and working in France, Mao pointed out that China could not afford the time for such gradualism; in any case, with both the schools and the press controlled by the capitalists, it was unlikely that change would ever occur if they meekly waited for it.[56]

Qu Qiubai himself, though steeped in Russell's works, missed the actual lectures because in October 1920 he received a lucrative offer to travel to the Soviet Union as a correspondent for the Beijing newspaper *Morning News* (*Chen bao*), an invitation that he decided to accept although it would interrupt his studies and possibly jeopardize his civil-service career. He took the gamble because he knew how little accurate knowledge there was in China about the Soviet Union; despite the small discussion group that Li Dazhao had set up in Beijing, and the formation of some cells of the Socialist Youth Corps in the summer of 1920, no informed Chinese observer had been to the Soviet Union since the Bolshevik revolution, and however vivid Russell's and Black's accounts might turn out to be, they would still be based merely on the limited experiences of a brief visit. Furthermore, information on Soviet society was sought not just by proto-Marxists; the *Morning News*, which would pay for the trip, had started out as the organ of Liang Qichao's Progressive Party about seven years earlier and had stayed linked to the group of influential Beijing intellectuals and politicians known as the Research Clique, of which Liang remained a prominent member. Qu was thus able to accept the assignment for practical and financial reasons, *and* in a pioneering spirit. Filled with excitement and alarm, he glorified the journey as a mission that would at last bring light to the Chinese people; at the same time he entered upon a protracted round of farewells to friends and relatives—including a visit to his father, whom Qu had not seen for several years—and put his youthful written works in order for posterity.[57]

On October 18 a large group came to the Beijing railroad station to see Qu off; in a farewell poem his radical uncle Qu Junong, with whom he had first tasted the joys of socialist activism the year before, invoked the spirits of Tagore and Bergson as evidence that there was a harmony to all existence that transcended mere physical separation.[58] Almost immediately, however, the journey bogged down, and Qu found himself rather anticlimactically stuck in the Manchurian city of Harbin, while the passengers waited for Soviet troops to clear the Siberian railway lines of the White Russian Cossack hetman Semënov's troops. November drifted into December, and still the train didn't proceed. Qu studied Harbin, where a Japanese industrial and economic presence was already massively apparent, watched Japanese arrogance at work, and began to piece together a collection of essays, poems, and observations that he would publish later as *Notes from the Land of Hunger*. (Qu chose this title in punning reference to the Chinese ideograph for "Russia," pronounced "E," and the Chinese ideograph for "hunger," also pronounced "E." Thus "E-guo," or "land of E," could be used to evoke, among educated Chinese, allusions both to the Soviet Union and to an incident from their own distant past, three millennia earlier, when two upright scholars starved themselves to death for principle, rather than serve under an amoral ruler, proving how self-sacrifice could bring the highest levels of spiritual reward.)[59]

One of Qu's poems, written on December 1, 1920, shows how he began the task of reconciling his Buddhist sense of the unreality of material life, and his sense of the world as in flux, with the very pressing "realities" of the world he was setting out to explore:

Life is indistinct,
A momentary sweeping light or fleeting shadow.
The morning is cool and cold dew freezes,
The tepid sun spreads like a disease
The dew melts—the wonderful mystery of life—
But the stream of inexhaustible treasury of meanings is not seen
And also the least particle in the mighty whirl.
Will you come to grasp, through the cracks, the meaning of all that?

The "ego" is limitless. The "other" is limitless, too.
Laughter and wrath, sorrow and joy will not end.
Who thinks of days filled with suffering?
When will come the time of deliverance from miseries?

Are you aware that the world is to be delivered?
To save oneself means also to save others.
For the sake of a thorough enlightenment I am going to the Land of Hunger.
The Land of Hunger will be limitless.[60]

In another passage, also written at Harbin, that was part essay, part chant, part vision, Qu Qiubai played with a number of ideas that his uncle had included in his October 18 farewell poem. Qu Junong had written the lines "See now, how your companions lie in drunken slumber in our land of sweet darkness, what can they accomplish? If you intend to make honey, gather the sweetness from the flowers and make the honey." Qu Qiubai developed this image into a prolonged metaphor about his country and his quest: China was the land of slumber, of "sweet darkness," because its people sought pleasure and comfort, and also because the rays of light had all been extinguished there: "Ever since my birth I have seen no ray, not the faintest ray, of sunshine. I don't even know what sunshine is. In such a place as that, I almost lost my powers to see." Now, however, a ray of sunshine had appeared in Russia, "a ray of light, red as blood, that illuminates the whole world. Everywhere, red flowers dyed with the blood of war radiate like red light, like evening clouds and morning mists." And in a piercing conclusion, Qu added: "That place of bright, red light, that is the place where, as punishment, you put the lunatics. It is the land of ice, of snow, of cold, of hunger.... Now you are punishing me, the lunatic, and I accept my punishment. I will not forget you all, I intend to open up for you a path of brightness."[61]

Even after the rail lines were finally cleared in December, the trans-Siberian journey was slow and laborious. The train had to pause at several railroad junctions on the edges of bleak and freezing provincial towns, where the misery Qu witnessed and conversations he had with disaffected Russians put considerable strain on his still-fledgling faith in the Soviet experiment. But all of this served to set the scene for the first hint of that "light" he claimed to be seeking; as he approached Moscow itself in early 1921, he perceived through the train window traces of brightness among the ranks of snow-covered winter trees: "The icy beams of the crystal moon struck in flashes through the windows of our compartment, and amidst these flashes and dancing lights our train pushed on, drawing ever nearer to Moscow."[62]

These icy moon-rays formed a fitting image indeed for Qu's sense of the Soviet Union in those days of famine and travail which marked the end of the first phase of the Bolshevik revolution before the opening of Lenin's New Economic Policy. In his second book, written during 1921 and entitled *History of My Mind in the Red Capital*, Qu continued to plumb different levels of dejection and euphoria, to experience both cold and heat. He did not try to hide the negative side that he had been warned of, of a socialist state that was "dreams, illusions, rifles, jails": he noted newspaper reports of starving Russian peasants eating corpses or burning themselves to death in despair in their houses; he followed the mutiny of the sailors at Kronstadt and its harsh suppression, experienced the taste of Russian black bread—"its bitterness and sourness, with an odor of rotten grass mixed with mud"—and watched with sympathy the Russian cadres unable to hide their yearning for the bread rolls made with white flour that the travelers from China had managed to obtain. He also fell seriously ill and began to suffer the deliriums of fever and the weakness of spreading tuberculosis that finally led to his hospitalization in a sanatorium near Moscow.[63]

Qu was often overwhelmed by homesickness for the remembered flowers, trees, friends, and landscapes of Jiangsu province and Beijing, though this nostalgia combined—as can be seen in a moving essay called simply "A Letter from Home"—with his growing ability to make sharp social analyses of Chinese society. In this essay Qu describes his feelings upon reading a letter from his younger brother, mailed from China in March 1921 and delivered to Moscow only in November; he is struck by his brother's phrase "everything is fine at home," and finally refuses to believe it—his own memories of home life and his sense of the role of the "scholar class" in China force him to reject the consolatory message. His love for his mother and the memory of how she died, the current fragmentation of his home and family, and the sense that they were all trapped in the world of the scholar class—all belied his brother's message. And Qu came to see that this class—neither clearly capitalist nor clearly feudal—had drawn its power from its spurious claims to control access to knowledge which in turn enabled it to "fleece" the ignorant peasantry; just so had foreign powers fleeced the indigenous Chinese capitalists. These reflections made Qu aware that he was a member of a class of "intellectual compradores," and left him bereft of thoughts as to how to proceed, save to offer the slogan "Proletarianize the scholars!" and to vow that "Such a day will come."[64]

Nevertheless, the Soviet Union enthralled him and offered him positive visions upon which to build his hopes, so that he could write: "Now, I am happy, for I have seen the lighthouse of the mind's sea. Even though it is but a single red ray, weak and indistinct, it is possible to see in it the approaching infinite progress."[65] Among experiences that Qu recorded with delight were the chance to walk on a sunny spring day to a park on the edge of Moscow and see the couples wander by, hand in hand; to be welcomed at an elementary school by little children singing and dancing and to teach them their first Chinese ideographs; to travel to Tolstoy's home at Yasnaya Polyana in the company of Tolstoy's granddaughter Sofya and to stroll in the woods, examine the library (which, he was happy to see, contained a copy of the great Daoist classic by Laozi, the *Daodejing*, in a bilingual English-Chinese edition), and visit the peasant homes on Tolstoy's estate; to see Lenin in person as he addressed a hall of assembled delegates; to hear Chaliapin sing musical settings of Pushkin's poems; and to grapple with the mixed emotions in his own heart and on the faces of the crowd at the funeral of the once-world-famous anarchist Peter Kropotkin.[66]

Among the occasions that impressed Qu most was a short talk with the Soviet commissar of education, Anatoly Lunacharsky, in the Kremlin, for despite its brevity Lunacharsky mentioned problems that had occurred in the Soviet Union after 1917 that must have produced answering echoes in Qu's head as he thought about China: How were you rapidly to "proletarianize" education when your school personnel and teachers not only were not members of the Communist Party but were in many cases members of the constitutional-democratic parties, or even saboteurs playing a deliberately reactionary role? Yet by concentrating on certain aspects of science and medicine the Russians had made such progress that some West European scientific academies had recently sent students to study in Russia. The ravages of war and civil war had played havoc with buildings and plant, and some of the problems were being circumvented ingeniously (because of the shortage of books and paper, for instance, some Russian books were printed in Germany); Lunacharsky also pointed to the Soviet Union's obvious interests in the culture and civilization of the Far East, partly because of the Soviet Union's geographical position, poised between Europe and the East, and partly because of the Russians' profound admiration for Eastern literature and philosophy. Everything would be done to foster these contacts, and for this very reason the Soviet Union had now founded its own University of the Far East.[67]

Qu Qiubai himself was a part of this process of development and exchange between the two countries, and as 1921 advanced he became valued in the Soviet Union as an interpreter for the growing number of Chinese students entering the country, and later as an instructor in that same University of the Far East, where only one of the staff knew any Chinese at all.[68] These were the years of the founding and initial growth of the Chinese Communist Party, a process in which experts from the Soviet Union were centrally important. Representatives from the Comintern—the Third International, founded by Lenin both to promote world revolution and to gain control over Communist organizations outside Russia's borders—arrived in China during 1920, meeting initially with Chen Duxiu and Li Dazhao. They made considerable headway, particularly because in that same year the Chinese learned that the Soviet government was willing to abandon many of the old Tsarist claims to treaty-port privileges and control over the Chinese Eastern Railway. Early Communist recruitment was slow and careful, building out through socialist clubs and study groups to form a small nucleus of Communist cadres: the first "national" congress of the Chinese Communist Party, which met in Shanghai in the summer of 1921—in an empty girls' school in the French section of the International Settlement, so as to be partially protected from the threats of raids by the troops of the local Chinese warlord—had thirteen delegates in all, speaking for a total membership of fifty-seven Communists in China and a small number in Japan. Two Comintern members were also present.[69]

From these quiet beginnings, the Chinese Communist Party grew slowly but steadily throughout 1922. Early in that year several radical Chinese students returned from France, having been deported by the French government for their attempts to disrupt the Sino-French headquarters of their work-study group in the University of Lyon. Among them were Mao Zedong's friend from Hunan, Cai Hesen, and Ding Ling's friend Xiang Jingyu; Cai and Xiang, who had married while in France, made their way to Shanghai and established contact with Chen Duxiu, the former *New Youth* editor and dean of students at Beijing National University, now secretary-general of the Communist Party. In July both were elected to the Central Committee. Xiang Jingyu was appointed director of a new women's department in the party, and began a successful program of organizing the women workers in the silk and cigarette factories of Shanghai. (A major strike of several thousand Shanghai women silk workers—many of whom labored in the summer over vats of boiling water in which the cocoons were softening, earning forty cents for a thirteen-hour day—which took place in August 1922, was the first major industrial action by women in China's history.) Cai Hesen was made director of the propaganda department and moved effectively to purge several of the more gradualist members of the party. In Hunan province such young leaders as Mao Zedong, Liu Shaoqi, and Li Lisan worked among miners and railway workers and helped organize strikes at the Anyuan collieries, on the Guangzhou–Hankou railroad, among the printing workers and the construction guilds of Changsha, and among the rickshaw pullers.[70]

By far the most important of these strikes, and the one that gave the greatest publicity to the potential strength of the labor movement, was the Hong Kong seamen's strike. The strike had started in the first days of 1922, in a demand for higher wages and for the rights of the seamen's union to be in charge of the signing on of new seamen, rather than having this done by often corrupt labor contractors, as in the past. By the end of January, as the various Hong Kong guilds of dockhands and coolies came out in sympathy, some thirty thousand men were involved and about one hundred and fifty ships immobilized. The situation became more serious when the coolies in Guangzhou refused to load ships sent by the Hong Kong government to obtain supplies. The strike spread to other major Guangdong ports and was aided by the activities of the Communist Labor Secretariat in Shanghai, which successfully prevented strikebreakers from being recruited on the waterfronts there. In late February, the strikers were joined by other sympathizers in Hong Kong, by vegetable sellers and tramway workers, by basket makers and domestic servants. On March

3, as the colony's economic life almost halted, the Hong Kong government gave in; it granted the seamen wage hikes of 15 to 30 percent, abolished the old labor-contract system, and annulled all orders for suppression of the unions.[71]

Following this success, there was a steady growth in the number of workers' clubs (which in turn often coalesced into unions) in various central China industries and on the railways—for example, the Hanyeping General Union, founded in December 1922 in the Wuhan tri-city area, combined workers from the coal and iron mines, foundries, steelworks, and the river-transportation systems.[72] Demands from these unions also grew more sophisticated, as their focus shifted from hours and wages to include plans for workers' compensation in case of sickness or injury, for the ending of private labor given on demand to overseers, for some forms of profit sharing, for rest-room and recreational facilities, and for death benefits.[73]

The strikes demanded considerable organizational skills, since the working members included artisans, members of trade guilds and social groups, and anarchists, as well as a scattering of members of the Communist Party. They also demanded courage, since repression was usually threatened and often practiced in the early 1920s: the government of Hunan province had executed two anarchist leaders of the workingmen's association after a strike in the Changsha cotton mill had led to window breaking and machine wrecking; just before the end of the Hong Kong seamen's strike, British police had fired on strikers leaving for Guangzhou; other strikers had been killed by Chinese troops during the southern railway strikes of 1922, and by foreign troops working in conjunction with company guards and warlord troops—this latter combination occurred late in 1922 at the huge British-run coalfield complex at Tangshan, southeast of Beijing, where British soldiers were backed by troops from one of General Wu Peifu's armies.[74]

General Wu was the most powerful warlord in east-central China, and from his base in the city of Luoyang he controlled much of the country between Beijing and Hankou. Although one of his subordinates had shared responsibility in breaking the Tangshan strike, General Wu himself was believed by Communist organizers to be a comparative liberal among warlords, and they thought he would cooperate with their endeavors to raise workers' living standards. Hence Li Dazhao and other Communists had been particularly active in working to form an amalgamated labor union out of the various workers' clubs along the Beijing–Hankou line. But as delegates from these clubs began to assemble in the northern railroad center of Zhengzhou in late January 1923, General Wu issued a ban on their meeting, and arrested several delegates when they refused to obey. Communist and union leaders called a general strike along the rail network on February 4. Such a strike was bound to be intolerable to General Wu, for it threatened his entire area of operations and the lifeline of his military-political organization. Working closely with other military leaders in the area, he ordered his troops to move against the strikers on February 7. About thirty workers were killed and many more wounded; and the union branch secretary from the Jiangnan depot was beheaded on the station platform in front of his union members for refusing to order them back to work.[75]

As if prompted by General Wu's violent action, other warlords and industrialists struck back at union organizations in Manchuria and Sichuan, in Tianjin and Shanghai.[76] The generally successful nature of this repression in early 1923 now made the Communists more interested in an alliance with Sun Yatsen and the Guomindang than they had been before. In Moscow, during the first Congress of the Toilers of the Far East in January 1922, which Qu Qiubai rose from his sickbed to attend, the executive head of the Comintern, Grigory Zinoviev, had presented a Communist alliance with the Guomindang as a matter of basic policy, arguing that the Communists in China should ally with the national bourgeoisie at this stage of the revolution in order to expel foreign imperialism and crush the forces of indigenous feudalism. Although this was a rather overblown formulation, in view of the fact that the Guomindang was still weak politically and militarily at this time, the second congress of the Chinese Communist Party had obediently adopted such a program during July 1922. Chen Duxiu, reelected secretary-general of the party at that same congress, traveled to Moscow later in the year for meetings with senior

Comintern representatives. He was persuaded of the correctness of the Soviet policy of alliance, as well as meeting (and being impressed by) Qu Qiubai, who acted as his interpreter.

Despite his recurrent illnesses, Qu had been excited by the possibilities offered to China by the Soviet Union, and he had himself joined the Chinese Communist Party in Moscow, probably early in 1922. He had never exactly claimed to be an objective journalist, and now he seemed to have found in Marxist belief a system that laid to rest his Buddhist doubts about the nature of reality, and promised him a meaningful role in life. Shortly before dawn on New Year's Day in 1922, he wrote some lines that show the way in which his journey to the "Land of Hunger" had triumphed as a search for light. "Moscow has suddenly moved nearer to the Far East," he exclaimed. "Look at the Far East, how bright the purple and red flames shine forth as they spin! The blazing clouds, just sprouting, how roaringly they shoot towards the firmament! How fierce, how dazzling, the wheel of light is spinning! Ah, morning glory, morning glory!"[77] His style sobered over the following months of work, writing, and study in Moscow, but his commitment remained firm, and it was just a question of finding the best place to serve. When, at the end of his visit, Chen Duxiu suggested that it was time for Qu to return to China, he agreed.

Though still only twenty-four years old, Qu had had more experience of life in a "revolutionary" society than any member of the Chinese Communist Party, and the prestige this brought him ensured that when he attended the third national congress of the party at Guangzhou in the summer of 1923, he was elected to the Central Committee. His background in Russian literature, his immersion in Soviet literary theory while in Moscow, and his studies of Soviet society also made him an attractive addition to the academic world, especially in a radical new school such as Shanghai University. By 1923 this university had become as exciting intellectually as Beijing National University had been a few years before: the labor organizer Cai Hesen taught historical sociology, the leftist critic and novelist Mao Dun was chairman of the literature department, the dramatist Tian Han taught English literature, and Qu's fellow townsman and schoolmate, Zhang Tailei, taught political science. Within a few months of his return from the Soviet Union, Qu Qiubai was offered the chairmanship of the social sciences department, and accepted it.[78]

From this new Shanghai base, Qu worked vigorously to introduce the basic premises of Marxist literary criticism to China, as well as a variety of writings by socialists, whether Robert Owen's early writings or Rosa Luxemburg's letters from jail.[79] Drawing mainly on Bukharin's theoretical works, Qu reiterated the fundamental Marxist premises concerning the place of art in society's "superstructure," and gave a brief survey of the ways that "progressive intellectuals" might initially help the proletariat to develop their own independent art forms. Thus instead of there being "art for art's sake," China would slowly develop to the stage where there was "art for life's sake." Qu mocked the claims that Kang Youwei and Liang Qichao still occasionally made to be discussing culture, and suggested that their discussions be enshrined along with the bound feet and the queues that the two scholars had battled a quarter of a century before.[80]

In other essays, Qu tried to widen the vocabulary open to post–May Fourth intellectuals by discussing the revolutionary uses that such Russian writers as Vladimir Mayakovsky and Boris Pasternak had made of symbolism as a weapon against traditionalist cultural forms, and also the significance of writers such as Sergey Semyonov, whose *Hunger* showed the potential of a literature written by proletarians for their own enrichment, a potential that would then be developed by the young writers enrolled in official Soviet cultural organizations. Qu's theoretical essays were ambiguous on the difficult question of whether writers in the superstructure could effect any changes in the economic base, and he implied that major cultural changes would come only *after* fundamental economic transformations. Thus Qu was not encouraging about that very vanguard role of intellectuals which he espoused in his own person.[81] In an essay entitled "In the Wasteland: Chinese Literature in 1923," which appeared in October of that year, Qu criticized other aspects of post–May Fourth culture. For example, though "Chinese Latin" (that is, the formal classical language) had been rejected by most contemporary Chinese writers, they still had great difficulties in reproducing a truly accurate vernacular (as opposed to an approximation full of literary overtones), and furthermore the admixture of too many elements from West European culture was leading to a new hybrid which Qu labeled "external classicism." This further muddied an already bad situation, in which most of Chinese literature continued to be socially irrelevant and emotionally affected—a matter of *"la valse"* and *"poésie"*—as well as dwelling endlessly on love. "Love really is not divine," wrote Qu, "love is human. Those who say it is divine are lying." As an alternative to such frivolous versifyings, Qu looked toward a future in which China's bourgeois writers would no longer think it a disgrace "to go into the coal pits."[82] Though he himself had not yet gone so far, he had tried to familiarize himself with the lot of Shanghai's industrial workers, and offered his own example of theoretically sound new verse in his poem "Iron Flower," published in a Shanghai paper on October 15, 1923:

> *I'm in no soft, smooth comfortable world,*
> *I'm perched in no glory and splendor;*
> *I'm in a smoke-filled somber factory*
> *Casting my iron flower in the forge, flames around me.*
>
> *Iron flowers get no reflected sunlight,*
> *Iron flowers get no moonbeam solace;*
> *In the furnace metals are fused in a typhoon of flame*
> *Which laughingly molds the emerging pistils.*
>
> *In that place the noise of clanging iron is raucous,*
> *In that place the sound of golden metal is urgent;*
> *It is like a copper tree withstanding the constant gales,*
> *This is my love, I won't reject it.*
>
> *Nobody here is waving a feather fan, engaged in a*
> *   stately dance,*
> *Here what you see are calluses—and strength;*
> *In the factory blaze unextinguishable jets of flame,*
> *Dazzling our stalwart unfrightenable chests.*

I breathe in the anger of the blast furnace workers,
I have a fantasy, a fantasy of the "Great Community":
A shrill song surges in my throat—I call out in
drunken laughter "The masses!"
Casting my iron flower in the forge, flames around me.[83]

That same autumn of 1923, like many other emancipated students from different parts of China, Ding Ling had taken the entrance exams and enrolled at Shanghai University. With her was one of her closest women friends from Changsha, Wang Jianhong, who had joined with her in the struggles to achieve coeducation in the Hunan schools and to win equal rights for women. The two young women—Ding Ling was now eighteen and Wang Jianhong twenty—could not, of course, match the range of Qu Qiubai's experiences, but like him they had left home in their teens, traveled across China on their own, and (like Qu in Wuhan and Beijing) spent several months living on their wits in Nanjing and Shanghai. They had tasted the frustrations of being unable to find work, whether as schoolteachers or as housemaids; they had learned something of labor organizations from new friends in Shanghai and something of journalism from volunteer work on the anarchist magazine *Free Man* and on the feminist *Women's Voice*. Qu Qiubai met them both in the fall of 1923 and charmed them with his erudition, his political involvement, and his declamation of Pushkin's poetry. By the year's end Wang Jianhong and Qu Qiubai were living together, and Ding Ling had moved her lodgings to be near them and Qu's younger brother Yunbai, with whom she had become close friends. The four were looked after by Qu's childhood nursemaid, who had left the family home in Jiangsu to be with him in Shanghai, and now cooked and washed for the whole group on a tiny weekly budget.

For a while it was a cozy life, but strains began to appear in the spring of 1924: Ding Ling's relationship with Qu Yunbai had not blossomed, and Qu Qiubai and Wang Jianhong seemed to be wearying of Ding's constant presence. As summer vacation approached, Ding Ling told her friends that she had resolved to leave Shanghai for good and that after making a trip inland to Hunan to see her mother she would proceed to

Beijing, where she would try to make a life on her own. Almost sixty years later she recalled that this news was received with equanimity, and that neither Qu Qiubai nor Wang Jianhong came to see her off on the Yangtze River steamer; in fact they didn't even bother to come to the door of their apartment. The old nursemaid, however, whose name was Adong, gave her a basket of fruit for the trip.[84]

·6·

EXTOLLING NIRVANA

In the mid-autumn days of 1923 Qu Qiubai sometimes took short trips into the countryside near Shanghai to meet with the poet Xu Zhimo, just back from England. Later, in 1925, when Ding Ling settled in Beijing, she, too, got to know Xu Zhimo; he helped her and her friends in some of their earliest literary ventures. Xu Zhimo was one of those young men for whom everything seemed always to have gone right. He was born in 1897 into a large and prosperous merchant family in Zhejiang province; not only did he not suffer during the 1911 revolution but his family grew ever richer, from commercial and banking ventures: Xu Zhimo's father, among other activities, supplied many of the guns for the revolutionary takeover in Hangzhou. Xu's education was not interrupted by the revolution or cut short soon after it, as Qu's had been; instead he progressed tranquilly through the fine modern schools in Zhejiang (he was precociously brilliant and named class president) and St. John's Baptist College in Shanghai before transferring to a small college in Beijing and finally into the school of law and politics at Beijing National University (for which neither Qu nor Mao had been able to afford the tuition). A marriage was arranged for him with Zhang Youyi, a girl from an influential family in the town of Baoshan, in Jiangsu province; in 1918, when he was twenty-one and she was eighteen, their first son was born. Even in his new relatives by marriage Xu Zhimo

seemed fortunate, for the Zhangs were an intelligent family, at
the forefront of the emerging "modern" consciousness of the
new China: one of Zhang Youyi's brothers was already regarded as being Shanghai's most effective and innovative
banker; another was a close confidant of Liang Qichao's, had
studied at the University of Berlin, and worked with Liang in
the constitutional movement and in editing reformist periodicals. Through Zhang family introductions, Xu met Liang Qichao, whose writings he had read voraciously as a schoolboy
and imitated in his own first essays. Liang admired Xu Zhimo
for his brilliance in classical Chinese and for his energy; Xu in
turn regarded himself as Liang's disciple.[1]

Xu Zhimo sailed to the United States late in the summer of
1918, to continue his higher education. He was fired by
dreams—perhaps in double emulation of his mentor, Liang
Qichao, and of his banking brother-in-law—of becoming the
Alexander Hamilton of the new China. And though he was as-
sailed by loneliness at leaving his wife and baby behind and by
fear of the unknown travails awaiting him in the United
States—just as Qu Qiubai approached the Soviet Union with
deep uncertainty—Xu Zhimo did not initially give vent to
the poetic ambiguities that marked Qu's first writings on the
"Land of Hunger"; instead, he stressed his heroic aspirations
in a long letter, written on shipboard in classical Chinese,
larded with historical allusions from his own and from Europe's past:

> Since the reforms of 1898, each year more and more of our
> countrymen have been going abroad in search of education.
> When they return, some go into political life, some go into
> the world of practical affairs, and some cannot decide what
> to do. Those in the first category have plenty of ability but
> are blinded in their search for profit; those in the second
> category have plenty of knowledge but cannot tell how
> to apply it; those in the third category either are help-
> less as fish on dry land or else are trying to find a right
> way in hopeless circumstances. Alas! These people are our
> nation's treasure, and yet their confusion and chaos has
> reached this extent. How can we have no true patriots,
> ready to rush forward and follow the path of the three

Italian heroes?* Instead, they wander around irresolute and follow the old ways. . . . They must understand that today's heroes and leaders cannot avoid the tempests [that surround them], and that even Kosciuszko couldn't protect Poland's ancestral lands. We youthful patriots must learn from this.

The only answer to this predicament, thought Xu, was to dedicate oneself to a life of hard work, self-denial, and an honest confrontation of reality without self-pity.[2]

Xu spent two years in the United States, first at Clark University in Worcester, Massachusetts, where he completed his work for the B.A. degree as a transfer student, and then at Columbia University, where he took an M.A. in political science. During this time he stuck to his ideals with real tenacity. He and a small circle of equally patriotic young Chinese students followed a rigorous schedule of early rising, study, and exercise, and met often to discuss their country's plight and stimulate their own ardor. Xu majored in history at Clark and also took a number of special courses in economics and banking; at Columbia he took more courses in economics, studied political theory, read up on early Owenite socialism and the history of the Russian Revolution, and wrote a thesis on the status of women in China (in which he asserted that missionary reports had exaggerated their plight).[3] Such studies make it appear he was preparing conscientiously to work in three capacities: as China's Hamilton, as a true disciple of Liang Qichao's, and as a filial son to his banking-magnate father.

Yet ambitious though this program of study seemed to be, Xu Zhimo began to be nagged by a sense that he was asking too little of life. He later recalled, "In America I kept busy attending classes, listening to lectures, writing exams, chewing gum, going to the movies, and swearing," but the basic levels of his thinking had not changed: "If I was a pure dunce when I came to America, I remained unchanged when I parted from the Lady of Liberty."[4] The impetus to leave the United States (and hence to abandon the Columbia Ph.D. program for which he

---

* Mazzini, Cavour, and Garibaldi, about whom Liang Qichao had written a popular and influential group biography.

had registered) came to Xu from the writings of Bertrand Russell, which seemed, in contrast to the other works he had been reading, like "the golden shafts of light—cold, sharp, swiftly moving—that break through the massed purple clouds piled up over the sea on a summer's evening." When Xu Zhimo thought of Russell, he wrote, he always associated these images of light and power with the counterimage of the Woolworth Building, which he had seen towering fifty-eight floors over the city of New York, an awe-inspiring symbol of the establishment and yet also a symbol of the mighty structures that could be brought crashing down by shafts of anger. Russell's former "incarnations," wrote Xu Zhimo, had been two: one was Voltaire, whose "cold, clear light" bore down for half a century on the "fifty-eight-story buildings" of eighteenth-century France before they came crashing down in 1789; the other was William Godwin—husband to Mary Wollstonecraft and father to Mary Shelley—who, though less famous than Voltaire, nevertheless seemed to Xu the true ancestor of modern socialism, a man who in his time managed "to destroy many false images and to knock down many a tall building."[5]

If Xu Zhimo was prompted to leave the United States partly because of such feelings of iconoclastic idealism, he was also the victim of powerful emotional pulls, which he later made some attempt to analyze:

> In the ups and downs of my life I have usually been tugged by the strings of deep emotion—we can take my search for education as one example. I went to England because I wanted to be a follower of Russell. (Russell's visit to China took place while I was in America.) There were rumors that he had died; they turned out to be false; but at the time I wept, and since my tears alone were inadequate I composed memorial poems in his honor. When I found he was not dead I was of course delighted: I canceled my registration as a dissertation student at Columbia and bought a boat ticket across the Atlantic, planning to apply myself wholeheartedly to studying with this twentieth-century Voltaire.[6]

It was an impetuous decision and it ended in an impasse: when Xu reached England in October 1920, planning to study with Russell at Cambridge, he discovered that Russell not only had not yet returned from China but had been expelled from his fellowship at Trinity College several years before because of the college fellows' disapproval of his pacifist views during the First World War and of his recent divorce.

So Xu Zhimo settled in London, with the stated intention of taking a doctorate in political science with Harold Laski at the London School of Economics. He canvassed with Mrs. Laski for elections down at the docks in Woolwich, and mailed Liang Qichao several essays on political topics for publication in Liang's magazines in China.[7] Yet Xu's heart was not in this political work. "It was a time," he wrote, "when I was feeling deeply depressed and searching for new directions." In a letter to his parents in November 1920, he told them that he was making some progress in his studies but that he kept on having the sense that what he achieved each year faded away as he began to learn fresh subjects: in this, London but repeated a cycle begun when he arrived at Clark from China, and continued when he left Clark for Columbia.[8] What the letter did not mention, for obvious reasons, was that he had fallen in love with Lin Huiyin, the sixteen-year-old daughter of Lin Changmin, director of the Chinese League of Nations Association.

Xu Zhimo had met the Lins, who were living temporarily in London, because they shared a mutual friend in Liang Qichao. Lin Changmin had worked with Liang on political and constitutional causes for a generation, and the two men had served together in a short-lived Progressive Party cabinet of 1917 that tried to bring back some order to China after the collapse of General Zhang Xun's restoration of Emperor Puyi. Lin was a gregarious and emotional man of romantic temperament, and he must have found the young Xu Zhimo an entertaining companion. Xu Zhimo, in turn, in his restless and excitable state, found in the young Miss Lin a soul mate who also happened to be a beautiful and widely traveled young woman. His own wife, Zhang Youyi, left behind in China with their baby more than two years before, had never traveled, indeed had only recently enrolled with a tutor so as to carry her education a step further, and doubtless would not compete in Xu's eyes with Lin

Huiyin's sophistication. Xu's surviving letters home convey little warmth toward his wife, though they do show real affection for his little son, whose changing face he knew only through photographs. In one letter, Xu asked his wife to spend a whole day following around the two-and-a-half-year-old boy, writing down his every word and action, and to send the complete record to him.[9]

London offered Xu Zhimo other diversions besides Miss Lin. One morning, for example, a couple of Chinese students arrived at his lodgings in a car and introduced Xu to H. G. Wells. Xu Zhimo and Wells became friendly and Wells invited him down to his country cottage; they lunched, walked in the park (to Xu's amazement Wells invited him to jump a fence; Xu politely complied, but Wells, following after, fell and tore his clothes), dined, and drank whiskey late into the night.[10] Another valuable contact in London was Goldsworthy Lowes Dickinson, whom Xu first saw on the platform with Lin Changmin at a League of Nations meeting. Later, Dickinson and Xu met at the Lins' for tea and became friends. Meeting Dickinson at this stage was crucial for Xu, since Dickinson promised to open many doors: he was a fellow of King's College, Cambridge, a lover of Chinese poetry and aesthetics, a man with wide contacts in literary London, and one ever eager to advance the career of an affable young companion. Sensing Xu's growing interest in literature, Dickinson urged him to transfer to Cambridge rather than stay on at L.S.E.; eager to comply, Xu applied to several Cambridge colleges but was turned down because it was too late in the academic year for a new admission to be processed. At some stage in these negotiations his life received further jolts when Miss Lin was sent off by her parents to study in Edinburgh and Xu's own wife, Zhang Youyi, made the sudden decision to leave China and travel halfway around the world, over rough winter seas, to be at her husband's side. Since Dickinson had managed to arrange for Xu to be admitted as a special student in his own college of King's, as soon as Zhang Youyi reached England she and her husband moved from London and settled, early in 1921, with one other friend, into a rented cottage in Sawston, a beautiful village some six miles from Cambridge and the university.[11]

Their life at Sawston was no idyll. This was not only because Xu continued to keep up an impassioned correspondence with Lin Huiyin, using the local Sawston grocery store as a poste restante for her letters; more important, it was because he felt his married life deprived him of his chance to get to know the "real" Cambridge and follow up on the opportunities that the university world seemed to offer. Xu felt that he was being prevented from unleashing the emotional and aesthetic forces that were burgeoning within him. Each day, early in the morning, he took the streetcar or bicycled to the university, and each evening he rode or pedaled back, but the days themselves brought no deep pleasure. "I spent the whole spring in this kind of life," he recalled three years later, "but I remained a mere stranger in Cambridge, I knew nobody there; one can say that I had absolutely no taste of real Cambridge life; all I knew was a library, some classrooms, and a few cheap restaurants. Dickinson was usually in London or on the Continent, so I didn't see much of him, either."[12]

There is no detailed record of what transpired in Sawston that spring and summer, but in the autumn of 1921, Xu's wife left him and went to pursue her studies at Berlin University; she had friends there and her brother was fairly close by, studying moral philosophy with Rudolf Euken at the University of Jena. That October, also, Lin Huiyin returned, with her father, to China.[13] "Late that autumn," wrote Xu, "I came back to Cambridge by myself; that was the year of my true education. That was the time I finally had the chance to draw close to the life of the real Cambridge, and at the same time I slowly began to 'discover' Cambridge. Never had I known such intense happiness."[14] For now he tasted "the honey-sweetness of being alone," as he phrased it; he could enjoy the three types of pleasure that his wife had denied him: those of being alone with his friends, alone with his own thoughts, and alone with nature. Now he was free to bask in the warm rays of Dickinson's high aestheticism, to be the favored recipient of a view of China that was idealized beyond all logic and yet stirring to the soul; for as Dickinson had written in his popular book *Letters from a Chinese Official*, back in 1901, pretending that these thoughts came from the pen of a Chinese scholar:

> To feel, and in order to feel to express, or at least to understand the expression of all that is lovely in Nature, of all that is poignant and sensitive in man, is to us in itself a sufficient end. A rose in a moonlit garden, the shadow of trees on the turf, almond bloom, scent of pine, the wine-cup and the guitar; these and the pathos of life and death, the long embrace, the hand stretched out in vain, the moment that glides for ever away, with its freight of music and light, into the shadow and hush of the haunted past, all that we have, all that eludes us, a bird on the wing, a perfume escaped on the gale—to all these things we are trained to respond, and the response is what we call literature. This we have; this you cannot give us; but this you may so easily take away.[15]

Xu Zhimo had read and admired this book, and Dickinson had reaffirmed the same sentiments after visiting China in 1913. Here was warm shelter, for Xu Zhimo, from the warlord humiliations of his homeland, or from the stirring injunctions to patriotism and duty of his mentor, Liang Qichao; and there was an extra twist, for although Xu was drawn to English culture and sensitivity, the very men who inspired him at this time found much to criticize in their own culture. The English were "divorced from Nature but unreclaimed by Art," Dickinson had written; "instructed, but not educated; assimilative, but incapable of thought."[16]

Xu Zhimo was also reading Shelley at that time; he took Shelley as his "guide" after learning the details of the poet's abandonment of his wife, Harriet, and his elopement with seventeen-year-old Mary Godwin (herself the daughter of that brilliant William Godwin whose works Xu so much admired). Shelley, both by his example and in his poems, must have given Xu Zhimo reinforcement as he planned to obtain his own freedom through divorce from the wife he had already driven away. At the same time, as he expanded his reading to include Keats and Byron, Xu began to ponder the freedom of the poet's soul, his defiance of all conventions; and as he read deeply in Walter Pater (whose work he discovered by chance while sheltering in a secondhand bookshop from a sudden storm of rain), his aesthetic ambitions were sharpened.[17] In his earliest surviving poem, the draft of which was dated November 23, 1921, Xu apostrophized his own emerging poetic self in the recently freed forms of Chinese verse:

> Oh Poet! How can springtime, that already has
>   reached out to other men,
> Still not release your
> Fountains of creative energy?
>
> Laugh, laugh aloud!
> The mountain ranges north and south have not yet
> spat out all their jewels,
> Nor the oceans east and west sprinkled all their pearls.
>
> Soft, soft the sounds of pipes, of strings,
> Drink deep the light of stars, sun, moon!
>
> Oh Poet! How can springtime, that already has
>   reached out to other men,
> Still not release your
> Fountains of creative energy?[18]

Xu's decision to end his marriage may have been briefly shaken by the news that his wife, after reaching Berlin, had discovered that she was pregnant; Xu's response, as if to test his own resolve to leave her to her own devices, was to translate into Chinese Wordsworth's "Lucy Gray, or Solitude" with its haunting last stanza,

> O'er rough and smooth she trips along,
> And never looks behind;
> And sings a solitary song
> That whistles in the wind.

This translation was finished on January 31, 1922, and in February he traveled to Berlin, where Zhang Youyi gave birth to a child, their second son, on the twenty-fourth. They named him Peter. In early March, having traveled to Weimar and Jena to stand on the home terrain of the two early giants of the romantic tradition, Goethe and Schiller—and perhaps to have a frank talk with his brother-in-law, Zhang Junmai—he finally wrote to his wife requesting a divorce.[19] Xu couched his letter entirely in formalized terms of the "higher emotions," speaking to the needs of their free spirits (as Shelley had done) rather than to any details of the couple's life together or their incompatibilities: "Real life must be obtained through struggle; real happiness must be obtained through struggle; real love must be obtained through struggle! Both of us have boundless futures; both of us have minds set on reforming society; both of us have minds set on achieving well-being for mankind. This all hinges on our setting ourselves as examples. With courage and resolution, and giving due respect to both our personalities, we must freely agree to divorce, thereby terminating pain and initiating happiness."[20] She agreed to the divorce, and Xu returned to England.

Back in Cambridge, Xu Zhimo found his true springtime—during those same months that Qu Qiubai in his Moscow sanatorium saw the lights in their true beauty for the first time, and joined the Communist Party. Now the already deep pleasures of the previous autumn grew richer, and Xu found himself in harmony with the universe: "That spring—alone in all my life, though I grieve to say this—was not spent in vain. For that spring alone my life was natural, was truly joyful!—even though it so chanced that that was also the time when I experienced most deeply the agony of life. What I did have then was leisure, liberty, the chance to be absolutely alone. However strange it may sound, it seemed for the first time then that I distinguished the light of stars and moon, the green of grass, the scents of flowers, the energy of flowing water. Shall I ever be able to forget that search for the coming of spring?"[21] That same spring he completed a short, joyful lyric, the earliest of his poems he chose to publish. Obviously trying to recapture in Chinese the short lines, simple words, and pure emotions of the *Lyrical Ballads* phase of English romanticism, Xu presented his vision of the English countryside:

> *Fragrant the southern breeze,*
> *Green the grass, the trees.*

Warm sunlight all across the land,
White clouds, yellow clouds, spread across the sky.
In the middle of that rippling wheatfield
Farm boys, farm girls, laugh and chatter.[22]

So the spring and summer passed, in conversation with friends, in lying on the banks of the River Cam gazing at the meadows of King's and at the bridge he loved so much in front of Clare College; in reading, in punting, in writing; in dreaming, or in riding his bicycle at frenzied speed into the light of the setting sun to extend for a few moments the length of the day that was passing. His friends were varied and fascinating: in Cambridge he moved in a circle that included Dickinson, E. M. Forster, I. A. Richards; in London he continued to see H. G. Wells and got to know John Middleton Murry, Bertrand Russell (now back from China), Roger Fry, and Arthur Waley. One late summer evening Murry invited him to Hampstead to meet his wife, Katherine Mansfield, whose short stories Xu revered. Despite the fact that she was already desperately ill, Xu was deeply moved by her "purity, grace, and brightness," and felt overwhelmed by her presence. They talked of literature, of course, and of translation, and as they parted she urged Xu never to waste his life in politics but to concentrate on art.[23] Yet all such periods must end, and in the fall of 1922 he at last returned to China, sailing into Shanghai harbor on October 15, to greet his parents and friends with "wildly beating heart."[24]

Xu Zhimo's treatment of his wife, and hers of him, had been dramatically "modern," a final response to the whole structure of arrangements and conveniences that had been under attack in China for two decades; for this, and for his equally modern poems—emotional, free-moving, dramatic in their imagery— he soon became widely known. Student organizations in China were eager to have him lecture on his chosen theme, "Art and Life," and the lectures (though initially he delivered them in English to his perplexed audience and filled them with references to Matisse and Picasso and with long quotations from Wells and Pater) became enormously popular. He taught a summer session in 1923 with Liang Qichao at Nankai University and was given a post at Beijing National University in

1924.[25] Yet to his seniors Xu's behavior also raised basic questions of human decency, especially after he began once again to court Lin Huiyin. This was a serious blow to Liang Qichao, for since Lin Huiyin's return to China, Liang had been striving to arrange a marriage between her and his own second son. In a long letter to Xu Zhimo in January 1923 (which he noted that he completed at three A.M.), Liang grappled with the personal dimensions of those questions of freedom and of choice that he had been debating in the political realm since the Hundred Days of Reform almost twenty-five years before:

> Two nights before he left, Junmai* told me of your doings, and made me very upset. Hitherto, because I thought that there had truly been basic incompatibilities between you and your wife (even if you don't want to call her that, I shall continue to do so), I hadn't wanted to pursue the matter further. But now I gather that since your return to China you have gone on writing to her and continue to sing her praises. Why then did you act as you did? It's really incomprehensible. I had also thought that perhaps, like Junmai, you would be quite happy to live alone, but now from what Junmai tells me I see that that is not so.

Liang then told Xu that he wished to get two fundamental points across to him. First, "it is the possibility of responding to other people emotionally that places humans above the other creatures, and we cannot seek to gain our own happiness if that is at the expense of someone else's sufferings"; therefore Xu was to be criticized for causing pain to his wife, to the senior members of the Zhang family, and to his own two sons, whom he was neglecting. Second, though "all the young people today want to talk most about the greatness of love (and I don't wish to stand against current attitudes), I am also aware that there are a great many other things on this earth, and to take this particular item as the only one is more than I can accept. Furthermore, this love is something that comes to you, it's not something you can go out and get, you can't just say 'I want such-and-such' and expect to get such-and-such." Liang ap-

---

* This was Zhang Junmai, brother to Xu Zhimo's divorced wife, Zhang Youyi, now returned to China after his studies in Jena.

pealed to Xu to curb his emotions and to avoid "overinvolvement," as Liang himself did.[26]

Xu responded, unchastened:

> I brave the adverse criticisms of society and struggle with all my energy, not so as to avoid the pains of a miserable lot but to seek the calm of my conscience, the firm establishment of my personality, and the salvation of my soul.
>
> Among men, who does not seek virtuous mediocrity? Who does not feel content with the status quo? Who does not fear difficulty and danger? Yet there are those who break loose and go beyond. I shall search for my soul's companion amidst the sea of humanity; if I find her, that is my fortune. If not, let that be my fate.
>
> Alas, my teacher! I have striven in the inner recesses of my soul to create a pure jewel out of my ideals; I nourish it with the hot blood that fills my heart, so that it will shine forth my deepest yearnings.[27]

Despite this rebuff, Liang retained his affection for Xu Zhimo, and he arranged for him to work on the literary supplement to the *Morning News* (the same newspaper that had sent Qu Qiubai to Moscow), as well as giving him living quarters in an old Qing dynasty building at Number 7, Stone Tiger Lane, where Liang kept much of his library of Chinese and foreign books. Here Xu Zhimo joined a number of Liang's friends and disciples—teachers at the university, philosophers, writers—as well as the irrepressible old Jian Jichang, a native of Guizhou province who had been Liang Qichao's companion and guide for many years, and whose convivial drinking sprees did not impair his capacious memory for Chinese scholarship, on which Liang constantly drew. Here the realities of China's political and economic life, and the crumbling Beijing government, could be forgotten, as Xu Zhimo showed in one of his loveliest poems, "Number 7, Stone Tiger Lane," written in the spring of 1923:

> *There are times when our little courtyard ripples*
> *with infinite tenderness:*
> *Winsome wisteria, bosom bared, invites the caress*
> *of persimmon leaves,*

From his hundred-foot height the sophora stoops
    in the breeze to embrace the wild apple,
The yellow dog by the fence watches over his
    little friend Amber, fast asleep,
The birds sing their latest mating songs, trilling
    on without cease—
There are times when our little courtyard ripples
    with infinite tenderness.

There are times when our little courtyard shades
    in the setting of a dream:
Across the green shadows the haze after rain weaves
    a sealed and silent darkness,
Facing my fading orchids, a single squatting frog
    listens out for the cry of a worm in the next garden.
A weary raincloud, still unspent, stretches above the
    sophora's top,
That circling flutter before the eaves—is it a bat
    or a dragonfly?
There are times when our little courtyard shades in
    the setting of a dream.

There are times when our little courtyard can only
    respond with a sigh:
A sigh for the times of storm, when countless red blossoms
    are pounded and pulped by the rain,
A sigh for the early autumn, when leaves still green
    fret free with regret from the branch,
A sigh for the still of night, when the moon has
    boarded her cloud-bark, over the west wall now,
And the wind carries a dirge for a passing, cold gusts
    from a distant lane—
There are times when our little courtyard can only
    respond with a sigh.

There are times when our little courtyard is
    inundated with joy:
In the dusk, after rain, the garden is shaded,
    fragrant, and cool,

Old Jian, the toper, clutches his great jar, his legs
    pointing to the sky,
And drains his cup, a pint, a quart, till warmth of wine
    fills heart and cheeks,
A mythical Bacchus-figure, swept along on the bubbling
    of laughter—
There are times when our little courtyard is inundated
    with joy.[28]

Nor could Liang resist introducing Xu Zhimo to his old teacher and friend Kang Youwei, now that the two men, political differences blurring if not forgotten, had reestablished relations. Liang described Xu Zhimo to Kang as "your disciple's disciple, a young man of exceptional intelligence, good at poetry and at classical prose; his grasp of English is even better, and the poems that he has written in English have been praised by foreign scholars." He added that Xu Zhimo was now translating Liang's study of early Chinese political thought into English (a project that Xu began but never completed).[29] What the three men talked of is not recorded—perhaps it was classical Chinese poetry, possibly contemporary politics; it is unlikely to have been European romantic poetry, or modern science, though by coincidence Xu, the passionate cyclist of the Cambridgeshire fens, was with two scholars who had both extended their knowledge of the awesome power of modern transportation within the preceding two weeks. Kang Youwei had just taken his first ride in an airplane, soaring up above the city of Baoding in Hebei province and seeing the great outer walls spread out below him "like a square dish, within which the buildings and pavilions were laid out like so many upturned cups."[30] And Liang Qichao had experienced the terrible drama of seeing his two younger sons seriously hurt in a car crash in Beijing, and had spent the last few days anxiously moving between home and hospital, waiting while doctors searched for internal injuries and gave their final reports. (Liang Qichao had learned that Liang Sicheng, his second son, and suitor for Lin Huiyin's hand, would be in the hospital at least two months; he had immediately prepared an imposing reading list so that his son would not waste that period of enforced leisure.)[31]

Since his return from Europe after the Paris Peace Conference, Liang had concentrated his energies on teaching and writing, content to lead a rather simple life with his wife and children and to wield political influence at a distance. The same was by no means true for Kang Youwei, who had returned to Shanghai in February 1918 after sheltering for almost seven months in the American legation in Beijing following the collapse of General Zhang Xun's restoration attempt. In Shanghai, Kang Youwei had to support an entourage that now included five consorts of various ages (he had added three new ones since the death of his beloved He Zhanli in 1914), six unmarried daughters, two young sons, ten maidservants and nurses, and thirty male servants.[32] To feed and house this number he had to generate an income of about two thousand dollars a month, which he did by selling his own calligraphy, dealing in rare books and art objects, dabbling in urban real estate (he owned property near Hangzhou and in Qingdao as well as in Shanghai), and by running (through agents) sizable estates in the Jiangxi countryside that produced tomatoes, onions, and tobacco as well as tea, timber, hogs, and chickens. The rural estates were particularly troubling, since dishonest tenants and local bandits were constantly wrecking his chances of making a respectable profit—further proof, if Kang needed it, that China had not benefited from the events of the revolution in 1911.[33]

In his search to bring order to China amidst the endless disruptions of warlord politics, Kang spent a very considerable part of his income—as much as half, according to one estimate—on telegrams and other communications with leading military and political figures.[34] Kang's goal, in all these protracted negotiations, was not only to try to restore a united China but also to ensure that Sun Yatsen be prevented from establishing a viable new power base. Kang's suspicion of Sun, and dislike of the methods and goals of the Guomindang, increased even more during 1922 and 1923, for in those years Sun was in Shanghai, seeking support for a reorganized Guomindang that he wished to establish in Guangzhou; Guangzhou would then become the springboard for future unification of the country.

As part of this reorganization, Sun had been trying to bring more rigor to his basic formulations concerning livelihood for the people, vigorous nationalism, and representative government. (By 1924 these principles were codified as the Three People's Principles and remained thereafter a central component of Guomindang ideology.) But Sun had found it hard to get any substantial military or economic support, and after being betrayed in turn by various Chinese warlord allies, and unable to gain substantial aid from either the Western powers or Japan, Sun had decided to form alliances with the Soviet Union and with a wider cross section of Chinese students and workers. To achieve this latter goal he decided to pursue the possibilities for a united-front strategy with the Chinese Communist Party. (This desire, of course, coincided with the decisions taken by the Comintern, and endorsed by the Central Committee of the Chinese Communist Party, to seek an alliance with the Guomindang.)[35]

Kang Youwei believed that the main hope of stopping the apparently Soviet-dominated Sun Yatsen lay with the northern warlord General Wu Peifu. Up until his massacre of striking railway workers in February 1923, Wu had been regarded as one of the most cultured and progressive warlords: he had expressed sympathy for the students in their May Fourth demonstrations, backed a promising cabinet of intellectuals that ruled briefly in 1922, sponsored plans for the peaceful reunification of China that included a potential leadership role for Sun Yatsen, and was also a painter and calligrapher of some expertise.[36] But though Wu's benign image was destroyed by his orders to kill the railway workers in February 1923, Kang continued to flatter him and to urge him to undertake his own massive reunification campaign, obviously quite undeterred by the widespread evidence of Wu's violence and unpredictability. In 1924 Kang expanded on his pleas to Wu, urging him now also to back General Zhao Hengti in Hunan, in a central China alliance that would prevent the southern armies that had declared their loyalty to Sun Yatsen from initiating a major campaign. One of Kang's actions shows how his eyes were now fixed on the rebellious youth of an earlier age, with earlier values, not those of 1924: he had no criticisms when General Zhao Hengti executed union organizers, threatened students, and forced Mao Zedong and his friends to flee Hunan province for the south; but when he found that the graves of Tang Cai-chang and the other martyrs of the 1900 risings were neglected and covered with weeds, he protested angrily and vigorously. His protests were effective, and the graves were restored at government cost.[37]

If such actions made the Kang of the 1920s seem out of touch with current realities, that did not mean that his own youthful writings or the example of his own courageous actions at the turn of the century had in any way become redundant. Indeed, if one remembers Kang in the 1890s for being absorbed with problems of China's national identity, with the fundamental content of education, with the analysis of the Chinese historical and cultural record, and with the value of Western science— then one sees how the intellectuals of the immediate post–May Fourth period were still very much aware of the same problem areas. Both for those who had just begun to adapt some segments of the Marxist analysis of society, and for those resistant to such analysis, China's past and future still presented troubling problems of definition.

As far as the omnipotence of Western scientific methodology was concerned, it was Liang Qichao who made the most telling criticisms. He wrote in one of his newspaper articles at the time of his 1919 visit to Europe:

> Those who praised the omnipotence of science had hoped previously that, as soon as science succeeded, the golden age would appear forthwith. Now science is successful indeed; material progress in the West in the last one hundred years has greatly surpassed the achievements of the three thousand years prior to this period. Yet we human beings have not secured happiness; on the contrary, science gives us catastrophes. We are like travelers losing their way in a desert. They see a big black shadow ahead, and desperately run to it, thinking that it may lead them somewhere. But after running a long way, they no longer see the shadow and fall into the slough of despond. What is that shadow? It

is this "Mr. Science." The Europeans have dreamed a vast
dream of the omnipotence of science; now they decry its
bankruptcy. This is a major turning-point in current world
thought.[38]

Yet Liang and his friend Zhang Junmai, through their Society
for Lectures on the New Learning, had brought such scholars as
John Dewey and Bertrand Russell to China; these visits certainly fostered—at one level—admiration for Western meth-
odologies of a "scientific" sort. The influential philosopher and
critic Hu Shi, who had studied with John Dewey at Columbia
University before returning to China and becoming one of the
most important spokesmen for Western thought, as well as a
popular teacher at Beijing National University during the May
Fourth Movement, urged a pragmatic, or "genetic," approach
to China's problems, and an abandonment of the facile belief
that any particular "ism" would have the power to address the
whole range of China's problems. Not surprisingly, such new
exponents of Communism as Li Dazhao and Chen Duxiu criticized both Liang Qichao and Hu Shi, pointing out that in an
economically stagnant country such as China one could not
solve problems without fundamental changes in the economic
structure, and that Marxist theories of class struggle and materialism were essential to such an analysis.[39] Chen himself, at
one stage, would gladly have scrapped the whole written structure of the Chinese language itself, since he felt that even the
allegedly "vernacular" written styles were impervious to
change and hence could not help usher in a new society: "The
Chinese script cannot communicate new things and new principles. It is, furthermore, the home of rotten and poisonous
thought. I have no regret in abandoning it."[40]

Moreover, lines of influence were by no means clear: students could continue to be influenced both by Kang Youwei's
ingenuity in historical analysis and by his search for meaning
in the past, while at the same time being deeply moved by the
young revolutionaries' sacrifices during the last years of the
Qing dynasty and drawn to Hu Shi's pragmatism and his application of Western historical methods to traditions of Chinese fiction and folklore. As one such student phrased his
quest in this period:

Of all the joyous emotions and fervent hopes, that we had heaped up in previous years, we now had left to us only melancholy memories. My mind was constantly so agitated that I could find peace only through the comforts and consolations of philosophy. By nature a wholehearted optimist, unable to adopt a negative attitude toward life or to seek consolation through the ascetic path of Buddhism, I had the notion that one might find a solution to life's problems in the study of psychology and sociology. Taught by increasing age and experience that the affairs of this world are confused and disordered, I cast about anxiously for some simple, underlying principle that would connect them all and help me to find a clue to the phenomena about me.[41]

The search for that "simple, underlying principle" could also, somewhat paradoxically, lead to a broader view of the diversity of human aspirations, as young Chinese made an attempt to get away from the dualisms that seemed implicit in Kang and Liang's thinking, and in that of the early Marxists. Often in the 1920s this took the form of seeing *three* great modes in world history: the Western, the Chinese, and the Indian. By identifying the last with either the Buddhist or quietistic elements in life, and the first with the scientific, a meaningful space could be cleared for China's past history and future aspirations. The poet Guo Moruo, as he sat on the beach with his son, Ah-ho, read *The Crescent Moon* by the Indian poet and 1913 Nobel Prize winner Rabindranath Tagore while he reflected on China's destiny, then drew Tagore's poem *into* his own:

> The lead-grey roofs of the fishermen's cottages
> Gleam darkly with a circle of red flame:
> Now crimson . . . now madder
> Now orange . . . now gold.
> It is as ever the white radiance of the moon.
> "On the seashore of endless worlds children meet.
> The infinite sky is motionless overhead and the
>   restless water is boisterous.
> On the seashore of endless worlds the children meet
>   with shouts and dances."*

* From Tagore's poem "On the Seashore," in *The Crescent Moon.*

Again I sit on the broken hulk on the shore.
My little Ah-ho
Joins with a troop of children;
They play together on the sands.
Reciting this poem of Tagore
I go and play with them.
Ah! If only I could become a pure child![42]

Guo further hoped that one might find a bond that the three civilizations shared, and he flirted briefly with the idea that a common "pantheism" at the heart of each culture might make such a meeting possible.[43]

The optimism of such pantheism was too facile for a man such as Liang Shuming (the son of the scholar Liang Ji, whose suicide in 1918 had shocked so many of his contemporaries); Liang Shuming advanced the idea that the three varying civilizations had been quite different in their growth, and that each represented a different stage of the will's adaptation to the natural environment. If the Western mode was currently dominant, through its mastery of struggle and its demand for conquest over environment, that did not mean there was no value or potential to Chinese ideas of harmony and adjustment; indeed, these would eventually triumph over the Western ways and blend material strength with a deeper understanding of nature and man's ethical nature. An Indian vision of the futility of all desires would, long after that, mark the final transformation of human civilization, as the will turned back into itself and sought its own negation. Liang Shuming spelled this out in simplified form: if one took the will's demand for shelter as one aspect of experience and the fact of a dilapidated house as the other, then the Western answer had been (and was) to demolish the old house and build a new one; the Chinese answer in similar circumstances would be to repair carefully the old house; while the Indian answer would be to extinguish the desire for housing.[44] Liang Shuming did not believe that one could "blend" cultures together creatively, as Liang Qichao (and Russell in his way) had suggested; in fact China should not be seen as "behind" in any sense, since it had had a completely separate developmental path—and one which proved that neither science nor democracy nor industrialization was in any intelligible way "inevitable." The danger of the current situation was that the three modes had now been forced into conjunction, and only one could ultimately survive; therefore, wrote Liang Shuming, in a rather tortuously arrived at solution, since China had "missed" the Western stage, it would have to go through it (as India would, too, sometime in the future); but by holding firmly to the Chinese attitudes to life as it did so, it would in fact be simultaneously transforming the nature of what had once been "Western."[45]

Liang Shuming's work had appeared under the title *Eastern and Western Cultures and Their Philosophies* in 1921, and despite its complexities and ambiguities it aroused considerable intellectual excitement. Two years later the direction of the argument shifted, and the controversy regenerated, with the publication of Zhang Junmai's lecture entitled "View of Life." Drawing from his prolonged studies of idealist philosophy in Germany, Zhang Junmai (a close friend of Liang Qichao's, and Xu Zhimo's former brother-in-law) launched a vigorous attack on the validity of "scientific method" as it was currently being applied by Chinese Marxists and others to China's social and economic problems. Man's view of life, Zhang insisted, could never be defined in "scientific" terms, for it was subjective, intuitive, and unique: personal psychological phenomena were beyond any laws of causality.[46] The resulting debates were prolonged and often vituperative, engaging philosophers, scientists, historians, and literary critics. Those who defended the "scientific" view were forthright, accusing Zhang Junmai of resurrecting a "Ghost Metaphysics," which, after "loitering" in Europe for two thousand years and finally being discredited, now turned up in China in this shopworn guise. It was obvious, they argued, that science had become omnipresent in the twentieth-century world, and "no knowledge can be recognized as knowledge if it is not critically and logically studied."[47]

Though the arguments on these questions swirled angrily in print all through the early 1920s, those who espoused differing sides could still be close friends—for they very often shared similar social backgrounds, had reached intellectual maturity in similar foreign university settings, and felt the same frustrations over China's weakness. Xu Zhimo's diary entries for the autumn of 1923 show how varied was this group of friends (both men and women) who gathered for an apparently endless round of talks, excursions, convivial meals, and drinking parties in the scenic surroundings of Hangzhou and Changzhou: there were former members of the Restoration Society who had known Qiu Jin, founding members of Sun Yatsen's Revolutionary Alliance, Guomindang politicians, activists in the fields of mass education and language reform, scientists, historians, dramatists, Marxist literary critics and poets as well as those who considered themselves disciples of John Dewey, Rudolf Euken, or Irving Babbitt. Qu Qiubai, too, would sometimes leave his work in Shanghai and come to join them, for his uncle Qu Junong (who three years before had seen him off from Beijing station with the haunting poem about life's sweetness) had become a good friend of Xu's.[48]

It is ironically apposite, in view of the utterly different intellectual directions that the two men had taken, that when Xu Zhimo and Qu Qiubai met during that October of 1923, it was in a garden, on a lazy afternoon after lunch, while Xu Zhimo was arguing with a group of friends about Walter Pater's theory of poetry. Xu was shocked to see how clearly the ravages of tuberculosis were marked on Qu Qiubai's features, and in his diary expressed dismay at the routine that kept Qu working from dawn until late into the night, with almost never a rest period. Qu Qiubai, in turn, thought that Xu Zhimo and his friends were living in a "fantasy" land, dominated by the sentimental works of Katherine Mansfield, their belief in the divine power of love, and the kind of fake bucolic philosophizing that was represented by their worship of Tagore. This life was particularly out of place in a world scarred by class exploitation and imperialist aggression. It was as if they felt the universe could be subsumed in the gorgeous settings of Hangzhou's West Lake. He had felt the pull of West Lake, too, wrote Qu, and for a wonderful moment it had filled his body with deep contentment. But the pull had to be resisted, for West Lake was not the genuine wilderness and its calm was delusory.[49]

A week before this particular meeting and just under two weeks before Qu published his poem "Iron Flower," Xu Zhimo, in the company of Qu's uncle and Zhang Junmai, had visited the Buddhist temple known as the Temple of Heaven's Stillness (the Tianning Si), outside the town of Changzhou. He had been enraptured by the setting and the rich and peaceful harmony of the chanting voices of the monks and the sounds of the drums, bells, and wooden clappers. "They combined," he wrote in his diary the next day, "to make a harmonious blend of extraordinary stillness and gentleness, and sent my emotions across unfamiliar boundaries."[50] The moment became a poem:

> *Like hearing, couched on one's back amid long-stemmed rioting grasses in the sunlight welcome as fire's warmth, the first summer call of the partridge which sounds from sky's edge up to the clouds and echoes from clouds back to the edge of sky;*

> *like hearing, through the tropic air eiderdown-soft of a desert night when the moonlight's tender fingertips stroke lightly one by one the scorched fragments of rock, hauntingly, hauntingly borne from afar the sound of a camel bell which nears, nears and again moves away . . . ;*

> *like hearing, in a sequestered valley of the hills where the bold stars of dusk alone illumine a world bereft of sunlight and the grasses and the trees are bowed in silent prayer, an old fortuneteller, a blind man led by a young boy, the clanging of whose gong reverberates through this realm of lowering dark;*

> *like hearing, on some ocean rock savagely struck by breakers tiger-fierce while a black cloudwrack bandages tight the sky, the sea in low and gentle tones confessing its every crime before the storm's menace;*

> *like hearing, among Himalayan peaks, echoing through innumerable ravines of shining snow the rush of clouds from beyond the sky driven by winds from beyond the sky;*

like hearing, from behind the scenes in the theater of life, the onstage symphony which blends laughter of vanity with screams of pain and despair, wild yell of rapine and massacre with shrill song of death wish and suicide;

I have heard the chant of intercession in the Temple of Heaven's Stillness!

Whence comes this godhead? Earth has no second realm such as this!

Sound of drum, sound of bell, sound of stone chime, sound of wood block, sound of the Buddha's name . . . as this music rolls and flows in stately measure through the great hall, stilled are the eddies of numberless conflicts, toned are the clashes of numberless bright tints, dissolved are the numberless hierarchies of men. . . .

This sound of Buddha's name, this sound of bell, sound of drum, sound of wood block, sound of stone chime (swelling in harmony filling the universe, loosing a speck of the dust of time) brings to fulfillment an endless number of karma centuries long;

whence comes this great harmony?—cessation of all movement, cessation of all disturbance in the radiant sea of the stars, in the pipe-song of the Thousand Earths, in the flood of Destiny;

to the limits of Heaven and Earth, in among the hall's lacquered pillars, on the brow of the Buddha image, in the wide sleeves of my robe, in my ears and at my temples, in the pit of my stomach, in my heart, in my dream. . . .

In my dream, this moment's revelation, blue sky, white water, warm soft maternal bosom of green grass, is this my birthplace, this the land of my belonging?

Shining of wings in infinity soaring!

Flow of joy from the source of Enlightenment, manifest now in this great, solemn calm, this calm of Release, harmonious, limitless calm!

O hymn Nirvana! Extol Nirvana![51]

This poem was written while Xu Zhimo, along with Liang Qichao and Zhang Junmai, was working to bring Tagore to China so that he could give a lecture series under the sponsorship of their Society for Lectures on the New Learning. Xu Zhimo had a deep admiration for Tagore's works and had even been willing to interrupt his own excursions and meditations in order to help with the arrangements.[52] After a whole series of delays and misunderstandings Tagore finally reached Shanghai on April 12, 1924, and was met at the dock by Xu Zhimo and Zhang Junmai. Zhang fell ill soon afterward and could not go along on the tour, but Xu Zhimo became Tagore's friend immediately, traveled everywhere with him, and acted as interpreter at most of the lectures, translating Tagore's English into Chinese. Though he was obviously overawed by the Indian poet, Xu's assiduousness in paying court may also have owed something to the fact that his cointerpreter was Lin Huiyin, who still had not married Liang Qichao's son (though she did the following year).[53]

In a series of lectures over the next month, Tagore delivered his message to the Chinese, of which the major thrust was as follows. It would be a mistake to abandon the central virtues of Asian culture by pursuing a Western civilization that had proved itself materialist and destructive; instead, the Chinese should cling fast to a number of "hopes." One hope lay with the poets, whose role in the world should be that of "capturing on their instruments the secret stir of life in the air and giving it voice in the music of prophecy." One hope lay in the individual, with his power of sacrifice, who could stand up against brute power and greed, "the individual with faith in the infinite, the invisible, the incorruptible, the fearless." One hope lay in the uniquely spiritual character of a united Asian civilization. One hope lay in man's eagerness to seek freedom from "the servitude of the fetish of hugeness, the non-human."[54]

The lectures were well attended by the public, Tagore was entertained at many smaller convivial gatherings, and obviously many students revered him; but from the very first his visit also drew taunts and protests. In China's current situation of subservience to foreign imperialism and domestic militarism there was something particularly distasteful in being preached to by an Indian, even if he had won the Nobel Prize. The day of Tagore's arrival in China the literary critic and novelist Mao Dun (a colleague of Qu Qiubai's at Shanghai University) wrote a newspaper article that gave some praise to Tagore for his support of the oppressed, his patriotism, and his poetic personality, but warned those Chinese who had lined up on the docks to welcome Tagore not to be overcome by his message concerning the value of "oriental civilization" and "paradise for the soul."

> Oppressed as we are, at this moment, by militarists within the country and by imperialists from without, this is no time for dreaming. To immerse ourselves in contemplating luminous visitors at this time will be no more effective for us than the technique of the literati long ago, as they tried to destroy bandits by chanting the Confucian classics at them. I suggest that a much better slogan for this hour is that of Wu Zhihui: "Reply to our enemies' machine guns with Chinese machine guns; answer their cannons with our cannons."[55]

The secretary-general of the Chinese Communist Party, Chen Duxiu, bluntly lumped Tagore with Liang Shuming and Zhang Junmai and mocked the group as one that sought to "destroy our railroads, our steamships, and our printing presses in order to return to wood-block printing, the canoe carved from a tree-trunk, the wheelbarrow, etc."[56] Qu Qiubai's own comments were even harsher, as might be expected from the man who had begun to protest Tagore's arrival six full months earlier: "India has already become a part of the British industrial economy, but Tagore, living in the world of the past, still dreams that the message of 'love and light' can win over the hearts of the English capitalist class. So he tries hard to ignore India's political struggle. India has already become modern India, but Tagore still seems to want to return to the abode of Brahma. No wonder he and India are moving in opposite directions—he has already retrogressed several hundred years!"[57]

Even Guo Moruo, who had quoted Tagore so lovingly in his poems to his little son, Ah-ho, had now swung decisively against him as he moved to a Marxist position; continuing the genre of medical metaphor that Lu Xun had used to such effect,

Guo wrote that "the decay of our East is a disease caused by the bondage of private property." Tagore's ideas, he added, were nothing but "the morphine and coconut wine of those with property and leisure" and his message of peace was false and dangerous: "Peace propaganda is the magic charm that protects the propertied class; it is the ball and chain that fetters the propertyless class."[58]

Radical Chinese students took up these ideas, or variants of them, as Tagore traveled from city to city. They distributed leaflets, asked hostile questions during his lectures, and disturbed his talks with chants of "Drive out the elephant" (picking up from a sarcastic parallel made by Chen Duxiu between the poet and the elephant—the largest, most self-important, most subservient, and "numbest" of the animals).[59] Student protests in Beijing were the most effective and the most biting. Broadsheets circulated there claimed that China's youth rejected Tagore's praise for an ancient China that debased women, engaged in war without reason, obeyed grotesque codes of filial piety, and fostered an apathetic people: "Our agriculture, which hardly feeds our peasants, our industry, which is strictly household industry, our carts and our boats, which go only a few miles a day, our monosyllabic language and our ideographic writing, our printing, which has remained at the stage of carved wood-blocks, our streets, which are latrines, and our deplorably dirty kitchens have made us lose our reputation throughout the world. And here Mr. Tagore comes to reproach us for our excess of material civilization! How can we fail to protest against him?"[60] Tagore was finally so disturbed by what he considered the deliberate distortion in these charges that he cut short his lecture series in Beijing and speeded up his visits to the remaining cities on his itinerary.

Xu Zhimo, who had fallen in love again (this time with Lu Xiaoman, the cultured and startlingly beautiful wife of a young Chinese military officer in Beijing), listened to this chorus of denunciations with dismay. His own heart was so full of generous thoughts, he was so set on living through Tagore's message of love and hope and of founding a community of his own in China to realize Tagore's principles, that the criticisms seemed to him appallingly misjudged, and he cried out in the Indian poet's behalf: "He advocates creative life, spiritual freedom, international peace, educational progress, and the realization of universal love. But they say he is a spy for the imperialists, an agent of capitalism, an exile from the enslaved people of a conquered country, a madman who advocates footbinding! There is filth in the hearts of our politicians and bandits, but what has this to do with our poet? There is confusion in the brains of our would-be scholars and men of letters, but what has this to do with our poet?"[61] And Xu Zhimo closed with an up-piling of epithets that exceeded even those he had accorded to Katherine Mansfield two years before:

> His great and tender soul, I dare say, is a miracle in human history. His unlimited imagination and broad sympathy make us think of Whitman; his gospel of universal love and zeal for spreading his ideas remind us of Tolstoy; his unbending will and artistic genius remind us of Michelangelo, the sculptor of Moses; his sense of humor and wisdom make us think of Socrates and Laozi; the tranquillity and beauty of his personality remind us of Goethe in his old age; the touch of his compassion and pure love, his tireless efforts in the cause of humanitarianism, his great and all-embracing message sometimes make us recall the Savior of mankind. His brilliance, his music, his grandeur, remind us of the Olympian gods. He cannot be insulted, he cannot be surpassed, he is a mysterious natural phenomenon.[62]

The exuberance was characteristically Xu's, the exaggeration was patent, and the roll call seemed bleakly lopsided to China's new nationalists, seeking reassurance as they were that Chinese resources could rescue the country from the dark ages foisted upon them by foreign guns. Even with the aid of Marx, they might well have asked, could Laozi be a match for Whitman, Tolstoy, Michelangelo, Socrates, Goethe, Christ, *and* the Olympian gods?

14. Zhou Enlai in Tianjin, 1917

15. The Changde group of seven, 1911. Xiang Jingyu, seated on ground at left; Ding Ling's mother, standing at right.

16. Xiang Jingyu
in France, 1920

17. Chinese women students in France, 1920. Standing at left, Cai Chang; seated on lower step (center), Xiang Jingyu.

18. Mao Zedong in 1918

19. Qu Qiubai's mother, shortly before her suicide in 1915

20. Qu Qiubai and his father, around 1909

21. General Wu Peifu in 1922, aged forty-eight

22. Qu Qiubai as a young man in the 1920s

23. Ding Ling with her mother in the mid-1920s

24. Xu Zhimo at Cambridge University, around 1922

25. Xu Zhimo's first wife, Zhang Youyi, around 1922

26. Lin Huiyin in Beijing, 1924

27. Kang Youwei with his consorts and children in Shanghai, 1921

·7·

WHOSE CHILDREN
ARE THOSE?

It was in 1921, while Xu Zhimo was in Cambridge and Qu Qiubai in Moscow, that Lu Xun wrote his most famous tale, "The True Story of Ah Q." In this story, which has come to be seen as a classic of modern Chinese literature, Lu Xun depicted Ah Q as a cowardly, selfish, and cunning man, capable of endless self-deception, who is finally shot in 1911 for claiming to be a revolutionary, when in fact he is no more than a braggart and a petty thief. Lu Xun deliberately kept the specific details of Ah Q's looks and background vague: "My method is to make the reader unable to tell who this character can be apart from himself," he explained, "so that he cannot back away to become a bystander but rather suspects that this is a portrait of himself as well as of all other Chinese."[1] Lu Xun could see little evidence that things had changed for the better since 1911, and continued to harp on his depressed images of China's "ancient spiritual civilization" as being inherently "cannibalistic"—in obvious contrast to the views of Liang Shuming, Zhang Junmai, and the overly gullible "Mr. Bertrand Russell, who praised the Chinese when some sedan-chair bearers smiled at him at the West Lake." All that had happened in 1911, Lu Xun now wrote, was that "the Manchus left the feast." Meanwhile beggars continued to "eat scraps by the roadside," "half-starved children are sold at eight coppers a pound," and "in the country men are starving to death." The conclusion? "Our vaunted Chinese civilization is only a feast of human flesh prepared for the rich and mighty. And China is only the kitchen where these feasts are prepared."[2]

In a letter of March 1925 to a friend who had suggested that perhaps things were not so bad as Lu thought, that it was possible that the Chinese acted as they did because they were "lazy," Lu Xun expanded on his earlier views in regretful dissent:

> This kind of behavior, I'm afraid, is not simply due to laziness, but in fact originates from vileness and cowardice. When the Chinese are confronted with power, they dare not resist, but use the words "taking the middle course" to put a good face on their real behavior so that they feel consoled. When they have power and realize that others cannot interfere with them, or when they are supported by the "majority," most of them are cruel, heartless, and tyrannical, just like despots; they then do not take the middle course. When they have lost power and cannot help taking the "middle course," they readily talk about its wisdom. As soon as they are totally defeated, they are ready to resign themselves to fate.[3]

And in an essay written partly in response to critics who felt the grand finale of the story, in which Ah Q is shot under the hungry eyes of the crowd, was overdrawn or inapposite, Lu Xun replied: "Of course, Ah Q could have come to all sorts of different ends, but I do not know what they would be. I thought, once, that I had exaggerated, but I do not think so now. If I were to describe events in China today exactly as they happen, they would appear grotesque to people of other countries or those of a future, better China." But then, as he had said in reference to Russell, "if chair-bearers could stop smiling at their fares, China would long since have ceased being the China she is."[4]

"Ah Qism" was a profoundly depressing allegory of China's fate, and whether one passed one's life in the spheres of high aestheticism or in trying to organize factory laborers, the situation seemed even bleaker in 1925 than it had in 1921, when Lu Xun first began to circulate his "humorous tale" (for it began as

Lu Xun's attempt at fun, commissioned by the editors to lighten the pages of the Beijing *Morning News,* though when they saw the second chapter they shifted it from the humor section to that on new literature).[5] By 1925, the remnants of the old republican regime had essentially disintegrated. A profoundly venal president, Cao Kun, had corrupted what was left of the National Assembly; and, perhaps even worse, one of the best-trained and most intelligent men ever to agree to serve in a cabinet position, the brilliant jurist Lo Wengan (who in 1922 had resigned his seat as chief justice of China's Supreme Court to attempt to bring some order and honesty to the Ministry of Finance), was himself framed, dismissed, and imprisoned.

With the ever-greater interference by northern warlords in the affairs of the waning central government, and with the concentration of power in southern and western China in the hands of a small number of regional commanders, each year saw more battles and heavier casualties. China was in danger of splitting permanently apart, most probably into nine separate units: these units in some cases coinciding with actual provinces, in others amounting to "macroregions" where combinations of economic and geographical factors gave the area a kind of logical cohesion. Three of the nine were in the south, three spread along the Yangtze River in central China, and three were in the north. In the easternmost of the southern regions, Sun Yatsen's regime in Guangdong province had to be sensitive to all political developments in the Guangxi region to the west and to the two Yangtze River regions immediately north of it. Any long-range planning for national reunification had therefore to anticipate a series of alliances that would enable Sun's Guomindang troops—still weaker than many of the warlord armies confronting them—to reach the Yangtze River via Hunan province, before moving downriver toward Nanjing, Shanghai, and the sea. There new alliances would have to be forged that might allow Guomindang forces to reach Beijing and gain ascendancy over the regimes in Shandong, Manchuria, and Shanxi. Even such a sketch suggests more solidity than there actually was, for massive armies like those of General Feng Yuxiang, which roamed across northern and northwest China, though without their own clear territorial base, were able on occasion to transform the northern power balance. In late 1924, for example, General Feng's troops had seized Beijing, forced President Cao Kun to resign, driven the deposed Emperor Puyi out of the Forbidden City and into sanctuary in the Japanese concession in Tianjin, and set up Duan Qirui (who had been premier four times, for brief periods, during the years of the First World War) as "provisional chief executive." In this rather nebulous position Duan went through the motions of drafting a new constitution for China and convening a new National Assembly, but no concrete achievements resulted. China ceased to have any clear focus of authority whatsoever.[6]

How could the situation improve? In a lecture to students in Beijing at the very end of 1923, Lu Xun had offered another of his bleak prognoses: "Unfortunately China is too hard to change: just moving a table or repairing a stove tends to involve bloodshed; and even after the blood has flowed there is no certainty that the change will be made. Unless a great whip lashes her on the back, China will never be willing to move forward of her own accord. I think such a whipping is bound to come; whether good or bad, it is bound to come, but where or how I do not know exactly."[7]

The whip did begin to fall on China's back in 1925; or perhaps it would be more accurate to say that it only began to sting unbearably in that year. For Lu Xun's metaphor makes sense if we define the whip as certain particular acts of foreign imperialism: to have their effect of "budging" China these had to be perceived as painful, and that perception had then to be acted upon. In this process industrial workers, merchants, idealistic students, and bourgeois intellectuals were all involved, while the members of the Communist Party, along with some radical members of the Guomindang, came to political prominence because of their ability to make the Chinese aware of the interconnections between foreign imperialist power and China's miserable economic condition. Li Dazhao, one of the cofounders of the Communist Party who had followed Comintern instructions by joining the Guomindang in 1923, had offered the analysis that foreign imperialism had "proletarianized" all the Chinese people: they were thus ripe for socialist revolution even though they had not gone through a highly developed capitalist phase and had only a few truly proletarian workers (China being still an almost totally agrarian society). Yet as Li Dazhao, Qu Qiubai, Xiang Jingyu, and other young Communists grew more familiar with the urban proletariat that did already exist, they found promising recruits, for work conditions in China were generally atrocious: workdays were often fourteen hours or more in a seven-day workweek, there were few holidays, use of child labor was widespread, and wages were pitifully low, at around a dollar a day per family; housing (often provided by the employer at low rents) was filthy, with densities of four or five people to each room, and there was no sanitation, and often no cooking facilities, either, so that scarce money had to be spent just buying hot water from street hawkers to cook an evening meal. For many workers' families, money was so short that less than a dollar a year per person was available for any paid entertainment or recreation, and the cheapest books or newspapers were beyond reach (even for the few workers who could read). Naturally, many of the factories that spawned these conditions were owned by Chinese entrepreneurs, but enough were controlled by Western or Japanese interests to give real force to antiforeign arguments.[8] By 1925 the three very different cities of Beijing, Shanghai, and Guangzhou were all, each in its own way, potential centers of violence, for though the manifestations of foreign imperialism might seem most obvious in Shanghai, Beijing had a large foreign presence in the legation quarters, as well as the enveloping Japanese threat in Shandong province to the east and in Manchuria to the north, while Guangzhou also had its foreign concession on Shameen Island as well as its Western business interests, and was close to Britain's crown colony of Hong Kong.

The first in a new series of strikes, directed at Japanese-owned cotton mills, was launched by the Communist-controlled West Shanghai Workers' Club in February 1925. The Shanghai strike received considerable support from students and patriotic businessmen, many of whom had already been moved to protest the widespread abuses of child workers in other plants. Further strikes took place that spring, and in mid-

May a Chinese striker was killed by his Japanese foreman; Communist leaders called for a demonstration of anti-imperialist solidarity to be held on May 30 to "revive the spirit of May 4." The demonstration took place as planned, but a clash erupted with British-led police in the International Settlement. The police fired into the crowd. Eleven marchers were killed and fifty or more injured.[9]

Within the following weeks, in much the same way as during the period after May 4, 1919, sympathy strikes and rallies spread out to other industries in Shanghai, though this time it was the students who joined the workers. In the city were a number of Communist Party leaders, including Li Lisan and Liu Shaoqi, who had worked with Mao Zedong in the 1922 Hunan strikes and, like him, been forced to flee from the province because of the violently anti-Communist warlord who was in control there. Liaison with the students was coordinated by Yang Zhihua, a student at Shanghai University who had divorced her husband and married Qu Qiubai after the death of Wang Jianhong in 1924. Qu himself supervised propaganda, edited an influential journal of the movement, *News of Bloodshed*, and prepared a major theoretical essay on the significance of the strikes, entitled "Nationalist Revolution and Class Struggle in the May 30 Movement." The violence, however, was far more pronounced than it had been six years before on May 4. Picket lines were effectively organized, armed with clubs, and given rudimentary military training; in response, Western and Japanese authorities mobilized volunteer corps, declared martial law in their concession areas, and in Shanghai brought in twenty-six gunboats and landed marines. Some sixty more students and demonstrators were killed in the first few days of June.[10] Rallies, protests, and strikes to show solidarity with the "spirit of May 30" now took place across China, often accompanied by boycotts of goods from British and Japanese firms and the wrecking of their factories. Violence was common and reprisals sometimes savage: in the city of Qingdao the Shandong warlord executed a union leader and the editor of a local newspaper sympathetic to the strikers; in Tianjin, workers took possession of a silk-reeling factory, and twenty were killed and perhaps as many as three hundred wounded when local troops fought prolonged battles to oust them.[11]

The news of the May 30 killings deeply moved the students in Beijing. Xu Guangping, one of Lu Xun's students at the Beijing Women's Normal College, wrote to him excitedly on June 5 to tell him that the "raging tide had swept up from Shanghai to Beijing"; now was the time for mass action by the Beijing students, she said, but though representatives from several campuses had duly assembled at the Gate of Heavenly Peace (as their forerunners had done on May 4, 1919), they had wasted their time bickering over who should be chairman of their projected "national committee" and had not come up with a coordinated program of action. Disgusted, Xu Guangping had left the meeting and was returning to her college when fortuitously she saw in the street the conservative principal of her college (who the year before had been forced out of her position by the radical students, only to be reinstated by the Ministry of Education). "As I saw that woman Yang," wrote Xu Guangping, "smiling her vague smile as she gazed at our group, I felt a kind of instantaneous heat rise up within me, and I yelled out, 'Down with Yang Yinyu, down with Yang Yinyu, away with Yang Yinyu!' Those with me took up the chant with loud shouts, and our voices reached to Yang's car until she had driven away. . . . My teacher, you can see that I'm the wild horse that leads the rest of the herd astray, I can't be reined in, I can't be kept under control. What's to be done about me?"[12]

Lu Xun would be generally sympathetic, Xu Guangping well knew, because he had mocked Yang Yinyu several times in his satirical essays, accusing her of "intimidating helpless students of her own sex," using "jackals and foxes" to maintain herself in her position of authority, behaving toward her students as if she were a tyrannical mother-in-law in the Chinese tradition and they were all "child-brides coming into her household," and being one of those murderous reactionaries who "strew filth over Aeolian harps."[13] Lu Xun answered Xu's letter just over a week later, apologizing for the delay caused by the number of things clamoring for his attention. Just because Xu Guangping was a favorite student of his—she had initiated a correspondence with him in March, and now signed herself with the affectionate diminutive "your little devil"—he was concerned and cautious about this kind of outspoken radicalism:

> I don't want this "little devil" to become transformed into a wild woman, or to have no control over her temper. Even though becoming a wild woman may not seem like much of anything to you yourself . . . when other people become aware of it that's the end of you. That's why, as far as I am able, I don't let myself grow really wild, though I have to admit that even though I don't get wild, people still insist on saying that I am mentally unstable—obviously there's nothing that can be done about that. If you are impetuous by nature, then of course it's easy to lose your temper; the best thing is to cool down that temper somewhat, otherwise you'll have to be on guard against being made a victim—for the China of today is a place where the secretive and the pliant win the victories.

Lu Xun also pointed out that student mass activism hardly seemed likely to succeed in this particular context: if the combined forces of Beijing National University had been unable to force the resignation of the unpopular minister of education, and the women students of the Women's Normal College had been unable to force out their principal, Yang Yinyu, what luck did they think they'd have against the British or the Japanese?[14]

One reason that Lu Xun had been too busy to reply earlier to his student was that he was preparing his own statement about the May 30 massacre for publication; it was finished on June 11. In this compassionate and rather curious piece, Lu Xun pointed to the burden that had now fallen on the younger generation of Chinese because of the ineffectuality of their seniors—seniors who "devoted so much energy to being mysterious and unfathomable, balanced and smooth, that they left all the real, difficult jobs for those after them." By firing on the Shanghai demonstrators the British had now proved that they would be tough antagonists, a good "whetting stone" for the Chinese, who must look forward to thirty years of struggle at the very least.[15]

Less than a month later Lu Xun had finished a short story in which he seemed to mock his own hesitations and to praise those who, like Xu Guangping, were willing to speak out boldly. Lu Xun had now almost abandoned the long and brilliantly observed tales that he had been writing between 1918 and 1923 in favor of brief, pungent satirical pieces, part prose-poem, part essay, part tract. He called this one (given here in its entirety) "Expressing an Opinion."

> I dreamed I was in a primary-school classroom preparing to write an essay, and I asked the teacher how to express an opinion:
>
> "That's hard!" Glancing sideways at me over his glasses he said: "Let me tell you a story—
>
> "When a son is born to a family, the whole household is delighted. When he is one month old they carry him out to display him to the guests—usually expecting some compliments, of course.
>
> "One says, 'This child will be rich.' He is heartily thanked.
>
> "One says, 'This child will be an official.' Compliments are paid him in return.
>
> "One says, 'This child will die.' He is given a thorough beating by the whole family.
>
> "That the child will die is inevitable, while to say that he will be rich or a high official may be a lie. Yet the lie is rewarded, whereas a statement of the inevitable earns a beating. You—"
>
> "I don't want to tell lies, sir, neither do I want to be beaten. So what should I say?"
>
> "In that case, say: 'Aha! Just look at this child! My word. . . . Did you ever! Oho! Hehe! He, hehehehe!' "[16]

Even before the story was finished, the British had shown once again how good a "whetting stone" they could be. In Guangzhou on June 23, when a massive demonstration of workers, students, and military cadets, expressing solidarity with the dead in Shanghai and the laborers in Hong Kong who had also come out on strike, marched toward the foreign-held island enclave of Shameen, British guards (joined this time by French forces) opened fire on the crowd when it was believed to be growing too threatening. Fifty-two marchers were killed and more than a hundred wounded.[17]

In 1922–23 General Wu Peifu's troops had held down the labor organizations for a full two years by their executions and reprisals, but the movement now had grown too strong to be restrained by this casual violence. Guangzhou, too, had been transformed under the influence of Sun Yatsen's reforming Guomindang. Comintern agents, working with Sun Yatsen, had developed the structure of his party so that it was well knit, disciplined, and committed to his revolutionary principles. Ironically this change came too late to benefit Sun himself, who died of cancer while in Beijing in early 1925, making a last attempt to get the northern warlords to agree to an alliance that would restore constitutional government to China; yet the reorganization enabled the party to hold together after his death while an assortment of leaders jostled for succession. Among this new generation was Chiang Kaishek; having aided Sun in a moment of grave personal danger during 1922, Chiang had been sent by the Guomindang to Moscow for military training in 1923, and on his return he had become head of the new army cadet academy established by Sun Yatsen at Whampoa, near Guangzhou, with Comintern funding and advisory personnel. (In line with the principles of the Guomindang-Communist alliance, the young Communist activist Zhou Enlai was appointed as his deputy in charge of political organization.) As the graduating military cadets brought new strength and cohesion to the southern armies, so did the labor secretariat bring greater strength to the local unions—the Hong Kong strike, for example, was to run for an unprecedented sixteen months, with the strikers being helped by contributions from Chinese and overseas Chinese workers, as well as being aided with housing, food, and educational needs.[18]

At the same time that this new attention was being given to Guomindang organization and to the miserable condition of China's industrial workers, Chinese intellectuals were for the first time carefully assessing and analyzing the resources, sufferings, and potential of rural China. In 1919 Li Dazhao had deeply influenced some Beijing students by suggesting they go to the country and investigate conditions at first hand, and similar groups had gone out from Shanghai in the 1920s; Mao Zedong and some school friends in Hunan had tramped across the province twice to gain experience of local conditions; but perhaps most significantly, a terrible famine had devastated

northern China during 1920 and 1921, millions of rural workers had lost their lives, and the details of this mass suffering
had been vividly recorded by international relief organizations
and the Chinese press.[19] But as was pointed out by Peng Pai, a
young Communist from a landlord background who had received his initial training in politics from Japanese socialists,
these "investigations" had their foolhardy and futile sides; the
cultural and economic gap between educated visitor and peasant tiller was so vast that misunderstandings over motives were
inevitable. Peng's own first revolutionary ventures, made in
eastern Guangdong province during the spring of 1921, had
been woeful: wearing his Western-style suit, Peng had approached a peasant spreading manure, who told him gravely
that he had no money to contribute to the theater troupe that
year. A second peasant, having asked what battalion Peng was
from, edged away with the remark that he "was not good
enough to be friends with you officials." A third asked him if
he had come to dun the villagers for payment of their debts. As
to the people in Peng's hometown, they assumed he had had a
nervous breakdown. Only slowly, after weeks of conversations
and arguments, enlivened with some public magic shows—
Peng was skilled at magic—did he begin to break through that
distrust and fatalism which had led one of his first peasant interlocutors to comment, "Each person's fate has long been determined in advance: a landlord will remain a landlord, and a
tenant will remain a tenant."[20] By 1925, however, Peng Pai not
only had formed several peasant associations in his home area
but directed a flourishing Peasant Training Institute, with joint
Guomindang and Communist leadership, in Guangzhou. (Mao
Zedong was appointed director for the 1926 class.)

If in Shanghai the political activity was mainly among the
urban workers, and in Guangzhou was beginning to include
rural workers, in Beijing in 1925 it continued to be concentrated among the intellectuals. While the warlord Feng Yuxiang
dominated the city, Li Dazhao was able to return from the
countryside where he had been living in retreat, and to resume
his proselytizing activities among faculty and students at the
Beijing and Tianjin universities. Li now had the prestige accru-
ing to a founding member of the Chinese Communist Party, to

which were added the experiences gained as a participant in the 1924 Comintern congress in Moscow and the wider base he enjoyed after his election to the executive committee of the reorganized Guomindang. Moreover, since General Feng also took a sympathetic stance toward labor unions, the northern branches of the Communist Party were able to proceed slowly to rebuild the system that had been shattered after the February 1923 killings.

The success of Li Dazhao and others in rebuilding the Chinese Communist Party was enough to alarm Wen Yiduo seriously when he returned to China in July 1925. Wen had been a May Fourth activist in 1919, when he was twenty, and during his ensuing three years of study in the United States—at the Chicago Art Institute, at Colorado College, and at Columbia University—he had become profoundly nationalistic, in part because he strongly felt the force of American racial discrimination. Yet Wen Yiduo was no more eager to have his Chinese nationalist beliefs coopted by the Communist Party than Kang Youwei had been to have *his* nationalism swept up in Sun Yatsen's republican rhetoric, and so Wen had joined the Great River Society (the Dajiang she), formed by Chinese students in the United States who supported the goal of a strong but nonsocialist China.

After returning to Beijing, Wen wrote on January 13, 1926, to a close friend with whom he had studied in Colorado that "in China the troubles caused by the Reds are violent and wild, which puts a heavy responsibility on the nationalists in our group; and progressing at all will get tougher and harder. In the very near future there is going to be a violent battle between Communism and Nationalism."[21] Wen added that he found most of the available non-Communist allies in Beijing to be bookish and rather ineffectual; only slowly was he able to locate some kindred spirits, who met at the new house he had leased in west Beijing, to discuss the problems of China's future. As he wrote in a letter to his Dajiang friends in the United States, this small band had met with members of other nationalist societies and forged a Federation of United Nationalist Groups for the purpose of lodging joint protests against Russian and Japanese encroachments in Manchuria and dispatch of troops there. Xu Guangping had told Lu Xun she found these meetings too tame, but to Wen Yiduo they were often disappointingly raucous, as taunts and insults (and occasionally furniture) flew through the air. Wen ascribed these excesses to "so-called Communists" to whom he continued to be bitterly opposed. But he was struck by the skill at invective of one woman student whose piercing yells cut through the crowd, astonishing all listeners; this same young female comrade, he was told, had been to the fore in the demonstrations against the May 30 massacre, marching boldly through the streets with banner aloft, so that awestruck Beijing citizens referred to her as the "Chinese Joan of Arc."[22]

Wen Yiduo's skepticism about young political activists echoed, in some respects, the cautious remarks of Lu Xun to his student Xu Guangping, but Lu Xun did not express similar anti-Communist sentiments. In his anti-Communism Wen was closer to Xu Zhimo, who had visited the Soviet Union in the early spring of 1925 and had been moved but not impressed. Xu's writings in the summer of 1925 show that he found none of the magic that Qu Qiubai had experienced in 1921 and 1922: for Xu Zhimo, Moscow was only leaden skies and snowy ground, a constant sense of a past destroyed without trace, memories of blood spilled in the search for a new order, sad faces in the streets, a lack of goods in the shops, shabby clothes on people's backs. In January 1926, as if trying to marshal his own values, Xu Zhimo published two pieces. The first was a careful response to the young Communist Chen Yi's enthusiastic encomium to Lenin; Xu saw Lenin as a "fanatic" who should never be taken as a model by a future developer of China, for he had brought too much destruction in his wake. Xu denied that China was susceptible to Marxist class analysis since "the children of our workers can become officials, and our peasants become merchants; not only can they pass across these divisions, but they have also never been completely separated."[23] The second piece, which he called "The Cambridge I Knew," presented the counterexample that he felt most expressed the choices to Soviet Russia or to warlord China. To present these emotions with the fullest force Xu Zhimo chose not the short lines and beautiful balance he had used to capture "Number 7, Stone Tiger Lane" in Beijing, not the matched long sentences with which he had caught the peace of "The Temple of Heaven's Stillness" in Changzhou, but the full grandeur of prose paragraphs in a Paterian mold:

> The sky's edge blurs in mist, and that sharp silhouette is the church of a nearby village. Listen, to the leisurely harmony of the bells that ring for matins. This region is the plain of the English Midlands, its topography a noiseless rise and fall like the swell of a calm sea; no mountains are in sight, only meadows, constantly green and fertile farmlands. If you look back from that hillock there, you see Cambridge as nothing but a verdant swath of woods close-set at one part and another with slender spires. Of the graceful Cam no trace is to be seen, but as your eye follows that brocade sash of trees you may imagine the course of its leisurely waters. Cottages and copses lie like checkers on this board; where there is a cottage there will be a patch of welcome shade, where there is a patch of shade there will be a cottage.
>
> This rising at dawn is the time to see the smoke from kitchen chimneys: as the dawn mists gradually ascend and draw back the gray-white curtain from the sky (best of all, after a light shower of rain), then the smoke from chimneys far and near, in threads, in strands, in coils, airily or sluggishly, thick gray or pale blue or white, gradually climbs through the tranquil dawn air and disappears, as though dawn prayers of men were fading raggedly into the halls of heaven. Only rarely is the dawn sun visible on these days of early spring. But when it does break through, the early riser knows no greater delight. In an instant the color of the fields deepens, a gold powder like a film of gauze dusts the grass, the trees, the roads, the farms. In an instant the land all about is tenderly suffused with the opulence of morning. In an instant your own heart drinks in its portion of the glory of the dayspring. "Spring!" the victorious air seems to whisper by your ear. "Spring!" your joyful soul seems to echo back.[24]

Wen Yiduo had no such retroactive visions of Chicago, Colorado City, or New York, but he could applaud Xu Zhimo's anti-Communist attitudes, and the two men shared a number of other attributes and experiences. Like Xu, Wen had been born into an affluent family (just to the east of the Wuhan tri-city area, in Hubei province) and had received an excellent classical education. Wen, also, was precocious, became an ad-mirer of Liang Qichao's writings, attended college in Beijing, and sailed to the United States after celebrating a marriage ar-ranged for him by his parents—Wen's first child, a girl, was born when he was already in Chicago, and was three years old before he even saw her. Both Wen and Xu discovered their true poetic vocation overseas, and as Xu wrote his first poems in the vernacular style while at Cambridge, so did Wen in Chicago; and though Wen never developed an admiration for Tagore (he wrote a critical essay at the time of Tagore's visit to China), he roamed in spirit with Xu through the realms of the higher aes-theticism, becoming an admirer of the drawings of Aubrey Beardsley and of the writings of Walter Pater. Wen taught for a brief period in the Beijing Art Institute, and this eclecticism found its expression in his studio apartment, which Xu Zhimo described as being painted entirely in black and highlighted with strips of gold, conveying an effect as of "a naked African beauty wearing only a pair of gold bracelets and anklets"; in one room a small marble replica of the Venus de Milo was placed in a wall niche, adding a touch of "dreamy suggestive-ness."[25]

In January 1926 Wen Yiduo was invited by Xu Zhimo to join with the group of poets who met informally as the Crescent Moon Society (named in honor of a famous collection of Ta-gore's poems); he accepted, though he did not at once recipro-cate by welcoming Xu into his own gatherings of young Chinese nationalists. (Perhaps he regarded Xu, who was at this time conducting his ecstatic love affair with the still-married Lu Xiaoman, as too notorious.) But by March 1926 Wen had agreed to run a poetry section for the literary supplement to the Beijing *Morning News*, which Xu Zhimo edited.[26]

By the kind of coincidence that had become a commonplace in China, the inaugural issue of what one might have expected to be a purely literary venture, dominated by the aesthetic theories and writings of Xu, Wen, and their friends, turned into a political document, since the third in a sequence of demon-strations-cum-massacre shook Beijing on March 18, just as the contents were being planned. The cause of the March 18 tragedy in Beijing was more complex than the previous year's May 30 Shanghai strike or the June 23 strikes in Hong Kong and Guangzhou, though again anti-imperialist anger was central, in this case the target being Japan rather than Britain or France. The crisis began with an incident in the fighting between rival warlord armies in the area of Tianjin: troops loyal to General Feng Yuxiang had mined the sea approaches to the city, so as to prevent Zhang Zuolin, the warlord who dominated Manchuria, from making a landing; the Japanese protested this interference with their trade and communications in an area they had come to regard as their own sphere of influence, and they ordered the harbor cleared. When nationalist students in Beijing, in demonstrations organized jointly by representatives of the Guomindang and the Communist Party, marched on the office of the chief executive (this being the title of the current head of state, so named by General Feng in the absence of a duly elected president) to demand that he reject the Japanese ultimatum, they were dispersed by government troops. The following day, March 18, another and larger group of demonstrators assembled near the Gate of Heavenly Peace. After listening to protest speeches, the crowd again moved off in the direction of the chief executive's office; police, barring the way, opened fire, and forty-seven of the marchers, mainly young students, were killed.

Far from reconfirming Wen Yiduo in his dislike of strident demonstrations, this event—so clear-cut in its initial motivation, so tragic to the young participants in its outcome—released his poetic voice from constraints that had made it almost impossible for him to write since his return to China. He at once began plans to use the *Morning News* poetry section as a forum to express his outrage, but even before that section could reach the printer, he had written a poem that Xu Zhimo printed in the literary supplement to the same newspaper on March 27. Wen Yiduo chose to use a rickshaw puller's imaginary monologue as the form in which to express his sorrow for the dead; like many contemporary intellectuals, he used the rickshaw puller's assumed simplicity of nature to make a complex statement about the human predicament. (Zhou Enlai had done the same in an early poem pointing up the inequities of the capitalist system, as had Xu Zhimo in a poem about the silence at the center of our mysterious journey across this earth.) Wen Yiduo named his poem, in memory of the location of the massacre, "The Gate of Heavenly Peace":

> *Good heavens, I was really scared today! Even now I can still feel my legs trembling. See there, see there, they are almost catching up with us, wouldn't anyone run as fast as I?*
>
> *Please, sir, just let me catch a breath, those things there, can't you see those pitch-dark things, some are headless, others hobbling, they frighten me, they keep on waving their white banners and calling out.*
>
> *There's nothing you can do nowadays, who could give you an answer? There's nothing men can do about it, let alone the ghosts. Ah, they are still holding their meetings, still not behaving properly! See there, whose children are those, they're hardly adolescents, are they? What's going on?*
>
> *Aren't those bayonet wounds on their heads? Sir, they say that people were killed yesterday, and those who died were foolish students. How strange things are nowadays, those students have all they need to eat and drink—my second uncle died at Yangliuqing, pushed by starvation to become a soldier—how can these ones sacrifice their lives like this?*
>
> *I'm no liar, I've just filled my lamp with two measures of oil, a full ladle's worth, how can I trudge on, trudge on, and fail to see the road? No wonder Little Baldy was scared out of his wits, and told us not to go through the Gate of Heavenly Peace at night. Ai! It's another blow for us rickshaw pullers. By tomorrow the city of Beijing will be full of ghosts!*[27]

Five days later, on April 1, the first issue of the poetry section appeared in Xu Zhimo's literary supplement. It contained a long essay by Wen Yiduo, in which he dwelt on the grim coincidence of the poetry section's being born while the blood of the dead students ran in the alleys near the Gate of Heavenly Peace. He hailed this as a true, even inevitable, conjunction, in which art and patriotism became one. The two occurred together because they were inseparable; the blood shed at the palace gate and in the alleys was the blood of patriotism that would flow from the new writers' brushes onto their paper: "Those worthies who died on March 18 were not just patriots, they were the grandest of poems."[28]

Another anguished observer of the March massacre was Lu Xun, though he did not share Wen's fancy that these young people's deaths constituted the "grandest of poems." For one thing, Lu Xun had feared too long and too vividly that something like this would happen, as we can see from his correspondence with his student Xu Guangping. Starting with his first letters to her in early 1925 he had warned her to be wary of violence; as for himself, he wrote, he had learned a lesson from the trench warfare of the Western Allies in the World War: if you were out in the open, you got hit, but secure in your trench you not only stayed alive but could "smoke, sing a little, play a game of cards, drink some wine and mount an occasional art show."[29] People did not adopt an attitude of "numbness" out of apathy alone, he added in another letter, but so as to avoid suffering further unbearable pain.[30] When Xu Guangping responded by praising the forceful example of the martyr Qiu Jin, and lamented that there were no more like her, Lu Xun replied that even though revolutionary change was obviously needed in a China that was "shut outside the gates of the Great Community," nevertheless overhasty change led only to "fire and sword," and neither Sun Yatsen nor Qiu Jin had been able to bring constructive change to the country.[31] Developing these ideas in other essays in the mid-1920s, he noted that in times of real trouble the teachers tended to disappear and most of the students slipped out of harm's way, leaving just a few to be the "scapegoats," who would be "slaughtered the moment they groan." The youngsters might think they would "kindle a fire in men's hearts and create a blaze which may revive the nation. But if men refuse to be kindled, sparks can only burn themselves out, just as paper images and carriages burn out on the street during funerals." Qiu Jin, after all, had died at the hands of informers: "Right after the revolution she was called a heroine, but this title is rarely heard now."[32]

The tragedy of March 18, 1926, therefore hit Lu Xun with the terrible force of a premonition realized. Xu Guangping was not among the dead, but two other students of his were, and a third was seriously wounded. One of the dead young women, Liu Hezhen, had been especially drawn to Lu Xun's writings, and he knew the poignant detail that despite her shortage of funds she had subscribed for a year to the magazine in which he wrote most often. At first his responses to March 18 were couched in generalized terms of outrage: he compared the government's act to Tsar Nicholas II's use of Cossacks to kill young Russian intellectuals, warned that blood debts would have to be paid in kind, mocked those who said the demonstration had been "Communist-inspired" when in fact there were no Communists among the leaders, and urged the young to realize that those who were doing the killing had no consciences, and so "our awakened youth should not be willing to die so lightly again."[33] When the Beijing students asked him to contribute something in writing to the memorial service held on March 25 for the murdered students, the sense of loss was still so strong that he couldn't do it; it was only on April 1, the same day that Wen Yiduo's essay appeared, that he was able to express his more personal feelings:

> Liu Hezhen, one of the more than forty young people killed, was my pupil. So I used to call her, and so I thought of her. But now I hesitate to call her my pupil, for I should present to her my sorrow and my respect. She is no longer the pupil of one dragging on an ignoble existence like myself. She is a Chinese girl who has died for China. . . .
>
> On the morning of the eighteenth I knew there was a mass demonstration before Government House; and that afternoon I heard the fearful news that the guards had actually opened fire, that there had been several hundred casualties, and that Liu Hezhen was one of the dead. I was rather skeptical, though, of these reports. I am always ready to think the worst of my fellow countrymen, but I could neither conceive nor believe that we could stoop to such despicable barbarism. Besides, how could smiling, gentle Liu Hezhen have been slaughtered for no reason in front of Government House? . . .

I did not see this, but I hear that Liu Hezhen went forward gaily. Of course, it was only a petition, and no one with any conscience could imagine a trap. But then she was shot before Government House, shot from behind, and the bullet pierced her lung and heart. A mortal wound, but she did not die immediately. When Zhang Jingshu, who was with her, tried to lift her up, she, too, was pierced—by four shots, one from a pistol—and fell. And when Yang Dezhun, who was with them, tried to lift her up, she, too, was shot: the bullet entered her left shoulder and came out to the right of her heart, and she also fell. She was able to sit up, but a soldier clubbed her savagely over her head and her breast, and so she died. . . .

Time flows eternally on: the streets are peaceful again, for a few lives count for nothing in China. At most, they give good-natured idlers something to talk about, or provide malicious idlers with material for "rumors." As for any deeper significance, I think there is very little; for this was only an unarmed demonstration. The history of mankind's battle forward through bloodshed is like the formation of coal, where a great deal of wood is needed to produce a small amount of coal. But demonstrations do not serve any purpose, especially unarmed ones.

Since blood was shed, however, the affair will naturally make itself more felt. At least it will permeate the hearts of the kinsmen, teachers, friends, and lovers of the dead. And even if with the flight of time the bloodstains fade, the image of a gentle girl who was always smiling will live on forever amid the vague sorrow. The poet Dao Jian wrote:

> My kinsmen may still be grieving,
> While others have started singing.
> I am dead and gone—what more is there to say?
> My body is buried in the mountains.

And this is quite enough.[34]

While teachers and poets mourned in Beijing, the two militarists who now controlled the city along with much of northern China—Generals Wu Peifu, breaker of the 1923 northern railroad strikes, and Zhang Zuolin, the deeply anti-Soviet ruler of Manchuria—made a concerted effort to drive both the Communists and the radical supporters of the Guomindang out of the city. Even the chief executive, against whom the students had tried to demonstrate on March 18, was forced to seek shelter in the Japanese concession in Tianjin, while General Feng Yuxiang—once a Guomindang supporter—sought refuge in the Soviet Union. Lu Xun initially stayed on, and attacked the northern militarists' logic with ebullient sarcasm, as in a mock "news report" entitled "Suppression of Reds": "Planes from Mukden bombed Beijing three times, killing two women and wounding one small brown dog. . . . Whether the two women killed by bombs and the small brown dog which was wounded were Reds or not, we common people cannot tell, since no decree has been issued."[35] But such taunts gained him more enemies, and he had to spend time in hiding; finally the danger to him became so great that in August 1926 he left Beijing altogether, accepting a temporary job at the provincial University of Amoy, on the coast, where life promised to be a little safer. His "little devil," Xu Guangping, also left Beijing, to continue her studies in Guangzhou.

But the south was no haven, for events were moving swiftly there, too. On March 20, only two days after the deaths of the Beijing students, Chiang Kaishek had moved to consolidate his own position in Guangzhou and within the Guomindang by striking against both Communists and Soviet advisers, imprisoning some and purging others from their party positions; these initial thrusts were ratified and strengthened by the Guomindang Central Committee at its meetings in May. Though these moves obviously acted against the long-term prospects for the Communists, and made many of them deeply uneasy, the political line to which they were committed by the Comintern, drawing its orders from Stalin, called for continuing the Guomindang alliance. Thus they could merely acquiesce when Chiang, having already personally taken over as head of the Political Organization Department, was installed in office on July 9 as supreme commander of the Nationalist armies. As supreme commander, Chiang now represented the leadership of a self-styled National Government of Guangzhou; continuities within the Guomindang were emphasized by having Sun Yatsen's surviving son hold his late father's portrait aloft as Chiang Kaishek received his new command.

Chiang's goal was to achieve the national reunification that had always eluded Sun Yatsen, and as head of a complex alliance that now included military allies (often former warlords) from the southern provinces of Guangdong, Guangxi, Hunan, and Yunnan, formed into eight field armies, with many of the officers trained and indoctrinated at the modern Whampoa Military Academy, he finally felt the goal could be achieved. Though the Communists thought that the attempt was premature, Chiang ordered the Northern Expedition, as it was termed, to begin in mid-July 1926, striking from Guangzhou through Guangdong and Hunan provinces to the tri-city area of Wuhan on the Yangtze River. The early phases of this military campaign were startlingly successful, as the Guomindang armies, moving among a sympathetic population and attracting ever new allies, marched north along the line of the Xiang River and on August 12 entered the city of Changsha, which had been seized for Chiang by a warlord ally commissioned as a Nationalist general. In September his troops pressed an assault on Wuhan: the cities of Hankou and Hanyang fell swiftly, and Wuchang followed, surrendering to the Nationalist armies on October 10, 1926, the fifteenth anniversary of that first mutiny that had sparked the revolution.[36]

At the end of 1926, when the Northern Expedition stalled briefly along the Yangtze River, new tensions and options appeared. After a split within the Guomindang itself the more radical members congregated in Wuhan; Chiang Kaishek and his key advisers, many of whom represented the more conservative and big-business-oriented side of the Guomindang, were now stationed in the city of Nanchang. Furthermore, Chiang made it clear that he intended to make a push downriver to Shanghai, rather than move immediately toward Beijing. Obviously this called for a cautious policy toward the foreign powers—there were some twenty-two thousand foreign troops in Shanghai alone and more than forty foreign warships stationed in or near the harbor. At the same time there were growing numbers of rural attacks on landlords and of urban strikes and protests against warlords and industrialists. In February 1927, the Communist-backed General Labor Union in Shanghai ordered a general strike to express solidarity with the Guomindang armies and to force the eviction of the warlord still dominating the city, Sun Chuanfang. They also sought the formation of a People's Government in the city, and a number of economic improvements. Though the strike brought out several hundred thousand workers on February 20 and silenced the major factories and transportation systems, it failed to gain the concerted support of the Chamber of Commerce or the shopkeepers' associations, and General Sun ordered troops in to suppress the strike. In a grim return to a Qing punishment for treasonous criminals, the heads of twenty executed strikers were displayed at public crossroads. A belated attempt at an armed rising by the General Labor Union two days later failed completely, in part because the Guomindang armies halted their own advance only twenty-five miles from the city while the mopping up was completed.[37]

In the rural parts of China, struggle was equally violent, and the numbers involved were immeasurably greater. In an article written in January 1926 for the Guomindang periodical *Chinese Peasant*, Mao Zedong had observed that even if one took only the tenth of a percent of the Chinese people who owned at least a hundred acres of land (a huge holding in the Chinese countryside) as constituting "big landlords," that still amounted to three hundred and twenty thousand people![38] Just over a year later, in February 1927, he observed the incredible development of peasant consciousness in his native province of Hunan: the peasant associations, some of which had been organized by Communist or Guomindang cadres, but many of which had sprung up spontaneously in response to unbearable abuses, now held power. "What was generally sneered at four months ago as the 'peasants' gang' has now become something most honorable. Those who prostrated themselves before the power of the gentry now prostrate themselves before the power of the peasants," wrote Mao. If one assessed roles in this revolution according to a ten-point structure, he continued, then the peasants deserved seven points and the "urban dwellers and the military" (that is, Guomindang and Communist troops and cadres) only three. He discussed the range of actions taken by peasant leaders: auditing landlord accounts to expose embezzlement and cheating; taking funds from them to set up rural credit agencies; parading local bullies in the streets in tall paper hats to identify and humiliate them; smashing clan authority and ancestral religious structures; and execution—"this punishment was invariably meted out to the biggest of the local bullies and evil gentry by request of the peasants and the people as a whole."[39]

On August 14, 1926, two days after Chiang Kaishek entered Changsha, Xu Zhimo gave a party in Beijing to celebrate his forthcoming marriage to Lu Xiaoman (now divorced). The reception was a lavish affair, attended by more than a hundred guests, as was suitable for the culmination of a dramatic and prolonged courtship, which had been conducted by Xu Zhimo in the glare of publicity and had been accompanied by numerous love letters, passionate poems, and self-revelatory diaries (which the couple were soon to publish). In Lu Xiaoman—famous in Beijing as a beauty, a good singer and painter, fluent in French, whose given name, curiously enough, was composed of the ideograph used to transcribe Katherine Mansfield's name, preceded by a diminutive, so that "Xiaoman" could in fact be translated as "little Mansfield"—Xu Zhimo was convinced that he had found that "soul's companion" whom he had told Liang Qichao that he would seek, at whatever cost.[40] Six weeks after the reception the pair held the wedding ceremonies. At Xu's request his old teacher Liang Qichao, promoted now out of politics into the chief post at the National Beijing Library, agreed to officiate and to make a speech in the couple's honor. To the astonishment of Xu and his guests, Liang used the occasion to blast the habits and morals of the young, suggesting that such a marriage between two recently divorced people was profoundly improper and that he and others had begged Xu not to proceed with it, but to no avail. "The newlyweds and the assembled guests who filled the hall," wrote Liang to his daughter the next day, "all turned pale; I fear this is an example of a wedding ceremony that has never been heard of before, either here or abroad, in antiquity or the present time." And after telling her that he'd send her a copy of his remarks at the reception, Liang continued:

> The youth make such a thing of love; they show no sense of moderation, but arbitrarily smash through the protective

nets of convention, and so fall into their own sorrowful snare. This is so very pitiable. Xu Zhimo is really intelligent; I love him; even though I saw him on this occasion sink so far beyond his depth, yet I never lost hope that I could extricate him from this predicament. Another thing that upsets me deeply is that all his old friends are profoundly disgusted by his behavior. If he insists on behaving like this and is then rejected by society, that will be his decision, freely arrived at, and one cannot blame him for it. Yet when I look at him I am filled with such pity for him, and worry that this is the kind of situation that leads to suicide.[41]

Xu, on the other hand, felt that he had overcome darkly negative forces. "I triumphed," he wrote to his friend Leonard Elmhirst in England, "triumphed against the deadly force of ignorance and prejudice in which all societies rest."[42] Yet the triumph, if such it was, was short-lived. Xu's parents had disapproved of his divorce and they disapproved of his new marriage, and when he took Lu Xiaoman with him to their home near Shanghai for two months, things went badly. Lu Xiaoman was ill much of the time and out of place in what she considered a provincial environment; and Xu's parents finally left Zhejiang, where some of their land had been seized by bandits and the family business was doing badly, and settled in Beijing with Xu Zhimo's ex-wife, Zhang Youyi, and the grandson she had borne to them in 1918 before Xu had left for the United States. (The other little boy, Peter, conceived in Cambridge and born in Berlin, had died at three, before Xu Zhimo ever had a chance to see him again.)[43] For good measure, Xu's father also denied him cashing privileges in his remaining bank accounts, and for the first time in his life Xu Zhimo was short of money; a new drama magazine that he had just founded folded, and he found himself so distressed and distracted that he was unable to write any more poetry.[44] In January 1927, as conditions grew more and more dangerous in the Zhejiang countryside, Xu and Lu Xiaoman left the family home and retreated to Shanghai "among the refugees," where he busied himself in setting up the Crescent Moon bookstore and another business to bring in some money—for he saw no chance of returning to teaching in Beijing. The area of Hangzhou, where Xu had been so happy in 1923, was now "half empty," he wrote in

English to Elmhirst, and "under great terror of all manners of calamity which civil wars always bring in their wake. Poor West Lake! Deserted and threatened." Dejected by close friends, who continued to show a "Panglossian" optimism in a world that seemed to be "fast tumbling into a nightmare of hideous passion and bestiality," Xu gave himself over to the completion of a project he'd been working on for more than two years: a translation of Voltaire's *Candide*.[45]

At the beginning of March, as Xu Zhimo completed the translation, police from the International Settlement in Shanghai, fearing renewed disruptions to business, began to identify and arrest potential strike leaders. In its turn the General Labor Union pressed ahead secretly with plans for another major strike that would finally open the city to the Guomindang.

On March 8, Kang Youwei celebrated his seventieth birthday in Shanghai. Xu Zhimo and Lu Xiaoman do not seem to have been invited to this large ceremonial affair, but Liang Qichao and some of Kang's former students came down from Beijing to pay homage to their former teacher, and the ex-Emperor Puyi, who had been living in sanctuary in the Japanese concession in Tianjin ever since being forced to flee the Forbidden City in 1924, sent Kang a present of a jade scepter and an honorific inscription.[46] For some time now, Kang had not corresponded with warlords about China's future; his only recent public pronouncement had been a general telegram to the various northern China warlords, urging them to restore to Puyi the stipends and the right to live in the Forbidden City that had initially been agreed to in 1912.[47] Instead, Kang was concentrating his thoughts on intergalactic travel. Ever since his airplane flight over Baoding, when, as he wrote in a poem, he had returned to earth feeling like a compassionate sage leaving the heavens to occupy himself with the measureless suffering of humankind, he had roamed the heavens in his mind. In 1926 in Shanghai he formally organized his Academy of Travel Through the Heavens, where he lectured and wrote of his journeyings, and of his dream of one day composing a Martian gazetteer that would be a counterpart to the voluminous local-history tradition of China. In some of his last poems, he reached for a new synthesis of the practical world of Western astronomical observation of the stars with the cumulative levels of the million-tiered heavens of traditional cosmology.

Look up at the glistening silver stream,
At the stretch of luminous whiteness,
Whose length spans sixteen degrees of heaven!
Two hundred million stars are gathered there
(Some say there are three billion)
Forming one family with our sun and the eight planets.

Our sun is but one star floating like an insect in the river,
Like a grain of sand in the Ganges;
Huge white stars with temperatures of myriad degrees,
Endlessly distant, are still its neighbors.
They help me onward with their dazzling light
As I roam afar and loudly sing.

In heaven's span of three hundred and sixty degrees
The width of the silvery stream takes merely ten;
Suspended in the extragalactic heavens
It is but one hundred and sixty thousandth part of the universe.
Up I ride in my celestial ship,
Ascending to the Milky Way and the abode of the blessed.[48]

Kang did not stay in Shanghai after his birthday, but left for the southern coast of Shandong province, where he had bought another house in Qingdao—the city once dominated by the Germans, now by the Japanese, and which had figured largely in the nationalistic protests of the late Qing and the May Fourth eras. Here he embarked on his final literary venture, a lengthy memorial of thanks for the birthday gifts given him by the deposed Emperor. Written with a shaking hand, yet in beautifully laid out and formed ideographs, the memorial recalled the turbulent events between 1895 and the 1917 restoration attempt. It was composed in full accordance with late Qing court etiquette, elevating the terms of heaven three characters above the text, and the Emperor's titles, two; Kang identified himself as "your obedient official," writing the ideographs that referred to himself with especially small brushstrokes, again as demanded by Qing ritual. On the last day of March 1927, ten days after a second general strike in Shanghai had brought down the warlord regime there and Guomindang troops had entered the city, Kang Youwei had his Qing court robes laid out on his bed, took a ritual bath, and sat upright beside the robes. Half an hour later he was dead, of a congestion in the brain.[49]

·8·

WAKE THE SPRING

The night before Kang Youwei died, Liang Qichao wrote to his two sons Sicheng and Siyong—who were studying in the United States, one at the University of Pennsylvania and one at Cornell—to express relief that they were not in the middle of the chaos. Though he was pleased that the alliance between the Guomindang and the Communist Party appeared to have broken down, and that Chiang Kaishek obviously was not drifting to the left (as some had feared he might, under the influence of his Soviet advisers), Liang was uneasy about what the Western reaction would be to the antiforeign demonstrations that had occurred in Nanjing and the probable condition of the China to which his sons would one day return:

> The Nanjing situation is in complete flux, and I am not completely sure what is going on. Outsiders are exaggerating everything, but though what happened was unavoidable, there is certainly a group within the army that is intent on stirring up trouble; one can have no doubt about that. Though we now have absolutely clear evidence that Chiang Kaishek and his people are not Communists, I fear that not even they themselves dare say whether or not they will have the capabilities of controlling the Communists. Shanghai at present is the prey being struggled over by both parties; it's an incredibly desperate situation. If the Communists emerge as the victors, then the rest of us won't

even know what our final fate will be. Beijing itself is like
an enormous powder keg, just waiting for something to set
it off.[1]

Within two weeks the question of who would seize the prey
had been answered: between April 11 and 13, troops loyal to
Chiang Kaishek, working closely with paramilitary groups and
local secret-society organizations, moved swiftly to arrest those
whom they knew to be Communists, to break up and disarm
the workers' pickets, and to seize the Shanghai headquarters of
the General Labor Union and all other left-wing strongholds.
Any attempts made by students or workers to show solidarity
with the leftists were savagely dispersed with machine-gun
fire. Though the Guomindang provided no toll of the dead,
contemporary estimates were that as many as five thousand
people in the city were killed.[2]

Behind these deaths lay months of political maneuvering:
among different factions within the Guomindang, and between
the Guomindang and different factions within the Chinese
Communist Party and the labor movement. The Communists,
under Chen Duxiu's leadership, had followed Comintern instructions to work with the Guomindang until the anti-imperialist phase of the revolution was completed; at the same time
they had naturally tried to strengthen their position among the
workers in each city the Guomindang occupied. Chiang Kaishek, aware of tension with these Communist "allies" and
among groups in his own party, at Wuhan and elsewhere, inevitably looked for more reliable allies and new sources of funds.
During March 1927 he had moved against the major labor organizations in Nanchang, Nanjing, and other cities whenever
they threatened his autonomy; at the same time he had pro-
cured loan offers in excess of six million dollars from business
interests in Shanghai who were alarmed by Communist power
there. The April attack was therefore the culmination of a con-
sistent swing to the right.

Communist Party morale was shaken by the events in
Shanghai, but though for the Communists Chiang Kaishek was
now proven to be a dangerous enemy, that did not mean that

their entire strategy of alliance with the Guomindang could be abandoned. In the first place, Chiang had not shown himself a true friend of the bourgeoisie, either, since he ruthlessly pressured them for funds, resorting to kidnapping and other forms of intimidation to get money for his armies. In the second, the northern warlords, except for Feng Yuxiang, had proved equally violent toward both Communists and striking workers, and they could not even make Chiang's claim that they were seeking national reunification. To those whose memories of General Wu Peifu's murder of the railway workers in 1923 might have blurred, the actions of the Manchurian warlord Zhang Zuolin in Beijing, also during April 1927, would have been a brutal reminder. General Zhang ordered his troops to break into the Soviet embassy in Beijing, where a score or more Chinese leftists had sought sanctuary during the previous year; once inside the embassy, his men seized all the Chinese hiding there, together with thousands of documents concerning Soviet involvement with the Chinese Communist Party. After a cursory examination, twenty Communists—among them Li Dazhao, leader of the May Fourth Movement, former head librarian of Beijing National University, and cofounder of the Chinese Communist Party—were hanged.[3]

Despite misgivings, the Chinese Communists continued to follow Stalin's orders, relayed through the Comintern, that they work with the more "left" elements of the Guomindang, who were now based in the Wuhan tri-city area, even though this entailed keeping a tight rein on peasant revolutionary movements lest they alienate their remaining supporters among the bourgeoisie. It was partly for this reason that much of Mao Zedong's Hunan report praising peasant activism was not published in official party periodicals until Qu Qiubai insisted on going ahead with his own edition. Qu was now working openly against Chen Duxiu and Chen's closest aides (although Chen was still secretary-general of the party); Qu felt that Chen and his faction overemphasized the role of the proletariat and underplayed the role of the petty bourgeoisie and the peasantry in the Chinese revolution. Picking up the language of polemic current in the Soviet Union, Qu accused Chen's leading colleague of "Trotskyism" as early as March 1927. Through the summer of that year he continued with his plans to have Chen dismissed as secretary-general, finally succeeding in ousting him at an emergency party conference in August. Qu, named chairman of the Political Bureau, now became de facto head of the Chinese Communist Party at the age of twenty-eight.[4]

While Qu had been maneuvering to obtain the leadership of the party, its general position had continued to deteriorate. For a time, in the spring and early summer of 1927, the Chinese Communists followed their instructions to work with the so-called left wing of the Guomindang, which was believed to be hostile to Chiang Kaishek and sympathetic to the long-term goals of the Communists. But the leaders of this allegedly leftist group of Guomindang politicians had to rely on independent military leaders in central China for their own survival, and since these militarists in turn had close ties with major landlords, the Communist Party had to mute the peasant associations that had been so active earlier in the year. The result was disastrous. The landlords, furious at the murders and humiliations wrought on their families or acquaintances, and determined to prevent any further Communist exploitation of rural grievances, used the local militarists (with Guomindang connivance and in the face of a hamstrung Communist Party) to smash the power of the peasant associations. In May and June 1927 more than ten thousand people were executed in the area around Changsha alone, and thousands more in Wuhan; those killed included peasant delegates to legitimately convened constituent assemblies, members of local peasant associations, and young radical women who bore the badge of cropped hair as a sign of their recently won emancipation.[5]

Finally responding to this savagery in midsummer, after the "left" Guomindang had broken all connections with the Communist Party and had returned in allegiance to the faction led by Chiang Kaishek, Stalin ordered the Chinese Communists to pursue an aggressive policy of fomenting both urban insurrections and rural risings. The combination, it was hoped, would once more build up the momentum of social revolution nationwide. The results, under the overall direction of Qu Qiu-bai, who had to interpret these instructions, were a series of catastrophes: the Autumn Harvest Risings in Hunan, which Mao Zedong was ordered to direct, ended in failure to seize either Changsha or a defensible area of countryside, and Mao, stripped of his party posts, retreated in disarray to the hills of Jinggangshan, on the Hunan–Jiangxi border; other Communist military units suffered heavy casualties and failed to gain their goals of Nanchang and Shantou; while a final concerted Communist effort to found a "commune" in Guangzhou during December 1927, to prove to the world (and to Stalin's critics) that there was still a "crest" to the revolutionary wave in China, ended in the massacre of even more workers by Guomindang-allied troops in that city. Early in 1927 the Communist leaders had claimed close to two million rural workers in their peasant associations and almost three million urban workers represented by delegates at the All-China Labor Congress; by the end of the year both groups of organizations had been effectively broken.[6]

Wen Yiduo had a chance to observe many of these developments at first hand, since he spent the latter part of 1926 and the early months of 1927 either working in Wuhan or at his family's home just east of the city, in Xishui, and the latter part of 1927 in or near Shanghai. In Wuhan the tragedies he witnessed led him to take up painting again, and he worked on a major composition designed to show the horrors of war; his sense of desolation at the political chaos was combined with personal loss, for his four-year-old daughter (born while he was a student in Chicago) died that winter.[7] In a brief introduction appended to his poem "The Deserted Village," dated May 1927, Wen cited reports concerning the bleakness of great stretches of Chinese countryside, where one never saw the smoke from a single kitchen fire, or a single light shining in a home at night, and peasants, who had already had their doors and window frames burned for fuel by warlord troops, hiding their precious last tools lest they, too, be burned or stolen and, in many cases, abandoning their land altogether, leaving any surviving animals to root among the untilled fields:[8]

Where did they go? How has it come to pass?
On stoves squat frogs, in ladles lilies bloom;
Tables and chairs float in fields and water ponds;
Rope-bridges of spiderwebs span room on room.
Coffins are wedged in doorways, rocks block windows;
A sight of strange gloom that rends my heart.
Scythes lie rusting away in dust,
Fishing nets, abandoned, rot in ash-piles.

Heavens, even such a village cannot retain them,
Where roses forever smile and lily leaves grow as big as umbrellas;
Where rice sprouts are so slender, the lake so green,
The sky so blue, and the birds' songs so like dew-pearls.
Who made the sprouts green and the flowers red?
Whose sweat and blood is it that is blended in the soil?
Those who have gone left so resolutely, unhesitatingly.
What was their grievance, their secret wish?

Now, somebody must tell them: "Here the hogs
Roam the streets, ducks waddle among the pigs,
Roosters trample on the peony, and cows browse on vegetable
  patches."
Tell them: "The sun is down, yet the cattle are still on the hills.
Their black silhouettes pause on the ridge, waiting,
While the mountains around, like dragons and tigers,
Close in on them. They glance about and shiver.
Bowing their heads, too frightened to look again. . . ."

Hurry now, tell them—tell Old Wang the Third,
Tell the Eldest Zhou and all his eight brothers,
Tell all the farmhands living around the Linhuai Gate,
And tell that red-faced blacksmith, Old Li.
Tell one-eyed Long and Xu the diviner,
Tell Old Woman Huang and all the village women,
Tell them all these things, item by item.
Call out to them, "Come back, come back!"
My heart is torn by this sight of gloom.
Heavens, that such a village cannot retain these people,
That such a paradise on earth should be without a living soul![9]

The poem gains extra poignance from the fact that Wen Yiduo, too, had joined the wanderers. Having left the Art Institute in Beijing because the situation there was so dangerous, he had also found Wuhan impossible to live in; shortly after friends got him a job teaching at the Political Science Institute in Wusong, near Shanghai, the institute was ordered closed by the Guomindang because of its leftist orientation; so Wen traveled to Hangzhou (which had seemed to Xu Zhimo shorn of its previous beauties) and then spent some of the summer of 1927 with Xu back in Shanghai, where they discussed the founding of a new journal that would be a forum for the work of the Crescent Moon group, now scattered from their former locus in Beijing. For a while Wen carved decorative seals, a delicate task to which he brought his artist's precision; he worked at an office job in Nanjing, which the Guomindang had named China's new national capital; and at Nanjing University he taught English and American drama and poetry. Committed to the pursuit of beauty in art, loving China deeply, Wen now had to reaffirm his faith in the possibilities of beauty in a world that seemed to make an utter mockery of it. During 1927 he worked on a collection of the verse that he had written since 1923; it was published in January 1928 in a black-and-gold binding (perhaps recalling the long-abandoned Beijing studio) by the Crescent Moon bookstore, which Xu Zhimo had founded the previous year in Shanghai. Wen called the collection *Dead Water*, and in the central stanzas of the poem of the same title, which set the mood for the volume as a whole, he made his strongest assertion of faith that beauty would stay alive, even if tremblingly, in the midst of ghastly conditions:

> *Perhaps scraps of brass may hue to turquoise,*
> *Peach blossoms flower from rusting cans,*
> *The greasy scum weave a texture of gauze*
> *And a tinted haze steam up from the germs.*
>
> *Let this dead water ferment into green wine*
> *Frothing with pearly beads of foam:*
> *Tiny beads chuckle, turn into big beads,*
> *Burst at the onslaught of raiding gnats.*

So this ditch of hopeless dead water
May well boast a certain splendor;
Then if the frogs can't bear the silence
Out of dead water a song will rise.[10]

To create this "certain splendor" in the midst of darkness was always Xu Zhimo's dream, too, and when he finally launched his journal *Crescent Moon* in March 1928 (with Wen as a coeditor) he wrote glowingly of the "creative idealism" that spurred him on, and with his customary sense of appropriate scale affixed two epigraphs to his opening manifesto, one from the Book of Genesis ("Let there be light") and one from Shelley ("If Winter comes, can Spring be far behind?"). For good measure, he claimed that his new review, standing for both "dignity" and "health," would forge onward, ready to "destroy all the bacteria that erode life and thought." In a tongue-in-cheek listing he identified thirteen categories of such "bacteria": sentimentalism, decadence, aestheticism, utilitarianism, didacticism, negativism, extremism, preciosity, eroticism, fanaticism, venality, sloganism, and "ism-ism."[11] Marxist writers, who now dominated the previously eclectic literary group called the Creation Society, saw themselves as the intended recipients of much of this critique (as indeed they were) and responded briskly that such "creative idealism" amounted to no more than "whimsical memory and fantasy," and that the "wheel of history would drag the Crescent poets to their graves."[12]

The conflict was of a kind to attract the attention of Lu Xun, who was getting ready to enter the public arena again after a long period of personal withdrawal. During much of 1927 he had had little to say; shocked by the violence meted out to the people—especially to the young women with bobbed hair, killed or mutilated by troops during the antileftist operations—he had resorted to innuendo or sarcasm. Nothing had raised his opinion of the Chinese people in the mass, and the eager crowds that jostled to see the naked bodies of beheaded female revolutionaries sickened him as much as those who had committed the initial violence.[13] Yet in personal terms he was probably happier than he had ever been before, for the long correspondence with his former student Xu Guangping, continued while he was in Amoy and she in Guangzhou, had developed through levels of friendship, to disarming frankness, and finally to love when in mid-1927 Lu Xun left Amoy to join her.[14] After living together for some months in Guangzhou, they left the city two months before the disastrous insurrection of December, and settled in Shanghai. (In 1929 she was to bear him a son, his only child.) Surely it was for love of her that Lu Xun wrote a brief aphorism on September 24, 1927: "Every woman is born with the instincts of a mother and a daughter. There is no such thing as wifely instincts. Wifely instincts come through the force of circumstances and are simply the combination of the instincts of mother and daughter." But that he had not drifted into sentimentality was shown by a complementary aphorism about Chinese men that he wrote at the same time: "The sight of women's short sleeves at once make them think of bare arms, of the naked body, the genitals, copulation, promiscuity, and bastards. This is the sole respect in which the Chinese have a lively imagination."[15]

The struggles between Creation Society Marxists and Crescent Moon romantic idealists struck Lu Xun as particularly absurd. The self-righteousness of many of the leftists both irritated and angered him: he jibed at those who sat in the International Settlement in Shanghai and wrote "revolutionary" poems that showed little more than the formative influence of "Shanghai film posters and advertisements for soya sauce," or else were merely fatuous:

> *Oh, steam whistle!*
> *Oh, Lenin!*

He mocked their muddled symbolism, too, giving as an example a "revolutionary" book jacket that bore the device of a trident with the hammer (of the Soviet hammer and sickle) stuck on its middle prong. "This juxtaposition means you can neither thrust with the trident nor strike with the hammer," observed Lu, "and merely shows the artist's stupidity—it could well serve as a badge for all these writers."[16]

Lu Xun was well aware that these same writers now regarded him as reactionary, as having egged on the youth to struggle by publishing the stories in his famous volume *A Call to Arms*, only to abandon them; he knew, too, that they had purposefully excluded him and several of his close friends from the revived Creation Society. Nevertheless, this didn't lessen his own sense of distance from the Crescent Moon experimenters such as Xu Zhimo and Wen Yiduo, for their pretensions were equally great, and he threw Xu Zhimo's list of "isms" back at him: "To write a good deal about yourself is expressionism. To write about others is realism. To write poems on a girl's leg is romanticism. To ban poems on a girl's leg is classicism. While:

> *A head drops down from the sky,*
> *An ox on the head stands high.*
> *Oh, my!*
> *At sea green thunderbolts fly! . . .*

is futurism."[17] Nor did he think much of their models: "Xu Zhimo has his Tagore, Hu Shi has his Dewey—oh yes, Xu Zhimo has Katherine Mansfield, too, for he wept at her grave."[18] In wanting to be left alone, Lu added, in accepting the harsh controls over society being imposed by the victorious Guomindang, as well as in condoning Guomindang violence, these writers were "skulking in the twilight of bourgeois culture" and could not see that they, too, might be destroyed. "After doing their utmost to preserve law and order, all that these critics in the Crescent Moon Society want is 'freedom of thought'—just freedom to think, not to realize their ideas. And yet there are now measures for the preservation of order which do not even allow you to think." Or, phrased another way, "John Stuart Mill declared that tyranny makes men cynical. He did not know that a republic makes them silent."[19]

On other occasions Lu Xun had pondered aloud whether young women, adrift in this "new China," would ever be able to survive. In a perceptive talk that he gave in 1923 to some of his students at Beijing Women's Normal College, with the apt title (in view of the popularity of Ibsen's *A Doll's House*) of "What Happens After Nora Leaves Home?" Lu Xun had pointed out that a Chinese Nora would have only three choices: to starve, to "go to the bad," or to return home to her husband.

Lu Xun apologized for the bleakness of this analysis, addressing his listeners with words that obviously recalled his earlier conversation with the *New Youth* editor about awakening the slumbering Chinese inside their iron house: "The most painful thing in life is to wake up from a dream and find no way out. Dreamers are fortunate people. If no way out can be seen, the important thing is not to awaken the sleepers." How could Nora evade the bleak choices facing her now that she was awakened? There was only one possible way, said Lu Xun: "To put it bluntly, what she needs is money."

How would women get money in China's society? Only by obtaining their full economic rights, both inside the family and outside in the world at large. How might this be done? Only by struggle, by long, slow, patient struggle, said Lu Xun, because "if you demand political rights you will not meet with much opposition, whereas if you speak about the equal distribution of wealth you will probably find yourself up against enemies, and this of course will lead to bitter fighting." He was not speaking of dramatic acts of self-sacrifice, he said, recalling Qiu Jin and perhaps the new radical women organizers of the Communist Party, for "I have assumed Nora to be an ordinary woman. If she is someone exceptional who prefers to dash off to sacrifice herself, that is a different matter. We have no right to urge people to sacrifice themselves, no right to stop them, either. . . . This choice of sacrifice is a personal one which has nothing in common with the social commitment of revolutionaries."[20]

Ding Ling had shown no inclination to embark on the path of sacrifice, though several of her friends from Changsha had thrown in their lot with the Communist Party, but neither did she achieve a level of economic self-sufficiency. After leaving Shanghai University in 1923 she had moved to Beijing, where she audited some of Lu Xun's classes and was kept going with the help of small stipends from home (Ding Ling's mother was by then an elementary-school principal in Hunan province) and by visits to the pawnshop. She was lucky, too, to have an understanding landlord, who would often let the rent go by unpaid in exchange for conversation about writers at home and abroad. She was also sustained by love and comradeship—by late 1924 Ding Ling, now aged nineteen, was living with a nineteen-year-old would-be writer named Hu Yepin.[21]

According to Ding Ling a few years later, this was a period of waiting and of experimentation for her: behind lay the stormy student activism of her Changsha days and the meetings with Shanghai and Nanjing radicals in the years up to 1923; still ahead was her period of political work for the Communist Party. In a letter to a dear friend Ding Ling wrote that in these Beijing days she and Hu were certainly in love, "but when we first met we were too young, we were like children making a stage play out of our love and out of our minor differences; once they were over we would rush off and start to play again in our splendid happiness. We feared nothing. We thought about nothing. By day we held hands and played games, at night we embraced and slept. We always seemed to be joyful. We had our own heaven and our own earth."[22]

Hu Yepin's early life, like hers, had been full of stress. Hu had run away from his home in the southern coastal province of Fujian at thirteen, some said after stealing a gold bracelet from a jeweler in whose shop he was apprenticed; he had had some schooling in Shanghai and at a naval academy in Shandong before ending up with a job on the literary supplement of the *Beijing News*. Other friends described Ding and Hu as being apparently carefree and utterly irresponsible during this period, although prey to violent swings of emotion: rushing along the streets in sheer delight on one day, lying in bed for hours on end and daydreaming on another when things went badly. When there was money, they would splurge on fine meals; when there was none they would stay in their tiny room, first near a temple in the Western Hills and later in a poor area of Beijing.[23] Shen Congwen, who had left his military life in western Hunan during 1923 and, determined to make his living as a writer, also drifted to Beijing, got to know the young couple in 1924, and described their lodgings as being similar to his own: "The bed is made of a hard wooden board; the earth floor is damp and musty. The walls are patched with old newspapers and the windows, pasted with paper, are covered with scratchy drawings." They also had the customary small private library of worn copies of translations—works on anarchism and revolution, Turgenev's *Fathers and Sons*, Dumas's *La Dame aux Camélias*, and Flaubert's *Madame Bovary* (which Ding Ling read again and again).[24]

Shen Congwen wrote of Ding Ling's character with perceptive affection:

> She showed a tendency toward quietness in her character and physical appearance, yet she had very strong emotions, sometimes unrestrained. The conflict between these two sides of her character, when apparent in her letters, appeared especially sincere and genuine. . . . She was not sociable and showed no talent in dealing with people at social gatherings as some women do. She did not know how to make conversation with strangers, but in front of old friends she could talk eloquently. She talked the way she wrote; whether at length or briefly, she always expressed herself clearly and never bored her listeners. In many ways she did not act like a woman, not having the usual feminine pretentiousness or the usual feminine delicacy. . . . Appreciating the ease between male friends, she wanted to enjoy that ease, too, and thus laid aside her femininity.[25]

The lack of social graces went along with the poverty, and most of Shen Congwen's own early stories from the mid-1920s dwelt on themes of social frustration and youthful malaise; but the young writers were able to help each other and to attract the attention of more established figures: for instance, Hu Yepin helped Shen place articles in the *Beijing News*, Xu Zhimo ran some of Shen's pieces in the *Morning News* along with Wen Yiduo's, and Shen also wrote for the same magazines as Lu Xun.[26]

Though Ding Ling, Hu Yepin, and Shen Congwen (the three had become inseparable friends by 1926) moved on the edge of university circles in Beijing, they do not seem to have played any part in the demonstrations of March 1926; nor were they forced to leave the city because of political pressure, as was the case with Lu Xun and Wen Yiduo. But once, when funds were running dangerously low, Ding Ling made a journey to Shanghai, hoping to get a job working in films; though she was unsuccessful, the visit gave her the incidental detail she needed to write her first story, "Meng Ke." It is the story of a provincial girl of that name, new to the city, patronized by urban relatives, and finally given a small part in a film in one of the big studios. In the course of the story Meng Ke meets hypocrisy or minor cruelty in various forms: rich girls, who sneer covertly at the poor, offer Meng Ke their stylish cast-off clothes; young radicals—who salute the startled Meng Ke as "China's Sofya"— preparing handbills and flags for a demonstration ask Meng Ke to join them before they know anything about her; a young student reads poetry to her and holds her hand although he is having an affair with someone else; the crass moguls at the studio who finally hire her treat her like an object. All this, refracted through the wide-eyed gaze of the Hunan girl Ding Ling had been only a few years before, proved irresistible to Shanghai readers, and the story was published late in 1927 in the prestigious *Fiction Monthly*.[27]

Perhaps what attracted readers most, and led to Ding Ling's instant success in a world jaded by war and violence and overcrowded with ambitious young writers trying to be both sensitive and modern, was her use of the cinema as a symbolic center for her story and her subtle linking of that symbol to elements in China's past. Midway through the story Meng Ke goes to the movies alone with a sophisticated young student, recently returned from a year in Paris. The movie that they see is a version of *La Dame aux Camélias* (which three years earlier, the reader is told, had made Meng Ke cry as she read it). Now that innocence disappears in the physical intimacy of the darkened theater, as Meng Ke sits pressed close to her friend amid the whispering couples.[28] A kind of Arcadia has been lost—as Meng Ke realizes also when she receives letters from her father describing the peaceful life in the rural area she has traded for Shanghai. When, at the end of the story, she goes off to get her first paying job (Nora leaving home at last, Lu Xun might have said), she is employed at a film studio, but this is not just any studio. In naming it the Full Moon Theater Company Ding Ling made an amusing comment on the bickerings between the Crescent Moon faction and their rivals: this, she is saying, is what we use today to shed our light.[29] And as Ding Ling ends her story, with the once retiring Meng Ke now known by her

stage name of Lin Lang, it is with a sideways look at the whole
Shanghai literary world, and with a sardonic echo of *A Call to
Arms*, the title chosen by Lu Xun for his first collection of
stories:

> And at present, probably in many newspapers and journals
> of a certain type, there must be quite a few of those self-ap-
> pointed literary giants of Shanghai, and dramatists, and
> directors, and critics, right down to their pitiable hangers-
> on issuing their own calls to arms, all using such phrases as
> "the most gorgeous woman" and "she who puts the moon
> and flowers to shame" as they make their claims to be rec-
> ognizing the talents of this Lin Lang despite her obscurity.
> For some, the reason they call her such an unparalleled and
> shimmering female star of the silver screen is that they
> would like to take advantage of her body so as to satisfy
> their own desires; for others, it is enough that they derive a
> certain satisfaction from being connected with her in some
> way.[30]

Within two months Ding Ling had finished another long
story, "Diary of Miss Sophie," which appeared in *Fiction
Monthly* in February 1928. This time Ding Ling's was one of the
five names featured on the magazine's cover. The title itself was
a brilliant choice, for the name initially evoked the heights of
revolutionary bravado as exemplified in the person of Sofya
Perovskaya—as the pre-1911 generation knew well, and as the
radicals had remembered in talking to Meng Ke in Ding Ling's
previous story. These echoes could then be distorted by Ding
Ling as she addressed new readers who had been children only,
if even born, at the time of the 1911 revolution. These readers
were growing, as young adults or adolescents, into a world
where revolution was becoming a euphemism for murderous
disappointment, and so the Sophie of 1928, as Ding Ling described her, was bored, ill, fretful, self-pitying, cruel, and emotionally uncontrolled. In a stream of first-person self-analysis,
as presented in the guise of diary entries between a certain December and March, we see a tubercular Sophie lying alone in a
small, mean room, wreaking her various vengeances against
those who love her. As in "Meng Ke" the cinema is an important motif, rendered pretentiously cosmic in the name of the

well-known Beijing theater to which Sophie goes, the Pure
Light Cinema. Just before entering it, however, Sophie is struck
with revulsion and abandons both her closest friends (who live,
suitably enough, in Youth Alley) and another group of young
women. In Ding Ling's powerful phrasing, Sophie saw the moment as follows: "It was still very early when we reached the
Pure Light, and in the lobby we ran into a group of young
women from my native place. How I loathed their compla-
cently smiling faces! I couldn't walk over and greet them, and
felt a rage beyond all reason at the sight of all those people
going to see the film." While her friends are momentarily distracted, Sophie slips away from the theater, to which *she* had
invited *them*, without even going in. She adds, in her diary,
"Nobody will be able to forgive me but myself."[31] By an irony
that Lu Xun would have liked, Sophie had read the advertise-
ment for the Pure Light Cinema among those for aphrodisiacs,
clothing sales, law-school courses, and "606," the venereal disease cure-all.[32] In 1918 Lu Xun had metaphorically suggested
"606" as a possible cure for China's deteriorated intellectual
state. For Ding Ling the prescription has been demoted to a
random spot in the back pages of a morning newspaper.
China's illness has become too generalized for any specific cure
to make sense.

Sophie's doubt is exacerbated by erotic longing, which she
dwells on but refuses to satisfy. "I feel there isn't any of him
that does not need the imprint of my lips," she writes of one
young man who calls on her. "I don't believe love can be rational and scientific," she writes of a couple who are in love but
sleep apart. "How is it that they don't feel the urge to embrace
each other's naked bodies?"[33] Sophie's own life, however,
lacks the fulfilled passion she criticizes others for avoiding, and
she is surrounded by inapposite memories: "The torn gloves.
The dresser drawer over there without perfume in it. The new
but strangely torn cotton gown, and the little old toys that have
been saved for so long."[34] The story ends, with ambiguous yet
startling force, after Sophie lets herself be kissed by the man
among her friends whom she finds the most handsome and
whom she despises the most:

After he was gone, I went over what had happened. I would like to tear out my heart and beat it with all my strength. Why could I endure the kisses of a man I despise? I do not love him, I mock him, yet I let him embrace me. Has this shell of a knight the power to pull me down so low?

In truth, it is I who have defiled myself, for one is one's own fiercest enemy. My heaven, how shall I begin to revenge and retrieve all I've lost? My life has been my own plaything; I've wasted so much of it already that it is of no material importance that this new experience has plunged me into a new abyss.

I don't want to stay in Beijing and I don't want to go to the Western Hills, I'm going to take the train southward, where no one knows me, and continue to waste what's left of my life. Out of the pain, my heart revives. And now I look on myself with pity and give a crazy laugh.

"Live and die your own way, unnoticed. Oh, how I pity you, Sophie!"[35]

With the success of this story in early 1928, Ding Ling and Hu Yepin (who had not been getting on together in Beijing) made their own way south, to Shanghai. There, in the next couple of years, she produced three volumes of short stories that consolidated her early fame. The stories almost all focused on the subject of women, and were narrated by women or related in diary form; they concerned women confronting the new society, trying, often unsuccessfully, to find a purpose in life, or else searching for something significant to write about. Sometimes they edged toward sharp social commentary: a young woman from a poor rural family is destroyed by her yearning for the life that she sees the rich live in their summer homes; a young prostitute's life is expressed through the daily humdrum details of her coping with a wearisome existence rather than through any high drama.[36] Yet Ding Ling stayed clear, during this period, of overt political statement, and made the sardonic point that at least for one man—Ou Waiou in her story "A Man and a Woman"—the sense of solidarity with his poor fellow creatures is stimulated only in those moments when he is walking through cold nights to an assignation with his lover, or with a prostitute, and sees the rickshaw men still waiting for their fares:

It is during those moments when he is walking, feeling lonely and suffering from the cold, that he can hate, hate the capitalists. It is in those moments that he can make himself feel like a revolutionary hero. It is not just for his own welfare that he feels revolution is necessary, not simply because he has no money with which to get married or to go to whorehouses. When he is walking on cold nights, he sees many rickshaw pullers in their worn-out shabby quilted clothes still running or looking for customers on the streets to make a little more money before they return to their wives and children. His conviction that the rich must be eliminated stems in a large part from seeing the rickshaw men. . . .[37]

While Ding Ling's writing flourished, that of Hu Yepin, with whom she was still living, went badly. His slight stories and poems had nothing to distinguish them in the competitive literary world. He had been given a job editing the literary page of the *Central Daily News*, and of another periodical, both of which he renamed the *Red and Black*. At the same time, he and Ding Ling formed their own little publishing company, the Red and Black Press, while Ding Ling and Shen Congwen founded yet another periodical, *The Human World*. The first volume of the press's grandly announced "Series of Collected Works" was a collection of Hu Yepin's poems. In a disarming preface to this little book (which was charmingly decorated with a red-and-black line on the front cover, a red-and-black semicircle—perhaps a sideways crescent moon?—on the back), Ding Ling wrote of their struggle to come up with enough money to publish fifty poems, and their final decision that they could print only twenty-two for now; the others would have to wait for a more favorable moment. Ding Ling wrote affectionately of Hu's being distracted from a life of poetry by his need to make a living, and of her inability to give him the leisure to write more poetry; she added that the task of selection was rendered more difficult by the fact that she was always drawn to choose those poems that he had originally written for her![38] But the book of nostalgic poems, even with Ding Ling's name on the title page, did not sell. The Red and Black Press folded, the magazine collapsed, Hu Yepin was replaced as editor. As he edged toward a socialist position, he began to read Lunacharsky and Plekhanov (in translation) and to write his own first novel, entitled *Moscow Bound;* in this short novel a young wife leaves her bourgeois husband after he has killed her Communist lover, and sets out to find a new life in the Soviet Union.[39] But writing was not bringing either of them much money, and to keep alive, Hu had to take some kind of a job— despite the success of Ding Ling's first two stories, the income they brought had been only about a hundred and forty dollars—and the one finally offered to him, which he accepted in late 1929, was as a high-school teacher in the city of Jinan, in Shandong province. Shen Congwen, also broke, got a job teaching in Wuhan.[40]

When Ding Ling, lonely and moody on her own in Shanghai, traveled to Shandong in the spring of 1930 to be with Hu, she wrote later, she was astonished: "I found him a different person. . . . He was the most radical man in the high school. All day long he preached Marxist historical materialism, Marxist literary theories translated by Lu Xun and Feng Xuefeng, and proletarian literature. When I saw him, still so young, surrounded and trusted by so many students, and talking calmly, confidently, and firmly, I was filled with indescribable joy."[41]

To be making such a public Communist commitment in such a year was a difficult and courageous act. The Communist Party was in disarray after the savage blows of 1927, and so dangerous had the situation become by 1928 that the sixth annual congress of the party had to be held in Moscow, the first time it had been convened outside China since the party's founding in 1921. At the Moscow meetings Qu Qiubai, who had criticized Chen Duxiu so violently for the "right-wing opportunism" of his alliance with the Guomindang, was now stripped of his senior party posts on the grounds of the "left-wing opportunism" of his urban and rural insurrections in late 1927 (both policies having been ordered initially by Stalin). While Qu stayed on in Moscow to study and write an analysis of the Chinese revolution, the party continued to move in three separate directions: the newly elected secretary-general (one of the few men in the hierarchy who had ever been an industrial worker) tried to hold the shattered union organizations together and keep some kind of power in the cities; the chief of his Propaganda Department, Li Lisan, worked hard to implement the stated Comintern policy of using an aroused peasantry and Chinese Red Army units to support proletarian risings against the Guomindang—this led to major Communist attacks on the cities of Changsha and Nanchang in the summer of 1930, though neither was successful; and Mao Zedong, though he did obey party orders to bring his troops into the Nanchang campaign for a brief period, consolidated his position in the mountainous and sparsely inhabited terrain between the borders of Jiangxi and Fujian provinces.[42]

Incessant foreign and Guomindang repression meant that the party continued to lose valued members: Ding Ling's friend Xiang Jingyu, who had been a leader among the women students sent to France in 1919, and had helped to organize the women workers in Shanghai before the May Thirtieth Movement of 1925, was arrested in the French concession of Hankou; after she led a hunger strike in the prison there, she was handed over to the Guomindang police and executed on May 1, 1928. Xiang's husband, Cai Hesen, who had been Mao's close friend at school in Changsha, was arrested by British police in Hong Kong and also handed over to the Chinese authorities there and killed. And Mao Zedong's young wife, Yang Kaihui, the daughter of his ethics teacher Yang Changji, and also one of Ding Ling's former schoolmates, was arrested with her two children after the failure of the 1930 attack on Changsha, and was shot.[43]

These arrests and executions were symptomatic of the Guomindang's control over the country; the Northern Expedition, after a hiatus in 1927, had been resumed in 1928 and brought to a conclusion in December of that year when troops loyal to Chiang Kaishek occupied Beijing and Zhang Zuolin's son (who had succeeded his father as the warlord controlling Manchuria) pledged his allegiance to the newly constituted National Government in Nanjing. Though Chiang Kaishek's power was regularly threatened by rival politicians in the Guomindang or by militarists allied with him, there was no successful challenge to his basic premise that the Communists must be eradicated as a political force before China could turn her attention to the problems of foreign imperialism (especially the constantly growing pressures from Japan). Chiang, like President Yuan Shikai before him in the early years of the Republic, was seeking to centralize his government and to modernize the economy, industry, education, and the army; and in some sense the Communists were to him what the Guomindang had been to Yuan: a political party of broadly based popular appeal whose demands for social justice, even if honestly put, had to be suppressed if they seemed to interfere with the public order that centralization demanded. Now, as before, the Japanese represented a very real threat that had to be placated until domestic dissidence was quelled.

Like Yuan, too, Chiang had a fairly shaky base in terms of territory, finance, and constitutional powers. Already commander of the Northern Expeditionary armies, he was named chairman of the Central Political Council in March 1928; in October of that year he was also appointed chairman of the National Government at Nanjing, with supervisory powers over the five branches into which the Chinese government had now been reorganized; but these titles were only as strong as he made them. Some of his power came from the army, and especially from the ranks of the cadets trained at Whampoa Military Academy, who regarded him as their personal leader. Other elements of support came from the political machine of the Guomindang training school, which was run by Chiang's closest associates in Nanjing. Yet others came from the factional alliances cemented by his marriage, at the end of 1927, into the powerful Soong family, which was linked, through education and Christianity, to the American and Chinese business establishments. Chiang's wife, Soong Meiling, had been educated at Wellesley College; one of her sisters had been married to Sun Yatsen and another to the financier H. H. Kung, a graduate of Oberlin and Yale; her brother, T. V. Soong, a Harvard graduate, had been director of the Guangzhou Bank under Sun Yatsen and was minister of finance for the Guomindang. Further power accrued to Chiang through connections with secret-society and underworld organizations in Shanghai; in the 1930s he consolidated power further by developing the elite Guomindang paramilitary organization of Blue Shirts and coordinating these supporters through the Guomindang secret-police apparatus.[44]

As anti-Communist repression became commonplace in Guomindang China, more and more Communist intellectuals congregated in Shanghai; in the International Settlement areas, despite what Lu Xun might say and despite the dangers of arrest and extradition, life was still far safer than in other Guomindang-controlled cities; also, the major industrial enterprises, the universities, the major publishing houses, and various newspapers and periodicals all gave encouragement and sustenance to Communist Party members. So it was back to Shanghai that Ding Ling and Hu Yepin fled when they were warned that his activities in Shandong were about to lead to his arrest. Here Hu Yepin plunged into a mass of party-related activities and was finally admitted to membership in November 1930. He became an energetic member of the League of Left-Wing Writers, a new consolidated organization that aimed to end the bickering between radical factions by drawing together the members of the Creation Society with those of a number of other leftist groups in which Lu Xun and others had once been active. Though Lu Xun did not join the party, he became a powerful spokesman for the League of Left-Wing Writers, as did Qu Qiubai, when he returned from Moscow that winter.[45]

If the intellectuals tended to bunch in Shanghai, the future hope for the Communist Party nonetheless lay mainly in remote rural areas where various Red Army groups had managed to establish soviets, carry through programs of land redistribution, and revolutionize family life by imposing new marriage laws that permitted free choice of partners and divorce to women. The largest of the eight soviets in existence in 1930 was the one known as the Jiangxi Soviet—on the mountainous borders between Jiangxi and Fujian provinces—which Mao Zedong had been largely responsible for establishing and preserving in the face of repeated Guomindang-led attacks. After Hu Yepin was elected to the executive committee of the League of Left-Wing Writers, he was also named as one of its delegates to a forthcoming congress in the Jiangxi Soviet.

Struck by what he had heard of the breakdown of traditional marriage customs in the Jiangxi Soviet after the party's dramatic August 1930 decree concerning sexual freedom, Hu wrote a brisk and cheerful story, "Living Together," about a peasant woman's decision to leave her husband of ten years and her two children to live with another man on the soviet. It is a story without climax, without tension, for the abandoned husband accepts the situation gracefully after being consoled by the president of the people's committee. As Hu described this new world:

> Conditions now are vastly changed. Men who were once harassed and poverty-stricken have become lively and merry. Even more striking is the gaiety and vivacity of the women. They used to live shut up in impoverished homes, going through the futile round of cooking, washing, caring for the children, feeding the pigs—shut up like prisoners in a jail without a ray of hope for the future. Now they are like birds soaring in the sky. Their life has become free. They are no longer persecuted or oppressed. Nor do they fear their husbands any more. They can make contacts with men as they choose. More than that, they are free to go with comrades to register at the district soviet, and so embark formally on a common life together. Even for the children to whom they give birth there is the provision of public care, so that the women are relieved of personal worry.[46]

In another story, written that same autumn or winter of 1930, Hu Yepin described a revolutionary young couple's decision to have an abortion rather than let a child interfere with their own political work. Again, there is no tension in the story, for the wife gladly accedes to the decision:

> "Don't feel sorry," she took his hand and said. "We do love each other. You are not to be blamed; you have already exercised enough self-control. I am responsible for it. Of course, if the circumstances were other than they are, the child should be brought up. But now, even though we could afford to bring it up, we should not allow it to see the light. Once there is a baby, our work will be hindered. We cannot have the baby."[47]

Whether there was tension in real life is a different matter, since throughout the spring and summer of 1930 Ding Ling was carrying Hu's child, and she gave birth to a boy in November. Almost all the short stories she wrote that year, as well as her novella, *Shanghai, Spring 1930*, hinged around the theme of a couple torn between a life of service to a revolutionary cause and a life of ordinary work and leisure inside the legally con-. stituted framework of society. Sometimes the man, and sometimes the woman, plays the revolutionary role, and it is possible to see in various stories echoes of Ding Ling's childhood friend Wang Jianhong (who had died so young while living with Qu Qiubai in 1924) as well as of her own predicament.[48] Undoubtedly Ding Ling herself began to query both the point of her present life and the significance of her current writing, for there is so much force in the long monologue by one of the characters in *Shanghai, Spring 1930* that it can surely be seen as an expression of her own deeply felt emotions:

As for writing, I sometimes feel that it would not be much of a loss if we gave it up entirely. We write, some people read, time passes, and there is no effect whatsoever. What is the meaning of it, then, except we've gotten paid for it? Even if some readers are moved by part of the plot or certain passages of writing—but who are these readers? Students of the petty-bourgeois class above high-school level who have just reached adolescence are most subject to melancholy. They feel that these writings fit their temper perfectly, expressing some melancholy they can feel but not really experience. . . . But in the end? Now I understand we have only done something harmful, we have dragged these young people down our old paths. The sort of sentimentalism, individualism, grumblings, and sorrows with no way out! . . . Where is the way out for them? They can only sink deeper and deeper day by day into their own gloom, not seeing the connection between society and their sufferings. Even if they could improve their language and produce some essays and poems that might win praise from some old writers, what good, I ask you, would it be to them? And what good to society? Therefore, with regard to writing, personally I am ready to give it up.[49]

From the summer of 1930 onward, Hu Yepin was secretive about the meetings he was attending in Shanghai. Ding Ling knew neither the agendas nor the locations, except that on occasion Qu Qiubai (living under an assumed name, and constantly changing his lodgings) was in attendance and that sometimes the Communists met on the third floor of a large town house with the windows sealed, while downstairs, for cover, an elaborate charade of a wealthy family's leisure afternoon, with games of Mah-Jongg and phonograph playing, was meticulously maintained.[50] On January 17, 1931, Hu went to yet another meeting. This one, at the Eastern Hotel on the Avenue Edward VII in the International Settlement, had been convened to discuss plans for the upcoming conference of delegates to be held in the Jiangxi Soviet later that year, and those attending were Communist writers and cadres of varying seniority. Security should have been very tight, since Chiang Kaishek's troops were currently engaged in a major campaign to smash the soviet, and even getting to Jiangxi would have been extremely dangerous; nevertheless somebody leaked the location of the Shanghai meeting, and perhaps a hint of the agenda, to the police in the International Settlement. (Rumors have persisted to this day that a fourth faction within the Communist Party, Comintern-backed and with a fresh Chinese leadership back from Moscow, tipped off the police so as to rid themselves of unwanted rivals.) The police raided the Eastern Hotel, arrested thirty-six of the meeting's participants (twenty-nine men and seven women), and handed them over to the Guomindang forces. After being manacled, the prisoners were sent down to the Shanghai-Wusong garrison command headquarters at Longhua, south of the city. A famous beauty spot— Xu Zhimo had visited there in springtime, after his marriage to Lu Xiaoman, and viewed the blossoms on the flowering peach trees—this was also the Guomindang marshaling area for arrested political prisoners.[51]

For a time there was confusion among the other radicals in Shanghai, since no one was sure how many people had been arrested, or for what. When Lu Xun heard the news—he was a close friend of one of those arrested—he burned much of his correspondence and moved, without telling anyone, with Xu Guangping and their baby to a hotel.[52] Shen Congwen had been planning to meet Hu that afternoon; when Hu didn't appear, Shen went to check with Ding Ling, and later they learned what had happened. The next three weeks were a nightmare of frenzied activity for both of them. Hu managed to smuggle a note out of prison begging for help, and they tried a whole range of friends and contacts—from Xu Zhimo and Cai Yuanpei to Chiang Kaishek's close aides and confidants Zhang Qun and Chen Lifu—in an attempt to procure Hu's release.[53] Their money trickled away in a ceaseless flow of small bribes and payments to messengers and intermediaries, but they could get no definite commitments of support. One freezing winter day, following up on a tip, they dressed as country folk and went down to Longhua, hoping to be allowed to see Hu, only to be told by the guards that Hu was in a special security category and had no visiting rights. Just before leaving they did catch a glimpse of him, and he of them. Hu raised his manacled hands to them in an ironical salute and Ding Ling, turning to Shen Congwen, said, "It's he, he seems happy, how brave he is, still like a young leopard!"[54] They did not get to see him again, and a few days later they learned that on the night of February 7 twenty-three of the arrested Communists had been executed by firing squad at Longhua. Among them was Hu Yepin. No public announcement was made of the executions, nor did any of the Shanghai newspapers carry the story. "Perhaps they didn't want to, or didn't think it worthwhile," wrote Lu Xun.[55]

In a novel finished just before his death, *Light Is Ahead of Us*, Hu Yepin had concentrated on the lives of three groups of characters set in the context of the May Thirtieth Movement of 1925: those already in the Communist Party; those whose socialism led them in a utopian or anarchist direction; and ivory-tower writers who believed in art for art's sake as opposed to the tenets of socialist realism. In the novel's resolution the latter two groups see their errors: the utopian socialists join the party and step out into "the bright sunshine"; the poetess, "pretty as a rose," who had, however, only written verses such as "Beautiful dreams are no more" and "Please kiss me again," finally begins to "emit red-hot flames" and persuades her ivory-tower novelist husband to join her in editing a new radical review, the *Blood Flower Weekly*.[56]

Xu Zhimo, however, underwent no such conversions; nor did his wife, Lu Xiaoman. The nearest he came to developing a formal social philosophy was in his espousal of the principles of shared craft-labor and companionship as exemplified by his English friend Leonard Elmhirst at Dartington Hall in Devonshire, and by Rabindranath Tagore at the community (established with Elmhirst's help) of Surul at Santiniketan. Xu visited both places in the summer and autumn of 1928, and wrote warmly to Elmhirst, in English:

> It would be interesting to compare Surul and Dartington. Both are your creation and both are inspired by the same ideals and worked out with a thoroughness all your own. Yet the impression I have of the one differs greatly from that of the other. Dartington as I once said is yet the nearest approach to an Utopia that I know. Nature is more kind and with love as the motivating force of your endeavour you are sure to reap a harvest of poetry wholly unadulterated with harsh notes. But the Indian soil is a different story altogether. Here Nature is as unkind as she is unyielding and, unless he is equipped with a knowledge as well as a resolute will necessary for his struggle for existence, man can scarcely hope to survive. The other day I stood for a long time contemplating the ruins of that deserted village where only 25 families are now left of once 500, and was touched with pity. Surul as a farming experiment is of course fairly established and with men like Lal, who I like very much, running it has yet a larger future before it. And yet what patience, what heroic effort, what sacrifice will be necessary for this great task of reconstruction which you have so admirably initiated and which nevertheless is barely begun considering the vastness of the country and even harder conditions elsewhere![57]

At the beginning of 1929 Xu was still hoping that he could, with Elmhirst's financial backing, set up some kind of similar community in China, perhaps in Zhejiang province; there, he felt, one could find people who "still retain some beauty of character which comes of close contact with nature and is yet unspoiled by modern influences."[58] But by March 1929 he had fallen into a deep depression and saw little hope that his plans could be realized. One contributing factor to his sadness was the death of Liang Qichao, which came on January 19 after a battle with kidney failure that had lasted many years. Liang, wrote Xu, had been "a much greater man than any of his contemporaries," for he had been at once a superb scholar and a perfect interpreter of Chinese traditional values; his great importance had lain "in effecting through one man's effort a complete mental revolution without which the last political one would have been impossible."[59] "It is an irretrievable loss to me," mourned Xu. Perhaps he was mindful of the verbal chastening he had received from Liang in 1923 when he insisted on pursuing Lin Huiyin, and in 1926 when he pressed on with his marriage to Lu Xiaoman. There was a touching paradox here, for it was Lin Huiyin, now Liang Qichao's daughter-in-law, who had looked after the dying man in his last months, while Xu's own marriage to Lu Xiaoman seemed to involve him either in rounds of unwelcome social engagements or in her endless petty maladies and casual extravagances. Xu's lengthy journeys abroad were all undertaken without her, and it was not long before she had plunged into the demimonde of the theater and was reputed to have taken a new lover.[60] Besides this, the battles within literary Shanghai over the issue of socialist realism versus aestheticism of differing kinds were wearisome: serious though both Xu Zhimo and his friend Wen Yiduo were about questions of style and the need for perfect form in art, and accomplished though their own work was, the controversies were enervating; after 1928 Wen Yiduo withdrew from poetry and painting into the world of classical scholarship. He did write one final poem, in 1930, at Xu Zhimo's request, but its central portion contained a haunting (and for Wen, definitive) skepticism about the work they had been engaged in:

> Who doesn't know
> How little these things are worth:
> A tree full of singing cicadas, a pot of common wine.
> Even the mention of misty mountains, valleys at dawn,
>   or glittering starry skies,
> Is no less commonplace, most worthlessly commonplace.

> *They do not deserve*
> *Our ecstatic surprise, our effort to call them in touching terms,*
> *Our anxiety to coin golden phrases to cast them in song.*
> *I, too, would say that to burst into tears because of*
> *an oriole's song*
> *Is too futile, too impertinent, too wasteful.*[61]

Xu's name had already been dropped from the masthead of his own *Crescent Moon* journal by more politically minded colleagues. Now, with Wen falling silent, he would have to content himself with the praise of young admirers.[62]

The Chinese scene depressed Xu Zhimo more deeply the more carefully he examined it. As he wrote to Elmhirst, again in English, in March 1929:

> All the more am I prone to a painful sense of nostalgia finding, as I cannot help finding, what daily surrounds me here: sordidness instead of nobility, hostility and mutual destructiveness rather than fellowship and cooperation, dead and infectious dogmas, not living principles, run wild, like stalking corpses, to plunge the whole nation into yet greater disaster and suppress the creative fountain of human spirit! Meanwhile whole provinces are dragging on in simply incredible conditions of existence. I myself have had glimpses of the starving North and my blood chills with the mere thought of it. Children that look no longer human actually fight over lichen and mosses that their bony fingers scratch off from the crevices of rocks and stuff into their mouths, in their desperate effort to assuage excruciating hunger and cold! Lord, wherefore such were caused to be born![63]

Yet he continued to write, sometimes dark and heroic intimations of death, sometimes visionary essays on the joys of flying, recalling what he had written of d'Annunzio when he first read him in 1925—"like the stormy sea that howls infinite profundities in the solitude of space; it is like clouds, enveloping earth"—as he urged onward his own dream of "soaring up in the sky to watch the earth roll like a ball in infinite space."[64] It was surely consonant with his own views concerning the untrammeled heart, and also perhaps with his realization that he was, at the age of thirty-four, China's most famous writer apart from Lu Xun (not to mention the fact that an admiring airline executive had given him a free pass), that he became a lover of flight, commuting between Nanjing, Shanghai, and Beijing for his various lecture and teaching assignments. The planes went with his passions, which he had now learned to express in deeper, stronger language. As he wrote in a poem (which, he noted, was completed at six in the evening of Christmas Day, 1930):

> *I looked only for a more enduring*
> *Measure of time to receive my breath,*
> *When the glittering stars should be my eyes,*
> *My hair, a sheen at the sky's edge,*
> *The disarray of the tinted clouds,*
> *And my arms, my breast, borne on the wind's*
> *Whirling, free against my brow,*
> *And the waves dashing my legs, from each*
> *Surging, rising a mystic aura.*
> *With these, the lightning for my thought,*
> *Flashing its dragon-dance on the horizon,*
> *My voice the thunder, suddenly breaking*
> *To wake the spring, to wake new life.*
> *Ah, beyond thought, beyond compare*
> *Is the inspiration, the power of love.*[65]

But flying remained a risky business in these early days of civil aviation in China. For instance, a small chartered plane en route from Nanjing to Beijing on November 19, 1931, smashed into the side of a mountain near Jinan, in Shandong province, in a heavy fog, and the lone passenger and the crew were killed. The passenger was Xu Zhimo.[66]

28. Rabindranath Tagore, with hand on Xu Zhimo's shoulder, and Leonard Elmhirst of Dartington Hall, in Beijing, 1924. (A friend's two children stand with them.)

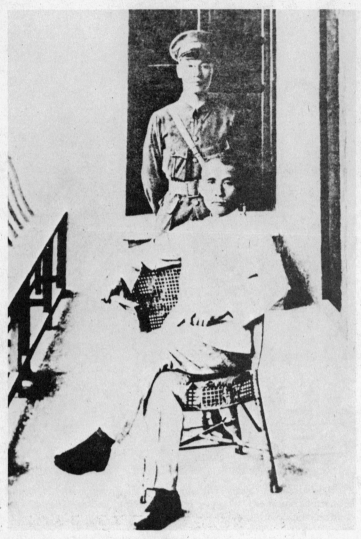

29. Sun Yatsen (seated) and Chiang Kaishek at the opening of Whampoa Military Academy, June 1924

30. Wen Yiduo as a student at the time of the May Fourth Movement

31. Mao Zedong in 1927

32. *Demonstration*, woodcut by Ye Fu

33. Xu Zhimo with Lu Xiaoman at their wedding in Beijing, October 3, 1926

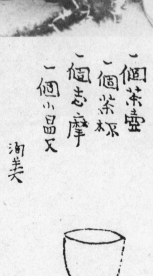

34. Drawing by Shao Xunmei, made after the wedding of Xu Zhimo and Lu Xiaoman. It is inscribed, "A teapot, a teacup; a Zhimo, a Xiaoman."

35. Xu Zhimo, around 1927

36. *Famine Survivors*, woodcut by Duan Ganqing

37. Lu Xun with his son, September 25, 1930. Lu Xun inscribed this, "Hai Ying and Lu Xun: aged one and fifty"

38. Lu Xun with Xu Guangping in Guangzhou, September 11, 1927

·9·

FAREWELL TO THE
BEAUTIFUL THINGS

"The China Aviation Company has dropped a bomb on the world of letters," wrote one high-school student in Tianjin after hearing the news of Xu Zhimo's death. "Who could have guessed that the poet-sage Mr. Xu would meet with death in the sky? It must be that God has erred, for in his lower realm he forgot to protect our most treasured poet; he destroyed our finest artist. Our poet-sage Mr. Xu is dead! It is a tragedy for Chinese culture, a tragedy for the poets coming after!" There were other fine Chinese poets, the young mourner acknowledged, but they had not held to their craft. They had drifted off into the world of philosophy, or sociology, or else lost their spirit, or remained immature. Xu alone had persevered, had struggled on, to end in death and immortality: "China now has her Mr. Xu as England has her Shelley. The question remains: whither has sped this bright lantern that shone above our circle of poets?"[1] But if such young men were distraught, and saw in Xu's death the end of a dream of pure and romantic individualism, others of Xu's generation were less moved. As Wen Yiduo put it (despite the years he had worked with Xu, and the works of his that Xu had helped to publish), Xu's entire life had "consisted of romantic stories. What can I write about him?"[2]

In terms of the times, it was Hu Yepin's death that seemed to pose the deeper questions. If Hu's revolutionary commitment had had something both casual and sentimental about it, his death brought him a new dignity. Lu Xun saluted Hu and the other Communists executed with him by reproducing a woodcut by Käthe Kollwitz—one called *Sacrifice*, in which a grieving mother is pictured giving up her son—in *Big Dipper*, a magazine of the League of Left-Wing Writers.[3] And in an essay in memory of the group of young martyrs, Lu Xun pointed out the irony that in China it always seemed to be the old who wrote the obituaries of the young, rather than the other way around. "During the last thirty years with my own eyes I have seen the blood of so many young people mounting up that now I am submerged and cannot breathe. All I can do is take up my pen and write a few articles, as if to make a hole in the clotted blood through which I can draw a few more wretched breaths. What sort of world is this? The night is so long, the way so long, that I had better forget or else remain silent."[4]

Yet Lu Xun did not cease to believe in the power of the pen, even though he saw both the fundamental difficulties of being a writer and the temptation to abandon an idealist political position. As he had told a gathering of the League of Left-Wing Writers in the spring of 1930:

> In my view, it is very easy for "left-wing" writers today to turn into "right-wing" writers. First of all, if you simply shut yourself up behind the windows of your study instead of keeping in touch with actual social conflicts, it is easy for you to be extremely radical, or "left." But the moment you come up against reality all your ideas are shattered. Behind closed doors it is very easy to spout radical ideas, but equally easy to turn "rightist." This is what is meant in the West by "salon socialists." . . . It is easy to become "right-wing" if you do not understand the actual nature of revolution. Revolution is a bitter thing, mixed with filth and blood, not so lovely or perfect as the poets think. It is eminently down-to-earth, involving many humble, tiresome tasks, not so romantic as the poets think. Of course there is destruction in a revolution, but construction is even more necessary to it; and while destruction is simple, construction is troublesome. So it is easy for all who have romantic dreams about revolution to become disillusioned on closer acquaintance, when a revolution is actually carried out.[5]

Such reflections led Lu Xun to try to define more accurately what valid social realism should be. He knew that exaggeration only led to ridiculous results and that petty-bourgeois writers and artists should not strive for false effect: "I personally think proletarians should be drawn realistically, just as they are—there is no need to make their fists bigger than their heads." He knew, too, that "none of our left-wing writers is of worker or peasant origin. One reason is that peasants and workers have always been too oppressed and ground down to have a chance to get any education. Another is that the Chinese ideographs—no longer recognizable for what they represent—make it impossible for workers and peasants to express themselves freely in writing even after ten years of study." The place of intellectuals in such a situation was obviously ambiguous, and Lu Xun felt that bourgeois writers would inevitably have a limited role in view of the current development of their consciousness; hence "the best we can hope for is the appearance of works showing the revolt of the petty bourgeoisie against their own class, or works that serve as exposés."[6]

It is not surprising that after his return from Moscow in 1931, Qu Qiubai should have become an ally of Lu Xun's and eventually a close friend. Now dismissed from his senior posts in the Communist Party, though still influential because of his knowledge of the Russian language and of Soviet politics, Qu had spent years on problems of literacy and language in the Chinese context, and had passed much of his time in Moscow drawing up plans to develop a phonetic script for Chinese so that a true proletarian literature would become possible. He joined with Lu Xun in attacking the shallowness of those who tried to prove that a valid national literary movement could take place under the Guomindang banner, and he insisted that literature remain a "fighting tool."[7] Yet Qu's disillusionment with the "Western" interpretations that Comintern agents insisted on giving to elements of the Chinese revolution grew so pronounced that it led him to reformulate the rejection of Western elements in China's new culture movement that he had originally aimed at Xu Zhimo in 1924. The vaunted vernacular (*baihua*) in which intellectuals were now writing was still inaccessible to the masses, since it retained old classical elements with an admixture of European grammatical structures and even vocabulary; the "new classical" language (*xin wenyan*) was controlled by (and gave control to) the elite, just as the old classical language had been:

> A Great Wall surrounds the working people, forming a barricade that completely cuts them off from cultural life. What is this Great Wall? It is simply the new classical language of the May Fourth period (the so-called *baihua* literature of today). Regardless of how much it is popularized, so long as it rests on the foundation of new classical language, all the scientific and artistic knowledge of the new period will only be able to reach ten or twenty thousand intellectual youth.[8]

Not only could the masses not read the works of Xu Zhimo, said Qu, but they were untouched by modern "revolutionary" writings as well. Qu put such arguments with formidable vigor, as in his own preface to a "proletarian" novel entitled *Spring*, written by a member of the League of Left-Wing Writers, which failed "even to achieve the goal of commonplace realism" and hence could not help readers "understand" the world, let alone "transform" it. Qu's conclusion was that such books nevertheless might advance the cause of revolution, and there was no need for writers to hold back. "Of course art cannot effect a transformation of the social system, and must be regarded from beginning to end as being regulated by the mode of production and class relations. But art can also influence social life, and *to a certain degree* advance or block the development of class struggle, changing somewhat the conditions of this struggle, and adding to or weakening the power of a given class."[9]

Qu's critique may have struck Lu Xun with particular force, since Lu's own writing style was difficult, filled with subtle phrasing and allusions, and more and more divorced from any accessible narrative line. Indeed, the novelist whom Qu most admired, Mao Dun, had noted regretfully that Lu Xun wrote only of "old villages" and that his landscapes had no big cities in them, nothing of the "beating hearts of city youth."[10] Perhaps for this reason Lu Xun devoted a great amount of time to the visual arts; he was especially drawn to the forceful simplicity and immediacy of the cartoon and the woodblock print, which he had long admired and now began to sponsor vigorously through the League of Left-Wing Artists, founded in the summer of 1930. Thus in the very years when he was debating lengthily with Qu Qiubai over Soviet literary theory and the Chinese proletarian position (and often sheltering Qu in his own home from the dangerous sweeps of the Guomindang police), Lu Xun was spending large sums of his own money in encouraging young artists to develop this powerful and direct means of visual communication in workshops and exhibits.[11]

Ding Ling's own response to the tragedy of Hu Yepin's death was to reaffirm the commitment that Hu had made. Borrowing money from friends in Shanghai she and Shen Congwen traveled across China to her mother's home in western Hunan. Just as Kang Youwei had concealed his brother's execution from their mother in 1898, so now did Ding Ling hide the truth about Hu Yepin's death from hers; entering into a complex charade with Shen Congwen, she arranged for letters in a copy of Hu Yepin's handwriting to be sent to Hunan, assuring the old lady that Hu was well and that she should have no anxieties about her family in Shanghai. Pretending that she was about to go on a long journey with Hu, Ding Ling persuaded her mother to look after the baby in their absence. After three days of intense and emotionally charged conversation with her mother, in which they ranged over memories of their life together before the May Fourth Movement and the changes that had taken place since then in the rural world and in their extended family, Ding Ling returned without her baby to Shanghai.[12]

In a short story written just after her return to Shanghai, in the summer of 1931, entitled "One Certain Night," she not only confronted the emotions aroused by Hu Yepin's death directly but also proved how far she herself had moved from simple optimism about the revolutionary cause. The story describes a small group of men and women prisoners as, chained together, they trudge through biting snow and wind to their last destination, stakes fixed in the cold ground. Though they have a chance to exchange final glances of trust and love, machine-gun fire drowns out their voices before they can finish the opening stanza of the "Internationale." In her closing words, "The night was ugly and forbidding. The huge snowflakes and the fine sleet drifted through. The wild wind of winter roared by, only to come roaring back again. The snow piled up on the hanging heads, to be blown off again by the gale. They were all dumb and motionless, fastened there. In some spots—in one, in two, in three spots—the blood trickled down and mottled the snow in the darkness. Will the sky ever grow light?"[13] Leftist readers responded enthusiastically: the League of Left-Wing Writers made her a member of their standing committee, she was appointed editor of one of the league's magazines, the *Big Dipper*, and head of the department of the league in charge of workers' and peasants' literature. Early in 1932 she joined the Communist Party.[14]

The experiences of Ding Ling during this period show how she struggled to find modes of expression that would give her own life some significance. Shortly after returning from Hunan in the spring of 1931, she gave an informal talk to the students at Guanghua University, in which she ranged over her past and her aspirations. Hu Yepin's death she referred to as "a certain unhappy experience," but she vigorously denied that it would make her retreat from society into a world of personal grief, or that it would make her stop writing—though she felt that much of her more recent work had not been successful. She did not feel that a writer should deal only with personal experiences, she told the students, but did set certain limits on what she felt she would attempt:

> I am certainly not going to write any more about love; I've recently been writing about things that have nothing to do with it. Nor do I want to write about workers or peasants, for I am neither a worker nor a peasant. So what can I write about? It occurred to me that most of my readers come from the ranks of the students, so that the content of my future writings should be directed toward them. It would not be any good for me to write about workers and peasants, but there is plenty of other material to write about in human society. I think I will write a long novel drawing on the material of my own family background.[15]

The novel that began to take shape in her mind was to be called, simply, *Mother* and would span the period from the last years of the Qing dynasty through the revolution of 1927, following the fate of her own mother within the context of their own enormous extended-family organization in Hunan province (which altogether embraced more than three thousand people scattered among numerous households). She wrote to her editor that she believed such a book would come out at three hundred thousand words and that she could write it at a speed of a thousand words a day, finishing the whole book in ten months. She intended to include in the novel details of rural tensions between peasants and landlords, the changes brought into small towns by the mechanization of local industries, and the effect on society of modern means of communication and aspects of modern commerce.[16]

In feeling ready to tackle such major themes in the form of a lengthy novel, Ding Ling was riding a new but dominant current. If the 1920s had been the time of the most extensive and successful experimentation with lyric verse forms and the short story, so the early 1930s was the great period of the emerging modern novel. Ba Jin's moving tale of three brothers' adaptation (or lack of it) to the pressures of modernization and marriage patterns in his home province of Sichuan, *Family*, had appeared in 1931. Mao Dun's massive Zolalike novel of the financial world of Shanghai, *Midnight*, appeared in 1933. Shen Congwen's poignant attempt to order his thoughts around the river life of western Hunan, where he had grown up and then been garrisoned as a soldier, appeared in 1934 as *Border Town*.

It was as if the dramas of the times were now taking place on such a massive scale that writers could find satisfaction only by striving for a similar grandeur. For as individual hopes continued to ebb, so the meaning of individual action in the political sphere seemed to diminish. In 1925 Lu Xun had gently chided Xu Guangping for thinking that students might affect foreign imperialists, but by 1932 his skepticism had been justified a dozen times. The Japanese, in particular, were stepping up the pace of their military and commercial involvement in the three areas of Manchuria, Shandong province, and Shanghai. Japanese army officers in China often acted independently of

Tokyo in their determination to force the Chinese into angry responses that would in turn justify further Japanese aggression; similarly, Japanese business firms on Chinese soil, even though they did not always make as much profit as was generally believed, pushed Chinese toleration to the limits by monopolizing sources of raw materials, exploiting Chinese labor, and demanding a wide range of preferential economic treatment that could only hurt Chinese manufacturers. Japanese officers directed the assassination of the Manchurian warlord Zhang Zuolin in 1928, and their armies in Shandong forced a major detour on the Northern Expedition's troops in that same year. In 1931 an alleged attack on Japanese troops by a Chinese unit near Mukden led to the occupation of large areas of Manchuria by the Japanese Army. In January 1932, Japanese forces invaded Shanghai and occupied part of the city following strikes and anti-Japanese riots; they withdrew only after unexpectedly bitter fighting by Chinese troops had inflicted heavy casualties. The Japanese also invited the ex-Emperor Puyi to leave his refuge in Tianjin to become the first "chief executive" of the state of Manchukuo, as Manchuria was now renamed. He agreed in March 1932, and after two years in office he was elevated to Emperor (this now being the third time, after 1908 and 1917, that he had assumed that title).[17]

It was during this period of the early 1930s that the Guomindang, under Chiang Kaishek's direction, made the fateful decision to suppress the sense of national outrage as best it could, fearing that new demonstrations by students or workers would only bring further reprisals from the Japanese or other foreign powers. Thus Chiang struck not only at the Communists but also at the new generation of liberal, often Western-educated or Western-influenced students, and moved his party back in the direction of a moralistic and simplified brand of Confucian authoritarianism, which he enforced through his ever-growing police and internal-security forces. Partly for this reason, and partly because of older antagonisms among Sun Yatsen's original band of followers from the days of the Revolutionary Alliance, Chiang Kaishek's power was never unquestioned, either within his party or among his military allies, who continued to dominate much of northern and western China. In 1930 Chiang faced a civil war with previously allied generals in northern China; in 1931 he was threatened both with a bolt from the right wing of the Guomindang and with the possible formation of an independent regime in Guangzhou; and during 1933 a major rising by dissident Nationalists erupted in Fujian province.

Chiang's survival was helped by the fact that the Communist forces themselves were fragmented and their leadership divided. Though the Comintern dominated the party in Shanghai until 1933, its generally urban orientation eventually proved inadequate, and power shifted to the Jiangxi rural base area, where Mao Zedong was de facto leader. But the Jiangxi Soviet was only one of several Communist bases scattered in the provinces of Guangxi, Hunan, Sichuan, Hebei, and Shaanxi, each of which had its own leaders and policies. Even in Jiangxi, moreover, there were constant minor shifts of line concerning how much violence should be permitted toward landlords, the pace at which land redistribution should proceed, the way that various subgroupings within the peasantry should be defined in class terms, and which repressive measures and guerrilla organizations should be used to withstand the regular Guomindang counterattacks.[18]

In the face of such developments, one response was to seize the tragic absurdity of the moment, and one of those who did this with the greatest brilliance was the novelist Lao She. Lao She was a Manchu whose father, a member of the Imperial Guards, had been killed during the Boxer Rising of 1900, while attempting to defend the Forbidden City against the allied forces sent to relieve the besieged foreign legations. (Those same allied forces had already defeated Shen Congwen's father and the armies seeking to defend the Dagu forts down on the coast.) At that time Lao She was only one year old, and he had grown up in near poverty with his widowed mother. Perhaps seeking to better his chances, he left China for England in 1924, and lived in London for five years, working as a language teacher, helping British scholars with their translations from the Chinese, and voraciously reading Dickens.[19] While in London he wrote three comic novels, which were published in China and well received; after his return to China in 1930—he was given a university teaching job in the city of Jinan in Shandong province—he was appalled by the evidence he saw of Japanese encroachments, and wrote a new novel about a Chinese family tragically involved in Japan's designs. As if to ram home the message of the novel, which he had completed during the summer vacation of 1931 and sent to his publishers in Shanghai, the only copy of the manuscript was destroyed in a fire when Japanese troops shelled Shanghai in their assault on the city in January 1932.[20]

Cat Country was Lao She's answer to this loss, and it was suffused with bitterness about himself, his own countrymen, and the foreign aggressors. Describing his state of mind at the time he composed *Cat Country*, Lao She mocked his own inadequacies, and the folly of his attempt, in a metaphor drawn from the barnyard: "An absolutely brainless man might find some nourishment in a dunghill; a brainy man wouldn't pay any attention to the dunghill in the first place. But it takes a half-brainy half-brainless clod like myself to come up with the idea of improving and preserving the dunghill. Such a man goes over and preaches at the flies that have gathered atop the turds, saying: 'Hey, come on! Let's keep this place in better shape!' "[21] It was as if he were struggling with all the elements in China's current crisis at once: the establishment of the puppet state of Manchukuo, the violence of the Japanese against helpless Chinese civilians, the myopic stance of the Guomindang, the internecine squabbles of the Communist Party, and the fact that tens of thousands of Chinese were becoming opium addicts to escape from the anguish of the times. In choosing the idea of a traveler marooned in an appositely allegorical country, Lao She was using an idea common to many authors of utopian and satirical literature; but one wonders if the opening lines of *Cat Country* were not inspired by some echoes of Xu Zhimo, who had translated *Candide* five years earlier and had been killed in a plane crash just outside Jinan, where Lao was now teaching:

> The aircraft was completely destroyed.
> My friend—the schoolmate of my childhood, who had just been my pilot for more than half a month—had no whole bones left in his body.

How was it possible that I was still alive? Why wasn't I dead? Perhaps the gods knew, but there was no sense in getting myself upset over it.

We had been on course for Mars, and according to my dead friend's calculations just before the plane crashed we had entered the atmosphere of Mars. So had I after all ended up on Mars? If that was truly so, then my friend's soul could rest in peace: To be the first Chinese on Mars— there was something worth dying for.[22]

The part of Mars where Lao She's narrator was stranded— which he came to call Cat Country after its feline inhabitants— was the home of cruel and lazy creatures. Possessed of a simple spoken language, a simpler written one, an endless appetite for opiates that kept them in a semipermanent state of stupefaction, unclean in their persons, chaotic in the organization of their urban conglomerations, fatalistic about death, hypocritical in their pretentious morality, the cat people filled the hero with dread as he compared them with the China that he had just left—a country that he praised as "great, glorious, and free." Cat poetry, as he became familiar with it, had at least a minimal dignity and had shown some signs of progress; for example, one cat showed the narrator a poem he had written entitled "Emotions after Studying Our History," which included the lines:

> *Precious leaf,*
> *Precious flower,*
> *Precious mountain,*
> *Precious cat,*
> *Precious stomach.*

According to this cat poet, the last line, "Precious stomach," was a recent poetic breakthrough that had lain awaiting its discoverer for twenty thousand years of cat poetry.[23] Cat politics, on the other hand, had no redeeming features. Insofar as the narrator could understand the system, it appeared that the cat people indulged in an endless series of government interactions, which they called "brawls"; nearly everyone joined in these unless they were too dazed by drugs to move. The domi-

nant ideology was "Everybody Shareskyism," which had risen
to its current position after a series of brawls had brought down
the cat emperors; but this ideology had failed to bring much solace to the nation, and the leader of the Everybody Shareskies
had ended up assuming the imperial mantle himself, and taking the honored title "Ruler of Ten Thousand Brawls."[24]

In the climax of the book, a group of "small people" (transparently a reference to the Japanese) invade Cat Country; unable to agree on any concerted policy, the cat people are systematically rounded up and slaughtered. One little group of ten
or so withdraws to an isolated mountain, but even there, temporarily safe from the invaders, they cannot agree to stand together, and when the small people capture the mountain there
are only two cat people still alive. "And even these two," wrote
Lao She, "were locked in mortal combat. Rather than killing
them, the enemy soldiers shut them up in a large wooden cage.
And there the two continued their struggle until they had bit-
ten each other to death."[25] The hero escapes, after this apoca-
lypse, by means of a French spacecraft which fortuitously lands
on Mars and returns him to China.

Cat Country was at once criticized by writers on the left, not
surprisingly in view of its message; Lao She himself said of it
that as a book it "was like a bird with cropped wings, unable to
leave the ground," for it lacked both the bitter power and the
humor needed in true satire, and was "full of negatives, for I
had no positive suggestions to advance."[26] Yet some of the
central questions Lao posed in the novel were similar to those
that had been plaguing both Lu Xun and Qu Qiubai for a decade: If direct political action led to such misery for China, did
that give more or less significance to words? And if so, was satire an effective tool?

Some of Lu Xun's thoughts on these topics were crystallized
for him during February 1933, when George Bernard Shaw
stopped off in Shanghai for the day during a tour of the Far
East. Lu Xun was invited to meet Shaw and gladly accepted.
The invitation came to Lu Xun from Cai Yuanpei; since retiring
as chancellor of Beijing National University, Cai had become
an influential leader in Guomindang educational circles and—
along with Sun Yatsen's widow—had founded the Chinese

League for the Protection of Human Rights, and it was this organization that was acting as Shaw's host in Shanghai.[27] Lu Xun, according to his own account, had little to say to Shaw, though he was pleased to be photographed in Shaw's company, but he was deeply impressed by Shaw's sincerity of manner, and by his composure in the face of the endless petty questions of crowds of Chinese journalists. When Qu Qiubai brought together a small book of descriptions of Shaw's visit to China, Lu Xun agreed to write the introduction. Shaw was a mirror, wrote Lu, in which the Chinese could see their true faces, and his greatness was proven by the accuracy of that reflection and by the fact that he offended everyone equally. Shaw refused to say what the various subgroups among Chinese intellectuals wanted him to say: "The lame hoped he would advocate using crutches, those with scabies hoped he would praise hat-wearing, those who used rouge hoped he would taunt sallow-faced matrons, and the writers of nationalist literature counted on him to crush the Japanese." Unable to accept Shaw's refusal to pander to them, the Chinese intellectuals turned against him: "He tells the truth, yet they say he is joking; they laugh loudly at him and blame him for not laughing himself." As a final defense they called him a "satirist," as if that might blunt the force of his analysis. But, as Lu Xun observed, "the end of the paradoxical Shaw, or the solution of Shaw's contradictions, will come only when the contradictions of society are solved, and that is no laughing matter."[28]

For Ding Ling and the few members of the Communist Party still in Shanghai during that spring of 1933—most had dispersed to other cities, been killed, been jailed, or else moved south to shelter in the Jiangxi Soviet—such words must have had a chilling ring. Ding Ling had been working hard for the party—at editorial tasks for the *Big Dipper*, on the executive committee of the League of Left-Wing Writers, and with the youth sections of the Communist Party. At the same time she wrote about a dozen short stories dealing with revolutionary themes and the anti-Japanese resistance movement. Though one of these, "Adolph the Poet," was a bleak sketch of the drifting life of a White Russian émigré, and one was a socialist projection of the saga of Peter Pan and Tinker Bell, most of the stories—in violation of her own disclaimers of 1931 delivered to the Guanghua students—were about peasants and workers in the revolutionary movement. She also worked hard on the projected novel *Mother*, and between the autumn of 1932 and the spring of 1933 she wrote almost a hundred thousand words, completing the first part of a projected trilogy, which she sent to the publisher in April.[29] While writing *Mother* she was living in a fourth-floor apartment on Kunshan Road in Shanghai, with a pale, rather sickly young writer and translator called Feng Da. (Shen Congwen, who met him and was unimpressed, thought that Feng looked like a clerk working for a foreign business firm.) On May 14, 1933, police broke into her apartment while she, Feng, and two Communist friends were talking. One of the friends, trying to climb over the balcony to reach another apartment, fell to his death; Ding and the others were arrested and completely disappeared from all contact with the world.[30] As far as her friends in Shanghai knew, she had been killed. In an attempt to find out whether she was still living, Yang Quan, secretary-general of that same League for the Protection of Human Rights which had recently entertained Shaw, issued a public protest at the arrest and demanded an explanation from the Guomindang. Yang had been hated by Guomindang leaders for months because of the vigorous denunciations that his league had been directing against them, and these new protests of his coincided with the dispatch of special Guomindang agents to Shanghai. On June 18, early on Sunday morning, as Yang was setting out for a drive with his son, four gunmen fired a volley of shots into the car. Yang was killed instantly.[31]

Later that same year Qu Qiubai completed his own plans to move to the Jiangxi Soviet, where Mao Zedong had invited him to serve as commissar of education, so that he could try to put his theories concerning mass education and literary realism into practice. He arrived in Jiangxi in January 1934 (having left his wife and daughter safe, he hoped, among friends in Shanghai), but conditions in the soviet were so primitive and life was so hectic under the constant military pressures of Chiang Kai-shek's "extermination campaigns" that Qu found most of his energies were taken up in training the illiterate in basic reading skills. Though Qu worked hard to innovate by incorporating dance and folk song into a proletarian art form, it was here perhaps that he encountered the full force of his own generalized statement (made in the summer of 1932) that educational work would be even harder among the peasantry than it was among the proletariat, for "the language of 'rural folk' is primitive and obscure," and still was dominated by those "obscure localisms" that the urbanized proletariat gradually sloughed off in the joint experience of urban work and life.[32] But here he had at least for a short while a chance to implement the dream of a Chinese written language that would reach the masses on their terms, not on the terms of the bourgeois elites, however defined:

> As for revolutionary popular literature and art, it is especially important that it begin by making use of the *most simple* proletarian street vernacular. On the surface of things, it will appear at the outset to be modeled on the vernacular of traditional fiction. But on no account should this be construed as a policy of surrender. It is a matter of the proletarian vanguard leading *all* the laboring people in the task of creating a new and rich *modern Chinese literature*. At times it will be necessary to use the various local dialects in writing, and in the future perhaps a special literature for Guangdong, Fujian and other places will be constructed.[33]

But little time was vouchsafed to Qu Qiubai to test these ideas. Under the steady pressure of the Guomindang troops the Communist forces in Jiangxi began to lose ground. Chiang Kaishek was directing a large and experienced army, and was being advised by senior German military officers who were veterans of the great battles of the First World War. By 1934 the war they conducted in Jiangxi had come to echo those earlier campaigns on the fields of Flanders, as Guomindang troops systematically advanced from prepared positions supported by blockhouses and trenches; at the same time they learned to identify the feints made by the Communist troops and to avoid the common disaster of those tackling guerrilla armies: overextending supply lines and fragmenting into small units that could be picked off by larger guerrilla groups. The Communist leaders, badly divided over what the correct military strategy should be, were pushed into a static and defensive position they could not long sustain. As they began to run out of food and ammunition in the spring of 1934 (they had never had anything in the way of medical supplies or sophisticated logistical support), they made contingency plans to abandon the soviet base area and strike out for new terrain where other Communist soviets had managed to survive—either in Sichuan province or in Shaanxi. By the end of the year, as retreat became imperative, about one hundred thousand Communists left the Jiangxi Soviet capital (brilliantly concealing their initial withdrawal from the Guomindang forces) to embark on the bitter and dangerous journey to the northwest that later was to be known as the Long March. A certain number of decoy troops remained behind in Jiangxi, along with the sick, the old, and the very young. Mao Zedong had to abandon the two children born to him by He Zizhen, with whom he had been living since he moved to the soviet area, though she accompanied him on the march.[34]

Qu Qiubai was too weakened by tuberculosis to attempt the march, and he stayed behind as well. Early in 1935 he started to make his way back to Shanghai, partly on foot, though some of the time he had to be carried by stretcher. In February the group with which he was traveling was caught by a patrol of Nationalist troops; initially Qu managed to conceal his identity, but after being named by an informer he was sent to Tingzhou prison at Changting in the mountains of western Fujian province.

During May 1935, Qu wrote a lengthy testament which he entitled "Some Superfluous Words"; after his death this document made its way out into the world by an unknown route and was later published. Though some of it had been seen by a journalist allowed to interview Qu in jail, it cannot be known how much the Guomindang censors may have cut from the original or even whether some of it was doctored. The Communist Party, in any case, felt that the self-deprecatory and sardonic tone of the testament was not a fitting tribute to his memory, and it was kept out of his official "collected works." Yet there are many echoes in it of the Qu who had journeyed to Moscow fifteen years earlier, though now he was grown ill and tired, feeling, at thirty-six, like an old man:

> Visualize for a moment a weak horse pulling a loaded wagon of several thousand pounds up a dangerous steep slope. Slowly it tries to move, but eventually the moment has to arrive when it is too exhausted to struggle forward and too frightened to beat a retreat. This was the way I felt during the time I was responsible for the Communist Party leadership. The feeling of despair that resulted from my inability to stop what I was doing had become an indescribable, unbearable weight upon my feeble self. This emotional weariness in connection with everything political made me long for a "sweet" rest when my mind would be devoid of thought and in fact would cease to function. Only emptiness has occupied my mind ever since the Fourth Conference of the Chinese Communist Party expelled me from the Political Bureau in January 1931.[35]

By "emptiness" Qu meant, probably, that he continued to be occupied with propaganda work, which, though it did interest him intellectually, was still no substitute for the study of Russian literature that had remained his own "true love": it had been "a historical error" that led him to a position of party leadership, he wrote, for "deep in my heart I knew that I was nothing but a carefree, unconventional and easy going 'man of letters,' " one of those "highbrow loafers" who contribute so little to the world.[36] As a Marxist theorist, wrote Qu, he had been superficial, picking up those elements that interested him and ignoring the rest. He had never read *Capital,* for example, since he had no interest in economics. But the randomness of this study did not mean that he was not a Marxist. Marxism had given him the context within which to place his thoughts, even if he had an admixture of Tolstoyan anarchism left from his earlier readings:

> As long as the Communist society of Marxism remains the freest of all societies, classless and stateless, I shall have no objection, since this kind of society conforms well with my anarchist ideal, where peace and love dominate the world and permeate all mankind. The difference between Marx-

ism and anarchism is a difference in method. The Marxists tell me that before their final goal is achieved, there has to be a most violent class struggle in order to establish the dictatorship of the proletariat, that is, the assumption by the proletariat of the governing power of the state. Likewise, before a state is eliminated, there has to be the establishment of a new state; before a true democracy comes about, there has to be a proletarian democracy. This seemingly contradictory and yet logically sound presentation—the so-called Marxist dialectics—really fascinated me.[37]

Elsewhere in the testament, Qu added, "You, dear comrades, are marching forward, constantly and indomitably. I envy you, and pray for your success; but I can no longer follow you."[38]

In the closing words of the testament, Qu described the terrible tiredness that had overwhelmed him for several years, a tiredness caused partly by his illness and partly by the nature of his political work. Now, for a few moments, he could enjoy the luxury of being frank before sliding into a permanent sleep. His regrets were varied: that he had not been able to transcend his class background and serve the Communist Party better; that he had not been frank, either with his comrades or with his wife, Yang Zhihua, whom he loved truly and deeply; that he had treated much of life like a "burlesque show" in which he had played too many shallow roles, as party leader, as college professor, as translator, as husband, as expert on elementary education; that he would never see his little daughter again.

> This world is still very beautiful to me. The young and the courageous are all marching forward. There are the flowers, the fruits, beautiful mountains and rivers, factories and their chimneys—how masculine and heroic they look to their beholders! Also the moon—how much I love the moon; she seems to be brighter tonight than she has ever been before. Farewell, farewell, you beautiful world!
>
> All my energy has been taken away from me. What I have now is only an empty frame. If I had any control over this empty frame, I would donate it to a laboratory of some medical school. I have heard that many hospitals and medical schools in China have great difficulties obtaining human bodies for experimental purposes. Since 1919 I have been infested with tuberculosis and have been X-rayed several times. I recall that in 1931 the physicians discovered many

scars on my lungs but could not diagnose their cause. I think that if they opened my body for a close examination, they would be in a better position to discover something new. This may in the future help other tuberculosis patients. My remark may sound amateurish or even ridiculous, since I do not know anything about medicine.

In short, this burlesque show has come to an end; now the stage is completely empty. What difference does it make anyway even if I were reluctant to leave? What I will have is a long, long rest. I do not even have any say as to how my body should be disposed of. Farewell, all the beautiful things in the world!

The Life of Klim Samgin by Gorky, *Rudin* by Turgenev, *Anna Karenina* by Tolstoy, *The True Story of Ah Q* by Lu Xun, *Vacillation* by Mao Dun, and *The Dream of the Red Chamber* by Cao Xueqin—those are all worth reading. The Chinese bean curd is the most delicious food in the whole world. Good-bye and farewell![39]

On June 18, 1935, he was executed by firing squad.

Just before leaving for Jiangxi in 1934, Qu Qiubai had written an affectionate preface for a new edition of Lu Xun's collected essays. After Qu's death, Lu Xun repaid the honor by working indefatigably to edit and see through the press the collected essays of Qu Qiubai—he evaded censorship of the volumes by having them published under a pseudonym, as he had done with so many of Qu's articles in the past.[40]

Some of the reasons for the close friendship that had developed between the two men must have lain in the range of their shared interests and experiences: their love of Russian literature, their marriages to radical young students, the fact that each had an only child for whose safety he constantly feared, their insomnia, their love of the essay form, the tuberculosis (which left Lu Xun, too, lying weak and motionless for days on end). As to factionalism, in the air of which Qu Qiubai had flourished in the late 1920s and been laid low in the 1930s, Lu Xun had always been an involved battler, and in 1935 and 1936 the storm around him intensified. Within the League of Left-Wing Writers, clashes of personality and differences over ideological direction had become commonplace. Through his friend the poet Hu Feng, Lu was dragged into a venomous bat-

tle with the leading Communist cadre in charge of cultural affairs, Zhou Yang. It had become a world, as Lu Xun wrote to
Hu Feng, in which "I always feel that I am bound in an iron
chain while a foreman is whipping me on the back. No matter
how hard I work, the whip will fall. When I turn my head and
ask what are really my faults, the man will clasp his hands and
politely shake them and say that I am doing an extremely fine
job; that he and I are surely the best of friends; and what a fine
day, ha, ha, ha." Or, as he wrote even more graphically to another friend, it was a world in which "to protect myself from
the rear, I have to stand slantwise."[41]

These new levels of tension between Lu Xun and various former friends or acquaintances in the Communist Party were
prompted by two factors: the growing power of the Japanese,
and the near-extinction of the Communist Party itself. By late
1935, the Japanese, not content with dominating Manchuria,
had taken over Chahar (to the north of Beijing) and had forced
the Guomindang to agree to keep large areas of Hebei province
free of Chinese troops—thus gaining more and more power
within China proper. At the same time the main body of the
Communist forces—after the yearlong retreat from the Jiangxi
Soviet that had taken them across almost four thousand miles
of country, fighting much of the way, in a great sweep down
through the southwestern province of Guizhou and then north
via the Tibetan borderlands and Gansu province to Shaanxi—
had managed to regroup around the township of Baoan. This
was a poverty-stricken and mountainous region of China, lying
between the Great Wall and the city of Xian (which, forty years
before, Kang Youwei had urged the Emperor Guangxu to make
the nation's capital). Here Mao Zedong and the seven thousand
survivors of the Long March joined a small Communist force
that had maintained a soviet in the region since 1931, and also
gained some extra recruits from Muslim communities in the
region and from local secret societies; but they remained extremely vulnerable.[42] Troops loyal to Chiang Kaishek had
already begun massing at Xian in order to conduct yet another—and, they hoped, final—extermination campaign. To
foment an anti-Japanese United Front on a nationwide basis
was thus a survival tactic for the Communists, and also one that

coincided with the general line presented by Stalin and the Comintern. It promised to have widespread popular support, for on December 9, 1935, students in Beijing had staged an immense anti-Japanese rally, which, in the passions it generated locally and the responses it aroused elsewhere in the country, echoed the great demonstrations of 1919, 1925, and 1926, and projected a new generation of student leaders to national attention.[43]

In this general context Lu Xun became enmeshed with Communist Party cadres in a battle of slogans, which grew more bitter in the spring of 1936 after the Central Committee ordered the dissolution of the League of Left-Wing Writers. Lu Xun, who had played such a vigorous part in the league's workings, was barely consulted. "To have the league dissolved like that," he told a friend, "as if it were not regarded as a battle line at all!" In its place an Association for Literature and Arts was founded, to assemble cultural workers under the slogan "Literature for National Defense." In angry opposition to this slogan, which they felt would defuse revolutionary fervor, Lu Xun and Hu Feng made the countersuggestion that writers rally under the slogan "Mass Literature of National Revolutionary War." In response Zhou Yang, speaking for the Communist leadership, insisted that "national defense" must become the central theme for all writings save those by "the nation's traitors"—an unpleasant and obvious reference to Lu Xun's stance.[44]

Already angry, Lu Xun was reduced to even greater rage after a mutual friend of his and Zhou Yang's wrote that Lu was "unwittingly strengthening the vicious tendencies" of men such as the poet Hu Feng. This mutual friend, under a veneer of elaborate politeness, cautioned Lu Xun at length about his position and its relevance to developments in world politics, from which China could not stand aside.[45] Lu Xun responded that of course he supported a rational stand for a United Front against Japan, but he believed that the motives of these young Communists who suddenly veered sharply in policy—as well as "planting their teeth in my flesh"—were primarily sectarian and narrow-spirited.[46]

These controversies seem to have restored some level of vitality and wit to Lu Xun, for at the end of 1935 he suddenly produced a long series of short stories that played with themes from China's past history, taking mythical or semimythical figures and placing them in incongruous settings where the dialogue was both funny and poignant, highlighting the pathos of these millennium-old beliefs and actions. The mythical rulers Shun and Yu, the faithful ministers Bo Yi and Shu Qi, who laid down their lives when the Shang dynasty fell, the philosopher Confucius and the Daoist sages Zhuangzi and Laozi—all entered this newly restructured world of Lu Xun's mind.[47] No longer merely the representatives of that "cannibalistic" culture Lu Xun had written of almost twenty years before, they were now touched with nostalgia, and their words have, on occasion, both shrewdness and the power to move. In the story called "Leaving the Pass," for example, the sage Laozi heads away from the world of the "court," which he senses will be dominated henceforth by Confucius, to pass through the Great Wall and on to the deserts of the northwest. As he nears his destination, traveling with his few possessions on the back of a dark ox, and already sees the sloping loess plateaus under a clear blue sky, he is stopped by a patrol that courteously but firmly brings him to their guardhouse so that he can deliver one last lecture before he continues on his way. As he starts to state his views, there is mild consternation:

> "The Way that can be told of is not an Unvarying Way;
> The names that can be named are not unvarying names.
> It was from the Nameless that Heaven and Earth
> sprang;
> The named is but the mother that rears the ten
> thousand creatures, each after its kind. . . ."

The listeners looked at each other. No one took notes. Laozi continued:

> "Truly, 'Only he that rids himself forever of
> desire can see the Secret Essence';
> He that has never rid himself of desire can
> see only the Outcomes.
> These two things issued from the same mold
> but nevertheless are different in name.

The 'same mold' we can but call the Mystery,
Or rather the 'Darker than any Mystery,'
The Doorway whence issued all Secret Essences."

Signs of distress were apparent on every face. Some seemed not to know where to put their hands and feet. One of the customs officers gave a huge yawn; the copyist fell asleep, letting slip his knives, brushes, and wooden tablets with a crash on to the mat.[48]

Puzzled by the lecture but eager to make a possible profit, the warden asks Laozi to write out his thoughts in a book; when the book is written, the warden sees with dismay that it is "the same old claptrap." Laozi is sent on his way to the desert, now with a small sack of supplies on the back of his dark ox, while the little book is placed on a shelf in the guardhouse, a shelf already "piled high with salt, sesame, cloth, beans, unleavened bread, and other confiscated goods."[49]

After these stories Lu Xun wrote no more fiction. He continued to edit Qu Qiubai's work, prepared an edition of Käthe Kollwitz's woodcuts, and worked to complete his translation of Gogol's *Dead Souls*. The rest of his time was occupied by the violent and exhausting polemics over the correct slogans for the current era of the United Front against Japan. Lu Xun's doctor was, in fact, Japanese, and though Lu Xun liked and trusted him, other friends arranged for him to have an examination by an American tuberculosis specialist in Shanghai. This doctor told Lu Xun that death was near, and added gracefully, as Lu Xun put it, that had Lu been a European he would already have been in his grave for five years. With one of his flashes of ironic humor, Lu Xun added, "I did not ask him to prescribe for me, feeling that since he had studied in the West he could hardly have learned how to prescribe for a patient five years dead."[50]

Lu's only near equivalent to the public testament that Qu Qiubai issued just before his execution was an essay of September 5, 1936, called, bluntly, "Death."

If I were a great nobleman with a huge fortune, my sons, sons-in-law, and others would have forced me to write a will long ago, whereas nobody has mentioned it to me. Still,

I may as well leave one. I seem to have thought out quite a few items for my family, among which are:

1. Don't accept a cent from anyone for the funeral. This does not apply to old friends.
2. Get the whole thing over quickly. Have me buried and be done with it.
3. Do nothing in the way of commemoration.
4. Forget me and look after your own affairs—if you don't, you are just too silly.
5. When the child grows up, if he has no gifts let him take some small job to make a living. On no account let him become a writer or artist in name alone.
6. Don't take other people's promises seriously.
7. Never mix with people who injure others but who oppose revenge and advocate tolerance.

There were other items, too, but I have forgotten them.

I remember also that during a fever I recalled that when a European is dying there is usually some sort of ceremony in which he asks pardon of others and pardons them. Now, I have a great many enemies, and what should my answer be if some modernized person asked me my views on this? After some thought I decided: Let them go on hating me. I shall not forgive a single one of them, either.

No such ceremony took place, however, and I did not draw up a will. I simply lay there in silence, struck sometimes by a more pressing thought: If this is dying, it isn't really painful. It may not be quite like this at the end, of course; but still, since this happens only once in a lifetime, I can take it.[51]

Lu Xun died in Shanghai on October 19, 1936.

Ding Ling had not been executed after her arrest in May 1933, but for the next three years she was kept in confinement by the Guomindang. As she was neither charged nor tried, and spent much of her time living in the houses of Guomindang officials (either in Nanjing or in Hangzhou), many of her former friends became convinced that she had become some sort of turncoat, had even, perhaps, betrayed her friends to the Guomindang or rejected her earlier Communist beliefs. Lu Xun, for example, dryly told friends that she "was being looked after by the Guomindang."[52] In fact the Guomindang's purpose in arresting her seems to have been to isolate her from her former friends rather than to punish her, and to force her to abandon all kinds of propaganda work for the Communist Party. She was allowed to be with her lover, Feng, and her mother (who must by now have learned what had happened to Hu Yepin) came from Hunan to be with her, bringing the child who had been left in her care after Hu's death. Sometime during 1935 Ding Ling had her second child, a daughter, fathered by Feng.

The whole situation was certainly most unusual in the prevailing context of the Guomindang-Communist struggle; a senior officer in the Guomindang's Investigation Bureau, who had given the original order for her arrest, commented later on Ding Ling's attitude, and hinted at some of the psychological pressure to which she was subjected:

> Her problem was not serious, since she had taken no part in violent and subversive activities. I hoped very much she would use her talent in creative writing and become a contributing cultural worker for our party. Right after her arrival in Nanjing I talked candidly with her. She expressed a decision to abandon her past and made a written statement of it. After the couple showed their willingness to begin a new life, I settled them in a quiet hotel. But after two weeks, because of the high expense at the hotel, they were moved to the house of one of my colleagues. . . . They were served comfortably inside the residence and provided with all the necessities but were not allowed to go out. Living in a big study, with a small garden outside, they could read, talk, or do anything they liked without interference. They were provided with bedding, sheets, clothing, books and periodicals, stationery, and food, all free of charge. She said she had never lived so comfortably when she was in Shanghai.[53]

But in fact, and not surprisingly, Ding Ling wrote very little in this curious and isolated environment. As she explained later, "I had absolute leisure time but I did not write. I only contemplated, contemplated so much that I became very restless. I simply hoped that one day I could be busy again so that I could squeeze in some time to write."[54] One of the stories that she did complete was about a prison guard, friendly in a clumsy way, who occasionally would offer her a cigarette and reminisce about his past exploits. Her obvious sympathy for this guard and some of his companions shines through the story, in clear contradiction to the developing argument in the Shanghai leftist world that class position must be meticulously related to character development. For Ding Ling, humane Guomindang jailors were not a contradiction:

> The days are too long. It seems that we are living on a desolate island, staying in that big hall all day long with nothing to do. I encourage them [the guards] to tell me their own stories. Their stories are touching, and I learn much from them. They have all continually braved the storms of life since they were born, and witnessed many strange things in their eventful past. After some time, a few of them regularly take lessons from us. One studies English. One learns Chinese and practices brush writing. Still another prefers to read novels; every day he asks about words he cannot understand.[55]

Perhaps just before, or just after, her arrest, Ding Ling returned to the character she had developed in "Diary of Miss Sophie," and began a continuation. In a moment of idleness, this older and wiser Sophie writes, she has been looking through the yellowing pages of her old diary and finds that she no longer has any relation to that earlier writer. No emotions are aroused by her former self; "those fantasies, those emotions, those wounds, those loves are all completely gone."[56] In this work (only a fragment of seven pages survives) Ding Ling associated herself totally with the new persona of Sophie, and wrote of Sophie's finding a nineteen-year-old lover and their passion for each other, of the slow changes in their lives in the years after they left Beijing, and of other developments:

> During that same time I became the mother of a son. We didn't want a child, it was not possible for us to keep a child, for a child would disrupt our lives too much. And yet, after all, we were commonplace people, we couldn't overcome our love for this little, responsive baby son; seeing his innocent red tender face as he slept in his cradle made some solace for all the troubles he had brought to his father and mother. He cried a great deal, and I suffered both in mind

and in body more than I ever have in my whole life. Yet I am a woman, not lacking the richness of maternal love, and had I wanted to keep the child by my side I certainly had the strength to be able to do so.[57]

But, said the Sophie of the new diary, she rejected the temptations this baby brought, and sent him off to his grandmother in Hunan, with never a tear. Because Ding Ling's disappearance had increased her fame, such fragments (regardless of literary merit) were published in well-known journals, increasing the sense of mystery and ambiguity that her name and Sophie's aroused.

During 1936, despite her apparent docility in captivity, Ding Ling was in fact laying careful plans to escape. Her common-law husband, Feng, was seriously ill with tuberculosis and had to be hospitalized at intervals; telling her Guomindang keepers that she was bored and depressed by his illness, and worn down by the endless demands of nursing and looking after her children, Ding Ling was given permission to make a trip to Beijing in May 1936. There she made contact with members of the Communist Party, and it was decided that she should return to Nanjing and try, later in the year, to make her way to the Communist base area of Baoan, to which a number of radical intellectuals had already escaped. Back in Nanjing that summer, Ding Ling made final plans with underground members of the party, and when all was ready, in September, she got permission from the Guomindang to go to Shanghai, on the grounds that she had to consult a Japanese medical specialist there. Once in Shanghai she was met by friends and taken into hiding. She stayed there about a month until transportation to the northwest could be arranged for her. The preparations were completed by the middle of October, and Ding Ling made her way to Xian, where she again hid out with friends, in the midst of the Guomindang armies.[58] On the last day of October 1936, she slipped out of the city on a cart and jolted her way toward the Communist base area. Drawing from the fiction she had written or read over the previous decade, one could see the young woman on that October day in three different guises: as Lao She's narrator joining the last ten guerrillas on their mountain in Cat Country; as Lu Xun's philosopher-sage moving beyond the passes to the clean blue sky shimmering above the eroded loess hills; or merely as an older, tired Sophie, determined, after all, not to waste what was left of her life in the south.

39. Mao Zedong's first wife, Yang Kaihui, and their sons, Anying (born 1921) and Anqing (born 1922). She was arrested and shot in 1930.

40. Sun Yatsen and his wife, Soong Qingling, in Tianjin, 1924

41. Chiang Kaishek and Soong Meiling at their wedding in Shanghai, December 1927

42. Hu Yepin, around 1930

43. Xu Zhimo and
Lu Xiaoman in 1931,
shortly before Xu's death

44. Ding Ling, her mother, and her baby, in Hunan in the spring of 1931, after Hu Yepin's execution

45. Lao She in the early 1930s

46. Lu Xun, George Bernard Shaw, and Cai Yuanpei (chancellor of Beijing University during the May Fourth Movement), after lunch at the home of Sun Yatsen's widow in Shanghai, February 17, 1933. "As we stood side by side," Lu Xun wrote six days later, "I was conscious of my shortness. And I thought, Thirty years ago, I should have done exercises to increase my height."

47. Qu Qiubai with his wife, the Communist leader Yang Zhihua, and their daughter, probably in Moscow, 1929

48. Qu Qiubai, with shaved head, in prison in 1935, shortly before his execution

49. Lu Xun in Shanghai, 1935

50. *Rickshaw Puller*, woodcut by Lan Jia

·10·

REFUGEES

In a self-deprecating preface to *Cat Country*, written during 1933, Lao She had included a snatch of imaginary dialogue with one of his readers: "He asked me, 'What school are you a writer for? What class do you belong to? What types of people do you claim to be speaking for? Are you, or are you not, a vertebrate? How much do they pay you?' I bought him ten pounds of apples to stop up his mouth; he asked me no more questions, and I, contented, went off to have a good sleep." The sleep was so deep, added Lao She, that when he awoke he no longer knew what year or month it was and hence could not append the date, as writers usually did, to the end of his preface.[1]

By early 1936 the experience of living in China had made Lao She realize that such questions could no longer be brushed aside as jokes. In two novels, written during the scorching Shandong summers of 1933 and 1934, in the long vacations from his teaching duties at the university in Jinan, Lao She had continued to explore the world of the modern Chinese middle class, and had grown ever more depressed by what he saw: no longer guided by the values of the old Chinese society, they had been unable to develop moral principles to help them in the new; aware of their unhappiness, they could not find the courage to act decisively to transform their situation. Whether beer-swilling pseudo-Marxists, satin-slippered phony Confucians, or the helpless poor caught up in social and military conflicts they couldn't understand, they were all defenseless. Like Lu Xun's men and women of 1911, rushing aimlessly from He market to Wu town, Lao She's characters could "never make out clearly who was fighting whom in these civil wars, nor were they concerned about who won or who lost." They merely prayed that all armies would stay away from where they lived, and when in doubt they flew the Japanese flag from their rooftops, hoping that that symbol at least would be respected by whatever army happened to be doing the invading.[2]

In early 1936, after he had failed to make his way as an independent writer in Shanghai and had returned to yet another teaching job in Shandong, this time in the city of Qingdao, Lao She decided to abandon teaching altogether for a year and to make one final attempt to write a successful, serious novel.

Rickshaw, which Lao She wrote during 1936 and began to publish in serial form in a magazine that September (as Ding Ling was making her way from Shanghai to Baoan, and Lu Xun lay dying), is the story of a young rickshaw puller, Xiangzi, nicknamed "Camel," who lives and works in Beijing; it is also (clearly though never crassly) an allegory of the fate of China during the decade following the Northern Expedition of 1926. As the novel opens, Xiangzi—young, strong, uneducated, yet full of hope—starts work in Beijing pulling a rented rickshaw; running swiftly and cheerfully, in all weathers and in all seasons, through the city in which he has come to know every gradient and alleyway, every restaurant and drainage gully, every play of light on wall or eddy of wind at street corner, he dreams only of the day when he can possess his own rickshaw, maintain it in oiled and polished splendor, and find an amiable wife to bear his children. Yet as an individual, despite the strength of his body and the simple clarity of his dreams, he cannot survive alone: the rickshaw, earned and bought at last, is commandeered by a wandering squad of soldiers and never returned; a new cache of money, saved with greater hardship the second time and with greater insensitivity to the needs of his fellow workers, is stolen from him by a crooked detective who claims to be seeking political subversives; Xiangzi marries a woman he does not love, in hopes of a life of ease, only to see her disinherited by her father; and after she dies in childbirth he rejects another young woman who could have offered him love and affection. At the novel's end, Xiangzi, sick, alone, and prematurely aged, lives by cadging loans, by marching in processions or demonstrations for hire, and by selling information on labor agitators to the Beijing police.[3]

Rickshaw gave Lao She's answers to the five questions posed by his imaginary interlocutor in the preface to *Cat Country* three years before. To take the last question first, the novel was written for money, and in obedience to the laws of the marketplace, it was longer rather than shorter: "Five thousand ideographs might well be better than one hundred thousand, since works of literature are not like pigs, where quality is a function of size. But that said, one must realize that for one hundred thousand ideographs one can get between three and five hundred dollars, whereas five thousand bring in only nineteen dollars. This determines one's reasons for not always emphasizing purely artistic criteria." Second, though Lao She wrote for no particular school, he had been influenced by socialist theories on the role of literature and the demands of realism; here there was none of the dazzling light that once brightened Qu Qiubai's hopes in Moscow, merely the quieter knowledge of a world in which an old man murmurs, "We are brothers, after all," or Xiangzi's wife before dying sees that life is "like strolling east when the sun is setting; the distant places are already dark but there is still a little light just ahead of you so you take advantage of it to go on a little further."[4] Third, Lao She saw himself clearly as a member of the bourgeoisie, endowed with some talent and some social conscience, a family man (he had married at last in 1934, after several earlier disappointments, and now had a baby) but without the means to change the world. The gentle character Cao, in *Rickshaw*, who employs Xiangzi for a while, seems to speak clearly for the author here:

> He was only an ordinary man who sometimes taught school by the hour and sometimes did other things. He thought of himself as both a socialist and an aesthetician, having been somewhat influenced by the writings of William Morris. He had no deep opinions about government and art but he did have one good point: what he believed in

could actually be acted upon in the small affairs of everyday life. He seemed to have realized that he had no talent that would astonish mankind and enable him to perform some earthshaking deed, and so he arranged his work and household according to his own ideals. Even though his ideals added nothing to society, at least he spoke and acted toward the same end and didn't go around passing off bravado as ability.[5]

Fourth, Lao She used the language of the Beijing streets in speaking both for the poor, whose individualism would avail them nothing in a harsh and unpredictable society, and for the Chinese of his day, who seemed incapable of intelligent collective action either for their own or for their nation's sake. The closing words of the novel make their political point with a colloquial force that surely would have pleased Qu Qiubai:

> The man in red beating the gong and the man with the silk flag urged the procession forward and used all the village slang they knew to swear at him.
> "You boy! I'm talking to you, Camel! Look sharp, you motherfucker!"
> He still seemed not to have heard. The gong beater came over and clouted him. He rolled his eyes and looked around in a daze. He paid no attention to what the gong man said. He concentrated on searching the ground to see if there were any cigarette butts worth picking up.
> Handsome, ambitious, dreamer of fine dreams, selfish, individualistic, sturdy, great Xiangzi. No one knows how many funerals he marched in, and no one knows when or where he was able to get himself buried, that degenerate, selfish, unlucky offspring of society's diseased womb, a ghost caught in Individualism's blind alley.[6]

Fifth, even for that most mocking of the questions, whether the author is a vertebrate or not, Lao She had now developed a kind of answer. For if upright posture was what distinguished humans from the other vertebrates and gave them what little dignity they could claim, then abandonment of that posture negated the distinction and erased the dignity. It is thus crucial to Xiangzi's melancholy story that he ceased to hold himself erect as he had at first, in youth's pride, even when between the shafts of his rickshaw. His experiences had cost him too dear; it was not only that fate had broken his spirit but that "his shoulders sagged deliberately." And as if that self-elected sagging were not enough, at times he doubled up at the pain caused by the venereal disease he had contracted from the concubine of one of his clients. Xiangzi knew nothing of the miracle cure arsphenamine, "606," which Lu Xun had urged on the nation twenty years before and Ding Ling's Miss Sophie had idly noted in the classified ads of her newspaper; even if he had known, he could not have afforded it: "He'd take a little medicine for the time being or he'd get through it grimly. He certainly didn't regard his illness as anything that mattered."[7]

During 1936, as Lao She was creating this dark picture of the individual's fate, and the Communist forces were endeavoring to hold out in their northwest base at Baoan, there was a slow resurgence of the nationalistic and patriotic mass sentiment that had been so central to the Chinese world of the 1920s. In March 1936 a National Student Union was formed once again, by delegates from sixteen cities meeting in Shanghai. In April the students in Beijing formed their own National Salvation Union, and in July they petitioned the Guomindang executive committee for an end to the anti-Communist fighting, for release of political prisoners, and for a pledge of anti-Japanese resistance. The Communist Party, which initially had played an inconspicuous part in the development of this nationalistic sentiment so favorable to its own interests, came out openly in support of the National Salvation Movement in August and invited them to send delegates to the northwest soviet area. After Japanese troops entered the province of Suiyuan (formerly a part of Inner Mongolia) in November 1936, the Communists began to publicize their demands for a United Front against the Japanese, and major demonstrations were held in Beijing, Shanghai, and Xian. (This United Front strategy was parallel in outline to that developed by the Soviet Union, during the same year, for use in the Spanish Civil War; some Chinese Communists emphasized this by comparing their actions in Yanan to those of the Loyalists holding Madrid.) Tensions grew greater at the end of the month after seven leaders of the National Salvation Union were arrested by the Guomindang in Shanghai. On December 4, as the northwest campaign against the Communists stalled—a major attack by troops loyal to Chiang Kai-shek, launched from Gansu province, had failed abysmally, and other troops, based in Xian, were refusing to fight any-more—Chiang flew to Xian to direct the campaign in person; eight days later he was arrested by his own mutinous troops. After two weeks of dramatic and tense negotiations, involving the Guomindang leaders, the Communists, and military leaders of various factions, Chiang was released on condition that he abandon the anti-Communist struggle and rally the whole na-tion behind him in an anti-Japanese United Front.[8]

Ding Ling had left Xian a couple of months before this anti-Chiang coup. Reaching the Communist base of Baoan in Octo-ber, she was warmly received by the Communist leaders, who were delighted to draw on her dual prestige as a writer and as an escaped Guomindang political prisoner. She had long talks with Mao Zedong, a fellow Hunanese, whose wife, Yang Kai-hui, executed in 1930, had been her schoolmate, and with Deng Yingchao, coordinator of the Tianjin students during the May Fourth Movement, now the wife of Zhou Enlai. A branch of the Association for Literature and Arts—whose existence Lu Xun had so vigorously protested the year before—was formed with Ding Ling at the center. At her own request she then went to inspect the military front area in western Shaanxi, on the Gansu border, where she spent December. By the time she re-turned, in January 1937, the Communists had moved to the larger town of Yanan, which was to be their base for the next decade. Here Ding Ling was appointed to a position supervis-ing political education, was assigned to work on editing the his-torical records of the Long March, and was asked to teach literature in a Yanan normal school.[9]

She could not but be struck by the zeal and simplicity of this Yanan life, where the Long March survivors, transformed by the Xian coup from traitors-on-the-run into patriots, were strengthening their defenses, attracting large numbers of new recruits, and preparing for a possibly protracted war against the Japanese. The contrasts with the three previous phases of her own life—as an almost penniless ex-student in Beijing, as a feted young writer in literary Shanghai, and as a hunted and then imprisoned Communist conspirator—were obvious and poignant. Now, told which roles to play—as administrator, propagandist, and teacher—and even given the lines to speak, she grew strong and put on weight, as she told a friend from Shanghai. She grew accustomed to walking long distances barefoot; she learned not to expect trains, or roads, or even mules to ride in the rough terrain over which she traveled; she held it no discomfort not to wash face or teeth for days on end, and dressed in simple army clothes, with a cap on the back of her head.[10]

During the spring of 1937 Ding Ling settled into the rhythms of Yanan life; the Communist Party leaders were working out the delicate details of their agreement with the Guomindang. The Communists agreed finally to make four concessions in return for their freedom from further Guomindang attacks: they would cease all further efforts to overthrow the National Government; they would place the approximately thirty thousand troops in the Red Army under Guomindang "guidance" and would no longer use the name "soviet" for the Yanan region and the one million people they controlled there; they would establish democratic procedures based on universal suffrage in which non-Communists would be eligible for office; and they would cease the confiscation of landlords' holdings. Seeking to reassure their followers that these "concessions" were not "surrender," but necessary actions in the face of mounting Japanese attacks, the Communists moved to implement all four of their gradualist policies, and in the summer of 1937 a final agreement was reached.[11]

The agreement was spurred on by the fact that on July 7, 1937, Japanese troops from the Tianjin garrison decided to take over the Marco Polo Railway Bridge, which spanned the Yongting River fifteen miles southwest of Beijing and provided the key communications link with Wuhan and central China; unexpectedly—in the context of the previous twenty years of accommodation or surrender—the Chinese troops there responded with fierce resistance. To help the Japanese troops in Tianjin—which numbered only ten thousand—the Japanese army command in Manchuria dispatched a further thirty thousand men as reinforcements, while other Japanese units launched a major attack on Shanghai. By August 1937 China and Japan were in a state of open warfare.[12]

In Yanan, the outbreak of anti-Japanese hostilities was greeted with delight. The Communists saw the resistance at Marco Polo Bridge as symbolic of the new spirit of the Chinese people, and Ding Ling wrote of it as opening a new era of heroic simplicity in which Yanan's spirit would encompass the nation. In one of her few attempts at poetry, dated three days after the Japanese attack and titled simply "July in Yanan," she underlined the contrast between Yanan and the world she had left—that abandoned world being, of course, the one the Japanese were now attacking:

> *What is this place?*
> *It is paradise.*
> *We've only been here for half a year*
> *And everything is not yet firmly built*
> *Yet streets are clean, verges lined with trees,*
> *There are no beggars, no women sell their smiles.*
> *You see no opium dens, no gambling halls,*
> *At all occupations people seem happy:*
> *The farmer has land,*
> *The workers an eight-hour day and good protection.*
> *So handsome are these workers, they come from*
> *Wuhan, Xian, Shanghai*
> *From the length and breadth of the land.*
> *Thousands of students, lively, intelligent,*
> *All of us sturdy descendents of the Yellow Emperor.*[13]

Five years earlier, at the end of a long and depressing conversation with a dispirited, shabbily dressed, run-down Ding Ling, Shen Congwen had said half-jokingly, "Our memories are still all so young, you shouldn't make yourself look so old while it's still so early!" And he recorded that she had responded, with a rather bitter smile, "When was I ever really young?"[14] Now, though she had had to travel halfway across China and leave behind her lover and her two children, she had recovered her sense of youth among the group of young women, drawn from all over the country, with whom she lived, traveled, and taught. Their common goal had been sought by her own mother thirty years before: the eradication of illiteracy, degrading poverty, and foot-binding—which was still practiced almost universally among the peasant women of the northwest.

From poetry she moved on to acting and playwriting, and after she was appointed head of the Northwest Battleground Service Corps, in late 1937, Ding Ling led a group of more than thirty artists and writers in Shanxi and Shaanxi, performing for troops and the local peasantry, working sometimes extemporaneously and sometimes from prepared scripts. The two plays she wrote at this time dealt, not surprisingly, with anti-Japanese themes: in one, a member of the Chinese resistance poses as a Japanese collaborator to help his lover in her underground work; in the other a captured Japanese soldier is led to see the true nature of his own countrymen's aggression and to sympathize with China's cause.[15]

If, by a curious irony, the outbreak of the Sino-Japanese War brought a measure of satisfaction and personal security to Ding Ling, the same was in no way true for those who had remained in eastern China, where the months after the incident at the Marco Polo Bridge brought a series of catastrophes. That same summer of 1937 the Japanese occupied Beijing and Tianjin; in November, Shanghai fell after heavy fighting, and in December, Nanjing. By the autumn of 1938 the Japanese had consolidated control over the cities of northeast China, advanced up the Yangtze River to seize the Wuhan tri-cities, and occupied Guangzhou. These first sixteen months of the war were marked by terrible losses for the Chinese armies: Chiang Kaishek, determined to try to hold his main bases in east-central China, had committed many of his best troops—often with orders to fight to the last man—to the defense of Shanghai and Nanjing. The Chinese lost more than 350,000 men in those battles, and a further 700,000 in the campaigns to hold a defensive perimeter around Wuhan in 1938. Loss of life among the civilian population was also high. Tens of thousands died as a consequence of military decisions made by Chiang's commanders—such as that to blow up the Yellow River dikes and flood the northern Chinese plain in order to slow down the Japanese advance, or to burn the entire city of Changsha lest it fall into enemy hands—but still more as a result of the savagery of Japanese troops. In Nanjing alone, during ten days in December 1937, an estimated 300,000 Chinese were killed and tens of thousands of women were assaulted or raped during an orgy of pillage and murder.[16]

The speed of the Japanese victories forced millions of Chinese who had any choice in the matter to make an urgent decision about where they were going to live. There were four possibilities: Japanese-occupied northern China, where a puppet regime under nominal Chinese control had been established in Beijing; the Yangtze Valley area in central China, where another puppet regime based in Nanjing (and headed after 1940 by the former Guomindang leader Wang Jingwei) ruled much of the richest area of China, including Shanghai; northwestern China, where the Communist base area at Yanan in Shaanxi—described now as a border-region government rather than as a soviet—had extended out through the neighboring provinces of Gansu and Ningxia and into Shanxi and Hebei; or the south and southwest, where political power was centered in Chiang Kaishek's wartime capital of Chongqing, in Sichuan province.

For many, of course, the question of location was decided by affiliation or sympathy: Lu Xun's brother, educated in Japan and married to a Japanese woman, chose to stay on at his Beijing home, and continued his life of writing and scholarship there throughout the war; though Nanjing had been almost destroyed, Shanghai remained a natural haven for many writers and artists as well as for those whose financial interests were centered there or who had landholdings in the area, and even after the International Settlement was occupied in 1942, the city formed a lively intellectual base where a group of talented writers lived and wrote for enthusiastic audiences.

For leftist and Communist writers, whether they had been friends or enemies of Lu Xun, it was logical to flee Shanghai and proceed to Yanan, where they were likely to be welcomed and promoted; but Zhou Yang's feted presence there—he was even named director of the Lu Xun Academy of Literature and Arts—was perhaps enough to keep a few leftist writers who had been close friends of Lu Xun's away from Yanan, and make them try their luck either in Chongqing or somewhere else in Guomindang-controlled territory. Such was the case with Feng Xuefeng (the Communist poet who had been instrumental in Ding Ling's escape from the Guomindang); and nothing would induce Chen Duxiu, the cofounder of the Communist Party, who for many years had been vilified as a Trotskyist by his former comrades, to go to Yanan even after Mao Zedong sent a special emissary to urge him to come to the northwest. Instead, Chen chose to live in a remote inland town, upriver from Chongqing, even though his two sons had been executed by the Guomindang in the 1920s and he himself had spent five years in Guomindang jails.[17]

Both Wen Yiduo and Lao She had to face similar decisions, despite the switches in their careers and aspirations, Wen having given up writing in order to teach, and Lao having at last (after the success of *Rickshaw*) given up teaching in order to write full-time.

For Wen Yiduo, who had been vigorous in his denunciations of Japanese imperialism and of the Communist Party, there was little choice but to go somewhere in central or southwestern China, despite his lack of enthusiasm for the Guomindang. Since 1928 Wen had found a measure of peace and financial security by teaching classical Chinese literature, first at Wuhan University, then at Qingdao, and after 1932 at Qinghua University in Beijing, where he himself had been a student before leaving for the United States in 1922. His energies were now focused on the earliest Daoist writings and on Tang dynasty poetry, as well as on the haunting and difficult cycle of poems from the third century B.C. written by Qu Yuan. Wen had become a popular and mildly eccentric lecturer: black-gowned, bushy-haired, informal in approach, smoking in class and inviting his students to do the same, starting his lectures in the evening and continuing far into the night. If students asked why he wrote no more poetry, he would sigh and say he could no longer do so; instead he wrote major articles illuminating the poetry of the past. He became politically passive, ignoring the demonstrations on December 9, 1935; and in 1936 he cautioned his students to stick to their work and not waste their energies in political agitation.[18]

Wen continued in this mood until July 1937. Then, as the Japanese advanced toward Beijing after the Marco Polo Bridge Incident, he hastily sent his wife and their five children (three others had died young during the civil war) off to what he hoped was safety at his parents' home near Wuhan, while he remained behind to pack his books and manuscripts and close the house in which he had found a few years of peace. He caught the pathos of the moment in a letter to his wife written just after her departure, on July 16:

> Everyone has now left. I am here alone in the house, it is so quiet, so very quiet, and I've been thinking of you, my beloved wife. I never thought I was such a helpless person, but since you left I've been like some wandering spirit; I can't get anything done. The other day I cursed out a student who wasn't studying properly because he was so much in love, but now I realize I am just the same. In the past few days I have been worrying about our country and missing my family, but what has made me most unhappy is that you were not here by my side. My dearest, I do not fear death, I only hope that we two may face it together.[19]

Later that month Wen left Beijing and joined his family near Wuhan, but he soon had to leave them again, as he moved farther south to Changsha, where his Qinghua students, in conjunction with refugees from two other Beijing universities, had reopened their school.

When the approaching Japanese armies forced the university to move yet again in early 1938, Qinghua students joined with those from Beijing and Nankai universities to form Southwest Associated University (abbreviated in Chinese as "Lianda"), in the city of Kunming, far to the southwest, in Yunnan province. The male students were instructed to walk from Changsha to Kunming, while the women and faculty were allowed to make the journey by train—traveling south as far as Haiphong, in Vietnam, whence they could backtrack up into Yunnan via the Indochina–Yunnan railroad, and so to Kunming. Wen Yiduo, however, despite his faculty status, chose to walk with his students. It turned out to be an important choice, a formative stage in his life, as these great marches across China were for so many Chinese in 1937 and 1938, giving them a sense of their country's grandeur and range, a less terrifying but on occasion almost equally arduous version of the Communists' Long March of 1934–35. On the sixty-eight-day journey, which lasted from February to April 1938, seven hundred miles as the crow flies but almost twelve hundred by the route they had to take through the mountainous and river-sliced terrain, Wen once more began to understand the hardships of the country that he had started to sense in 1927.

Wen and his students traveled across western Hunan province and passed through the town of Yuanling, where Shen Congwen had grown up. Shen was there, as it happened, having escaped the fighting farther east, and he greeted Wen and the two hundred students traveling with him and helped them to find food and shelter for a few days. Like Shen, Wen learned to admire the Miao people of the area and tried to understand their culture. For the first time in many years Wen was sketching again, and in impromptu lectures to his students at rest periods he elaborated on the mythology and history of the lands they were passing through. In the 1920s Shen Congwen had made a selection from six hundred Miao songs his army friends had gathered, introducing to the Beijing literary world something of the elegance, wit, and bawdiness of the living tradition of Miao folk songs. Now one of Wen's own students collected more than two thousand songs from these same regions and from those farther southwest in Guizhou and Yunnan provinces, and prepared them for publication.[20]

Wen and his students learned to dole out scarce food supplies and to survive in villages where there was simply no extra food to be had; and to cope with the anger that flared easily. He found poverty and conservatism deeper than any that he had seen in Hunan and Hubei during the 1927 fighting: young women too poor to own clothes; men doubled like beasts beneath colossal loads; hillsides covered with opium poppies and patrolled by bandits; children untouched by the faintest trace of modern education, still kowtowing before the tablet of Confucius while they recited the Confucian classics.[21]

For the first few months in Kunming, Wen battled with a host of problems. Tens of thousands of refugees jammed into the city, rents shot up, and all essential items grew scarce. Hot water replaced tea except on rare occasions, and the previously chain-smoking Wen found cigarettes almost unobtainable. As food prices rose, his teacher's salary looked more and more inadequate, and the school itself was constantly moving as one military organization or another demanded their facilities. For a time they camped in a deserted graveyard, sleeping on the mud floors of straw huts or curled in holes in the ground. Some worked part-time as water carriers or janitors; others, to Wen's distress, began to make fast money as smugglers.[22] Wen's letters to his wife during that summer of 1938 were full of such details: the desperate search for money and the anxious reading of newspapers to see which railway lines or roads might still be open, what airfields still took passenger planes, what cities were still safe to live in as the Japanese advanced ever farther east and south.[23]

The affection obviously shared by Wen and his wife, even though theirs had been an arranged marriage, fixed by their parents in the early 1920s, serves to show how certain elements of the old China could still have value in the new. At the same time their example reminds us of the other human casualties bruised in the emancipated world of the revolution: Chiang Kaishek's first wife, abandoned so that he could marry Meiling Soong; Lu Xun's first wife, still living with her mother-in-law in Beijing while Xu Guangping looked after Lu Xun's baby and saw to his literary estate; Xu Zhimo's ex-wife, Zhang, living with their only son while Xu's second wife, Lu Xiaoman, edited his diaries; Mao Zedong's second wife, He Zizhen, who had had to leave their two children behind in Jiangxi and had been pregnant on the Long March, abandoned in Yanan by Mao so that he could marry the film starlet Jiang Qing. For Wen, at least, as he circled the city of Kunming, looking for villages where there still were rooms for rent, and brooding where the next blow would fall, his greatest dream was to be reunited with his wife so that they could "eat bitterness together."[24] In anxiety-torn letters to his father Wen begged his parents to reconsider their decision to stay on in their ancestral home, the only problem being to decide where—as the warfare spread—a safe haven was to be found. That September, after Wen had met his wife and their five children at the railhead in Guiyang, and returned with them to Kunming, accompanied by his younger brother and his family, the eleven of them moved into two rooms above a packhorse station in a village northwest of Kunming, sleeping on the floor like the students, and using borrowed utensils and furniture.[25]

In such a stressful atmosphere, as was the case with Ding Ling in Yanan, Wen's work and health flourished. He rediscovered the physical vitality and patriotism that had animated him during the time of the Beijing demonstrations in March 1926 but that he had lost thereafter. Now, in wartime Kunming, for a time there were no more bitter and ingrown literary fights, only problems of getting enough to eat, of surviving the Japanese planes that once almost killed Wen as he was bringing the children back from school, and of carrying out his own basic teaching duties in a stripped-down and simplified world.[26] Though he no longer wrote poetry, he could still express his feelings for the new China in his scholarly works—one such occasion being provided by the publication of the Miao folk songs his students had collected on their march from Changsha to Kunming. In a preface he composed for this book in March 1939, Wen wrote: "You say these [poems] are primitive and savage. You are right, and that is just what we need today. We've been civilized too long, and now that we have nowhere left to go we shall have to pull out the last and purest card, and release the animal nature that has lain dormant in us for several thousand years, so that we can bite back." The war against Japan, continued Wen, would give the Chinese a final and much-needed chance to prove themselves. In words that echoed those of Liang Qichao writing to his friends from Paris in 1919, Wen proclaimed: "This is a chance that comes once in a thousand years, to let us see whether there still exists in our blood the motive power of the ancient beasts; if not, then we had better admit that as a people we are spiritual eunuchs, and give up trying to survive in this world."[27]

Lao She followed a rather similar route of intellectual change, though unlike Wen he ended by institutionalizing his patriotism. In the late summer of 1937 Lao She had fled from his home in Shandong province and traveled southwest to join the Guomindang forces in their temporary wartime capital at Wuhan. There, in the spring of 1938, he was elected chairman of the All-China Anti-Japanese Writers' Federation and made editor of the federation's journal, *Literature for National Resistance*. He doubtless owed these posts to the fact that, despite his mordant critique of Everybody Shareskyism on the one hand, and his bitter denunciation of the exploitation of the poor on the other, both Communist and Guomindang supporters could admire his integrity as an artist and be pleased at his attacks on the opposition, however critical he seemed to be of themselves. His duty, in these joint posts, was to rally writers of all ages behind the slogans of the Chinese war effort, and he worked hard to this end, first in Wuhan and then, after the Japanese Army forced the evacuation of Wuhan in the summer of 1938, in Chongqing. While he struggled to hold together the literary arm of the United Front, he also tried to set an example by writing a steady stream of patriotic plays and ballads that were designed to rally troops and civilians alike behind the Chinese war effort. But both the passion and the ironic humor of his earlier works were muted in these overtly propagandistic pieces; and he fared even worse when he tried to recapture his old mastery of the novel form. *Cremation*, which he finished in 1943, was transparently designed to denigrate Chinese who collaborated with the Japanese and to show that, even though they high-mindedly claimed to be saving their fellow countrymen's lives, they would merely be displaced by Chinese traitors of darker hue; the only hope for their nation lay in the guerrilla forces loyal to the Guomindang, who would continue their struggle relentlessly until the invaders had been expelled from Chinese soil.[28] In his preface to *Cremation* Lao She expressed uneasiness about the novel, and candidly noted that "in prewar times I would have destroyed the manuscript." He acknowledged his ignorance of war in all its technical aspects—tactics, weaponry, transportation—and added that he didn't even know much about the interior of China where he was now living: "What, then, should people write? How could they write?"[29]

In these apparently casual remarks Lao She was underlining a profound problem about life in Chongqing, indeed about life in all the Guomindang-occupied areas of "Free China" from 1938 onward. After the bloody campaigns of that year, both the Japanese and the Chinese armies were exhausted, and they settled into a period of uneasy stalemate as each tried to regenerate itself for the next stage of the fray. The Chinese, having lost almost all their planes and heavy military equipment, and based now in poor inland areas with minimal industrial plant, had become largely dependent on the supplies that could reach them from the West over the Burma Road. Thus they could not undertake a major offensive against the Japanese. In this period of enforced calm, old animosities between the Guomindang and the Communists began to flare anew: clashes between guerrilla troops claiming different loyalties were common, for the Communists, from their base in Yanan, steadily extended a series of border-region governments behind Japanese lines, encouraged mutinies among armies of northern militarists previously loyal to Chiang Kaishek, and enlarged their armies and expanded their operations accordingly. Each party tried to infiltrate the organizational apparatus of the other with intelligence agents. Guomindang spokesmen claimed that the Communists were making cynical use of United Front slogans to increase their own sphere of operations, while the Communists insisted they were deprived of essential military supplies and of any meaningful voice in government. In January 1941, Guomindang units, alleging that Communist forces operating in the area of southern Anhui were disobeying orders, openly attacked the Communist New Fourth Army and killed thousands of troops; a few months later the Yanan base area was attacked from the northwest by Chinese Muslim troops apparently acting under Guomindang instructions. A broad-based coalition of Chinese politicians and intellectuals from a number of third parties tried desperately to reestablish some form of national reconstruction league and pressed for a reconvening of the old National Assembly to bring back a measure of unity. In March 1941 they formed a Federation of Chinese Democratic Parties, but their initiatives were not successful in healing the rift. By the time of the Japanese bombing of Pearl Harbor in December 1941, and the establishment by President Franklin Roosevelt of a major American command center at Chongqing under the direction of General Joseph Stilwell, the Chinese United Front was already showing signs of disintegration.[30]

One upshot of this situation was a particular disparity between Western and Chinese perceptions of what was happening in Chongqing: Western political leaders and editorial writers praised "Free China" and spoke of Chiang Kaishek as a truly national leader, whose country could be considered one of the major allies in the anti-Japanese war effort, but critics within China pointed bitterly to the muddle and bureaucratic inefficiency at the capital, to the poorly run army, to the flagrant corruption that accompanied the accounting and disbursement of the huge American loans that had been made to Chiang's government, and to the renewed censorship and political intimidation that the Guomindang was directing at anyone suspected of being "left." One of Wen Yiduo's students, who had moved to Chongqing around the time Wen went to Kunming, and had kept up a regular correspondence with his former teacher, caught this aspect of the times with chilling brevity in a poem entitled "Arrest":

> *A feeble struggle*
> *Like that of a small bird*
> *Gripped in a huge hand.*
> *Confused footsteps*
> *Pass through the tiny courtyard.*
> *Torchlights flash beyond my window.*
> *Frightfully, for a moment,*
> *An old woman's piercing, sad wail,*
> *Like the ripples on a sea of darkness*
> *Where someone has just cast a pebble,*
> *Gradually recedes afar,*
> *Gradually fades.*[31]

Other writers sought to capture the mingled frenzy, callousness, and corroded, semi-Westernized morality of wartime Chongqing in their verses. Particularly successful was Yuan

Shuipai, in "Headline Music"; he used a montage of current
political slogans, advertisements, and newspaper headlines to
memorialize the hundreds of refugees trampled to death in the
summer of 1941 during a panicked scramble for shelter as Japanese planes bombed the city. This poem, not surprisingly,
could not be published in Chongqing and eventually appeared
in Hong Kong:

Seven days and seven nights eating, sleeping, defecating
   on top of a freight car
From one hundred to three hundred swept up at the entrance to the tunnel
Big fire, Big fire, Big fire
Bodies, Bodies, Bodies
>   *The suggestive pictures on the walls*
>   *Musclemen pushing their way forward*
>   *Leg, Leg, Leg*
>   *Curve, Curve, Curve*
A pair of eyes protruding from the flames
And the flames shooting out from the eyes
City follows city, the rail line
From village to village, narrow trails and cavalries
>   *Infinite joy, when the moon is again full*
>   *Lots of people lose their hats in the thumping crowd*
>   *If the air-raid siren sounds, full Technicolor*
>   *First prize is definitely here, hurry up and get rich*
Tense, Tense, Tense
Bullish, Bullish, Bullish
Four thousand million dollars tumble in the gold market
Change, No change, Don't discuss national affairs
>   *Every tune grand, elegant, and elevating*
>   *Every scene full of exquisite music and dance*
>   *Sing in honor of schoolmates joining the army*
>   *Dance for benefit of the refugees.*[32]

Obviously Yanan benefited from the contrast with Chongqing, and the inspiring sense of cutting through the complexities of life to some cleaner, clearer center dominated the Communist world there and had an inspiring effect not just on the
Chinese intellectuals such as Ding Ling who moved to Yanan

but on almost all the visiting Western journalists and military personnel who managed to reach the Communist base area. This was partly because luxuries were simply unavailable—the mere fact that Ding Ling owned a can of coffee at one point was a subject for extended conversation—and partly because Communist ideology was in a flexible and pragmatic state following the acceptance of a national United Front policy. Furthermore, given the poor economic condition of Yanan, almost any Chinese ally, regardless of class, was welcome in the struggle against the Japanese.[33] Mao Zedong's own writings of the late 1930s emphasized the need for constant learning through practice and for understanding the contradictions inherent in any given situation, and eulogized the creative work of the Guomindang in its thirty years of leadership since the last years of the Qing. Mao pointed up the need for "the sinification of Marxism—that is to say, making certain that in all its manifestations it is imbued with Chinese peculiarities," but he insisted at the same time that the broadest possible range of forces should be studied: this was essential if the Chinese were not to become "either Don Quixotes or Ah Qs."[34] Ding Ling's feelings at the time can be gauged from a brief dialogue between two women in the Communist base area which appears in one of her 1939 stories:

> "You always look so pleasant," Liusu said, "I cannot understand, Weidi. It seems that you have never been affected by any kind of trouble in life. How do you cultivate such a spirit?"
> "Don't think I have always been like this. I was an unhappy girl in the past; I worried a lot. Since coming here, I feel reborn spiritually. I can follow my own interests, plan my own work, and dare to say and do as I want. Collective life suits me well. I am conscious of my existence, however insignificant it may be."[35]

Yet even by 1940 this air of optimism was growing hard to sustain. The New Fourth Army clash with the Guomindang in 1941 and the death of so many Communist troops was a serious setback, as had been the savage Japanese counterattacks that followed hard upon the major Hundred Regiments Offensive which the Communists mounted in northern China during 1940. In their campaign, which had the grim name "Three Alls" (standing for "burn all, loot all, kill all"), the Japanese made a systematic attempt to root out northern Chinese resistance through terror. Scores of villages were destroyed and their civilian populations either shot or transported to work in Japanese industrial plants in Manchukuo. Though one response to this terror was a flood of new recruits to the Chinese Communist Party, various developments forced the Communist leadership to rethink their strategy. In particular, the economic blockade by the Guomindang, combined with a cutoff of subsidies, led to massive inflation and supply shortages; the need to tighten party morale and discipline became paramount; and party leaders began to place renewed insistence on the importance of the "Mass Line" and a greater emphasis on the need for solidarity within the ranks of those intellectuals who claimed adherence to Communism.[36]

Ding Ling felt these pressures along with everyone else, and after 1940 she stopped writing the euphoric resistance stories that had kept her busy the previous two years. It is a curious coincidence—and one that perhaps helps explain this shift in her mood—that she and some of her friends had recently acquired copies of Qu Qiubai's sardonic testament, "Some Superfluous Words," and had been arguing over its message. Ding, who had known Qu very well, was sure that the document was genuinely his, though other cadres denied its authenticity.[37] In a new group of four stories, written during 1940 and 1941, she began to probe deeply into the problems of harshness, hypocrisy, and disillusionment that she discerned behind the apparently cheerful face of Yanan Communism. In one of these stories a newspaper reporter, longing for the richer life of the Guomindang base areas, is at last confronted with true hardship and true courage, but instead of being enriched by the experience he dreams only of exploiting this chance to write it up and vaunt his own role. In another, entitled "When I Was in Xia Village," a girl, abducted by the Japanese and repeatedly raped by them until she is sickened by humiliation and weakened by venereal disease, is persuaded by the Communists to continue having assignations with Japanese men so that the party underground can gain vital information; unable to explain her actions publicly, the young woman is of course vilified and distrusted by her fellow villagers, though she never loses her faith that the party doctors will eventually be able to cure her disease. In a third story, a man vaulted into a responsible rural office that he doesn't want, and unhappy in his childless marriage to a much older wife, worries over his sexual frustrations and his political incompetence; the dominant thought in his mind as his wife, enraged at his apathy, pounds on the side of their bed is that she may break the family crock of bean sprouts that is balanced there. He loves bean sprouts.[38]

If some might have seen in that ironic ending an echo of the last line of Qu Qiubai's "Some Superfluous Words," and found that echo reprehensible, it was her fourth story, "In the Hospital," that was the frankest, the most meticulously documentary, and ultimately the most damaging to the party. For in this depiction of a young woman eager for revolutionary service, sent to work in a small clinic in the Yanan base area, Ding Ling presented a world in which Communist heartlessness and incompetence led to a state of affairs that could barely be distinguished, in any rational way, from the capitalist world elsewhere. Ding Ling acknowledged the reality of the wartime shortage of equipment and services in any base-area hospital, where there was no coal for stoves, no clean bedding, one hypodermic needle for the whole unit, and almost no anesthetics or medicines; but what she added was a sense that these conditions were made worse, not better, by the particular attitudes of the cadres and their staff. Those most devoted to their work are slowly frozen into silence or else forced into a frenzied and ultimately self-defeating round of complaints. The story ends with the protagonist, a young nurse named Lu Ping, applying for and being granted transfer to another unit.

The deep ambiguity of Lu Ping's motives for joining the party and her intrinsic sense of the weakness of her party discipline are spelled out in a passage of interior monologue, delivered by Lu Ping not long after her arrival at the hospital. Here she reflects on the way the party had ordered her to give up her hopes of becoming a senior official, and had ended her college education so that she would become a nurse in the hinterland:

> She argued, saying that she didn't have the right disposition
> for such work, and that she would do anything else, no
> matter how significant or insignificant. She even dropped a
> few tears, but these arguments weren't enough to shake the
> chief's determination. She couldn't overturn this decision,
> so she had no choice but to obey.
> The party branch secretary came to talk to her and the
> section leader wouldn't leave the subject alone. Their tactics
> irritated her. She knew the rationale behind all this. They
> simply wanted her to cut herself off from the bright future
> which she had been dreaming of for the past year and to
> return to her old life again. She knew she could never become
> a great doctor and was nothing more than an ordinary
> midwife. Whether she was there or not made no difference
> at all. She was full of illusions about her ability to break out
> of the confines of her life. But now that the iron collar of
> "party" and "needs of the party" was locked about her
> neck, could she disobey party orders? Could she ignore this
> iron collar which she had cast upon herself?[39]

Ding Ling gave a powerful portrait of the muddle and fright
that lay at the heart of Nurse Lu Ping's thinking: after assisting
at one protracted operation, where she finally faints because of
the accumulated fumes from the coal brazier in the cave where
the team is working, she lies in bed, crying and feverish, longing
only to be with her mother once again, so that she can cry
her heart out on her bosom:

> The realities of life frightened her. She wondered why
> many people had walked by her that night, yet not a single
> one of them had helped her. And she thought about the fact
> that the director of the hospital would endanger patients,
> doctors, and nurses just to save a little money. She looked
> back on her daily life. Of what use was it to the revolution?
> Since the revolution was for the whole of mankind, why
> were even the closest of comrades so devoid of love? She
> was wavering. She asked herself: "Is it that I am vacillating
> in my attitude toward the revolution?" The neurasthenia
> which she had had of old gripped her once again. Night
> after night she could not sleep.
> People in the party branch were criticizing her. They

capped her with labels like "petty-bourgeois consciousness," "audacious and liberal intellectualism," and many
other dangerous doctrines; in short, they said that her party
spirit was weak. The director of the hospital called her in
for a talk.

Even the patients were cool and distant toward her, saying she was a romantic. Yes, she should struggle! But whom
should she struggle against? Against everyone?[40]

It was not a very encouraging question for Ding Ling to be asking, in this time and place, even through a fictional character;
and if she meant the answer to be in the affirmative, as she certainly seemed to be implying, then she was offering the kind of
challenge that the party could not afford to ignore.

·11·

RECTIFICATIONS

Ding Ling was treading on dangerous ground in 1942, and other writers in Yanan were not deterred from doing the same. One of her friends, picking up her critical attitude, invoked the memory of Lu Xun in writing a number of *zawen*—the short, sharp, critical essays that had been Lu Xun's stock-in-trade during the last years of his life, and in which he mocked or parodied aspects of the Communist style. Other Yanan intellectuals followed suit, and in her position as editor of the literary page of the Yanan paper *Liberation Daily*, to which she had been appointed in the spring of 1941, Ding Ling actively encouraged this trend:

> . . . It is said that this is not a suitable place for the writing of the *zawen* and that what is needed here is only the reflection of democratic life and great construction.
>
> It may be in human nature to be intoxicated with small successes or to hate to be told that one is sick or that one needs to see a doctor about it. But that is also a sign of indolence and cowardice.
>
> Lu Xun is dead. Customarily we say to ourselves that we should do this or that in order to live up to him. But we have not sufficiently acquired his courage in sparing no details. I think it will do us most good if we emulate his steadfastness in facing the truth, and his fearlessness. This age of ours still needs the *zawen*, a weapon that we should never lay down. Raise it, and the *zawen* will not be dead.[1]

Several writers responded, pointing out that there was darkness over Yanan as well as over Chongqing, and that the cadres were "inflicting scars" on those they sought to suppress: Lu Xun's "dagger" had been rusting in the ground, it must be dug up and sharpened. Others wrote that the party had not rooted out corruption and indifference, and its leaders separated themselves out from the masses and the young by enjoying a whole range of special privileges.[2] Xiao Jun, a young Manchurian writer who had been a highly praised protégé of Lu Xun's and had arrived at Yanan in 1940, amplified these doctrines, claiming that "the wine of comradely love" was being "diluted" in Yanan, and that some overzealous cadres behaved like runners in spiked shoes who "stamped on the faces" of their rivals in the race.[3] By January 1942, Xiao Jun had begun to reintroduce the old theme of "heroic individualism" (once espoused by Xu Zhimo), in which he championed the goal of all people to "strengthen themselves and strive to be first"; though Xiao placed Marx and Lenin in his individualistic pantheon, he wrote that the reason he found them worthy of love was that they "were truly poets," and he put them in the context of Homer, Socrates, Byron, Beethoven, and Rodin.[4]

More searching and subtle was Ding Ling's essay of March 1942 entitled "Thoughts on March 8," in which she reflected on the situation of women in Yanan in the general context of International Women's Day. (Inaugurated in 1910, this day had first been celebrated in China in 1924.) Ignoring the instructions issued by the party's Central Committee, which stated that International Women's Day should be devoted to celebrating the anti-fascist United Front, promoting unity in China, and extolling the active roles of women within the revolution, Ding Ling took her own tack.[5] It might be true that things were better for women in Yanan than in other parts of China, she wrote, but there was still no need for people to envy them unduly. Women continued to lead a difficult life, in fact, because of the double standard of the men around them.

> People all pay attention when a woman comrade gets married, but they don't leave it at that. It's difficult for a woman to have a fairly close relationship with any comrade, and

impossible to do so with several. She will be satirized by cartoonists who ask, "So the section head is to marry, is she?" As the poets have said of women:

> *In Yanan only the horseriders are the political bosses,*
> *There are no artists as bosses.*
> *An artist in Yanan is one who hunts for a pretty*
> *girl in vain.*

And the women have to put up with words like these at various gatherings: "Dammit, you may sneer at us old cadres, and say we are 'country bumpkins,' but if it wasn't for us bumpkins you wouldn't even be in Yanan!"

But most women here have to get married. (Not to get married is a greater crime, for then they will be the subject of all sorts of rumors and constantly reviled.) If they don't marry one of those who ride on horseback, then it'll be one wearing straw sandals; if not an artist, then the general affairs section chief.

What was especially ironical, Ding Ling continued, was that having been forced by pressures within Yanan society to give up their party careers, to marry, and to bear children, these women were then sneered at as "Noras who came home"; if they so much as left their babies with a sitter to go out dancing once a week, the whole world started to gossip about them. Some married women tried to avoid having children and sought abortions, or else tried to find full-time nursemaids so they could get back to political work—but if they did, they were accused of being "backward." Divorce was no solution, either: made easy for men, it was always criticized if undertaken by a woman. As for a woman's ultimate fate, said Ding Ling, whether she is "backward" or not, the physical laws of life remain unchanged and only the terminology has been altered to show that women live in the modern age: "Their skin soon starts to wrinkle, their hair begins to thin, the vexations of their daily life take from them the last vestiges of their beauty. They are trapped among these misfortunes as if they were totally natural. And yet in the old society people could at least have said they were to be pitied or were ill-fated, whereas today we say it's 'her own doing' or 'serves her right.' " In a central passage of the essay, Ding Ling asked the party to take a more generous view of women's problems:

> I am a woman myself, and I understand women's short-comings better than anyone. But I also understand their sufferings. Women cannot transcend their times, they are not ideal, they are not made of steel. They are unable to resist all of society's temptations and silent oppressions, they have all had a history of blood and tears, they have all felt grand emotions (no matter whether they have been elated or depressed, whether they are lucky or unlucky, whether they are still struggling on their own or have entered the stream of ordinary life), and this is all the truer for the women comrades who have managed to reach Yanan. How I sympathize with all those women who have been cast down and called criminals! I wish that men, especially those in positions of power, as well as women themselves, would see women's shortcomings in the context of social reality.[6]

A couple of months later Mao Zedong was reported to have given up the seat of honor in a group photograph to Ding Ling, with the quip, "We don't want to be rebuked again on March 8."[7] But in fact, by then the first major Communist "rectification" campaign was almost over, and as things transpired, Ding Ling was not to write again with such frankness for almost four decades.

The stated aim of the 1942 rectification movement was to improve party organization and tighten discipline during a time of rapid expansion of party membership due to the flood of refugees to Yanan and the immense pressures being placed on Yanan by both the Japanese and the Guomindang. The fundamental strategy was based on theories that Mao Zedong had first experimented with in the Jiangxi Soviet during the late 1920s, in an attempt to resolve party conflicts by peer-group pressure and by intensive study rather than by purges or physical violence; in 1939 and 1940 this method had been used on four thousand students and cadres in the Yanan area, who were given a directed course of readings in Marx, Lenin, Stalin, and the works of Mao Zedong and Liu Shaoqi. In early 1942 Mao announced a new campaign to be directed at two sets of problems: on the bureaucratic front, the targets were to be "subjectivism, sectarianism, and commandism"; in the cultural world, "realism, sentimentalism, and satire."[8] A speech that Mao gave in February 1942 set the tone: the rectification campaign had an ambiguous side to it, and could be seen as being directed against the cadres criticized by Xiao Jun and Ding Ling, or against Ding Ling and Xiao Jun themselves, or indeed against anyone with only book learning who could not till the soil, fight, or understand the real nature of revolutionary theory. "We do not study Marxism-Leninism because it is pleasing to the eye or because it has some mystical value," said Mao. "Marxism-Leninism has no beauty, nor has it any mystical value. It is only extremely useful." The relationship between Marxism-Leninism and the Chinese revolution was the same as that between an arrow and a target, he went on. If it made no sense to shoot arrows carelessly into space, neither did it make sense to "take the arrow in hand, thrust it back and forth, and say again and again in praise, 'excellent arrow, excellent arrow,' " and never shoot it at all. At this stage of China's experience, however, so Mao claimed, the archer should not be punished for inaccuracy or for a lack of comprehension of the arrow's true function: "Our object in exposing errors and criticizing shortcomings is like that of a doctor in curing a disease. The whole purpose is to save people, not to cure them to death."[9]

Mao's criticisms of the Yanan intellectuals' shortcomings prompted those same intellectuals to a vigorous counterattack. Ding Ling's essay on International Women's Day may be seen as one such response—a reassertion of the need for feminist arguments in a world where Communist cadres had been claiming that feminist concerns must yield to the interests of proletarian solidarity—but there were scores of others, many of which she published on the literary page of *Liberation Daily*. Perhaps the bitterest pieces were those by Wang Shiwei, a Communist activist who had studied in Moscow during the 1920s, won some reputation as a translator of Marxist works, and was currently employed as an instructor of Communist theory at the Central Political Institute in Yanan. In a two-part essay, "Wild Lily," which Ding Ling published in mid-March 1942, Wang mourned a young woman friend who had been executed by the Guomindang in 1928. He contrasted her world of political passion and activism with the complacency of the cadres at Yanan, who kept well away from the "sea of carnage" that was the reality elsewhere in China. Wang wrote that he had entitled his piece "Wild Lily" for two reasons: one, because this flower, which grew in such profusion around Yanan, made "a fitting dedication" to his friend's "pure memory"; two, because its bulb, when eaten, was said to be rather bitter to the taste. Those who had tasted the bulb claimed it had medicinal value, said Wang (an obvious reference to Mao's speech of a month before), "but I myself am not so sure of this." If Yanan was nevertheless a rare spot of light in a sea of darkness—and Wang admitted that on the whole it was—then there was all the more need "after having recognized the inevitability of such darkness, to prevent its reemergence in the guise of Bolshevik activism."[10]

The spate of criticism came to an end in April, when Ding Ling was removed from her editorial position; on May 2, after an address by Mao ordering the Yanan intellectuals to reflect on their attitudes toward the Communist Party and the audience for whom they were writing, both writers and cadres were ordered to conduct a protracted series of meetings, some in small sessions and some in public forums.[11] After three weeks of debate, Mao gave a second address, in which he spelled out his views on the function of art in much greater detail. Drawing from his own sense of what he felt to be the vitality of "popular" cultural forms, as well as from Soviet theorists and from the later writings of Qu Qiubai, Mao presented the basic rules under which writers were to operate henceforth in the Communist-dominated border regions: literature and art were to be for the masses, and the class stand was to be that of the proletariat, not that of the petty bourgeoisie. To this end, writers and artists must learn from the workers, peasants, and soldiers, and then popularize only what was needed and could be "readily accepted" by those same groups. Though one might learn from past or foreign literatures, these literatures could never be uncritically transplanted. The masses provided "literature and art with an inexhaustible source, their only source"; thus there could be no theory of "human nature" that was independent of class, and what some writers alleged to be a true human nature beyond class was in fact no more than bourgeois individualism. If a Yanan intellectual were to avoid becoming "the kind of useless writer or artist that Lu Xun in his will earnestly instructed his son never to become," said Mao, that intellectual must "definitely destroy feudal, bourgeois, petty-bourgeois, liberalist, individualist, nihilist, art-for-art's sake, aristocratic, decadent, pessimistic, and other kinds of creativity that are alien to the popular masses and the proletariat."[12] In another section of his talk, Mao directed himself specifically to Ding Ling's remarks of 1941 on the need for maintaining Lu Xun's *zawen* essays, and the spirit that had motivated them:

> "It is still the age of essays, and we still need the Lu Xun style." If we take the essay and the Lu Xun style just to mean satire, then this view is only correct when it applies to enemies of the people. Lu Xun lived under the rule of the forces of darkness, where there was no freedom of speech, and it was therefore absolutely correct of Lu Xun to use the essay form, with its cold ridicule and burning satire, to do battle. We also have a need for sharp ridicule to direct at fascism and Chinese reactionaries, but in anti-Japanese bases in the Shaanxi–Gansu–Ningxia border areas and elsewhere behind the enemy lines, where revolutionary writers and artists are given complete democratic freedom and only counterrevolutionary and Special Branch elements are denied it, the essay should not take the same form as Lu Xun's; it can shout at the top of its voice, but it shouldn't be obscure or devious, something that the popular masses can't understand. When it came to the people themselves and not their enemies, Lu Xun even in his "essay period" never ridiculed or attacked revolutionary people or parties, and his style in these essays was completely different from the style he employed against the enemy. I have already said above that the people's shortcomings must be criticized, but we must speak from genuine identification with the people and total devotion to their protection and education. If we treat comrades with the ruthless methods required against the enemy, then we are identifying ourselves with the enemy.[13]

On May 27, four days after this speech of Mao's, the Central Political Institute began a new series of meetings, called specifically to attack Wang Shiwei for "Wild Lily" and other writings. By early June these meetings had become more like mass rallies, with a thousand or more in attendance. Wang was charged with saying that "politics follows art" and that literature could reveal the universal aspects of human nature. He offered to give up his party membership but refused to recant, even when "big-character posters" denouncing him as a Trotskyist began to appear on the walls. Ding Ling, now subject to heavy pressures by party members who disliked her short story "In the Hospital," joined in the criticism of Wang; and on June 10 the Central Political Institute condemned him for being a "hidden Trotskyist" and expelled him from the party. He disappeared from public view while, it was said, he "applied himself to political problems." (Twenty years later, Mao reported that Wang had been executed in 1947.)[14]

Ding Ling was unable to save herself by her opposition to Wang. Increasingly strident attacks against her, some of them printed in *Liberation Daily*, denounced her as being just like her character Lu Ping in "In the Hospital"; the story itself was described as a work that ignored the masses and used old-fashioned realist techniques. In line with Mao's remarks of May 23, it was said that she had improperly used the tools of criticism against members of the Communist Party. The day after the condemnation of Wang was announced, she gave in: admitting that the charges against her were just, she added that she had also been mistaken in the views about women she presented in "Thoughts on March 8"; though she had "poured out blood and tears" in the essay, her attitudes represented an outdated feminism in the world of Yanan, where unity in the face of class struggle must transcend differences between the sexes.

Ding Ling's controversial earlier stance on women and this subsequent recantation prompted a flurry of comments about the role of "Noras" in the modern world. While at least one writer argued that Qiu Jin had been the true Nora, abandoning family for an uncertain future of revolutionary activism, others pointed out that in Yanan, at least, Nora would have acknowledged her responsibility to the masses as being the essential prerequisite for realizing her own true individuality. In Ding Ling's case, the verdict was left dangling: in late June she was ordered to leave Yanan and go to the rural areas to "study" with the peasantry. On the way, however, she was encouraged to write a long story on Red Army soldiers' heroism by the commander-in-chief of the Communist forces, Zhu De; Zhu invited her to his headquarters at Taolin and gave her access to combat reports. Her dutiful story, called "The Eighteen," was published in *Liberation Daily* on July 9, 1942. A few days later she left Taolin and went to work in the countryside, where she was to remain for the next two years.[15]

During these two years of Ding Ling's enforced withdrawal from the political and literary world of Yanan, the balance of forces in China between the Guomindang and the Communists began to shift dramatically. The American entry into the combat sphere in East Asia (as far as the Chinese were concerned, the Second World War had been in progress since 1937, with the outbreak of war against Japan, not merely since Hitler's invasion of Czechoslovakia in 1939 or the Japanese attack on Pearl Harbor in 1941) had conveyed far less advantage to Chiang Kaishek than he had hoped. Though the United States made massive loans to the Guomindang government, sent General Stilwell and a task force of advisers to Chongqing, and promised large supplies of Lend-Lease war matériel to the Chinese, the fall of Singapore to the Japanese and the sudden and catastrophic collapse of the British armies in Malaya during the spring of 1942 altered everyone's calculations about the probable speed of the Japanese advance in Southeast Asia; in the summer of 1942, after Chiang Kaishek's troops—to the fury of General Stilwell—had failed to check the Japanese advances in Burma, resulting in the closing of the Burma Road, China's last outlet to the ocean was lost. Thereafter, Chiang was to be dependent on the few supplies that could be ferried into southwestern China over the dangerous Himalayan airlift route from India known as "the Hump." Churchill and Stalin naturally gave priority to the campaigns against the German forces commanded by General Rommel in North Africa and to the defense of Stalingrad, rather than to the China theater, and since President Roosevelt's own interests lay in the Western theater also, he acceded to Churchill's requests that war matériel previously designated for China be shipped instead to Europe. Holding Stilwell personally responsible for this "betrayal," and resenting his attempts to push through sweeping reforms of the Nationalist army's tactical-training and command structure, Chiang Kaishek tended to follow the advice of General Claire Chennault that China try to defeat Japan from the air rather than on the ground. But the construction of major new airfields in southwestern China, often at an agonizing expense of labor and suffering, from which Japanese supply lines could be bombed, led predictably to a counterattack by a force of more than four hundred thousand Japanese troops during 1944. The Japanese captured Changsha, Guilin, and finally the strategic city of Guiyang, from which they could threaten Chongqing itself; Chiang's armies suffered casualties in excess of two hundred thousand men and a corresponding collapse of morale.[16]

In the latter part of 1943 and in 1944, by contrast, the Communist government in Yanan had made startling progress. Learning from the guerrilla experiences of the other border-region governments, and less and less restricted by United Front gradualism, the Yanan leadership adopted so-called Mass Line policies that included large-scale peasant mobilization, the pooling of mutual resources in poor areas, increasing domestic production in small industries and handicrafts, working in homes, schools, and youth groups to introduce socialist theory, extending the network of guerrilla operations against the Japanese into areas previously dominated by the Guomindang, and involving the peasants themselves in campaigns to confront landlords with demands for rent reduction. The combined effect of these efforts was the spread of Communist bases across the whole of northern China and the incorporation of more than one hundred million people into areas where there was at least some Communist presence.[17]

The levels of honesty, competence, and dedication among the Communist cadres who had brought about these results— whatever criticisms of their insensitivity or arrogance Ding Ling might have had—compared favorably with the behavior of those administering the Guomindang regions, whose venality and cruelty was widely known and widely feared. The Communists' ability to hold down prices in the border regions, after the bad experiences of 1941, also contrasted with the Guomindang's inability to control inflation, which by 1944 was catastrophic in Chongqing. Fully aware of the propaganda value of these contrasts, the Communists did everything they could to underline them. Ding Ling probably owed her return to Yanan from the countryside in the summer of 1944 to the fact that she was such an invaluable interviewee to present to foreign journalists: when they saw her there, ebullient and smiling, visibly relaxed, growing her own vegetables on a little plot outside her cave, spinning her own cotton thread, she appeared to be a living testimonial to the rightness of the Yanan way. The characters in the stories she wrote at this time were hardworking, unassuming, obedient to the party's call to service, and ready to apply all their skills to mobilize the peasantry for the war of resistance and to identify future party recruits. She adopted the folk idioms of northern Shaanxi province and abandoned the more convoluted sentence patterns—partly based on adopted European grammatical models —of her earlier stories. Mao Zedong expressed satisfaction with her new writings, which fitted admirably into the conception of Communist literary work that he had been developing.[18]

This combination of expanding Communist influence and Guomindang demoralization prompted Chinese Nationalists in Chongqing and Kunming to make a last attempt to establish some alternative political focus. The result was the establishment in October 1944 of the China Democratic League, which was committed to a program of civil liberties, avoidance of civil war, nationalization of the Chinese armed forces, and convocation of a representative National Assembly. Such a program, which would not have seemed farfetched to Kang Youwei in the 1890s, was too extreme for many of the embattled leaders of the Guomindang, and from its inception the league met with harassment, censorship, police interference, and sporadic acts of violence.[19]

Even though the Democratic League was active in Kunming, one might not have expected Wen Yiduo to take much interest in its work. In 1944 he was forty-five years old, and his days of student radicalism were twenty years behind him. With singular success he seemed to have managed to forge a life for himself that was beyond war and beyond politics. Deeply absorbed in the upbringing of his children, passionately devoted to his wife (friends took note of the way they arranged their time to be together and managed to make loving rituals of the daily meetings and partings ordained by the rhythms of his university teaching life), and close to his students, he had also immersed himself in the life of scholarship and had entered a period of extraordinary productivity. He was publishing steadily on the topic of his favorite "Songs of the South" by the third-century B.C. poet Qu Yuan, exploring the social background of such Confucian classics as the *Book of Poetry* and the *Book of Changes*, writing on Tang dynasty poetry, and compiling a major anthology of modern Chinese poetry. He was surrounded by compatible colleagues: his younger brother was in Kunming teaching French literature, Shen Congwen (who had developed a scholarly passion for the world of the sixth century B.C.) had moved south from Hunan and was living nearby, another friend was studying and teaching the works of Verlaine and Mallarmé, and yet another friend, the poems of Rilke and Goethe. Wen himself, although true to his decision to write no more poetry, had nevertheless found an outlet in the word settings he designed as supplements to Qu Yuan's poems, for Wen had begun the project of re-creating the world in which he believed these songs had been chanted and enjoyed twenty-two hundred years before:

> Under the thick shadowy foliage of a bamboo grove on a hillside there is a cart drawn by a leopard. The animal has a bright orange coat; beside it lies a fox, its body dotted with patches of gold and copper. Behind the bamboos in the background we can see the Goddess Peak, towering like a screen and forever hiding itself in the cloud and mist—the most beautiful and bashful among the Twelve Peaks of the Wu Mountain. The monotonous chirping of insects in the woods sounds like the buzzing in our ears. Suddenly a voice splits the silence, "It seems there is someone over there, in that fold of the hill." And the echoes, like countless concentric ripples on water, spread wider and wider toward the cliffs on all sides—"The hill—the hill—the hill—"[20]

His only prescription for China's illness, he told a close friend in a letter of November 25, 1943, was to compile a vast history of Chinese poetry or perhaps to compose a long historical poem which might pacify those spirits he had invoked so long ago in *Dead Water*: "I never forget that as well as our todays we are the possessors of those two or three thousand years of yesterdays."[21]

It seems to have been his growing awareness of the corruption and callousness in the Guomindang army that broke Wen Yiduo away from his scholarship and his poetic re-creations. By 1944 his three sons were in their teens, and when a national conscription program became more likely after the Japanese victories in southwestern China, Wen thought with horror of the life his children could expect. For years his own students had been torn in their allegiances, as some went to Yanan and some to Chongqing, and he knew that the youth of China were being forced into a situation where they would end up fighting one another rather than their common enemy, the Japanese. Now Wen began to see conscripts outside Kunming chained together, sometimes dying by the roadside, human jettison denied food or medicine or pay. At the same time his salary was being eroded by inflation at so swift a rate that he could feed his family on it for only a few days each month; he had to make up the difference by teaching at a second school and by carving decorative seals late into the night.[22]

One of the members of a small poetry club at the university, who sometimes walked to Wen's little house in the countryside outside Kunming, has recorded what was probably the breaking point. It was April 9, 1944, a sunny day; Wen had taken his eight-year-old daughter by the hand and, accompanied by a dozen students, sat on a patch of grass near some trees, where he and his students talked about poetry for two or three hours. After the session he strolled back with them to a bridge near the main road, where they came across another group of conscripts. "We've just got to do something about it," Wen told them. "Each time I see these 'able-bodied recruits' starved to death at the side of the road it's as if I myself suffered their punishments. Look at them there, tied together, dragged along, driven at gun point, every one of them emaciated to such an extent that their legs are no larger than this"—and Wen held up his right hand, finger touching thumb, to show the pitiful thinness of their limbs. "They trudge on, trudge on, and one of them falls to the ground. They trudge on again. Down goes another."[23]

In the course of the next few weeks Wen produced a series of politically oriented essays in which he lashed out at Chinese Confucian values of "moderation" for having induced the population to accept a "life between hunger and death," and blamed Chinese faith in the family for having destroyed the possibilities of true patriotism. He urged the adoption of progressive Western ideals, the abandonment of a self-centered "antiquarianism" that ignored current problems, and a total rejection of Confucian "thievery" and Daoist "escapism."[24] In July he talked at a student rally, challenging the students to revive the spirit of May 4, 1919, and December 9, 1935. In August, in company with several of his colleagues, he told a group of army officers who had invited them to discuss China's future that he was dismayed by the state of the Chinese armed forces and felt "revolution" might be the one remaining solution to China's problems. That autumn, as Chiang Kaishek finally triumphed over General Stilwell's attempts to force reform of the Chinese Nationalist army and got President Roosevelt to recall Stilwell to the United States, Wen Yiduo joined the newly formed Kunming branch of the Democratic League, helped organize a major rally in Kunming, and established a new political weekly. In a burst of redirected intellectual energy he began to read Lunacharsky and Plekhanov, the poems of Mayakovsky, the critical works of Lu Xun, and any of Mao Zedong's materials that he could obtain.[25]

Wen Yiduo's radical commitment and sense of personal frustration grew ever deeper during 1945. Once again the land war against the Japanese in China had reached a stage of stalemate: overextended after their 1944 counterattacks into southwestern China, the Japanese were now mustering all their resources to withstand the American forces in the Pacific. Chiang Kaishek used this time—aided by General Albert C. Wedemeyer, Stilwell's more tactful successor as commander in the China theater—to reorganize his armies and improve their training; the Communist forces in the north moved similarly to expand their areas of control through campaigns of mass education and guerrilla mobilization. Wen's response, in this mood of retrenchment, was to throw himself with greater energy into the work of the Democratic League and to spur the Chinese on to national reform through his writings.

His approach had much of the flavor of the May Fourth Movement in 1919, in which he had participated as a student, for clearly all its aims of eradicating old cultural and social values had not yet been achieved. Uneasy about his own long years of immersion in classical studies, Wen remarked that the motive for his study of such works was now "to bleed their poisonous boils and expose their sinister sides." To friends who reminded him of his former high poetic standards and insistence on rigid form, he responded that "this is a time when drummers are needed. . . . As to chamber music players, our need of them is secondary." Wen's specific reference here was to the school of young Chinese poets drawn to emulate the Soviet poet Mayakovsky, whose "drumbeat style" suggested a call to arms. Colleagues remonstrated with Wen, pointing out the inappropriateness and personal danger of his conduct, and he replied, "I don't understand politics, but is today the time for us to worry about our personal safety? I appreciate your concern very much. But I still want to be a man, and I still have a conscience."[26]

The poet Qu Yuan, whose death by suicide while an exile in the southwest twenty-two hundred years before had rich historical resonance for Wen, now came to seem "symbolic of man's struggle for life with honor." One must assume that Wen talked lengthily about this theme with Guo Moruo when Guo visited Kunming in the summer of 1945. Guo Moruo had recently finished his own historical play based on Qu Yuan's life and had been translating Qu's difficult poetry into vernacular Chinese; furthermore Guo, a committed member of the Communist Party since he had shed his infatuation with the poetry of Tagore and left Xu Zhimo's circle back in the mid-1920s, and well acquainted with the situation in Chongqing, where he had been serving in the Propaganda Department, must have reinforced Wen's sense of the urgency of the need for political reform in China.[27]

The slow reorganization of the Guomindang armies, and their plans for eventual reunification of the country, were predicated on a probable collapse of Japan during 1946; because the Chinese were unaware of the development of the atomic bomb, no one expected an earlier Japanese surrender. Thus when the Japanese armies were ordered by Emperor Hirohito to lay down their arms in China in mid-August 1945, after the bombings of Hiroshima and Nagasaki, over much of China the Guomindang were quite unprepared at any formal level to receive the Japanese surrender. Accordingly, Communist troops moved into the vacuum, both accepting surrender and seizing Japanese arms and munitions, bolstering their own armed forces and ordering their troops to occupy portions of Manchuria. The American mediation efforts, led first by General Patrick Hurley and then by General George C. Marshall, succeeded in getting Mao Zedong to fly to Chongqing for talks with Chiang Kaishek in late 1945, and in getting both sides to agree to convene a Political Consultative Conference in January 1946 that would combine Communist, Guomindang, and the various "Third Force" democratic parties into discussions of China's future. Wen Yiduo worked hard in Kunming, through speeches and writings, to ensure that the conference would have a substantive effect on China's future, but his efforts were first undercut and then made increasingly dangerous by Chiang's decision to replace the various wartime regional commanders—some of whom, in line with the still official United Front policy of accommodation, had been moderately tolerant of political dissent—with men of proven political loyalty to Chiang himself. The results in Kunming were immediate: student demonstrations were fired upon, and gangs of toughs, dressed in civilian clothes or as coolies, roamed through schools and colleges, smashing windows and equipment, beating up Lianda students, and even throwing hand grenades. Three students and one music-school teacher were killed and one other student lost a leg in a grenade explosion; in defiance of the authorities the students placed the coffins of these four "martyrs" in the university library, surrounded by funeral scrolls and burning incense. In March 1946, during processions and memorial services for the four, the Kunming students called a student strike, which soon spread to other campuses around the country.[28]

Later in that spring of 1946 further mediation efforts failed, and civil war between the Communists and the Guomindang erupted yet again; the Lianda students and faculty slowly began to move back toward their campuses in the north. Wen Yiduo stayed on in Kunming to continue working for the Democratic League and to tidy up bits of university business. Sympathetic friends, worried about his chances of survival in this tense political world, had helped to clear an academic appointment for him at the University of California, but he declined to go, even when his wife added her pleas to those of his colleagues. On July 11 one of his closest friends in the Democratic League, Li Gongpu, was shot and killed in the street a few blocks from Wen's home. Wen insisted on holding a memorial service for Li, even though warned that the act was sheer folly.

His insistence reminds one of his emotional state in 1922, after he heard that a young Chinese friend of his had been killed in a car crash in Colorado: "This news makes me think of bigger questions—the meaning of life and death—the great puzzle of the universe. The last several days I have been very absentminded. They say I am losing my mind. But isn't the man who cannot lose his mind over such big questions the one who is truly senseless?"[29] The memorial ceremonies for Li Gongpu were held on July 15, 1946, and Wen himself addressed the crowd, praising Li's example and daring the secret agents who had killed his friend to shoot him, too. At five o'clock that evening, as he left the office of the Democratic League's newspaper in the company of his nineteen-year-old son, who had come to walk him home, a group of men across the street opened fire. Wen fell to the ground with three bullets in his head and died instantly. (His son, seriously wounded in the chest and legs, survived.)[30]

Though Wen's friends in Kunming did not dare to protest after his death as he had protested after Li's, the matter swiftly became a national *cause célèbre*. The Democratic League formed a commission of inquiry, headed by Liang Shuming, the controversialist of the 1920s who was now a nationally respected philosopher and political activist; the commission's report concluded that members of the Kunming garrison command had been responsible for the murder, though direct links to the senior Guomindang leadership could not be proved. Wen Yiduo's name became a symbol across China for the need to stand up for intellectual and personal freedom against the repressive measures of the Guomindang.[31]

One of the league's demands, reemphasized by the Political Consultative Conference in 1946, had been for an end to "foreign involvement" in China's civil war, a clear reference to the aid the United States had been giving to the Guomindang. This aid, in late 1945 and early 1946, had included the patrolling of certain key harbors in northern China by the United States Marines, and the airlifting of large numbers of Chiang Kaishek's troops to Manchuria, so as to prevent the whole area's falling into Communist hands. The league also protested the scale of the American sales of war surplus equipment to Chiang (some $900 million worth by the summer of 1946). In December of that year the alleged rape of a Chinese woman student at Beijing National University by two American Marines raised the excitement and anger of the students, so recently returned from Kunming, to new and dramatic levels, and clumsy government attempts to discredit the young woman's story by questioning her morality only inflamed the situation further. Guomindang repression of dissent, American military aid to Chiang Kaishek, the American presence in China, and the act of rape itself fused together in the public mind. Protest rallies and demonstrations in Beijing spread to other cities: to Tianjin, to Shanghai, to Chongqing, to Guangzhou, even to Taibei, in Taiwan, now restored to Chinese sovereignty for the first time since its loss in 1895 had sparked Kang Youwei's earliest protests. Chambers of Commerce and women's groups joined the movement. Only a year after the war's end, the Guomindang seemed as incapable of meeting the needs of the Chinese people as the warlord regimes of the past, and the Americans were already replacing the Japanese as the key symbol of imperialist aggression. Wen Yiduo, who had played his part in the May Fourth Movement of 1919 by writing heroic couplets in beautiful classical calligraphy shortly before leaving for Chicago, would certainly have been grimly amused.[32]

At the war's end, some one hundred thousand troops from the Communist base areas, commanded by General Lin Biao, a thirty-eight-year-old veteran of the Jiangxi Soviet campaigns and the Long March, moved north into Manchuria. There they made contact with Russian troops (who had entered the area in August 1945) and accepted the surrender of both the Japanese Manchurian armies and the forces of the former Manchukuo puppet regime; with the massive new supplies of captured arms now available to them, the Chinese Communist forces were prepared to hold Manchuria—especially the area north of the Sungari River—against any Guomindang forces sent against them. Ding Ling left Yanan late that same summer, though she did not get as far as Manchuria. Instead she settled a hundred miles northwest of Beijing in the city of Zhangjia-kou, once an important garrison city on the Great Wall, now one of the bastions of the Communist base area in northern China. Here she spent a few peaceful months with her friend the writer Chen Ming, whom she had met while working in Yanan, and with her son and daughter, abandoned during her flight from Shanghai a decade earlier, now reunited with their mother. Then in July 1946—the same month that Wen Yiduo was shot in Kunming—she moved out into the Hebei countryside near Zhuolu, on the Sanggan River, to join the Communist cadres and local villagers in the work of land reform.[33]

The patterns of land reform that were to be followed in the countryside marked a dramatic and deliberate abandonment of the more moderate policies of "rent reduction" practiced in Communist areas during the United Front period of the war against Japan; they were detailed in a directive of May 4, 1946, an intraparty document intended to set policy for such provinces as Shandong, Hebei, and Shanxi in northern China, where the Guomindang had not been able to reestablish effective power. (In the south, the Guomindang was generally too strong; in Manchuria the complexities of the situation caused by the American airlift of tens of thousands of Guomindang troops, as well as the ongoing Soviet presence, made coherent planning difficult.) The policy directive took care to distinguish between different types of landlord, different levels within the peasantry, and differing degrees of Communist control in a given area. Big landlords and Japanese collaborators, if guilty of major crimes, were to be beaten or killed; those who had been less exploitative were to be left enough land for subsistence and the rest was to be confiscated. In areas where the party was strong, smaller landlords and rich peasants were to be persuaded through "arbitration and agreement" to sell or donate their surplus landholdings to the poorer members of the community, but their industrial and commercial enterprises would be left untouched. The middle peasants—those who held enough land for their own sustenance but did not hire much extra *labor*—were to be treated with the greatest care and "absorbed into the movement," and their land was not to be "encroached" upon. All land accumulated through sales, confiscation, and "donations" would then be distributed by the Communist-organized peasant associations among landless rural workers, poor tenants, the poorest peasants, and families of the war dead. Toward intellectuals and those landlords who had escaped from their villages during the war but now sought to return home and work productively, there was to be a "conciliatory attitude." In areas where Communist control was less strong, land reforms were to stop at the level of rent and interest reduction, as they had in Yanan, and not proceed to land redistribution.[34]

In addition to the peasant associations, several other mass organizations were called upon for service: militia units at the county level, to guard supply lines and occupy areas captured by the line troops in the Communist army; local self-defense corps at the village level, to transport grain and military supplies and handle village defense, a task demanded of all men between the ages of sixteen and fifty-five; women's associations, to maintain sentry systems, check all travelers, help with first aid, and develop handicrafts and local women's educational systems. Naturally, this document presented an ideal model rather than reality, and variations existed in every village, from the number of landlords and their exploitativeness down to the numbers of tenants and the ability of available cadres; the general trend, however, was toward ever greater radicalism, accompanied by much random violence and terror, and by the summer of 1947 total redistribution of land among all villagers—women and men alike—was widely advocated, even if that meant seizing middle peasants' land as well.[35]

The tension and excitement caused by these Communist programs, which promised land ownership—even if only of small plots—to tens of millions of peasant families who had lived in the bleakest poverty all their lives, was immense. Ding Ling was at once caught up in the drama of what these changes meant, and of how the poor reacted, by their moments of caution as well as by their excesses. Though there was of course no guarantee that the reforms would be permanent, for fighting between Communist and Guomindang forces continued over much of Manchuria and northern China, the peasants involved in the mass discussions and the mass activism of the land-reform process were permanently changed by it. Ding Ling was affected by her experiences with the peasants, and also saw those experiences as the raw material for her own writing:

> I found I was deeply concerned about them, though not because they possessed certain lovable qualities. I was extremely tolerant of their shortcomings. I felt restless and sleepless, and gradually found that my earlier devotion to land-reform work became channeled into another kind of ardor. Many characters crowded into my mind. I discussed my ideas with them, argued with them. Sometimes so much came to mind that there was too much for me to handle; other times there was too little to write. Anyway, the memories and my aroused imagination excited me and drove me on, making me nervous yet also strong. I lived in their world, immersed in clouds of colorful new possibilities. I was eager to do something, saying to myself, "Start; don't wait!"[36]

Supplementing those areas in which there was "too little to write" by wide reading in the filed reports of Communist cadres, to which she was given special access, Ding Ling started a new novel early in 1947. In the summer of 1948 she finished *The Sun Shines over the Sanggan River* (or, more exactly, as with *Mother* thirteen years before, she finished the first part of an initially projected trilogy, which was destined to stand on its own as a completed work).[37]

Ding Ling set her novel in the countryside near the Sanggan River where she had been living during 1946, focusing on a fictional village she called Nuanshui (which can be literally translated as "Genial Stream"). She was not going to repeat the mistakes she had made in 1942 by criticizing Communist cadres unnecessarily, and the senior cadre in Nuanshui, named Zhang Bin, sent in briefly to supervise the trickiest phase of the land reform, is presented as a superhero, with "eyes like a hawk and the speed of a deer," a man who can live for months on raw maize or salted turnip, or sleep in holes in the ground in deepest winter (wakening at intervals to jump up and down to prevent frostbite). His judgments are always fair, shrewd, kind.[38] One should add that the other cadres in the story are recognizably human: some young and energetic, preys to temptation; many corruptible, subject to fears and doubts. One, like Ding herself, has given up his work among the books at the base library since he believes "the rural areas were a great living library in which he could study more realistically";[39] another, named Wen Cai (literally, "Highly Cultured") doubtless embodied certain elements of the "self-criticism" that Ding had learned to make during the rectification programs in Yanan. She described Wen as being still too bookish, too engrossed in theory, to have learned how to study from the masses, though his intentions are good:

> Now he was joining in land reform, claiming to be studying China's land problem and rural economy. The party considered more experiences would be good for him, and therefore wanted him to take part in the work. But after he reached the district the authorities there, not knowing him and impressed by his fine talk and apparent learning, were exceptionally polite to him, and trusted him enough to make him leader of a work team sent by the district party committee to take charge of the land reform in Nuanshui with its two hundred–odd families.[40]

Not surprisingly, Wen makes a number of mistakes that have to be corrected by more experienced cadres.

The landlords and villagers of Nuanshui are also shown to be multifaceted people, caught up by vast forces they understand only dimly, struggling to retain or seize what they believe to be rightfully theirs. The village women of Nuanshui, in particular, are well drawn: the worried leader of the local women's group, the beguiling wife of landlord Li, the pretty young niece of landlord Qian, the thin, proud, bitter shepherd's wife who in the past could show her anger only by insulting her already poor and hardworking husband until the land reform gave her a voice and a role. Ding Ling kept away from feminist ideas of the kind presented in her "Thoughts on March 8," but her depictions were still vivid, as in the case of an old woman, half-crazed by the griefs of a long life of poverty, now trembling on the edge of uncomprehended joy; when the cadres encounter her, as they prepare for a climactic meeting with the richest of the landlords, she is sitting on the raised-earth sleeping platform (*kang*) of a dispossessed landlord's house:

> When the few of them managed to squeeze together to talk things over, they found no place to go, and Yumin took them into a side room. There was an old woman there, a toothless, deaf old crone who could hardly walk, but her face was pressed to the glass window, and she was chuckling gleefully as she watched the masses outside, tears standing in her eyes. When the men burst in she was taken aback for a moment, then suddenly seemed to catch on, crawled over from the other end of the *kang*, shaking her head again and again, holding up her hand and opening her mouth; but instead of saying anything she just laughed, laughed and laughed until tears began pouring down her cheeks. Hu, who was standing by the *kang*, hurried over to put an arm round her, and she leaned on his shoulder and started to sob like a child. Hu patted her, and after she'd cried for some time, she raised her head to look at them all, wiping her tears with one hand, leaning against the wall with the other, then crawled back to the corner of the *kang*. Once more she flattened her face against the windowpane.[41]

According to many records of land-reform activities, from those witnessed by Mao Zedong and recorded in his Hunan report of 1927 down to those of twenty years later, a vital moment in every village occurred when the time had come to identify and punish the most powerful of the local landlords—a moment intended to make the landlord so humiliated that he would never dare tyrannize again, and a time to involve all the village in an act of group violence that would physically and emotionally commit them to the procedures of revolutionary change. In a central passage of her new novel, Ding Ling portrayed the villagers' attacks on their hated landlord, Qian:

> When the chairman began to read the statement, the crowd grew tense again and shouted, "Let him read it himself!"
>
> Qian knelt in the middle of the stage, his lined gown hanging in shreds, shoeless, not daring to meet anyone's eyes. He read: "In the past I committed crimes in the village, oppressing good people—"
>
> "That won't do! Just to write 'I' won't do! Write 'local despot, Qian.'"
>
> "Yes, write 'I, the local despot Qian.'"
>
> "Start again!"
>
> Schemer Qian began to read again: "I, Qian, a local despot, committed crimes in the village, oppressing good people, and I deserve to die a hundred times over; but my good friends are merciful—"
>
> "Who the devil are you calling your good friends?" An old man rushed forward and spat at him.
>
> "Go on reading! Just say all the people of the village."
>
> "No, why should he call us his people?"
>
> "Say all the gentlemen."
>
> "Say all the poor gentlemen. We don't want to be rich gentlemen! Only the rich are called gentlemen."
>
> Qian had to continue: "Thanks to the mercy of all the poor gentlemen in the village—"
>
> "That's no good. Don't say poor gentlemen; today we poor people have stood up. Say 'the liberated gentlemen,' and it can't be wrong."
>
> "Yes, liberated gentlemen."
>
> Someone chuckled. "Today we're liberated gentlemen!"
>
> "Thanks to the mercy of the liberated gentlemen, my unworthy life has been spared—"
>
> "What? I don't understand." Another voice from the crowd interrupted Qian. "We liberated gentlemen aren't going to accept all this literary stuff. Just put it briefly: say your dog's life has been spared."
>
> "Yes, spare your dog's life!" the rest agreed.

Qian had to go on: "Spare my dog's life. In future I must change my former evil ways completely. If I transgress in the slightest or oppose the masses, I shall be put to death. This statement is made by the local despot Qian, and signed in the presence of the masses. August 3."[42]

The Sun Shines over the Sanggan River had a simple enough narrative line, as the times demanded. However, Ding Ling managed to enrich its aesthetic structure with some haunting interior echoes. Some of these ranged back across time to Ding Ling's own childhood memories of her mother's first days at school, as she wrote of the peasant women in Nuanshui teetering in pain on their bound feet, or sitting out on the sidelines to massage them, as the villagers' accusations against landlord Qian dragged on. Other echoes were literary: the crows fly cawing over the head of the old peasant Gu, not now to some unknown horizon as in Lu Xun's "Medicine" but to a horizon nevertheless clouded with socialist uncertainties, for Gu, a hardworking middle peasant, has been "carelessly classified as a rich peasant"; and as the peasants begin to shout their charges aloud, a thin crescent moon is seen to hang above the stage on which the landlord stands, evoking memories of literary battles in the days of Xu Zhimo.[43] Other passages contain implied criticism of Communist violence: for example, a scene in which the cadres debate whether there is any villain in Nuanshui village so prominent that they should start the assault with him is balanced by a vignette of a little boy who plays casually with a locust whose wings he has torn off. The novel's ending is both subtle and sad, as the villagers crowd to watch the new defense corps recruits march cheerfully off to defend Yanqing city against the advancing Guomindang troops of General Fu Zuoyi, straining their eyes until their friends pass around a curve in the road and out of sight. The reader remembers that the same language was used of the thin wife of the shepherd, after she has fought and made up with her husband, watching him trudge to the end of the road with his little flock on a cold dawn.[44]

The passage gains extra force from the fact that General Fu Zuoyi's troops were real enough; indeed, elements of his armies captured Zhangjiakou itself and took over much of the Zhuolu district on the Sanggan River in October 1946, while another Guomindang general captured Yanan—which the Communists had managed to evacuate safely—in March 1947. Such armies inevitably tried to reverse the patterns of land reform that the Communists had achieved, and often the reversal was carried through with terrifying ferocity. Especially in Jiangsu province, in recaptured areas near Chiang Kaishek's capital (his government was now reestablished in Nanjing), but also in the northern areas where Ding Ling had worked, the families of landlords who had been beaten to death or publicly humiliated took revenge by jailing, shooting, and even—in many documented cases—burying alive their erstwhile peasant expropriators.[45]

Many of the original peasant models for Ding Ling's Sanggan River villagers may have died in these reprisals, but for Ding Ling herself the novel brought new recognition and preferment in Communist circles. She had now officially rectified the mistakes for which she had been censured in 1942, and as if to show how totally her change of heart was accepted by the party, she was chosen to be a member of the Chinese Communist delegation to the Second Democratic Women's Federation, held in Budapest in late 1948; taking copies of her just-published book, she traveled to Hungary and thence to Moscow. It was the first time in her life that she had traveled outside China's borders.[46]

51. Ding Ling in the Yanan
Communist base area, 1938

52. Mao Zedong (right),
General Zhu De (center),
and Zhou Enlai in
Shaanxi province in
late 1936,
after completing
the Long March

53. *Refugees Crowding onto Trains Bound for Guilin,* woodcut by Cai Dizhi

54. Chiang Kaishek
addressing an
anti-Japanese rally
in Chongqing
in the early 1940s

55. Wen Yiduo
in Kunming
in late 1945

56. *Dunning for Debt*, woodcut by Wu Zha

57. Ding Ling sketching her teenage daughter, Zuhui, in Beijing, 1954

58. Cartoon mocking Ding Ling for "one-bookism," 1957

59. Lao She in Beijing in the early 1960s

60. Students weeping at memorial services for Premier Zhou Enlai, in front of the Gate of Heavenly Peace, April 5, 1976

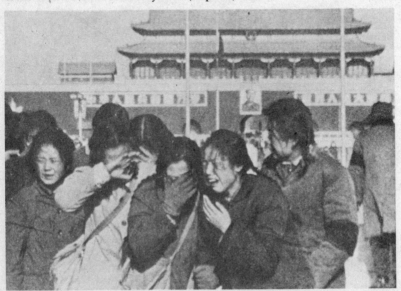

61. Wei Jingsheng as a soldier in the People's Liberation Army, 1973

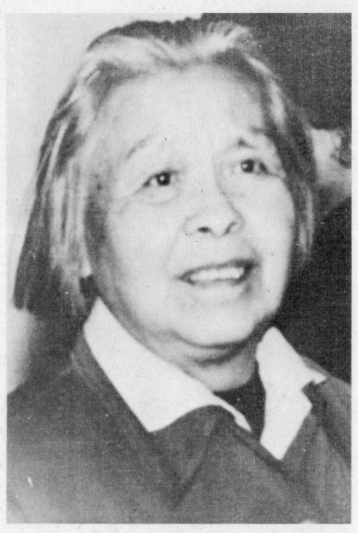

62. Ding Ling in Beijing after her release, December 1979

·12·

A NEW ORDER

Ding Ling's civil-war experiences contrasted sharply with those of Xiao Jun, the young Manchurian writer who had been befriended by Lu Xun in 1935 and had joined with Ding in criticizing the Yanan cadres during 1942. In late 1945, when Ding was sent to Zhangjiakou to observe land reform, Xiao Jun had been permitted to accompany Lin Biao's troops back to his homeland. Since, with the sole exception of Lao She, Xiao was undoubtedly Manchuria's most famous literary native son, especially well known for his novel *Village in August* (first published in 1935), which described the struggles by Communist guerrillas in Manchuria against Japanese invaders, the Communist Party must have expected that he would be a propaganda asset, especially now that he had experienced "rectification." Accordingly, they appointed him editor of a new magazine, *Cultural Gazette*, which was intended to be a focal point for the rallying of radical intellectuals in the northeast. The job was significant, since the battle for China's future was being fought in Manchuria, between the Communist forces (strong north of the Sungari River, and scattered through the countryside in the south) and the Guomindang forces (which were struggling to reestablish control of the Nanjing regime); in this battle, the party felt, intellectuals had their role to play as surely as the peasantry or the troops of the newly named Northeast Democratic Allied Army.[1]

After almost a year's careful preparatory work, Xiao Jun

brought out the first issue of the *Cultural Gazette* on May 4, 1947, a date obviously chosen to suggest continuity with the cultural struggles of the original May Fourth Movement of 1919. Those who might have thought this to be a purely symbolic choice were soon disillusioned, for almost from the first, Xiao Jun used the *Cultural Gazette* as a forum for a number of views that were anathema to the fledgling Communist cultural establishment. As he had in Yanan, he now criticized the Communist cadres operating in Manchuria for their insensitivity and overbearing ways, equating their treatment of the local population with a clown's treatment of an audience, both derisive and hypnotic: the people clapped loudly at the show, wrote Xiao, not realizing that they were being ridiculed and humiliated. In an obvious reference to Mao Zedong's 1942 rectification speech, he accused the party of a mass of "isms," including "Ah Qism" and "Don Quixoteism," while broadening the list (as both May Fourth Movement intellectuals and Xu Zhimo had done long before) to include such made-up terms as "so-soism" and "eat-well-and-do-nothing-ism."[2] But he also went far beyond his 1942 stance, and criticized the whole landreform program as "unkind and heartless," an "unprecedented act of robbery." He wrote of the party's renewed mass campaigns to "reform" the thoughts of Chinese intellectuals as "mechanical" and counter to the creative spirit of the Chinese people. He condemned the ongoing civil war as a senseless tragedy and argued that efforts should be made to end the fighting and work for a united democratic China. And he attacked and criticized the Russians in Manchuria, both for their uncouth behavior and for the fact that they had shipped muchneeded industrial matériel back to the Soviet Union to make up for their own losses in the war against Germany, thereby seriously hindering China's attempts at economic reconstruction.[3]

Certainly there was self-aggrandizement behind Xiao's charges as well as honest indignation, for at the same time he published his own autobiography in the *Gazette* (he was now thirty-nine) and wrote at length of his own "grand defiance" and his desire to "be indomitable." He also published the various letters Lu Xun had written to him in 1935 and 1936, with elaborate glosses, and took to writing poems in the classical mode. His unwillingness to accept rigorous party discipline was so obvious that it can only have been his local prestige that kept him in his editorial post—or perhaps the party leaders were interested in seeing how far he would choose to go. But by the end of 1948 they had decided to use him as a negative example, and they inaugurated a new rectification campaign, designed to instill obedience among the bourgeois intellectuals of unproven loyalty who were trying to join the Communist Party now that the Guomindang seemed sure to lose the civil war.

Xiao Jun was an ideal target, since his outspoken criticisms of the party could be used as firm proof of the need to shift those who had espoused the old anti-Japanese nationalism to a new level of socialist class struggle. A number of articles attacking Xiao began to appear in late 1948, and these led in turn to "criticism meetings" in Harbin at schools, factories, and party assemblies. From Harbin, the criticism meetings spread through Manchuria. Influential individuals were called in to make fresh charges, among them Ding Ling, on her return from Budapest. In a public statement she urged Xiao "to correct his mistakes, study the workers, peasants, and soldiers, and follow the party." Others accused him of trying to "make friends with our enemies" and brought back his novel *Village in August* for scrutiny, arguing that the author had failed to show how the power of the peasantry was guided by "the party and the proletariat," and had neglected to discuss the "class character" of the enemy. Still others accused him of equating the old Russian imperialism of the seventeenth century with Soviet behavior in the present. How could he believe, they asked, that a country such as the Soviet Union, based on Marxist-Leninist principles, could ever become "an oppressor nation over other oppressed nations"? When he steadfastly refused to make any form of public recantation, the *Cultural Gazette* was closed down. Xiao Jun himself was sent to work with the miners in the southern Manchurian collieries at Fushun—in perhaps unwitting adherence to Qu Qiubai's injunction of 1923 that writers who wished to understand the proletariat should go down into the mines.[4]

The Communists' decisiveness in disciplining Xiao was a

corollary of their growing military success against the Guomindang. At the end of 1948, city after city fell to the Communists in Manchuria; they gained control of Shandong province and captured several cities in Henan province; the collapse of the Guomindang in Nanjing could be safely predicted. Chiang's government was suffering from labor unrest, low military morale, spreading bureaucratic corruption, and an ever-worsening inflation that had passed the stage of wiping out savings and was now reducing people to shopping with boxes full of bank notes, as they had done in the Germany of 1923.

Disastrous as the effects of inflation were on workers' salaries, however, and harsh as conditions were on the land for the peasantry, now dominated again by the landlords who had fled during the war or been dispossessed during the first phase of Communist land reforms, those on government pay fared almost as badly, particularly the teachers at the state-financed schools and universities. In 1943 Wen Yiduo had complained in Kunming that his bushel of rice cost 4,000 Chinese national currency dollars (CNC$), and he had to teach in a second school and carve seals in order to make ends meet. The Chinese dollar had once had near-parity with the American dollar, and even during the early years of the Second World War the official exchange rate had been around twenty to one. By early 1946, inflation had taken the Chinese national currency into a sphere all its own: salaries for college professors were about CNC$60,000 a month, slightly ahead of women garment workers' wages but only a third of the sum being earned by skilled carpenters or machinists in Shanghai industries. By the spring of 1947, as inflation worsened and more and more paper money was printed, government salaries were raised to the region of CNC$200,000 a month, but even so, they did not cover both rent and food. In the spring of 1948 a civil servant whose income had risen to CNC$3,100,000 a month could not afford the rent on the hut he lived in if the landlord wanted it paid in rice instead of in cash. The result of such a collapse of living standards and erosion of all faith in the currency was to blur any sense that a Communist victory might be a threat, and to make the bourgeoisie look toward the Communist base areas with more sympathy, since in many cases they felt they had already been reduced to "proletarian" status. As one association of university professors observed, they were now being paid less than coolies or the men who shoveled manure in the countryside.[5]

Shen Congwen caught the mood prevailing among intellectuals in a letter he sent in December 1948 to a young student who had asked him for advice. Even Shen's language was already changing to suit the needs of the time:

> The present government is corrupt and paralyzed in every respect and continues to be incorrigible. We writers of this age, the age beginning with the May 4 uprising thirty years ago, have used our pens in the democratic and scientific spirit, and have toiled unselfishly. We have done our best, particularly in cultural areas. Our burgeoning society demands sacrifices from young stalwarts like you. Regardless of political fluctuations, the construction of a new country depends on honest and diligent youth. You ask what you, personally, can do to offset the status quo. . . . I can only remind you that it is futile to escape. Since we are here to stay, we have to dedicate ourselves to learning from our past mistakes. We can no longer afford to seek protection behind our old shield: we must stop being bookworms.[6]

Shen Congwen had been back in Beijing since 1946, teaching Chinese literature, and had certainly had a chance to size up the situation and try to guess how it might affect him. His personal decision that escape was futile, and his feeling that he would be safe under a Communist regime, may have been due to his confidence that his writings had either been nonpolitical or, in the case of some of his wartime works, actually critical of the Guomindang's alleged "reform programs" in the Hunan countryside.

In January 1949, the month after Shen wrote this letter, the Guomindang General Fu Zuoyi surrendered Beijing to the Communists, who started immediate preparations to make the city China's new capital, transferring senior personnel and establishing the bureaus and protoministries—so long on the move—in permanent homes. Among the new appointees was Ding Ling (her loyalty proven afresh by her criticisms of Xiao Jun), named in February to be a member of a committee charged with reorganizing the world of Chinese culture. She and Shen Congwen had not spent any time together in Beijing since they were young writers in 1927, she living with Hu Yepin and writing the "Diary of Miss Sophie," and he exploring the literary possibilities of his years with the Hunan militarists.[7] Now, in this shaken China of 1949, she could not help him—or chose not to. On February 1 anonymous attacks on Shen began to appear in the form of wall posters displayed around Beijing University that reproduced various criticisms of Shen which had been written by Guo Moruo and other Communist Party spokesmen. These accused Shen of being reactionary, immoral, a "literary prostitute." Items of mail arriving at his home contained threats of physical violence, drawings of bullets, and other warnings. In an atmosphere not unlike the one that Wen Yiduo had experienced in Kunming three years before, Shen grew nervous and upset; he gave away much of his library to students and friends, saying to one of them, "It seems that I may have to die, but these books have done nothing wrong, there is no reason why they should be wiped out along with me." Finally the anxiety became too great, and he slipped away from the faculty residences of Beijing University to stay with friends near the Qinghua campus, where his family joined him.[8]

While Shen sought anonymity, Ding Ling continued to flourish in the limelight, her swift rise following hard upon the astonishing successes of the Chinese Communists in the civil war. Chiang Kaishek resigned as president of China (a title he had selected himself but had held for less than a year) in January, after the fall of Beijing. By the time Ding Ling's committee had formulated the cultural structure known as the All-China Federation of Literary and Art Circles, in March, Communist troops had moved through central China to the Yangtze River. They crossed the river and took Nanjing in April, when Ding Ling was in Czechoslovakia representing China at a World Congress to Defend Peace; when she returned in July for the inaugural meetings of the All-China Federation, at which Mao Zedong and Zhou Enlai both spoke, Communist troops had taken Shanghai and Wuhan. In the next two months, as she took up her duties as a member of the All-

China Federation's standing committee of twenty-one artists and writers and was named editor of the *Literary Gazette*, designed to be the central voice of the new Communist literary establishment, Chinese Communist armies routed the last of Chiang's southern supporters. Mao Zedong declared the official foundation of the Chinese People's Republic on October 1, 1949, two weeks before Guangzhou fell. Ding Ling was again out of the country—this time in Moscow as head of a Chinese delegation to celebrate the thirty-second anniversary of the Bolshevik October Revolution—when Chongqing and Kunming fell into Communist hands, and the civil war was essentially over.[9]

Almost no one had guessed that the victory of the Communist forces would be so swift, or that the agony of further protracted civil war would be avoided. Though China was faced with a barrage of problems such as terrible inflation, millions of refugees, a partially begun land reform, inexperienced cadres catapulted to national office, and an isolated position in the international world, most Chinese surely felt euphoric now that the long struggle was over. Among the celebrators was Hu Feng, Lu Xun's friend and ally in the 1936 literary battles of Shanghai, who had spent the war years in Chongqing and who was now back in Beijing. His 1949 poem "Song of Joy" was at once a summary and a benediction:

> *My comrades at arms,*
> *My brothers,*
> *I have seen you*
> *Dying in a dank and stench-filled prison,*
> *Starving and freezing in a deserted village.*
> *You—you and the peasants—have fed lice with your flesh,*
> *Have drunk bloody water on the battlefield with your friends.*
> *You have endured repeated hammerings, repeated trials.*
> *You have conquered pain and death.*
> *During these*
> *Many, many years,*
> *Your hope stayed alive*
> *And your will stayed alive.*

And today,
At this very moment that stirs you,
Forget all the past,
Except that the past
Has purified you, like a newborn child
Lying in a warm cradle
His untainted heart overflowing with the blessing of new life.[10]

Lao She, however, was not so ebullient. He had spent the three years of the civil war in the United States, for in early 1946—just at the time Wen Yiduo refused the offer of a teaching position in California—Lao had accepted an invitation from the U.S. State Department's cultural exchange program. Lao's sojourn in the United States was full of ironies. Some were minor, such as his attempt to be pleasant to the locals, which led to his being cheated out of fifty dollars in cash by a confidence man at the Taft Hotel in New York, shortly after his arrival in America. Others were more significant, as in the case of his newfound fame. In 1945 a translation of his novel *Rickshaw* had been published in New York. It was a Book-of-the-Month Club selection and became a best-seller. But any gratification Lao She might have felt about its success disappeared when he looked closely at the translation—which he had never authorized: the entire shape of the novel had been altered, presumably to suit the American need to feel solidarity with a wartime ally and the public's desire for a happy ending to all entanglements, domestic and social. Whereas Lao She had left the reader with the portrait of the rickshaw puller Xiangzi broken in spirit and hunched in body with the pain of gonorrhea, his girl friend a suicide, and himself selling dissidents' names to the police for cash, the translator expunged Xiangzi's venereal disease, brought the girl back to life, purified Xiangzi's conduct, and even transformed a betrayed dissident into an influential official. In Lao She's own last paragraph Xiangzi was shuffling along the streets, looking for cigarette butts, a victim of his own naive hopes that individualism could lead to fulfillment; the American translator's last paragraph presented a powerful Xiangzi sweeping his beloved into his arms and racing across the countryside to a new dawn: "In the mild coolness of summer evening the burden in his arms stirred slightly, nestling closer to his body as he ran. She was alive. He was alive. They were free."[11]

Lao She mentioned his intense irritation about these alterations to his Chinese friends, though he took no steps to seek legal redress; he did, however, apply himself with extraordinary care to locating (and then working closely with) translators for his wartime novels, two of which were published in English but without the popular acclaim that had greeted *Rickshaw*. During the three years he spent in the United States he grew more and more critical both of Americans and of the Guomindang. Perhaps the roots of his anger lay in Chongqing, where he had lived during the war, writing Guomindang propaganda, while his wife and child were in Beijing; now, oddly enough, his family were living in Chongqing (where they had moved toward the end of the war) while he was in New York, and Lao She must have worried about the difficulties they faced from the renewed civil war and the mounting inflation. The melancholy thoughts about Chinese culture that had been so obvious in *Cat Country* surfaced again, as he spoke angrily of prominent Chinese intellectuals of the May Fourth generation who had swung to open support of the Guomindang against the Communists; but at the same time, his criticism of Communism yielded to his displeasure at American attempts to intervene in China's civil war. Lao was especially critical of the visit to China made by General Wedemeyer in 1947. In Chongqing during 1945, Wedemeyer had warmly supported Chiang Kaishek, and his visit two years later was obviously designed to encourage further American aid to the Guomindang's military forces to help them in their battles with the Communists in Manchuria and northern China.

By 1949, Lao She's irritation with things American had spread across a wide range, from the filmed version of *The Great Gatsby* starring Alan Ladd and Betty Field to ice cream and Coca-Cola.[12] Yet the final decision to return to China, which he made in the autumn of 1949, as the evidence of the Communist victory became irrefutable, was not an easy one. It could not be, to one who had writtern so bitingly of Everybody Shareskyism, and who held so clear a view of the manipulative nature of radical revolutionaries. A friend of his in San Francisco recalled seeing Lao She, a few days before his boat sailed, sitting on a grassy knoll in Golden Gate Park, silent in his own thoughts, as a light breeze brought the sound of a brass band toward him from somewhere in the direction of the zoo.[13] Lao told this same friend that when he reached China he would practice a "Doctrine of Three Nos"—no political discussions, no participation in meetings, no speechmaking—but in the intensely political world to which he chose to return, this doctrine was quite impossible to follow. By February 1950, Lao She had joined Ding Ling as a member of the standing committee of the All-China Federation of Literary and Art Circles and had published an essay in *People's Culture* in which he analyzed America's "decline into Fascism" and the "two great camps" to one or the other of which all Chinese, whether at home or overseas, must declare their allegiance.[14]

That same month, Mao Zedong returned from Moscow, where he had spent nine weeks negotiating with Stalin, with a treaty between Russia and China embracing mutual security, trade agreements, and the promise of a certain amount of Soviet technical assistance; but there were no major promises of help and no effusive signs of Soviet joy at the recruitment of this giant country into the Communist camp.

During the rest of the year, virtually all Chinese were swept up in the program of land reform. Building on the experience gained in northern China during the 1940s, the party mobilized hundreds of thousands of cadres to work in the villages, to establish peasant associations, and to lead the poor and middle peasants against their landlords. The cadres, often starting work in a "keypoint" village that would later become the model for the surrounding countryside, taught the poorer peasants and landless laborers how to evaluate the different levels of wealth within their communities, encouraged them to "speak bitterness" about the degrading poverty they had suffered in the past, and led them in public demonstrations—often similar to those so vividly described by Ding Ling—in which the landlords were denounced, humiliated, and sometimes beaten or killed.

The process was difficult, violent, and full of unexpected

problems: landlords hid their money and grain supplies, gave away land in an attempt to hide their real status, killed livestock or chopped down orchards to reduce their apparent prosperity, or sought simply to frighten the poor out of taking any action by spreading rumors that the Guomindang forces would soon return and take vengeance. Nevertheless, by the end of 1951 the old landlord and rich-peasant dominance of rural China had been effectively destroyed, and the land and material possessions (beyond the little that each family needed for bare subsistence) had been parceled out among one hundred million or more poorer families. If the amount such poor families received was small—perhaps about one-fifth of an acre per capita in densely populated areas, an acre or two in sparsely inhabited or infertile areas—nevertheless this mass involvement of the Chinese people in such a radical redistribution of private property effectively ended the old order of life throughout the country, even though it did not remove land from private ownership.[15]

This land-reform program was accompanied by the promulgation of a comprehensive 1950 Marriage Law designed to release women from the tyranny of imposed marriage and to open up the possibilities of divorce for them, as well as to give children certain protections under the law that would end infanticide and the sale of minors. Though bitterly opposed by many men, these policies were effective. Especially in areas where a high percentage of males were absent, fighting in the civil war, or after late 1950 in the Korean War, women were important to the land reform, and in becoming so, they reopened the question broached by Ding Ling in 1942: whether a woman's identity as a woman might not transcend the demands of economic revolution. The close to one million divorces granted within a year of the enactment of the Marriage Law testify to the tensions that many women had felt.[16]

But the Chinese Communist Party, striving to build up a viable government after twenty-eight years spent largely on the move or in actual combat, could not afford to institute radical change in all sectors of life. In Chinese industry, the policy was cautious, designed to encourage key capitalist managerial personnel to stay on in their posts, regardless of their previous connections with the Guomindang or with foreign imperialists, so that China's production could move ahead. Here the priorities were to check the disastrous inflation of the previous decade by fixing wages and prices and controlling food distribution. This entailed, in addition to the establishment of the necessary bureaucracy, the structuring of a union system loyal to the party which could break the hold of secret-society lodges and criminal elements on the transportation workers, coolies, and dockers, and disperse the gangs that dominated prostitution and the opium trade.[17]

The approach that Mao Zedong took in enrolling the educated elite behind these policies, and that he presented at party meetings and at gatherings of the People's Consultative Conference (which continued to meet under the People's Republic), was that China had now entered a "mature stage" of coalition in which workers and peasants would join with the "petty bourgeoisie and the national bourgeoisie" in a new united front described as a "people's democratic dictatorship." Rights would be denied only to certain major landlords and to the "bureaucratic bourgeoisie," representatives of the Guomindang militarists who had fostered domestic terror and had collaborated with American imperialism. As a corollary to the economic campaigns in the countryside, Mao launched a program of "thought reform"; building on the experiences of the Yanan movement of 1942 and the anti–Xiao Jun campaigns of 1948, this program was designed to correct and mold the thinking of the intelligentsia, who by virtue of their basic class position were obviously not ready to understand the necessities for sacrifice demanded of the members of the new society.

The prime aim of this new rectification movement was the eradication of those elements in Chinese culture that looked too strongly to the West, that refused to see the revolutionary urgency of suppressing "ivory-tower" escapism, or that basked in their own "decadence" or in "melancholia." In 1949, on the thirtieth anniversary of the May Fourth Movement, before the People's Republic had even been officially inaugurated, the critic Mao Dun, who had once so bitterly attacked Xu Zhimo for his homage to Rabindranath Tagore, and was now working with Ding Ling and Guo Moruo in the Federation of Literary and Art Circles, gave a speech in which he lumped all such attitudes together as being "compradore culture"—that is to say, as being like the old economic system under which Chinese merchants had worked for Western trading companies, unwittingly helping in the development of foreign imperialist power:

> Compradore culture, which might well be termed the godchild of imperialism, has relied on our big cities as its base camps and has sent out its probing attacks from there. The petty bourgeoisie is the hothouse soil most conducive to compradore culture, a soil in which it will always take root. The worshipping of Western people, the intoxication with European and American life, the notion that "the moon shines brighter abroad than here at home"—or, to put it more succinctly, the sowing of the seeds of an inferiority complex in the minds of our people—this is the specialty of compradore culture. Most odious are those who carefully select out some of the decadent and unsavory feudalistic customs of China (adopting the approach of those who traffic in phony antiques) in order to write whole books merely to win a laugh and earn some paltry largesse from their Western masters; and all this for the purpose of satisfying their material desires![18]

These ideas became central preconceptions of Communist policy in 1950, when Mao Dun was named in turn vice-chairman of the Federation of Literary and Art Circles, chairman of the Writers' Union, and minister of culture; and they were pursued with renewed urgency after October 1950, when the Chinese decision to intervene in the Korean War, after American and United Nations troops approached the Yalu River, threw the entire country back onto a war footing against an external enemy, led to a speedup and intensification of various domestic campaigns, and brought a corresponding growth in the size and power of the secret-police and public-security apparatus. The first of the campaigns, that against "counterrevolutionaries," led to the trial and execution of perhaps a million people who had been members of the Guomindang or had worked with foreigners before 1949; in addition to that, the party launched a "Three-Anti Campaign" to speed the elimination of corruption, waste, and overbureaucratization within its ranks, as well as to purge Guomindang elements; while a "Five-Anti Campaign" was directed mainly at the alleged abuses of those financiers and managers who had stayed on in China after 1949 to help with the economic recovery and were now accused of bribery, tax evasion, fraud, and theft of government property and state economic secrets. The "thought-reform program," based on principles of self-examination and confession under party guidance, combined with intensive study of Mao Zedong's writings, was an important corollary to these overlapping systems of economic change and internal "cleansing."[19]

Despite his misgivings at the time of leaving the United States, Lao She responded to these new pressures with apparent aplomb. He did not make an outcry when the film version of one of his earlier short stories, "This Life of Mine"—a pessimistic tale of the corruptions and tragedies of twentieth-century China as seen through the eyes of a Beijing policeman—was given an upbeat ending on the party's orders. This action, in its way so reminiscent of his American translator's unauthorized revision of *Rickshaw*, had to be accepted if Lao She was to flourish as a writer in the People's Republic, and his swing toward the new demands of socialist realism was rapid and successful. The new play he wrote in 1950, *Dragon's Beard Ditch*, described the miserable life of poor people living on the banks of a sewage-filled canal in Beijing. The theme was a perfect one to suggest the contrasts between pre- and post-Communist China: the canal dwellers' lives before 1949 were presented as a nightmare round of disease, accidental death from drowning, degradation at the hands of local thugs, and exploitation by a grasping Guomindang government that levied a sanitation tax on the already desperate people; the Communists, by contrast, cleaned the canal, found jobs for the poor, and removed the thugs—literally and figuratively purifying the canal dwellers' world.[20] In an even more striking assertion of his solidarity with the Communist regime, Lao She chose, in celebration of the second anniversary of the founding of the People's Republic in October 1951, to write an essay on the excitement generated in his own head by a "struggle" meeting against dissident intellectuals. It was duly published in *People's Culture*:

The meeting started. The platform announced the purpose of the meeting and the crimes committed by the evil bullies. At appropriate intervals one group after another of the crowd, front and back, left and right, yelled out slogans: "Down with the Evil Bullies! Support the People's Government!" When the whole crowd then took up the cry the noise rose in a mighty tide. The people's voice is the people's strength, a strength sufficient to make the evildoer tremble. . . . Men and women, old and young, one after another came on to the platform to make accusation. When a speech reached its climax of feeling many in the audience would shout, "Beat them!" I myself, like the intelligentsia sitting by me, yelled out involuntarily, "Beat them! Why don't we give them a beating?" As police restrained those who went forward to strike the bullies, my own voice mingled with the voices of hundreds roaring, "They've asked for it! Beat them!" And this roar changed me into a different man! I used to be a man of pretensions to cultivation. To be sure, I hated evil bullies and wicked men; but had I not been at that accusation meeting, how could I have brought myself to yell ferociously, "Beat them!"? The people's indignation so stirred me that I became one of them. Their hatred was my hatred also; I could not, would not "look on with hands folded."[21]

In an official "self-criticism" statement, written the following year, Lao She wrote that he would "forever try to advance step by step in accordance with Chairman Mao's instructions, as well as to rectify all my faults in thought and life."[22]

Shen Congwen, by contrast, found the new pressures almost unbearable. Though in 1949 he had been allowed to keep his job at Beijing University, criticisms continued to be directed at him, and special committees of cadres and students were sent to "cleanse" his thoughts and to "counsel" him; in 1950 he was dismissed from his job and made to enroll in a "revolutionary course of study." One of his friends, who later left China, reported that domestic tensions grew high as Shen's wife became politically more active, and their two children, with the encouragement of their teachers, wrote essays in which they recorded their own and their mother's correct social stance, while regretting their father's "reactionary" point of view. Shen's younger son, in one such essay, called his father a "so-called" writer

who had fallen sick in the People's Republic because his comprehension was blurred, and declared that the other three
members of the family spent their evenings after work or
school trying to reform him.[23] At some stage in this cycle of experience, the same friend reported, Shen made a bungled attempt at suicide, swallowing a quantity of kerosene and cutting
his throat and wrists. When he was hospitalized, he initially
believed the institution was a jail. For some weeks after his release he remained a pitiable figure, his face and eyes puffed up
and his nose bleeding continually. When questioned about his
experiences, Shen delivered this melancholy outburst:

> How am I meant to understand this? Those writers who
> grew up so comfortably and had the money to go off and
> study abroad, and lived in the top levels of our society, now
> celebrate some bigwig's birthday one day and go off to
> some other great man's party the next. The Communists
> have now taken over, yet those people are still living in the
> top levels of society. I was an army private for years and am
> from country stock; even granting that my political indoc-
> trination in the past was limited and that I have lagged be-
> hind up to now, why am I not given any opportunity to
> rejoin the team? What specific crime have I committed?
> What have the Communists in store for me? If they'd only
> be clear about what they want, I would certainly follow
> their orders. Death doesn't frighten me, but why this vague
> campaign of vilification toward me personally? Several of
> my old friends are in the Communist Party, for example,
> Ding Ling, and a lot of my former students.[24]

Ding Ling, however, was not overly helpful to Shen. She had
her own party orthodoxy to prove, and was eager to avoid any
action that might weaken her power base at the *Literary Gazette.*
One of the ways she validated her revolutionary credentials
was by extolling her former lover Hu Yepin, since his status as
a revolutionary martyr was now confirmed by the party's action in exhuming his body, along with those of the other Communists executed in February 1931, from the mass grave at
Longhua and transferring them to the new "revolutionary martyrs'" cemetery outside Shanghai. The party also authorized a
collected edition of his works and chose Ding Ling to supervise

the project.[25] In the preface she wrote for this edition, dated November 1950, she criticized her own past "petty-bourgeois illusions" and her "moroseness," and "ennui," and "eccentricity," and then went on to denigrate Shen Congwen in what seems to have been a gratuitous way:

> Fundamentally, Yepin was different from Shen Congwen and me. Unlike me, who can be self-indulgent and fanciful, Yepin was a pragmatist always, never permitting himself, as did Shen Congwen, to appease the upper class. Yepin was firm, forever at odds with the rulers. From the very beginning, Shen Congwen was enamored of the genteel, and this led to his affiliation with the Crescent Moon Society and the Modern Critic School. He was not content with the modest lot of a struggling writer; no, he had to become a professor; he had to teach at the institute in Wusong. Unconsciously, he was afraid of those who originated the Proletarian Literary Movement.[26]

Such an assessment would carry considerable weight, for Ding Ling's prestige was approaching its apogee in 1951; that year she was awarded a Stalin Prize for her novel *The Sun Shines over the Sanggan River*, which had been translated into Russian two years earlier. She had also been permitted to organize a Central Literature Institute in Beijing for the purpose of training young writers, which brought her the power of patronage over a new generation of younger intellectuals, as well as being given a senior post in the party's Propaganda Department. Thus when in 1951 she invited Shen to contribute an essay to her magazine, he clearly felt unsure of her motives, telling her: "I have lost contact with the new literary periodicals. It would be better if you were to give me two readable articles so I'll know what to write."

The essay he wrote during that year obviously showed his attempt to cope with the current literary dogmas and to assess his failure to be a revolutionary activist. His early experience in the warlord armies had made him "despair of politics," he admitted, and therefore in the 1920s and 1930s he had "taken the liberal attitude of an old intellectual, thinking that it was impossible, unnecessary, and erroneous for literature to be

attached to politics." Accidentally, therefore, his work "benefited the unbroken feudal rule of the old Guomindang" and
had "abetted the small group of scum" gathered around
Chiang Kaishek, especially his in-laws, the notorious Soong
family. Shen Congwen's formal summary of his own earlier
writing life read as follows:

> After 1928, my life was spent in schools and happened to
> have stronger ties to intellectuals of the Anglo-American
> school who were battling for democracy and freedom. Al-
> though my work habits remained the same, my way of life
> gradually changed, and I became a half-intellectual: in one
> respect, my contact with society did not extend beyond stu-
> dents and colleagues; in another, the scope of my reading
> became more diffuse. Then, I was an energetic and prolific
> writer, about to help establish a new publishing enterprise.
> Readers were to be found not only in schools but among
> members of other modern enterprises. My work received
> encouragement and stimulation; I became an intimate
> member of the short-story-writer group. Most of what I
> produced within the previous twenty-year period was rela-
> tively progressive, but some reflected a weakness of the
> wandering intellectual: my language was flowery, but my
> thoughts were confused; I had a style but no sense of life.
>   Most of my writing was of no use to the people's revolu-
> tion, it had a detrimental effect on youth, and it numbed
> their will to progress. The stories I wrote that I had adapted
> from the Buddhist classics reveal the muddled nature of my
> encyclopedic learning. I confused Buddhist nihilism with
> my own exotic feelings and the various studies of the
> Spring and Autumn Era anthologies with which I was famil-
> iar. The confusion produced very sick, paganistic, and un-
> healthy books like *The Seven-Color Nightmare*. Works that
> stimulated my development obviously included the writ-
> ings of Freud and Joyce, whose incomplete and shattered
> reflections could be seen in my own work.[27]

The sentiments expressed here seem to have satisfied the
cadres investigating Shen, and after a brief period of further
ideological training he was assigned to a new post. As if to em-
phasize the past-oriented nature of his thinking, he was put to
work not at teaching or creative writing but on the cataloging of

antiquities in the former imperial palace, now the Beijing Palace Museum.

In the next few years, Shen slowly made himself into an expert on early Chinese silk designs and the bronze mirrors of the Tang and Song dynasties; Lao She wrote several more plays, was sent to Korea on a goodwill mission, and was named vice-chairman of the Writers' Union; Ding Ling grew experienced in spearheading critical attacks against erring intellectuals. This period of time, between late 1952 and 1955, was a comparatively relaxed and peaceful one in China: the armistice ending the Korean War in 1953 left the Chinese government free to concentrate on its domestic programs, and though the Taiwan issue was perforce unresolved, since the United States Seventh Fleet continued to patrol the Taiwan Strait and no Communist amphibious operation could be attempted even had it been desired, the death of Stalin that same year eased the overwhelming pressures the Soviet Union had exerted over China. The post-Stalin leadership also agreed to return Port Arthur and Dalian to Chinese control. At international forums the Chinese played a conciliatory role: Zhou Enlai served as a mediator between the French and the Vietnamese at the conclusion of their bitter war in 1954, while at the meetings of non-SEATO countries held the following year at Bandung, Indonesia, he was a moderating influence in discussions of Far Eastern strategy. At home, the first Five-Year Plan for development of China's industry seemed successful. The gradual expropriation of foreign assets was accomplished without bloodshed; nationalization of domestic industries was carried through without violence and in the context of long-range state planning. The first thorough census in China's modern history was taken in 1953, yielding a population figure of 582,600,000. With Soviet technical assistance a major series of hydroelectric projects was initiated, particularly on the Yellow River, while the army was reequipped and its staff system reorganized so as to avoid any repetition of the mistakes that had led to heavy Chinese casualties during the Korean War. The war itself, along with the economic reconstruction that followed, provided material for much of the country's literature, plays, and films, and a chance to sharpen the definitions of a current "socialist patriotism."

In the realm of agriculture the changes went even deeper. Party leaders began to introduce a complex system of state credit bureaus and rural marketing cooperatives; these, when used in conjunction with the "mutual-aid teams" in which the poorer peasants were encouraged to gather, were designed to make private farming decreasingly profitable, and thus prepare the way for a system of collectivized agriculture.[28] The process was not going to be easy, given the passionate belief of Chinese peasants that land ownership was the main key to a happy life for oneself and one's children. In *The Sun Shines over the Sanggan River* Ding Ling had caught this mood perfectly, by depicting the moment when a tenant farmer named Hou, who has spent his life in desperate poverty, is finally given land title deeds by his former landlord; so inured is he to his fate that at first he thinks he should return the deeds, but after the members of his village peasant association and his own son have argued with him, he realizes finally that the land is his to keep:

> Someone else praised him: "He's too straightforward, this old fellow. He's been trampled all his life, but now at last he's coming to his senses!"
>
> Young Hou laughed too and said, "Father, Buddha has nothing to do with us. We burned incense every year, but he never paid the least attention. Yet as soon as Chairman Mao gave the order, people came here to give us land. Chairman Mao is our Buddha. In the future if we worship anyone it should be Chairman Mao. Don't you agree, Father?"
>
> Tenant Hou only grinned silently. Finally somebody asked him, "You'll have your share of the land. Will you give it back again?" He shook his head vigorously, and answered: "No! No! Didn't that mass meeting yesterday bring me to my senses?" He chuckled.[29]

By 1953, however, the government's economic policies were being carefully adjusted to encourage the transition to agricultural producers' cooperatives; and although in these early cooperatives the principle of land ownership was retained—along with various socioeconomic distinctions, since each peasant still received returns in proportion to the land and draft animals he or she contributed to the cooperative—all of that changed in mid-1955. For in that summer Mao Zedong and the party leadership—alarmed by the fact that agricultural surpluses were too small to maintain the pace of industrial development they aimed for (the peasants, producing more, were also eating more), and also alarmed that rich peasant families were once again drawing ahead of the poorer peasants in most rural communities—ordered an immediate switch to a pattern of full collective agriculture. Abolishing the validity of title deeds to land meant that the individual or family would be left only a small plot of private property on which some extra vegetables, or perhaps hogs and chickens, could be raised. The transition took place with amazing speed. By the early summer of 1956 seventy-four million households in China (61.8 percent of the total) were enrolled in collectives, and by the end of the summer the figure was 90 percent.[30]

This new stage in the Chinese revolutionary process, impressive though it was, proved infinitely harder to dramatize (either with political rhetoric or in literature) than the more violent phase of initial land reform had been, and most major writers, including Ding Ling, remained silent on the issue. The government's own statements inevitably glossed over the tensions that this giant transformation engendered, especially since throughout China there were other endemic regional and generational conflicts: as northern cadres moved into the newly liberated south, as urban cadres entered rural areas, or as millions of newly enrolled Communist Party members began to compete for positions with those who had joined the party before 1949, before 1945, or, in the case of the true elite of Long March veterans, before 1934. Two of the most powerful figures in the entire party had already been purged, for reasons that are still not entirely clear: one, Gao Gang, was accused of attempting to develop his own "independent kingdom" in the heavily industrialized region of southern Manchuria and of "engaging in conspiratorial activities"; the other, Rao Shushi, was charged with "shameless deceit" during the war years in Yanan and in postliberation Shanghai, and with forming an "antiparty alliance" with Gao Gang while the two of them were on the State Planning Committee. Gao committed suicide in 1954, and Rao was removed from all his posts and disappeared from view during the same year.[31]

Similar types of conflict occurred in the upper echelons of the cultural bureaucracy, where factional divisions were bitter and memories apparently even longer. In the early 1950s Ding Ling seemed to have near-parity with Zhou Yang, Lu Xun's antagonist from the Shanghai of 1936 and her opponent during the Yanan rectification of 1942. From 1953 on, however, her career began a slow slide, as she yielded up various editorships and committee posts and saw the literary institute she had founded pass into other hands. Though vigorous in opposing writers—some of them formerly her close friends—for their lack of attention to the needs of the masses, she herself remained a perfectionist, urging writers to strive for the creation of the perfect book, holding up Lu Xun's stories and Cao Xueqin's eighteenth-century *Dream of the Red Chamber* as stylistic models, and urging party literary cadres not to adopt a stance of "parental authority" to the writer that would end up stifling creativity. Unable to write anything herself except for a few short journalistic pieces, she found solace in publicly championing the importance of the writer's role in society. Finally she was brought to the forefront of the political world, despite herself, as the *Literary Gazette* she had once controlled became itself an analogue of those "independent kingdoms" allegedly established in Shanghai and Manchuria.[32]

Before criticism brought Ding Ling low, the party focused on the writers Hu Feng and Feng Xuefeng. Both men were tenacious revolutionaries and former friends of Lu Xun's (as Feng was also of Ding Ling's) who had spent the war years mainly in Chongqing, where they had been critical of the Yanan Communists' attempt to dominate culture and had founded their own magazine to oppose that tendency.[33] In the early 1950s both were criticized for continuing to harbor bourgeois ideas. Then in late 1954 the party attacks on Hu's literary views were replaced by political charges, and in 1955 he was arrested and jailed for being a counterrevolutionary, a Guomindang agent, and the leader of an anti-Communist underground network.

Ding Ling, anticipating that those who hated Hu would also hate her, began to make a series of self-criticisms at party meetings in late 1954—these were neither released to the public nor accepted. She retreated, briefly, to a sanatorium; but when, in 1955, the party named a special team to investigate her case, she left that temporary refuge and tried to withdraw altogether from literary and political Beijing and to live quietly in the suburbs west of the city, not far from where she had lived with Hu Yepin in student poverty thirty years before. The attempt at withdrawal failed: in 1956 the powerful cultural leader Zhou Yang attacked her personally and at length for having been "anti-Party" all her life.[34] Again she made a lengthy self-criticism, again it was not released, but from fragments of essays she wrote then (one of them dedicated to the memory of Hu Yepin), one can tell the direction of her thoughts. Because she had suffered so much in her youth, she wrote, it was true that her stories were "full of contempt for society and full of the stubbornness of the individual's lonely soul." And the people of the May Fourth era who had shaped her thinking most profoundly and entered into her writings as characters were all people "under heavy pressure, helpless, feeling entirely alone, but still striving to find a way to go on."[35]

These appeals for sympathy were ineffective, but the development of national policies brought Ding Ling a brief respite in mid-1956, anyway, for in May of that year, worried that the highly accelerated rural collectivization movement was running into serious problems because of cadres' caution and ingrained habits of "bureaucratism," and therefore eager to rally the intellectuals more effectively behind him, Mao Zedong announced a new mass movement, this time to let "a hundred flowers bloom and a hundred schools of thought contend." The aim of this movement was to restore confidence to those who felt their skills were not valued by the state, whether in the realm of the creative arts and humanities (the flowers) or in the areas of scientific research and practice (the schools of thought).[36]

The response of many Chinese to this new campaign was an understandable caution, but others believed that the party was truly opening up new avenues of criticism. As Huang Qiuyun, who had once translated Romain Rolland's *Jean Christophe*, wrote in the autumn of 1956:

> No one can deny that in our country at present there are still floods and droughts, still famine and unemployment, still infectious diseases and the oppression of the bureaucracy, plus other unpleasant and unjustifiable phenomena. . . . A writer with an upright conscience and a clear head ought not to shut his eyes complacently and remain silent in the face of real life and the sufferings of the people. If a writer does not have the courage to reveal the dark diseases of society, does not have the courage to participate positively in solving the crucial problems of people's lives, and does not have the courage to attack all the deformed, sick, black things, then can he be called a writer?[37]

Lao She had already begun to rise to the type of challenge discussed by Huang. He had completed, early in 1956, a play based on the life story of an impostor named Li Wenming, who had managed to infiltrate the Communist Party in the early 1950s by posing as a wounded war hero; since Li had been fawned upon by Communist cadres, some of whom even sought to ride on his coattails, and had received many favors, he was the perfect foil for satire directed against the party.[38] By later 1956, like other Chinese writers, Lao She was trying to decide how far the new freedoms were really meant to extend. As he wrote in a letter to a friend, "In the western chamber young Miss Zhou is listening to a broadcast of new poetry read in a clear voice. Can this be called the blooming of a hundred flowers?"[39] "The western chamber" was an elegant and elliptical reference either to China's perennially popular fourteenth-century drama of romantic love *The Dream of the West Chamber* or to the renewal within China of an interest in Western strains of literature that had been so popular in the 1920s and the 1930s. Deciding to explore the changing effects of outside influence in China, Lao She proceeded to write his most remarkable play, *Teahouse*.

Building on ideas that he had begun to explore in the story "This Life of Mine," filmed eight years before, Lao She now set out to summarize the great events of China's recent history by focusing on three time periods—each of which takes an act of the play—as these are lived through and discussed by the customers and owners of a Beijing teahouse, changing over time but still recognizably the same. Act 1 is set in the early autumn of 1898, just after the Hundred Days of Reform, the flight of Kang Youwei, and the executions of his brother, Guangren, and his disciple Tan Sitong; Act 2 takes place on a summer afternoon in 1917, the year after the death of President Yuan Shikai, the same summer that Zhang Xun staged his unsuccessful coup to restore the ex-Emperor Puyi; Act 3 is set on an autumn day "after the victory over the Japanese, while Guomindang forces and American troops were occupying Beijing," though the exact year is not specified. In this play, jammed with characters from all social strata, Lao She celebrated the city that he seemed always to have loved above all others, and also hailed the wit and the courage of the Chinese people as he had not attempted to do since *Rickshaw.* At the same time there was a profound ambiguity about the play's message, for the villain of the piece was government—cruel, insensitive, inept, and omnipresent government—and if there was a logical historical progression among the acts, from Qing to warlords to Guomindang, it took little imagination to see the Communist cadres as another possible focus for the same critiques.[40]

Huang and Lao were members of an older generation, which had been raised on Western literature during the May Fourth period, but their message was taken up with even greater force by those who had been born in the mid-1930s and were now—at the age of twenty or so—finishing their university studies or embarking on their first jobs under the Communist regime. A novella by the young writer Wang Meng entitled *The Young Man Who Has Just Arrived at the Organization Department,* published by *People's Literature* in September 1956, was an example of these emerging voices. The novel's protagonist is a twenty-two-year-old Communist Party member (as was Wang Meng himself in real life), eager to serve his party and his country; to his dismay, he finds on his first assignment that his superiors are often lazy, ineffective, hypocritical, or domineering. They live in a world where one has to wait until someone "embezzles some money or rapes a woman before the higher echelons finally sit up and take notice." In the atmosphere of boredom and mutual suspicion that permeates the work station, it is only rarely—for instance, while relaxing for a moment, chastely, with a young woman comrade, and listening to the music of Tchaikovsky's *Capriccio Italien*—that the hero can attain a sense of coherence and emotional fulfillment in his troubled heart.[41]

There was still no massive response to Mao Zedong's request for open criticism, however, and in January 1957 Mao arranged for publication of his own poems, all of which were written in the old classical style, apparently in order to reassure those who were worried that their "old-style" writings would be condemned. And to silence critics of the Hundred Flowers policy within the party, Mao delivered his celebrated speech of February 1957, "On the Correct Handling of Contradictions Among the People," in which he gave a forceful warning that only through creative struggle and daring would the Chinese be able to deepen the revolution and attain higher levels of political and social life.[42] In the late spring of 1957, Mao's promise to protect greater freedom of expression was finally accepted by a majority of intellectuals, and during May and June a host of students, writers, teachers, painters, medical workers, and members of religious groups sought to recapture some of the frankness and iconoclasm that had once marked the intellectuals of the May Fourth Movement, invoking almost-forgotten names and cultural modes: universities began to offer courses on Bertrand Russell and John Maynard Keynes; a student at Beijing University, demanding the right to read Byron rather than an endless diet of second-rate Soviet writers, signed his manifesto in Latin; another placed the Hu Feng case of 1955 in the same context as the Dreyfus case of 1894–1906 and observed that the French people were to be congratulated for "reversing the verdict" which they themselves had wrongfully imposed.[43]

As the new generation found its voice, younger leaders appeared. Lin Xiling, a law student at Beijing University who had already published articles on Balzac and Tolstoy and served briefly in the People's Liberation Army, was only twenty-one in May 1957 when she became famous for her powerful campus speeches. Referring to herself as "a little devil" (just as the student Xu Guangping had to her teacher Lu Xun more than thirty years earlier), Lin observed that Mao Zedong's remarks at the Yanan forum of 1942 were no longer germane to China, since intellectuals had now become workers, peasants, and soldiers; it was their duty to show that China still had a feudal foundation and was undemocratic—Lin herself, having worked in district courts during her law training, had seen how alleged counterrevolutionaries were treated, and she estimated that more than seven hundred thousand people had been executed on rigged charges in the early years of the revolution, and that public-security forces had tampered with the court records to prevent systematic review. Claiming that all Chinese should insist on their right to be dissatisfied with society, whether now or five hundred years in the future, Lin Xiling presented Titoist "socialist democracy" as one valid model that might help China in her present plight.[44]

As if this were not enough, wall posters were hung up in public, asking more and more troubling questions: Why had the two party leaders Gao Gang and Rao Shushi been suppressed? What had happened to Wang Shiwei, the friend of Ding Ling and author of the "Wild Lily" essays back at Yanan in 1942? Had not Mao Zedong eaten well in those days while the peasants starved? Should not Mao, perhaps, be addressed as "Your Majesty" because of his imperial pretensions? The circle of complainers broadened rapidly. Urban workers began to express dissatisfaction by means of strikes, demands for better work conditions, slowdowns, and phony sick calls; peasants withdrew from the new collectives or tried to withhold taxes, claiming that the party was extracting more than landlords had ever done.[45] Mao Zedong, placed in an incredibly difficult position because of his initial sponsorship of the criticism movement, decided to end it in late June 1957, and inaugurated a new "antirightist" campaign, claiming in his own defense that he had "let the demons and hobgoblins come out of their lairs in order to wipe them out better, and let the seeds sprout to make it more convenient to hoe them."[46]

This shift in direction came at the worst possible time for

Ding Ling, for the earlier stages of the Hundred Flowers Movement had seemed like a good time for her to battle for a reinstatement within the cultural bureaucracy and to end the dominance of her rival, Zhou Yang. In a series of party meetings convened in the summer of 1957 as the antirightist moves gathered strength, she bitterly denied the charges that she had betrayed Communist comrades to the Guomindang between 1933 and 1936, or that she had slandered the party in 1942 by her remarks on International Women's Day. Ding Ling argued that in all the protests she had directed against party personnel she had never deviated from correct party procedures. She apparently also attempted to lead a bolt from the Writers' Union so as to prove her influence and prestige, but she failed, and the opposition toward her hardened. At daily meetings convened throughout July, often with two hundred or more present, she and one of her former *Literary Gazette* colleagues, Chen Qixia, were criticized and questioned about their party loyalty. Chen Qixia broke first, on August 3, when he confessed to various antiparty "crimes," handed over all the correspondence he and Ding Ling had exchanged over the previous years, and accused Ding of attempting "to seize the leadership of literary circles." The effects of these charges can be gauged from a press release by the official party news agency in Beijing issued on August 7, 1957:

> An anti–Communist Party clique, headed by the writers Ding Ling and Chen Qixia, opposing Party leadership in literary work and striving for personal power has been revealed at the current meeting here called by the Communist Party Committee in the Union of Chinese Writers, the *People's Daily* reports today. . . .
>
> The basic position of this clique included: rejecting leadership and supervision by the Party and its policies, principles and directives on literary work; building an anti-Party alliance in violation of Party principles; destroying Party unity through provocations; propagating bourgeois individualism and advocating hero worship.
>
> It was also disclosed that this anti-Party clique had planned to launch an all-out attack against the Party and divide the writers at the coming national writers' and artists' conference scheduled for this October. They also schemed

> to use their followers to turn the organ of the Chinese Writ-
> ers' Union—*The Literary Gazette*—into their mouthpiece. . . .
>   Chen Qixia admitted his crimes against the Party at the
> meeting, but Ding Ling has still refused to.[47]

Ding Ling's refusal to admit the validity of the charges
against her was particularly resented in the party, especially as
renewed emphasis was put on party loyalty following the
traumas of Khrushchev's denunciations of Stalin in Russia, and
an awareness of the ways intellectuals had gathered together to
oppose the state (in the so-called Petőfi Circles) during the
Hungarian revolution of 1956. By late September her case had
been carried through a further twenty-seven separate meetings,
and criticisms of her came from more and more influential literary figures: Lao She accused her of having a "superiority
complex" and of constantly looking down on other writers;
Mao Dun, author of *Midnight*, whom she had vigorously criticized in 1952, charged her with being self-centered and indulg-
ing in "bourgeois individualism"; Lu Xun's lover and former
student, Xu Guangping, charged her with "one-bookism," a
complex intellectual crime that implied a writer was selfishly
trying to produce a perfect literary work at the expense of the
other demands of life and the party, a charge in which Guo
Moruo, now president of the Chinese Academy of Sciences,
concurred.[48] Cartoons of the time showed a fat Ding Ling laz-
ing under a money tree, propped on a bulky volume entitled
"One-Bookism." The charge was particularly ironic in view of
her failure to produce any prolonged piece of work since 1948,
but this route of criticism was followed back into her past;
moreover, it was given a deeply personal aspect, as in the eyes
of her Communist critics Ding Ling ended up *becoming* the characters she had once so brilliantly created. This trend was exemplified by the party official Yao Wenyuan (later to be a
member of the "Gang of Four"), who accused her of writing
pornography in her early attempts to describe the lives of
prostitutes, and lumped her together with Miss Sophie and the
Yanan nurse Lu Ping in a biting essay entitled "The Freedom
Kingdoms of the Miss Sophies."[49] Finally, a special number of

the *Literary Gazette* in January 1958 was given over to reprinting and criticizing her Yanan essay "Thoughts on March 8" and her story "In the Hospital." In an editorial comment in the same issue, she was accused of fostering Japanese imperialism and Guomindang reactionaries in her work, and of becoming an agent for the Guomindang during her Nanjing imprisonment. As the author of an article entitled "Miss Sophie in Yanan" expressed it, "Ding Ling, Sophie, and Lu Ping are merely three different names for the same cruel-natured woman. All of them share the same special viewpoint, which is to beautify the soul-destroying nature of their own extreme individualism. What she hates is not just some specific aspect of Yanan, but Yanan itself. She attacks not certain specific people but everyone at Yanan. She negates not only some specific worker, peasant, or soldier, but the entire mass of workers, peasants, and soldiers."[50]

Ding Ling might not have seen all these later attacks, for in September 1957, still refusing to admit her guilt to the satisfaction of the party authorities, she was stripped of all her remaining posts and committee assignments, expelled from the Writers' Union and the party, and sent to redeem herself through labor at a farm outside the little town of Tangyuan, on the northern bank of the Sungari River, in China's most northerly province, Heilongjiang, not far from the Soviet border.

In 1958, Mao Zedong pushed China toward the Great Leap Forward, that astonishing and visionary plan by which the seven hundred thousand existing agricultural cooperatives, which had an average membership of about a thousand people, were condensed and combined into some twenty-four thousand communes, each with populations of thirty thousand or more. These new units were designed to incorporate agriculture, local industry, education, defense, and health functions, making for both decentralization and self-sufficiency, while at the same time, claimed Mao, moving China a gigantic step forward toward communism. In the cities, too, commune organization was to foster production by destroying what traces of traditional family structures and individualism remained and by concentrating on the total organization of the workers' intellectual and physical environment. As food was to be produced on every scrap of spare urban land, so in the countryside private plots and kitchens were to be abandoned in the interests of the collective, while every rural subgroup would create its own small blast furnaces for the production of the iron needed for China's industrial development.[51]

The impetus for attempting the Great Leap Forward came from a combination of several factors: the general success of the first Five-Year Plan, together with the rural cooperativization and the nationalization of industry, encouraged a certain faith in the inherent powers of the Chinese economy; the Soviet Union's launching of its space satellite, *Sputnik*, seemed a symbol of the superiority of the socialist world over the capitalist West; and Mao's own differences of opinion with his senior colleagues, which had already been apparent in the 1955 movement to collectivize agriculture and the 1956–57 attempt to foster criticism of the party, prompted him to push in a more radical direction so as to prevent stagnation. The same factors in their negative form marked the collapse of the Great Leap Forward in 1959 and 1960: bad natural conditions, an overextended work force, and hopelessly erratic statistics led to serious shortfalls in the major economic goals; Soviet criticism of the plan's impetuousness was severe, prompting bitter Chinese rejoinders; and recriminations and purges within the Chinese Communist Party sundered the leadership and led to policy reversals. In the spring of 1959 Mao Zedong stepped down as chairman of the People's Republic (though he continued as chairman of the Communist Party), yielding the position as head of state to Liu Shaoqi; that summer the defense minister, Peng Dehuai, who was a believer in the appropriateness of Soviet technological methods for both army and the government as a whole, strongly criticized the Great Leap Forward. Mao rallied enough support to have Peng purged from his senior party position and sent to work at hard labor.

During this period Ding Ling was assigned to duty in the chicken coops of Tangyuan. She has recorded that she grew absorbed in the task of raising the fowl and expert at looking after the ailing chickens, some of which she nursed back to health on the heated *kang* in her own hut. It was almost fifty years since she had witnessed her family servant's attempts to supplement the family income by raising a hundred chicks, and Ding Ling noted with resigned humor that her own experiences of life had brought her a natural sympathy for the plight of sick chickens. She began to take a genuine interest in the problems of developing the best methods for raising a healthy flock, and during her spare time even built models of an ideal chicken complex, using the cardboard from old toothpaste containers or any other material she could find. She was also asked to help with local education and plunged into a mass of teaching assignments, including teaching reading to the elderly on the commune.[52]

In 1960 Ding Ling was allowed to participate in a junior capacity in a conference at Beijing, and she must have learned something there of the major political repercussions that followed the backtracking away from the Great Leap Forward. After a succession of bad harvests led to terrible hardship in rural China, the number of communes was increased back up to about seventy thousand, significantly reducing the number of people in each; collective cooking arrangements were abandoned; and, the locally produced iron and steel being found substandard, the communal blast furnaces were dismantled. Liu Shaoqi grew stronger after these setbacks to Mao's policies and to Mao's personal sway within the party, and the rift with the Soviet Union steadily widened following Khrushchev's 1959 visit to Camp David to talk with President Eisenhower. But Ding Ling has recorded the days only through the poignant and significant detail that during the years 1961 and 1962 food was so short in Tangyuan that she could not mount a serious education program—the peasants were too tired and hungry to concentrate. Instead, she told them whatever stories she could remember of her days in Yanan and elsewhere, drawing eager listeners after the sparse midday meal and distracting them from their other worries. Poor and bleak though this life appears, she was to remember it with nostalgia later in her life. Chen Ming, who had been living with her as common-law husband since her days in Yanan, had been allowed to accompany her, and they were able to find something "romantic" even about this life of theirs in the far northeast: "Life during those years had its agreeable moments," she wrote later, "such as going down to the riverbank to wash out the clothes, or on a snowy night during winter walking back home with Chen Ming after seeing a movie, no one else around, just the night scene whitened by the snow." She had been through greater hardships in the Yanan days, she said, reporting from the front in the war against Japan; the Tangyuan peasants were often kind to her despite her "rightist" label and the shadow cast over her by the allegations of unspecified crimes committed at equally unspecified times.[53]

·13·

THE NOISE OF THE RENEGADES

In the period that followed the Hundred Flowers Movement and the Great Leap Forward, the party struggled to find adequate compromises. The restraints on intellectuals and peasantry were loosened: Chinese writers and artists who had been forced to hew rigorously to a socialist-realist line, to use only acceptable material concerning revolution and class struggle, and to portray all characters unambiguously in terms of their "good" or "bad" class background, now began to explore some of the real ambiguities in the Great Leap; and Chinese peasants, after being caught up in the fervors of collectivization for two years, were once again permitted to farm their own plots of land. The government's strict controls over the marketing of privately grown farm produce were relaxed, and a greater measure of local autonomy was given to the communes' leadership. More than a touch of pragmatism was in the air as the Communist party tried to steer rural and urban workers of all classes back to realizable production goals, a pragmatism neatly encapsulated by a remark made by Deng Xiaoping, secretary-general of the party, that it did not matter whether a cat was black or white so long as it was good at catching mice.

Along with this economic retrenchment came a renewed

bureaucratization, for cautious planning was now recommended in the place of those heroic acts of collective will on which Mao Zedong had so greatly relied to make the Chinese transform themselves and their society. Among members of the Communist Party itself—who numbered some seventeen million by 1961—struggles broke out between local cadres, often recruited from the poorer sectors of society and sympathetic to Mao's vision of violent transformation, and the more highly educated and disciplined cadres who held senior posts in the regional planning bureaus. Alarmed at the new patterns of caution and routinization, Mao Zedong attempted in 1962 to institute a major "Socialist Education Campaign" that would reemphasize the values of class struggle within China by encouraging the poorer peasants once again to identify their class enemies among the former landlords and rich peasants, as well as compel rural cadres to work on the land in person for a certain time each year.[1]

The central thrust of this new movement was to come from large work teams, composed of experienced Communist cadres, which were to be dispatched to the countryside, where they would "take root" among the peasants, gain their trust, and then expose examples of malfeasance or backsliding among the local leadership. Almost from the start, however, this procedure led to problems: the work teams sometimes abused their power, falsely identifying conscientious cadres as extremists, as well as increasing—by the sheer weight of their own numbers—the amount of interference in rural work patterns. So at least Mao believed, especially after Deng Xiaoping and Liu Shaoqi (Mao's successor as head of state) redrafted the basic directives under which the investigating cadres operated. Instead of emphasizing the importance of class struggle, these new directives seemed often to persecute radical peasant activists while protecting the upper levels of an already ossifying bureaucracy. Mao's fears were exacerbated by the example of one county in Hebei province, where Liu Shaoqi's wife, Wang Guangmei, personally led a work team, and concluded that 85 percent of the local cadres were either corrupt or practicing "spontaneous capitalism." Wang Guangmei reported that the whole local organization "basically does not belong to the Party," but was "a two-faced counterrevolutionary regime," and suggested radical changes in the local leadership.[2]

Mao, feeling that such judgments would wreck the morale of genuine peasant revolutionaries and showed a complete failure to comprehend the difference he had so painstakingly established between "contradictions among the people" (which should be handled gently) and "contradictions with the enemy" (where violent action was warranted), endeavored through various newspaper and propaganda outlets to spread the news about those rural production brigades which, he felt, had shown spectacular success, such as Dazhai, in a poor and mountainous part of Shanxi province; yet though Mao instituted a national campaign of praise for this unit, which had moved so swiftly first to form mutual-aid teams in the late 1940s and then to organize collectives in the early 1950s, a "cleanup" unit dispatched to Dazhai concluded that the unit's successes were much less than they seemed, since its vaunted local leaders had falsified both acreage reports and grain-production figures.[3]

It may well have been after talking personally to the head of the Dazhai brigade, in late 1964, that Mao decided that elements within his party were now openly seeking to undermine everything he stood for, but he had already begun to order the press to publicize impressive examples of individual rural poverty and sacrifice so as to reinforce the Dazhai picture. The instruction Mao issued in 1963 to "learn from Lei Feng" was an example of this tactic: Lei Feng was a young soldier, born in 1939 to a poor peasant family in Hunan, who became in turn tractor driver, steel worker, and People's Liberation Army soldier before dying in an accident in 1962. Lei's simple and undramatic life underscored Mao's commitment to the ordinary poor of China; his membership in the army hinted at Mao's decision to use the army and its loyal defense minister, Lin Biao, as the base for an assault on party "rightists," and his alleged adoration of Mao's written works prepared the country for a new and higher stage of the cult of Mao's personality.[4]

By the time that cult came to its apogee in 1966, with Lin Biao leading the army in distribution and praise of Mao's sayings, collected now in the "little red book," with Mao hailed as the "great helmsman," the "great, great leader," and "the red, red sun in our hearts," there was little that intellectuals such as Lao She could do but anticipate a new period of restriction and wait out these developments in patience. Admittedly, some high officials, such as Shao Quanlin in 1962, had quite forcefully broached the notion of allowing intellectuals to broaden out from the strictest tenets of socialist realism to include what he called the "middle character"—that is, figures who could be found in the center of the spectrum that had pure People's Liberation Army soldiers and intrepid poor peasants as examples of purest virtue on one end, and vile landlords and Guomindang collaborators on the other. As Shao presented his ideas to a conference held in Dalian:

> The two tips of a pole are small, while the middle area is large. The heroes and the backward elements are the two tips; those situated in the middle are the majority, so we ought to write about the various kinds of richly complex psychological states of such people. The chief educational target of literature is the middle character. There is no need to indoctrinate those who are the most progressive and the most advanced. It is true that depicting heroes establishes a model; however, we should also pay attention to depicting characters who are situated in the middle. If we only depict the heroic models and not the contradictory and complex characters, then realism in fiction will be inadequate. When creating characters in fiction, the most important thing is to rely upon the character's own actions and psychology to reflect his or her contradictions. The fact that it was revisionists who wrote about the darkness of people's inner lives has caused us to shy away from doing the same thing. But the dark, inner life *is* something we can write about; it is only writing about darkness for the sake of darkness that is wrong.[5]

Shao's views were rejected, however, and Ding Ling was one of those "rightists" whose past works were unearthed and quoted to show Shao the error of his ways, even though Shao himself had been one of Ding's fierce opponents.[6]

Yet a man such as Lao She, despite his "correct" performance in writing *Dragon's Beard Ditch*, was not the kind of writer who could ignore the inner need to analyze a character's "own actions and psychology to reflect his or her contradictions," of which Shao had spoken. As early as 1957, when Lao She finished *Teahouse*, readers must have seen the reemergence of something shrewd and sarcastic, something linked to *Cat Country* and *Rickshaw*. "Who is Tan Sitong?" asks a character near the end of Act 1 of *Teahouse*, after hearing the news that Tan has been executed by the Manchus for being a follower of Kang Youwei's reform faction in 1898. "It seems I have heard his name somewhere," responds a friend. "Anyway, he must have committed a grave crime, or else he would not have been beheaded."[7] With remarks like this, Lao She kept alive a view of the state's recurrent abuse of its power and the citizens' silent acceptance of that abuse, and in circling back from the Hundred Flowers Movement to Kang Youwei, he implied a blessing on activists such as Qiu Jin, with her poems of anguish, on Lu Xun, with his ceaseless messages of warning against man's tendency to keep quiet in the face of injustice, and even on Xiao Jun and Ding Ling, whatever their current political status. At other times his comments, presented in the guise of literary criticism, took on a deadpan seriousness that must have seemed—at least to those among his readers who could remember the "heroic" example of poetry he had cited in *Cat Country*—truly hilarious. As Lao She wrote in one such essay:

> *"The East is Red,*
> *The Sun is rising,*
> *In China Mao Zedong has appeared!"*

This poem also uses fast beats, but what a wonderful poem it is! If one seeks purity in a poem, how lovely is the discipline of that single sentence. The poet doesn't expand his theme by writing:

> *"It has already been bright a long time and the eastern regions*
> *are already filled with redness.*
> *The sun is just about to come out completely.*
> *Ah, Mao Zedong can indeed be compared to China's sun, ah yes!"*

He writes his sentence with disciplined economy, yet how great is the spirit, how great is the range of that sentence, how deep is its feeling, how sonorous its rhythms! It is a joy to read, a joy to chant![8]

The joke might become labored if pushed too far, but Lao She inserted such passages in longer essays where they were unnoticed by many readers; he did not attempt the sustained criticism of the party leadership by means of historical allegories that other scholars were writing in the 1960s, in the form of newspaper articles or historical plays, such as Wu Han's *Hai Rui Dismissed from Office*. This latter work, interpreted by Communist cadres and eventually by Mao himself as a criticism of Mao's handling of the Great Leap Forward and a tacit eulogy to Mao's now-disgraced colleague Marshal Peng Dehuai, was used as one of the triggers for the final stage of a "Socialist Education Campaign." This new political campaign, launched in 1966, came to be called the Great Proletarian Cultural Revolution, and it brought literally millions of radicalized youths from all over China to Beijing, where they were reviewed in great parades by Mao Zedong at the Tiananmen Square in front of the Gate of Heavenly Peace.

For those seventeen or younger, who had been born since the Communist takeover of China in 1949, this was the chance to re-create something of the experience of the famous Long March of 1935. Though Mao intended the young Red Guards, as they were called, to exert pressures on the educational and party bureaucracies of China, they represented an almost endless variety of stances and pursued divergent goals: some were peasants or proletarians who believed they had been denied a fair chance for education or advancement by entrenched conservative forces; some were children of people who had been branded as "rightists," who felt they were denied access to the same goods because of their parents' faults; some had been sent away from their hometowns to work in the countryside and used this chance to return home; some were idealistic youth encouraged to march by ambitious party cadres who wanted to consolidate their own power. Within rural communes, within universities, within factories, the claim of "redness" came to be universal, hard to dispute and hard to prove; some "waved the red flag to attack the red flag," while others sought to preempt attacks on their previous lethargy by speeding the revolutionary pace. The Red Guards who burned the British legation in Beijing to the ground, beat up "former capitalists," struck for higher wages, smashed art objects, changed "reactionary" street signs, kidnapped representatives of the Central Committee, bombed one another's campuses, established new worker-managed communes, and cried out in unison to Mao as the "red, red sun in their hearts" were, for a heady space, at once the manipulated and the masters.[9]

It is hard to recapture the excitement and anger of those days in 1966 and 1967, the deadly seriousness with which enemies were hunted down, the sense that all the conventional institutions of China—cultural, political, economic—were about to fall. The awareness that Chinese youth had been liberated to attack the old intoxicated other young people around the world, in Japan and the United States, in England, France, and West Germany, and brought frightened moments to those country's leaders; within China the effect was all the greater, for it was Chairman Mao Zedong himself who backed the movement, the regular army that condoned or encouraged it, and a new emergent group of Shanghai party leaders that spurred on the young. Deng Xiaoping, Liu Shaoqi and his wife, Wang Guangmei, and a host of other senior party leaders were publicly humiliated and toppled from power. Zhou Enlai was briefly in danger, and Mao himself was criticized for trying to restrain the momentum of the Cultural Revolution. Old reputations were refurbished or obliterated in new ways: some students formed a Lu Xun Corps to battle with the entrenched elite and the favored children of senior cadres; others turned on the dead Qu Qiubai because he had once written those defeatist "Superfluous Words" which seemed to belittle party activism, and smashed the memorial tablets to him in the Beijing revolutionary martyrs' cemetery and defiled his grave.[10] At the same time Red Guard groups turned on each other: those from worker or peasant backgrounds who were trying to rise within the party hierarchy cried out against those from highly educated families who dominated the university entrance exams and slipped into the fatter jobs; they mocked the well-connected young party hacks for having their "hearts set on a small car, a little modern house, a white coat, a laboratory," and in language that sounded like the youthful Zou Rong's mockery of the Manchus in 1903 they cried out against the "old and young gentlemen" of the People's Republic: "Formerly you were in a privileged position, sat on our heads and let your excrement fall on us to show that you were superior. Today you are under dictatorship and you suffer." Well-connected students struck back to protect themselves and their families' good names; they were joined by those from landlord and Guomindang backgrounds who had been prevented from having any party careers at all. Often they broke into government offices to ransack the hated records that held the key to their family antecedents and thus to their future lives.[11]

It is not clear precisely how or why Lao She became a target. He was of course well known for his recent plays, but most Red Guards would have been too young to see the film *This Life of Mine*. Did they know of his love for the novels of Charles Dickens? Had someone read *Cat Country* and caught the defamation of Everybody Shareskyism? Had his sarcastic comments on the new poetry been picked up by the young? Perhaps it was enough—as it was for so many who suffered at this time—that he was old and famous and had absorbed enough foreign culture to be considered Westernized. Many must have sensed he was not deeply committed ideologically. As he had told a couple of Western interviewers in May 1966, "I can understand why Mao Zedong wishes to destroy the old bourgeois concepts of life, but I cannot write about this struggle because I am not a Marxist, and therefore I cannot feel and think as a Beijing student. . . . We old ones can't apologize for what we are. We can only explain why we are and wave the young ones on their way to the future."[12] In the summer of 1966 he had turned back to his own distant past and was working on an autobiographical novel about life among the old Manchu military families at the end of the Qing dynasty. He remembered with amusement how fashionable it had been to have everything Western in those days—the last lines of the draft dealt wryly with characters assembling in a Qing dynasty pavilion windowed in glass where all was in the Western mode—Western crockery on the table, Western rugs on the floor, a Western lamp swinging overhead. . . .[13]

During August 1966 Lao She was ordered to attend a number of "study sessions" with members of the revolutionary committee in Beijing. He had been having trouble with his health—he was now sixty-seven, his leg pained him, and he had bronchial bleeding—and was given a few days at home, with his wife and four children (one daughter was a physicist and one son a carpenter), to recuperate. During this time he phoned his friend the poet Zang Kejia to discuss his situation; Zang had known Lao since 1935 and, as a close friend of Wen Yiduo's and as the author of "Arrest," written in wartime Chongqing, would be able to understand what Lao She was going through. Lao, in a distraught voice, told Zang: "I am getting quite an education!" On August 23 Lao She was summoned to another meeting, this time a full "struggle session" with a group of middle-school students in the Red Guards; there he was forced to stand for hours holding aloft a placard stating he was a counterrevolutionary and a criminal. According to some reports he also was forced to wear a dunce's hat on his head and was beaten with some of the wooden props used for making scenery in the theater. While he was at the meeting, his house was ransacked and many of his books and possessions destroyed. The next day he was summoned to another round of meetings and beaten again. That night he died in the Taiping Lake, near the southwest corner of the old Manchu city, either a suicide by drowning or else having been beaten insensible and then thrown into the lake by his interrogators. Immediate cremation was ordered by the local authorities and no thorough examination of the body was possible.[14]

Ding Ling escaped the harsh fate of Lao She and others in the major cities, perhaps by virtue of being far to the north, in Heilongjiang province, but she still had a bleak time of it. In fact the softer side of her collective-farm experiences had ended before the Cultural Revolution, in 1964, when she and Chen Ming were transferred from Tangyuan to the county of Lobei, even farther to the north. Here she was made to do hard manual work, forced to live apart from Chen Ming, and denied writing materials. Rival teams from the two communes of Lobei and Tangyuan made her go through "struggle sessions" that involved mental strain and physical abuse. Ding Ling told an interviewer later that she believed some friends from Tangyuan had pretended to be stern with her so as to deflect the genuine cruelties that the radical cadres at Lobei wished to inflict on her;[15] but after the summer of 1966 Ding Ling was taken over entirely by the Lobei radicals. Humiliated in group-criticism sessions, she was kicked and pummeled and made to stand for long periods in the painful "airplane" position (legs straight, and torso bent forward into a right angle, arms extended to the side). The draft of a long novel that she had been working on while in Tangyuan—a kind of sequel to *The Sun Shines over the Sanggan River*, dealing with the fate of those peasant revolutionaries left behind in Zhangjiakou after General Fu Zuoyi recaptured the area in 1946—was taken from her and destroyed. She was ordered out of the dormitory where she had been living and made to sleep on her own in a cowshed. Even in this situation, she claimed later, she was convinced that some of those abusing her did so in fact only to protect her from worse treatment, a complex act of courage and deceit that won her gratitude.

But they were long, dark days, and her only solace came from tiny notes, scrawled to her by Chen Ming on the corners of scraps of wastepaper, on matchboxes, on cigarette packets, even on the dried-out leaves of the maize they ate, which he would drop on the ground when they passed, or somehow smuggle to her. Even after the notes were confiscated and burned by Red Guards, Ding Ling did not despair, for she had forced herself to remember all of them in case of just such an eventuality: "They might take away the physical strength from your body," Chen wrote in one of the notes, "but they can never destroy the strength of your mind. You are a white sail far out across the sea, there is hope even as the waves crash against each other. I am gazing out after you! Others join me in raising our voices to you." And again, "Dark nights pass and dawn comes. Bitter-cold days will turn to spring breezes. If wild winds and rain didn't beat down on soft shoots, how would mighty trees ever grow?" Or again, "We are not alone. How many talented officials, able scholars, had times of grief and were charged with crimes? We are but seeds of grain on the ocean, we mustn't grieve too much. Spread out your wings, hoard your supplies, so that you can avail yourself of the grand future that is coming. Never, never despair!"[16]

Although there were many thousands of personal tragedies like Ding Ling's or Lao She's, the Cultural Revolution did not succeed in completely reversing the old political order; in the face of mounting domestic chaos Mao was compelled to call in the army so as to calm down the students, settle the battles between rival Red Guard factions, and get both peasants and urban dwellers back to work. But the old intellectual order remained fundamentally changed for a decade, as Mao's wife, Jiang Qing, took control of cultural affairs and projected a vision of a purely Chinese socialist art that would be untainted by traces of Western influence or by elitist holdovers from the earlier "feudal" society. Elements of folk art and dance, peasant tales, People's Liberation Army triumphs, and Communist Party heroics were blended to provide a new national culture that became compulsory fare for China. The Gate of Heavenly Peace, from the terrace of which Mao had saluted the marching columns of Red Guards week after week in late 1966, remained the symbol of revolution to the young long after they had been deflected back to their fields and factories. Once, Wen Yiduo had applied the newly discovered techniques of vernacular poetry to hymn a rickshaw puller's fear and the ghosts of students shot down by warlord guns at that gate in 1926; now hundreds of young workers could use their newfound literacy to salute their own party at the same site:

> Cheers, the thousands of mountains and rivers, all liberated now,
> Unfurl the glowing red flag with five gold stars
> Chairman Mao waves his hand at the Gate of Heavenly Peace;
> In an instant, history has rolled away so many centuries.
>
> You Gate of Heavenly Peace, solemn and majestic,
> You've lived through hundreds of war storms,
> Embodying the seven hundred million people's triumphant joy;
> On the eastern land, you stand, straight and proud.
>
> Radiating from you is the Party's brilliance,
> Peerless and invincible, shouting orders to the elements.
> It has met, head-on, the vicious storms from the Pacific,
> And smashed the encroaching cold front from Siberia. . . .

Look, flowers of uncounted colors decorate the Gate, look—
They reflect the red of the three flags that roll and
*   unroll with the spring wind.*
The footsteps before the Gate, forever marching forward, command
*   us to listen—*
And hear, oh, hear, how they drown out the noise of all
*   the renegades.*[17]

One assumes that the young woman textile-factory worker named Lu Ping who wrote this poem—her name, by chance, an echo of the one Ding Ling had given the unhappy heroine of "In the Hospital"—knew little or nothing of Ding Ling the writer, but her line on drowning out the renegades fitted Ding Ling's current situation well enough, as if anticipating the next downward drop in Ding Ling's fortunes. Even as the Cultural Revolution seemed to wane, the rancor harbored toward a broad group of intellectuals since Yanan days by Mao's wife, Jiang Qing, who had emerged during the Cultural Revolution as China's leading cultural commissar, grew in strength. Jiang's hostile attitudes were reinforced by Yao Wenyuan, the bureaucrat who had criticized Ding Ling's works with such thoroughness and hostility in the antirightist period after the Hundred Flowers Movement and had now become one of the four people, along with Jiang Qing, who seemed to have gained the most power from the Cultural Revolution. When Ding Ling was summoned from Lobei to Beijing in April 1970 by the Cultural Revolutionary Small Group, she initially thought that "rescue was at hand." Her optimistic expectations, however, were immediately shattered. She was taken to a maximum-security prison on the outskirts of the city and locked in a small cell. In that one small room, as she later recalled, she "ate, urinated, defecated, and slept," and read the works assigned to her: the four volumes of Mao's *Selected Works* the first year; the six-volume party-approved set of selections from Marx and Lenin the next year; thereafter a wider choice that included Engels and Stalin, as well as the Communist theoretical organ *Red Flag* and the *People's Daily*.[18] She was allowed into the open air for exercise once a month, and cut off totally from all contact with Chen Ming or other friends. "If I happened to want to write something," as she described the experience,

> I had no pen, I had no paper. If I had something that I wanted to say to someone, there was no one else in the room but myself. It was isolation, complete and absolute isolation. From the day of my birth I had never experienced isolation like that. Before, during the Cultural Revolution, if during the daytime I had been abused or beaten or was forced to suffer in some other way, still at nighttime I could return to my own shed; and if Chen Ming was there we could share our experiences, offer each other some comfort, and give each other support. The bitter tears could flow out; one didn't have to hold in all the bile. But shut up alone in that room, from daytime to nighttime, from nighttime to daytime, one had the choice of sitting facing the wall or of pacing about between the walls. That loneliness was like a poisonous snake, gnawing away at my heart.[19]

Lu Xun had used the same metaphor of a snake coiled around his heart to describe his own loneliness in the warlord years before the May Fourth Movement, when he could reach no one, find no one, see no hope. He had only the flickering chance of reaching some new fighter "galloping on in loneliness," and even that was denied Ding Ling. All she could cling to was the memory of the jailers in her long period of house arrest in Nanjing in the mid-1930s, when their humanity shone through their duty. As she said of her second imprisonment in the 1970s:

> It may seem funny, but during that time I kept having one completely confident idea, one truly "romantic" fantasy: I imagined that one day a good-hearted jailer—just like those good-hearted prison guards one always saw in the old plays and operas—would take pity on me in my loneliness, and in a good-hearted way would bring me a letter from my husband; in that letter Chen Ming would write a few words to comfort me and cheer me up. I waited with longing day after day, and day after day sadly saw my hopes not realized; I continued to hope for one thousand and eight hundred days, but never did that yearned-for letter arrive.[20]

Ding Ling mentioned that not a single friend came to visit her during the five years she spent in prison, but possibly this was because they had no idea she was there, and not out of callousness or fear. "People like her are doing all right, you don't need to worry," Shen Congwen told one of his former students who visited Beijing in May 1973. Though Shen hadn't seen Ding Ling for nine years, he believed she was still in Heilongjiang, "in good spirits and in good health." The mistake was doubly poignant in view of Shen's own comparatively good situation at this time. His interviewer found him happy and vigorous, working steadily in the Beijing Palace Museum on the old textile collections. He had done no more creative writing since some little poems written at the scene of Mao Zedong's 1928 guerrilla base at Jinggangshan, which the party had sent him to visit in 1962 (the site was now a national shrine to the memory of those days of revolutionary struggle and survival), but he seemed pleased to be publishing historical materials. Furthermore, he stated, his two sons were working contentedly as machine-tool operatives, while the favors bestowed on the family could be gauged from the fact that even during the Cultural Revolution he had been allowed to vacation at a little house out in the Hubei countryside.[21]

Shen's interviewer, who had been a student of Wen Yiduo's as well, was one of the first Chinese American visitors to travel to the People's Republic following the resumption of diplomatic relations between China and the United States after China's 1971 admission to the United Nations and President Nixon's 1972 visit to China. Yet despite this new Sino-American relationship, China continued to be shaken by the uncertainties that followed the death of Lin Biao, which had come in 1971 (after he had allegedly tried to kill Mao in an assassination plot); in addition, China was faced with ongoing threats of war with the Soviet Union and American pressures in Vietnam. Furthermore, the whole structure of university research was still disrupted after years of closure; there were continued massive shifts of urban youth out to the countryside so as to prevent urban unemployment; and crisis levels of population growth were reached as the nine-hundred-million mark was passed. The growing power of the four new leaders who had emerged from the turmoil of the Cultural Revolution in the shadow of an ailing Mao Zedong had not brought political stability, since at the same time Deng Xiaoping (purged in 1966) was regaining power with the backing of Premier Zhou Enlai, himself ill with cancer.

In a curious mass campaign in 1974, the movement to "criticize Confucius and criticize Lin Biao," the party sought to purvey the idea that Lin was a reactionary parallel to Confucius, in that Lin had opposed Mao just as Confucius had stood against the politically centralizing and economically progressive policies of the emerging feudal and antiaristocratic states of the fifth century B.C. By a similar historical leap, Mao Zedong could be compared to the third-century B.C. Emperor Qin Shi Hoangdi, who had done so much to unify China. Behind these rather strained formulations lay the fact that Mao was seriously ill, and that the millions of revolutionary youth who had been wrought up to a pitch of great excitement only a few short years before had little sense of where national policy was heading. They were fully aware, however, that there were still profound inequalities in the way cadres were chosen—the balance had swung decisively *against* those with any form of advanced Western training or with parents who had been in the pre-1949 elites—and knew that the party's policy of massive relocation of urban youth into the countryside was a dismal failure.[22]

These stresses were picked up and encapsulated by three former Red Guards in Guangzhou, a city that had been one of the most volatile centers of the Cultural Revolution. All three young men had been in favorable circumstances in 1966: one had just graduated from the Guangdong College of Fine Arts, and the other two were cadres' sons in middle school. None of them had found satisfactory jobs or anything to replace the excitement of those years. During 1973 and 1974 the three friends worked on a manifesto, which they finally posted on a street wall in Guangzhou on November 7, 1974; signed with a pseudonym that was composed of one ideograph from each of their real names—Li-Yi-Zhe—the document was written on sixty-seven sheets of newsprint pasted together, and stretched for almost a hundred yards. Claiming to be speaking on behalf of Marxism and against the "Lin Biao system" and the regressive policies of Deng Xiaoping, Li-Yi-Zhe wrote that the party, having hosed down the old revolutionary wall posters, was now instituting a "new bourgeois mode of possession" by "changing the public into private under the conditions of socialist ownership of the means of production." In other words, access to scarce goods and resources was becoming a perquisite of a limited group of cadres, while the rest of China was expected to perform a "grotesque loyalty dance," to work long hours for low pay, and to offer "morning prayers and evening penitence." Lin Biao's "feudalistic semifascist autocracy" had killed forty thousand people in Guangdong province alone and herded hundreds of thousands more into "scum-hole types of cow pens"; how could one distinguish such actions from those of foreign imperialists, the warlords, or the Guomindang on those once famous dates, May 30, 1925, March 18, 1926, or April 12, 1927?[23]

During the years of the Cultural Revolution, continued the three authors, China's legal system had disintegrated and the people "had acquired new chains" (a mocking reversal of the last lines of Marx's *Communist Manifesto*). Implored to be courageous and to "go against the tide," the youth of China could not even partake of the courage of a Lu Xun, for Lu Xun had had Japanese friends to help him publish works when he was desperate, whereas in the People's Republic the youth of the 1970s had nowhere to turn if the party banned their articles. The people of China had become "just like a traveler from the well-rivered south, who treasures water only when he comes to the desert"; Li-Yi-Zhe called on the Fourth National People's Congress, which was just about to meet (the last congress, the third, had met in 1964), to restore some levels of socialist democratic rights.[24]

In the event, Li-Yi-Zhe could gather little solace from the People's Congress, which finally convened in January 1975. For in the new Constitution which that congress promulgated—replacing the Constitution of 1954—though declaring grandly that China had now moved from being a "people's democratic state" (in the 1954 formulation) to a "socialist state of the dictatorship of the proletariat," that "Marxism–Leninism–Mao Zedong thought" was the "theoretical basis guiding the thinking of our nation," and that the commune was to be considered the basic form of political and economic organization, the congress deleted the various clauses in the earlier Constitution granting freedom to engage in scientific research and literary and artistic creation, and freedom of residence and movement. It would remain to be seen if the new clause 13—"speaking out freely, airing views fully, holding great debates, and writing big-character posters are new forms of carrying on socialist revolution created by the masses of the people"—would be honored in the breach or the observance. The initial party response, after all, had been to jail Li-Yi-Zhe's three authors, and they were still behind bars.[25]

A few months after the congress, however, Ding Ling was released from prison as suddenly as she had been arrested five years before. She and Chen Ming, still labeled "counterrevolutionaries," were sent to Changzhi city, in Shanxi province, to help look after the elderly. In Changzhi, allowed to write again, Ding Ling began to reconstruct the scenes of her destroyed draft novel, which she titled *In the Bitter Cold Days*; she was cheered by people's cautious friendliness, a wonderful change from the atmosphere of Lobei. This briefly restored sense of well-being was shattered by the news of Premier Zhou Enlai's death in January 1976, for Ding was convinced that he had been one of those who had protected her from Jiang Qing. With him gone, her own continued survival seemed to her even more problematical than in the past. She wrote later that she set up a little memorial altar to Zhou in her house and pasted a copy of Deng Xiaoping's eulogy to the dead premier on her wall; that done, she waited in trepidation.[26]

The vast outpouring of grief in China over Zhou Enlai's death was sincere and unanticipated by the government, which tried to mute the response. But in April, during the Beijing observances of the annual spring rites for the departed, hundreds of thousands of men and women converged on the memorial to revolutionary heroes in the huge square outside the Gate of Heavenly Peace, bringing poems and garlands of flowers to place on the monument in Zhou's memory. Grief slipped over into outrage, and demonstration edged toward riot, as they had so many times before in the 1920s and 1930s. Police and troops were called out. The authorities arrested many participants;

there were beatings; property was set afire; people were badly hurt. Deng Xiaoping was blamed and dismissed from all his posts.[27]

These tortured twists of domestic politics were growing commonplace in China, and inasmuch as they echoed the old divisiveness of earlier dynasties, it was appropriate that imperial imagery (at least in the sense of drawing parallels with the ruthless founding Emperor of the third century B.C., Qin Shi Hoangdi) had been accepted during his last years by Mao Zedong. It seemed equally fitting that in the few weeks between the death of Mao's greatest general, Zhu De, and the death of Mao Zedong himself in September 1976, one of the severest earthquakes in China's history laid waste the area around the northern city of Tangshan and killed three quarters of a million people, as if in solemn echo of the portents that had reverberated at moments of great political change through China's past. Mao's last will and testament, or at least the version of it released by the Communist Party's Central Committee just after his death, lambasted, among others, the long-dead Qu Qiubai and the sequestered Deng Xiaoping for their divisiveness and their attempts to wreck the Chinese Communist Party. Yet within a few weeks the presumed authors of the "will," the Gang of Four, had been removed from their offices by a counterfaction; neatly airbrushed out of the photographs of Mao's funeral obsequies, they were banished by modern technology from having paid homage to the man they claimed to revere.[28]

One by one, the most vilified figures of China's recent past began to be plucked back, alive or dead, from the shades: if alive, to be replaced in office; if dead, to have memory and a measure of honor restored. The party now blamed all the setbacks in China's performance on the Gang of Four, and a restored Deng Xiaoping urged the Chinese on to the path of Four Modernizations—in industry, in science and technology, in agriculture, and in military affairs—which would, it was hoped, propel China yet again toward the modern age. A Communist Party congress in August 1977 officially declared the closing of the Cultural Revolution and the inauguration of a new period of Great Unity. If the phrase recalled Kang Youwei's youthful dreams, the contents were also couched in his basic formula of self-strengthening through Western scientific technology: a Ten-Year Plan of sustained national growth was proposed in which one hundred and twenty major projects would be completed; among these would be ten iron and steel plants, nine plants for processing nonferrous metals, eight coal mines, ten oil and natural-gas fields, six trunk rail lines, five harbors, thirty power stations. In each year of the first eight years of the plan, agricultural output was to rise 4 to 5 percent and industrial output by more than 10 percent. At the end of the development cycle, China would possess fourteen separate industrial areas, each of which would be strong in its own right.[29] In three consecutive articles of a new Constitution (promulgated by the Fifth National People's Congress, in March 1978), the role of scientists was boosted: Article 12 declared that the state would "devote major efforts to developing science, expanding scientific research, and promoting technical innovation and technical revolution"; Article 13 spoke about raising the "cultural and scientific level of the whole nation"; and Article 14 stated that the principle of "letting a hundred flowers bloom and a hundred schools of thought contend" was to be a basic matter of state policy, though the context for that blooming and contending remained one in which "all cultural undertakings" must serve the cause of socialism.[30]

In a speech on March 18, 1978, to the audience assembled at a national science conference, Deng Xiaoping made a determined attempt to reassure technically skilled personnel that they would not be discriminated against on the grounds of the old distinctions (which Mao himself had so often made) between "mental" and "manual":

> In a socialist society, brain workers trained by the proletariat itself differ from intellectuals in any exploiting society in history. . . . Generally speaking, the overwhelming majority of them are part of the proletariat. The difference between them and the manual workers lies only in a different role in the social division of labor. Those who labor, whether by hand or by brain, are all working people in a socialist society. With the advancement of modern science and technology and progress toward the four modernizations, a

great deal of heavy manual work will gradually be replaced by machines. Manual labor will steadily decrease, for workers directly engaged in production and mental work will continuously increase. Moreover, there will be an increasing demand for more people in scientific research and for a larger force of scientists and technicians. The "Gang of Four" distorted the division of labor between mental and manual work in our socialist society today, calling it class antagonism. Their aim was to attack and persecute the intellectuals, undermine the alliance of the workers, the peasants and intellectuals, disrupt the social productive forces, and sabotage our socialist revolution and construction.[31]

These words of Deng Xiaoping's, when coupled with the promise in the preamble to the new Constitution that the party would seek to create "a political situation in which there are both centralism and democracy, both discipline and freedom, both unity of will and personal ease of mind and liveliness," brought immediate responses in the intellectual sphere. Indeed, the nearest parallel to the outpouring of new essays and poems, new study societies and new magazines, would lie not in the Hundred Flowers activities of twenty-one years before but rather in the period around the May Fourth Movement of 1919, or in the Shanghai and Japan inhabited by late Qing dynasty students.[32] But the circumstances of those pleading for greater human rights continued to be difficult; though things were not so bad as the Li-Yi-Zhe group had claimed in 1974 (all three of those former students, incidentally, were released in 1978), it was still almost impossible to buy paper in bulk, to get enough ink, to find space for editorial offices or time off from regular jobs to get the editorial work done. Rather nostalgically, the young authors appealed to Deng Xiaoping to remember his own youth as a "Doctor of Mimeography"—a reference to his student days in France in the 1920s when he had edited the mimeographed Communist weekly *Red Light*.[33]

The assemblies that took place in late November 1978, near the former Forbidden City, at what had become known as the Xidan Democracy Wall, led to discussions of extraordinary excitement and frankness. On December 15 a former Red Guard activist named Wei Jingsheng—now a twenty-nine-year-old electrician working in the Beijing zoological gardens—posted on the wall a lengthy statement entitled "The Fifth Modernization," appending his name and address and inviting interested persons to come to visit him at his lodgings; in Wei's action a wide spectrum of dissidents, many of them young men and women in their late twenties from that same Red Guard generation and whose own lives and educations had been violently disrupted, found a focus and an inspiration.[34] Wei had declared that the Fifth Modernization—by which he meant democracy—was essential if the Four Modernizations proposed by Deng Xiaoping were to have any meaning. Other young activists began to criticize Deng for stating that judgments on Mao Zedong must be left to later generations. Did that mean, they asked rhetorically, that young Chinese should limit their discussions to the policies of eighteenth-century rulers such as Kangxi and Qianlong?[35]

Criticism of Mao Zedong now became common in these debates and magazines. As one "former intellectual," now a worker, said of Mao: "He became introspective, and with his small-producer background, too many ancient books around, and flattering voices in his ears, he was unable to see the rapid development of science abroad and unable to hear the urgent appeals of the people." The result was that a whole generation of youth had been "fooled and cheated."[36] Other young writers drew on language and metaphors that had been central to Lu Xun. Though Lu Xun had been made into a cult figure by the Gang of Four, and at times in the early 1970s had been almost the only Chinese writer besides Mao whose books one could find on sale, he had then been transformed by Deng's leadership into a prescient critic of the Gang of Four's own future machinations![37] Eschewing both overpraise and overinterpretation, the youth of 1979 returned to Lu's medical metaphors, claiming that the "medicine of importing technology" was not enough for China, since the "root illness" of the nation remained an ideological one. Only by transforming consciousness throughout the whole "upper structures of our country" (as Kang Youwei and Liang Qichao had tried to do in the 1890s, added one writer) could China escape paralysis and transformation back into the "sick man of the East."[38]

Lu Xun's more compassionate side had not been lost sight of, either, and the language of his elegy to the students gunned down in March 1926 shines through the lines written in April 1979 to commemorate a young student, Yu Luoke, who had been shot by the government in 1970 for insisting that China was corrupted by the omnipresence of the "Theory of Class Origin" which bound all younger generations to the party's view of the sins of their parents: "On March 5, 1970, a bullet that should have been aimed at an enemy went through the body of a twenty-seven-year-old fighter who had upheld truth and was brave and unyielding. His body, a frail body, fell, but his heroic image, in the search for and in defense of truth, stood majestically in people's minds."[39] And one hears echoes of the young student Lu Xun looking at the lantern slides of an execution in the 1979 words of another protester: "If we look stupefied as others are being subjected to prosecution, we will not be qualified to be a civilized people."[40]

Images and inspiration were sought not just in China's recent past. Like the young nationalists of the late Qing period, these writers rediscovered Voltaire and Rousseau, presenting them as powerful seers who had championed human rights and equality and attacked religion, economic oppression, and spiritual enslavement. An article of January 29, 1979, invoked the image of the bound feet of an earlier time to make the point that China, like eighteenth-century France, must have its own Enlightenment:

> At the present stage of human development on this tiny planet, many countries have entered the modernized and electronic age at different times, while our country is still groaning in the prison of feudalism that has existed for thousands of years. People are still fooled by feudal ideas, tied up by feudal shackles, and subjected to feudal autocratic persecution. The Republic, which has overthrown an old regime, has been severely restrained by feudal autocracy and obscurantism, as by a pair of small tight shoes, throughout thirty years of development. They feel as though they live in the age of the Yellow Emperor, the age of feudalism. They are suffering great discomfort from the small, tight shoes and know that the shoemakers have no idea whatsoever of their suffering. The progress of the Republic has slowed down and ground to a halt. If China

wants to accomplish the Four Modernizations, it must first get rid of the shoe of feudal autocracy. People will become their own masters with democracy and human rights. Then, after the acquisition of knowledge, the second shoe, that of obscurantism, will be removed. This is the prerequisite as well as the guarantee for accomplishing the Four Modernizations. Without the measures, the Four Modernizations will become just empty talk.[41]

In the March 11, 1979, number of his underground periodical *Explorations*, which he edited with a friend (a physicist named Yang Guang) and sold at Democracy Wall, Wei Jingsheng described life for those held in Beijing's maximum-security prison, Qincheng (the one where Ding Ling had almost certainly been incarcerated). Drawing from firsthand accounts (one of his sources may well have been his girl friend's father, who was imprisoned there for nearly a decade), Wei described the isolation, bad food, tiny cells, and lack of opportunity for exercise inside China's "twentieth-century Bastille," as well as the physical abuse to which the prisoners were constantly subjected; he also reported on attempted suicides and the use of torture. "The irony is," he added parenthetically of the victims, in the midst of his bleak account, "that these unusually gifted individuals joined the Communist Party to fight for the freedom and well-being of China and of mankind, and consequently devoted the better part of their lives to obtaining and maintaining the party's political dominance." He concluded his essay by commenting on the procedures arranged by the party to enable former prisoners to move slowly back to life in society (this might explain Ding Ling's lengthy stay in Shanxi), and by adding some reflections on political life in general:

In 1975 Deng Xiaoping suggested releasing Qincheng's political prisoners. Going along with the "reversal of verdicts" movement of the time, many old party members were freed. To them this was an altogether unexpected piece of luck.

But a sudden overwhelming emotion of joy can sometimes be dangerous. To "insure safety and health," the Central Committee adopted a policy of exile. In 1975, all who left Qincheng had to first spend some time at a hospital to absorb the shock of going back into the world. After

1977, the hospital was no longer considered necessary. Instead the prisoners were sent to distant, out-of-the-way villages whose quiet surrounding supposedly served just as well to soften the violent shock of liberation. . . .

Before leaving, you are made to shoulder a number of groundless accusations. A final summary of your case is then drawn up showing why your ten or fifteen years of imprisonment were well deserved. . . .

We must permanently get rid of Qincheng Prison. We must permanently get rid of political persecution and imprisonment. It is not the few unfortunate victims but the basic political and personal rights of the entire people that are at stake. We might ask the high cadres who have come out of Qincheng: When you suppressed the rights of others to express freely their political views, did you secure your own? When you persecuted others using political pretexts, did you foresee yourselves being subjected to the same kind of persecution?[42]

Wei Jingsheng was himself arrested on May 29, 1979, accused of a variety of crimes that included passing military secrets concerning China's invasion of Vietnam on to foreign newsmen, a charge of high treason that could bring the death penalty. In October he was tried at the Beijing Intermediate People's Court. The state prosecutor insisted that Wei was a "running dog of Vietnam" and "a scum of the nation." In pushing for the Fifth Modernization he had "tried his best to vilify Marxism–Leninism–Mao Zedong thought as a prescription only slightly better than that peddled by charlatans." He also had called the Chinese political system "a feudal monarchy disguised as socialism." The prosecutor concluded:

Our Constitution clearly stipulates extensive democratic rights. However, our democracy should be a democracy protected by law. It does not mean absolute freedom for one to do as one likes. . . . Freedom of speech of the individual citizen must be based on the four basic principles of insisting on the socialist road, the dictatorship of the proletariat, the leadership of the party, and Marxism–Leninism–Mao Zedong thought. The citizen has only the freedom to support these principles and not the freedom to oppose them. . . .

The defendant Wei Jingsheng hid his criminal aim of overthrowing the dictatorship of the proletariat and chang-

> ing the socialist system under the guise of democracy. If
> such individualistic freedom of the minority is allowed to
> run rampant, the freedom of the majority will be lost. The
> people will sink into misery and the nation will be
> doomed.[43]

Waiving the right to counsel, Wei spoke in his own defense,
basing it on Article 45 of the 1978 Constitution, which granted
Chinese citizens the rights of speech, assembly, publication, association, and freedom to write big-character posters. He denied that he had access to any secret military information about
the Vietnam invasion, and claimed that far from being counterrevolutionary his idea of the Fifth Modernization was that
without democracy the other Four Modernizations could never
be attained. His journal *Explorations* had as its sole goal that of
"exploring China and making it rich and powerful. We believe
that only by free, unrestrained, and practical exploration is it
possible to achieve this purpose." In defending himself against
the charges of denigrating Mao Zedong's thought, he stated
calmly that Marxism, like everything else, changes. There was
Kautskyism as well as Leninism, Trotskyism as well as Stalin-
ism, Mao Zedong's thought along with Eurocommunism. In the
Soviet Union and in Vietnam, as in the Gang-of-Four China, a
government allegedly in the hands of the dictatorship of the
proletariat had degenerated into "fascism," with a minority
"exercising dictatorship over the broad masses of the working
people." In such a global context, "the fate of Marxism is like
that of many schools of thought in history. Its revolutionary
essence was emasculated after its second and third generations.
Some of the ideals of its teachings have been used by rulers as
the pretext for enslaving people. Is this not a prescription that
is only slightly better than the medicine peddled by charlatans?"[44]

Wei concluded with a defense of his basic right to speak:

> The indictment states that I "waved the banner of so-
> called freedom of speech and the demand for democracy
> and human rights to agitate for the overthrow of the dicta-
> torship of the proletariat." I must point out that freedom of
> speech is not a wild allegation but is stipulated in black and

white in the Constitution. It is a right which every citizen should enjoy. The tone in which the prosecutor talks about that right shows not only that he is prejudiced in his thinking but that he has forgotten his responsibility to protect the democratic rights of citizens. . . .

The prosecutor accuses me of trying to overthrow the socialist system. . . . In the course of my editing, our publication *Explorations* has never been involved with any organization engaged in conspiracy or violence. *Explorations* is a journal of theoretical investigation on public sale. It has never taken the overthrow of the government as its aim. . . .

The prosecutors perhaps do not agree with my theories. In my several conversations with them we have talked about this. I would just like to add a point. The Constitution gives the people the right to criticize leaders because they are human beings and not deities. Only through criticism and supervision by the people can they reduce their errors. . . .

Criticism cannot possibly be nice and appealing to the ear or entirely correct. To require that criticism be entirely correct and to inflict punishment if it is not is the same as prohibiting criticism and reforms and elevating the leaders to the position of deities. Is it really true that we must again take the old path of modern superstition of the Gang of Four?[45]

Wei was sentenced to fifteen years in prison, and his appeal for leniency was rejected by the High Court on November 6, 1979. However, the editors of another Beijing underground journal, *April 5 Forum* (named for the day on which the Beijing masses had assembled to pay homage to Zhou Enlai in 1976), obtained a transcript of Wei's testimony and printed nearly six hundred copies, which they put up for sale at Democracy Wall; they justified their action by saying that the party authorities had been even more secretive about Wei Jingsheng's trial than the Qing officials had been about disseminating news concerning Zou Rong and the defendants in the *Subao* case back in 1903. The editor and the sellers of *April 5 Forum* were in turn arrested. On December 8, the right to hang posters at Democracy Wall on Xidan Street was withdrawn by government order, and only a spot in Yuetan Park, three miles away, was made available to those who had cleared the contents of their writings, and registered their names and addresses, with the authorities. On January 17, 1980, as the announcement came that Deng Xiaoping's son would be leaving China for the United States to study advanced physics at the University of Rochester, Deng himself announced that the wall-poster clause would be withdrawn from the Constitution at the next suitable occasion. The privilege had been "abused by ultra-individualists."[46]

The arrest and trial of Wei Jingsheng coincided with the release and rehabilitation of Ding Ling. It was around the time of the promulgation of the 1978 Constitution that Ding Ling, still working in Shanxi, had her "rightist" label removed; in February 1979 she was summoned back to Beijing; and that July she was cleared of all the charges made against her in 1957 and 1958. Though she had been ill for some time, she agreed to address the writers and artists assembled for their national congress, which was held in late October and early November 1979. She blamed no individuals for what had happened, said Ding Ling, since there was no single villain, but rather an entire social phenomenon, involving the whole of society. This view came through powerfully in her statement, highlighted by her subtly chosen use of pronouns:

> It has been fifty-two years since I began writing stories in 1927, though after 1958 there was a gap of twenty years. In the 1930s the Guomindang banned my books; after 1958 we ourselves banned my books. . . .
>
> Most of those who were struck down during the Great Cultural Revolution were good people, as everyone knows full well; and those struck down by the Gang of Four were also mostly good people; they have now been endowed with a special fragrance by all the people. But what of those who were criticized in 1957? They were purged and treated like dung. But did they all really deserve to be treated like dung? I have been asking myself repeatedly whether I should speak out about these things, which I felt so deeply. I am well over seventy, I've spent time in a Guomindang prison, and during the Great Cultural Revolution I spent time in a Gang of Four prison, so should I not follow the advice of my good-hearted friends who urged me not to ask questions about such matters, not to talk about them, and

just to muddle along as best I can? But am I the kind of person who doesn't worry about such matters? Am I without emotion? No, I can never be like that, for I know that those who claim to be spurning the vanities of real life are the truly selfish people.[47]

Ding Ling seemed to agree with those who claimed that there were still "feudal" elements in Chinese society; but since she pointed out that feudalism had been blamed for most of the ills of China ever since she was a girl of fifteen, one could guess that she did not take the claim too seriously. Instead, she said, the Chinese should see the fault as lying within a system that permitted power to fall into the hands of those who had special interests to protect and advance. She reiterated her faith in the youth of China, and mentioned her real regret about the two decades during which her books had been suppressed: there was now an entire generation of Chinese in their thirties who had never read her works at all.[48]

Ding Ling's implied criticism of China's cultural and political leaders was printed in the official Communist newspaper *Red Flag*; this alone guaranteed that her remarks would be read and digested everywhere in China. Yet, though politically courageous (and also neatly geared to the steady buildup of evidence that was being assembled for the forthcoming trial of the Gang of Four), Ding Ling's speech did not touch at all on her life as a woman, a subject she had last addressed specifically in her remarks on International Women's Day just before the Yanan forum of 1942, thirty-seven years earlier. Her failure to deal with the topic was not surprising, in a China where many women denied the claims of the party to be advancing the cause of women generally, and still felt circumscribed by traditional occupational and family patterns, and at the mercy of their male counterparts in industry, the armed forces, and politics.[49] Yet her omission had a poignant side, too, for at the same time Ding Ling was addressing the assembled dignitaries, a highly questionable, even brutal examination was being carried out into the activities of Fu Yuehua, a young woman of that same dislocated generation as Wei Jingsheng.

Fu Yuehua had married when she was comparatively young,

and seems to have had a fairly happy life until 1971, when the exigencies of state planning separated her from her husband: he was sent to work in Hebei province while she was assigned to work in a construction company in the Xuanwu district of Beijing. The following year, the head of Fu Yuehua's work unit made sexual advances to her; when she refused to reciprocate, he threatened to accuse her of being a counterrevolutionary and subsequently, according to her own graphic testimony, raped her. Leaving her job, unable to get references for a new one, suffering spells of mental breakdown and prolonged financial hardship, she brought rape charges against the unit chief, but they were thrown out of court. She became a liaison worker with peasants, protesting their low living standards in the areas around Beijing, and at just about the time that Deng Xiaoping traveled to Washington, D.C., in January 1979 to press for American help with China's Four Modernizations, Fu Yuehua led a peasant demonstration through the streets of Beijing. She was arrested ten days later, and after a series of investigations and trials that took up an entire year, was sentenced to a year in prison for libeling her former boss and for disrupting public order. In remarks at the trial, the judge referred to her as "morally degenerate," just as the villagers had referred to the raped girl in the tale "When I Was in Xia Village," told by Ding Ling thirty-seven years before.[50]

The only people to take up Fu's case, besides the members of her own family, were the editors of the surviving unofficial journals. But many of these writers were now judged guilty, by association, with Wei Jingsheng and his friends. Commenting on these protests in an editorial of October 1979, the official party newspaper, *People's Daily*, was stern: "We want to warn all counterrevolutionaries that no matter how fashionable your banner is, no matter how cunning your ways, in the end you will not escape the net of the people's justice."[51]

But was it really "people's justice" that was the net? Might it not be life itself that was the net for these young people, as they struggled to survive in a world of constantly shifting party pronouncements, where Deng Xiaoping, ascendant for the third time, was placing Mao's wife and closest advisers on public trial, while senior party intellectuals (among them Ding Ling) competed to write fulsome articles that would restore Qu Qiubai to posthumous glory? After so many years of intense study of foreign imperialism and the shortcomings of the feudal past, how was one meant to react to the elaborate trade arrangements being made with the United States and Japan, and how was one to view the delegations of distinguished Chinese academics who met to ponder the early writings of Kang Youwei, the character of Emperor Guangxu, and the lessons of the 1898 reforms during China's attempts at modernization almost a century before?[52] What was to happen to love, as the party, confronted by a Chinese population moving inexorably toward the one-billion mark, began to plan for one-child households on a nationwide scale and inevitably intruded into the most private personal spheres, backing their prescriptions with economic and educational sanctions?[53] Were art and poetry to move out of party control, and if so, where? Back to abandoned Western domains of cubism, symbolism, romanticism, where a new generation of Xu Zhimos might feel at home? Had China's long revolution really settled their lives, or would they have to define its elusive messages anew, trying to create for themselves and their country something that had been so often promised for almost a century and yet so seldom grasped?

Ding Ling, at least, was free, and so was the writer Wang Meng, critic of the party in the Hundred Flowers Movement, after having been made to spend twenty years in Xinjiang. Shen Congwen, too, was well, and was given an exit visa to visit his sister-in-law, who taught Chinese calligraphy at Yale University. Lao She's *Teahouse* was revived, to intense public and critical applause. Did these facts balance out in some way, as Fu Yuehua and Wei Jingsheng entered on their life behind bars? A Chinese poet signing himself "Bei Dao" wrote a poem for the underground journal *Today*, giving the closest approximation to an answer he could find.[54] He called his poem "Notes from the City of the Sun":

Life
The sun still rises.

Love
Stillness. Wild geese fly over
virgin waste land.
Old trees topple with a crack.
Sharp, salty rain sprays the air.

Freedom
Float.
Torn scraps of paper.

Child
A balloon lifts its cradle
and flies up and up into the blue.

Girl
A shimmering rainbow
collects birds' colored feathers.

Youth
Red waves
drench solitary oars.

Art
Millions of shining suns
are reflected in a broken mirror.

The People
The moon has been torn into many glistening ears of grain,
sown into honest sky and earth.

Labor
Hands. Enfold the globe.

Fate
Children at random hit railings.
Railings at random hit the night.

Faith
A flock of sheep spill beyond the limits of their pasture,
the shepherd still plays his same old tune.

Peace
In the shop window of a food store
a silent chocolate cannon revolves.

The Motherland
*She was engraved on a bronze shield
which leaned against a partition in a museum.*

Living
A net.

Notes

The word "following" placed before a cited translation signifies that while I have relied heavily on that translation, I have chosen to make fairly considerable changes in it after consulting the original Chinese text. When the changes involve merely definite articles, tenses, or shifts from Wade-Giles to Pinyin romanization, I have added the phrase "with minor changes" after the citation.

CHAPTER 1 / AROUSING THE SPIRITS

1. Kang Youwei, *Nianpu*, p. 129; Lo Jung-pang, ed., *K'ang Yu-wei, a Biography and a Symposium* (hereafter cited as Lo, *Symposium*), p. 63.
2. Examples drawn from *Peking Gazette*, 1895, pp. 8, 55, 71, 72, and the *Guangxu Shilu* [Veritable Records] of the Guangxu reign, twenty-first year. A vivid and amusing picture of the chaos of these late examinations was presented by Chen Duxiu, later secretary-general of the Chinese Communist Party; see Richard Clark Kagan, "The Chinese Trotskyist Movement and Ch'en Tu-hsiu," Appendix, pp. 193–96.
3. Kang Youwei, *Memorial*, p. 146.
4. Hsiao Kung-chuan, *A Modern China and a New World*, p. 9, note 36; Lo, *Symposium*, pp. 28–33.
5. Kang Youwei, *Nianpu*, p. 109; Lo, *Symposium*, pp. 26–27.
6. Lo, *Symposium*, p. 31.
7. Ibid., p. 34.
8. Ibid., p. 35.
9. Ibid., pp. 36–37.
10. Ibid., pp. 54–56.
11. See Kang's comments on Cao Tai (Ts'ao T'ai) in Lo, *Symposium*,

pp. 57, 62; and on Chen Qianqiu (Ch'en Ch'ien-ch'iu) in ibid., p. 63.

12. Kang, *Nianpu*, pp. 117–18, following Lo, *Symposium*, pp. 40–42. Lo, *Symposium*, pp. 75–76, gives Kang's dating of this section as 1895.

13. The enormous mass of material on this "self-strengthening" period of China's history is conveniently summarized in John K. Fairbank, ed., *The Cambridge History of China*, vol. 10. In her essay "The Image of the Empress Dowager Tz'u-Hsi," Sue Fawn Chung has reassessed that formidable lady's approach to reform in a more favorable light.

14. *Wuxu bianfa*, 2/154–55; Liang Qichao, *Nianpu*, p. 23; Kang, *Nianpu*, p. 130; and Lo, *Symposium*, pp. 63–66.

15. Kang, *Memorial*, pp. 135–37.

16. Ibid., pp. 138–39. For some technical antecedents for this discussion by Kang, see Thomas Kennedy, "Mausers and the Opium Trade," especially pp. 120–21 on quick-firing gun production.

17. Kang, *Memorial*, pp. 140–43.

18. Ibid., p. 143.

19. Ibid., pp. 143–45.

20. Ibid., p. 145.

21. Ibid., p. 150. The "universality" of Confucian doctrine (and its parallel to the West's claims to universality) as preached by Kang Youwei and other later Qing reformers is discussed by Wong Young-tsu in "The Ideal of Universality in Late Ch'ing Reformism," pp. 150–54. On Leibniz and the Confucian missions cf. Donald Lach, *The Preface to Leibniz' Novissima Sinica*, p. 69; and Adolf Reichwein, *China and Europe*, pp. 80–81. Zhang Zhidong (Chang Chih-tung) had also suggested having Confucian academies overseas, in 1886: see Michael Godley, "The Late Ch'ing Courtship of the Chinese in Southeast Asia," p. 366.

22. This period of Kang's life is described in Lo, *Symposium*, pp. 68–74.

23. Chu's memorial and the Emperor's response are given in *Guangxu Shilu*, 369/22b and 371/6b–7, and in *Peking Gazette* for 1895, p. 109 under August 11. Kang's opinion of Chu is given in Lo, *Symposium*, p. 73. Specific examples of overseas Chinese involvement with the Qing are given in Michael Godley, "Overseas Chinese Entrepreneurs as Reformers: The Case of Chang Pi-shih," pp. 49–53; and in Godley, "The Late Ch'ing Courtship," especially p. 363 on Ding Richang and p. 367 on Xue Fucheng. From Ch'eng I-fan's work on Wang Xianqian one can see how use of merchants overseas blended in with even a conservative view of the "collectivity": cf. Ch'eng's "*Kung* as an Ethos in Late Nineteenth Century China," p. 178.

24. Harold Schiffrin, *Sun Yat-sen and the Origins of the Chinese Revolution*, chapter 2. For migration patterns from Kang and Sun's home

areas in Guangdong province see June Mei, "Socioeconomic Origins of Emigration," especially p. 475.

25. Schiffrin, *Sun Yat-sen*, chapter 3.

26. Schiffrin, *Sun Yat-sen*, chapter 4; and Eve M. B. Armentrout-Ma, "Chinese Politics in the Western Hemisphere, 1893–1911," pp. 126–40. On Sun's forged birth certificate see Robert L. Worden, "K'ang Yu-wei, Sun Yat-sen, et al. and the Bureau of Immigration," pp. 6–7. An excellent introduction to the recruitment and rituals of these secret societies is given in Fei-ling Davis, *Primitive Revolutionaries of China*, chapters 5 and 7. The societies' general role during the revolution is analyzed in John Lust, "Secret Societies, Popular Movements and the 1911 Revolution," pp. 177–84.

27. Lo, *Symposium*, pp. 63–75.

28. Ibid., pp. 76–83.

29. Ibid., pp. 83–84. The Manchu was Ronglu, a grand secretary and president of the Board of War.

30. Ibid., p. 74.

31. Letter to daughter in Kang Youwei, *Wanmu*, p. 776. See also Lo, *Symposium*, p. 79; and Kang, *Nianpu*, p. 144. The "first minister" in 1897 is a reference to Weng Tonghe.

32. Lo, *Symposium*, p. 95; Kang, *Nianpu*, p. 145.

33. Lo, *Symposium*, p. 98.

34. Kang, *Wanmu*, p. 776.

35. See especially Kang's biographical poem in Kang, *Shiji*, 5/99–101, and Lo, *Symposium*, p. 148, note 22.

36. Lo, *Symposium*, pp. 101, 103; and family letters in Kang, *Wanmu*, pp. 773–75, 777.

37. Lo, *Symposium*, pp. 104, 115.

38. Kang, *Nianpu*, p. 156; Lo, *Symposium*, p. 117. (One can also find descriptions of large posters in the Kangxi reign and the Taiping rebellion.) A preliminary attempt to gauge the Emperor's motives is made by Wong Young-tsu, "The Significance of the Kuang Hsü Emperor to the Reform Movement of 1898."

39. On Tan Sitong's career and writings cf. Luke S. K. Kwong, "Reflections on an Aspect of Modern China in Transition: T'an Ssu-t'ung (1865–1898) as a Reformer," and Richard Shek, "Some Western Influences on T'an Ssu-t'ung's Thought." Some of Tan's writing on study associations is translated by Ronald Robel in "T'an Ssu-t'ung on Hsüeh Hui or 'Study Associations,'" pp. 172–76; and there are helpful comments on the *Renxue* (*Jen-hsueh*) in Frederic Wakeman, Jr., *History and Will*, pp. 128–29. Huang Chang-chien in his essay "On the Hundred Days Reform," p. 308, points also to the anti-Manchu strain in Tan's *Renxue*. The young Guangdong reform chairman was Lin Xu. For sources on Lin, and the others selected as secretaries, see Hsiao, *Modern China*, p. 270, note 23.

40. Kwong, "Reflections," p. 189; and Kang in Lo, Symposium, p. 121, on the unpromising physiognomies of the group.

41. Kang, Nianpu, p. 159; Lo, Symposium, pp. 122–23.

42. Kang's dramatic account of these events is translated in Lo, Symposium, pp. 126–42. Tan's last poems and reflections are in Wuxu bianfa, 4/349. Huang Chang-chien, "Hundred Days Reform," pp. 308–309, discusses the evidence that Kang and Liang did, indeed, plan a countercoup. Lao She, in the first act of his play Teahouse, brilliantly reconstructs the mood of Beijing at this time; cf. Hsu Kai-yu and Ting Wang, eds., Literature of the People's Republic of China, pp. 749–61.

43. Lo, Symposium, p. 135.

44. Kang, Shiji, 4/7. The poem is densely erudite and not susceptible to the literal translation; I follow the version and glosses provided by Hellmut Wilhelm, "The Poems from the Hall of Obscured Brightness," in Lo, Symposium, pp. 326, 337.

45. Kang, Nianpu, p. 167, following Lo, Symposium, p. 138.

46. Lo, Symposium, p. 226; Li Yunguang, Kang Youwei jiashu kaoshi, p. 2.

47. Lo, Symposium, pp. 178, 253–55.

48. Ibid., pp. 255–56. On Kang's inability to enter the United States see Worden, "Bureau of Immigration," p. 3.

49. Armentrout-Ma, "Chinese Politics," pp. 98, 142–48; Lo, Symposium, p. 256.

50. Kang, Shiji, 4/54, following Wilhelm, "Poems," p. 330.

CHAPTER 2 / VISIONS AND VIOLENCE

1. Harold Schiffrin, Sun Yat-sen and the Origins of the Chinese Revolution, pp. 218–19; Lo, Symposium, pp. 182–86; Liang Qichao, Nianpu, p. 103.

2. On Tang, see Charlton M. Lewis, Prologue to the Chinese Revolution, pp. 100–104; Hsiao Kung-chuan, A Modern China and a New World, p. 236, note 152; Lo, Symposium, pp. 184–86, 263, note 19; and Howard Boorman and Richard Howard, eds., Biographical Dictionary of Republican China (hereafter cited as BDRC), 1/93a, 2/347–48. Tang's capture may have been speeded by conservative local scholars who bitterly distrusted both Kang's politics and his iconoclastic views on Confucian scholarship and had publicly decried his immorality: cf. Lewis, Prologue to Chinese Revolution, and BDRC, 4/36b, citing Yeh Te-hui as an example. On Yeh (Ye Dehui) see also Angus W. McDonald, Jr., The Urban Origins of Rural Revolution, pp. 63–67.

3. Schiffrin, Sun Yat-sen, chapter 5; Martin Bernal, Chinese Socialism to 1907, pp. 56–57. Sun's belief in interventionist state socialism combined with private capital, and his nationalist thrust within a context of "delayed industrialization," are examined by James A.

Gregor and Maria Hsia Chang, *"Nazionalfascismo and the Revolutionary Nationalism of Sun Yat-sen,"* pp. 22–28.

4. Schiffrin, *Sun Yat-sen*, chapter 8, gives a detailed account of the Huizhou (Waichow) risings. The cited slogans are given in Schiffrin, pp. 242, 244. See also Edward Rhoads, *Chinese's Republican Revolution: The Case of Kwangtung, 1895–1913*, pp. 43–46.

5. Kang Youwei, *Shiji*, 5/38.

6. Quoted in Eve M. B. Armentrout-Ma, "Chinese Politics in the Western Hemisphere, 1893–1911," p. 159.

7. Ibid., pp. 180, note 72, and 205–206.

8. Yen Ching Hwang, *The Overseas Chinese and the 1911 Revolution, with Special Reference to Singapore and Malaya*, pp. 56, 80, note 132; Schiffrin, *Sun Yat-sen*, pp. 219, 223 (using "Ch'iu Shu-yuan" as the romanization for Khoo Seok-wan); Lo, *Symposium*, pp. 186–89. For other cases see Michael Godley, "Overseas Chinese Entrepreneurs as Reformers" and "The Late Ch'ing Courtship of the Chinese in Southeast Asia."

9. Yen, *Overseas Chinese*, pp. 39–40; and Lo, *Symposium*, pp. 264–65, note 22.

10. There is a fascinating account of these activities in Yen, *Overseas Chinese*, pp. 41–51. For Sun's skillful supporter You Lie (Yu Lieh) cf. also Schiffrin, *Sun Yat-sen*, pp. 303–304.

11. On the "Gongyang" and "Liyun" traditions cf. Hsiao Kung-chuan (trans. F. W. Mote), *A History of Chinese Political Thought*, pp. 124–42; Wolfgang Bauer (trans. Michael Shaw), *China and the Search for Happiness*, pp. 302–303; and Lo, *Symposium*, pp. 190–92. Kang's discussion of the need for gradualism can be found in his *Wanmu*, pp. 187–89. Kang and his followers were of course indebted to other scholars—perhaps most centrally to Gong Zizhen (Kung Tzu-chen), who also admired the "Gongyang" commentaries; see Judith Whitbeck, "Three Images of the Cultural Hero in the Thought of Kung Tzu-chen," pp. 26–27. The major "Liyun" and "Gongyang" themes are also analyzed and helpfully diagrammed in Frederic Wakeman, Jr., *History and Will*, pp. 130–36. Philip A. Kuhn, "Local Self-government under the Republic," pp. 272–75, discusses Kang's concurrent preoccupations with local assemblies and representation.

12. Hsiao, *Modern China*, pp. 497–513.

13. Bernal, *Chinese Socialism*, pp. 22–28, quotation p. 25.

14. See the long colophon in Kang, *Shiji*, 5/84–85, on the completion of the cycle of memorial poems to the six martyrs.

15. Kang Youwei, *Datongshu*, p. 2, following Lawrence G. Thompson, ed. and trans., *Ta T'ung Shu: The One World Philosophy of K'ang Yuwei*, p. 63.

16. Kang, *Datongshu*, p. 3.

17. Ibid., pp. 4–5, following Thompson, *One World*, pp. 65–66.

18. Thompson, *One World*, pp. 73–75.

19. Ibid., pp. 79–127.
20. Kang, *Datongshu*, pp. 355–56, following Thompson, *One World*, p. 213. Thompson, p. 229, note 10, suggests that the phrase "blood and iron" might be a deliberate reference to Bismarck's policies.
21. Kang, *Datongshu*, p. 180, following Thompson, *One World*, p. 143.
22. Thompson, *One World*, pp. 140–48.
23. Discussed in Hsiao, *Modern China*, p. 402; and Thompson, *One World*, pp. 234–35.
24. Huang Zunxian, *Renjinglu shicao jianzhu*, 4/132, following Ramon L. Y. Woon and Irving Y. Lo, "Poets and Poetry of China's Last Empire," p. 353. A biography of Huang is in Arthur W. Hummel, ed., *Eminent Chinese of the Ch'ing Period* (hereafter cited as *ECCP*), pp. 350–51; see also Godley, "Late Ch'ing Courtship," p. 368, on Huang's nationalism.
25. Kang, *Datongshu*, p. 390, as translated by Thompson, *One World*, p. 234.
26. Thompson, *One World*, pp. 236–60. (There are striking parallels here to the tasks given to the leaders in Hermann Hesse's novel *Magister Ludi*.)
27. Thompson, *One World*, pp. 169–86, for general arguments, and pp. 187–209 for specific institutions.
28. Lo, *Symposium*, p. 50.
29. On his children and consorts see Li Yunguang, *Kang Youwei jiashu kaoshi*, p. 2, note 4; and Lo, *Symposium*, pp. 42–43, 53.
30. Kang, *Shiji*, 6/38; Hsiao, *Modern China*, pp. 9–11.
31. Kang, *Datongshu*, p. 193, following Thompson, *One World*, pp. 149–50.
32. Thompson, *One World*, pp. 151, 167, 191, 194, 248–52.
33. Discussed in ibid., p. 26.
34. Lo, *Symposium*, pp. 193–99, for Kang's travels in this period. A photostat of his two-page travel visa to the United States is given in Li Yunguang, *Kang Youwei jiashu*, p. 216.
35. Sun's letter to a student of 1903, quoted (with minor changes) from Bernal, *Chinese Socialism*, p. 58; and Schiffrin, *Sun Yat-sen*, p. 137.
36. Chang Hao, *Liang Ch'i-ch'ao and Intellectual Transition in China, 1890–1907*, pp. 163, 165, 192; the introduction of social Darwinist ideas is beautifully described by Benjamin Schwartz in *In Search of Wealth and Power*.
37. Chang, *Liang*, pp. 193, 221–22.
38. Ibid., pp. 239–40.
39. Ibid., pp. 242–43.
40. Cited in Don C. Price, *Russia and the Roots of the Chinese Revolution, 1896–1911*, p. 130; see also ibid., p. 131, and p. 251, note 39.
41. Ibid., p. 130.
42. Ibid., pp. 122–23, discussing the work of Kemuyama Sentarō.
43. Armentrout-Ma, "Chinese Politics," pp. 215–20; Lo, *Symposium*,

pp. 136, 184, 260, note 11; Rhoads, *China's Republican Revolution*, pp. 47–48.

44. Price, *Russia and the Roots*, pp. 106–107; Lo, *Symposium*, p. 259, note 10; Yen, *Overseas Chinese*, pp. 55–56.

45. Cited in Price, *Russia and the Roots*, p. 125. On Han see Lo, *Symposium*, pp. 53, 184, 191.

46. Vera Broido, *Apostles into Terrorists*, pp. 75–81, 183–205. A sample Chinese popular biography of Sofya, dated 1907, is given in Li Yu-ning and Chang Yü-fa, eds., *Jindai Zhongguo nüchuan yundong shiliao*, pp. 346–50. Roxane Witke, "Transformation of Attitudes toward Women During the May Fourth Era of Modern China" (hereafter cited as "Transformation of Attitudes"), pp. 53–54, discusses Sofia (Sofya) and other heroines.

47. On Kang and assassination see Armentrout-Ma, "Chinese Politics," p. 143; the attempt on the Empress Dowager by Liang Tiejun is in Lo, *Symposium*, p. 204; the attempt on the Guangxi governor Wang Zhijun was made by Wan Fuhua, see Mary Backus Rankin, *Early Chinese Revolutionaries*, p. 102.

48. Price, *Russia and the Roots*, pp. 149–51; Rankin, *Early Chinese Revolutionaries*, pp. 106–108. The Japanese-based trainer of assassins was Yang Dusheng.

49. Rankin, *Early Chinese Revolutionaries*, pp. 69–81, quotation, p. 80; *ECCP*, p. 769; the early education reforms are well described in Rhoads, *China's Republican Revolution*, pp. 50–56.

50. Zou Rong's biography is in John Lust, ed., *Tsou Jung, The Revolutionary Army*, pp. 18–21; and *ECCP*, p. 769.

51. Zou Rong, *Gemingjun*, pp. 1–2, following Lust, ed., *Tsou Jung*, p. 58. For a general assessment of Zou see Michael Gasster, *Chinese Intellectuals and the Revolution of 1911*, pp. 37–42.

52. Lust, ed., *Tsou Jung*, pp. 78–80; quotation in Zou Rong, *Gemingjun*, p. 20. For Zou Rong in the context of Chinese "racialist" thought of the 1900s see Joshua A. Fogel, "Race and Class in Chinese Historiography," pp. 362–65.

53. Lust, ed., *Tsou Jung*, p. 106.

54. Ibid., pp. 123–24.

55. Ibid., p. 126.

56. *ECCP*, p. 769; John Lust, "The Su-pao Case"; Y. C. Wang, "The Su-pao Case."

57. Yen, *Overseas Chinese*, pp. 59–63; Armentrout-Ma, "Chinese Politics," p. 280.

58. *Qiu Jin ji*, pp. 4–5; also included in Li Yu-ning and Chang Yü-fa, eds., *Jindai Zhongguo nüchuan*, p. 423. Examples of similar rhetoric, and of Liang Qichao's influence on feminist writing, are given in Charlotte L. Beahan, "Feminism and Nationalism in the Chinese Women's Press, 1902–1911," pp. 390–91.

59. A good summary of these developments is given in Charlotte L. Beahan, "The Women's Movement and Nationalism in Late

Ch'ing China"; Rhoads, *China's Republican Revolution*, pp. 55–56, 64–65; Paul A. Cohen and John E. Schrecker, eds., *Reform in Nineteenth-Century China*, pp. 245– 51.

60. *Qiu Jin ji*, pp. 72, 92, 97, 106; Mary Backus Rankin, "The Emergence of Women at the End of the Ch'ing," pp. 52–53. The tradition of Chinese women writers is surveyed in Marián Gálik, "On the Literature Written by Chinese Women Prior to 1917"; and by Paul S. Ropp, "The Seeds of Change." These areas are also discussed in Witke, "Transformation of Attitudes," pp. 55–62.

61. *Qiu Jin ji*, p. 36.

62. Ibid., p. 106; Gálik, "Literature Written by Chinese Women," p. 93.

63. *Qiu Jin ji*, p. 36.

64. *ECCP*, pp. 169–70; Rankin, "The Emergence of Women," pp. 47–50, and *Early Chinese Revolutionaries*, pp. 40–42. Qiu Jin's daughter has left a moving account of how miserable her childhood was after her mother abandoned her to a succession of friends, nursemaids, and grandparents; see Qiu Canzhi, *Qiu Jin geming zhuan*, pp. 30–31, 156–61.

65. *Qiu Jin ji*, p. 85.

66. Ibid., p. 73. On the students in Japan see Philip Huang, "Liang Ch'i-ch'ao," pp. 76–79.

67. *Qiu Jin ji*, pp. 78–79, for her poem praising Wu Yue. For the Zhejiang student journal in Japan and the praise of Sofya Perovskaya and assassination see Price, *Russia and the Roots*, p. 210; and Robert A. Scalapino, "Prelude to Marxism," pp. 196, 200.

68. Rankin, *Early Chinese Revolutionaries*, pp. 41, 254, notes 99, 100; Qiu Canzhi, *Qiu Jin geming zhuan*, p. 34.

69. *Qiu Jin ji*, p. 76.

70. Ibid., p. 33. (This is the first in a series of nine extant letters to her brother Qiu Yuzhang.)

71. Rankin, *Early Chinese Revolutionaries*, p. 104, referring especially to the work of Cai Yuanpei and Chen Chimei; and Rankin, "The Revolutionary Movement in Japan: A Study in the Tenacity of Tradition," pp. 331–34. The theoretical underpinnings of the boycott are discussed in Akira Iriye, "Public Opinion and Foreign Policy," especially p. 224.

72. *Qiu Jin ji*, pp. 185–86; Qiu Canzhi, *Qiu Jin geming zhuan*, p. 9.

73. See the works in *Qiu Jin ji*, pp. 163–75, and comments in ibid., p. 186. Rankin, "The Emergence of Women," pp. 53–57, summarizes her Shanghai years.

74. *Qiu Jin ji*, p. 83. Beahan, "Feminism and Nationalism," pp. 400–402, also discusses this dichotomy between political activism and feminism, as does Witke, in "Transformation of Attitudes," pp. 60–61. Rankin, "The Emergence of Women," pp. 57–58, discusses Qiu Jin's draft novel about five rebellious women friends.

75. Rankin, *Early Chinese Revolutionaries*, p. 104, gives the fascinating

account of one other backer, the anarchist and tycoon Zhang Renjie.

76. These reforms are well covered in Rhoads, *China's Republican Revolution,* chapter 4; and in Mary C. Wright, *China in Revolution,* chapters 3, 4, 8. On the emerging social forces see Wright's introduction, and also Frederic Wakeman, Jr., *The Fall of Imperial China,* pp. 230–39. For the Qing state and the New Armies see Stephen R. Mackinnon, "The Peiyang Army, Yüan Shih-k'ai, and the Origins of Modern Chinese Warlordism," pp. 406–409; and Anita O'Brien, "Military Academies in China, 1885–1915."

77. Rankin, *Early Chinese Revolutionaries,* pp. 164–66.

78. Ibid., pp. 169–73, 177, 285, note 11.

79. *Qiu Jin ji,* pp. 21–25.

80. Ibid., p. 186.

81. Ibid., p. 64.

82. Rankin, *Early Chinese Revolutionaries,* pp. 174–75.

83. Ibid., pp. 183–184.

84. Ibid., pp. 180–184.

85. *Qiu Jin ji,* p. 91.

CHAPTER 3 / WANDERINGS

1. Lu Xun, *Selected Works* (hereafter cited as *SW*), 1/410–11. A basic biography of Lu Xun, the pen name used for the whole of his writing career by Zhou Shuren (Chou Shu-jen), is in *BDRC,* 1/416–24.

2. For Lu Xun on Xu Xilin see *SW,* 1/414; on Qiu Jin see William A. Lyell, *Lu Hsün's Vision of Reality,* pp. 83–84, 183.

3. *Lu Xun Quanji,* 2/405, following Lyell, *Vision,* pp. 47–48, and Leo Ou-fan Lee, "Genesis of a Writer," pp. 170, 426, note 45. Yan Fu's work on Huxley is discussed in Benjamin Schwartz, *In Search of Wealth and Power,* pp. 98–112.

4. See C. T. Hsia, "Yen Fu and Liang Ch'i-ch'ao as Advocates of New Fiction," pp. 244, note 26, and p. 245, note 28. Also Leo Ou-fan Lee, *The Romantic Generation of Chinese Writers,* pp. 51–56. Details of Lu's early education and reading program are given in Zhou Zuoren, *Guatou ji,* pp. 212–24.

5. Hsia, "Yen Fu and Liang Ch'i-ch'ao," p. 256.

6. These details all in Lyell, *Vision,* pp. 12–20, 45–46.

7. Hsia, "Yen Fu and Liang Ch'i-ch'ao," pp. 222–23.

8. Lyell, *Vision,* pp. 65–68. Lu Xun's essay on Sparta is in his *Quanji,* 7/374–84. The growth of Liang's thought in Japan is detailed by Philip Huang in "Liang Ch'i-ch'ao," pp. 81–95.

9. Lu Xun describes such a speech by Wu Zhihui in *SW,* 4/274.

10. Following Lu Xun, *SW,* 1/402.

11. *BDRC,* 1/319, on Chiang; Charlton M. Lewis, *Prologue to the Chi-*

nese Revolution, p. 98, on Zhang; Lu Xun, *SW*, 4/276, on Huang.

12. Huang Hsin-chyu, trans., *Poems of Lu Hsun*, pp. 1, 61, also following Lyell, *Vision*, p. 56, and Lee, "Genesis," p. 173; the reference to Lara is in Lyell, *Vision*, p. 56, note 11. Lu Xun mentioned the "inconvenience" of the queue in *SW*, 4/276.

13. Following Lu Xun, *SW*, 1/2, and Lin Yü-sheng, *The Crisis of Chinese Consciousness*, p. 106.

14. Lin, *Crisis*, p. 109, note 11.

15. Lyell, *Vision*, p. 20.

16. Lin, *Crisis*, p. 108. "Sickness" metaphors generally, from Zhu Xi through Liang Qichao to Mao Zedong, are discussed in Frederic Wakeman, Jr., *History and Will*, pp. 35-37.

17. His studies are summarized in Lyell, *Vision*, p. 72.

18. Lu Xun, *SW*, 1/407-408.

19. Ibid., 1/3.

20. Lyell, *Vision*, pp. 32-33; 9, note 2; 105.

21. Irene Eber, "Images of Oppressed Peoples and Modern Chinese Literature," p. 129, and Eber, *Voices from Afar*, pp. 24-33.

22. Lyell, *Vision*, pp. 80, 86, 91; Eber, "Images," p. 130; Patrick Hanan, "The Technique of Lu Hsün's fiction," pp. 57-58.

23. Lu Xun, *SW*, 4/267-68, for his views of Zhang generally; Joshua A. Fogel, "Race and Class in Chinese Historiography," p. 347, discusses Lu and Zhang's style. Michael Gasster gives a careful examination of Zhang's ideas in *Chinese Intellectuals and the Revolution of 1911*, chapter 6.

24. Cited in Eber, "Images," p. 130.

25. This theme of "Mara" poetry is discussed by several scholars, including D. W. Fokkema, "Lu Xun," p. 90; Lee, "Genesis," p. 181; Harriet Mills, "Lu Xun," p. 192; and Lyell, *Vision*, pp. 91-92.

26. *Lu Xun Quanji*, 1/41, following Mills, "Lu Xun," p. 194, and Lee, "Genesis," p. 181.

27. Cited in Mills, "Lu Xun," p. 192.

28. See the excellent exposition in ibid., pp. 192-94; the quotations are on pp. 192, 193. On p. 194 Mills points to Lu's echoing of Tolstoy. See also Lyell, *Vision*, pp. 92-93.

29. Lyell, *Vision*, pp. 95-96; Lin, *Crisis*, p. 114, note 21; Zhou Zuoren, *Guatou ji*, pp. 233-36: Tokyo sales were 21 and 20, print orders 1,000 and 500. Projected third and fourth volumes were abandoned. For Lu Xun's plan to use the girl in George Watts's "Hope" as the cover picture for *New Life* see Fujii Shozo, "The Origins of Lu Xun's Literature and Philosophy," pp. 10-12.

30. Chang Hao, *Liang Ch'i-ch'ao and Intellectual Transition in China, 1890-1907*, pp. 222-24; C. T. Hsia, "Yen Fu and Liang Ch'i-ch'ao," pp. 252-54 and 252, note 44, on Liang and Bellamy. For Liang and Datong see Kang Youwei, *Shiji*, 1/3.

31. This society, the Zhengwenshe, is discussed in Lo, *Symposium*, especially p. 273, note 42; Akira Iriye, "Public Opinion and For-

eign Policy," pp. 226–27, notes the connection with merchant groups. On nomenclature and other groups see also Eve M. B. Armentrout-Ma, "Chinese Politics in the Western Hemisphere, 1893–1911," pp. 269–70, 303.

32. Armentrout-Ma, "Chinese Politics," pp. 300–301.

33. Lo, *Symposium*, pp. 199, 271, notes 33 and 34; Armentrout-Ma, "Chinese Politics," pp. 285–86 for Los Angeles and 293–97 for Kang's troubles with Homer Lea. A passage of one of Kang's songs is given in Hsiao Kung-chuan, *A Modern China and a New World*, pp. 242–43. See also the cycle of patriotic poems in Kang, *Shiji*, 1/6–15.

34. Lo, *Symposium*, pp. 207, 273, note 39.

35. Iriye, "Public Opinion," pp. 227, 235; Lo, *Symposium*, p. 270, note 32; Armentrout-Ma, "Chinese Politics," p. 299.

36. Lo, *Symposium*, p. 213, on the political demands; Ernest P. Young, "The Reformer as a Conspirator," p. 243, for the strong impact on Liang of the Qing order to close the Political Information Society.

37. Lo, *Symposium*, p. 200.

38. Ibid., p. 272, note 37.

39. For details on his finances see ibid., pp. 202–208, 215.

40. Ibid., passim, on his travels. On his new consort, He Zhanli, see ibid., pp. 210, 214; Hsiao, *Modern China*, p. 10; and Li Yunguang, *Kang Youwei jiashu kaoshi*, p. 2.

41. Paris and balloon, Kang, *Shiji*, 7/71–74; Netherlands and Constantinople, Lo, *Symposium*, pp. 197, 212.

42. Kang's long poem on the Wailing Wall is in Kang, *Shiji*, 11/49–56. Some sections are excerpted and translated in Ramon L. Y. Woon and Irving Y. Lo, "Poets and Poetry of China's Last Empire," pp. 357–58. The four verses I translate here are drawn from Kang, *Shiji*, 11/50, lines 1 and 2; p. 51, lines 2 and 3; p. 55, lines 4 and 5; p. 56, lines 4–6.

43. Joseph Esherick, *Reform and Revolution in China*, pp. 58–65; BDRC, 3/211 (under T'an Chen); Lewis, *Prologue to the Chinese Revolution*, 185–90.

44. K. S. Liew, *Struggle for Democracy*, pp. 61–65, includes details on the planning (such as it was) and the financing. The operation was attempted by Song Jiaoren (Sung Chiao-jen).

45. Edward Rhoads, *China's Republican Revolution*, pp. 110–21, and BDRC, 2/194 (under Huang Hsing).

46. Rhoads, *China's Republican Revolution*, pp. 186–89, and BDRC, 2/194.

47. Rhoads, *China's Republican Revolution*, pp. 114, 196.

48. Armentrout-Ma, "Chinese Politics," pp. 344–47, for expansion, and p. 359 for translator.

49. Ibid., pp. 372–75.

50. Rhoads, *China's Republican Revolution*, pp. 197–203; secret-society backing from Triads and others in the Huizhou (Waichou) area is

documented in Winston Hsieh, "Triads, Salt Smugglers, and Local Uprisings," pp. 148, 164.

51. The best summary of the revolutionary elements is in Mary C. Wright's introduction to *China in Revolution*. There have been numerous analyses of the centralizing and railway policies—a clear introduction of the stakes involved is given in Albert Feuerwerker, *China's Early Industrialization*, pp. 66–70, 80–82; see also Frederic Wakeman, Jr., *The Fall of Imperial China*, pp. 237–39, 247–48. A good account of the various social and economic tensions in the late-Qing reformist center of Changsha is given by Arthur L. Rosenbaum, "Gentry Power and the Changsha Rice Riot of 1910"; on Ye Dehui's role there see ibid., pp. 697, 707.

52. The tri-city risings and the sociopolitical backgrounds to them are vividly presented in Esherick, *Reform and Revolution*, chapter 6; a day-by-day account of the risings is given in Vidya Prakash Dutt, "The First Week of Revolution: The Wuchang Uprising."

53. For Guangxi province see *BDRC*, 2/447 (under Lu Jung-t'ing), and Diana Lary, *Region and Nation*, pp. 27–29; for Yunnan province, *BDRC*, 3/286 (under Ts'ai O).

54. For Hunan see *BDRC*, 3/221 (under T'an Yen-k'ai); Angus W. McDonald, Jr., *The Urban Origins of Rural Revolution*, pp. 22–24. For Hubei, *BDRC*, 2/346 (under Li Yuan-hung); Dutt, "The Wuchang Uprising," pp. 404–413. For Shanghai and Zhejiang, Mary Backus Rankin, *Early Chinese Revolutionaries*, pp. 198, 210, 217. Ch'i Hsi-sheng, *Warlord Politics in China, 1916–1928*, chapter 1, discusses the pervasiveness of this local fragmentation.

55. On Chiang Kaishek, see Pichon P. Y. Loh, *The Early Chiang Kaishek*, pp. 20–26; Rankin, *Early Chinese Revolutionaries*, pp. 211 and 297, note 39, and Loh, p. 27, discuss Chiang's willingness to assist Chen Chimei by killing a key Restoration Society leader. For Mao in Changsha, see Stuart Schram, *Mao Tse-tung*, pp. 32–34.

56. A good summary is given by Ernest Young, "Yuan Shih-k'ai's Rise to the Presidency." See also Stephen R. Mackinnon, "The Peiyang Army," p. 419, on the high desertion rates and lack of political consciousness among the troops.

57. Kang, *Shiji*, 12/19, 12/32.

58. Cited in Liang Qichao, *Nianpu*, p. 342.

59. Hsiao, *Modern China*, p. 246, and Liang, *Nianpu*, p. 342.

60. Lo, *Symposium*, p. 218.

61. Liang, *Nianpu*, p. 339.

62. Lo, *Symposium*, p. 219, and Hsiao, *Modern China*, p. 247.

63. Young, "Reformer as Conspirator," pp. 249–59, for the northern China coup and Manchurian visit; ibid., pp. 259–65, for the southern plan; also Liang, *Nianpu*, pp. 344–45.

64. For Kang's suggestions, see Hsiao, *Modern China*, pp. 247–48; in Liang, *Nianpu*, p. 384, Liang's disciple Ding Wenjiang places the rift in April or May 1912.

65. Liang, *Nianpu*, p. 406, letter dated Oct. 8, 1912.
66. Rankin, *Early Chinese Revolutionaries*, pp. 214–19.
67. Lu Xun, *SW*, 1/416 (with minor changes). The structure of Shaoxing society, and of Lu Xun's view of it, is discussed in James Cole, "The Shaoxing Connection."
68. Translated in Lyell, *Vision*, p. 322. The story, later given a title by Lu's brother, has been also analyzed by Jaroslav Prusek, who called it a "pure" and "clinical" case study: see Prusek's "Lu Hsün's 'Huai-chiu,'" p. 170.
69. Lyell, *Vision*, p. 325.
70. Ibid., p. 321.
71. Ibid., p. 327 (with minor changes).

CHAPTER 4 / THE FAR HORIZON

1. Shen Congwen, *Congwen Zichuan*, p. 28; Jeffrey C. Kinkley, "Shen Ts'ung-wen's Vision of Republican China," p. 402, note 10, gives the reasons for placing Shen's birth in 1902.
2. Shen, *Zichuan*, pp. 26–27.
3. Ibid., pp. 28–29, following Nieh Hua-ling, *Shen Ts'ung-wen*, pp. 21–22.
4. As translated in Nieh, *Shen*, p. 22 (with minor changes); Shen, *Zichuan*, pp. 29–30.
5. Shen, *Zichuan*, chapter 3, and extensive passages in Kinkley, "Shen," and Nieh, *Shen*.
6. Kinkley, "Shen," p. 422, note 22, on the family connections; *BDRC*, 2/108, and Lo, *Symposium*, pp. 142 and 204 on Xiung.
7. Kinkley, "Shen," pp. 109, 111.
8. Shen, *Zichuan*, pp. 6–7.
9. Ibid., pp. 31–33. This pattern of tightened elite control at local levels has been well documented by Philip A. Kuhn in "Local Self-government under the Republic"; for the gentry dominance of the revolutionary process see also Ichiko Chūzō's forceful argument in "The Role of the Gentry."
10. Lu Xun, *SW*, 1/418.
11. See Ernest Young, "Yuan Shih-k'ai's Rise to the Presidency," pp. 436–41, for a convincing rebuttal of the argument that Yuan himself engineered these mutinies.
12. K. S. Liew, *Struggle for Democracy*, pp. 182–90; *BDRC*, 3/194–95. On Kang and the name Guomindang see Lo, *Symposium*, p. 222.
13. Liang Qichao, *Nianpu*, p. 418, letter to daughter of Mar. 18, 1913.
14. Ibid., p. 418, first parenthesis in Mar. 18, 1913, letter to daughter. On election problems see also Guy Alitto, *The Last Confucian*, pp. 47–48.
15. *BDRC*, 2/108–109, 4/87 (under Hsiung Hsi-ling and Yuan Shih-k'ai).

16. *BDRC*, 2/350 (under Liang Ch'i-ch'ao).
17. Yuan's centralizing goals and their cost are carefully analyzed in Ernest Young, *The Presidency of Yuan Shih-k'ai*, passim, and especially pp. 150–55. For various aspects of the costs of reforms and resentment toward them see R. Keith Schoppa, "Local Self-Government in Zhejiang 1909–1927," pp. 508–509; Joseph Esherick, *Reform and Revolution*, pp. 117–23; Angus W. McDonald, Jr., *The Urban Origins of Rural Revolution*, pp. 23–25.
18. On the Twenty-one Demands see Young, *The Presidency of Yuan Shih-k'ai*, pp. 186–89.
19. Lo, *Symposium*, pp. 222–26.
20. Ibid., pp. 226–27.
21. Ibid., p. 229; *BDRC*, 2/448 and 2/456 (under Lo Jung-t'ing and Lung Chi-kuang). *BDRC*, 3/289, for Cai E (Ts'ai O).
22. Kang Youwei, *Wanmu caotang yigao waibian*, p. 612.
23. Nancy T. Lin, *In Quest, Poems of Chou En-lai*, Chinese text p. 42, following English translation in Lin, p. 7.
24. Kang Youwei, *Shiji*, 14/2.
25. Lo, *Symposium*, p. 233; the poem, dated following the old-style calendar as on the thirteenth day of the fifth month, is in Kang, *Shiji*, 14/3. For the military aspects of Zhang's coup, see Ch'i Hsi-sheng, *Warlord Politics in China, 1916–1928*, pp. 17–18, 136–38.
26. Hsiao Kung-chuan, *A Modern China and a New World*, p. 255; Lo, *Symposium*, p. 234.
27. Kang, *Shiji*, 14/4–5.
28. Lo, *Symposium*, p. 235, and Kang, *Shiji*, 14/6. For the immediate decision to use the restoration fiasco to restructure the parliament and for fascinating details on the ensuing elections see Andrew J. Nathan, *Peking Politics 1918–1923*, pp. 91–103.
29. A broad typology of warlordism has been given by Ch'i Hsi-sheng in *Warlord Politics*; among many case studies see Diana Lary, *Region and Nation*, on the background of the "Guangxi Clique"; Robert A. Kapp, *Szechwan and the Chinese Republic*, on the warlords of Sichuan; James E. Sheridan, *Chinese Warlord*, on the remarkable background of Feng Yuxiang; and Edward Friedman, *Backward Toward Revolution*, for the vivid portrayal of bandit leader/militarists such as White Wolf. A good overview of all the various sources is given by Diana Lary in "Warlord Studies."
30. Shen Congwen, *Zichuan*, chapters 9, 10, 16. Details from those chapters and from Shen's fiction are assembled in the very fine third chapter of Kinkley, "Shen." Ch'i Hsi-sheng, *Warlord Politics*, chapters 4 and 5 on recruitment and training, confirm the general accuracy of Shen's descriptions.
31. Shen, *Zichuan*, pp. 131–32, following the translation by William McDonald in Cyril Birch, ed., *Anthology of Chinese Literature*, 2/284–85.
32. Kang's assessment is given in Lo, *Symposium*, p. 226; a general sur-

vey of nineteenth-century levels of violence is offered by C. K. Yang, "Some Preliminary Statistical Patterns of Mass Actions in Nineteenth-Century China."

33. Alitto, *Last Confucian*, pp. 63–65.

34. For Lu Xun on Liang in his story "White Light" see Alitto, *Last Confucian*, p. 69. On the syphilis image in Lu's writings see Lin Yü-sheng, *The Crisis of Chinese Consciousness*, pp. 116–17; on p. 116, note 27, Lin discusses Zhou Zuoren's possible coauthorship of this essay.

35. *Lu Xun Quanji*, 1/274. Lin, *Crisis*, p. 118, identifies the interlocutor "Jin" in this anecdote as Qian Xuantong; for Qian, see *BDRC*, 1/368 (under Ch'ien Hsuan-t'ung).

36. *Lu Xun Quanji*, 1/272, following Lu Xun, *SW*, 1/4.

37. Lu Xun, *SW*, 1/6.

38. Lin, *Crisis*, pp. 70–71, 75. For this period of "cultural search" as opposed to the later Marxist theory and political movement stages of *New Youth* see Lawrence Sullivan and Richard H. Solomon, "The Formation of Chinese Communist Ideology in the May Fourth Era"; tables on pp. 128–29.

39. Cited in Lin, *Crisis*, p. 76. Chen's writings on youth and patriotism from 1914 to 1916 are translated in Kevin Fountain, ed., *Ch'en Tuhsiu*, documents 2–4.

40. As cited in Lin, *Crisis*, p. 59, with minor changes. For the force of provincialism and the frailty of "nationalism" in this period see R. Keith Schoppa's analysis of Zhejiang in "Province and Nation," pp. 665–66.

41. Perry Link, "Traditional-style Popular Urban Fiction in the Teens and Twenties," pp. 330–34, 339; Link has also translated a fascinating tale from this period, of love and revenge springing from the passion between a Chinese woman and a young Englishman; cf. Zhou Shoujuan, "We Shall Meet Again."

42. Lu Xun, *SW*, 1/6, and discussion in Lin, *Crisis*, p. 118.

43. Lu Xun, *SW*, 1/400–401. For a discussion of the levels of memory and reality in such passages see William A. Lyell, *Lu Hsün's Vision of Reality*, passim, and especially chapter 10.

44. Lu Xun, *SW*, 1/1.

45. On Lu's work see especially Lyell, *Vision*; Lin, *Crisis;* the essays in Hsia Tsi-an, *The Gate of Darkness*; and C. T. Hsia, *A History of Modern Chinese Fiction 1917–1957*, pp. 28–54.

46. *Lu Xun Quanji*, 1/307–310, following George Kennedy's translation in Harold Isaacs, ed., *Straw Sandals*, pp. 21–24, Lu Xun, *SW*, 1/29–39, and C. T. Hsia, *History of Modern Chinese Fiction*, p. 35. For further analysis of the story's structure see Milena Doleželová-Velingerová, "Lu Xun's 'Medicine,'" Lyell, *Vision*, pp. 252, 276–80, and Patrick Hanan, "The Technique of Lu Hsün's Fiction," particularly pp. 62–66 on Andreyev's influence. Qiu Jin's childhood alternate name had been that same "Yu" used by Lu

Xun for his revolutionary martyr; see Qiu Canzhi, *Qiu Jin geming zhuan*, p. 3.

47. These roots can be traced through Martin Bernal, *Chinese Socialism to 1907*, and Don C. Price, *Russia and the Roots of the Chinese Revolution*; on workers in France, see Jean Chesneaux (trans. H. M. Wright), *The Chinese Labor Movement, 1919–1927*, pp. 138–40; McDonald, *Urban Origins*, p. 120; Shirley Garrett, *Social Reformers in Urban China*, pp. 154–56.

48. These 1918 loans are generally referred to as the "Nishihara loans."

49. Liang Qichao, *Nianpu*, pp. 554–55.

50. Ibid., p. 556.

51. Ibid., p. 556, postcard to daughter of Mar. 7, 1919.

52. Ibid., pp. 557, 560. Liang's lack of success at this time is discussed by Joseph R. Levenson, *Liang Ch'i-ch'ao and the Mind of Modern China*, pp. 184–90, 196–201.

53. The poem comes from Guo Moruo, *The Goddesses*, pp. 32–33. Benjamin Schwartz cautions against seeing the May Fourth Movement as being any more than "a somewhat higher range in a long stretch of complex mountainous terrain" (see Schwartz, ed., *Reflections on the May Fourth Movement: A Symposium*, p. 4); nevertheless it seems to me that the extent of the emotional transformation was so great that it truly inaugurated a new phase in China's history. See also Charlotte Furth in Schwartz, *Reflections*, p. 59.

CHAPTER 5 / THE LAND OF HUNGER

1. Chow Tse-tsung, *The May Fourth Movement*, pp. 106–109.

2. *BDRC*, 3/299–302, and Chow, *May Fourth*, p. 102, note v; detailed background on Cao's Japanese connections and financial dealings is given by Madeleine Chi, "Bureaucratic Capitalists in Operation," pp. 678–81, 685–86.

3. Chow, *May Fourth*, p. 132. A good sidelight on the Tokyo riots through the medium of Peng Pai's career can be found in Pang Yong-pil, "Peng Pai: From Landlord to Revolutionary," pp. 309–11.

4. Chow, *May Fourth*, pp. 126–27.

5. Ibid., pp. 128, note m, 141–43; Jean Chesneaux (trans. H. M. Wright), *The Chinese Labor Movement 1919–1927*, p. 152.

6. See the summary of his chancellorship in Chow, *May Fourth*, pp. 47–51, and his resignation message in ibid., p. 135, note q; a broader survey of his career in this period is given by William J. Duiker, *Ts'ai Yüan-p'ei*, pp. 53–73.

7. Chow, *May Fourth*, pp. 143-44.
8. On Xu Shichang see *BDRC*, 2/136-40 (under Hsu Shih-ch'ang).
9. Quoted in Chow, *May Fourth*, p. 173, note b.
10. Ibid., pp. 150-51 and 150, note e.
11. Chesneaux, *Chinese Labor Movement*, pp. 152-53; Chow, *May Fourth*, pp. 129-30, 141, 157. An excellent analysis of the impact on Shanghai is given in Joseph T. Chen, *The May Fourth Movement in Shanghai*, chapter 5.
12. Chow, *May Fourth*, pp. 129-30, 151.
13. Ibid., pp. 165-66.
14. A range of journals is listed in ibid., pp. 178-79.
15. As translated in ibid., pp. 174-75 (with minor changes).
16. A good summary of such business ventures is in Charlotte L. Beahan, "The Women's Movement and Nationalism in Late Ch'ing China," chapter 6, "Women in Groups." On women in the army and Miss Tang Qunying's agitation in the Nanjing Assembly see Chen Dongyuan, *Zhongguo funü shenghuo shi*, pp. 355-60, and Roxane Witke, "Transformation of Attitudes," pp. 62-64, 68-71. See also Elisabeth Croll, *Feminism and Socialism in China*, pp. 70-72, and Chow, *May Fourth*, p. 258, note c.
17. Beahan, "Women's Movement," pp. 350, 357-58, and *BDRC*, 2/232.
18. Statistics on student numbers are given by Chen Dongyuan, *Zhongguo funü*, pp. 349, 389-92. The shift in local attitudes is well shown in Ding Ling, *Muqin*, pp. 140-41, 144, 155. A wide range of new women's organizations is listed by Bobby Siu, *Fifty Years of Struggle*, pp. 71-79.
19. Chen Dongyuan, *Zhongguo funü*, pp. 365-72; on Lu Xun, Hu Shi, and others who encouraged the reading of Ibsen, see Elisabeth Eide, "Ibsen's Nora and Chinese Interpretations of Female Emancipation"; Chang Jun-mei, *Ting Ling*, pp. 18-19; and Witke, "Transformation of Attitudes," pp. 164-66. Suzanne Leith, "Chinese Women in the Early Communist Movement," p. 58, discusses the difficulties in overcoming the women's natural inhibitions regarding activism and protest.
20. "Ding Ling" was the pseudonym adopted for the whole of her adult life by Jiang Bingzhi. There are conflicting records of her birthdate; I adopt the year 1905 since Ding Ling herself, in "Jiang yidian xinli hua," says she was fifteen *sui* in 1919, and in "Xiang Jingyu tongzhi," p. 184, says she was seven *sui* in 1911. For a detailed discussion of her childhood see Gary Bjorge, "Ting Ling's Early Years," pp. 9-22. Bjorge prefers the birthdate 1906. Zong Chen and Shang Xia, in "Ding Ling zaoqi de shenghuo he chuangzuo," give her birthdate as Oct. 12, 1904.
21. *Ding Ling pingzhuan*, p. 223; Ding Ling, *Muqin*, pp. 226, 235-39.
22. Ding Ling, *Muqin*, p. 211; Chang, *Ting Ling*, p. 3; *Ding Ling ping-*

zhuan, p. 223, on the size of the ancestral home; Bjorge, "Ting Ling's Early Years," pp. 11–14.

23. Charlton M. Lewis, *Prologue to the Chinese Revolution,* pp. 47–59; Witke, "Transformation of Attitudes," pp. 284, 297.

24. For Ding Ling's account of the composition of the biographical and autobiographical novel *Muqin* [Mother] see *Ding Ling ping-zhuan,* pp. 127–30.

25. Ding Ling, *Muqin,* p. 159.

26. Ibid., p. 187.

27. Ibid., pp. 189, 191.

28. Ding Ling, "Xiang Jingyu tongzhi liugei wo de yingxiang," p. 184, col. 2, describes this band of seven. An account of a similar group is in *Muqin,* pp. 198–203.

29. Ding Ling, *Muqin,* p. 194.

30. Ibid., pp. 80–81, has a graphic passage on these male-female differences, and on the raising of the chickens.

31. There is a lengthy description of this scene in ibid., pp. 137–47.

32. Ibid., pp. 160–61.

33. Chang, *Ting Ling,* pp. 2–4; Ding Ling, "Xiang Jingyu tongzhi," p. 185, col. 1.

34. Ding Ling, "Xiang Jingyu tongzhi," p. 185. A slightly different listing of schools is given in Bjorge, "Ting Ling's Early Years," pp. 16–19.

35. On Xiang Jingyu see *BDRC,* 2/86–87 (under Hsiang Ching-yu), and *BDRC,* 3/283–86 (under Ts'ai Ho-shen); on the work-study program, Angus W. McDonald, Jr., *The Urban Origins of Rural Revolution,* pp. 94–95; on the schools, Witke, "Transformation of Attitudes," pp. 247–48, 284, 296–300; on Xiang's travels and talks, Ding Ling, "Xiang Jingyu tongzhi," p. 185. On the dramatic levels of pro-Hunan sentiment felt by Mao and many other young radicals in 1920 see Angus W. McDonald, Jr., "Mao Tse-tung and the Hunan Self-Government Movement, 1920," pp. 756–58. Mao Zedong's very early writings (of 1917 on the Changsha night school) have been translated by M. Henri Day in *Mao Zedong 1917–1927, Documents,* Documents M3 and M4, pp. 39–41. (For a parallel example of pro-Zhejiang sentiment see R. Keith Schoppa, "Province and Nation," p. 665.)

36. A range of such discussions on marriage and love are graphically presented in Witke, "Transformation of Attitudes," pp. 159–61, 177–81; on Ding Ling's own canceled marriage and her politics, see Chang, *Ting Ling,* pp. 3–7, and Bjorge, "Ting Ling's Early Years," p. 20. On Yang Kaihui as a member of the same group, see *Mao Zhuxi yijia liu lieshi,* p. 9. One of Xiang Jingyu's earliest letters from France is in *Jinian Xiang Jingyu tongzhi yingyong jiuyi wushizhounian,* pp. 43–44; see also Leith, "Chinese Women," pp. 50–51.

37. There is a remarkable example of such a "mathematical" proof in Chow, *May Fourth*, pp. 185, note f, and pp. 257–58.
38. Lu Xun, *SW*, 2/14.
39. Ibid., 2/17 and 20.
40. Ibid., 2/24. Witke, "Transformation of Attitudes," pp 117–19, discusses Lu Xun on chastity; also the Japanese source for his views (ibid., pp. 111–13) and the similar writings by his two brothers (ibid., pp. 112, 158).
41. On Yang Changji see *BDRC*, 4/2; Witke, "Transformation of Attitudes," pp. 90–92, 294–95; Frederic Wakeman, Jr., *History and Will*, pp. 157–63.
42. Stuart Schram, *The Political Thought of Mao Tse-tung*, pp. 155, 158, 160. Schram has made a detailed study of this work; see his *Mao Ze-dong: "Une Étude de l'éducation physique."*
43. Schram, *Political Thought*, pp. 234–37. A detailed discussion of this case is in Roxane Witke, "Mao Tse-tung, Women and Suicide in the May Fourth Era," pp. 137–44.
44. Background vividly described in Hsia Tsi-an, *The Gate of Darkness*, pp. 9–11.
45. Li Yu-ning and Michael Gasster, "Ch'ü Ch'iu-pai's Journey to Russia 1920–1922," p. 540.
46. These recollections from his 1935 "confession" have been translated in Dun J. Li, *The Road to Communism*, p. 161.
47. Hsia, *Gate of Darkness*, p. 15.
48. Maurice Meisner, *Li Ta-chao and the Origins of Chinese Marxism*, pp. 72–73; Hsia, *Gate of Darkness*, pp. 11, 15.
49. Meisner, *Li Ta-chao*, pp. 65, 68.
50. Hsia, *Gate of Darkness*, p. 15.
51. Li, *Road to Communism*, p. 160.
52. As translated by Hsia, *Gate of Darkness*, p. 16 (with minor changes); Qu, *Wenji*, 1/23.
53. Hsia, *Gate of Darkness*, pp. 16–17; Shirley Garrett, *Social Reformers in Urban China*, chapter 5, "The Y.M.C.A. and Community Action."
54. Qu Qiubai, *Wenji*, 1/26, on Russell; general discussion in Chow, *May Fourth*, pp. 233–38; details on Russell's relation to Qu's concerns are given in Marián Gálik, "Studies in Modern Chinese Intellectual History: II, Young Ch'ü Ch'iu-pai," pp. 103–109.
55. Chow, *May Fourth*, p. 192 on the Russell societies and pp. 233–38 on the China tour. Dora Black's contributions are discussed by Witke, "Transformation of Attitudes," pp. 168–75.
56. Schram, *Political Thought*, pp. 296–99.
57. Hsia, *Gate of Darkness*, pp. 20–21.
58. Qu, *Wenji*, 1/30–31; Hsia, *Gate of Darkness*, p. 22.
59. Li and Gasster, "Ch'ü's Journey," pp. 543–44; Gálik, "Young Ch'ü," pp. 86–87; Hsia, *Gate of Darkness*, pp. 18–20.

60. As translated in Gálik, "Young Ch'ü," pp. 109–110 (with minor changes); Qu, Wenji, 1/6–7. For Buddhist elements in Qu's thought see Gálik, "Young Ch'ü," especially p. 95.

61. Qu, Wenji, 1/3–5; Li and Gasster, "Ch'ü's Journey," pp. 544–45.

62. Qu, Wenji 1/84, following Hsia, Gate of Darkness, p. 32. On the Siberian journey, Hsia, Gate of Darkness, pp. 28–31, and Li and Gasster, "Ch'ü's Journey," p. 549.

63. Negative side, Hsia, Gate of Darkness, p. 32; starvation, Qu, Wenji, 1/132; Kronstadt, Qu, Wenji, 1/107–108; black bread, Hsia, Gate of Darkness, p. 31; cadres' hunger, Qu, Wenji, 1/109; sickness, Qu, Wenji, 1/130. For other possible translations of the title of History of My Mind in the Red Capital, see Gálik, "Young Ch'ü," pp. 85–86.

64. Qu, Wenji, 1/162–64.

65. Gálik, "Young Ch'ü," pp. 102–103; Qu, Wenji, 1/91.

66. For these moments, in order, see Qu, Wenji, vol. 1, pp. 120 (park), 103 (children), 142–48 (Tolstoy's house), 128 (Lenin), 127 (Chaliapin), 100–101 (Kropotkin).

67. Ibid., 1/103–104.

68. Hsia, Gate of Darkness, p. 38.

69. Stuart Schram, Mao Tse-tung, pp. 64–67.

70. Chesneaux, Chinese Labor Movement, pp. 179–80; further details on Shanghai women's strike in Witke, "Transformation of Attitudes," pp. 265–67; an analysis of guild components among the laborers in these strikes is given by Lynda Shaffer, "Mao Ze-dong and the October 1922 Changsha Construction Workers' Strike"; the Anyuan miners' strike and the railroad strike are described in McDonald, Urban Origins, pp. 166–79, and in Linda Shaffer, "Anyuan." Useful data on women strikers are presented in Bobby Siu, Fifty Years of Struggle, pp. 80–99.

71. Chesneaux, Chinese Labor Movement, pp. 181–85.

72. Ibid., p. 189, and McDonald, Urban Origins, pp. 166, note 34, and pp. 170–71.

73. Chesneaux, Chinese Labor Movement, pp. 190–93.

74. Ibid., pp. 180, 184, 193.

75. McDonald, Urban Origins, pp. 195–97; Chesneaux, Chinese Labor Movement, pp. 192, 208–209.

76. Examples in Chesneaux, Chinese Labor Movement, pp. 212–13.

77. Qu, Wenji, 1/178; Hsia, Gate of Darkness, p. 41.

78. On Shanghai University see BDRC, 4/76 (under Yü Yu-jen), and 3/249 (under Teng Chung-hsia); Chang, Ting Ling, pp. 8–9; Mao Dun, "Huiyi Qu Qiubai," p. 35.

79. Qu, Wenji, 1/216–21.

80. Paul G. Pickowicz, "Qu Qiubai's Critique of the May Fourth Generation," pp. 356–58; on Kang and Liang see Qu, Wenji, 1/239–40. For Qu on Bukharin and historical materialism see Arif Dirlik, Revolution and History, pp. 23, 31.

81. On this difficult theoretical point see the discussion by Pickowicz,

"Qu's Critique," pp. 357–61, and the same author's "Ch'ü Ch'iu-pai and the Chinese Marxist Conception of Revolutionary Popular Literature and Art."

82. Qu, *Wenji*, 1/231; Pickowicz, "Qu's Critique," pp. 362–64.
83. Qu, *Wenji*, 1/222–23.
84. Ding Ling gives a very detailed description of this phase of her life and her relations with Wang Jianhong and the Qu brothers in her long article "Wo suo renshide Qu Qiubai tongzhi," pp. 157–58; this article was written in the spring of 1980. See also her shorter essay "Wo dui 'Duoyu de hua' de lijie," and *BDRC*, 1/479 and 3/272–73; Chang, *Ting Ling*, pp. 8–9; Bjorge, "Ting Ling's Early Years," pp. 22–30.

CHAPTER 6 / EXTOLLING NIRVANA

1. On Xu family background see Leo Ou-fan Lee, *The Romantic Generation of Chinese Writers*, pp. 124–27, and Gaylord Kai-loh Leung, "Hsü Chih-mo: A Literary Biography," pp. 54–55, notes 1 and 10. On Xu and Liang, see Xu Zhimo, *Quanji*, 1/562–63. On the Zhang family, *BDRC*, 1/26 and 1/31 (under Chang Chi-ao and Chang Chia-sen [Carsun Chang]).
2. Text in Liang Shiqiu, *Tan Xu Zhimo*, p. 20, and Xu Zhimo, *Quanji*, 6/100. Another section of the same letter is translated in Lee, *Romantic Generation*, p. 127.
3. The disparate accounts of Xu's education have now been clarified in Leung, "Hsü Chih-mo," pp. 14, 45, and 56, note 21, after checking with college records at Clark and Columbia. See also Lee, *Romantic Generation*, pp. 128–30, and Xu Zhimo, *Quanji*, 1/565–70.
4. Quoted from Lee, *Romantic Generation*, p. 132 (with minor changes); Xu, *Quanji*, 3/239.
5. Quotations from Xu's essay on Russell, Xu, *Quanji*, 6/161–62.
6. Xu, *Quanji*, 3/243.
7. Leung, "Hsü Chih-mo," pp. 17–18; for three of his submissions to Liang's *Gaizao* magazine see Xu, *Quanji*, 1/636.
8. Quotations in Xu, *Quanji*, 3/244 and 1/569.
9. Xu's letter to parents, Xu, *Quanji*, 1/569. On Zhang's education, ibid., 1/566. On the Lin family see Lee, *Romantic Generation*, p. 133; Leung, "Hsü Chih-mo," pp. 19–23; *BDRC*, 2/368–72 (under Lin Ch'ang-min).
10. Xu's reminiscences of Wells are in Xu, *Quanji*, 6/152–54, transcribed from a lecture given later at Nankai University.
11. Xu letter home of Nov. 26, 1920, in *Quanji*, 1/570; ibid., 3/244, on Sawston; Lee, *Romantic Generation*, pp. 131–32; Leung, "Hsü Chih-mo," pp. 20 and 60, note 45, for Lin in Edinburgh.

12. Xu, *Quanji*, 3/245. Lee, *Romantic Generation*, p. 133, calls this an "idyllic atmosphere"—Xu's sense seems rather to be that this was a time of deep frustration.
13. *BDRC*, 1/31; Xu, *Quanji*, 1/572; Leung, "Hsü Chih-mo," p. 23.
14. Xu, *Quanji*, 3/245 and 3/250.
15. For the context of this piece see Jonathan Spence, "The Explorer Who Never Left Home—Arthur Waley," p. 33.
16. Ibid., p. 33.
17. Xu, *Quanji*, 3/315; Lee, *Romantic Generation*, pp. 164–65.
18. Xu, *Quanji*, 1/137 and 1/143–44.
19. Lucy Gray translation, and date, Xu, *Quanji*, 1/157–62. For the whole 1922 Berlin sequence see ibid., 1/573–74.
20. As translated in Lee, *Romantic Generation*, p. 134.
21. As translated in Cyril Birch, ed., *Anthology of Chinese Literature*, 2/343; Xu, *Quanji*, 3/256.
22. Xu, *Quanji*, 1/163–68, last stanza, p. 168. The draft was dated Apr. 30, 1922, and published in the *Shishi xinbao* in March 1923.
23. Xu, *Quanji*, 5/177–203, for the Mansfield meeting, and Lee, *Romantic Generation*, pp. 166–67. Other friends in Lee, *Romantic Generation*, p. 132, and Xu, *Quanji*, 4/386. Cambridge life in Xu, *Quanji*, 3/243–61, and selections translated in Birch, *Anthology*, 2/341–47. According to Xu's comment in his essay on his son, "Wode Bide," *Quanji*, 3/461, he saw Peter for the last time just before the child was four months old—so Xu may have gone briefly to Berlin in early June.
24. Xu, *Quanji*, 1/578.
25. Leung, "Hsü Chih-mo," p. 35, 65, note 106, and pp. 81–83.
26. Both the facsimile and transcript of Liang's long letter are given in Xu, *Quanji*, 1/125–36 (the quoted passage is from pp. 133–34); Lee, *Romantic Generation*, p. 136, also translates part of it. Liang Qichao urged the need for his son to marry Miss Lin quickly in Liang, *Nianpu*, p. 632.
27. As translated in Lee, *Romantic Generation*, pp. 137–38 (with minor changes), and rearranged in accordance with the original, Xu, *Quanji*, 1/361–62, as cited by Hu Shi.
28. Xu Zhimo, *Quanji*, 2/105–107, as translated by Birch, *Anthology*, 2/348–49, except for the third line of the last stanza, where my retranslation is based on Jiang Fucong's discussion of the role "Jian the toper"—Jian Jichang—played in Liang's life and at "Number 7." Cf. the discussion in Xu, *Quanji*, 1/582–83 and 1/591. The metrical structures of Xu's poems in the 1920s have been analyzed by Cyril Birch, "English and Chinese Metres in Hsü Chih-mo," and by Julia C. Lin, *Modern Chinese Poetry*, pp. 103–108.
29. For Xu and Kang see Liang Qichao, *Nianpu*, p. 644.
30. Kang Youwei, *Shiji*, 15/73–74.

31. Liang, *Nianpu*, pp. 641–44, letters to daughter of May 8 and May 11, and to son in mid-May.

32. Li Yunguang, *Kang Youwei jiashu kaoshi*, introductory section pp. 16 and letters p. 2 list the full entourage; Lo, *Symposium*, pp. 235–37, for his stay in the American legation.

33. On income and estates see Li Yunguang, *Kang Youwei jiashu*, introductory section, pp. 10–11 and 16; letters pp. 18 and 48.

34. Estimate by Li Yunguang, ibid., introductory section, p. 16.

35. Detailed analysis of this is provided by C. Martin Wilbur, *Sun Yat-sen: Frustrated Patriot*, chapter 6.

36. BDRC, 3/444–50; Wilbur, *Sun Yat-sen*, p. 129; Wu Peifu's interests in national centralism and his anti-Japanese aspects are discussed in Odoric Y. K. Wou, "The Military and Nationalism," pp. 118–20.

37. Lo, *Symposium*, pp. 242–45. For a flattering poem see Kang, *Shiji*, 15/66; and for examples of Wu's view of Confucianism as an integrating national force see Wou, "The Military and Nationalism," pp. 123–24.

38. As translated in Chow Tse-tsung, *The May Fourth Movement*, p. 328.

39. Ibid., pp. 218–19, 328–29; the details of Hu Shi's stance on this question are discussed by Jerome Grieder in *Hu Shih and the Chinese Renaissance*, pp. 178–84.

40. Quoted in Lin Yü-sheng, *The Crisis of Chinese Consciousness*, p. 77. Several related texts on the Chinese script are translated in M. Henri Day, *Mao Zedong 1917–1927, Documents*, Document Sl, pp. 61–69.

41. This student was Gu Jiegang (Ku Chieh-kang), who became one of China's leading historians; the passage is translated in Arthur Hummel, ed., *The Autobiography of a Chinese Historian*, p. 60.

42. Guo Moruo, *The Goddesses*, p. 56; David Roy, *Kuo Mo-jo: The Early Years*, p. 65, discusses Guo's first reading of "On the Seashore" during 1915, when Guo was living in Japan.

43. See his "Three Pantheists" poem in *The Goddesses*, p. 23, and the discussions by Lee, *Romantic Generation*, pp. 181–86; Roy, *Kuo Mo-jo*, pp. 69–70, 85–89; and Bonnie S. McDougall, *The Introduction of Western Literary Theories into Modern China, 1919–1925*, pp. 125–36.

44. Guy Alitto, *The Last Confucian*, p. 83.

45. Ibid., pp. 87–88; Chow, *May Fourth*, pp. 329–32.

46. As summarized in Chow, *May Fourth*, pp. 333–35. The intellectual background on the question of "national essence" is thoroughly analyzed by Lawrence Schneider, Martin Bernal, and Charlotte Furth in Furth, ed., *The Limits of Change*, chapters 3, 4, and 5.

47. Chow, *May Fourth*, p. 334, citing Ding Wenjiang (Ting Wen-chiang).

48. Xu Zhimo, "Xihu ji," in Xu, *Quanji*, 4/485–515, spanning the pe-

riod Sept. 7–Oct. 28, 1923. At this time, the diary shows that Xu's friends included Sophia Chen, Wang Jingwei, Hu Shi, Zhang Junmai, Ren Hongjun, Tian Han, Guo Moruo, Zhang Dongsun, Tao Xingzhi (then named Tao Zhixing), and Zhu Jingnong.

49. Xu, *Quanji*, 4/498–99, entry of Oct. 11, 1923; Qu Qiubai, *Wenji*, 1/223–24, 231.

50. Xu Zhimo, *Quanji*, 4/495, entry of Oct. 4, 1923.

51. As translated in Birch, *Anthology*, 2/353–55; Leung, "Hsü Chih-mo," pp. 136 and 179, note 290, discusses this poem in terms of Xu's relationship with his new love, Lu Xiaoman.

52. Xu Zhimo, *Quanji*, 4/510, entry of Oct. 21, 1923, where Xu laments giving up a moon-viewing outing because of being so involved with the impending Tagore visit.

53. On Tagore's visit see Stephen Hay, *Asian Ideas of East and West*, pp. 142–70; Léon Wieger, S. J., "Visite de Sir R. Tagore," *Chine Moderne*, 5/66–83. On Xu's general admiration for Tagore see Leung, "Hsü Chih-mo," p. 116 and notes on pp. 163–64.

54. The passages cited are from Hay, *Asian Ideas*, pp. 150, 154, 157, 169.

55. Text in Léon Wieger, *Chine Moderne*, 5/66; see also Hay, *Asian Ideas*, pp. 200–201. The context of Mao Dun's intellectual growth in the early 1920s is well described in Marián Gálik, *Mao Tun and Modern Literary Criticism*, chapter 5.

56. Hay, *Asian Ideas*, p. 227.

57. Ibid., p. 231.

58. Ibid., p. 203; Wieger, *Chine Moderne*, 5/78–79. The growing quarrels of 1923 between Xu and Guo are described in Gálik, *Mao Tun*, pp. 100–101.

59. Hay, *Asian Ideas*, p. 228.

60. Ibid., p. 170.

61. Ibid., p. 195. On Xu and Tagore's meetings with the Shanxi warlord Yan Xishan, and hopes of backing, see Leung, "Hsü Chih-mo," p. 123. For Xu's initial meetings with Lu Xiaoman see Lee, *Romantic Generation*, pp. 139–40; Liu Xinhuang, *Xu Zhimo yu Lu Xiaoman*, chapter 8, reviews all the relevant sources on their relationship.

62. Hay, *Asian Ideas*, pp. 195–96.

CHAPTER 7 / WHOSE CHILDREN ARE THOSE?

1. Cited in Lin Yü-sheng, *The Crisis of Chinese Consciousness*, p. 124.

2. Lu Xun, *SW*, 2/139–40; Lin, *Crisis*, p. 123.

3. As translated in Lin, *Crisis*, pp. 128–29 (with minor changes).

4. Lu Xun, *SW*, 2/311 and 2/140 (with minor changes).

5. Lu Xun, *SW*, 2/309.

6. The growing geographical extent and fatalities in warlord con-

flicts are presented in tabular form in Ch'i Hsi-sheng, *Warlord Politics in China, 1916–1928*, pp. 137–38; for Feng and Duan see James E. Sheridan, *Chinese Warlord*, pp. 133–48; the concept of Chinese "macroregions" is developed at length in G. William Skinner's essays in *The City in Late Imperial China* (an introductory framework is presented in ibid., pp. 211–22). A brief biography of Lo Wengan (Lo Wen-kan) appears in *BDRC*, 2/438–41, and his case is analyzed in Andrew J. Nathan, *Peking Politics 1918–1923*, pp. 195–200; on Lo and Cai Yuanpei see also William J. Duiker, *Ts'ai Yüan-p'ei*, pp. 75–76. On the final republican debasement see Nathan, *Peking Politics*, chapter 7.

7. Lu Xun, *Quanji*, 1/151, following Lu Xun, *Silent China*, pp. 153–54.
8. Conditions of work for the year 1925 are presented with the most convincing detail by the British consular officers in China in *Papers Respecting Labour Conditions in China*; the percentage of foreign holdings and output is tabulated in Albert Feuerwerker, *Economic Trends in the Republic of China, 1912–1949*, pp. 30–37; harrowing and apparently accurate statistics for social conditions among workers in Shanghai (during 1930–31) were compiled by the social scientists Simon Yang and L. K. Tao, *A Study of the Standard of Living of Working Families in Shanghai*, especially pp. 38–40, 57–58, 68. Li Dazhao's concept of "proletarianization" is analyzed by Maurice Meisner, *Li Ta-chao and the Origins of Chinese Marxism*, chapter 6.
9. Jean Chesneaux, *The Chinese Labor Movement, 1919–1927*, pp. 262–63; Nicholas R. Clifford, *Shanghai, 1925*, pp. 14–34.
10. Chesneaux, *Chinese Labor Movement*, pp. 262–65, and Sima Lu, *Qu Qiubai zhuan*, pp. 43–45.
11. Chesneaux, *Chinese Labor Movement*, p. 276. On the formidable Shandong warlord Zhang Zongchang (Chang Tsung-ch'ang) see *BDRC*, 1/122–27; Lin Yutang's brilliant and venomous profile, "The Dog-meat General," anthologized in Edgar Snow, *Living China*, pp. 222–25; and Gavan McCormack, *Chang Tso-lin in Northeast China, 1911–1928*, pp. 105–106 and 153–54.
12. Lu Xun, *Quanji*, 7/103, letter of June 5, 1925.
13. Lu Xun, *SW*, 2/146, 156, 160, 161.
14. Lu Xun, *Quanji*, 7/107, letter to Xu of June 13, 1925. The minister of education was Zhang Shichao.
15. Lu Xun, *SW*, 2/163–67, quotation p. 166.
16. As translated in Lu Xun, *Silent China*, p. 126 (with minor changes).
17. Chesneaux, *Chinese Labor Movement*, p. 291.
18. Ibid., pp. 290–95.
19. Meisner, *Li Ta-chao*, pp. 80–89; description in *The North China Famine of 1920–21*; Ross Terrill, *Mao, A Biography*, pp. 31–32, 73–74.
20. Anecdote and translation in Dun J. Li, *The Road to Communism*, pp. 72–73. The general history of this early Chinese rural soviet is

given by Eto Shinkichi in "Hai-lu-feng—the First Chinese Soviet Government," and also by Roy Hofheinz in *The Broken Wave*, part 3. On Peng's early radicalism see Pang Yong-pil, "Peng Pai," pp. 317–18; on the training institute, Gerald W. Berkley, "The Canton Peasant Movement Training Institute," pp. 163, 166, discusses Mao's special subjects; on Peng's extraordinary charismatic power among the peasantry see Robert B. Marks, "The World Can Change!" pp. 94–96.

21. Wen Yiduo, *Quanji*, "Nianpu," p. 48, letter of Jan. 13, 1926, to Liang Shiqiu; Hsu Kai-yu, "Wen I-to," p. 82; *BDRC*, 3/409. The basic source I have used on Wen Yiduo's life is the dissertation by Hsu Kai-yu, "The Intellectual Biography of a Modern Chinese Poet: Wen I-to (1899–1946)," cited here and in following pages as "Wen I-to." A revised version of this study, entitled *Wen I-to*, was published in 1980. (All page references here to "Wen I-to" are to the dissertation, not to the recent published edition, though interested readers will find the major references quite easily in the latter.) A valuable selection of Wen Yiduo's poems from *Red Candle* (1923) and *Dead Water* (1928) has been translated by Tao Tao Sanders, and is listed under Wen Yiduo in the bibliography. On Columbia University as a focus for Chinese student nationalists see Barry Keenan, *The Dewey Experiment in China*, pp. 18–21.

22. Wen Yiduo, *Quanji*, section "geng," p. 40, letter undated but written after Jan. 23 and before March 18, 1926.

23. Xu Zhimo, *Quanji*, 3/536–39, on the Soviet Union, and ibid., 3/127–40, on Lenin; quotation on p. 135. Xu's anti-Soviet stance is analyzed by Gaylord Kai-loh Leung, "Hsü Chih-mo," pp. 195–98.

24. As translated in Cyril Birch, ed., *Anthology of Chinese Literature*, 2/344–45, with minor changes and adding one dropped sentence according to the version in Xu Zhimo, *Quanji*, 3/257–58.

25. Wen Yiduo, *Quanji*, "Nianpu," p. 50; Hsu, "Wen I-to," p. 85; *BDRC*, 3/409. Wen on Tagore, and citing Pater, in Wen Yiduo, *Quanji*, section "ding," pp. 275–79.

26. Wen Yiduo, *Quanji*, section "geng," p. 39, letter of Jan. 23, 1926. On Wen's initial reluctance to invite Xu see Leung, "Hsü Chih-mo," p. 210; Hsu, "Wen I-to," pp. 84–85, has a different emphasis, pointing to Wen's desire to meet more literary people.

27. The poem from Wen's collection *Dead Water* is in Wen Yiduo, *Quanji*, section "ding," pp. 27–28. See also Wen Yiduo, *Red Candle*, pp. 48–49, for a translation by Tao Tao Sanders. On the date of the poem's appearance see Wen Yiduo, *Quanji*, "Nianpu," p. 49. Xu Zhimo's rickshaw poem entitled "Shei zhidao?" is in Xu Zhimo, *Quanji*, 2/114–20, and is discussed briefly in Leung, "Hsü Chih-mo," p. 132. A translation of Zhou Enlai's rickshaw poem is in Nancy T. Lin, *In Quest, Poems of Chou En-lai*, p. 19, under the title "The Indolence of Life-in-Death." These three poems by Wen, Xu, and Zhou could be added to the list of "rickshaw works" of-

fered by Yi-tsi Feuerwerker in "The Changing Relationship Between Literature and Life," p. 302. Wen Yiduo's close friend Liang Shiqiu later mocked the whole "rickshaw-boy school"; see Marián Gálik, "Studies in Modern Chinese Literary Criticism: VII, Liang Shih-ch'iu and New Humanism," p. 43. The realities of rickshaw-pulling life are well presented by David Strand and Richard R. Weiner, "Social Movements and Political Discourse in 1920's Peking," pp. 139, 156–60.

28. Wen Yiduo, *Quanji*, section "ding," pp. 239–40.

29. Lu Xun, *Quanji*, 7/31, Lu letter of Mar. 11, 1925, to Xu.

30. Ibid., 7/42, Lu letter of Mar. 23, 1925, to Xu.

31. Ibid., 7/53, Xu to Lu of Apr. 6, 1925; and 7/56, Lu to Xu of Apr. 8.

32. Three quotations in order, Lu Xun, *SW*, 2/161–62, 2/176, 2/212.

33. Ibid., 2/248–53.

34. As translated in ibid., 2/258–62 (with minor changes).

35. Ibid., 2/267. For the warlord jostlings in Beijing see *BDRC* (under Feng Yü-hsiang, Tuan Ch'i-jui, Wu P'ei-fu, and Chang Tso-lin).

36. On the Northern Expedition see Donald A. Jordan, *The Northern Expedition*, especially chapter 19, and *BDRC* (under Chang Fa-k'uei, Chiang Kai-shek, and T'ang Sheng-chih). The role of the mass organizations in Hunan is analyzed by Angus W. McDonald, Jr., *The Urban Origins of Rural Revolution*, pp. 264–70.

37. Chesneaux, *Chinese Labor Movement*, pp. 349–51, 355; Harold Isaacs, *The Tragedy of the Chinese Revolution*, chapter 8; Jordan, *Northern Expedition*, chapter 12.

38. Stuart Schram, *The Political Thought of Mao Tse-tung*, p. 241, and discussion in McDonald, *Urban Origins*, pp. 259–64.

39. Schram, *Political Thought*, pp. 250, 252, 256–57; Roy Hofheinz, *The Broken Wave*, pp. 31–35, offers the challenging suggestion, hard to accept, that the whole report was "an utter fantasy." Philip Huang, "Mao Tse-tung and the Middle Peasants, 1925–1928," pp. 281–85, discusses this report in detail; an extremely shrewd analysis is also given by McDonald, *Urban Origins*, pp. 264–79, 281–83.

40. On the courtship see especially Leo Ou-fan Lee, *The Romantic Generation of Chinese Writers*, pp. 139–44; Xu–Elmhirst Letters, pp. 7–8, letter of Hu Shi to Elmhirst, Dec. 26, 1926; the couple's diaries in Xu Zhimo, *Quanji*, vol. 4; and Liu Xinhuang, *Xu Zhimo yu Lu Xiaoman*, pp. 125–28. For the reception, see Xu Zhimo, *Quanji*, 1/621.

41. Liang Qichao, *Nianpu*, p. 710, letter to daughter of Oct. 4, 1926.

42. Xu–Elmhirst Letters, p. 10 (letter of Jan. 5, 1927).

43. Xu–Elmhirst Letters, p. 7, Hu Shi to Elmhirst, Dec. 26, 1926; Xu letter to Zhang Youyi of Dec. 14, 1926, in Xu, *Quanji*, 1/68–69 and 1/624–25; Leung, "Hsü Chih-mo," p. 279. On Peter's death see Xu letter to Lu Xiaoman of Mar. 26, 1925, in Xu, *Quanji*, 4/380, and his moving prose elegy "Bide" in *Quanji*, 3/457–66.

44. Leung, "Hsü Chih-mo," pp. 226, 279, 341, note 31 on magazine and money; Xu–Elmhirst Letters, p. 14, Xu letter of Apr. 1, 1927, to Elmhirst says, "I have been dumb for half a year already."

45. Xu Zhimo, *Quanji*, 1/626–27; Xu–Elmhirst Letters, p. 10 (Jan. 5, 1927), on West Lake; pp. 13 and 14 (Apr. 1, 1927) on Hu Shi as Pangloss. Xu, *Quanji*, 5/211–417, for *Candide* translation.

46. Liang Qichao, *Nianpu*, p. 729; Li Yunguang, *Kang Youwei jiashu kaoshi*, p. 77, note 3; Kang Youwei, *Shiji*, 15/97–101. Xu Zhimo makes no mention of any invitation in his diary of this month, *Quanji*, 4/534–35.

47. Lo, *Symposium*, p. 248.

48. *Kang Nanhai zhutian jiang*, 8/1b–2, following Hsiao Kung-chuan, "K'ang Yu-wei's Excursion into Science," p. 383. For the plane-flight poem see Kang, *Shiji*, 15/75. The inscription for the academy had also been donated by Puyi; see Li Yunguang, *Kang Youwei jiashu*, p. 54, note 4.

49. Lo, *Symposium*, pp. 249–52. Full memorial, in facsimile, in *Qingji mingren shouzha*, pp. 1095–1136. The purchase of the Qingdao home is detailed in Li Yunguang, *Kang Youwei jiashu*, pp. 44–46.

CHAPTER 8 / WAKE THE SPRING

1. Liang Qichao, *Nianpu*, p. 727, letter of Mar. 30, 1927.

2. Wu Tien-wei, "Chiang Kai-shek's April 12th Coup of 1927"; Harold Isaacs, *The Tragedy of the Chinese Revolution*, chapter 11. Chiang Kai-shek's continuing violence to the wealthy Shanghai bourgeoisie is detailed in Parks M. Coble, Jr., "The Kuomintang Regime and the Shanghai Capitalists, 1927–1929," especially pp. 8–11; for the long-range effect on a Chinese firm see also Sherman Cochran, *Big Business in China*, pp. 188–95.

3. Maurice Meisner, *Li Ta-chao and the Origins of Chinese Marxism*, pp. 257–59 (the Chinese officer who arrested Li was identified and executed by the Chinese Communist government in 1951). For an analysis of the seized documents see C. Martin Wilbur and Julie Lien-ying How, *Documents on Communism, Nationalism, and Soviet Advisers in China, 1918–1927*.

4. BDRC 3/73–75 (under P'eng Shu-chih); Richard Clark Kagan, "The Chinese Trotskyist Movement and Ch'en Tu-hsiu," pp. 87–88; Arif Dirlik, *Revolution and History*, p. 69, note 28, shows that the Trotsky-Bukharin-Stalin arguments were well known in Wuhan.

5. Angus W. McDonald, Jr., *The Urban Origins of Rural Revolution*, pp. 312–16; Isaacs, *Tragedy of the Chinese Revolution*, chapter 14.

6. Roy Hofheinz, *The Broken Wave*, pp. 53–63, marshals a host of reasons for the failure of the Autumn Risings; Stuart Schram,

Mao Tse-tung, pp. 118–25; Lyman P. van Slyke, *Enemies and Friends,* pp. 22–37. The military side of the Nanchang rising has been described by J. Guillermaz, "The Nanchang Uprising"; an intriguing sequel to that essay is C. Martin Wilbur's account in "The Ashes of Defeat"of how the Communist Party then analyzed the rising.

7. Wen Yiduo, *Quanji,* "Nianpu," pp. 50–52; Hsu Kai-yu, "Wen I-to," pp. 99–100.

8. Wen Yiduo, *Quanji,* section "ding," p. 24.

9. As translated by Hsu Kai-yu, *Twentieth Century Chinese Poetry,* pp. 60–61 (with minor changes); Wen Yiduo, *Quanji,* section "ding," pp. 24–26. Another good rendering, by Tao Tao Sanders, is in Wen Yiduo, *Red Candle,* pp. 44–46.

10. As translated in Cyril Birch, ed., *Anthology of Chinese Literature,* 2/356. For Wen's life at this time see Wen Yiduo, *Quanji,* "Nianpu," pp. 51–52, and Hsu, "Wen I-to," pp. 99–102; Hsu, pp. 102–107, analyzes the general nature of the *Dead Water* collection. The poem's structure is analyzed by Julia C. Lin in *Modern Chinese Poetry,* pp. 85–87.

11. Cited in Leo Ou-fan Lee, *The Romantic Generation of Chinese Writers,* p. 148.

12. Hsu, "Wen I-to," p. 107 (with minor changes).

13. Lu Xun, *SW,* 2/334–36, 3/41–43.

14. The development of their relationship can be followed through their letters of late 1926 and 1927 in Lu Xun, *Quanji,* vol. 7.

15. Lu Xun, *SW,* 2/338.

16. Ibid., 3/47–48, 76. For Lu Xun's continuing lack of sympathy for the party in this period see Harriet Mills, "Lu Hsün and the Communist Party," pp. 18–20.

17. Lu Xun, *SW,* 3/24.

18. Ibid., 3/45.

19. Quotations (in order), ibid., 3/79, 3/54, and 2/337.

20. Lu Xun, *Silent China,* pp. 148–54. The contexts of that and other Nora parallels are given by Elisabeth Eide, "Ibsen's Nora and Chinese Interpretations of Female Emancipation," pp. 140–144, 150–151.

21. Chang Jun-mei, *Ting Ling,* pp. 15–16; Gary Bjorge, "Ting Ling's Early Years," pp. 31–32.

22. See "Buxuan qingshu," in *Ding Ling pingzhuan,* p. 237.

23. Chang, *Ting Ling,* p. 11; Hsia Tsi-an, *The Gate of Darkness,* p. 184; "Meizi" in *Ding Ling pingzhuan,* p. 185; *Ding Ling ziliao ji,* pp. 4–5. Bjorge, "Ting Ling's Early Years," pp. 32–47, gives useful details on this Beijing period.

24. Cited in Chang, *Ting Ling,* pp. 13–14.

25. As translated in ibid., pp. 14–15.

26. Jeffrey C. Kinkley, "Shen Ts'ung-wen's Vision of Republican China," pp. 145–50 and 170; Gaylord Kai-loh Leung, "Hsü Chih-mo," p. 306.

27. "Meng Ke" appears as the first story in *Ding Ling xuanji*; the story is discussed by Chang in *Ting Ling*, pp. 23–27, and by Yi-tsi Feuerwerker, "The Changing Relationship Between Literature and Life," p. 289.

28. *Ding Ling xuanji*, pp. 23–25.

29. Ibid., pp. 46–47.

30. Ibid., p. 56.

31. "Shafei nushi," in *Ding Ling xuanji*, p. 61. The story is translated in its entirety in Harold Isaacs, ed., *Straw Sandals*, pp. 129–69. For a vehemently negative view of Ding Ling's talents as a writer see C. T. Hsia, *A History of Modern Chinese Fiction*, pp. 268–69. In his *Twentieth Century Chinese Stories*, introduction, p. xi, Hsia notes that he decided not to include "Diary of Miss Sophie" because it was "very much dated and therefore unusable"; however, Yi-tsi Feuerwerker in "Women as Writers in the 1920s and 1930s," pp. 159–63, gives a sympathetic analysis of the confessional form and its "emotionalism." A reversal of previous Communist hostility to the story can also be seen in Zong Chen and Shang Xia, "Ding Ling zaoqi di shenghuo he chuangzuo," pp. 43–44.

32. *Ding Ling xuanji*, p. 58.

33. Isaacs, ed., *Straw Sandals*, p. 140, 142.

34. Ibid., p. 162 (with minor changes).

35. Ibid., p. 169 (with minor changes).

36. For a rather different interpretation of Ding's relationship with Hu Yepin, and other useful details, see Bjorge, "Ting Ling's Early Years," p. 47, note 46. For plot summaries and discussion see Chang, *Ting Ling*, pp. 32–37.

37. Translated in Chang, *Ting Ling*, p. 38. The passage is also given in Yi-tsi Feuerwerker, "Changing Relationship," p. 302.

38. Hu Yepin, *Yepin shixuan*, pp. 1–6, introduction by Ding Ling.

39. Discussed in Chang, *Ting Ling*, p. 46, and Hsia, *Gate of Darkness*, p. 183.

40. Chang, *Ting Ling*, pp. 24–25.

41. Ibid., p. 47. Lu Xun's role in publishing volumes by Plekhanov and Lunacharsky is discussed by Leo Ou-fan Lee, "Literature on the Eve of Revolution," pp. 300–301. For Shen Congwen's view of the political naiveté of both Ding and Hu, see Hsia, *History of Modern Chinese Fiction*, p. 267.

42. BDRC, 2/87–88 (under Hsiang Chung-fa); James P. Harrison, "The Li Li-san Line and the CCP in 1930"; Kagan, "The Chinese Trotskyist Movement and Ch'en Tu-hsiu," pp. 96–98; Philip Huang, "Mao Tse-tung and the Middle Peasants, 1925–1928," pp. 285–92, details the Jinggangshan period in terms of Mao's understanding of the "intermediate class." The mass mobilization techniques in the Jiangxi Soviet are described by Ilpyong J. Kim, *The Politics of Chinese Communism*, chapter 5, and Mao's agrarian policy by John E. Rue, *Mao Tse-tung in Opposition, 1927–1935*, chapter 9.

43. See biographies in *BDRC*; and, for Yang Kaihui, *Mao Zhuxi yijia liu lieshi*, pp. 31–33.

44. The closing phases of the Northern Expedition are detailed in Donald A. Jordan, *The Northern Expedition*, chapters 16 and 17. See also *BDRC*, 1/63 and 1/327 (under Chang Hsueh-liang and Chiang Kai-shek), and 3/137 (under the Soong family); on the party machinery and the secret organization of the "Blue Shirts" see Lloyd E. Eastman, *The Abortive Revolution*, chapter 2; on the pseudonyms, false names, and constantly changing magazine titles used by various leftists to avoid Guomindang censorship see Lee-hsia Hsu Ting, *Government Control of the Press in Modern China, 1900–1949*, pp. 80–83. Guomindang ideology of the period and its relationship to Sun Yatsen's ideas of tutelage are in Robert E. Bedeski, "The Tutelary State and National Revolution in Kuomingtang Ideology, 1928–31," especially p. 324. Arif Dirlik, "The Ideological Foundations of the New Life Movement," p. 954, quotes Chiang's language on the dirt and laziness of the Chinese, which eerily echoes the young Lu Xun; see also ibid., p. 949, on the "mass participation" side of the Guomindang.

45. Some early examples of Guomindang attacks on Communists even in the international areas are mentioned by Coble, "Kuomintang Regime and Shanghai Capitalists," p. 11; see also Y. C. Wang, "Tu Yueh-sheng (1888–1951)," for examples of underground violence. On Hu Yepin and Lu Xun at this time see Hsia, *Gate of Darkness*, pp. 110–17, 176–77.

46. As translated in Isaacs, ed., *Straw Sandals*, pp. 207–208 (with a minor change). The Jiangxi Soviet marriage laws are summarized and analyzed by Mariam Darce Frenier, "Women and the Chinese Communist Party, 1921 to 1952," pp. 41–51. Hu Chi-hsi, "The Sexual Revolution in the Kiangsi Soviet," p. 479, discusses the specific effects of the August 1930 decree; ibid., pp. 484–89, also details negative reactions in the Soviet to the 1931 marriage law. See also Delia Davin, "Women in the Liberated Areas," p. 74.

47. As translated by Hsia, *Gate of Darkness*, p. 178.

48. Chang, *Ting Ling*, pp. 9–10, and plot summaries in ibid., pp. 52–55; Hsia, *Gate of Darkness*, pp. 175–76.

49. As translated by Yi-tsi Feuerwerker, "Changing Relationship Between Literature and Life," pp. 301–302 (with minor changes). Other versions can be found in Hsia, *Gate of Darkness*, p. 188; Lee, *Romantic Generation*, pp. 271–72; and Bjorge, "Ting Ling's Early Years," pp. 206–207.

50. Chang, *Ting Ling*, p. 49; Hsia, *History of Modern Chinese Fiction*, pp. 264–65; Mao Dun, "Huiyi Qu Qiubai," p. 36.

51. Meeting and rumors discussed in Hsia, *Gate of Darkness*, pp. 164, 218–19, 230–33; Xu Zhimo, *Quanji*, 4/539; and Chang, *Ting Ling*, p. 52.

52. Lu Xun, *SW*, 3/209; Paul G. Pickowicz, "Lu Xun through the Eyes of Qu Qiubai," pp. 333–34.

53. Shen Congwen, *Ji Ding Ling xuji*, p. 47, 53, 58; Hsia, *Gate of Darkness*, p. 231, note 155.

54. Shen Congwen, *Ji Ding Ling xuji*, p. 78.

55. Lu Xun, *SW*, 3/202; Hsia, *Gate of Darkness*, pp. 164–65.

56. Cited by Hsia, *Gate of Darkness*, pp. 183 and 186–87.

57. Xu-Elmhirst Letters, pp. 28–29, letter of Oct. 23, 1928. A great deal of useful material on the Elmhirst-Whitney relationship, some of it of immediate value to a study of the Xu-Elmhirst ties, is contained in the Dorothy Whitney Straight Elmhirst Collection at Cornell University. One example in file 3725, not too flattering to Xu, is contained in Gretchen Green's letter of summer 1924 to Dorothy Straight, warning Mrs. Straight what would happen if she rejected Elmhirst's hopes for marriage: "If you say no, it means Shansi, it means wandering about with the Poet, it means no stability of purpose, it means a barren life." (I am grateful to Ingeborg Wald for this reference.)

58. Xu–Elmhirst Letters, p. 32, letter of Jan. 7, 1929.

59. Ibid., p. 36, letter of Mar. 5, 1929.

60. Lee, *Romantic Generation*, p. 144, and Liu Xinhuang, *Xu Zhimo yu Lu Xiaoman*, chapter 11.

61. "Miracle," translated in Hsu Kai-yu, *Twentieth Century Chinese Poetry*, p. 67. For this as Wen's last poem see Hsu, "Wen I-to," pp. 114–18.

62. Lee, *Romantic Generation*, p. 148.

63. Xu–Elmhirst Letters, p. 34, letter of Mar. 5, 1929 (correcting the phrase "of assuage" to read "to assuage").

64. Cited in Lee, *Romantic Generation*, pp. 165 and 172.

65. As translated in Cyril Birch, ed., "English and Chinese Metres in Hsü Chih-mo,"p. 285; also cited in Lee, *Romantic Generation*, p. 162. For the poem's date see Xu Zhimo, *Quanji*, 2/573.

66. Xu Zhimo, *Quanji*, 1/663–64; Lee, *Romantic Generation*, pp. 155, 172–74.

CHAPTER 9 / FAREWELL TO THE BEAUTIFUL THINGS

1. The student was Tang Eryou; his letter is printed in Xu Zhimo, *Quanji*, 1/453–55.

2. Cited in Gaylord Kai-loh Leung, "Hsü Chih-mo," p. 220.

3. Hsia Tsi-an, *The Gate of Darkness*, p. 179; Shirley Hsiao-ling Sun, "Lu Hsun and the Chinese Woodcut Movement," pp. 126–35, details Lu's interest in Käthe Kollwitz.

4. Lu Xun, *SW*, 3/212–13.

5. Ibid., 3/93–94 (with minor changes).

6. Ibid., quotations in order, 3/17, 3/112, 3/124.

7. Marián Gálik, *Mao Tun and Modern Literary Criticism*, pp. 119–21. Qu's friendship with Lu Xun is described in Paul G. Pickowicz, "Lu Xun through the Eyes of Qu Qiu-bai."

8. Paul G. Pickowicz, "Qu Qiubai's Critique of the May Fourth Generation," pp. 366–72, quotation p. 372.

9. Ibid., pp. 374, 376, 381.

10. Discussed in Gálik, *Mao Tun*, pp. 101–104.

11. Sun, "Chinese Woodcut Movement," pp. 69–76. An illustrated edition of the woodcuts Lu Xun collected between 1931 and 1936 has been printed: *Lu Xun shoucang zhongguo xiandai muke xuanji*.

12. Shen Congwen, *Ji Ding Ling xuji*, pp. 121–24; Chang Jun-mei, *Ting Ling*, p. 52; *Ding Ling pingzhuan*, pp. 128–29, "Guanyu Muqin"; Gary Bjorge, "Ting Ling's Early Years," pp. 63–67.

13. As translated in Harold Isaacs, ed., *Straw Sandals*, p. 260.

14. Chang, *Ting Ling*, pp. 56–57.

15. "Wode zibai" in *Ding Ling pingzhuan*, pp. 215–33, quotation pp. 222–23.

16. Ibid., pp. 130, 223, and 128–29 (letter to her editor of June 11, 1932, in "Guanyu Muqin").

17. See biographies in *BDRC* (under Chang Tso-lin, P'u-yi, and Ts'ai T'ing-k'ai [the commanding general of the Nineteenth Route Army, which led the defense of Shanghai in 1932]. Japanese motives for killing Zhang Zuolin are assessed by Gavan McCormack, *Chang Tso-lin in Northeast China, 1911–1928*, pp. 246–48, and Takehiko Yoshihashi, *Conspiracy at Mukden*, pp. 41–50. The commercial effects of Japan's economic policies in Manchuria at this time (especially overconcentration on the soya bean crop, patterns of tenantry, and incidences of banditry) are studied in Herbert P. Bix, "Japanese Imperialism and the Manchurian Economy, 1900–31," pp. 430, 433–36. An excellent example of Japanese business methods in China, in this case in Shandong between 1921 and 1937, is given by Tim Wright, "Sino-Japanese Business in China"; table I, ibid., p. 723, shows that in several years the Luda Company in fact *lost* money in China. The "Mukden Incident" of 1931 is exhaustively studied in Yoshihashi's *Conspiracy at Mukden*, chapter 6.

18. The most illuminating treatment in English of Chiang's political struggles is Tien Hung-mao's *Government and Politics in Kuomintang China*. See also Ch'ien Tuan-sheng, *The Government and Politics of China, 1912–1949*, especially chapters 23 and 24 on "Political Parties" and "Party Politics." The Communist Shanghai leadership struggles are well summarized in Benjamin Schwartz, *Chinese Communism and the Rise of Mao*, especially chapter 10, "Changsha and the Li Li-san Line," and given detailed study in Richard Thornton, *The Comintern and the Chinese Communists, 1928–1931*. The Jiangxi Soviet is analyzed by Ilpyong J. Kim, *The Politics of Chinese Communism*, and John E. Rue, *Mao Tse-tung in Opposition, 1927–1935*.

There are valuable data on the Guangxi Soviet (and on Deng Xiaoping's early activities there in 1929) in Diana Lary, *Region and Nation*, pp. 104–107; and on He Long (Ho Lung), later leader of the Hunan Soviet, in Jeffrey C. Kinkley, "Shen Ts'ung-wen's Vision of Republican China," chapter 4, especially pp. 103–104, 120, 140. The abortive Hebei Soviet is examined by Linda Grove, "Creating a Northern Soviet."

19. Background on Lao She (the pseudonym used throughout his writing life by Shu Qingchun) is given by Prudence Sui-ning Chou in chapter 1 of her "Lao She: An Intellectual's Role and Dilemma in Modern China," and by Ranbir Vohra, *Lao She and the Chinese Revolution*, chapters 1 and 2. Lao She himself gave a fictionalized account of his Manchu family upbringing in his *Zhenghongqi xia* (published posthumously in 1979). See also King Hu, "Lao She in England," and the introductions by William A. Lyell, Jr., and Paul Bady to their translations of *Maocheng ji* and *Lao niu po che*.

20. See Chou, "Lao She," chapters 2 and 3, on his earliest novels; also Paul Bady, trans., Lao She, *Lao niu po che*, pp. 37–42, and Vohra, *Lao She*, p. 60, on the lost novel.

21. Cited in William A. Lyell, Jr., trans., *Cat Country*, introduction p. xl. The whole of the essay "How I Came to Write *Cat Country*" has been translated into French by Paul Bady, in Lao She, *Lao niu po che*, pp. 43–49.

22. Lao She, *Maocheng ji*, p. 2, following Lyell, trans., *Cat Country*, p. 3.

23. Lao She, *Maocheng ji*, pp. 37–38; Lyell, trans., *Cat Country*, pp. 41–43.

24. Lyell, trans., *Cat Country*, chapter 21.

25. Ibid., p. 294 (with minor changes).

26. Paul Bady, "Death and the Novel—On Lao She's 'Suicide,' " p. 11, note 27, gives some of these earliest critiques; Bady, trans., *Lao niu po che*, p. 45, gives Lao She's own dismissive remarks. Chou, in "Lao She," pp. 63–70, analyzes and defends the novel, seeing it as a "successful satire."

27. On the League for the Protection of Human Rights see William J. Duiker, *Ts'ai Yüan-p'ei*, pp. 94–95. Lu Xun describes the lunch in *SW*, 3/218–20.

28. Preface to Qu's anthology, *SW*, 3/222–24; "Who Is the Paradox," *SW*, 3/214–16 (quotation with minor changes).

29. Stories summarized in Gary Bjorge, "Ting Ling's Early Years," pp. 213–44 (the Peter Pan rendition being on pp. 242–44); and in Chang Jun-mei, *Ting Ling*, pp. 65–67. Ding Ling, *Muqin*, concluding note following p. 239.

30. Chang, *Ting Ling*, pp. 60–61.

31. *BDRC*, 4/6 (under Yang Ch'uan). The background and the killing of Yang are discussed by Chen Shaoxiao in *Heigang lu*, pp. 71–75. (I am grateful to Michael Lestz for this reference.)

32. Paul G. Pickowicz, "Introduction to Qu Qiubai's 'Who's "We"?' and 'The Question of Popular Literature and Art,' " p. 50; Dun J. Li, *The Road to Communism*, p. 173.

33. Pickowicz, "Introduction to 'Who's "We"?' " p. 50.

34. The most detailed account of the extermination campaign, and the roles of German officers, is in F. F. Liu, *A Military History of Modern China, 1924–1949*, chapters 7–10. The secrecy was such that even senior Communist cadres in Jiangxi knew nothing of the party's retreat plans; see Jerome Ch'en, "Resolutions of the Tsunyi Conference," pp. 29–30. On the unsuccessful CCP responses to Chiang's Fifth Encirclement Campaign strategies, and the role of the Comintern agent Otto Braun, see Hu Chihsi, "Hua Fu, the Fifth Encirclement Campaign and the Tsunyi Conference" (especially p. 40); for Lin Biao's crucial contributions see Hu Chihsi, "Mao, Lin Biao and the Fifth Encirclement Campaign," pp. 268–69.

35. Li, *Road to Communism*, p. 163. Questions of the testament's authenticity are carefully considered by Hsia in *Gate of Darkness*, pp. 44–52; he concludes that it is genuine, as did Ding Ling later.

36. Li, *Road to Communism*, pp. 163, 169–70.

37. Ibid., pp. 165–67, quotation p. 165 (with minor changes). This seems a reprise to Qu's *New Youth* essay of Mar. 26, 1926, on socialism and classes—see Arif Dirlik, *Revolution and History*, p. 60.

38. Li, *Road to Communism*, p. 174.

39. Ibid., pp. 175–76 (with minor changes); Sima Lu, *Qu Qiubai zhuan*, pp. 160–61. The intellectual attenuation, so vivid here, was also expressed less than a month later by Tao Xisheng; see the discussion in Dirlik, *Revolution and History*, p. 221.

40. For Qu's analysis and editing of Lu's work see Pickowicz, "Lu Xun through the Eyes of Qu Qiubai," pp. 342–55. For Lu's publishing of Qu in 1936, Hsia, *Gate of Darkness*, p. 128, note 72.

41. Quotations cited in Hsia, *Gate of Darkness*, pp. 113 and 114; see Yang I-fan, *The Case of Hu Feng*, pp. 28–29, on the Lu–Hu correspondence.

42. For detailed descriptions of the Long March see Anthony Garavente, "The Long March," and Dick Wilson, *The Long March, 1935*, part 2. On settlement in Baoan and the countryside and alliances there see Stuart Schram, *Mao Tse-tung*, pp. 192–99. Mark Selden, *The Yenan Way in Revolutionary China*, chapters 1 and 2, gives a graphic picture of social conditions in Shaanxi, and the fluctuations of the various Communist groups there in the 1930s.

43. Lyman P. van Slyke, *Enemies and Friends*, chapter 4; for the December 9 demonstrations see John Israel and Donald W. Klein, *Rebels and Bureaucrats, China's December 9ers*, passim, and especially pp. 57–59 on Lu Cui (Lu Ts'ui), the students' new "Joan of Arc."

44. As quoted in Hsia, *Gate of Darkness*, pp. 121 (with minor changes) and 131; see also Yang I-fan, *Case of Hu Feng*, pp. 30–32.

45. Hsia, *Gate of Darkness*, pp. 135–36.
46. Ibid., pp. 138–41.
47. See Lu Xun, *Quanji*, 2/485–505, "Li Shui," November 1935; 506–532, "Cai Wei," December 1935; 561–75, "Chu Guan," December 1935; 593–608, "Qi Si," December 1935. *BDRC*, 2/246, discusses Lu Xun's mockery of Gu Jiegang in "Li Shui."
48. Lu Xun, *Silent China*, pp. 81–82.
49. Ibid., pp. 84–86.
50. Lu Xun, *SW*, 4/295.
51. Ibid., 4/295–96.
52. *Lu Xun shuxin ji*, p. 769, letter to Xiao Hong. Bjorge, "Ting Ling's Early Years," pp. 89–97, discusses details of Ding Ling's arrest.
53. Chang, *Ting Ling*, p. 62 (with minor changes).
54. Ibid., p. 69 (with minor changes).
55. Ibid., p. 71.
56. *Ding Ling pingzhuan*, p. 227.
57. Ibid., p. 230.
58. Details of her flight are given in Chang, *Ting Ling*, pp. 64 and 72.

CHAPTER 10 / REFUGEES

1. Lao She, *Maocheng ji*, preface, p. 2.
2. See plot summaries and discussion of *Divorce* and *Niu Tianzi zhuan* (*Niu T'ien-tzu chuan*) in Ranbir Vohra, *Lao She and the Chinese Revolution*, pp. 70–97 (quotation on p. 86), and C. T. Hsia, *A History of Modern Chinese Fiction, 1917–1957*, pp. 176–81.
3. An excellent new translation of the novel is Jean James's *Rickshaw*. Lao's own account of the writing of *Rickshaw*—"Wo ziyang xie 'Loto xiangzi' "—is included in the volume of his works, edited by his widow, Hu Xieqing, *Lao She shenghuo yu chuangzuo zishu*, pp. 65–71, and is also translated as "How I Came to Write the Novel 'Camel Hsiang-tzu.' " There, Lao says the idea for the novel came from two casual anecdotes told him by a friend: in one, a Beijing rickshaw man loses the vehicle after saving up for it for a long time; in the other, a dispossessed rickshaw man steals some soldiers' camels. (This explains the novel's title, and perhaps the lack of integration between the camel episode and the rest of the plot.) Lao also notes that serialization of the novel began well before he had completed it. See also Prudence Sui-ning Chou, "Lao She," pp. 80–93, for discussion of the novel's structure and impact.
4. On writing for money see Lao She (trans. Paul Bady), *Lao niu po che*, p. 65, and Vohra, *Lao She*, p. 98; the passages on the old man and the wife are in Lao She (trans. Jean James), *Rickshaw*, pp. 93 and 164. C. T. Hsia gives the highest accolades to the craftmanship, integrity, and content of this novel in his *History of Modern*

Chinese Fiction, pp. 181–88. See also Vohra, *Lao She*, chapter 5, and Cyril Birch, "Lao She," pp. 50–54.

5. Lao She (trans. Jean James), *Rickshaw*, p. 60; the passage is also cited and discussed in Vohra, *Lao She*, p. 113; and Chou, "Lao She," pp. 91–92.

6. Lao She (trans. Jean James), *Rickshaw*, p. 249. (In the best-selling American "translation" of the novel, this ending was abandoned without Lao She's permission, and replaced by a happy "boy gets girl after all" conclusion.)

7. Ibid., p. 211, for his "deliberate" stoop and acceptance of the disease.

8. The most careful study of the kidnapping is Wu Tien-wei's *The Sian Incident*. Detailed coverage of the National Salvation organizations and the Xian arrest is also given by Lyman P. van Slyke, *Enemies and Friends*, pp. 68–91. For details on the student movement see also John Israel, *Student Nationalism in China*, especially pp. 129–38. On the important role of the Communist Youth Leagues in the 1936 and 1937 salvation movements see Klaus H. Pringsheim, "The Functions of the Chinese Communist Youth Leagues (1920–1949)," pp. 82–84. On Yanan and Madrid see Carl E. Dorris, "Peasant Mobilization in North China and the Origins of Yenan Communism," p. 702.

9. Chang Jun-mei, *Ting Ling*, p. 73.

10. *Ding Ling zai xibei*, p. 74, and preface by Shi Tianxing, ibid., p. i.

11. Van Slyke, *Enemies and Friends*, pp. 90–93. On Mao's appeals to the Gelao hui and other possible allies in the area see Stuart Schram, "Mao Tse-tung and Secret Societies."

12. A very detailed analysis of the follow-up to the Marco Polo Bridge Incident is given by James B. Crowley in *Japan's Quest for Autonomy*, pp. 324–42. On the various goals of the occupying armies see also Lincoln Li, *The Japanese Army in North China 1937–1941*, chapters 2 and 6.

13. *Ding Ling zai xibei*, pp. 44–45. Gary Bjorge, "Ting Ling's Early Years," p. 19, notes that she had published two poems in Hunan during 1919.

14. Shen Congwen, *Ji Ding Ling xuji*, p. 185.

15. Chang, *Ting Ling*, pp. 75–76. The first play, "Chong feng," was printed in *Ding Ling zai Shaanxi*, and the second, "Henei yilang," as a separate book in 1938. See also Bjorge, "Ting Ling's Early Years," pp. 98–105.

16. Japanese War Crimes Tribunal, as cited in Dun J. Li, *The Road to Communism*, pp. 207–215; F. F. Liu, *A Military History of Modern China, 1924–1949*, pp. 145 and 198 on casualties; BDRC, 1/247; Edward M. Gunn, *Unwelcome Muse*, pp. 110–15 on Shanghai theater, chapter 4 on Zhou Zuoren (Chou Tso-jen) and Beijing literary life in the occupation.

17. For major figures see the relevant biographies in *BDRC*. The war-time intellectual life in Beijing and Shanghai is well described by Gunn in his *Unwelcome Muse*. See also Theodore D. Huters's remarkable study of Qian Zhongshu, "Traditional Innovation," pp. 150–52 and chapters 4 and 5. Richard Clark Kagan, "The Chinese Trotskyist Movement and Ch'en Tu-hsiu," pp. 97, 155–61, discusses the decision of Chen Duxiu.

18. Hsu Kai-yu, "Wen I-to," pp. 111–25.

19. Wen Yiduo, *Quanji*, section "geng," p. 59, letter of July 16, 1937.

20. The Wuhan interlude, the journey to the southwest, and the meeting with Shen are detailed in Wen Yiduo, *Quanji*, "Nianpu," pp. 60–63. Shen's interests in Miao culture are described in Jeffrey C. Kinkley, "Shen Ts'ung-wen's Vision of Republican China," especially chapter 8.

21. Hsu, "Wen I-to," pp. 126–27.

22. Ibid., pp. 130–31, 150. Wen Yiduo, *Quanji*, letters in section "geng," pp. 60–65.

23. Wen Yiduo, *Quanji*, section "geng," p. 59, letter of July 16, 1937.

24. Ibid., pp. 62–63, letters of June 22 and June 27, 1938. (Biographical information on the other figures is in *BDRC*; William A. Lyell, *Lu Hsün's Vision of Reality*; Ross Terrill, *Mao: A Biography*; Gaylord Kai-loh Leung, "Hsü Chih-mo.")

25. Hsu, "Wen I-to," p. 130. Wen Yiduo, *Quanji*, "Nianpu," p. 65, and ibid., section "geng," p. 79, letter of June 13, 1938.

26. Wen Yiduo, *Quanji*, "Nianpu," p. 65, for one such Japanese air strike on Kunming in September 1938.

27. Ibid., section "ding," p. 229; part translated in Hsu, "Wen I-to," p. 128.

28. A detailed account of Lao She's life is given in Chou, "Lao She," chapter 5. For plot summary and analysis of *Cremation* see also Birch, "Lao She," p. 55, and *BDRC*, 3/134. Lao She's wartime plays are discussed in Vohra, *Lao She*, pp. 131–38.

29. Quoted in C. T. Hsia, *Modern Chinese Fiction*, p. 367 (with minor changes).

30. On Communist expansion and mutual infiltration see van Slyke, *Enemies and Friends*, pp. 135–42, 162–64; on New Fourth Army and Muslim raids, F. F. Liu, *Military History*, p. 206; *BDRC*, 4/38 (under Yeh T'ing). The Democratic and third-party activities are analyzed in van Slyke, *Enemies and Friends*, pp. 170–77.

31. Translated in Hsu Kai-yu, *Twentieth Century Chinese Poetry*, p. 288. For letters between Wen and the poet Zang Kejia (Tsang K'o-chia) see Wen, *Quanji*, section "geng," pp. 53–57.

32. Hsu, *Twentieth Century Chinese Poetry*, pp. 402–403.

33. Chang, *Ting Ling*, p. 74. For the impact on Westerners see Kenneth Shewmaker, *Americans and Chinese Communists 1927–1945*, especially chapter 8 on the period 1939–44.

34. Stuart Schram, *The Political Thought of Mao Tse-tung*, pp. 190–201

on contradictions, p. 228 on Guomindang, pp. 172–73 on Ah Q and sinification.

35. Chang, *Ting Ling*, p. 78 (with minor changes).
36. Mark Selden, *The Yenan Way in Revolutionary China*, chapter 5; Chalmers A. Johnson, *Peasant Nationalism and Communist Power*, pp. 55–56 on the "Three Alls" (*sankō-seisaku*) campaign.
37. See the remarkable section of Ding Ling's 1980 essay, "Wo suo renshide Qu Qiubai tongzhi," p. 162, col. 1.
38. These three stories are, in order, "Enlisted," "When I Was in Xia Village," and "Night." Plot summaries are given in Chang, *Ting Ling*, pp. 79–81. "When I Was in Xia Village" has been translated by Kung Pu-sheng (as "When I Was in Sha Chuan") and commented on by Yi-tsi Feuerwerker—see Feuerwerker's "Discussion" in *Signs*. For Ding Ling's fiction in Yanan at this time see Bjorge, "Ting Ling's Early Years," pp. 253–56.
39. Ding Ling, "In the Hospital," p. 126; "Zai yiyuan zhong," p. 13, col. 1.
40. Ding Ling, "In the Hospital," p. 137; "Zai yiyuan zhong," p. 16, col. 1. The story is analyzed by Bjorge in "Ting Ling's Early Years," pp. 126–34.

CHAPTER 11 / RECTIFICATIONS

1. Quoted in Hsia Tsi-an, *The Gate of Darkness*, p. 251. Her assumption of the editorship is discussed in Chang Jun-mei, *Ting Ling*, p. 87.
2. Merle Goldman, *Literary Dissent in Communist China*, pp. 24–26; Wang Hsueh-wen, *Chinese Communist Education*, p. 195.
3. Goldman, *Literary Dissent*, p. 43.
4. Leo Ou-fan Lee, *The Romantic Generation of Chinese Writers*, pp. 238–39.
5. On International Women's Day, and the party instructions, see Mariam Darce Frenier, "Women and the Chinese Communist Party 1921 to 1952," p. 62n., and Hsia, *Gate of Darkness*, p. 251, note 45.
6. Ding Ling, "Sanbajie yougan," p. 8. Discussions of her essay and partial translation are given in Yi-tsi Feuerwerker, "The Changing Relationship Between Literature and Life," p. 299; Frenier, "Women and the Chinese Communist Party," p. 105; and Wang Hsueh-wen, *Chinese Communist Education*, p. 199. A full translation is given by Gregor Benton in "The Yenan 'Literary Opposition,'" pp. 102–105. For a careful analysis of Ding Ling's feminism see Gary Bjorge, "Ting Ling's Early Years," pp. 136–37 and chapter 9.
7. Hsia, *Gate of Darkness*, p. 255.
8. On the 1929 and 1939 programs see Mark Selden, *The Yenan Way in Revolutionary China*, pp. 190–93. On 1942, Selden, *Yenan Way*,

pp. 193–200; Hsia, Gate of Darkness, pp. 238–41; Goldman, Literary Dissent, chapter 2; and Boyd Compton, ed. and trans., Mao's China. For contrast with the "Kangda" model of the internationalist wing, and the role of army rectification at the same time, see David Leroy Liden, "Party Factionalism and Révolutionary Vision," chapter 7.

9. Compton, Mao's China, pp. 15, 21, 31.

10. Benton, "Yenan 'Literary Opposition,'" translates the whole "Wild Lily" essay; the quotations are from ibid., pp. 96 and 100 (with minor changes). See also Chang, Ting Ling, pp. 91–92; Goldman, Literary Dissent, pp. 25–27; D. W. Fokkema, Literary Doctrine in China and Soviet Influence, pp. 11–19; and Gary Bjorge, "Ting Ling's Early Years," pp. 138–39.

11. For Ding Ling's April dismissal and replacement by Ai Siqi see Hsia, Gate of Darkness, p. 247.

12. Bonnie S. McDougall, Mao Zedong's "Talks at the Yan'an Conference on Literature and Art," gives a meticulous introduction to and translation of the original version of these important speeches of Mao's. On Lu Xun's son see ibid., p. 70, and see p. 83 for the list of things to be destroyed.

13. Ibid., pp. 80–81.

14. Chang, Ting Ling, pp. 95–96; Goldman, Literary Dissent, pp. 37–42; Bjorge, "Ting Ling's Early Years," pp. 139–59.

15. Goldman, Literary Dissent, pp. 38–43; Chang, Ting Ling, pp. 97–98. For the 1942 essays on Nora (one of them by Guo Moruo) see Roxane Witke, "Transformation of Attitudes," pp. 166–67. The story "The Eighteen" is discussed in Bjorge, "Ting Ling's Early Years," pp. 160–63.

16. The story of this American-Chinese relationship is summarized in Jonathan Spence, To Change China, chapter 9. The most important body of new material on the conflict is presented in Christopher Thorne, Allies of a Kind. See also F. F. Liu, A Military History of Modern China, 1924–1949, pp. 145 and 220–22, for the casualties and the southwestern campaigns.

17. See particularly Selden, Yenan Way, chapter 6, and the modifications to Selden's discussion suggested by Carl E. Dorris in "Peasant Mobilization in North China and the Origins of Yenan Communism," especially pp. 699–700. See also Lyman P. van Slyke, Enemies and Friends, pp. 144–53. For the campaign in education (and the collapse of the attempt to use a romanized script) see Peter J. Seybolt, "The Yenan Revolution in Mass Education," pp. 653–55.

18. Chang, Ting Ling, pp. 98–100. The summer 1944 writings are in Ding Ling, Yanan ji, pp. 1–18, 168–230. Ding's own evaluation is in ibid., pp. 231–35.

19. Van Slyke, Enemies and Friends, pp. 177–84; Anthony Joseph Sha-

heen, "The China Democratic League and Chinese Politics, 1939–1947," chapter 6, especially p. 216 for the Kunming branch.

20. As cited in Hsu Kai-yu, "Wen I-to," p. 134, with one small addition from original; Wen Yiduo, *Quanji*, section "jia," p. 328. For the Kunming group see Hsu, "Wen I-to," pp. 140, 160, 202, 229. On Wen and his wife see Wen Yiduo, *Quanji*, "Nianpu," p. 68 (under the entry for October 1941).

21. This remarkable letter, written "by lamplight" to the poet Zang Kejia, is cited at length in Wen Yiduo, *Quanji*, "Nianpu," pp. 70–71. See also the discussion by Hsu Kai-yu, "The Life and Poetry of Wen I-to," p. 171.

22. Hsu, "Wen I-to," p. 150. The appalling recruitment practices are detailed in F. F. Liu, *Military History*, especially pp. 137–39; see also Suzanne Pepper, *Civil War in China*, pp. 163–67.

23. Wen Yiduo, *Quanji*, "Nianpu," p. 72; part translated in Hsu, "Wen I-to," p. 152.

24. Contents summarized in Hsu, "Wen I-to," pp. 165–69; the April dates are of articles cited in ibid., notes 40, 51, 52, 54.

25. Wen Yiduo, *Quanji*, "Nianpu," pp. 74–77, on the various meetings; Hsu, "Wen I-to," pp. 153–54, on the political activities, and pp. 156–57 on his reading program. Hsu, "Life and Poetry," p. 177, cites Wen's change of heart about the value of Lu Xun's critical writings.

26. Quotations in order from Hsu, "Life and Poetry," pp. 173 and 170, and Hsu, "Wen I-to," p. 175.

27. Hsu, "Wen I-to," p. 135, on Qu Yuan. Guo Moruo's play *Qu Yuan (Ch'ü Yuan)* was completed in 1942, and translated into English in 1953. For Wen Yiduo's uses of Qu Yuan in the tradition of Chinese nationalism see the analysis by Laurence A. Schneider, *A Madman of Ch'u*, pp. 120–24.

28. On Kunming student activities see Pepper, *Civil War*, pp. 47–52.

29. Cited in Hsu, "Life and Poetry," p. 142.

30. Hsu, "Wen I-to," pp. 177–78. Wen's widow later dictated a moving account of their last days together, and his determination to fight on to the end; this was transcribed by her daughter and printed in 1972 under her maiden name, Gao (Xiao) Zhen, as "Yiduo xisheng qian hou jishi."

31. The report by the league was published in late 1946 under the title *Li-Wen an diaocha baogao shu*.

32. On the rape and protests, see Pepper, *Civil War*, pp. 52–57.

33. Chang, *Ting Ling*, pp. 103–104; F. F. Liu, *Military History*, pp. 240–45; *BDRC*, 2/376.

34. This May Fourth Directive is summarized in Pepper, *Civil War*, pp. 246–48.

35. Ibid., p. 292; for the growing radicalism in 1947, and the general agreement between Liu Shaoqi and Mao Zedong, see Tanaka

Kyoko, "Mao and Liu in the 1947 Land Reform," especially pp. 569, 583, and Frederick C. Teiwes, "The Origins of Rectification," pp. 33–46.

36. Quoted in Chang, *Ting Ling*, p. 104 (with minor changes).
37. Ding Ling, *The Sun Shines over the Sanggan River*, author's foreword. For this novel in its late 1940s context see Cyril Birch, "Fiction of the Yenan Period," pp. 9–11, in which he summarizes such works as being of a "sparkling mediocrity."
38. Ding Ling, *Sanggan River*, pp. 232–35.
39. Ibid., p. 55.
40. Ibid., p. 66.
41. Ibid., p. 275.
42. Ibid., pp. 292–93 (with minor changes); compare with the very similar scene in William Hinton, *Fanshen*, pp. 136–37. For discussion of the Qian scene, and contrasts with land reform themes as handled by the novelist Eileen Chang, see C. T. Hsia, *A History of Modern Chinese Fiction*, pp. 486–87 and 427–29. Such a scene as Qian's humiliation highlights the problem of trying to assess the degree to which landlords in the 1930s and 1940s had exploited their tenants. For examples of landlord callousness and excesses see Ralph Thaxton, "On Peasant Revolution and National Resistance," pp. 28, 41–42, 52; a counterargument to Thaxton's is advanced by Ramon H. Myers in "North China Villages During the Republican Period, Socioeconomic Relationships."
43. Ding Ling, *Sanggan River*, p. 284 on bound feet; pp. 299 and 302 for Gu and horizon; p. 252 for the crescent moon.
44. Ibid., pp. 104 and 111 on violence and the locust, pp. 73 and 332 for the shepherd's wife and the defense corps. C. T. Hsia, *Modern Chinese Fiction*, pp. 488–91, gives detailed analysis of other relationships.
45. Pepper, *Civil War*, pp. 300–305.
46. Chang, *Ting Ling*, pp. 104–105. For Chang's analysis of the novel see ibid., pp. 105–117.

CHAPTER 12 / A NEW ORDER

1. On the army in the region see Suzanne Pepper, *Civil War in China*, pp. 202–203.
2. Merle Goldman, *Literary Dissent in Communist China*, p. 76, and Leo Ou-fan Lee, *The Romantic Generation of Chinese Writers*, p. 241.
3. Goldman, *Literary Dissent*, pp. 74–78; Lee, *Romantic Generation*, p. 241.
4. Lee, *Romantic Generation*, pp. 241–42, assesses Xiao's character; Goldman, *Literary Dissent*, pp. 79–85, details the campaigns.
5. Pepper, *Civil War*, pp. 126–29; Wen Yiduo, *Quanji*, "Nianpu," p. 70.

6. Cited in Nieh Hua-ling, *Shen Ts'ung-wen*, p. 111.

7. On Shen's writings critical of the Guomindang "New Life Movement" see Jeffrey C. Kinkley, "Shen Ts'ung-wen's Vision of Republican China," pp. 372–79 and 389, and C. T. Hsia, *A History of Modern Chinese Fiction 1917–1957*, pp. 361–65; on Ding see Chang Jun-mei, *Ting Ling*, p. 121. (Shen and Ding may have met in Beijing briefly in 1936, as she prepared for her flight to Yanan.)

8. Ma Fenghua, "Huainian Shen Congwen jiaoshou," pp. 13–14; Nieh, *Shen Ts'ung-wen*, pp. 111–12.

9. Chang, *Ting Ling*, pp. 121–23; F. F. Liu, *A Military History of Modern China, 1924–1949*, pp. 266–70; Pepper, *Civil War*, pp. 385–90.

10. Hsu Kai-yu, *Twentieth Century Chinese Poetry*, pp. 380–81.

11. George Kao, "Lao She in America," pp. 69–70; for this "conclusion" see Evan King, trans., *Rickshaw Boy*, p. 384. Other cited episodes in King, ibid., pp. 359, 375, 378.

12. Kao, "Lao She in America," pp. 71–72; and Ranbir Vohra, *Lao She and the Chinese Revolution*, pp. 140–42. The background and results of the Wedemeyer mission are discussed in Jonathan Spence, *To Change China*, pp. 265–80.

13. Kao, "Lao She in America," p. 75.

14. Cyril Birch, "Lao She," pp. 55–56; Kao, "Lao She in America," p. 74.

15. The first phase of land reform and the concept of keypoint villages has been analyzed in the greatest detail by Vivienne Shue in *Peasant China in Transition*, chapters 1 and 2, taking the case study of Hunan province. See also Robert Ash, "Economic Aspects of Land Reform in Kiangsu, 1949–52," for a careful study of Jiangsu province; estimates of overall land availability are given in ibid., Part 2, p. 521. The major land-reform documents are printed in Mark Selden, *The People's Republic of China*, Part 1, sections A and B.

16. The role of women within land reform is discussed by Mariam Darce Frenier in "Women and the Chinese Communist Party, 1921 to 1952," chapter 6; see especially pp. 202, 217, 229. Prior stages in Yanan and the civil war in the development of the Marriage Law and the problem of women laboring in agricultural production are discussed in K. C. Ho, "The Status and the Role of Women in the Chinese Communist Movement, 1946–1949," pp. 110 and 181–83. Delia Davin, "Women in the Liberated Areas," p. 86, mentions that 40 percent of 464 recorded women's deaths in 1948 were suicides or homicides arising from divorce arguments. The text of the 1950 Marriage Law is in Selden, *People's Republic*, pp. 193–200. Examples from fiction of the early 1950s showing the effects of landholding on the women, and the hostility this aroused among men, are given in Irene Eber, "Images of Women in Recent Chinese Fiction," pp. 28–29, 31–33.

17. See Maurice Meisner, *Mao's China*, pp. 84–99, for general urban

problems. Kenneth Lieberthal, "The Suppression of Secret Socie-ties in Post-Liberation Tientsin," gives a graphic description of this process between 1949 and 1951 within Tianjin. Transitional problems in Shanghai are analyzed by Lynn T. White, "Workers' Politics in Shanghai," pp. 101–106; those in the Guangdong area by Ezra F. Vogel, *Canton under Communism*, chapter 2.

18. As translated by John Berninghausen in Hsu Kai-yu, ed., *Literature of the People's Republic of China*, pp. 40–41.

19. Programs summarized in Stuart Schram, *Mao Tse-tung*, pp. 268–73. A shrewd assessment of the scale of repression is given in Meisner, *Mao's China*, pp. 76–82.

20. According to a note appended to the summary of the film pre-pared by the Chinese Cultural Foundation of San Francisco, the party pressured the director, Shi Hui, to have a happier ending in which the old father was reunited with his son before his death, but Shi refused. On *Dragon's Beard Ditch* see Vohra, *Lao She*, pp. 154–55; Birch, "Lao She," p. 58.

21. Translated by Birch, "Lao She," p. 56.

22. Ibid., p. 57.

23. Ma Fenghua, "Huainian Shen Congwen jiaoshou," p. 15.

24. Ibid., p. 14, following Nieh, *Shen Ts'ung-wen*, pp. 112–13.

25. Hsia Tsi-an, *The Gate of Darkness*, p. 165.

26. Nieh, *Shen Ts'ung-wen*, p. 59, and Hsia, *Gate of Darkness*, p. 184 (with minor changes).

27. As cited in Nieh, *Shen Ts'ung-wen*, pp. 115–16 (with minor changes).

28. Shue, *Peasant China in Transition*, especially chapters 5 and 6.

29. Ding Ling, *Sanggan River*, p. 305.

30. Shue, *Peasant China in Transition*, chapter 7, p. 287, statistics show-ing speed of the transition; Kenneth R. Walker, "Collectivisa-tion in Retrospect," pp. 30–31 on speed-up decision, pp. 39–40 on cadre analysis of income increases. Illuminating contrasts with the Soviet Union's 1929–30 collectivization attempts are given in Thomas P. Bernstein, "Leadership and Mass Mobiliza-tion in the Soviet and Chinese Collectivisation Campaigns of 1929–30 and 1955–56," especially p. 11 on extent of CCP branches and p. 28 on the "three constants" designed to reassure the peasantry.

31. See their biographies in *BDRC*, 2/216 and 2/235, and in Donald Klein and Ann Clark, *Biographical Dictionary*, pp. 408–411 and 431–36. Also John Israel and Donald Klein, *Rebels and Bureaucrats*, pp. 59, 264–82.

32. Merle Goldman, *Literary Dissent*, pp. 93–100; Chang, *Ting Ling*, pp. 128–31; Yi-tsi Feuerwerker, "The Changing Relationship Between Literature and Life," p. 306.

33. Goldman, *Literary Dissent*, pp. 55–58, on Feng, Hu, and *Hope* mag-azine.

34. Chang, *Ting Ling*, pp. 130–34; Goldman, *Literary Dissent*, pp. 150, 208–210.

35. See summary by Yi-tsi Feuerwerker, "Changing Relationship," p. 290.

36. The most detailed account of this period is given in Roderick MacFarquhar, *The Origins of the Cultural Revolution*, passim. See also Goldman, *Literary Dissent*, pp. 160–65; D. W. Fokkema, *Literary Doctrine in China and Soviet Influence*, chapters 2 and 3; and John Bryan Starr, *Continuing the Revolution*, pp. 195–97.

37. Cited from Goldman, *Literary Dissent*, pp. 167–68 (with minor changes). The whole of Huang's essay "Do Not Close Your Eyes to the Suffering of the People" is translated in Nieh Hua-ling, *Literature of the Hundred Flowers*, 1/72–74.

38. *Look Westward to Ch'ang-an*, analyzed in Vohra, *Lao She*, pp. 155–56, and discussed by Vincent C. Y. Shih, "Lao She a Conformist?" pp. 314–15.

39. Vohra, *Lao She*, p. 153 (with minor changes). An essay on "Freedom and the Writer" by Lao She, dated Jan. 1, 1957, is translated in Nieh, *Literature of the Hundred Flowers*, 1/44–51.

40. Lao She, *Chaguan*, stage directions and character lists. Analysis of the play is in Vohra, *Lao She*, pp. 157–63; the entire play was translated by Ying Ruocheng for *Chinese Literature* in 1979. (Act I is included in Hsu Kai-yu and Ting Wang, eds., *Literature of the People's Republic*, pp. 749–61.) On the background to the play see Ying Ruocheng's "Lao She and His 'Teahouse.'"

41. The novella is translated in Nieh, *Literature of the Hundred Flowers*, 2/473–511, along with Wang Meng's self-criticism of May 8, 1957 (ibid., pp. 511–17), and a comprehensive selection of public critiques of Wang (ibid., pp. 518–63). Sections of the novella have also been translated by Gary Bjorge in Hsu, *Literature of the People's Republic*, pp. 229–41; see also Merle Goldman, *Literary Dissent*, pp. 179–80, and Fokkema, *Literary Doctrine*, pp. 99–103.

42. MacFarquhar, *Origins of the Cultural Revolution*, pp. 179–80, on Mao's poetry decision.

43. See especially René Goldman, "The Rectification Campaign at Peking University," p. 144; Roderick MacFarquhar, *The Hundred Flowers*, p. 119; Dennis J. Doolin, *Communist China: The Politics of Student Opposition*, p. 55. The changing nature of the faculty and student body at Beijing University has been analyzed in Sidney Leonard Greenblatt, "Organizational Elites and Social Change at Peking University," pp. 467–70; the party's attempts to influence such students can be followed in James R. Townsend, "Revolutionizing Chinese Youth," particularly pp. 453–58.

44. Doolin, *Student Opposition*, pp. 14, 24–28, 37–41.

45. MacFarquhar, *Hundred Flowers*, chapter 13, on peasants and workers; Doolin, *Student Opposition*, pp. 60–64, for other bitter questions.

46. On Mao's dilemma see MacFarquhar, *Origins of the Cultural Revolution*, pp. 278–81. Quotation from ibid., p. 279, with minor changes.

47. Xinhua News Agency release, series 2725, Aug. 8, 1957, no. 080712; also cited in MacFarquhar, *Hundred Flowers*, p. 188; see also *Ding Ling ziliao ji*, pp. 9–15, and Fokkema, *Literary Doctrine*, pp. 154–62, for other details of the campaign against Ding and Chen.

48. Chang, *Ting Ling*, p. 142; Merle Goldman, *Literary Dissent*, p. 216; *Ding Ling ziliao ji*, pp. 18–20. Several criticisms of Ding are translated in Nieh, *Literature of the Hundred Flowers*, 2/266–72.

49. Chang, *Ting Ling*, pp. 143–44; see also the analysis by Yi-tsi Feuerwerker in "Discussion," pp. 270–79. The cartoon is printed in *Ding Ling shiliao*, p. 1.

50. Zhang Guangnian, "Shafei nushi zai Yanan," p. 11; also *Wenyi bao*, no. 2 (1958), p. 2, editorial; and ibid., no. 3 (1958), pp. 22–24, for an attack on her "When I Was in Xia Village."

51. An excellent summary is given in Meisner, *Mao's China*, pp. 230–41; see also Byung-joon Ahn, "The Political Economy of the People's Commune in China," pp. 632–37.

52. Bai Jieming, "Ding Ling," pp. 90–91.

53. Ibid., p. 91, and Liu Wenyong, "Fang Ding Ling," p. 76.

CHAPTER 13 / THE NOISE OF THE RENEGADES

1. Richard Baum, *Prelude to Revolution*, gives an excellent summary of Chinese politics in the early 1960s. On the problems of will and voluntarism in Maoism see the analysis by Frederic Wakeman, Jr., of Mao's debt to Friedrich Paulsen in *History and Will*, pp. 202–205. On perpetual struggle see ibid., pp. 320–26, and John Bryan Starr, *Continuing the Revolution*, pp. 300–308.

2. Baum, *Prelude to Revolution*, pp. 56–57, and chapter 4 on the "T'aoyüan Experience."

3. Ibid., pp. 117–21. On Dazhai's earlier history and the role of its leader Chen Yonggui, see Mitch Meisner, "Dazhai: The Mass Line in Practice," pp. 30–45, and Byung-joon Ahn, "The Political Economy of the People's Commune in China," p. 647.

4. The Lei Feng cult has been analyzed by Mary Sheridan in "The Emulation of Heroes," pp. 48–51, and Ewa Chomczyńska, "Chinese Youth Personality Models in the Sixties," pp. 103–107. An excellent example of Mao's reminiscent yet revolutionary style in 1964 is in Mao Zedong, *Chairman Mao Talks to the People*, pp. 197–211.

5. Cited in Hsu Kai-yu, *Literature of the People's Republic of China*, p. 645. On Shao see also D. W. Fokkema, "Chinese Criticism of Humanism," pp. 77–78, and two essays by Merle Goldman: "The

Unique 'Blooming and Contending' of 1961–62," pp. 69–70, and "The Chinese Communist Party's 'Cultural Revolution' of 1962–1964," pp. 246–51.

6. Shao's earlier attacks on Ding Ling are discussed in Merle Goldman, *Literary Dissent in Communist China*, pp. 226, 239; see also Hsu, *Literature of the People's Republic*, p. 651.

7. Cited in Hsu, *Literature of the People's Republic*, p. 759.

8. Lao She, *Fuxing ji*, p. 32, following the translation in Vincent C. Y. Shih, "Lao-she a Conformist?," p. 318. Ibid., pp. 312–13, presents examples of Lao She's attacks on his colleagues as also being high sarcasm. This is a difficult area of analysis, and of course most spokesmen in the People's Republic claim Lao She was consistently loyal to Chairman Mao. Lao She's wife points out they had indeed been treated well by the state; see Hu Xieqing, *Lao She shenghuo yu chuangzuo zishu*, p. 557.

9. For a very detailed analysis of the first year of the Cultural Revolution see Lee Hong Yung, *The Politics of the Chinese Cultural Revolution*. Useful essays are collected in Thomas W. Robinson, ed., *The Cultural Revolution in China* (see especially Robinson's own essay on Zhou Enlai's involvement). On the links between the Red Guard struggle and the youths' own families, see David Raddock, "Between Generations," pp. 523–24; for the packing of the party with new members see Lynn T. White, "Workers' Politics in Shanghai," p. 114. On the new "post-Lei Feng generation" of Cultural Revolution heroes, their class backgrounds, military service and dramatic deaths, see Chomczyńska, "Chinese Youth Personality Models," pp. 112–13. Mary Sheridan, "Young Women Leaders in China," pp. 76–83, shows how women exemplars failed to get included at these more dramatic levels.

10. Lee Hong Yung, *Politics of the Chinese Cultural Revolution*, p. 173, note 127, on the Lu Xun Corps; on Qu Qiubai's tomb see Ding Ling, "Wo suo renshide Qu Qiubai tongzhi," p. 162, and the excellent coverage in Li Yu-ning, "The Vicissitudes of Chinese Communist Historiography," pp. 253–56.

11. John Israel, "The Red Guards in Historical Perspective," p. 10, and *China News Analysis* no. 636 (Nov. 11, 1966), pp. 3–4. On the importance of personnel files generally, see Lee Hong Yung, *Politics of the Chinese Cultural Revolution*, pp. 50–51. Andrew G. Walder gives a meticulous account of Shanghai contradictions in *Chang Ch'un-ch'iao and Shanghai's January Revolution*.

12. Interview with Roma and Stuart Gelder, cited in Ranbir Vohra, *Lao She and the Chinese Revolution*, p. 164, and Paul Bady, "Death and the Novel," p. 13.

13. See the last lines of Lao She's *Zhenghongqi xia*, printed in Hu Xieqing, *Lao She shenghuo*, p. 350. (The uncompleted draft first appeared in *Renmin wenxue* in spring 1979.) Bady, "Death and the Novel," p. 9, points out that Lao She knew the purged Beijing

mayor Peng Zhen and the disgraced army chief of staff Lo Rui-qing, and had defended Wu Han.

14. The evidence for his death is meticulously sifted by Bady in "Death and the Novel," pp. 8, 17–20; Bady points out that many inconsistencies remain in the various versions. Bady, p. 19, also translated a section of Zang Kejia's important memoir, "Lao She yongzai," which gives a detailed account of the friendship of the two men; Zang Kejia, p. 90, records their final phone conversation. Lao She's wife, Hu Xieqing, gives a moving account of their last days together, and her discovery of the body after an anonymous phone call, in *Lao She shenghuo*, pp. 558–61.

15. Bai Jieming, "Ding Ling," p. 91. The violent disruptiveness of the Cultural Revolution in Heilongjiang is examined by Margie Sargent, "The Cultural Revolution in Heilungkiang," especially pp. 27–28, 45–46.

16. See her interview with Liu Wenyong, "Fang Ding Ling," p. 78 (Liu cites several of Chen's notes which were published in issue no. 3 [1979] of *Shiyue*), and her own reminiscence "Guanyu Du Wanxiang," which has moving passages on a labor heroine in the Lobei area and on the unfair treatment Du received.

17. Translated by Hsu Kai-yu (from *Thousands of Songs Dedicated to the Party*, pp. 32–33) in *The Chinese Literary Scene*, pp. 259–60; cited with minor changes. An even-handed assessment of visual art in the Cultural Revolution is Ralph Croizier's "Chinese Art in the Chiang Ch'ing Era"; Jiang Qing's own views are expressed at length in Roxane Witke, *Comrade Chiang Ch'ing*.

18. Liu Wenyong, "Fang Ding Ling," p. 77, and Bai Jieming, "Ding Ling," p. 91.

19. Liu Wenyong, "Fang Ding Ling," pp. 77–78.

20. Ibid., p. 78. I accept this version over her more cheerful and briefer account in Bai Jieming, "Ding Ling," p. 91.

21. Interview of May 11, 1963, in Hsu, *Chinese Literary Scene*, pp. 132–39. Nieh Hua-ling, *Shen Ts'ung-wen*, cites his 1962 poem.

22. Merle Goldman, "China's Anti-Confucian Campaign, 1973–74"; the historiographical dimensions of the Qin Shi Hoangdi model are examined by Li Yu-ning in *The First Emperor of China*; see especially pp. 180–90, "Why Did Lin Piao Revile Ch'in Shih-huang?" For sending the youth to the countryside see D. Gordon White, "The Politics of *Hsia-hsiang* Youth"; and Thomas P. Bernstein, *Up to the Mountains and Down to the Villages*, pp. 96–112, on the perceived unfairness of the selection process.

23. Li-Yi-Zhe, "Concerning Socialist Democracy and Legal System," pp. 114–20. Background on the authors is given in ibid., pp. 110–11, and in Wang Hsueh-wen, "Revolutionary Youth and the Li I-che Poster," p. 80. On their background in the Guangzhou context see Stanley Rosen, "The Radical Students in Kwangtung During the Cultural Revolution," especially pp. 393–95. I was first

led to consider the important question of "special access" as being parallel to a class phenomenon by Frederic Wakeman, Jr., "The Use and Abuse of Ideology in the Study of Contemporary China," p. 145, note 2; a more detailed discussion of this Chinese "embourgeoisement" is given in John Bryan Starr, *Continuing the Revolution*, pp. 116–28.

24. Li-Yi-Zhe, "Concerning Socialist Democracy," pp. 134, 140, 148. The official party rebuttals of their stance have been translated by "Xuan Jiwen" ("Collected Propaganda Essays") under the title "Criticizing 'Concerning Socialist Democracy and Legal System.' "

25. Summary in Maurice Meisner, *Mao's China*, pp. 374–79; text of the 1974 Constitution in Mark Selden, *The People's Republic of China*, pp. 571–75, quotation p. 575.

26. Bai Jieming, "Ding Ling," pp. 91–92, and Liu Wenyong, "Fang Ding Ling," p. 75.

27. There were many recordings of this scene. Nearly four hundred of the eulogies and poems to Zhou, along with photos of the ceremonies, were printed in *Bingchen Qingming shichao*. An analysis of Beijing students' responses is given by David S. Zweig in "The Peita Debate on Education and the Fall of Teng Hsiao-p'ing," pp. 146, 155–58.

28. The Central Committee's assessment of Mao's "Will" is printed in *China Quarterly* 68 (December 1976): 875–78. All members of the "Gang of Four" had been removed from the photos of the funeral ceremonies when these were released later in October, although earlier press photos clearly showed them all as having been present. Witke, *Comrade Chiang Ch'ing*, gives a good selection of anti–Jiang Qing posters. On the Tangshan earthquake and the damage and casualty estimates see the report by Walter Sullivan in *The New York Times*, June 11, 1979, p. 2.

29. Selden, *People's Republic*, pp. 688, 699. For essays analyzing the scope of the proposed changes see Richard Baum, ed., *China's Four Modernizations*, and especially the essay by Thomas Fingar, pp. 61–101.

30. Ibid., p. 694.

31. *Peking Review*, no. 12 (Mar. 24, 1978), pp. 11–12 (cited with minor changes); also cited in Selden, *People's Republic*, p. 703.

32. James D. Seymour, ed., *The Fifth Modernization*, p. 291, lists thirty such new organizations and periodicals. A wide selection of translations is given in David S. G. Goodman, ed. and trans., *Beijing Street Voices*; facsimiles of the late 1978 and early 1979 underground magazines, along with tables of contents and sample excerpts, appeared in a special number of *China Monthly* (*Zhongguo ren*, vol. 1, no. 5); Howard Goldblatt also gives an introduction to the range of materials in "Underground Literature in Contemporary China." The complexity and range of many other authors of

theoretical essays (besides Wei Jingsheng) can be seen from the selections in *Translations from Beijing Unofficial Journals*—for example, the essays in *Sea Spray (Hailanghua)*, on pp. 67–73, 74–85, and 86–105. The preamble to the Constitution is from Selden, *People's Republic*, p. 691.

33. Seymour, *Fifth Modernization*, p. 251, citing the magazine *Beijing Spring* for Jan. 27, 1979.

34. A vivid first-person account of the November 1978 forums and the effect of Wei's poster is given by Lu Lin, "The Story of *Exploration* Magazine." Lu Lin in "The Masses and the Criminal Law," *Translations from Beijing Unofficial Journals*, pp. 30–34, also gives detailed biographical material on Wei. Lee Ta-ling and Miriam London, "A Dissenter's Odyssey Through Mao's China," have published a version of Wei's own account of his turbulent Red Guard years.

35. Lu Lin, "Masses and Criminal Law," p. 38. Wei Jingsheng's "Fifth Modernization" is printed (in translation) in its entirety in Seymour, *Fifth Modernization*, pp. 47–69. The concept of generations in this recent period of Chinese history is explored by Michael Yahuda, "Political Generations in China," especially pp. 802–803, and by David M. Raddock, "Between Generations."

36. Cited in *SPEAHRhead*, 6/7, pp. 36–37.

37. Author's observation of Beijing and Shanghai bookstores in 1974 during the "Pi Lin pi Kong" campaign; on the use of Lu Xun as a premature critic of the Gang of Four see Frederic Wakeman's discussion of Lu, Zhang Chunqiao, and Yao Wenyuan's father in "Historiography in China after 'Smashing the "Gang of Four," ' " pp. 899–900.

38. Cited in *SPEAHRhead*, 6/7, pp. 44–45, from *Democracy and Modernity*, March 1979.

39. Cited in *SPEAHRhead*, 6/7, p. 37, from *April 5 Forum*, Apr. 1, 1979.

40. Cited in *Translations from Beijing Unofficial Journals* (from *Exploration*, Sept. 9, 1979), p. 23.

41. Cited in *SPEAHRhead*, 6/7, p. 33, from *Enlightenment*, Jan. 29, 1979.

42. English translation in Seymour, *Fifth Modernization*, pp. 219–21. For Chinese text see Wei Jingsheng et al., *Kending ziyou, kending minzhu*, pp. 35–40. Wei's friend Pingui and her imprisoned father (he was of Tibetan stock) are discussed by Zhuang Mei in "Wei Jingsheng de nüyou."

43. Trial transcript in *Translations from Beijing Unofficial Journals*, pp. 45–46. The complete Chinese transcript is given in Wei Jingsheng et al., *Beijing zhi chun shiwen xuan*, pp. 188–253.

44. *Translations from Beijing Unofficial Journals*, pp. 50–51.

45. Ibid., pp. 51–53.

46. Stories carried in *The New York Times*, Nov. 12, Nov. 13, and Dec. 19, 1979, and Jan. 18, 1980. *Subao* example is in *Translations from Beijing Unofficial Journals*, p. 55.

47. Ding Ling, "Jiang yidian xinli hua," pp. 51–52. On the fourth writers' congress see *China Quarterly* 81 (March 1980): 166–67. Much of Ding's speech is translated by Nieh Hua-ling in her introduction to *Literature of the Hundred Flowers*, 1/xliv–xlv.

48. Ding Ling, "Jiang yidian xinli hua," p. 52.

49. The slowness of the change in women's status is discussed in Kay Ann Johnson, "Women in China"; see especially p. 297 on the situation in 1957–58, and p. 308 on the early 1970s. On certain heroic attributes granted to women's status in the 1960s see Mary Sheridan, "Young Women Leaders in China"; Phyllis Andors, "Politics of Chinese Development," pp. 105–110, shows an increase in certain *inequalities*. In *Feminism and Socialism in China*, chapter 10, Elisabeth Croll discusses the problems of women in the Cultural Revolution, while her 1977 essay "A Recent Movement to Redefine the Role and Status of Women" illustrates the ongoing perceptions of problems in the mid-1970s. On slowness of change within the rural family unit see William L. Parish, "Socialism and the Chinese Peasant Family," p. 620.

50. For background on Fu Yuehua (which gives less significance to the sexual aspects of the case than do other sources) see Arlette Laduguie, "The Human Rights Movement," pp. 19–20. Trial accounts were given in *The New York Times*, Nov. 8, 1979, and Jan. 8, 1980. A good analysis of the case is made by Gong Zhiyan in "Fu Yuehua anjian"; protests on behalf of Fu Yuehua in unofficial journals are cited by Seymour, *Fifth Modernization*, pp. 102–104, 256–59. See also Wei Jingsheng et al., *Kending ziyou*, pp. 125–39.

51. Cited in Laduguie, "Human Rights Movement," p. 26.

52. The proceedings of a number of conferences on the Sino-Japanese War of 1894–95, problems of modernization, and the 1898 reform movement appeared in various 1980 numbers of the *Foreign Broadcast Information Service* (*FBIS*): see *FBIS* (PRC-80), no. 148 (July 30, 1980) (L11–L17) on the Sino-Japanese War; no. 132 (July 8, 1980) (L4–L8) and no. 141 (July 21, 1980) (L7–L9) on 1898; and no. 157 (L13) and no. 162 (L13) on Westernization, frontier defense, and comparisons with the Meiji reforms.

53. A good summary of the latest birth-control regulations is provided by Pedro Pak-tao Ng, "Planned Fertility and Fertility Socialization in Kwangtung Province," on implementation of the "late, sparse and few" programs. Recent reports from China detail the incentives (negative and positive) given to late marriage, efficient (supervised) birth control, and one-child families. An important study on the background of the program is Janet Salaff, "Institutionalized Motivation for Fertility Limitation."

54. Translated in David S. G. Goodman, "Poems of the Democracy Movement," p. 29. Other poems from the same magazine, *Jintian* (*Today*), are given in Wei Jingsheng et al., *Beijing zhi chun*, pp. 346–56.

SOURCES OF ILLUSTRATIONS

Frontispiece: *Zikai manhua quanji*, vol. 4, *Minjian Xiang*, no. 59. #1: *Guofu yu Jiang Zongtong huazhuan* (Taibei, 1976), p. 20. #2: *Qingji mingren shouzha*, p. 829. #3: Li Yunguang, *Kang Youwei jiashu*, p. 208. #4: Chang P'eng-yüan, *Liang Qichao yu Qingji geming* (Taibei, 1964), frontispiece. #5: John Lust, ed. and trans., *Tsou Jung*, facing p. 51; from *Min-pao*, no. 7 (July 1906). #6: *Lu Xun 1881–1936*, plate 8. #7: *Qiu Jin Shiji*, p. 1. #8: *Lu Xun 1881–1936*, plate 13. #9: *Guofu yu Jiang Zongtong huazhuan*, p. 54. #10: *Guofu yu Jiang Zongtong huazhuan*, p. 65. #11: Sekiya Jūrō, *Yuan Shikai*, frontispiece. #12: *Qingji mingren shouzha*, p. 851. #13: Lo Jung-pang, *Symposium*, p. 250. #14: *Jinian Zhou Enlai Zongli* (Beijing, 1978), plate 3. #15: *Shouhu*, no. 1 (1980), p. 186. #16 and #17: *Jinian Xiang Jingyu tongzhi*. #18: *Shaoshan Mao Zedong*, plate 23. #19 and #20: Qu Qiubai, *Wenji*, vol. 1. #21: Okano Masujiro, *Wu Peifu*. #22: Qu Qiubai, *Wenji*, vol. 3, frontispiece. #23: *China Pictorial*, no. 10 (Nov. 1, 1980), p. 9. #24, Xu Zhimo, *Quanji*, vol. 1, p. 37. #25: Xu Zhimo, *Quanji*, vol. 1, p. 48. # 26: Stephen Hay, *Asian Ideas of East and West*, facing p. 111, courtesy of Rabindra-Bhavana, Visva-Bharati. #27: Li Yunguang, *Kang Youwei jiashu*, p. 209. #28: Rabindranath Tagore and Leonard Elmhirst, *Rabindranath Tagore, Pioneer in Education*, frontispiece. #29: *Guofu yu Jiang Zongtong huazhuan*, p. 115. #30: *Wen Yiduo Quanji*, vol. 1. #31: *Shaoshan Mao Zedong* (Beijing, 1978), plate 42. #32: *Lu Xun shoucang . . . muke*, no. 23. #33: Xu Zhimo, *Quanji*, vol. 1, p. 58. #34: Xu Zhimo, *Quanji*, vol. 4, p. 550. #35: Xu Zhimo, *Quanji*, vol. 1, p. 43. #36: *Lu Xun shoucang . . . muke*, no. 73. #37: *Lu Xun 1881–1936*, plate 69. #38: *Lu Xun 1881–1936*, plate 54. #39: *Shaoshan Mao Zedong*, plate 54. #40: *Jianguo da gang*, ninetieth anniversary volume (Beijing), Renmin Meishu Chubanshe, 1956. #41: *Guofu yu Jiang Zongtong huazhuan*, p. 132. #42: *New Masses*, vol. 7, no. 1 (June 1931), p. 14. #43: Xu Zhimo, *Quanji*, vol. 1, p. 62. #44: *Ding Ling pingzhuan*, facing p. 1. #45: Lao She, *Lao niu po che*, Paul Bady, ed. and trans., frontispiece. #46: *Lu Xun 1881–1936*, plate 80. #47: *Chengming*, no. 31 (May 1, 1980), p. 16. #48: Qu Qiubai, *Wenji*, vol. 4, frontispiece. #49: *Lu Xun 1881–1936*, plate 95. #50: *Lu Xun shoucang . . . muke*, no. 49. #51: *China Pictorial*, no. 10 (Nov. 1, 1980). #52: *Jinian Zhou Enlai Zongli*, p. 45. #53: *Woodcuts of Wartime China 1937–1945*, no. 25. #54: *Yonghuai lingxiu*, Li Ming Cultural Enterprise Co. (Taibei), p. 57. #55: *Wen Yiduo Quanji*, vol. 1. #56: *Lu Xun shoucang . . . muke*, no. 16. #57: *Kaixiang*, 2:5 (December 1979), pp. 27–28. #58: *Ding Ling shiliao*, p. 1. #59: *Wangshi yu aisi* (Shanghai, 1979), p. 34. #60: *Bingchen Qingming Shichao*. #61: *Mingbao*, no. 167 (November 1979), p. 97. #62: *Mingbao*, no. 169 (January 1980), frontispiece.

Bibliography

Ahn, Byung-joon. "The Political Economy of the People's Commune in China: Changes and Continuities," *Journal of Asian Studies* 34 (May 1975): 631–58.

Alitto, Guy S. *The Last Confucian: Liang Shu-ming and the Chinese Dilemma of Modernity.* Berkeley, 1979.

Andors, Phyllis. "Politics of Chinese Development: The Case of Women, 1960–1966." *Signs: Journal of Women in Culture and Society* 2:1 (1976), pp. 84–119.

Armentrout-Ma, Eve M. B. "Chinese Politics in the Western Hemisphere, 1893–1911: Rivalry Between Reformers and Revolutionaries in the Americas." Ph.D. dissertation, University of California at Davis, 1977.

Ash, Robert. "Economic Aspects of Land Reform in Kiangsu, 1949–52. Part 1, *China Quarterly* 66 (June 1976): 261–92; part 2, *China Quarterly* 67 (September 1976): 519–45.

Bady, Paul. "Death and the Novel—On Lao She's 'Suicide,'" and "Rehabilitation: A Chronological Postscript." Both in *Renditions*, no. 10 (Autumn 1978), pp. 5–20.

———. See also Lao She, *Lao niu po che.*

Bai Jieming (Geremie Barmé). "Ding Ling: Manhua ershinian zaoji" [Ding Ling: A Discussion of Twenty Difficult Years]. *Qishi niandai,* no. 8 (1979), pp. 90–92.

Bauer, Wolfgang. *China and the Search for Happiness: Recurring Themes in Four Thousand Years of Chinese Cultural History.* Translated by Michael Shaw. New York, 1976.

Baum, Richard. *Prelude to Revolution: Mao, the Party, and the Peasant Question, 1962–66.* New York, 1975.

————, ed. China's Four Modernizations: The New Technological Revolution. Boulder, Colo., 1980.

BDRC: Biographical Dictionary of Republican China. Edited by Howard Boorman and Richard Howard. 4 vols. New York, 1967. Vol. 5, A Personal Name Index, compiled by Janet Krompart. New York, 1979.

Beahan, Charlotte L. "Feminism and Nationalism in the Chinese Women's Press, 1902–1911." Modern China 1 (1975): 379–416.

————. "The Women's Movement and Nationalism in Late Ch'ing China." Ph.D. dissertation, Columbia University, 1976.

Bedeski, Robert E., "The Tutelary State and National Revolution in Kuomintang Ideology, 1928–31." China Quarterly 46 (April–June 1971): 308–30.

Benton, Gregor. "The Yenan 'Literary Opposition.' " New Left Review 92 (July–August 1975): 93–106.

Berkley, Gerald W. "The Canton Peasant Movement Training Institute." Modern China 1 (1975): 161–79.

Bernal, Martin. Chinese Socialism to 1907. Ithaca, N.Y., 1976.

Bernstein, Thomas P. "Leadership and Mass Mobilization in the Soviet and Chinese Collectivisation Campaigns of 1929–30 and 1955–56: A Comparison." China Quarterly 31 (July–September 1967): 1–47.

————. Up to the Mountains and Down to the Villages, The Transfer of Youth from Urban to Rural China. New Haven, 1977.

Bingchen Qingming shichao [Poems from the Qingming Festival in 1976]. Hong Kong, 1978.

Birch, Cyril. "English and Chinese Metres in Hsü Chih-mo," Asia Major, N.S. 8:2 (1961), pp. 258–93.

————. "Fiction of the Yenan Period." China Quarterly 4 (October–December 1960): 1–11.

————. "Lao She: The Humourist in His Humour." China Quarterly 8 (October–December 1961): 45–62.

————, ed. Anthology of Chinese Literature. Vol. 2, From the Fourteenth Century to the Present Day. New York, 1972.

Bix, Herbert P. "Japanese Imperialism and the Manchurian Economy, 1900–31." China Quarterly 51 (July–September 1972): 425–43.

Bjorge, Gary John. "Ting Ling's Early Years: Her Life and Literature Through 1942." Ph.D. dissertation, University of Wisconsin, 1977.

Broido, Vera. Apostles into Terrorists: Women and the Revolutionary Movement in the Russia of Alexander II. New York, 1977.

Buxbaum, David C., and Frederick Mote, eds. Transition and Permanence: Chinese History and Culture. A Festschrift in Honor of Dr. Hsiao Kung-ch'üan. Hong Kong, 1972.

Chan, F. Gilbert, and Thomas H. Etzold, eds. China in the 1920s: Nationalism and Revolution. New York, 1976.

Chang Hao. Liang Ch'i-ch'ao and Intellectual Transition in China, 1890–1907. Cambridge, Mass., 1971.

Chang Jun-mei. *Ting Ling: Her Life and Work*. Taipei, 1978.

Chen Dongyuan. *Zhongguo funü shenghuo shi* [History of Women in China]. Shanghai, 1937.

Ch'en, Jerome. "Resolutions of the Tsunyi Conference." *China Quarterly* 40 (October–December 1969): 1–38.

Chen, Joseph T. *The May Fourth Movement in Shanghai: The Making of a Social Movement in Modern China*. Leiden, 1971.

Chen Shaoxiao. *Heigang lu* [History of Guomindang Secret Operations]. Hong Kong, 1966.

Ch'eng I-fan. "*Kung* as an Ethos in Late Nineteenth-Century China: The Case of Wang Hsien-ch'ien (1842–1918)." In Cohen and Schrecker, eds., *Reform in Nineteenth-Century China*, pp. 170–80.

Chesneaux, Jean. *The Chinese Labor Movement, 1919–1927*. Translated by H. M. Wright. Stanford, 1968.

————, ed. *Popular Movements and Secret Societies in China, 1840–1950*. Stanford, 1972.

Ch'i Hsi-sheng. *Warlord Politics in China, 1916–1928*. Stanford, 1976.

Chi, Madeleine. "Bureaucratic Capitalists in Operation: Ts'ao Ju-lin and His New Communications Clique, 1916–1919." *Journal of Asian Studies* 34 (May 1975): 675–88.

Ch'ien Tuan-sheng. *The Government and Politics of China, 1912–1949*. Stanford, 1970.

Chomczyńska, Ewa. "Chinese Youth Personality Models in the Sixties." *Asian and African Studies* (Bratislava) 15 (1979): 101–116.

Chou, Prudence Sui-ning. "Lao She: An Intellectual's Role and Dilemma in Modern China." Ph.D. dissertation, University of California at Berkeley, 1976.

Chow Tse-tsung. *The May Fourth Movement: Intellectual Revolution in Modern China*. Cambridge, Mass., 1960.

Chung, Sue Fawn. "The Image of the Empress Dowager Tz'u-Hsi." In Cohen and Schrecker, eds., *Reform in Nineteenth-Century China*, pp. 101–110.

Clifford, Nicholas R. *Shanghai, 1925: Urban Nationalism and the Defense of Foreign Privilege*. Michigan Papers in Chinese Studies, no. 37. Ann Arbor, 1979.

Coble, Parks M., Jr. "The Kuomintang Regime and the Shanghai Capitalists, 1927–1929." *China Quarterly* 77 (March 1979): 1–24.

Cochran, Sherman. *Big Business in China: Sino-Foreign Rivalry in the Cigarette Industry, 1890–1930*. Cambridge, Mass., 1980.

Cohen, Paul A., and John E. Schrecker, eds. *Reform in Nineteenth-Century China*. Cambridge, Mass., 1976.

Cole, James H. "The Shaoxing Connection: A Vertical Administrative Clique in Late Qing China." *Modern China* 6 (July 1980): 317–26.

Compton, Boyd, ed. and trans. *Mao's China: Party Reform Documents, 1942–44*. Seattle, 1966.

Croizier, Ralph. "Chinese Art in the Chiang Ch'ing Era." *Journal of Asian Studies* 38 (February 1979): 303–11.

Croll, Elisabeth. *Feminism and Socialism in China.* London, 1978.

———. "A Recent Movement to Redefine the Role and Status of Women." *China Quarterly* 71 (September 1977): 591–97.

Crowley, James B. *Japan's Quest for Autonomy: National Security and Foreign Policy, 1930–1938.* Princeton, 1966.

Davin, Delia. "Women in the Liberated Areas." In Marilyn Young, ed., *Women in China,* pp. 73–91.

Davis, Fei-ling. *Primitive Revolutionaries of China: A Study of Secret Societies in the Late Nineteenth Century.* Honolulu, 1977.

Day, M. Henri. *Mao Zedong 1917–1927, Documents.* Orientaliska Studier, no. 14. Stockholm, 1975.

Ding Ling. "Guanyu Du Wanxiang" [On the Life of Du Wanxiang]. *Beifang wenxue* 3 (1980): 49–52.

———. "In the Hospital." Translated by Susan M. Vacca. *Renditions,* no. 8 (Autumn 1977), pp. 123–35.

———. "Jiang yidian xinli hua" [Some Words from the Heart]. *Hongqi (Red Flag)* 12 (1979): 51–52.

———. *Muqin* [Mother]. Shanghai, 1933.

———. "Sanbajie yougan" [Thoughts on March 8]. *Wenyi bao,* no. 2 (1958), pp. 8–10.

———(Ting Ling). *The Sun Shines over the Sangkan River.* Translated by Yang Hsien-yi and Gladys Yang. Beijing, 1954.

———. "When I Was in Xia Village." Translated by Kung Pu-sheng as "When I Was in Sha Chuan (Cloud Village)." Reprinted in *Signs: Journal of Women in Culture and Society* 2:1 (1976), pp. 270–79.

———. "Wo dui 'Duoyu de hua' de lijie" [My Interpretation of "Superfluous Words"]. *Guangming Ribao,* March 21, 1980.

———. "Wo suo renshide Qu Qiubai tongzhi" [The Qu Qiubai That I Remember]. *Xinhua yuebao* [Literary Supplement], no. 5 (1980), pp. 155–63.

———. "Xiang Jingyu tongzhi liugei wo de yingxiang" [Xiang Jingyu's Lasting Influence on Me]. *Shouhu,* no. 1 (1980), pp. 184–86, 232.

———. *Yanan ji* [Records from Yanan], Beijing, 1954.

———. *Yige xiaohongjun de gushi* [The Story of a Little Red Soldier]. Shanghai, 1956.

———. *Zai yanhan de rizi li* [In the Bitter Cold Days]. Part 1, *Qingming* 1:1 (1979), pp. 4–92.

———. "Zai yiyuan zhong" [In the Hospital]. *Wenyi bao,* no. 2 (1958), pp. 11–16.

Ding Ling pingzhuan [Essays by and About Ding Ling]. Edited by Zhang Baiyun. Shanghai, 1934.

Ding Ling shiliao [Historical Materials on Ding Ling]. Hong Kong, 1976.

Ding Ling xuanji [Selected Stories of Ding Ling]. Beijing, 1951.

Ding Ling zai xibei [Ding Ling in Northwest China]. Edited by Shi Tianxing. Hankou, 1938.

Ding Ling ziliao ji [Collected Materials on Ding Ling]. Collection 1. Hong Kong, June 1971.

Dirlik, Arif. "The Ideological Foundations of the New Life Movement: A Study in Counterrevolution." *Journal of Asian Studies* 34 (August 1975): 945–80.

———. *Revolution and History: The Origins of Marxist Historiography in China, 1919–1937.* Berkeley, 1978.

Doleželová-Velingerová, Milena. "Lu Xun's 'Medicine.'" In Merle Goldman, ed., *Modern Chinese Literature*, pp. 221–31.

Doolin, Dennis J. *Communist China: The Politics of Student Opposition* [a translation of "Look, What Kind of Talk Is This?" dated June 14, 1957]. Hoover Institution, Stanford University, 1964.

Dorris, Carl E. "Peasant Mobilization in North China and the Origins of Yenan Communism." *China Quarterly* 68 (December 1976): 697–719.

Duiker, William J. *Ts'ai Yüan-p'ei: Educator of Modern China*, University Park, Pa., 1977.

Dutt, Vidya Prakash. "The First Week of Revolution: The Wuchang Uprising." In Mary C. Wright, ed., *China in Revolution*, pp. 383–416.

Eastman, Lloyd E. *The Abortive Revolution: China Under Nationalist Rule, 1927–1937.* Cambridge, Mass., 1974.

Eber, Irene. "Images of Oppressed Peoples and Modern Chinese Literature." In Merle Goldman, ed., *Modern Chinese Literature*, pp. 127–41.

———. "Images of Women in Recent Chinese Fiction: Do Women Hold Up Half the Sky?" *Signs: Journal of Women in Culture and Society* 2:1 (1976), pp. 24–34.

———. *Voices from Afar: Modern Chinese Writers on Oppressed People and Their Literature.* Michigan Papers in Chinese Studies, no. 38. Ann Arbor, 1980.

ECCP: Eminent Chinese of the Ch'ing Period [1644–1912]. Edited by Arthur W. Hummel. 2 vols. Washington, D.C., 1943.

Eide, Elisabeth. "Ibsen's Nora and Chinese Interpretations of Female Emancipation." In *Modern Chinese Literature and Its Social Context*, edited by Göran Malmqvist, pp. 140–51. Nobel Symposium, no. 32. Stockholm, 1977.

Esherick, Joseph. *Reform and Revolution in China: The 1911 Revolution in Hunan and Hubei.* Berkeley, 1976.

Eto Shinkichi. "Hai-lu-feng—the First Chinese Soviet Government." Part 1, *China Quarterly* 8 (October–December 1961): 161–83; part 2, *China Quarterly* 9 (January–March 1962): 149–81.

Fairbank, John K., ed. *The Cambridge History of China.* Vol. 10, *Late Ch'ing, 1800–1911*, part I. New York, 1978.

Feng Zikai. *Zikai manhua quanji* [Collected Drawings]. 6 vols. Vol. 2, *Ertong xiang*: vol. 4, *Minjian xiang*: vol. 5, *Dushi xiang*. Shanghai, 1948.

Feuerwerker, Albert. *China's Early Industrialization: Sheng Hsuan-huai (1844–1916) and Mandarin Enterprise*. Cambridge, Mass., 1958.

———. *Economic Trends in the Republic of China, 1912–1949*. Michigan Papers in Chinese Studies, no. 31. Ann Arbor, 1977.

Feuerwerker, Albert, Rhoads Murphey, and Mary C. Wright, eds. *Approaches to Modern Chinese History*. Berkeley, 1967.

Feuerwerker, Yi-tsi M. "The Changing Relationship Between Literature and Life: Aspects of the Writer's Role in Ding Ling." In Merle Goldman, ed., *Modern Chinese Literature*, pp. 281–307.

———. "Discussion" (accompanying the translation of Ding Ling's "When I Was in Xia Village"). *Signs: Journal of Women in Culture and Society* 2:1 (1976), pp. 270–79.

———. "Women as Writers in the 1920's and 1930's." In Wolf and Witke, eds., *Women in Chinese Society*, pp. 143–68.

Fogel, Joshua A. "Race and Class in Chinese Historiography: Divergent Interpretations of Zhang Binglin and Anti-Manchuism in the 1911 Revolution." *Modern China* 3 (1977): 346–75.

Fogel, Joshua A., and William T. Rowe, eds. *Perspectives on a Changing China: Essays in Honor of Professor C. Martin Wilbur on the Occasion of His Retirement*. Boulder, Colo., 1979.

Fokkema, D. W. "Chinese Criticism of Humanism: Campaigns Against the Intellectuals, 1964–1965." *China Quarterly* 26 (April–June 1966): 68–81.

———. *Literary Doctrine in China and Soviet Influence* [1956–60]. The Hague, 1965.

———. "Lu Xun: The Impact of Russian Literature." In Merle Goldman, ed., *Modern Chinese Literature*, pp. 89–101.

Fountain, Kevin, ed. "Ch'en Tu-hsiu: Lifetime Oppositionist." *Chinese Law and Government* 12:3 (Fall 1979).

Frenier, Mariam Darce. "Women and the Chinese Communist Party, 1921 to 1952: Changes in Party Policy and Mobilization Techniques." Ph.D. dissertation, University of Iowa, 1978.

Friedman, Edward. *Backward Toward Revolution: The Chinese Revolutionary Party*. Berkeley, 1974.

Fujii Shozo. "The Origins of Lu Xun's Literature and Philosophy: Watts' and Petofi's 'Hope.'" *Modern Chinese Literature Newsletter* 5:1–2 (Spring–Fall 1979), pp. 8–16.

Furth, Charlotte, ed. *The Limits of Change: Essays on Conservative Alternatives in Republican China*. Cambridge, Mass., 1976.

Gálik, Marián. *Mao Tun and Modern Literary Criticism*. Wiesbaden, 1969.

———. "On the Literature Written by Chinese Women Prior to 1917." *Asian and African Studies* (Bratislava) 15 (1979): 65–97.

————. "Studies in Modern Chinese Intellectual History: II, Young Ch'ü Ch'iu-pai (1915–1922)." *Asian and African Studies* (Bratislava) 12 (1976): 85–121.

————. "Studies in Modern Chinese Literary Criticism: VII, Liang Shih-ch'iu and New Humanism." *Asian and African Studies* (Bratislava) 9 (1973): 29–51.

Gao Zhen. "Yiduo xisheng qianhou jishi" [A Record of Events Around the Time of Wen Yiduo's Death]. *Xinwenxue shiliao*, no. 2 (1972), pp. 55–69.

Garavente, Anthony. "The Long March." *China Quarterly* 22 (April–June 1965): 89–124.

Garrett, Shirley. *Social Reformers in Urban China: The Chinese Y.M.C.A., 1895–1926.* Cambridge, Mass., 1970.

Gasster, Michael. *Chinese Intellectuals and the Revolution of 1911.* Seattle, 1969.

Godley, Michael R. "The Late Ch'ing Courtship of the Chinese in Southeast Asia." *Journal of Asian Studies* 34 (February 1975): 361–85.

————. "Overseas Chinese Entrepreneurs as Reformers: The Case of Chang Pi-shih." In Cohen and Schrecker, eds. *Reform in Nineteenth-Century China*, pp. 49–59.

Goldblatt, Howard. "Underground Literature in Contemporary China." *Modern Chinese Literature Newsletter* 5:1–2 (Spring–Fall 1979), pp. 1–7.

Goldman, Merle. "China's Anti-Confucian Campaign, 1973–74." *China Quarterly* 63 (September 1975): 435–62.

————. "The Chinese Communist Party's 'Cultural Revolution' of 1962–1964." In Chalmers Johnson, ed., *Ideology and Politics in Contemporary China*, pp. 219–54.

————. *Literary Dissent in Communist China.* Cambridge, Mass., 1967.

————. "The Unique 'Blooming and Contending' of 1961–62." *China Quarterly* 37 (January–March 1969): 54–83.

————, ed. *Modern Chinese Literature in the May Fourth Era.* Cambridge, Mass., 1977.

Goldman, René. "The Rectification Campaign at Peking University: May–June 1957." *China Quarterly* 12 (October–December 1962): 138–53.

Gong Zhiyan. "Fu Yuehua anjian" [The Case of Fu Yuehua]. *Qishi niandai* 122 (March 1980): 64–66.

Goodman, David S. G., ed. and trans. *Beijing Street Voices.* London, 1981.

————, ed. and trans. "Poems of the Democracy Movement." *Index on Censorship* 9 (February 1980): 27–31.

Greenblatt, Sidney Leonard. "Organizational Elites and Social Change at Peking University." In *Elites in the People's Republic of China*, edited by Robert A. Scalapino, pp. 451–97. Seattle, 1972.

Gregor, A. James, and Maria Hsia Chang. "*Nazionalfascismo* and the

Revolutionary Nationalism of Sun Yat-sen." *Journal of Asian Studies* 39 (November 1979): 21–37.

Grieder, Jerome. *Hu Shih and the Chinese Renaissance: Liberalism in the Chinese Revolution, 1917–1937.* Cambridge, Mass., 1970.

Grove, Linda. "Creating a Northern Soviet." *Modern China* 1 (July 1975): 243–70.

Guangxu Shilu [The Veritable Records of Dezong, The Emperor Guangxu]. Tokyo, 1937.

Guillermaz, J. "The Nanchang Uprising." *China Quarterly* 11 (July–September 1962): 161–68.

Gunn, Edward M. *Unwelcome Muse: Chinese Literature in Shanghai and Peking, 1937–1945.* New York, 1980.

Guo Moruo. *The Goddesses.* Translated by John Lester and A. C. Barnes. Beijing, 1978.

Hanan, Patrick. "The Technique of Lu Hsün's Fiction," *Harvard Journal of Asiatic Studies* 34 (1974): 53–96.

Harrison, James P. "The Li Li-san Line and the CCP in 1930." Part 1, *China Quarterly* 14 (April–June 1963): 178–94; part 2, *China Quarterly* 15 (July–September 1963): 140–59.

Hay, Stephen. *Asian Ideas of East and West: Tagore and His Critics in Japan, China and India.* Cambridge, Mass., 1970.

Hinton, William. *Fanshen: A Documentary of Revolution in a Chinese Village.* New York, 1967.

Ho, Kuo Cheng. "The Status and the Role of Women in the Chinese Communist Movement, 1946–1949." Ph.D. dissertation, Indiana University, 1973.

Hofheinz, Roy. *The Broken Wave: The Chinese Communist Peasant Movement, 1922–1928.* Cambridge, Mass., 1977.

Hsia, C. T. *A History of Modern Chinese Fiction, 1917–1957.* New Haven, 1961.

—————. "Yen Fu and Liang Ch'i-ch'ao as Advocates of New Fiction." In *Chinese Approaches to Literature from Confucius to Liang Ch'i-ch'ao,* edited by Adele Rickett, pp. 221–57. Princeton, 1978.

Hsia, C. T., and Joseph S. Lau, eds. *Twentieth Century Chinese Stories.* New York, 1972.

Hsia Tsi-an. *The Gate of Darkness, Studies on the Leftist Literary Movement in China.* Seattle, 1968.

Hsiao Kung-chuan. *A History of Chinese Political Thought. Vol. 1, From the Beginnings to the Sixth Century* A.D. Translated by F. W. Mote. Princeton, 1979.

—————. "K'ang Yu-wei's Excursion into Science: *Lectures on the Heavens.*" In Lo Jung-pang, ed., *Symposium,* pp. 375–407.

—————. *A Modern China and a New World: K'ang Yu-wei, Reformer and Utopian, 1858–1927.* Seattle, 1975.

Hsieh, Winston. "Triads, Salt Smugglers, and Local Uprisings: Observations on the Social and Economic Background of the Waichow

Revolution of 1911." In Jean Chesneaux, ed., *Popular Movements*, pp. 145–64.

Hsu Kai-yu. *The Chinese Literary Scene: A Writer's Visit to the People's Republic.* New York, 1975.

———. "The Intellectual Biography of a Modern Chinese Poet: Wen I-to (1899–1946)." Ph.D. dissertation, Stanford University, 1959.

———. "The Life and Poetry of Wen I-to." *Harvard Journal of Asiatic Studies* 21 (1958): 134–79.

———. *Wen I-to.* Boston, 1980.

———, ed. and trans. *Twentieth Century Chinese Poetry: An Anthology.* Ithaca, N.Y., 1970.

Hsu Kai-yu and Ting Wang, eds. *Literature of the People's Republic of China.* Bloomington, Ind., 1980.

Hu Chi-hsi. "Hua Fu, the Fifth Encirclement Campaign and the Tsunyi Conference." *China Quarterly* 43 (July–September 1970): 31–46.

———. "Mao, Lin Biao and the Fifth Encirclement Campaign." *China Quarterly* 82 (June 1980): 250–80.

———. "The Sexual Revolution in the Kiangsi Soviet." *China Quarterly* 59 (July–September 1974): 477–90.

Hu, King. "Lao She in England." Translated by Cecilia Tsim. *Renditions*, no. 10 (Autumn 1978), pp. 46–51.

Hu Xieqing, ed. *Lao She shenghuo yu chuangzuo zishu* [Lao She on His Life and Writings]. Hong Kong, 1980.

Hu Yepin. *Yepin shixuan* [Selected Poems of Hu Yepin]. Introduced by Ding Ling. Shanghai, 1929.

Huang Chang-chien. "On the Hundred Days Reform." In Cohen and Schrecker, eds., *Reform in Nineteenth-Century China*, pp. 306–309.

Huang Hsin-chyu, trans. and annotator. *Poems of Lu Hsun.* Hong Kong, 1979.

Huang, Philip. "Liang Ch'i-ch'ao: The Idea of the New Citizen and the Influence of Meiji Japan." In Buxbaum and Mote, eds., *Transition and Permanence*, pp. 71–102.

———. "Mao Tse-tung and the Middle Peasants, 1925–1928." *Modern China* 1 (1975): 271–96.

Huang Zunxian. *Renjinglu shicao jianzhu* [Annotated Edition of Huang's Collected Poems]. Shanghai, 1957.

Hummel, Arthur, ed. and trans. *The Autobiography of a Chinese Historian, Being the Preface to a Symposium on Ancient Chinese History.* Taipei, 1972.

Huters, Theodore David. "Traditional Innovation: Qian Zhong-shu and Modern Chinese Letters." Ph.D. dissertation, Stanford University, 1977.

Ichiko Chūzō. "The Role of the Gentry: An Hypothesis." In Mary Wright, ed., *China in Revolution*, pp. 297–317.

Iriye, Akira. "Public Opinion and Foreign Policy: The Case of Late

Ch'ing China." In Albert Feuerwerker et al., eds., *Approaches to Modern Chinese History*, pp. 216–38.

Isaacs, Harold. *The Tragedy of the Chinese Revolution*. 2d rev. ed. Stanford, 1961.

———, ed. *Straw Sandals: Chinese Short Stories 1918–1933*. Cambridge, Mass., 1974.

Israel, John. "The Red Guards in Historical Perspective: Continuity and Change in the Chinese Youth Movement." *China Quarterly* 30 (April–June 1967): 1–32.

———. *Student Nationalism in China* [1927–37]. Stanford, 1966.

Israel, John, and Donald W. Klein. *Rebels and Bureaucrats, China's December 9ers*. Berkeley, 1976.

Jinian Xiang Jingyu tongzhi yingyong jiuyi wushizhounian [Fiftieth Anniversary Memorial of the Courageous Comrade Xiang Jingyu]. Beijing, 1978.

Johnson, Chalmers A. *Peasant Nationalism and Communist Power: The Emergence of Revolutionary China*. Stanford, 1962.

———, ed. *Ideology and Politics in Contemporary China*. Seattle, 1973.

Johnson, Kay Ann. "Women in China: Problems of Sex Inequality and Socioeconomic Change." In *Beyond Intellectual Sexism*, edited by Joan I. Roberts, pp. 286–319. New York, 1976.

Jordan, Donald A. *The Northern Expedition: China's National Revolution of 1926–1928*. Honolulu, 1976.

Kagan, Richard Clark. "The Chinese Trotskyist Movement and Ch'en Tu-hsiu: Culture, Revolution and Polity, with an Appended Translation of Ch'en Tu-hsiu's Autobiography." Ph.D. dissertation, University of Pennsylvania, 1969.

Kang Youwei. *Datongshu* [Book of the Great Community]. Shanghai, 1935. (See also Thompson, *Ta T'ung Shu*.)

———. *Wanmu caotang yigao waibian* [Supplementary Materials by Kang Youwei, 2d Collection]. Compiled and edited by Jiang Guilin. 2 vols. Taipei, 1978.

Kang, *Memorial*: see Kang Youwei, "Shang Qingdi dier shu" [Kang's Memorial of Guangxu 21/4/8]. In *Wuxu bianfa*, vol. 2, pp. 131–66.

Kang, *Nianpu*: Kang Youwei, *Kang Nanhai zibian nianpu* [Kang's Autobiography up to 1898]. In *Wuxu bianfa*, vol. 4, pp. 107–169.

Kang, *Shiji*: Kang Youwei, *Kang Nanhai xiansheng shiji* [The Collected Poems of Kang Youwei]. 15 zhuan (1927), Wenhai chubanshe reprint. Taiwan, n.d.

Kang Nanhai xiansheng moji [Calligraphy of Kang Youwei]. In *Qingji mingren shouzha*, pp. 811–1150.

Kang Nanhai zhutian jiang [Kang Youwei's Lectures on the Heavens]. 15 zhuan. Shanghai, 1930.

Kangzhan banian muke xuanji [Selected Woodcuts from the Eight-Year Anti-Japanese War]. Shanghai, 1949.

Kao, George. "Lao She in America—Arrival and Departure." *Renditions*, no. 10 (Autumn 1978): 68–75.

Kapp, Robert A. *Szechwan and the Chinese Republic: Provincial Militarism and Central Power, 1911–1938*. New Haven, 1973.

Keenan, Barry. *The Dewey Experiment in China: Educational Reform and Political Power in the Early Republic*. Cambridge, Mass., 1977.

Kennedy, Thomas L. "Mausers and the Opium Trade: The Hupeh Arsenal, 1895–1911." In Fogel and Rowe, eds., *Perspectives on a Changing China*, pp. 113–35.

Kim, Ilpyong J. *The Politics of Chinese Communism: Kiangsi under the Soviets*. Berkeley, 1973.

King, Evan (pseudonym), trans. *Rickshaw Boy* by Lau Shaw [*sic*]. New York, 1945.

Kinkley, Jeffrey C. "Shen Ts'ung-wen's Vision of Republican China." Ph.D. dissertation, Harvard University, 1977.

Klein, Donald, and Ann Clark, eds. *Biographical Dictionary of Chinese Communism, 1921–1965*. Cambridge, Mass., 1971.

Kuhn, Philip A. "Local Self-government under the Republic: Problems of Control, Autonomy and Mobilization." In Wakeman and Grant, eds., *Conflict and Control*, pp. 257–98.

Kwong, Luke S. K. "Reflections on an Aspect of Modern China in Transition: T'an Ssu-t'ung (1865–1898) as a Reformer." In Cohen and Schrecker, eds., *Reform in Nineteenth-Century China*, pp. 184–93.

Lach, Donald. *The Preface to Leibniz' Novissima Sinica*. Honolulu, 1957.

Laduguie, Arlette. "The Human Rights Movement." *Index on Censorship* 9 (February 1980); 18–26.

Lao She. *Cat Country, A Satirical Novel of China in the 1930's*. Translated by William A. Lyell, Jr. Columbus, Ohio, 1970.

———. *Fuxing ji* [Collected Essays]. Beijing, 1958.

———. *Lao niu po che*. Edited and translated by Paul Bady. "Essai autocritique sur le roman et l'humour." *Bulletin de la Maison Franco-Japonaise*, n.s. 9, nos. 3–4, Paris, 1974.

———. *Lao She juzuo xuan* [Selected Plays of Lao She]. Beijing, 1978.

———. *Maocheng ji* [Cat City]. Xiandai shuzhu. Shanghai, 1933.

———. *Rickshaw, The Novel Lo-t'o Hsiang Tzu*. Translated by Jean M. James. Honolulu, 1979.

———. *Teahouse* (A Play in Three Acts). Translated by Ying Ruocheng. *Chinese Literature*, no. 12 (1979), pp. 16–96.

———. *Zheng hongqi xia* [In the Plain Red Banner]. In Hu Xieqing, ed., *Lao She shenghuo*, pp. 179–350.

Lao Sheh [*sic*]. "How I Came to Write the Novel 'Camel Hsiang-tzu.' " Translated in *Chinese Literature*, no. 11 (1978), pp. 59–64.

Lary, Diana. *Region and Nation: The Kwangsi Clique in Chinese Politics, 1925–1937*. New York, 1974.

———. "Warlord Studies." *Modern China* 6 (October 1980): 439–70.

Lee Hong Yung. *The Politics of the Chinese Cultural Revolution: A Case Study.* Berkeley, 1978.

Lee, Leo Ou-fan. "Genesis of a Writer: Notes on Lu Xun's Educational Experience, 1881–1909." In Merle Goldman, ed., *Modern Chinese Literature*, pp. 161–88.

———. "Literature on the Eve of Revolution: Reflections on Lu Xun's Leftist Years, 1927–1936." *Modern China* 2 (1976): 277–326.

———. *The Romantic Generation of Chinese Writers.* Cambridge, Mass., 1973.

Lee Ta-ling and Miriam London. "A Dissenter's Odyssey Through Mao's China." *New York Times Magazine*, Nov. 16, 1980, pp. 134–43.

Leith, Suzanne. "Chinese Women in the Early Communist Movement." In Marilyn Young, ed., *Women in China*, pp. 47–71.

Leung, Gaylord Kai-lóh. "Hsü Chih-mo: A Literary Biography." Ph.D. dissertation, London University, School of Oriental and African Studies, 1972.

Levenson, Joseph R. *Liang Ch'i-ch'ao and the Mind of Modern China.* Cambridge, Mass., 1959.

Lewis, Charlton M. *Prologue to the Chinese Revolution: The Transformation of Ideas and Institutions in Hunan Province, 1891–1907.* Cambridge, Mass., 1976.

Li, Dun J. *The Road to Communism: China since 1912.* New York, 1969.

Li, Lincoln. *The Japanese Army in North China, 1937–1941: Problems of Political and Economic Control.* New York, 1975.

Li-Wen an diaocha baogao shu [Report of an Investigation of the Li Gongpu and Wen Yiduo Cases]. Compiled by Liang Shuming and Zhou Xinmin. Minzhu chubanshe, n.p., 1946.

Li-Yi-Zhe. "Concerning Socialist Democracy and Legal System." Translated in *Issues and Studies* 12 (January 1976): 110–48.

Li Yunguang. *Kang Youwei jiashu kaoshi* [A Study of Kang Youwei's Family Correspondence]. Hong Kong, 1979.

Li Yu-ning. "The Vicissitudes of Chinese Communist Historiography: Ch'ü Ch'iu-pai from Martyr to Traitor." In Fogel and Rowe, eds., *Perspectives on a Changing China*, pp. 237–58.

———, ed. *The First Emperor of China: The Politics of Historiography.* White Plains, N.Y., 1975.

Li Yu-ning and Chang Yü-fa, eds. *Jindai Zhongguo nüchuan yundong shiliao* [Documents on the Feminist Movement in Modern China, 1842–1911]. 2 vols. Taipei, 1975.

Li Yu-ning and Michael Gasster. "Ch'ü Ch'iu-pai's Journey to Russia, 1920–1922." *Monumenta Serica* 29 (1970–71): 537–56.

Liang Qichao. *Nianpu: Liang Rengong xiansheng nianpu changbian chugao* [Draft Chronological Biography of Liang Qichao]. Compiled by Ding Wenjiang. Taipei, 1959.

Liang Shiqiu. *Tan Xu Zhimo* [About Xu Zhimo]. Taipei, 1958.

Liden, David Leroy. "Party Factionalism and Revolutionary Vision: Cadre Training and Mao Tse-tung's Effort to Consolidate His Control of the Chinese Communist Party, 1936–1944." Ph.D. dissertation, University of Michigan, 1978.

Lieberthal, Kenneth. "The Suppression of Secret Societies in Post-Liberation Tientsin." *China Quarterly* 54 (April–June 1973): 242–66.

Liew, K. S. *Struggle for Democracy: Sung Chiao-jen and the 1911 Chinese Revolution.* Berkeley, 1971.

Lin, Julia C. *Modern Chinese Poetry: An Introduction.* Seattle, 1972.

Lin, Nancy T., trans. *In Quest, Poems of Chou En-lai.* Hong Kong and Cambridge, Mass., 1979.

Lin Yü-sheng. *The Crisis of Chinese Consciousness: Radical Antitraditionalism in the May Fourth Era.* Madison, Wis., 1979.

Link, Perry. "Traditional-style Popular Urban Fiction in the Teens and Twenties." In Merle Goldman, ed., *Modern Chinese Literature*, pp. 327–49.

Liu, F. F. *A Military History of Modern China, 1924–1949.* Princeton, 1956.

Liu Wenyong. "Chuanqi de wenxue nu qiangren: fang Ding Ling, tan pihai" [The Drama of a Strong Woman Writer: An Interview with Ding Ling Concerning Her Hardships]. *Chung Pao Monthly*, no. 3 (March 1980), pp. 73–79.

Liu Xinhuang. *Xu Zhimo yu Lu Xiaoman* [Xu Zhimo and Lu Xiaoman]. Taipei, 1965.

Lo, *Symposium:* Lo Jung-pang, ed. *K'ang Yu-wei, a Biography and a Symposium.* Tucson, 1967.

Loh, Pichon P. Y. *The Early Chiang Kai-shek: A Study of His Personality and Politics, 1887–1924.* New York, 1971.

Lu Lin. "The Story of *Exploration* Magazine." Translated by Joint Publications Research Service, report no. 4764. Reprinted in *SPEAHRhead*, no. 6/7 (1980), pp. 38–40.

Lu Xun (Lu Hsün). *Selected Works.* Translated by Yang Hsien-yi and Gladys Yang. 4 vols. Beijing, 1957.

———. *Silent China.* Selected writings edited and translated by Gladys Yang. New York, 1973.

Lu Xun, 1881–1936 [Photographic Studies of Lu Xun]. Beijing, 1976.

Lu Xun Quanji [The Collected Works of Lu Xun]. 20 vols. Shanghai, 1973.

Lu Xun shoucang zhongguo xiandai muke xuanji, 1931–1936 [A Selection from Lu Xun's Collection of Modern Chinese Woodcuts]. Beijing, 1963.

Lu Xun shuxin ji [The Collected Letters of Lu Xun]. 2 vols. Beijing, 1976.

Lust, John. "Secret Societies, Popular Movements, and the 1911 Revolution." In Chesneaux, ed., *Popular Movements*, pp. 165–200.

———. "The Su-pao Case: An Episode in the Early Chinese Nationalist Movement." *Bulletin of the School of Oriental and African Studies* 27:2 (1964), pp. 408–429.

————, ed. Tsou Jung, *The Revolutionary Army: A Chinese Nationalist Tract of 1903*. The Hague, 1968.

Lyell, William A. *Lu Hsün's Vision of Reality*. Berkeley, 1976.

Ma Fenghua. "Huainian Shen Congwen jiaoshou" [Thinking of Professor Shen Congwen]. *Zhuanji wenxue* 2:1 (1957), pp. 6, 13–16.

McCormack, Gavan. *Chang Tso-lin in Northeast China, 1911–1928: China, Japan, and the Manchurian Idea*. Stanford, 1977.

McDonald, Angus W., Jr. "Mao Tse-tung and the Hunan Self-Government Movement, 1920: An Introduction and Five Translations." *China Quarterly* 68 (December 1976): 751–77.

————. *The Urban Origins of Rural Revolution: Elites and the Masses in Hunan Province, China, 1911–1927*. Berkeley, 1978.

McDougall, Bonnie S. *The Introduction of Western Literary Theories into Modern China, 1919–1925*. Tokyo, 1971.

————. *Mao Zedong's "Talks at the Yan'an Conference on Literature and Art": A Translation of the 1943 Text with Commentary*. Michigan Papers in Chinese Studies, no. 39. Ann Arbor, 1980.

MacFarquhar, Roderick. *The Hundred Flowers*. London, 1960.

————. *The Origins of the Cultural Revolution, I: Contradictions among the People, 1956–1957*. New York, 1974.

Mackinnon, Stephen R. "The Peiyang Army, Yüan Shih-k'ai, and the Origins of Modern Chinese Warlordism." *Journal of Asian Studies* 32 (May 1973): 405–423.

Mao Dun. "Huiyi Qu Qiubai." Transcribed from *Hongqi*, no. 6 (1980). *Dongxi fang (East and West)* 17 (May 10, 1980): 35–37.

Mao Zedong. *Chairman Mao Talks to the People: Talks and Letters, 1956–1971*. Edited by Stuart Schram. New York, 1974.

————. *Selected Works*. 5 vols. Beijing, 1967–77.

Mao Zhuxi yijia liu lieshi [Six Martyred Heroes in Chairman Mao's Family]. Compiled by the "New Hunan" (Xinxiang) Study Group. Hunan, 1978.

Marks, Robert B. "The World Can Change! Guangdong Peasants in Revolution." *Modern China* 3 (January 1977): 65–100.

Mei, June. "Socioeconomic Origins of Emigration: Guangdong to California, 1850–1882." *Modern China* 5 (1979): 463–501.

Meisner, Maurice. *Li Ta-chao and the Origins of Chinese Marxism*. Cambridge, Mass., 1967.

————. *Mao's China: A History of the People's Republic*. New York, 1977.

Meisner, Mitch. "Dazhai: The Mass Line in Practice." *Modern China* 4 (1978): 27–62.

Mills, Harriet. "Lu Hsün and the Communist Party." *China Quarterly* 4 (October–December 1960): 17–27.

————. "Lu Xun: Literature and Revolution—From Mara to Marx." In Merle Goldman, ed. *Modern Chinese Literature*, pp. 189–220.

Myers, Ramon H. "North China Villages During the Republican Period. Socioeconomic Relationships." *Modern China* (July 1980): 243–66.

Nathan, Andrew J. *Peking Politics 1918–1923: Factionalism and the Failure of Constitutionalism.* New York, 1976.

Ng, Pedro Pak-tao. "Planned Fertility and Fertility Socialization in Kwangtung Province." *China Quarterly* 78 (June 1979): 351–59.

Nieh Hua-ling. *Shen Ts'ung-wen.* New York, 1972.

———, ed. and co-trans. *Literature of the Hundred Flowers,* 2 vols. New York, 1981.

The North China Famine of 1920–1921. Report by the Peking United International Famine Relief Committee. Beijing, 1922.

O'Brien, Anita M. "Military Academies in China, 1885–1915." In Fogel and Rowe, eds., *Perspectives on a Changing China,* pp. 157–81.

Pang Yong-pil. "Peng Pai: From Landlord to Revolutionary." *Modern China* 1 (1975): 297–322.

Papers Respecting Labour Conditions in China. China, no. 1. H. M. Stationery Office, London, 1925.

Parish, William L. "Socialism and the Chinese Peasant Family." *Journal of Asian Studies* 34 (May 1975): 613–30.

Peking Gazette [translations of *Jingbao,* published by the *North China Herald*]. Shanghai, 1872–1911.

Pepper, Suzanne. *Civil War in China: The Political Struggle, 1945–1949.* Berkeley, 1978.

Pickowicz, Paul G. "Ch'ü Ch'iu-pai and the Chinese Marxist Conception of Revolutionary Popular Literature and Art." *China Quarterly* 70 (June 1977): 296–314.

———. "Introduction to Qu Qiu-bai's 'Who's "We"?' and 'The Question of Popular Literature and Art'" [includes translation of these two essays]. *Bulletin of Concerned Asian Scholars,* January–March 1976, pp. 45–52.

———. "Lu Xun through the Eyes of Qu Qiu-bai: New Perspectives on Chinese Marxist Literary Polemics of the 1930s." *Modern China* 2 (1976): 327–68.

———. "Qu Qiubai's Critique of the May Fourth Generation: Early Chinese Marxist Literary Criticism." In Merle Goldman, ed., *Modern Chinese Literature,* pp. 351–84.

Price, Don C. *Russia and the Roots of the Chinese Revolution, 1896–1911.* Cambridge, Mass., 1974.

Pringsheim, Klaus H. "The Functions of the Chinese Communist Youth Leagues (1920–1949)." *China Quarterly* 12 (October–December 1962): 75–91.

Prusek, Jaroslav. "Lu Hsün's 'Huai-chiu': A Precursor of Modern Chinese Literature." *Harvard Journal of Asiatic Studies* 29 (1969): 169–76.

Qingji mingren shouzha [Calligraphy by Late Qing Notables]. 2 vols. Reprint. Taiwan, 1966.

Qiu Canzhi. *Qiu Jin geming zhuan* [The Revolutionary Biography of Qiu Jin]. Reprint. Taipei, 1955.

Qiu Jin ji [Collected Works of Qiu Jin]. Beijing, 1960.

Qiu Jin shiji [Historical Materials on Qiu Jin]. Shanghai, 1958.

Qu Qiubai. *Wenji* [Collected Literary Works]. 4 vols. Beijing, 1954.

Raddock, David M. "Between Generations: Activist Chinese Youths in Pursuit of a Political Role in the *San-fan* and in the Cultural Revolution." *China Quarterly* 79 (September 1979): 511–28.

Rankin, Mary Backus. *Early Chinese Revolutionaries: Radical Intellectuals in Shanghai and Chekiang, 1902–1911.* Cambridge, Mass., 1971.

———. "The Emergence of Women at the End of the Ch'ing: The Case of Ch'iu Chin." In Wolf and Witke, eds., *Women in Chinese Society,* pp. 39–66.

———. "The Revolutionary Movement in Japan: A Study in the Tenacity of Tradition." In Mary Wright, ed., *China in Revolution,* pp. 319–61.

Reichwein, Adolf. *China and Europe: Intellectual and Artistic Contacts in the Eighteenth Century.* London, 1925.

Rhoads, Edward. *China's Republican Revolution: The Case of Kwangtung, 1895–1913.* Cambridge, Mass., 1975.

Robel, Ronald R. "T'an Ssu-t'ung on *Hsüeh Hui* or 'Study Associations.'" In *Nothing Concealed, Essays in Honor of Liu Yü-yün,* edited by Frederic Wakeman, Jr., pp. 161–76. Taipei, 1970.

Robinson, Thomas W., ed. *The Cultural Revolution in China.* Berkeley, 1971.

Ropp, Paul S. "The Seeds of Change: Reflections on the Condition of Women in the Early and Mid Ch'ing." *Signs: Journal of Women in Culture and Society* 2:1 (1976), pp. 5–23.

Rosen, Stanley. "The Radical Students in Kwangtung During the Cultural Revolution." *China Quarterly* 70 (June 1977): 390–99.

Rosenbaum, Arthur L. "Gentry Power and the Changsha Rice Riot of 1910." *Journal of Asian Studies* 34 (May 1975): 689–715.

Roy, David. *Kuo Mo-jo: The Early Years.* Cambridge, Mass., 1971.

Rue, John E. *Mao Tse-tung in Opposition, 1927–1935.* Stanford, 1966.

Salaff, Janet. "Institutionalized Motivation for Fertility Limitation." In Marilyn Young, ed., *Women in China,* pp. 93–144.

Sargent, Margie. "The Cultural Revolution in Heilungkiang." In *The Cultural Revolution in the Provinces,* edited by M. Sargent et al., pp. 16–65. Cambridge, Mass., 1971.

Scalapino, Robert A. "Prelude to Marxism: The Chinese Student Movement in Japan, 1900–1910." In Albert Feuerwerker et al., eds., *Approaches to Modern Chinese History,* pp. 190–215.

Schiffrin, Harold. *Sun Yat-sen and the Origins of the Chinese Revolution.* Berkeley, 1968.

Schneider, Laurence A. *A Madman of Ch'u: The Chinese Myth of Loyalty and Dissent.* Berkeley, 1980.

Schoppa, R. Keith. "Local Self-Government in Zhejiang, 1909–1927." *Modern China* 2 (1976): 503–530.

———. "Province and Nation: The Chekiang Provincial Autonomy Movement, 1917–1927." *Journal of Asian Studies* 36 (August 1977): 661–74.

Schram, Stuart. *Mao Tse-tung.* London, 1966.

———. "Mao Tse-tung and Secret Societies." *China Quarterly* 27 (July–September 1966): 1–13.

———. *Mao Ze-dong: "Une Étude de l'éducation physique."* Paris, 1957.

———. *The Political Thought of Mao Tse-tung.* Rev. and enl. ed. New York, 1972.

Schwartz, Benjamin. *Chinese Communism and the Rise of Mao.* Cambridge, Mass., 1958.

———. *In Search of Wealth and Power: Yen Fu and the West.* Cambridge, Mass., 1964.

———, ed. *Reflections on the May Fourth Movement: A Symposium.* Cambridge, Mass., 1972.

Selden, Mark. *The People's Republic of China: A Documentary History of Revolutionary Change.* New York, 1979.

———. *The Yenan Way in Revolutionary China.* Cambridge, Mass., 1971.

Seybolt, Peter J. "The Yenan Revolution in Mass Education." *China Quarterly* 48 (October–December 1971): 641–69.

Seymour, James D., ed. *The Fifth Modernization: China's Human Rights Movement, 1978–1979.* Human Rights Publishing Group, Stanfordville, N.Y., 1980.

Shaffer (Womack), Lynda. "Anyuan: The Cradle of the Chinese Workers' Revolutionary Movement, 1921–1922." In *Columbia Essays in International Affairs,* edited by Andrew Cordier. Vol. 5, pp. 166–201. New York, 1970.

———. "Mao Ze-dong and the October 1922 Changsha Construction Workers' Strike: Marxism in Preindustrial China." *Modern China* 4 (1978): 379–418.

Shaheen, Anthony Joseph. "The China Democratic League and Chinese Politics, 1939–1947." Ph.D. dissertation, University of Michigan, 1977.

Shek, Richard. "Some Western Influences on T'an Ssu-t'ung's Thought." In Cohen and Schrecker, eds., *Reform in Nineteenth-Century China,* pp. 194–203.

Shen Congwen. *Congwen zichuan* [Autobiography]. Kaiming shudian, 1943.

———. *Ji Ding Ling xuji* [Further Reminiscences Concerning Ding Ling]. Shanghai, 1939.

Shen Tseng-wen [*sic*]. *The Chinese Earth.* Translated by Ching Ti and Robert Payne. London, 1947.

Sheridan, James E. *Chinese Warlord: The Career of Feng Yü-hsiang*. Stanford, 1966.

Sheridan, Mary. "The Emulation of Heroes." *China Quarterly* 33 (January–March 1968): 47–72.

———. "Young Women Leaders in China." *Signs: Journal of Women in Culture and Society* 2:1 (1976), pp. 59–88.

Shewmaker, Kenneth. *Americans and Chinese Communists, 1927–1945: A Persuading Encounter*. Ithaca, N.Y., 1971.

Shih, Vincent C. Y. "Enthusiast and Escapist: Writers of the Older Generation." *China Quarterly* 13 (January–March 1963): 92–112.

———. "Lao-she a Conformist? An Anatomy of a Wit under Restraint." In Buxbaum and Mote, eds., *Transition and Permanence*, pp. 307–319.

Shue, Vivienne. *Peasant China in Transition: The Dynamics of Development Toward Socialism, 1949–1956*. Berkeley, 1980.

Sima Lu (Smarlo Ma). *Qu Qiubai zhuan* [Biography of Qu Qiubai]. Hong Kong, 1962.

Siu, Bobby. *Fifty Years of Struggle: The Development of the Women's Movements in China, 1900–1949*. Hong Kong, 1975.

Skinner, G. William, ed. *The City in Late Imperial China*. Stanford, 1977.

Snow, Edgar, ed. *Living China: Modern Chinese Short Stories*. New York, 1936.

Snow, Helen. *Women in Modern China*. The Hague, 1967.

SPEAHRhead (Bulletin of the Society for the Protection of East Asians' Human Rights, P.O. Box 1212, Cathedral Station, New York, N.Y. 10025). Double Issue, nos. 6 and 7 (Northern Summer–Autumn 1980).

Spence, Jonathan. "The Explorer Who Never Left Home—Arthur Waley." *Renditions*, no. 5 (Autumn 1975), pp. 32–37.

———. *To Change China: Western Advisers in China, 1620–1960*. New York, 1980.

Starr, John Bryan. *Continuing the Revolution: The Political Thought of Mao*. Princeton, 1979.

Strand, David, and Richard R. Weiner. "Social Movements and Political Discourse in 1920's Peking: An Analysis of the Tramway Riot of October 22, 1929." In *Select Papers from the Center for Far Eastern Studies*, no. 3, edited by Susan Mann Jones. Chicago, 1978–79.

Sullivan, Lawrence, and Richard H. Solomon. "The Formation of Chinese Communist Ideology in the May Fourth Era: A Content Analysis of *Hsin ch'ing nien*." In Chalmers Johnson, ed., *Ideology and Politics in Contemporary China*, pp. 117–60.

Sun, Shirley Hsiao-ling. "Lu Hsun and the Chinese Woodcut Movement: 1929–1936." Ph.D. dissertation, Stanford University, 1974.

Tagore, Rabindranath, and L. K. Elmhirst. *Rabindranath Tagore, Pioneer in Education, Essays and Exchanges between Rabindranath Tagore and L. K. Elmhirst*. London, 1961.

Tanaka Kyoko. "Mao and Liu in the 1947 Land Reform: Allies or Disputants?" *China Quarterly* 75 (September 1978): 566–93.

Teiwes, Frederick C. "The Origins of Rectification: Inner-Party Purges and Education before Liberation." *China Quarterly* 65 (March 1976): 15–53.

Terrill, Ross. *Mao: A Biography*. New York, 1980.

Thaxton, Ralph. "On Peasant Revolution and National Resistance: Toward a Theory of Peasant Mobilization and Revolutionary War with Special Reference to Modern China." *World Politics* 30 (October 1977): 24–57.

Thompson, Laurence G., ed. and trans. *Ta T'ung Shu: The One World Philosophy of K'ang Yu-wei*. London, 1958.

Thorne, Christopher. *Allies of a Kind: The United States, Britain, and the War against Japan, 1941–1945*. New York, 1978.

Thornton, Richard. *The Comintern and the Chinese Communists, 1928–1931*. Seattle, 1969.

Tien Hung-mao. *Government and Politics in Kuomintang China: 1927–1937*. Stanford, 1972.

Ting, Lee-hsia Hsu. *Government Control of the Press in Modern China, 1900–1949*. Cambridge, Mass., 1974.

Townsend, James R. "Revolutionizing Chinese Youth: A Study of *Chung-kuo Ch'ing-nien*." In *Chinese Communist Politics in Action*, edited by A. Doak Barnett, pp. 447–76. Seattle, 1969.

Translations from Beijing Unofficial Journals. China Report, Political, Sociological and Military Affairs, no. 42. Joint Publications Research Service, report no. 74764. Arlington, Va., Dec. 13, 1979.

Van Boven, P. Henri. *Histoire de la littérature chinoise moderne*. Peiping [Beijing], 1946.

Van Slyke, Lyman P. *Enemies and Friends: The United Front in Chinese Communist History*. Stanford, 1967.

Vogel, Ezra F. *Canton under Communism: Programs and Politics in a Provincial Capital, 1949–1968*. Cambridge, Mass., 1969.

Vohra, Ranbir. *Lao She and the Chinese Revolution*. Cambridge, Mass., 1974.

Wakeman, Frederic, Jr. *The Fall of Imperial China*. New York, 1977.

———. "Historiography in China after 'Smashing the "Gang of Four."'" *China Quarterly* 76 (December 1978): 891–911.

———. *History and Will: Philosophical Perspectives of Mao Tse-tung's Thought*. Berkeley, 1973.

———. "The Use and Abuse of Ideology in the Study of Contemporary China." *China Quarterly* 61 (March 1975): 127–52.

Wakeman, Frederic, Jr., and Carolyn Grant, eds. *Conflict and Control in Late Imperial China*. Berkeley, 1975.

Walder, Andrew G. *Chang Ch'un-ch'iao and Shanghai's January Revolution*. Michigan Papers in Chinese Studies, no. 32. Ann Arbor, 1977.

Walker, Kenneth R. "Collectivisation in Retrospect: The 'Socialist High Tide' of Autumn 1955–Spring 1956," *China Quarterly* 26 (April–June 1966): 1–43.

Wang Hsueh-wen. *Chinese Communist Education: The Yenan Period.* Taipei, 1975.

———. "Revolutionary Youth and the Li I-che Poster." *Issues and Studies* (February 1976): 80–93.

Wang, Y. C. "The Su-pao Case: A Study of Foreign Pressure, Intellectual Fermentation, and Dynastic Decline." *Monumenta Serica* 24 (1965): 84–129.

———. "Tu Yueh-sheng (1888–1951): A Tentative Political Biography." *Journal of Asian Studies* 26 (May 1967): 433–55.

Wei Jingsheng et al. *Beijing zhi chun shiwen xuan* [Selection of Poems and Essays from the Beijing Spring]. Hong Kong, 1980.

Wei Jingsheng et al. *Kending ziyou, kending minzhu* [Hope for Freedom and Democracy]. Taipei, 1979.

Wen Yiduo. *Quanji* [Collected Works]. 8 sections in 4 vols. Shanghai, 1948.

———. *Red Candle.* Translated by Tao Tao Sanders. London, 1972.

Whitbeck, Judith. "Three Images of the Cultural Hero in the Thought of Kung Tzu-chen." In Cohen and Schrecker, eds., *Reform in Nineteenth-Century China,* pp. 26–30.

White, D. Gordon. "The Politics of *Hsia-hsiang* Youth." *China Quarterly* 59 (July–September 1974): 491–517.

White, Lynn T., III. "Workers' Politics in Shanghai." *Journal of Asian Studies.* (November 1976): 99–116.

Wieger, Léon, S.J., ed. *Chine Moderne.* Vol. 5, *Nationalisme, Xénophobie, Antichristianisme.* Tianjin, 1924.

Wilbur, C. Martin. "The Ashes of Defeat: Accounts of the Nanchang Revolt and Southern Expedition, August 1–October 1, 1927, by Chinese Communists Who Took Part." *China Quarterly* 18 (April–June 1964): 3–54.

———. *Sun Yat-sen: Frustrated Patriot.* New York, 1976.

Wilbur, C. Martin, and Julie Lien-ying How, eds. *Documents on Communism, Nationalism, and Soviet Advisers in China, 1918–1927: Papers Seized in the 1927 Peking Raid.* New York, 1956.

Wilhelm, Hellmut. "The Poems from the Hall of Obscured Brightness." In Lo Jung-pang, ed., *Symposium,* pp. 319–40.

Wilson, Dick. *The Long March, 1935: The Epic of Chinese Communism's Survival.* New York, 1973.

Witke, Roxane. *Comrade Chiang Ch'ing.* Boston, 1977.

———. "Mao Tse-tung, Women and Suicide in the May Fourth Era." *China Quarterly* 31 (1967): 128–47.

———. "Transformation of Attitudes toward Women During the May Fourth Era of Modern China." Ph.D. dissertation, University of California at Berkeley, 1970.

Wolf, Margery, and Roxane Witke, eds. *Women in Chinese Society.* Stanford, 1975.

Wong Young-tsu. "The Ideal of Universality in Late Ch'ing Reformism." In Cohen and Schrecker, eds., *Reform in Nineteenth-Century China*, pp. 150–59.

————. "The Significance of the Kuang Hsü Emperor to the Reform Movement of 1898." In Buxbaum and Mote, eds., *Transition and Permanence*, pp. 169–86.

Woon, Ramon L. Y., and Irving Y. Lo. "Poets and Poetry of China's Last Empire." *Literature East and West* 9:4 (1965), pp. 331–61.

Worden, Robert L. "K'ang Yu-wei, Sun Yat-sen, et. al. and the Bureau of Immigration." *Ch'ing-shih wen-t'i* 2:6 (June 1971), pp. 1–10.

Wou, Odoric Y. K. "The Military and Nationalism: The Political Thinking of Wu P'ei-fu." In Chan and Etzold, eds., *China in the 1920s*, pp. 108–126.

Wright, Mary Clabaugh, ed. *China in Revolution: The First Phase, 1900–1913.* New Haven, 1968.

Wright, Tim. "Sino-Japanese Business in China: The Luda Company, 1921–1937." *Journal of Asian Studies* 39 (August 1980): 711–27.

Wu Tien-wei. "Chiang Kai-shek's April 12th Coup of 1927." In Chan and Etzold, eds., *China in the 1920s*, pp. 147–59.

————. *The Sian Incident: A Pivotal Point in Modern Chinese History.* Michigan Papers in Chinese Studies, no. 26. Ann Arbor, 1976.

Wuxu bianfa [The Reform Movement of 1898]. Edited by Qian Bocan et al. 4 vols. Shanghai, 1953.

Xu-Elmhirst Letters. Series of letters between Xu Zhimo and Leonard Elmhirst, covering the years 1925–1928, given to Professor Leo Ou-fan Lee by Leonard Elmhirst.

Xu Zhimo. *Xu Zhimo Quanji.* Edited by Jiang Fucong and Liang Shiqiu. 6 vols. Taipei, 1969.

"Xuan Jiwen" [Collected Propaganda Essays]. "Criticizing 'Concerning Socialist Democracy and Legal System.'" Translated in *Issues and Studies* 12 (February 1976): 109–135.

Yahuda, Michael. "Political Generations in China." *China Quarterly* 80 (December 1979): 793–805.

Yang, C. K. "Some Preliminary Statistical Patterns of Mass Actions in Nineteenth-Century China." In Wakeman and Grant, eds., *Conflict and Control*, pp. 174–210.

Yang I-fan. *The Case of Hu Feng.* Hong Kong, 1956.

Yang, Simon, and L. K. Tao. *A Study of the Standard of Living of Working Families in Shanghai.* Peiping [Beijing], 1931.

Yen Ching Hwang. *The Overseas Chinese and the 1911 Revolution, with Special Reference to Singapore and Malaya.* Kuala Lumpur, 1976.

Ying Ruocheng. "Lao She and His 'Teahouse.'" *Chinese Literature*, no. 12 (1979), pp. 3–11.

492 · The Gate of Heavenly Peace

Yoshihashi, Takehiko. *Conspiracy at Mukden: The Rise of the Japanese Military.* New Haven, 1963.

Young, Ernest P. *The Presidency of Yuan Shih-k'ai: Liberalism and Dictatorship in Early Republican China.* Ann Arbor, 1977.

———. "The Reformer as a Conspirator: Liang Ch'i-ch'ao and the 1911 Revolution." In Albert Feuerwerker et al., eds., *Approaches to Modern Chinese History,* pp. 239–67.

———. "Yuan Shih-k'ai's Rise to the Presidency." In Mary Wright, ed., *China in Revolution,* pp. 419–42.

Young, Marilyn B., ed. *Women in China: Studies in Social Change and Feminism.* Michigan Papers in Chinese Studies, no. 15. Ann Arbor, 1973.

Zang Kejia. "Lao She yongzai" [Lao She Is Always with Us]. *Renmin wenxue* 228 (September 1978); 82–90.

Zhang Guangnian. "Shafei nüshi zai Yanan" [Miss Sophie in Yanan]. *Wenyi bao,* no. 2 (1958), pp. 9–11.

Zhou Shoujuan. "We Shall Meet Again." Translated by Perry Link. *Bulletin of Concerned Asian Scholars,* Special Issue (January–March 1976), pp. 15–19.

Zhou Zuoren. *Guatou ji* [Collected Essays]. Hong Kong, 1969.

Zhuang Mei. "Wei Jingsheng de nüyou" [Wei Jingsheng's Girl Friend]. *Dongxi fang (East and West)* 17 (May 10, 1980): 26–27.

Zong Chen and Shang Xia. "Ding Ling zaoqi di shenghuo he chuangzuo" [The Life and Creative Work of Ding Ling in Her Early Years]. *Dongbeishida Xuebao* 3 (1980): 41–47, 130.

Zou Rong. *Gemingjun [The Revolutionary Army].* See edition under Lust, ed., *Tsou Jung.*

Zweig, David S. "The Peita Debate on Education and the Fall of Teng Hsiao-p'ing." *China Quarterly* 73 (March 1978): 140–59.

Index

Wade-Giles romanizations for certain names and places that may still be more familiar in that earlier form are placed in parentheses following the new Pinyin transcriptions.

Grateful acknowledgment is made to the following for permission to reprint copyrighted material:

George Allen & Unwin Ltd.: Selections from *Ta T'ung Shu: The One World Philosophy of K'ang Yu-wei,* edited and translated by Laurence G. Thompson, 1958.

Cyril Birch and China Quarterly: Selections from "Lao She: The Humourist in His Humour," by Cyril Birch, from *China Quarterly* 8 (October–December 1961).

Marion Boyars Publishers Ltd.: "Notes from the City of the Sun," from *Beijing Street Voices,* edited and translated by David S. G. Goodman, 1981.

Bulletin of Concerned Asian Scholars: Selections from Paul G. Pickowicz's "Introduction to Qu Qiu-bai's 'Who's "We"?' and 'The Question of Popular Literature and Art,' " from *Bulletin of Concerned Asian Scholars,* January–March 1976.

Cheng Wen Publishing Company: Selections from *The Autobiography of a Chinese Historian, Being the Preface to a Symposium on Ancient Chinese History,* edited and translated by Arthur Hummel.

China Book Company: Photographs 1, 9, 10, 29, 40, and 41 from *The Photographic Biography of Dr. Sun and President Chiang.*

Doubleday & Company, Inc.: "The Deserted Village" and excerpts from "Arrest," "Headline Music," "Miracle," and "Song of Joy," from *Twentieth Century Chinese Poetry,* edited and translated by Hsu Kai-yu. Copyright © 1963 by Hsu Kai-yu.

Grove Press, Inc.: Selections from *Anthology of Chinese Literature, Volume II,* edited by Cyril Birch. Copyright © 1972 by Grove Press, Inc.

Harvard University Press: Selections from *Asian Ideas of East and West: Tagore and His Critics in Japan, China and India,* by Stephen

N. Hay, 1970. From *Modern Chinese Literature in the May Fourth Era*, edited by Merle Goldman, 1977. From *Literary Dissent in Communist China*, by Merle Goldman, 1967. From *The Romantic Generation of Chinese Writers*, by Leo Lee, 1973. From *The May Fourth Movement: Intellectual Revolution in Modern China*, by Chow Tse-tsung, 1960.

Hsu Kai-yu: Selections from "The Intellectual Biography of a Modern Chinese Poet: Wen I-to (1899–1946)." Ph.D. dissertation, Stanford University, 1959.

Human Rights Publishing Group: Selections from *The Fifth Modernization: China's Human Rights Movement, 1978–1979*, edited by James D. Seymour. Copyright © 1980 by Earl M. Coleman Enterprises, Inc.

Indiana University Press: Selections from *Literature of the People's Republic of China*, edited by Hsu Kai-yu and Ting Wang, 1980.

Institute of International Relations: Selections from *Ting Ling: Her Life and Work*, by Chang Jun-mei, 1978.

Literature East and West: Selections from "Poets and Poetry of China's Last Empire," by Ramon L. Y. Woon and Irving Y. Lo, from *Literature East and West* 9:4 (1965).

Litton Educational Publishing, Inc.: Selections from *The Road to Communism: China since 1912*, by Dun J. Li. Copyright © 1970 by Litton Educational Publishing, Inc. Used by permission of Van Nostrand Reinhold Company.

Lund Humphries, London: Selections from "English and Chinese Metres in Hsü Chih-mo," by Cyril Birch, from *Asia Major* 8:2 (1961).

The MIT Press, Cambridge, Massachusetts: Selections from *Straw Sandals: Chinese Short Stories 1918–1933*, edited by Harold Isaacs. Copyright © 1974 by Harold Isaacs.

John Murray Publishers, Ltd., London: Photograph 28 from *Rabindranath Tagore, Pioneer in Education,* by Rabindranath Tagore and L. K. Elmhirst.

Ohio State University Press: Selections from *Cat Country: A Satirical Novel of China in the 1930's,* by Lao She. Translated from the Chinese by William A. Lyell, Jr. (Columbus: Ohio State University Press, 1970).

Oxford University Press, London: Selections from *Silent China: Selected Writings of Lu Xun,* edited and translated by Gladys Yang. Copyright © 1973 by Oxford University Press.

Rabindra-Bhavana Development Committee, Tagore Trust Fund: Photograph 26 courtesy of Rabindra-Bhavana, Visva-Bharati.

Random House, Inc.: Selection from "Heavenly Peace Gate" by Lu Ping, from *The Chinese Literary Scene,* by Hsu Kai-yu. Copyright © 1975 by Hsu Kai-yu.

Renditions: Susan Vacca's translation of Ting Ling's "In the Hospital," from *Renditions,* a Chinese-English Translation Magazine, no. 8, Autumn 1977, published by the Comparative Literature and Translation Centre, The Chinese University of Hong Kong.

Twayne Publishers, a Division of G. K. Hall & Co., Inc.: Selections from *Shen Ts'ung-wen,* by Nieh Hua-ling. Copyright © 1972 by Twayne Publishers.

University of Arizona Press: Selections from *K'ang Yu-wei, a Biography and a Symposium* (Association for Asian Monograph No. XXIII), Lo Jung-pang, editor. Copyright © 1967 by the University of Arizona Press.

University of California Press: Selections from *Lu Hsün's Vision of Reality,* by William A. Lyell.